Purity in Print

Print Culture History in Modern America
James Danky and Wayne Wiegand, *General Editors*

Paul Boyer
*Purity in Print: Book Censorship in America from the Gilded
Age to the Computer Age*

Purity in Print

BOOK CENSORSHIP IN AMERICA FROM
THE GILDED AGE TO THE COMPUTER AGE

Paul S. Boyer

Second Edition

THE UNIVERSITY OF WISCONSIN PRESS

The University of Wisconsin Press
1930 Monroe Street
Madison, Wisconsin 53711

www.wisc.edu/wisconsinpress/

3 Henrietta Street
London WC2E 8LU, England

Printed in the United States of America

Library of Congress Cataloging-in-Publication Data
Boyer, Paul S.
    Purity in print : book censorship in America from the Gilded Age to
    the Computer Age / Paul S. Boyer.—2nd ed.
    pp. cm.—(Print culture history in modern America)
    Includes bibliographical references and index.
    ISBN 0-299-17584-7 (paper : alk. paper)
    1. Censorship—United States—History.   2. Obscenity (Law)—
United States.
I. Title. II. Series.
KF4775 .B6   2002
363.3′1′0973—dc21   2002001066

For ann, once again

Contents

List of Illustrations

Preface to the Second Edition

Although the fact is probably not of consuming interest to anyone but me, the beginnings of *Purity in Print* can be traced to the fall of 1961 when, in a graduate seminar at Harvard led by Professor Frank Freidel, I opted to write my research paper on book censorship in Boston. A revision of that seminar paper, appearing in the *American Quarterly* (Spring 1963), constituted my first scholarly publication. Further revised, it became a chapter in my 1966 Ph.D. dissertation, which in turn became the basis of this book.

I hope that not merely vanity or authorial self-indulgence lies behind my willingness to contemplate a new edition of a book whose origins are now so far in the past. Were I approaching the topic afresh today, I have no doubt that in some respects I would treat it differently and emphasize additional themes beyond those I highlighted in the 1960s. Particularly, I would certainly today give considerably more attention to gender issues; to questions of readership; to a critical analysis of language; to cross-cultural comparisons, and to the broader phenomenon of censorship of all media, not just print materials. No doubt many other issues that loom larger today than they did a generation ago would make this a very different book had I started work on this topic in the later 1990s rather than the early 1960s.

Nevertheless, on rereading the original work, and focusing my attention on these issues once again, I find that the research holds up and that my overall treatment still seems valid and worthwhile. As a historian about to retire, I can say that I still generally agree with the young historian of the 1960s who was just beginning to gain experience in historical research and writing, even if certain features of his prose style and occasionally his jejune tone differ from what I would strive for were I writing the book today. (Others may well disagree, of course: the continuing effort to make sense of the past is a social process, not an individual endeavor.)

Essentially what I tried to do in my doctoral dissertation, and thus, in the first edition of *Purity in Print*, was to appropriate a topic—book censorship—that had been primarily the domain of journalists, polemicists, lawyers, and constitutional scholars, and reclaim it for American history, broadly understood. Specifically, I felt that the story of book censorship in America could best be understood if embedded within the larger cultural and social history of the decades that I had chosen to focus on: the 1870s through the 1930s. Viewed from this perspective, I found that censorship history became considerably more complex and less black-and-white, the battle lines more blurred, the villains less villainous, and the heroes a tad less heroic than was the case in much of the existing literature on the topic.

Since, despite my reservations and caveats, I remain fairly confident about the research that went into the original book, and its structure and argument, I decided not to revise the original work (chapters 1–9 of the present edition), except to move several paragraphs that looked beyond the 1930s from chapter 8 into chapter 10, where they now more logically belong. I have also let stand unrevised the introduction to the first edition, as a document revealing the crosscurrents of thinking on censorship issues (including my own) in the late 1960s.

This new edition has two new chapters (10 and 11), and this requires a bit of explanation. The first edition of *Purity in Print* ended with the 1930s, the decade of several landmark censorship rulings, notably federal judge James M. Woolsey's 1933 decision in a U.S. Customs case clearing James Joyce's long-banned classic *Ulysses*. This was also the decade when dictatorial governments abroad, particularly the Hitler regime in Germany, engaged in savagely repressive campaigns against the printed word, most notoriously in the Nazi book burnings of May 1933. Since the original edition has been out of print for some years, a simple reprint of the original book, ending the story in the 1930s, would probably have been justifiable—and certainly would have involved less work for me! Nevertheless, in contemplating a second edition, I could not resist the opportunity to carry the story forward, examining developments in the area of print-censorship in America from World War II to the dawn of the twenty-first century.

I had, of course, followed developments in this field in a general way over the years, and occasionally written and lectured on them (see "Acknowledgments to the Second Edition"), even as my own evolving scholarly interests had carried me far afield from the subject of book censorship. As I immersed myself in this topic once again in preparation for writing these new chapters, I found myself fascinated by the sometimes tortuous and unpredictable course of censorship in the post-1940 decades. I also found, to my pleasure, that my original approach still proved helpful: censorship history becomes most interesting, and I think most persuasive, when the activities of the censors and their opponents are placed within a broader conceptual framework that includes cultural, political, social, and even technological components.

In the introduction to the 1968 edition, reprinted below, I described American society at that moment as "engaged in a major reëxamination and reformulation of . . . attitudes toward the problems of literary freedom and censorship." The First Amendment absolutist position, which held that "obscenity" was largely a figment of prudish minds, and that nearly any censorship was by definition to be deplored—a position that had appeared to be gaining momentum for several decades—was, I observed, "being sharply challenged from many quarters." And I proceeded in that introduction to discuss some of those challenges, not only from predictable religious quarters, but also across a broad intellectual spectrum.

As I now document in chapter 10, this process continued and even accelerated in the years after 1968, as a larger conservative shift, including the political mobilization of the religious right, reoriented American culture and politics. As time went on, other developments shaped attitudes toward obscenity as well, including a sharp feminist critique of the classic liberal hostility to censorship mounted by Catharine MacKinnon, Andrea Dworkin, and others. Meanwhile, technological changes, especially the revolution in information technology and the explosive growth of the World Wide Web, profoundly affected attitudes toward censorship of the printed word. These developments frame the discussion in chapter 11, with which this new edition concludes.

In short, this revised version of an old book is admittedly something of a hybrid: the first nine chapters are redolent of the 1960s, the concluding two chapters reflect an early twenty-first century perspective. Nevertheless, I hope the work coheres intellectually, both as a narrative account of an important and neglected strand of American cultural and intellectual history, and as an argument making the case for the deeply embedded presence of censorship history within the larger culture, whether one is looking at the Gilded Age, the Progressive Era, the 1920s, the 1950s, or our own day.

The experience of revisiting a topic of historical inquiry after forty years and re-immersing myself in issues that first engaged me as a graduate student has been enormously stimulating and rewarding. I hope readers of this book will find it worthwhile as well, both as a work of historical scholarship and as a contribution to contemporary discourse on an issue that—albeit in different guises—remains almost as contentious for Americans of the twenty-first century as it was for Americans of earlier generations.

Acknowledgments to the First Edition

I should like to express my sincere thanks to the persons who kindly granted personal interviews or otherwise answered my queries, including Roger N. Baldwin, Gordon Cairnie, Fred Dicker, Morris Ernst, Charles B. Everitt, Walter Willard (Spud) Johnson, Alfred A. Knopf, Louis Lyons, Charles W. Morton, Allan Nevins, Mary U. Rothrock, Henry W. Simon, Upton Sinclair, Dwight S. Strong, and Edward Weeks. My thanks to five men must be given posthumously: Raymond Calkins, Donald Friede, B. W. Huebsch, Delcevare King, and Arthur M. Schlesinger, Sr.

Many other individuals and institutions were helpful in various ways. These include Miss Irene Goodsell of the Civil Liberties Union of Massachusetts; Richard Hart of the Enoch Pratt Free Library, Baltimore; David C. Mearns of the Manuscript Division of the Library of Congress; John Mullane of the Public Library of Cincinnati and Hamilton County; Virgil W. Peterson of the Chicago Crime Commission; Miss Irene Peterson of the Chicago Public Library; and Alan Reitman of the American Civil Liberties Union. Milton R. Merrill of Utah State University kindly gave permission to quote from his doctoral dissertation on Reed Smoot, and Roger N. Baldwin did the same for his reminiscences in the Oral History Library at Columbia University. Zechariah Chafee III graciously granted access to his father's papers in the Harvard University Archives. The Department of History of Harvard University provided special funds for additional research in Albany and Princeton.

I should like also to thank Janet Beal, who generously aided in the task of proofreading, and Thomas J. Davis, III, History Editor at Charles Scribner's Sons. Professor Frank Freidel, who has seen this study grow from a graduate seminar paper into a book, gave warm encouragement and sound advice at all stages. Dr. Edward T. James, editor of *Notable American Women, 1607–1950*, on whose staff I served for several years while revising and rewriting my own manuscript, provided encouraging evidence that a scrupulous regard for accuracy need not preclude a gracious literary style. My wife Ann Chapman Boyer has played a greater role than I can well acknowledge here, but her more immediate contributions included several careful and critical readings of the entire manuscript.

Is it necessary to add the conventional disclaimer? None of the above persons should in any way be held responsible for the lapses and errors which inevitably remain.

PAUL S. BOYER

Hadley, Massachusetts
March, 1968

Acknowledgments to the Second Edition

After the publication of the first edition of *Purity in Print* in 1968, my scholarly interests turned in other directions. Though I continued to work in the general area of American thought and culture, I did not pursue research or publish on book censorship and First Amendment issues as a primary focus. Nevertheless, I was asked from time to time to speak on this topic, review books on censorship, respond to the queries of younger scholars working on this topic, or contribute essays on censorship to reference works. In this way the subject remained on my radar screen, as it were, as I periodically had occasion to reflect on it, generalize about it, and consider its current manifestations in American society. (The first such invitation, somewhat to my amazement, came in the fall of 1968, shortly after the book was published, when I appeared on NBC-TV's *Today* show to discuss book censorship with Barbara Walters and Joe Garagiola!)

I would, then, like to express my thanks to those responsible for keeping this topic in the realm of my awareness—even despite myself, I might say. Of the more recent such opportunities, the Minneapolis Public Library asked me to speak in September 1985 on "Censorship and Libraries," as the keynote lecture in its centennial celebration. Thanks, also, to the editors of the *Dictionary of American History* (1976) and the *Encyclopedia of American Political History* (1984), in which my essays on censorship appeared. More recently, the Friends of the Library at the University of Wisconsin–Madison, in conjunction with the University's Center for the History of Print Culture in Modern America, invited me to lecture on this topic. That lecture appeared in the Fall/Winter 1997 issue of the Friends' *Messenger Magazine*. A September 2001 seminar on book censorship, which I gave at the University of Wisconsin's Institute for Research in the Humanities at the invitation of director Sally Banes, led to a stimulating discussion and helpful exchanges with colleagues from various disciplines.

I am particularly grateful to professors Carl Kaestle and Janice Radway, editors of the forthcoming volume four of the *History of the Book in America*, a collaborative project of the American Antiquarian Society and Cambridge University Press, for the invitation to contribute a chapter on censorship. In preparing and writing that extended essay, I found myself reengaging with this topic in a quite new and serious way, as I not only drew upon my own and others' published work on the late nineteenth and early twentieth century period, but also reflected on how the censorship of books and periodicals had evolved in America in the eventful decades since the 1930s, where I had left the topic in the first edition of *Purity in Print*.

Several Wisconsin colleagues were especially helpful. Louise S. Robbins, director of the School of Library and Information Studies, generously shared her extensive knowledge of library-censorship issues as well as primary source documents and the photograph of librarian Ruth Brown that appears in this book. Donald A. Downs of the Political Science department, whose *The New Politics of Pornography* I found especially valuable, has provided thoughtful comments and helpful suggestions as well. My thanks, also, to two fine historians who make their academic home in the School of Journalism and Mass Communication. Stephen Vaughn provided a thoughtful reading of my "Censorship" essay for the *History of the Book in America* project. James Baughman generously shared a highly useful draft chapter from his forthcoming work on the history of television in the 1950s, and brought to my attention other scholarly work directly relevant to my interests.

Ralph Ginzburg not only supplied interesting information in a telephone interview, but also provided his penitentiary "mug shot" for reproduction and gave me permission to reprint an *Eros* cover. Catharine A. MacKinnon of the University of Michigan Law

School incisively critiqued my discussion of the antipornography ordinance she and Andrea Dworkin drafted in 1983. Brett Gary of the Modern History and Literature Department at Drew University gave permission to quote from a conference paper and read a portion of my manuscript based on his work. Louise Robbins, Louis Galambos and Janet R. Brugger, editor and associate editor of the Eisenhower Papers, and Barbara Krieger, an Archival Specialist in the Special Collections division of Baker Library at Dartmouth College, all assisted in my somewhat compulsive quest to discover what President Eisenhower actually said in his famous "don't join the bookburners" comments at the Dartmouth commencement on June 14, 1953.

The immediate impetus for this new edition of the book came from my friends and colleagues James Danky of the Wisconsin Historical Society, and Wayne Wiegand of the School of Library and Information Studies, co-editors of the University of Wisconsin Press's newly established Print Culture History in Modern America series. My warm thanks to them, as well as to press director Robert Mandel and associate director Steve Salemson, for their encouragement and support.

Adam Mehring of the press's editorial department shepherded the manuscript through the editorial process with efficiency and professional skill. Sharon M. Van Sluijs, the highly competent copyeditor, demonstrated preternatural patience with my last-minute changes as she worked under a tight deadline. Her final e-mail message dealing with the latest of my revisions was composed at 10:14 P.M. the night before the manuscript was due back at the press!

Pembroke Herbert and Sandi Rygiel of Picture Research Consultants & Archives, Topsfield, Massachusetts, provided efficient and productive photo research, again under tight deadlines. Robin Rider, director of Special Collections at the University of Wisconsin Memorial Library, and the staff of the library's Digital Content Group were most helpful with the *Eros* magazine cover illustration. Bill Barrow and JoAnne Cornelius of the Cleveland State University Library helped me acquire a photograph of Nico Jacobellis.

And I would be remiss not to mention Jan Miernowski of the UW French and Italian Department, who passed along Wislawa Szymborska's wonderfully witty poem "An Opinion on the Question of Pornography," which begins: "There's nothing more debauched than thinking. / This sort of wantonness runs wild like a wind-borne weed / on a plot laid out for daisies."

Finally, as in the original 1968 edition, I want to express my gratitude to Ann Chapman Boyer for her unfailing support and tolerance of my rather meandering succession of scholarly interests, and, specifically, once again, for taking time from her own busy schedule to read the two new chapters with her keen eye for typos, gaffes, and infelicities.

PAUL S. BOYER

Madison, Wisconsin
March, 2002

Introduction to the First Edition (1968)

It seems clear that we in the United States are at the present mo
ment engaged in a major reexamination and reformulation of our attitudes toward the problems of literary freedom and censorship. For
years it has been widely assumed that the new freedom of sexual expression in literature was a "good thing"—an encouraging sign of
our society's increasing maturity and healthy-mindedness and the
harbinger of a literary renaissance which would be marked by ever
more sensitive explorations of the human condition. Any effort by
society to limit this freedom was denounced as a dangerous symptom of incipient totalitarianism or residual Victorian prudery.

This position is being sharply challenged from many quarters.
In 1957 the United States Supreme Court denied to "obscenity" the
Constitutional guarantee of freedom of the press, and since then the
courts have been engaged in a sometimes confusing effort to define
the precise limits beyond which First-Amendment protection does
not extend. In one recent attempt to deal with this issue, the
Ginzburg decision of 1966, the Supreme Court significantly broad-
ened the legal definition of obsenity by upholding Ginzburg's conviction on the basis of the "pandering" manner in which he had advertised his publications.[1] And in April 1968 the High Court, in a
6–3 ruling, upheld a New York statute, enacted in July 1965, aimed
at protecting minors from the presumed evils of pornography.[2]

On the legislative side, Congress late in 1967 authorized the creation of a Presidential advisory commission to study the traffic in obsenity, to examine its alleged role in fomenting anti-social behavior, and to recommend possible legislation.[3] The report of this Commission, when it becomes available, may give important clues as to the nation's future course in the realm of book censorship. This official activity has been matched on the popular level by numerous movements aimed at alerting the public to the dangers of obscenity.

Perhaps an even more significant straw in the wind is the deluge of essays in recent months by writers, critics, and scholars seriously confronting the implications of the present massive output of pornographic and erotic works. This high-level debate, carried forward in *Partisan Review*, *Encounter*, and the *New York Review of Books,* and similar periodicals, has engaged such varied individuals as Susan Sontag, George P. Elliott, Howard Moody, Richard Schechner, Ernest van den Haag, Sidney Hook, Pamela Hansford Johnson, Gore Vidal, Norman Mailer, and Georger Steiner. [4]

In reading these essays, I have been struck by the contrast they reveal between the attitudes of today's intellectuals (if the above list may be considered in any way a representative sampling) and their counterparts of the 1920s. Today's group is far less ready to defend uncritically the proposition that any book dealing "frankly" with sex is *a priori* evidence of the author's emotional maturity and freedom from crippling inhibitions. The reason for the shift, I suppose, is clear. In the 1920s, most of the "shocking" books which aroused the censors treated sexual relations, whether heterosexual or homosexual, in a context of love, tenderness, and respect for human dignity. *Ulysses*, *Lady Chatterley's Lover*, and *The Well of Lonliness* illustrate my point. Whatever erotic emotions these novels may arouse, they are clearly humane and "life-affirming" in intent. In defending such books, the anti-censorship champions waxed eloquent over the clear gains for the human spirit which their free circulation would entail.

Today the censorship fight has moved to another arena altogether. Romantics like D. H. Lawrence and Radclyffe Hall have been left far behind. It is now writers like William Burroughs, Hubert Selby, Jr., "Pauline Réage," and—ultimately—the Marquis de Sade for whom one must take a stand. Under these circumstances, the old cheerful faith in the obvious desirability of complete permissiveness has faded. The pornographic carnival is now revealed to have not only an exciting midway and titillating sideshows, but also a rather chilling chamber of horrors—a fact rarely faced up to by the anti-censorship enthusiasts of the 1920s. A few doughty individuals—Hugh Hefner, Maurice Girodias, Wayland Young, and the industrious editors at Grove Press—remain touchingly loyal to the old faith, but many others are deeply troubled. The nature of their concern is suggested by the proposal of the Rev. Mr. Howard Moody (no prude, incidentally) who urges that *obscenity* be redefined as "material, whether sexual or not, that has as its basic motivation and purpose the degradation, debasement, and dehumanization of persons."

In "Night Words," a celebrated essay which originally appeared in *Encounter* in October 1965, the critic George Steiner passionately deplores the current outpouring of mass-produced pornography for its "unutterable monotony" and its debasement of the intensely private erotic vocabulary:

> The new pornographers subvert this last, vital privacy; they do our imagining for us. They take away the words that were of the night and shout them over the rooftops, making them hollow. The images of our love-making, the stammerings we resort to in intimacy, come pre-packaged. . . . [T]he present danger to the freedom of literature and to the inward freedom of our society is not censorship or verbal reticence. The danger lies in the facile contempt which the erotic novelist exhibits for his readers, for his personages, and for the language. Our dreams are marketed wholesale.

Pamela Hansford Johnson's attack on pornography, *On Iniquity*, while less subtle, is no less passionate. Reminding us that Ian Brady, the mastermind of the appalling "moors murders" in England, was an admirer of de Sade's works, she turns this fact into an indictment of "our libertarian intellectuals, who are the new tyrants." Miss Johnson quotes from the trial manuscript a passage which is a grotesque echo of countless glib anti-censorship arguments from days gone by. Brady has been asked about his collection of pornographic books:

> "They cannot be called pornography. They can be bought at any bookstall."
> "They are dirty books, are they not?"
> "It depends on the dirty minds."

Richard Schechner, editor of the *Tulane Drama Review*, rejects Miss Johnson's line of attack, but he is equally dismayed about the immanence of pornography in our culture. Denying that the reading of pornography is likely to lead to anti-social action, Schechner contends instead that its more typical effect is to induce a state of monumental passivity. The present massive consumption of erotica, he suggests, merely reflects an effort by Americans to reduce the tension they feel between their own inertia and the vast possibilities for meaningful involvement which lie all about.

Susan Sontag, in a brilliant *Partisan Review* essay, criticizes the prevailing tendency to see pornography solely in terms of individual or social pathology. *Some* pornography, she believes, demands serious consideration as literature. (Among the books she discusses is *Story of O,* a standing refutation to the facile contention that the line between pornography and "true" literature is a distinct and easily recognized one.) Yet Miss Sontag concludes her essay by acknowledging that without "subtle and extensive psychic preparation" the widening of consciousness which pornography entails may well be "destructive for most people" and result in the "brutalization of the morally innocent."

I find the present critical attitude toward pornography richer in nuance and far more subtle than the shallow affirmations of an earlier generation of libertarians. That generation was simply not candid with itself about the full implications of its enthusiastic support of untrammelled sexual candor.

As a corollary to their more skeptical attitude toward the literary and social merits of the "new" pornography, some of today's intellectuals are also viewing censorship in a more tolerant light. In the 1920s, most intellectuals followed Mencken's lead and greeted the mere suggestion of censorship with derisive contempt. This is not the case today. The ridicule is now more often directed at the "muddleheaded sentimentalism" (Sidney Hook) or "destructive nihilism" (George P. Elliott) of those who oppose censorship. "[I]n social life the moral criterion has primacy over all other values," Hook declares rather sententiously, "and therefore can legitimately mediate and set limits to them." Elliott firmly believes that even for adults the "decent hypocrisy" of "unenforced laws" should be retained to keep the consumption of pornography furtive and clandestine. Pamela Hansford Johnson, concluding her gruesome account of the moors atrocities, cries: "What price would we pay to prevent the torturing of one helpless child? The price of restricting art? I don't answer this question. I simply ask it."

Perhaps the most outspoken champion of cnesorship among the figures I have mentioned is Ernest van den Haag, professor of social philosophy at New York University. "If we induldge pronography, and do not allow censorship to restrict it," he asserts, "our society at best will become ever more course, brutal, anxious, indifferent, de-individualized, hedonistic; at worst its ethos will disintigrate altogether." Such apocalyptic prophecies are of course difficult to refute, but the scanty evidence which is available suggests that Mr. van den Haag has overstated his case. In June 1967, for example, the Danish Parliment, by overwhelming vote, abolished *all* legal barriers against printed obscentiy. The result has been a startling *decline* in the criculation of pornography—more then 50%, according to some reports.[5]

Not all the critics of pornography share the sympathy for censorship. Susan Sontag, while professing herself "uncomfortable" about the increasing availability of pornography, enters the explicit disclaimer that she is willing to express her views only "in the privacy of serious intellectual debate, not in the courts." Bu even those who reject censorship tend to do so for narrowly pragmatic reasons, rather then on the sweeping ideological grounds of former years. George Steiner, for example, notes in passing that censorship is futile because "those who really want to get a hold of a book will do so somehow"—hardly a ralling cry to send libertarians to the barricades.

Clearly, then, the issues bening debated today are ones about which serious-minded persons may differ. Having read many books, polemical essays, legislative acts, and judicial opinions on the subject of censorship and the First Amendment, I confess that I have not yet resolved the issue to my own satisfaction. But perhaps such a final resolution is undesirable. Perhaps the wisest postion *is* the uncertain one, in which one remains deeply committed to literary freedom, yet *not quite*, willing to subordinate all other considerations to even so high a good as this.

I do, however, find myself skepical of those critics like Pamela Hansford Johnson who postulate a direct casual link between pornography and gross anti-social behavior. Despite the "common sense" appeal of this belief, I do not think it has yet been empiri cally proved. As Richard Schechner points out, it tends to identify as cause and effect that are in fact two symptoms. Those who speak of a more general deadening of sensitivity and debasement of language seem to me much more persuasive. As Gore Vidal suggests, perhaps the worst thing to be said about the reading of pornography is that it leads to the reading of more pornography. If this is true, are we really faced with a problem which demands massive legal remedies?

One of the thorniest problems facing those who advocate censorship is the practical one. If censorship is not to do more harm than good, it must be administered in the most careful and sensitive fashion. Yet the very people most qualified to render such judgments are precisely the ones most unwilling to be identified with censorship. When *Last Exit to Brooklyn* was recently suppressed in England, the author of a slashing review of Selby's novel in *Time* was shattered to learn that his piece had been quoted to good effect by the prosecution at the trial. Both Sidney Hook and George P. Elliott propose to resolve this dilemma by setting up panels of distinguished citizens—clergy, critics, writers, social workers, etc.—who would assume the censorship burden. Aside from the Constitutional barriers to such an extralegal scheme, the abortive efforts to inaugurate such plans in the 1920s (see Chapter IV) strongly suggest their fundamental impracticality.

We must simply face the fact that while intellectuals discuss the theoretical merits of censorship, it is not the intellectuals who are doing the censoring. Censorship, *as actually practiced in American cities today,* is too often directed against worthwhile publications, while the "brutalizing" works which the intellectuals rightly deplore are left undisturbed. For example, two young men were recently arrested in Northampton, Massachusetts, for peddling *Mother of Voices,* a struggling but well-regarded "underground newspaper" which occasionally makes use of taboo words. It is also intensely critical of the local and national power structures and of the war in Vietnam. The arrests were instigated and loudly applauded by the mayor, a patriotic gentleman and dedicated foe of "Hippies" who is also the owner of "Wally's Spa," a soda and magazine emporium which offers a large selection of trashy tabloids and pornographic paperbacks.

My purpose thus far has been simply to suggest something of the current mood in the United States on the issue of censorship.

Much scattered evidence—from the bench, the legislatures, the intellectual community, and the grassroots level—suggests to me that we may be on the threshold of a period of greatly intensified censorship activity. If this is correct, it would seem worthwhile to pause and examine with some care the last great cycle of suppressive enthusiasm, which reached its peak in the 1920s.

It might be asked if yet another study of book censorship in America is needed. At first glance it does seem that the subject has been fully explored. Yet in my perhaps biased view, many of the existing studies appear superficial, written more to entertain than to promote understanding. Others are wholly polemical, intent upon exposing and discrediting "the censors" in all their many guises. Such works serve a useful purpose, but in pursuing a laudable goal their authors sometimes wander from the path of accuracy. Typically, for example, they portray the founders and supporters of the vice societies as hopeless neurotics or amiable clowns who appear only long enough for their misguided activities and foolish assumptions to be roundly denounced. I can fully understand those who find ridicule the only possible response to the vice-society champions. Having plowed through volumes of their reports, I heartily sympathize with Thomas Beer's comments in *The Mauve Decade* about the "minor moralist" who "challenges no belief, imposes no new value . . ., and ends nowhere." Yet it seems to me that the vice-society supporters do merit reëxamination. They were not quite as absurd as a subsequent mythology suggests.

A further weakness of some of the censorship literature, it seems to me, is its easy assumption that we are moving inexorably toward a "frank" and permissive literary Promised Land where censorship shall be no more. I find this assumption naïve and fundamentally ahistorical. The fact that Maurice Girodias was recently hounded out of Gaullist France after that country had had no censorship prosecutions for more than a century should be enough to cast serious doubt upon the visions of those who foresee a sure and inevitable movement from dark repression to bright permissiveness. Although my own account closes with the censors in defeat and dismay, I would not therefore suggest that this situation was permanent or irreversible.

Other authors—usually lawyers—treat censorship history exclusively as a sub-category of legal history, concentrating narrowly

on the "landmark" judicial rulings which resulted in liberalization of
the obscenity laws. Clearly book-censorship history is, in part, a
record of changing legal formulae, but works which treat it *exclusively* as such, sealing off the courtroom from the rich welter of its
enveloping social milieu, prove singularly thin and unsatisfying to
the person seeking to comprehend the total cultural phenomenon.
Shifting legal standards will be noted in the pages which follow, but
they do not lie at the heart of the study.

My central aim has been to place in historical perspective the
so-called "vice societies" of New York, Boston, and other cities—the
organizations which were the source and target of so much of the
censorship and anti-censorship activity of the 1920s. In the pages
which follow I have tried to trace the circumstances which spawned
these groups, maintained them for decades, and finally destroyed
them.

As a historian, I hope this study will be helpful in illuminating
a significant aspect of America's social and cultural history. As a
believer in an open, rational, and humane society, I hope my account
of an earlier cycle of earnest suppressive effort will provide a certain perspective on, and suggest intelligent responses to, the renewed
demands for censorship increasingly heard today.

IN THE BEGINNING:

Literary Criticism in Cincinnati, 1828–29

On one occasion . . . I passed an evening in company with a gentleman, said to be a scholar and a man of reading; he was also what is called
a *serious* gentleman, and he appeared to have pleasure in feeling that
his claim to distinction was acknowledged in both capacities. . . . To
me he spoke as Paul to the offending Jews; he did not, indeed, shake
his raiment at me, but he used his pocket handkerchief so as to answer the purpose; and if every sentence did not end with "I am clean,"
pronounced by his lips, his tone, his look, his action fully supplied the
deficiency.

Our poor Lord Byron, as may be supposed, was the bull's-eye
against which every dart in his black little quiver was aimed. I had never
heard any serious gentleman talk of Lord Byron at full length before,
and I listened attentively. It was evident that the noble passages which
are graven on the hearts of the genuine lovers of poetry had altogether
escaped the serious gentleman's attention; and it was equally evident
that he knew by rote all those that they wish the mighty master had
never written. I told him so, and I shall not soon forget the look he gave
me.

Of other authors his knowledge was very imperfect, but his criticisms very amusing. Of Pope, he said, "He is so entirely gone by that in
our country it is considered quite fustian to speak of him."

But I persevered, and named "The Rape of the Lock" as evincing
some little talent, and being in a tone that might still hope for admittance
in the drawing room; but, on the mention of this poem, the serious gentleman became almost as strongly agitated as when he talked of Don Juan;
and I was unfeignedly at a loss to comprehend the nature of his feelings,
till he muttered with an indignant shake of the handkerchief, "The very
title!"

At the name of Dryden he smiled, and the smile spoke as plainly
as a smile could speak, "How the old woman twaddles!"

"We only know Dryden by quotations, Madam, and these, indeed,
are found only in books that have long since had their day."

"And Shakespeare?"

"Shakespeare, Madam, is obscene, and thank God, *we* are sufficiently advanced to have found it out!" . . .

> —Mrs. Frances Trollope, *Domestic Manners of the Ameri-
> cans*, Donald Smalley, ed. (Vintage ed., N.Y., 1960), pp.
> 91–92.

ONE

The Vice Societies in the
Nineteenth Century

When Americans of the 1920s grew bored by Mah-Jongg, Lindbergh, or Wall Street, they frequently turned for diversion to the seemingly endless series of book censorship cases which punctuated the decade. D. H. Lawrence, James Branch Cabell, H. L. Mencken, and James Joyce—not to mention Voltaire, Petronius, Boccaccio, and Rabelais—all at one time or another fell under the ban, to a full accompaniment of fervent approval and outraged protest.

Many of these censorship efforts proved upon examination to be the work of self-constituted organizations dedicated to the suppression of vice—particularly when "vice" appeared between the covers of a book. Gradually these vice societies, as they were called, came to typify mindless, prudish hostility

to creative literary endeavor. As these groups became the butt
of ridicule, a somewhat distorted version of their history won
general acceptance. According to this version, Americans until
shortly after the Civil War enjoyed all manner of printed
ribaldry in Edenlike innocence, untroubled by the serpent of
censorship. But then, for reasons never fully explained, misguided groups of fanatics, busybodies, and repressed individuals had banded together to impose on the nation, by a
variety of underhanded maneuvers, a rigid censorship which
harrassed American literature for over fifty dark years.

One may as well grant at the outset that the most famous
early champion of the vice-society movement sufficiently resembles this caricature to lend it a certain plausibility. Anthony
Comstock, who ranks with Thomas Bowdler in that select
company of men whose names have become common nouns,
was a centrally important vice-society figure whom students
of book censorship ignore at their peril. Born in 1844 to devout
Connecticut farm parents, this child of destiny arrived in New
York City in 1867, a Civil War veteran with five dollars in
his pocket. He tried his hand at clerking in a dry-goods store,
but in 1872 realized his true calling when he noticed the
shocking books and pictures his fellow-employees were sur-
reptitiously passing about. Securing the arrest of one purveyor,
Comstock at once began to publicize his awful findings.
Wealthy patrons rallied to his support and in 1873 joined
him in founding the New York Society for the Suppression of
Vice, the organization he led for over forty eventful years
until his death in 1915.

In the course of these four decades Anthony Comstock
earned a permanent niche in the gallery of American folk
heroes. His outlandish appearance—potbelly, thick neck, jut-
ting jaw, mutton-chop whiskers—and vivid prose, lush with
"Base Villains" and "Pathetic and Awful Cases," are legendary.
He was devoid of humor, lustful after publicity, and vastly
ignorant. Still remembered are his impromptu belly-dance
before a roomful of reporters in 1893 (to illustrate the evils
of the Chicago World's Fair) and his 1906 Art Students'

League raid, which culminated in the daring arrest of a fright-
ened young secretary. His 1913 attack on an obscure and
charmingly innocent painting known as "September Morn"
was parlayed into a fortune by shrewd promoters. Even the
genuinely dramatic chapters in Comstock's life had their ludicrous tinge; his enemies once mailed him a package of small-
pox scabs, but the ominous gift proved upon examination
sterile and completely harmless.[1]

Comstock's towering reputation seems in little danger of
fading away. As recently as 1953 Margaret Anderson wrote
that a 1917 issue of her *Little Review* had been "suppressed
by Anthony Comstock." The magazine was censored, all right,
but not by Comstock. In 1917 the venerable vice-hunter had
been in his grave for two years![2]

It seems clear that this man from New Canaan has so
dominated our thinking about book censorship that we must—
regretfully—leave his colorful personality aside in order to
obtain a fresh view of the vice-society movement and the men
behind it. We should be clear about the early history of these
organizations, if only to comprehend fully the magnitude of
their later fall.

The vice-society movement was, in essence, a response
to deep-seated fears about the drift of urban life in the post-
Civil War years. The origin of Comstock's New York Society
for the Suppression of Vice, the first organization of its type
in America, is illustrative. Throughout the nineteenth century,
as today, New York City possessed a magnetic attraction for
ambitious and restless young men from other parts of the
country. The metropolis which held so much promise for
these youths, however, was also somehow threatening. The
familiar sources of guidance and support—family, church,
close-knit community—had been left behind, and often it
seemed that the city offered nothing in their place. Many of
these transplanted provincials went on to amass great fortunes,
but this merely made it more difficult for them to develop

organic ties to the burgeoning metropolis they now called
home. Typical was the attitude of Charles Loring Brace, a
New York businessman turned philanthropist, who in 1855
warned that the thousands of children roaming the streets of
New York must be brought under control lest they join the
ranks of "the great lower class of our city" and "poison society
all around them."[3] One solution offered by Brace's Children's
Aid Society was to transport these street urchins to western
farms where they might enjoy the moral and physical ad-
vantages of a rural upbringing.

The Civil War draft riots which swept New York City in
July 1863 intensified the apprehensions of men like Brace. For
nearly a week mobs armed with hammers, pitchforks, and
bricks roamed the streets, killing eighteen people and sacking
shops, armories, and private houses—including the mayor's.
Federal troops summoned by desperate authorities shot and
killed over 400 demonstrators before a semblance of order
returned to the city. "Nothing that we could say," declared
the 1864 Children's Aid Society report,

> could add to the impressiveness of the lesson furnished by
> the events of the past year, as to the needs and the dangerous
> condition of the neglected classes in our city. Those terrible
> days in July . . . were the first dreadful revelations to many
> of our people of the existence among us of a great, ignorant,
> irresponsible class . . . [and of] the fires of a social revolution
> . . . just beneath their feet.[4]

Even with the return of peace, the memory of this cata-
strophic social breakdown remained vivid. In 1872 Charles
Brace could still ask rhetorically: "Who will ever forget the
marvelous rapidity with which . . . a ruffianly and desperate
multitude . . . crept from their burrows and dens to join in the
plunder of the city . . . ?" A book of 1887 retold the story,
stressing that such "social volcanic forces" had not disappeared
from New York in the intervening years. As late as 1892 the
wartime uprising inspired a children's book which vividly
recreated the "nightmare feeling" which had gripped the city.[5]

The mere possession of great wealth did not immunize one from such anxieties—quite the contrary!—but it did suggest possible means of combatting the threatened disorder. Perhaps money and pooled social influence could create some substitute for the shared values and common moral code which had bound together the communities where many wealthy New Yorkers had grown up, but which seemed missing from the great, seething city. From such a train of thought, only partially articulated, sprang the New York Society for the Suppression of Vice.

The immediate impetus was an 1866 Y.M.C.A. survey of New York's young workingmen which described the rootless anonymity of those who once would have lived "directly under the eye" of their employers but who now resided in rented rooms and boardinghouses, devoid of restraint or guidance. As evidence of their abandoned lives the report mentioned not only their weakness for poker and prostitutes, but also for "vile weekly newspapers" and "licentious books." To fight at least two of these evils, the Y.M.C.A. at once launched a campaign for a stricter state obscenity law and in 1872, under the added impetus of young Comstock's fervor, created a committee for the suppression of vice. In 1873 this committee became an independent organization possessing an impressive charter from the New York legislature.[6] Later that year a group of ministers gathered in Boston's historic Park Street Church to organize the New England Society for the Suppression of Vice, a body which was to win immortality as the New England Watch and Ward Society, the name it adopted a few years later. Similar groups soon appeared in St. Louis, Chicago, Louisville, Cincinnati, and San Francisco.[7] The vice-society movement had been launched.

If the founders of these organizations were moral fanatics, as the later mythology had it, they were at least highly successful ones. J. P. Morgan and the copper magnate William E.

Dodge are merely the best known in a list of New York Vice
Society incorporators that reads like a *Who's Who* of the day—
bankers, attorneys, a realtor, a book publisher, the proprietor
of a leading metropolitan newspaper, even a well-known
ophthalmologist.[8]

The first president of the New York Vice Society, who
served until his death in 1898, was Samuel Colgate, head of the
family's New Jersey soap business. Other early officers included
Alfred S. Barnes, a native of New Haven who had become a
successful New York textbook publisher; Killaen Van Rensselaer, scion of one of the state's most prestigious families; and
William C. Beecher, a lawyer of Connecticut background and
the son of Henry Ward Beecher.[9]

The most influential of the founders, a man in many ways
typical of the group, was Morris Ketchum Jesup. Forty-one
years old in 1873, Jesup was a native of Westport, Connecticut,
where he had grown up in a strict and devout home, deeply
influenced by his grandfather, a Congregationalist minister.
His father was wiped out in the Panic of 1837 and died soon
after, whereupon his mother brought the family to New York
City. Jesup went to work at the age of twelve, and by 1873
(the year the vice society began) was well launched on the
career as a merchant, banker, and railroad financier which
made him a multimillionaire and in 1899 won him the presidency of the New York State Chamber of Commerce. Jesup
was not only the largest single contributor to the Vice Society
and a vice-president until his death in 1910, he was also
Comstock's unfailing friend, adviser, and confidant.[10]

Such men, of course, were *not* abnormal by any meaningful definition of the word, but simply representative figures
of their time. In the full vigor of early middle age in the 1870s,
most of them had been bred in the pious atmosphere of a
small town or farm, often in families dominated by the
ministerial strain. Faced with the apparent lack of cohesiveness
in a rootless urban population, they yielded to the plausible
notion that by money and influence they could impose upon

their present "neighbors" the moral precepts and taboos that had pervaded their own earlier years.

A similar pattern emerges in other cities. The founder and principal backer of Cincinnati's Western Society for the Suppression of Vice was William J. Breed (1835–1908), a native of the fishing village of Fairhaven, Massachusetts, who came to Cincinnati as a young man and made a fortune manufacturing metallic burial cases and undertakers' supplies.[11] In Boston a comparable group of successful young businessmen rallied behind the Watch and Ward Society—the head of the city's Central Bank was an early president, but in the New England organization the clerical element was more directly in evidence. Early vice-presidents included Phillips Brooks, famed rector of Boston's Trinity Church; Edward Everett Hale, an equally distinguished Unitarian divine; and the presidents of Yale and Dartmouth and four other New England colleges—preachers all.[12] The dominant figure in the Watch and Ward Society, and Boston counterpart to Morris K. Jesup, was Frederick Baylies Allen, a highly respected Episcopal priest who served for a time as Phillips Brooks's assistant at Trinity Church and then founded the Episcopal City Mission, which he headed for many years. (He was also, interestingly enough, the father of Frederick Lewis Allen, the sophisticated editor and social chronicler of the Jazz Age.)[13]

The money which financed the vice societies came from families whose social standing matched that of the founders. The Watch and Ward contributors' list for 1889—to pick a year at random—is almost a roll call of the Brahmin aristocracy,[14] including such names as:

Abbott	Cabot	Farnsworth	Lawrence
Ames	Coolidge	Fletcher	Lee
Appleton	DeWolf	Forbes	Leverett
Beebe	Dexter	Ginn	Lodge
Bradford	Eliot	Holmes	Loring
Bunker	Endicott	James	Lowell

Lyman	Phelps	Sewell	Tufts
Paine	Pickering	Shattuck	Thorndike
Palfrey	Pierce	Shaw	Weld
Peabody	Saltonstall	Thayer	Wigglesworth

The fears troubling such people are evident throughout the vice-society literature. "Into this great city comes a vast crowd of people daily. What becomes of them? Where do they go?" asks a vice-society speaker in Boston.

> Young men and young women come from the country. They are known in the community where they have always lived; everyone recognizes them, and that knowledge of them is a kind of restraint. . . . When they come to the city that whole bulwark is swept away. They are lost in the crowd.

In New York, William E. Dodge suggested to his Vice Society colleagues that they had been "raised up by Providence to look after particular matters in which citizens are deeply interested, but which they feel powerless to control."[15]

Not all these apprehensions were externally directed. The vice-society backers were uneasy also about their own families. Would the temptations of wealth seduce their children from the stern morality by which they themselves had been reared? Here again the vice society, with its unqualified commitment to the traditional standards, offered reassurance. Men like Frederick Allen seemed the very embodiment of old-fashioned rectitude, while Anthony Comstock's whole manner reminded his wealthy patrons of their youthful piety. His very prayers, writes his minister and laudatory biographer, exuded "the simple, childlike Christian faith that the New England boy breathed in at his mother's knee."[16] Comstock's greatest asset, and the quality which helped him keep the loyalty of his supporters through all his bumbling escapades, was the way in which he personified the unambiguous moral code of an earlier day. He sensed this strength and did not hesitate to unleash stern warnings upon his own supporters. "Elegant dress, lavish expenditure, proud position, and arrogant ways—none of them makes a pure mind, a noble character, nor prevents the evils of lust from exerting themselves upon the inner nature," he thundered. "Those who have money to gratify every wish and hide their crookedness are often the ones most susceptible to these influences." "Parents are mourning," Comstock wrote elsewhere, "over the distaste of their children for all that is sensible and useful."[17]

With their blue-ribbon backing as a recommendation, the vice societies won influential support. In New York City the major newspapers, including the *Tribune* and the *Times* (both before and after its purchase by Adolph Ochs in 1896), were generally approving. In 1876 the mayor attended a vice-society gathering, contributed $100, and offered best wishes "in words as earnest as they were simple and unaffected."[18] In Boston, the influential and socially impeccable *Transcript* warmly endorsed the Watch and Ward Society. "We have been especially gratified at the manner in which our work . . . has been regarded by the community," reported the Reverend Mr. Allen in 1895.[19]

This is not to suggest that the vice societies were ever universally popular. The tighter postal obscenity law of 1873 (passed after vigorous lobbying by Comstock) generated some pained newspaper editorials, and the grim intensity of Comstock's personal vendettas against obviously well-intentioned sexual reformers like Ezra H. Heywood gave rise to sporadic protest.[20] The sharpest attacks came from the National Liberal League founded by Colonel Robert G. Ingersoll in 1876, and the National Defense Association established three years later to "investigate all questionable cases of prosecution under what are known as the Comstock laws, State and National, and to roll back the wave of intolerance, bigotry and ignorance which threatens to submerge our cherished liberties."[21] By 1878 Ingersoll had 50,000 signatures on a petition demanding repeal of the postal obscenity law as "unconstitutional . . ., ill-advised, contrary to the spirit and progress of our age, and almost certain in the end to defeat any beneficial objects intended."[22]

Despite their ringing words, these movements never won

a significant following. Ingersoll's support came principally
from the militant agnostics whose ideas he championed. His
petition, presented to the House of Representatives, was buried
in committee and promptly forgotten.[23] Whatever the cumulative effect of this undercurrent of anti-vice-society sentiment,
it had little noticeable impact upon the public favor enjoyed
by these organizations in the closing decades of the nineteenth
century. When Comstock in 1891 prosecuted the editor of
Christian Life for some now-forgotten editorial lapse, the influential *Woman's Journal* chided him—but most gently, "because the objects of the [Vice] Society are so excellent and its
general work so valuable."[24]

   While the day-to-day vice-society chores were performed
by salaried functionaries—Comstock in New York and the
dimmer Henry Chase in Boston—the eminent founders, officers, and financial angels always hovered in the background.
By assiduously publicizing the names of these persons, the
vice societies constantly reminded the public of the pooled
social influence which underlay their efforts. In any court test
the presumption was in their favor (as evidenced by a conviction rate of well over 90% throughout this period),[25] but
rather than depending merely on the law, the vice societies
preferred a more subtle blend of legal pressure and informal
coercion. In the words of a founder, they tried to "frown
down and drive away" the evils of city life.[26] The vice society,
one might say, was the institutional embodiment of the dis-
approving stare.
   An early Watch and Ward campaign against crime books
and "degrading" magazines like the *Police Gazette* is illustrative. In the opening skirmish in 1879, a petition pointedly
suggesting a literary cleanup of railway stations was signed by
300 "leading citizens" and sent to all the railroads operating
in New England. The offending books and periodicals were at
once withdrawn. The vice society's next target was the corner

news-vendor. In 1880 the Massachusetts legislature passed a Watch and Ward bill prohibiting the sale of publications "manifestly tending to corrupt the morals of youth." In 1885, to supplement this measure, the vice society drew up a still more stringent bill that forbade the sale to minors of books or magazines featuring "criminal news, police reports, or accounts of criminal deeds, or pictures and stories of lust or crime." The bill even outlawed the *display* of such vaguely defined publications *"within the view* of any minor child." The Watch and Ward called for "the earnest personal effort of the best citizens" on behalf of this amendment, and in 1886 reported that thanks to the intervention of "many distinguished citizens" the bill had been enacted into law. Under this Draconian statute the vice society in 1892 obtained convictions and heavy fines against seven hapless Boston and Lowell booksellers, and at once notified all Massachusetts bookdealers that sale of the condemned titles would bring a similar fate.[27]

For a time, at least, purity reigned. By a subtle combination of social pressure, legislation, and selective court action, the vice society had imposed an effective statewide control. "[T]he chief value of these convictions," commented Frederick Allen, "is not in the fact that a few individuals are punished . . . but in the fact that others throughout New England reading the account in the daily papers are deterred from doing the same." "Wherever purity enters," noted another Watch and Ward speaker complacently, "it helps to purify . . . the whole country, and gives a new tonic to every part."[28]

A little incident related in the Watch and Ward report for 1899 similarly illustrates the importance of informal social pressure in achieving vice-society goals:

> A hawker was selling upon the streets a very improper picture, an advertisement of a certain brand of cigarette. The [Watch and Ward] agent, judging from past experience, felt that any effort to prevent it would be useless, till several respectable gentlemen . . . complained of it. The agent replied: "If I can have the support of such men I may hope for success."

By carefully deploying the influence at their command,
the vice organizations achieved impressive results against the
suggestive pictures, obscure erotic books, and ephemeral crime
magazines they had set out to combat. As early as 1885 the
Watch and Ward reported that obscene books had been "sub-
stantially suppressed." In 1899 it added that the struggle
against improper, if nonindictable, publications had also been
won, "nothing further being needed but constant watchful-
ness."[29] Success was never so complete in New York City,
but there, too, gratifying results were achieved.

Surprising as it may seem to a later generation, the vice-
society movement was initially welcomed as a natural and
valued expression of the late-nineteenth-century philanthropic
impulse. One can understand that Anthony Comstock's tireless efforts to expose a variety of mail frauds, crooked gambling
schemes, and dishonest advertisements should have won praise
from everyone except the shady characters whose nefarious
plans were frustrated,[30] but it is also a fact that the vice-society
activity which later aroused such bitter opposition—the suppression of "obscene" books, magazines, and newspapers—
won broad and enthusiastic support from precisely those groups
and individuals who are usually thought of as having represented a valuable strain of social awareness in a hurly-burly
generation often marked by a heedless disregard of human
values. The New York Vice Society was regularly listed
in the New York Charities Directory; Anthony Comstock
was discussed favorably in the Encyclopedia of Social Reform
in 1898; and in 1897 the National Mothers' Congress (fore-
runner of the P.T.A.) respectfully heard Comstock's address on
the baneful effect of impure literature on children. In 1884
the Woman's Christian Temperance Union (still in this period
a wide-ranging reformist organization) gave Comstock a warm
reception at its national convention, having the year before set
up a Department for the Suppression of Impure Literature.[31]

In Boston, the Watch and Ward Society and its efforts to "cleanse our common life" won high praise in 1898 from Francis G. Peabody, the Harvard professor known for his innovative course in social ethics. Peabody compared the vice-society movement, in its emphasis on collective action by concerned private citizens, with the Abolitionist crusade of the generation before, finding both movements typical of "the American way . . . in social reform." The Watch and Ward, he said in a pungent metaphor, was like a sewer "unobtrusively working underground, guarding us from the pestiferous evil which at any time may come up into our faces, into our homes, into our children's lives."[32]

The affinity between the vice-society movement and the broader current of urban philanthropy is evident in the wide-ranging reform interests of the founders. To them, vice-society work seemed a perfectly natural corollary to their efforts on behalf of prison reform, children's aid, and poor relief. Cornelius Agnew, the New York ophthalmologist, for example, was also the founder of two hospitals, president of the New York City school board, and a trustee of the state institution for the insane at Poughkeepsie. Another New York Vice Society founder is remembered (dimly) as the man who persuaded Manhattan to establish a street-cleaning department. And Morris Jesup, Comstock's great patron, greatly reduced his business activity in 1884 to devote himself to such charities as the Slater Fund for the Education of Freedmen, the Five Points House of Industry, and the New York Institute for the Deaf and Dumb. He is primarily known today as the founder and million-dollar benefactor of the American Museum of Natural History.[33]

William J. Breed, the Cincinnati coffin maker and vice-society champion, had a noteworthy career in philanthropy, beginning with his Civil War work with the Christian Commission and continuing through the 1880s and 1890s with long service as president of the Cincinnati Associated Charities. "He was born to wealth and to a place in the com-

munity, and he shirked none of the responsibilities that were
thus put upon him"—so noted his Commercial Club obituary
approvingly.[34]

A similar catholicity of reform interest pervaded the
Watch and Ward Society, on whose executive committee sat
men who were at the same time busily helping the poor and
needy through workingmen's housing movements, free clinics
and dispensaries, and adult-education programs.[35] Frederick
B. Allen, for his part, was a veritable Paul Bunyan of philanthropy. He established not only the Episcopal City Mission,
but also Sailors' Haven in nearby Charlestown, St. Mary's
Home for Sailors in East Boston, "Mothers' Rest" at Revere
Beach, the Massachusetts Prison Reform Association, and
numerous children's playrooms in Boston's North End.[36]

Such were the stalwarts of the vice-society movement in
the nineteenth century. With considerable justice the Reverend
Dr. Raymond Calkins, who became active in the Watch and
Ward Society in the 1890s, has characterized his colleagues
as "some of the most intrepid as well as the most intelligent
social workers whom I have ever known."[37]

The vice-society activists themselves had little doubt that
they were acting as an "enlightened civic conscience." The
Watch and Ward, proudly proclaiming itself a "philanthropic
association," declared:

> [W]hile others endeavor to remedy the effects of crime, we
> strive to remove the causes. . . . [E]very successful blow at
> immoral literature, the brothel, or the gambling-hell goes far
> to remove the necessity for the hospital, the asylum, and the
> charity home. . . .[38]

To the few who challenged their activities on libertarian
grounds, they merely offered the familiar reformist argument:
"[P]rivate interests must be subservient to the general interests
of the community."[39]

Perhaps the author of an obituary tribute to Frederick
Allen best summed up the outlook which could turn men of
Allen's calibre into staunch vice-society champions:

Those who injured others for their selfish gain aroused his burning indignation. It was this passion for justice which led him to organize and serve the Watch and Ward Society. . . . He would do what he could to see that everyone had his rightful heritage of a clean and wholesome environment.[40]

In 1929, during a bitter book-censorship case involving the Watch and Ward, a young district attorney declared scornfully:

It is inconceivable, with all the misery that exists in every city, that contributors, instead of bestowing funds on the poor and unfortunate, consider it their duty to contribute to a private organization that hires paid snoopers to watch over the morals of the general public.[41]

His was the voice of a brash generation that did not remember the days when the vice societies had been looked up to as leaders in the fight against misery, crime, and social injustice.

A recent book about censorship discusses the founding of the vice societies under the heading: "Tragedy Comes to American Literature."[42] Some evidence does support the view that these much-maligned organizations had a stranglehold over late-nineteenth-century literary expression. In 1882, for example, when a Boston district attorney, prodded by the Watch and Ward, complained about a planned edition of Walt Whitman's *Leaves of Grass*, the offending publisher, James R. Osgood, simply cancelled his contract with the poet. One discerns the hand of Comstock, similarly, in an 1890 postal ban on a newspaper serialization of Tolstoy's *Kreutzer Sonata*, a book about prostitution.[43]

In general, however, the vice societies during these years paid scant attention to books published for general circulation by known houses. Although they occasionally indulged in sweeping verbal assaults on "modern novels," their actual suppressive attempts were usually limited to furtively circulated erotica such as *The Lustful Turk* and to the troublesome stream of "vulgar" and "degrading" crime books and magazines.

These attacks were not thought particularly oppressive or alarming—except, of course, by those unlucky enough to be directly affected—because the vice societies, the literary community, and society's influential upper stratum were in sweet accord as to what constituted a "bad book." The nation's fictional fare in this period was largely determined by a small and ingrown group of venerable publishing houses supported by an interlocking network of powerful critics and literary monthlies. Men like Richard Watson Gilder of *Century Magazine* and Henry Mills Alden at *Harper's* were bulwarks of a code which permitted only coy hints that a physical attraction might exist between the sexes. "A painted girl glanced at him as he moved away," was enough to bring the editorial blue pencil—wielded in this instance by Alden—rapidly into action. Walter E. Houghton, in his perceptive study of Victorian thought, has suggested that in the nineteenth century, with its social turmoil, economic conflict, and industrial upheavals, "the home" provided the sole haven of peace, security, and stability and thus had to be preserved—both in reality and in literature—at all costs. The resultant effort to purge books of any erotic aspect, he writes, "was natural enough at a time when so white a purity was demanded that only extreme measures seemed capable of preserving it from taint or corruption." The result is summed up in George Moore's bitter comment about Britain in the 1880s: "Respectability has wound itself about society, a sort of octopus, and nowhere are you quite free from one of its suckers."[44]

The genteel literary code was reaffirmed with tiresome regularity by the panjandrums of American society in the Gilded Age. Good literature, explained the United States Commissioner of Education in 1897, is that which "educates man's insight into the distinction of good from evil, reveals to him his ideals of what ought to be, and elevates the banner of his march toward the beautiful good and the beautiful true."[45] Some years before, Julia Ward Howe, perhaps the most famous and beloved woman of her day, had offered a similarly inspiring, if nebulous, definition. Literature, she declared, "must bring pure and beautiful ideals to . . . the human mind. The brutal, the violent, the excessive, do not need to be increased and multiplied in the pages of a book. . . . All that is loud, violent, harsh, extravagant does damage to the public. . . ." "[I]t becomes the guardians of society to keep a watchful eye upon the press," Mrs. Howe assured her audience, the prestigious members of the Association for the Advancement of Women. "It becomes the faithful and good everywhere to league together against the evil and unscrupulous agencies which corrupt the current of literature, and through it the mind of the age. . . . I can imagine nothing more important than the careful and rigid enforcement of the [obscenity] laws. . . ." A feminist as well as a purity champion, Mrs. Howe had only one implied complaint against the vice societies: they were dominated by men. "[W]omen should have their part in the guardianship of the press," she said. "They will be more strict and scrupulous than the average of the other sex. . . ." Evangelists from Finney to Moody denounced improper novels, and the influential arbiter of etiquette Mrs. H. O. Ward declared that in good society "the flashy novels, the unclean novels, the novels that glow with the fires of impure passions, are to be relentlessly proscribed." Physicians were in agreement with this judgment. Dr. Abraham Jacobi, who served as president of both the New York Academy of Medicine and of the American Medical Association in the course of a distinguished career, was convinced that dime novels were among the significant causes of crime, and the highly respected Elizabeth Blackwell, America's first woman M.D., wrote in a book of advice to parents:

> The dangers arising from vicious literature of any kind cannot be overestimated by parents. . . . The permanent and incalculable injury which is done to the young mind by vicious reading, is proved by all that we know about the structure and methods of growth of the human mind.

The Comstock organization, Dr. Blackwell added, was doing noble work in combatting this evil.[46]

Although there were a few rare exceptions (some of which loom large in retrospect), the vast majority of authors worked comfortably within these limitations. As for the occasional transgressor, he was usually dealt with by the publishing fraternity itself. When a chapter of Henry James's translation of a Daudet novel was omitted from a *Harper's* serialization, Henry Mills Alden explained disarmingly to the puzzled James that since some readers might have taken offense he had simply followed the "usual rule in such a case" and dropped the chapter altogether. A Scribner's editor wrote in the same vein about some "questionable" passages in Gorky. "[T]he fact that they suggest debate," he told the translator, "is of itself enough to menace misconception, and we feel inclined to omit this episode." And in an 1889 rejection letter William S. Walsh of Lippincott's explained that the manuscript's frankness would have made it a "dangerous experiment, commercially speaking." "I am very much afraid," he concluded, "we shall have to go back to the conventional lies of modern fiction and leave such books . . . to other publishers." Who these others were to be, he did not specify.[47]

Even those writers who seemed most contemptuous of the code remained powerfully under its sway. Mark Twain could boast flippantly that Louisa May Alcott's famous attack on *Huckleberry Finn* ("If Mr. Clemens cannot think of something better to tell our pure-minded lads and lasses, he had better stop writing for them") would boost sales by 25,000 copies, but the author of the ribald classic *Conversation, As It Was by the Social Fireside in the Time of the Tudors* was the same man who earnestly advised his sweetheart to avoid *Gulliver's Travels* and *Don Quixote* so as to remain "untainted, untouched even by the impure thoughts of others." Twain could entertain a male audience in Paris with "Some Thoughts on the Science of Onanism" while fuming in his private journal that a Titian Venus at the Louvre was "bestial" and "grossly obscene."[48]

The fate of the early exponents of naturalistic fiction offers further testimony to the power of the genteel standard. *Maggie: A Girl of the Streets* was rejected by several publishers, including Harper's and Century, before Stephen Crane himself in 1893 printed a small and quickly forgotten pseudonymous edition. Only after the success of *The Red Badge of Courage* did Appleton's agree to publish *Maggie*, and then not until the language had been toned down. "I have carefully plugged at the words which hurt," Crane wrote his editor in 1896, while this expurgation was in progress. "[T]he book wears quite a new aspect. . . ." Even this purified version was severely criticized, the *Library Journal* assailing its "imbruted vulgarity."[49]

The familiar story of Theodore Dreiser's discouraging early experiences as an author is another case in point. Dreiser's first novel, *Sister Carrie*, was accepted for publication in 1900 by Walter Hines Page of Doubleday, but when the redoubtable Frank Doubleday (and his even more redoubtable wife) read the proofs upon returning from a European holiday, they were repelled. "The feeling has grown upon us," Page dutifully informed Dreiser, that *Sister Carrie* would debase the Doubleday imprint. "[T]o be frank," he wrote, "we prefer not to publish the book, and we should like to be released from my agreement with you."[50] When Dreiser insisted, Doubleday fulfilled the letter of its contract by printing (and quietly storing away) 1,000 copies. Dreiser's efforts to take the book elsewhere were rebuffed by eight leading publishers. ". . . I cannot conceive of the book arousing the interest or inviting the attention, after the opening chapters, of the feminine readers who control the destinies of so many novels," wrote a Harper's editor.[51]

The point is that few of these suppressions, expurgations, and evasions involved the vice societies. With the literary market firmly in the hands of men who shared their background and outlook, the vice-society leaders rarely had to concern themselves with general trade books. Nor did the lesser cogs in the book-distribution machinery present many

problems. "Respectable booksellers give us their sympathy and
cooperation . . . ," observed the Watch and Ward Society in
1886.[52] When the vice societies did stray into the domain of
"respectable" literature, their forays were accepted as salutary.
When the Postmaster General banned *Kreutzer Sonata* in 1890,
Jeanette Gilder, the influential editor of *The Critic,* observed:
"I do not see how he could take any other course. . . . I believe
the book to be harmful in its effect. . . ."[53]

"Book censorship" in the late Victorian era was not primarily a matter of obscenity laws or of suppressive attacks
by specific groups. It was simply the sum total of countless
small decisions by editors, publishers, booksellers, librarians,
critics, and—occasionally—vice societies, all based on a common conception of literary propriety.

This happy unanimity was more apparent than real, however, for, as between the book world and the vice societies,
it was based on fundamentally different points of view. To
the literary community, after all, the genteel code was little
more than a vague sense of the "fitness of things" coupled with
a rough estimate of what the reading public would accept at
any given moment. The average editor or publisher knew a
"bad book" when he saw one, but he didn't waste much time
brooding over precisely what made it bad or what the nature
of its baneful impact might be. The vice-society leaders, by
contrast, feeling that such questions fell within the range of
their professional competence, conscientiously attempted to
answer them. In so doing, they became dangerously addicted
to sweeping generalizations about the horrid effect of improper
books. These assertions soon acquired the status of received
truth, and were documented and elaborated in loving detail.
"[B]ad books are worse, far worse, than bad companions,"
declared a Watch and Ward spokesman. The printed page,
agreed Comstock, was Satan's chief weapon in his effort to
"ruin the human family."[54] In pursuing this sinister goal, de-

clared Comstock, the "Spirit of Evil" made use of sensual
books and art objects to "hang upon the walls of the chamber
of imagery in the heart (of young men particularly) seductive
pictures . . . for secret entertainment." Even the briefest of
stimulating passages could plunge the helpless reader into
that "state of excitement in which principle is overcome by
passion and nothing but opportunity is wanted for unbridled
indulgence." Books, in short, produce lust, *the boon companion of all other crimes*" and source of all manner of wrongdoing, including the dread "secret entertainment." Lust, declared Comstock, in full cry, "defiles the body, debauches the
imagination, corrupts the mind, deadens the will, destroys the
memory, sears the conscience, hardens the heart, and damns
the soul." All these dire sequelae were summed up in the word
"corruption," a mental and spiritual state as different from
purity and innocence as a healthy human body is different
from one "infected with a loathsome disease." To avoid "corruption," only stern measures would suffice: "The mind must
not be permitted to dwell for a moment upon improper subjects. All reading and conversation must be of the most pure
and elevating character."[55]

Persuaded by their own eloquence, the vice societies
gradually evolved a far more grandiose view of their role.
Indecent literature—originally simply one symptom of a threatening social and moral climate in the large cities—now became
the epitome of evil, a Hydra to be attacked from all angles.
Not only "erotic books" but "classics [and] standard literature"
had to be scrutinized for possible taint. As Comstock observed,
"Garbage smells none the less rank and offensive because
deposited in a marble fount or a gold or silver urn."[56]

The sweeping implications of such a view did not become
apparent so long as the vice-society standards and those of
the broader American community remained comparable. In
later years, however, when the prevailing conception of literary
propriety had vastly altered, the vice societies were held fast
in the grip of their own rhetorical excesses and could only

mechanically reiterate archaic and irrelevant jargon. The gap between twentieth-century reality and the world of vice-society rhetoric eventually loomed so large that ridicule became the only possible public response.

Such a day seemed remote indeed, however, as the 1890s drew to a close. Respected as worthwhile philanthropies, ostensibly in tune with the prevailing moral and literary outlook, the vice societies rested secure in national esteem and goodwill. A Watch and Ward speaker, surveying the landscape in 1899, was completely optimistic. "[T]he whole movement stands upon a firm basis in the approval of the best people," he noted. "[I]t has public sentiment behind it, which is heavier than any penalty of law." Looking into the crystal ball, he saw every reason to assume that the "rich people and religious people" of America would continue their invaluable support.[57] His listeners saw little cause to doubt that the dawning century would prove the truth of his hopeful prophecy.

The Vice Societies in the Progressive Era

The surge of enthusiasm for social justice and civic regeneration which swept America in the early years of the twentieth century seemed, at first, a great boon to the vice societies. Their long-standing interest in ridding the cities of moral hazard was fully in tune with the Progressive desire to remedy the evils and injustices piled up through decades of helter-skelter urbanization and industrial growth.

The vice societies had traditionally placed heavy stress on the welfare of the child—"We are fighting . . . to protect the young," the Watch and Ward Society had declared in 1898[1]—and this solicitude proved highly appealing to a generation that worked for child-labor laws, applauded a White House Conference on Children, and created a Federal Children's Bureau. Even the lurid rhetoric of the vice-society

23

ideology seemed less blatant amid the emotional, quasi-re-
ligious fervor of Progressivism.

The link between Progressivism and the vice societies
may seem tenuous in retrospect, but to the reformers of the
day it was real enough. In 1903 Robert A. Woods, Boston
settlement-house leader and social worker, warmly praised
the Watch and Ward Society as "a sort of Moral Board of
Health" that was making a "profound contribution to the work
of every uplifting agency. . . ." Similarly, William Forbush's
The Coming Generation (1912) ranked the New York Vice
Society with child-labor laws and juvenile courts as forces
"working for the betterment of American young people." The
aged Charles William Eliot, lately retired as president of
Harvard, in 1911 offered the ultimate Progressive accolade
when he praised the Watch and Ward as "a thoroughly scientific charity."[2]

At the heart of Progressive reform lay the dual convictions
that human misery and social disorder were rooted in en-
vironmental maladjustments, and that these could be corrected
by men of good will. Books and magazines obviously were as
much a part of the urban environment as were sweatshops
and adulterated food, and if these latter evils were valid
objects of social control, then certainly a movement dedicated
to the surveillance of the printed page was equally defensible.
Implicit here were two assumptions: that "obscenity" was as
dangerous as the other evils against which the reformers
battled, and that its presence could be ascertained with sufficient precision to justify censorship. These assumptions were
rather casually made in the Progressive period. Later, when
statistics, surveys, and elaborate investigation came to be considered essential prerequisites to social action, the difficulty
of defining "obscenity" and of proving its bad effects dampened
the censorship ardor of most social reformers.

For a time, however, the vice societies were welcomed
within the capacious Progressive tent. The president of the
Boston School for Social Workers was only one of a long
succession of reformers who appeared at the annual Watch

and Ward meetings to endorse its work. When E. T. Devine praised the campaign against "salacious literature" at the National Conference of Charities and Corrections in 1906, the evidence suggests that he voiced the feelings of the great majority of his colleagues.[3]

The vice societies, for their part, proved highly skilled at stating their goals in the Progressive idiom. "The old idea of 'charity,'—of giving alms to the poor, healing the sick, providing for the orphan and the aged," declared the Watch and Ward in 1915, "has gradually given way to a larger conception: . . . to prevent . . . the moral diseases which lead to misery and crime." The vice societies (continued this analysis) fully shared this new conception, for they sought "to eliminate from our social system those who for pecuniary profit would pander to the passions of the vicious, provide temptations for the weak, and coin character into tainted money."[4]

The bond between Progressivism and the vice societies involved personnel as well as pronouncements. As the preachers and philanthropic businessmen who had sustained the vice-society movement in its infancy passed from the scene, their places were taken not only by younger men of commerce— John H. Storer and Godfrey Cabot in Boston, for example— but also by reformers who were involved in a great variety of good causes. By 1910 the Watch and Ward's officers included such men as Charles Birtwell, secretary of the Children's Aid Society; William Cole, a social worker at Boston's South End House; Joseph Lee, president of the Playground Association of America; and Edwin D. Mead, founder of the World Peace Foundation.[5] The increasing eccentricity of Anthony Comstock prevented reformers from identifying themselves quite so closely with the New York Vice Society, but Comstock did his best to adapt to the Progressive mood. "[T]here is no work of reform of a higher order . . ." he said of his own labors in 1903.[6]

The branch of Progressive reform most sympathetic to the vice-society movement was that concerned with sexual

morality. As the Progressives gingerly poked into the dark
corners of American life they soon realized that, despite the
emotional "white slave" crusades of the late nineteenth century, prostitution still flourished in the great urban centers.
The Social Evil in New York (1910), *The Social Evil in
Chicago* (1911), and similar reports in many other cities exposed and interminably documented the sordid truth. The
Mann Act of 1910 was one outgrowth of this Progressive
assault on prostitution.[7]

Another was the American Social Hygiene Association,
founded in 1914 to combat prostitution and venereal disease
by compiling accurate statistics on the problem, promoting
stricter legislation, and educating youth about sex and the
dangers of promiscuity. The new organization at once won
impressive support; Charles William Eliot was the first president, and he was succeeded by the head of Northwestern
University.[8]

To the social hygienists, prostitution and social disease
were preëminently *moral* problems. In the words of the president of the Pacific Coast Sex Hygiene Federation, the primary
goal of the movement was to reassert "the control of moral
and spiritual law over sex impulses." And in 1918 the Reverend
William Lawrence, an Episcopal leader and an active social
hygienist, declared: "Defilement of the body drives out spiritual
power: an infected body leads to an infected soul."[9] The
scientific approach to sexual matters was valued only insofar
as it reënforced the moral argument for chastity. "In all
previous effort to safeguard the morality of youth," declared
one social hygienist, "the ethical barrier was alone available"
and "the situation seemed . . . hopeless." But, he concluded
triumphantly, when medical science linked VD with promiscuity, "[s]exual morality, long an ethical ideal, became
grounded upon the most convincing scientific facts."[10]

Rigidly moralistic beneath their scientific façade, the
social hygienists were highly vulnerable to the vice-society
contention that books and brothels were linked in an unholy

alliance. As early as 1882 William W. Sanger had asserted in his monumental *History of Prostitution* that "obscene and voluptuous books" were a factor in the survival of the world's oldest profession, and the social hygienists of thirty years later fully agreed.[11] They invariably couched their own writings in a depressingly dull and impersonal jargon, avoiding any hint that sex might be a source of pleasure, and they expected others to do the same. In his influential *Problems and Principles of Sex Education* (1915), a study of how 948 college men had acquired their sex knowledge, Dr. M. J. Exner included among the "bad" sources any printed matter or conversation that caused "vulgarized or sensualized" thinking or generated "a desire for sexual intercourse." The great need, declared Exner, "is to lift the whole subject into a fine, inspiring atmosphere. . . ."[12] In the same vein, the first annual report of the American Social Hygiene Association urged parents and teachers to "banish prurient curiosity" from the minds of the young "by diverting the imagination to emotions joyous and clean . . ., by inspiring the soul with the highest religious and family and civic ideals."[13]

As had Comstock a generation before, the social-hygiene enthusiasts soon recognized that some of the reading matter in circulation was hardly calculated to arouse emotions joyous and clean. "Probation officers connected with the Juvenile Court testify," reported *The Social Evil in Chicago*, "that a great many delinquent girls have been influenced for evil by improper literature. . . ," A 1914 Wisconsin investigation of the "White Slave Traffic" similarly condemned "suggestive novels" and "plays that suggest immoral conduct and entirely lack an ethical standard."[14] A few years earlier, 400 Chicago ministers and social workers had founded the Illinois Vigilance Association with the dual aims of fighting prostitution and working for "the suppression of indecent pictures, magazines, and books."[15]

President Eliot, in his maiden address before the American Social Hygiene Association in 1914, minced no words on this subject. The A.S.H.A., he said, "should always be ready to take part in the prosecution of men or women who make a profit out of obscene publications. . . ." Following Eliot's lead, *Social Hygiene* included state obscenity laws in its 1916 summary of "Social Hygiene Legislation."[16]

There was no lack of scholarly support for those who took this dire view of questionable literature. The psychologist G. Stanley Hall, in his important 1904 work *Adolescence,* censured "erotic reading" and observed in passing that "legislation is sadly needed for the protection of youth."[17]

As suggested above, the oft-repeated vice-society warnings that bad reading could have direct and alarming physiological consequences seemed timely indeed to the champions of purity who rallied to the social hygiene and antiprostitution banners. As early as 1895 the National Purity Congress (an early mobilization of the antiprostitution forces) had listened respectfully to a speech by Anthony Comstock dwelling on the evils of erotic books. In 1914 Comstock addressed the same body in San Francisco—by now it had become the *International* Purity Congress and Comstock was the official American delegate by appointment of President Wilson—and an eyewitness later reported that of the 4,000 delegates "there were probably not two persons who did not unreservedly share his point of view."[18]

Just as they identified themselves with the wider Progressive impulse, so the vice societies took pains to underline their common bond with the social-hygiene movement. In 1895 the Watch and Ward devoted its annual report to an address entitled "How Shall a Great City Deal with the Social Evil?" In 1909 the Watch and Ward elected G. Stanley Hall as its president—an honor he readily accepted. The New York Vice Society joined in as well. "[W]e heartily commend the work of the national and local Social Hygiene Societies," said the New York organization in 1916, adding that it, too, was dedicated to shielding "the minds of the young and susceptible from those impressions which lead to degrading and devitalizing thoughts and practices."[19]

The many links uniting Progressivism and social hygiene with the vice societies helped maintain their reputation at a high level throughout this period. The contributors' lists of the vice organizations still sparkled with eminent names—as late as 1916, Andrew Carnegie, W. Bayard Cutting, Cleveland H. Dodge, Mrs. Russell Sage, Louis C. Tiffany, John Wanamaker, Joseph H. Choate, Charles Olmstead, and several hundred only slightly less distinguished names adorned the New York Vice Society's list of donors. In Boston, large and fashionable crowds faithfully turned out for the yearly Watch and Ward gathering to hear exhortations from the likes of Julia Ward Howe, former governor Curtis Guild, G. Stanley Hall, President Alice Freeman Palmer of Wellesley, and the ubiquitous Charles W. Eliot. In 1901 the principal address was given by the Reverend Edward Cummings of Cambridge, father of the poet E. E. Cummings.[20]

Undeniably, Anthony Comstock became something of a figure of fun even while the vice-society movement as a whole was held in continued respect. "Comstockery!" was George Bernard Shaw's retort in 1906 after the vice-society champion had ungraciously called him "a foreign writer of filth"—and a delighted public at once incorporated the word into the language.[21] Nevertheless, when the venerable Comstock died of pneumonia nine years later, he was widely eulogized. The *New York Times* reviewed his career in a front-page story and praised him editorially as a "benefactor and a hero" who had "served a good cause with tireless devotion." The *New Republic*, while duly noting that on occasion Comstock had "conspicuously made an ass of himself," lauded the "vast amount of good" he had done. *Survey*, the social-work weekly, agreed: "Viewing the bulk of Comstock's work over forty-seven years," it said, "there is much that every rational being must approve." "No one knew . . . his 'blind side' better than his friends," added *Outlook*, "but in their opinion the

warfare he was waging was much more important than his
blunders of taste, and they stood by him to the end."[22]

As the laudatory tributes to Comstock rolled in, the newspapers noted, in passing, that one John S. Sumner, a thirty-
nine-year-old stockbroker turned lawyer, had been chosen as
his successor. The Episcopal son of a high-ranking naval officer,
Sumner lived on Long Island with his wife and daughter,
indulging his taste for golf and motoring.[23] From all reports
he possessed a remarkably equable disposition, although not
everyone was impressed by the spirit of reasonableness and
good humor which he brought to his new job. (Henry F.
Pringle was later to observe that under attack Sumner's smile
remained "as genial, if as synthetic, as that of a YMCA secretary meeting a squad of doughboys returning uproariously
from a bordello.")[24] The general feeling, however, was that
Sumner gave every promise of carrying on the good work
while avoiding the embarrassing idiosyncrasies of Comstock.

THE VICE SOCIETIES AND
THE LITERARY WORLD

The genteel literary code, though under pressure, remained powerful through the Progressive years. A characteristic and winning spokesman for the dominant viewpoint was
Henry Van Dyke, poet, essayist, critic, Presbyterian minister,
and Princeton English professor. Nearly forgotten today—
except perhaps as the man who gave *The First Christmas Tree*
to the world of letters—Van Dyke was a weighty figure in
pre-First World War America. As a literary arbiter, Van Dyke
threw his influence firmly on the side of books that transcended
the "tangle and confusion" of the mundane world to rise into
a "loftier and serener region." The only enduring literature, he
wrote in 1905, "is that which recognizes the moral conflict as
the supreme interest of life, and the message of Christianity
as the only real promise of victory."[25]

Similar lofty standards prevailed in every corner of the

book world. The publisher J. Henry Harper, while scouting
the idea that he favored "censorship," nevertheless in 1912
dismissed "unwholesome" books as "deserving the severest
censure" and added that if possible they should be "suppressed
altogether." A year later Paul Elmer More, patrician editor of
the *Nation,* sharply criticized writers who failed to recognize
that readers "still require such old themes as home and mother
and love's devotion." Somewhat earlier, an admirer had written
in a similar vein to Alice Hegan Rice, author of the 1901 best-
seller *Mrs. Wiggs of the Cabbage Patch:*

> I am old-fashioned or sentimental or something about books.
> Whenever I read one I want in the first place to enjoy myself,
> and in the next, to feel that I am a little better and not a
> little worse for having read it . . . I do not want people to
> shirk facts, or write what is not so, and it is often necessary
> to dwell on painful things; but I feel that they should be dwelt
> upon in proper fashion and not for the sake of giving a kind
> of morbid pleasure.[26]

In this, as in so many other areas, Theodore Roosevelt neatly
summed up the prevailing spirit of his generation.

As for the librarians of America, a group which was to
play such a significant role in the anticensorship fights of the
later 1920s, they were in this period mainly concerned with
keeping "bad books"—a broad and infinitely flexible category—off their shelves. In 1908 the president of the American
Library Association, Arthur Bostwick, urged the suppression
of all books of an "immoral tendency" and warned that American literature was "menaced" by immigrants whose "standards
of propriety are sometimes those of an earlier and grosser age"
and by the *nouveaux riches* "with little background of heredi-
tary refinement to steady them." The librarian, cried Bostwick,
must declare to this "menacing tide" of books: " 'Thus far shalt
thou go and no farther.' "[27]

Inspired by this Canutelike exhortation, the *Library
Journal* announced a symposium on the question, "What Shall
the Libraries Do About Bad Books?" From librarians across

the country came letters telling how they avoided buying "doubtful" fiction, or of their stratagems for keeping it from the reading public. An Atlanta librarian proudly described how she had placed the novels of "one of the continental authors" in the *Literature* section of the library, "with the idea that this would restrict their use." When the offending books nevertheless gained an "unprecedented popularity," she concluded, they were "removed from the shelves, and will finally be discarded." The Wisconsin Library Commission reported that no book by a "modern degenerate" could find a place in its traveling libraries, while a spokesman for the New York Public Library observed that "immoral" classics were strictly forbidden to anyone requesting them for "unworthy" reasons.[28]

Several years after this survey, one librarian undertook to define more precisely the elusive "bad book" that she and her sisters found so troublesome. Immoral literature, she wrote, is that which "degrades our intellect, vulgarizes our emotions, kills our faith in our kind, and in the Eternal Power . . . which makes for righteousness. . . ."[29] Thus enlightened, librarians continued to guard their patrons from any taint of corruption. As a British visitor observed, "The moral tap must be kept running, the arts can only defy its cleansing at their peril."[30]

With such standards still prevailing, the vice societies' grandiose image of themselves as the moral arbiters of all literature only infrequently had to stand the acid test of practicality. Their day-to-day preoccupation continued to be with the furtive publication and hapless peddler whose obscure fate aroused slight interest or concern. On the rare occasion when a book issued by a known publisher for open circulation *did* transgress the code, the vice societies usually experienced little trouble in suppressing it, as is illustrated by the unhappy fate of three widely differing novels: *Three Weeks, Homo Sapiens,* and *The "Genius."*

Elinor Glyn's frothy romance *Three Weeks* streaked vividly across the gray publishing skies in 1907. Published first in England, it was issued in the United States by Duffield and Company. Sales quickly reached 50,000 copies, and by January 1908 the book was the leading seller in many cities. The plot, improbable in the extreme, involves a fleeting, idyllic Venetian romance between a callow English youth, Paul Verdayne, and a beautiful mysterious woman in her mid-thirties, wife of a dissolute Russian potentate. This description of their first night of love is a fair sample of Mrs. Glyn's prose:

> "Beautiful, savage Paul," she whispered. "Do you love me? Tell me that?"
> "Love you!" he said. "Good God! Love you! Madly, and you know it, darling Queen."
> "Then," said the lady in a voice in which all the caresses of the world seemed melted, "then, sweet Paul, I shall teach you many things, and among them I shall teach you how—to— LIVE."
>
> .   .   .   .   .
>
> And outside the black storm made the darkness fall early. And inside the half-burnt logs tumbled together, causing a cloud of golden sparks, and then the flames leapt up again and cracked in the grate.

The dreamy interlude ended, the unhappy woman returns to her Eastern kingdom where, some months later, she delights the realm by presenting her husband with an heir—her love child. The following summer, about to be reunited with her beloved, she is murdered by her husband in a drunken frenzy.[31]

Reviewers were not particulary scandalized, but neither were they much impressed. "[Y]ou laugh a little and yawn a little and are not shocked at all, but only rather bored by a vulgar and extremely silly story," was a typical verdict.[32] Some readers took comfort in the fact that the heroine did, after all, die for her wrongdoing, but Mrs. Glyn, on a New York promotional trip, explicitly denied that the book's ending implied

divine retribution. "God is above such action," she declared.
"He does not make men pay."[33]

Such a calculated nose-thumbing at the genteel code could
hardly go unchallenged, and the directors of the New England
Watch and Ward Society voted to proceed against the book.
They were encouraged in this course by a Boston municipal-
court judge who assured them that *Three Weeks* would likely
be held obscene if it came to trial in Massachusetts. A warning
notice went out to booksellers, and the novel disappeared from
the shelves.[34]

The publisher showed unusual spunk for the period. He
tried to offer *Three Weeks* for sale by mail, but his advertisements were cancelled by the Boston newspapers after a warning from the Watch and Ward. In February 1908, in a pre-
arranged test case, a Duffield representative named Joseph
Buckley sold a copy of the book to a Boston police officer and
was arrested. A Superior Court jury promptly found him
guilty under the obscenity law, and levied a stiff fine.

On appeal, the conviction was upheld by the Massachusetts Supreme Court in a January 1909 decision that sums
up the current thinking on obscenity. Rejecting the defendant's
claim that such words as "obscene" are impossibly vague, the
court said: "They are common words and may be assumed
to be understood in their common meaning by an ordinary
jury." The further assertion by the defense that Mrs. Glyn's
delicate language saved her from obscenity under any reasonable meaning of the word was also rejected. *Three Weeks*,
said the court, "disclosed so much of the details of the way to
the adulterous bed . . . that not the spiritual but the animal,
not the pure but the impure, is what the general reader will
find as the most conspicuous thought. . . ."[35] The Watch and
Ward Society, reporting this outcome with quiet pride, drew
the obvious conclusion: "Boston has well-defined literary standards, and its average citizen feels himself cultured enough to
apply them in the interests of morals."[36]

Little protest was heard from the literary community

over this banning of a best-seller. "The best newspapers and the best magazines uphold the decision," noted the Watch and Ward. Some months later *Publishers' Weekly* reaffirmed not only "the necessity of a clear-cut stand for decency in literature" but also, with regret, "the occasional necessity of defining that stand in concrete instances."[37] The Massachusetts booksellers most immediately affected were similarly philosophical. Primarily interested in avoiding notoriety, they protested vice-society action if it came without due warning—as in 1903 when the Watch and Ward unexpectedly prosecuted four booksellers for selling Boccaccio and Rabelais[38]—but if the rules of the game were observed, as in the *Three Weeks* case, the bookmen were little troubled by the occasional vice-society suppressions. Soon after the Glyn decision, the Boston booksellers joined the Watch and Ward in a system of "self-censorship" based on blacklists drawn up by the Watch and Ward in consultation with two or three of the most conservative booksellers.[39] This plan, as we shall see, remained in full force well into the 1920s.

In contrast to the Glyn masterpiece, *Homo Sapiens* was anything but a best-seller. Published in the United States in the autumn of 1915, this intense and introspective work by the Polish writer Stanislaw Przybskewski attracted a devoted, but very small, circle of admirers.

Among the readers—if not admirers—was John S. Sumner. On Christmas Eve, 1915, a short notice deep in the *New York Times* reported: "The examination of Alfred A. Knopf, 23 years old, a publisher . . ., was begun before Magistrate Simms in Jefferson Market Court yesterday. . . ."[40] It was as the publisher of *Homo Sapiens* that Knopf had been hailed into court. In Sumner's opinion, the book was obscene. The confrontation in dingy Jefferson Market Court was a portentous one: Knopf, recently out of Columbia, was in his first year as a publisher; Sumner had been installed as secretary of the

vice society only a few months before. Each, in his chosen
field, would go far.

The hearing was brief. Knopf defended *Homo Sapiens*
as a work of art which had been well reviewed and openly
sold. His attorney suggested an adjournment to permit Magistrate Simms to read the book, but Assistant District Attorney
Van Castile protested. "His Honor should not be subjected to
such cruel punishment," he expostulated. "The book is utterly
stupid as well as indecent."[41] An adjournment was arranged,
however, and Knopf's well-connected father contacted his
lawyer, Wilson E. Tipple, who happened also to be a vice-
society director. A subsequent meeting between Knopf and
Sumner resulted in total capitulation by the young publisher.
Knopf withdrew *Homo Sapiens* and melted down the plates,
and in return Sumner withdrew his complaint. In a letter
to *Publishers' Weekly*, Knopf said that the book had been
"smirched," and that he did not deign to satisfy the prurient
demand which had been created. ". . . I will print no further
edition and will accept no more orders for it."[42]

One of the few who paid any attention to the incident was
Margaret Anderson, publisher of the *Little Review* and a
great admirer of Przybskewski. "*Homo Sapiens* will no longer
be circulated in this country," she burst forth excitedly in the
Little Review. "[I]t is the most inexcusably ridiculous thing
that has happened for many months. It is incredible!"[43] Incredible or not, John Sumner had won his first skirmish with
the Borzoi.

The last in this series of prewar vice-society successes
pitted Sumner against a somewhat less pliant antagonist. An
author in Poland could scarcely make effective protest if his
American publisher chose to yield to the censors without a
fight, but Theodore Dreiser, living in New York City and
embittered by his *Sister Carrie* experience, fought back vigor-

ously when his publisher opted for strategic retreat. The outcome, however, was very much the same.

Dreiser's *The "Genius,"* a novel containing large autobiographical elements, was published in 1915 by the John Lane Company, a British firm which had opened an American branch some years before. The book's hero, Eugene Witla, is a commercial artist who achieves success in New York City but, after a nervous collapse, vows to pursue art as a path to self-understanding rather than financial gain. A succession of romantic entanglements punctuate the novel. Marriage proves unrewarding, and Witla reacts to his wife's death in childbirth with something like relief. The book closes on a note of halfhearted resolve and opaque philosophical rumination buttressed by lengthy quotations from Herbert Spencer.

The descriptions of sexual encounters in *The "Genius"* are rather breathless but, by latter-day standards, almost Victorian in their restraint:

> She accepted first the pressure of his arm, then the slow subtlety with which he caressed her. Resistance seemed almost impossible now for he held her close—tight within the range of his magnetism. When finally she felt the pressure of his hand upon her quivering limbs, she threw herself back in a transport of agony and delight.
>
> "No, no, Eugene," she begged. "No, no! Save me from myself. Oh, Eugene!" [etc.][44]

Witla is staggered when one young lady, a concert singer, coolly weighs the pros and cons of having an affair with him.

> To hear an artist of her power, a girl of her beauty, discussing calmly whether she should sacrifice her virtue to love; whether marriage in the customary form was good for her art; whether she should take him now when they were young or bow to the conventions and let youth pass, was enough to shock his still trammelled soul.[45]

It was enough to shock the still-trammelled souls of most reviewers as well. "Passion reduced to the prose of daily entry bookkeeping," thundered *Bookman*. "[P]ersonal details that even a Zola would avoid," sniffed the *Boston Evening Transcript*. "All very realistic—and very depressing and unpleasant," added the *New York Times*. Stuart P. Sherman joined the attack in the *Nation*, and Mrs. Elia W. Peattie, the influential *Chicago Tribune* critic, reviewed the book under the headline: "Mr. Dreiser Chooses a Tom-Cat for a Hero."[46]

In the face of such unanimous critical denunciation, how could the vice societies fail to see their duty? In Cincinnati, the Western Society for the Suppression of Vice and the "Law and Order Committee" of the local church federation, having counted eighty-seven "lewd" pages and seventeen "profane" pages in The *"Genius,"* secured its removal from all the city's bookstores.[47] In New York, meanwhile, John Summer had received in the mail several pages of The *"Genius"* ripped from a library copy by an irate borrower, and on July 25, 1916, he warned J. Jefferson Jones, head of Lane's New York office, that criminal proceedings would begin unless the book was withdrawn. "[F]emale readers of immature mind," he explained later, would be harmed by the "vivid descriptions of the activities of certain female delinquents who do not, apparently, suffer any ill consequences from their misconduct. . . ."[48]

Jones immediately capitulated. He not only banned further shipments of the book, but instructed bookstores to return all unsold copies. Legally, affairs were at an impasse. The mere threat of court action had been sufficient to suppress The *"Genius,"* yet without a trial an authoritative judgment as to its standing under the law could not be secured.[49]

Incensed, Dreiser toyed with the idea of a dramatic gesture. ". . . I may go to jail for mailing a copy," he wrote his friend H. L. Mencken. "Only the hot weather deters me." The heat evidently continued, for Dreiser did not carry out his threat. Instead, he issued a newspaper statement denouncing the "literary reign of terror" by "a band of wasplike censors . . . attempting to put the quietus on our literature which is at last showing signs of breaking the bonds of puritanism. . . ."[50]

Mencken, meanwhile, had brought the matter before the Authors' League of America, an organization founded in 1912 to look after the interests of writers in copyright and royalty matters. Late in August 1916, the League's executive committee voted to condemn the Vice Society and to defend *The "Genius."* Mencken, Dreiser, and Harold Hersey, an Authors' League secretary, collaborated in circulating a protest petition, while Mencken wrote personal appeals to "the more important, respectable, and conservative authors." Of the several hundred who responded favorably, wrote Mencken, many were "painfully seduced into signing by all sorts of artifices."[51]

Many authors refused to sign. Among the abstainers were William Dean Howells, Agnes Repplier, Ellen Glasgow, Hamlin Garland, Brander Matthews, Joyce Kilmer, Mark Sullivan, Rex Beach, George Barr McCutcheon, Owen Johnson, Augustus Thomas, and William Allen White. Indeed, a group of Authors' League dissidents, led by Hamlin Garland, threatened to resign because of the League's involvement in the case. Not for years would the Authors' League again take a stand in a censorship fight.[52]

Even H. L. Mencken, scourge of the comstocks in the 1920s, prudently warned Dreiser against pushing his claims to literary freedom too far. In the midst of the *"Genius"* controversy, Mencken exhorted Dreiser not to publish *The Hand of the Potter*, his recently completed play about sexual perversion and incest, arguing that this would "forfeit the respect of all intelligent persons." Explicit treatment of such themes, Mencken argued, "is banned by that convention on which the whole of civilized order depends." "[T]here are certain rules that can't be broken," he went on, "and I am disinclined to waste time trying to break them when there is so much work to do in places where actual progress can be made."[53] Dreiser was not impressed. "Could Anthony do better . . . ?" he jeered. "Why not have asked me to be safe and sane?"[54]

The "Genius" remained effectively suppressed until well into the 1920s. Its fate, added to that of *Three Weeks* and

Homo Sapiens, offered persuasive rebuttal to any who doubted that the vice societies could, when necessity arose, still act decisively to enforce the teetering genteel taboos.

CLOUDS ON THE HORIZON

The vice societies' satisfaction in these successes was tempered, however, by the emergence of distinct signs that their power was soon to face far more serious challenges.

The publishing world no longer presented the monolithic façade of the 1890s. Despite the fate of Glyn, Pryzbskewski, and Dreiser, their novels *had* appeared under respectable imprints. "Knopf" was only one of a number of unfamiliar names beginning to crop up in the pages of *Publishers' Weekly*. These newcomers—who were to make the 1920s a time of such yeasty ferment in the book-publishing industry—were eager to satisfy the needs of writers and readers who felt increasingly hedged in by the genteel code. "I am told," wrote a *Putnam's* columnist apprehensively during the *Three Weeks* furore, "that the manuscripts that have been received by the publishers of that book since its appearance make even its coarsest pages seem as innocuous as a Sunday School publication."[55] How long could the line be held?

Disregarding all signs and portents, the vice societies clung doggedly to the hoary nineteenth-century ideology in which their entire philosophy was rooted. Imperceptibly, they began to diverge from the mainstream of American thought. The bonds of shared values and common purpose which had linked them to the broader community strained and grew taut. The vice societies' conviction rate remained high, but a rapid increase in the number of prosecutions—300% in Boston from 1903 to 1911—forecasted stormy weather ahead.[56]

Equally disturbing, from the vice-society point of view, was the growing discussion over the legal implications of literary censorship. So long as the genteel code had held full sway, the occasional role of the courts in enforcing it had gone largely unexamined. A dictum uttered in 1868 by Lord Chief Justice Cockburn of Great Britain was cited repeatedly in obscenity cases as a *carte blanche* justifying the suppression of any work considered morally repugnant. The "test" of obscenity, Cockburn had declared, was "whether the tendency of the matter charged as obscenity is to deprave and corrupt those whose minds are open to immoral influences and into whose hands a publication of this sort may fall."[57] As the Victorian era drew to a close, however, such formulaic mumbo-jumbo began to be examined more critically, and the word "censorship"—often prefaced by "prudish" or some other harsh epithet—was heard in the land.

A central figure in this development, indeed the man who did the most to advance this pre-World War One censorship debate, was a now-forgotten lawyer named Theodore Schroeder. Schroeder was born in Wisconsin in 1864, some years after his Lutheran father had fled from Germany in the aftermath of the revolutionary unrest of 1848. His Catholic mother had been disowned for marrying a Protestant, and young Schroeder, absorbing her bitterness, became vociferously anticlerical. As a boy he attended lectures by the agnostic Colonel Robert G. Ingersoll, whose contempt for Anthony Comstock he came to share. Graduating from the law school of the University of Wisconsin in 1889, he moved to Salt Lake City where he at once founded a violently anti-Mormon newspaper, *Lucifer's Lantern*. This publication aroused understandable opposition in Zion and involved its publisher in at least one obscenity prosecution.

Tiring of Utah, Schroeder around 1900 came to New York City, where he devoted the rest of his long life to a single-minded fight for free speech and a free press. In 1911 he founded the Free Speech League to propagate his views. Although its directors included Lincoln Steffens, Hutchins Hapgood, and Brand Whitlock, the League in reality was a one-man operation, its headquarters wherever Schroeder happened to be at any given moment. In a dizzying torrent of books,

pamphlets, articles, and manifestoes, he rang the changes on
the basic theme expressed in his January 1914 *Forum* article:
"Our Prudish Censorship Unveiled."[58]

In his weightiest book, *"Obscene" Literature and Constitutional Law* (1911), Schroeder offers a witty, vigorous, and
remorselessly logical statement of the anticensorship position—
a position totally at variance with the prevailing consensus.
Rejecting Cockburn's ponderous certitudes and Comstock's
lurid rhetoric, Schroeder ridicules the notion that "obscenity"
causes moral decay. Obscenity exists, he says, "only in the
minds of those who believe in it." He points out the absurdity
of the fact that certain words describing wholly normal human
functions should be categorized as lewd. Why does no one
object to the phrase "the initial act for the investiture of a
human life," he asks innocently, while its four-letter equivalent
is the *ne plus ultra* of obscenity?[59] Pursuing the argument,
Schroeder pronounces all obscenity laws in violation of the
First Amendment because they discriminate "according to the
subject matter discussed" or "according to differences of literary style in expressing the same thought." Postal censorship
he dismisses as an effort "to use the mails as a means to control
the psycho-sexual condition of postal patrons." The only
grounds for banning a book, he concludes, should be if a
specific illegal act can be proven to have been directly incited
by a reading of that book.[60]

Fascinated by his theories, Theodore Schroeder rarely
involved himself in specific censorship cases, and his massive
output on a single theme arouses a suspicion of monomania.
Nevertheless, his exhaustive formulation of the anticensorship
position helped give shape to a discontent that was beginning
to stir in this prewar period. If few of his readers were willing
to accept his suggestion that the obscenity laws should simply
be junked, many realized for the first time that the issue was
considerably more complex than their parents had imagined.
The arsenal of libertarian arguments carefully assembled by
Schroeder lay ready for battle when the time should come, and

his probing dissection of the vice societies' activities and assumptions helped bring that time steadily nearer.

Gradually, the vice societies were forced to recognize the fact that beneath the reassuring evidences of continued power and influence were disturbing signs that all was not well. The network of institutions and individuals with which they shared a common outlook no longer held absolute sway. Once-impregnable standards were beginning to totter. "As the twentieth century swings into its second decade," declared a Watch and Ward speaker in 1909, "the tone of much of its clever fiction is depressing; it is unbelieving; it seems to be written in a spirit of revolt against the old ideals of chivalry and chastity."[61]

To meet this situation the vice societies stiffened themselves with muscular exhortation. "We need moral quarantine, and we need men who have got the stuff to enforce it, in spite of public ridicule," exclaimed a vice-society speaker in 1906.[62] *Force* began to assume a more important place in their thinking. "The police today are better friends than they have ever been," the Watch and Ward secretary noted with satisfaction in 1903. Several years later, with unconscious irony, he declared: "This has been in some respects one of our most successful years. We have prosecuted more cases than in any other year of our history." By 1909 the vice-society leaders were thinking of themselves as "sentinels on the walls . . . and outposts in the trenches." Even the normally self-assured Frederick B. Allen of the Watch and Ward Society began to speak harshly of "slick lawyers who get large fees for doing the devil's dirty work. . . ."[63]

Sensing their growing isolation, the vice-society champions tried to persuade themselves that this was merely the price of moral leadership. "In order to keep the moral average even as it is, some people must be above the average. Now is it any shame to be above the average? Don't we need some people to keep up high standards . . . ?" So asked a vice-society spokesman rather plaintively in 1906.[64]

Clearly, the vice societies were in no mood for legal
quibbles. Their response to Schroeder and other critics was to
profess total incredulity at the idea that book censorship could
involve constitutional issues. "When we interfere with the
murderer and lock him up for life . . ., that is an interference
with personal liberty, if you like, but we call it the salvation
of society," asserted Professor William T. Sedgwick of M.I.T.
defending book censorship in a 1906 Watch and Ward address.[65] Another speaker that year dismissed the matter with
an equally facile analogy:

> We are quarantined today by the state against all germs of
> disease that hurt our bodies. But there are other germs. . . .
> We call them words and ideas. They enter through the eye
> and the ear and feed upon the brain-cells and destroy the
> very tissue of the immortal soul.[66]

"The cry is 'Personal liberty endangered!' " mocked a Watch
and Ward speaker in 1908. "Capitalized vice means by that
cry . . . that it is in danger of losing its freedom to enslave
the souls of men."[67]

Murderers, germs, "the very tissue of the immortal soul"—
such imagery was so much more satisfying than the prosaic
reality of a banned book! These arguments, feeble and irrelevant as they often were, constituted the vice societies' sole
answer to criticism. Unwilling to face the issue of censorship
candidly, they retreated, squidlike, behind an inky stream of
arguments and analogies that became less persuasive with each
passing year.

The most serious challenge to the vice societies in the
Progressive era did not come from critics like Theodore
Schroeder, but, ironically, from within the reform movement
itself. No matter how circumspectly conducted, the antiprostitution and social-hygiene crusades could hardly avoid discussing sex, and thereby ripping a hole in the genteel code.
"[S]ensational reformers and giddy humanitarians," growled

Paul Elmer More in the *Nation,* ". . . are accustoming thought-less minds to the contemplation of vice in all its hideous forms, and deadening the right sensibility of the public while at-tempting to awaken it."[68]

The social hygienists needed no reminding of the awk-wardness of their position. In New York City, a Cornell medical professor became so embarrassed while lecturing on venereal disease to a social-hygiene gathering that he simply sat down in the middle of his speech, unable to continue.[69] The sex reformers devoted much thought to this dilemma. Charles W. Eliot recommended that social-hygiene literature be "public and frank" yet "high-minded and free from suggestions which might invite youth to experiment in sexual vice"; Dr. M. J. Exner urged that sex instruction be conducted in "a fine, inspiring atmosphere"; and G. Stanley Hall reported that in Europe cadavers were being used to teach children about sex, "so that in the presence of death, knowledge may be given without passion."[70]

But, willy-nilly, the antivice crusade acted as a corrosive solvent upon the genteel sex taboos. Prostitution, as the object of so much reformist attention, inevitably became grist for the literary mill. And, in contrast to the difficulties which Stephen Crane and Theodore Dreiser had encountered with their books on the subject, prostitution novels linked to the sex-reform movement readily found publishers and a wide reading public. Undeniably "erotic," they could nevertheless be read with a satisfying sense of social concern. The prostitute, once a wicked pariah, now became a "somewhat romantic object of charity, compassion, and sympathetic understanding."[71] "A wave of sex hysteria and sex discussion seems to have invaded this country," declared *Current Opinion* in 1913. "[N]ovels and plays . . . fairly . . . reek with sex."[72]

Many uplifters seemed strangely undisturbed by this development, so long as the authors' intent was laudable. As early as 1890 Benjamin O. Flower, editor of the reform maga-zine *Arena,* had characterized the suppression of books dealing with prostitution as "conservatism protecting vice by assailing all who seek to purify life. . . ."[73]

Unmoved by such arguments, the vice societies invoked the familiar code and set out to suppress these well-intentioned books. This was a mistake. In three important cases from 1913 to 1919 the New York Vice Society attacked books about prostitution—and twice it met decisive defeat. The books at issue were *Hagar Revelly*, *Susan Lenox*, and *Madeleine*.

The author of *Hagar Revelly* was Daniel Carson Goodman, a thirty-year-old St. Louis physician and social hygienist who was moved to take up the pen because of a desire to teach "the innocent youth of the land . . . the wiles of vice."[74] His earnest novel tells the story of two sisters in New York City. One of them, Thatah, is the spokesman for what appear to be Goodman's own ideas about sex: "Virtue is not an affair of the body, it's an affair of the mind"; "Nowadays it is only hypocrisy that the world calls virtue." The other sister, Hagar, however, is the one who actually goes wrong, largely through naiveté. Seduced by her employer, a department-store manager, she turns for comfort to an honest-seeming laborer, but soon finds herself pregnant and abandoned. Narrowly escaping a life of prostitution, she sees no alternative but to accept her employer's long-standing offer to become his mistress.

The language of the novel is stilted and restrained. Perhaps its most daring passage is that describing the effect of Hagar's fatal first drink and her consequent ruin:

> For only a moment did Greenfield watch the drooping lashes, the quivering lips, the tremulous pulsation of her bosom. Then he lifted her into his arms, and despite a moment of slight resistance—carried her into the next room. [End of chapter][75]

Hagar Revelly appeared in 1913 under the imprint of Mitchell Kennerley, a young Britisher of advanced views and somewhat shady business ethics who had entered book publishing in New York in 1905. Reviews were generally favorable. The *Boston Evening Transcript* described the book as "a very significant piece of work." The *Review of Reviews* praised the "high plane" of Goodman's prose.[76]

Anthony Comstock, however, found the whole thing "rotten." Securing an indictment, he led a force of United States marshals in a raid on Kennerley's offices. The publisher was arrested and the entire stock and plates of *Hagar Revelly* seized.[77] Kennerley's attorney at once petitioned for a dismissal of the indictment. In a ruling rejecting this plea (on the principle that a jury should pass upon the obscenity question), Judge Learned Hand nevertheless took occasion to observe that the prevailing definition of obscenity, "however consonant . . . with mid-Victorian morals," bore little relation "to the understanding and morality of the present time. . . ." Barely concealing his distaste for individuals who professed to be shocked at passages that were "honestly relevant to the adequate expression of innocent ideas," Hand suggested that legal obscenity be defined not in terms of moral corruption, but simply as "the present critical point in the compromise between candor and shame at which the community may have arrived here and now."[78]

With these words of wisdom, Hand passed the case to a federal court jury which heard it in February 1914. Defending Kennerley and *Hagar Revelly* was John Quinn, a distinguished member of the New York bar. Quinn, born about 1870 into an impoverished Ohio Irish-Catholic immigrant family, had risen by way of Harvard Law School to become a very wealthy Tammany lawyer. He used his fortune to satisfy a deep love of literature and art; at his death in 1924 he left a large collection of Impressionist paintings and a quarter-million-dollar library of literary manuscripts and first editions. This same aesthetic bent also drew him, rather reluctantly at times, into a number of important censorship cases.[79]

In the *Hagar Revelly* trial, Quinn shrewdly stressed Goodman's reformist intent. An appreciative letter from the muck-

raking journalist Ida Tarbell was read to the jury. Defense
witnesses included Norman Hapgood, editor of *Collier's* in its
reformist heyday, and Jeremiah Jenks, a Columbia sociologist
given to writing inspirational pamphlets with such titles as
"Life Questions of High School Boys." Quinn's aim was to
assure the jury that *Hagar Revelly* was in the mainstream of
the social-hygiene movement—and he succeeded. After five
hours of deliberation, the jury acquitted Kennerley.[80]

Understandably elated, Daniel Carson Goodman declared
that the verdict signaled "a direct change in public sentiment." "Only recently," he wrote, "have people begun to
understand that if the shadowy recesses of an alleyway need
to be pointed out, it is better to illuminate the alley than to
board up each end."[81]

In contrast to Goodman's book, *Susan Lenox: Her Fall
and Rise* was the work of a seasoned and established novelist.
Inspired by New York's "white-slave" furore of the 1890s,
David Graham Phillips had started the book in 1902, working
on it intermittently until his death in 1911. It is the story of
an illegitimate small-town girl who runs away from home to
escape the marriage to a coarse farmer insisted upon by an
uncle; drifts into and out of several romances; lives for a time
as a prostitute; and by the end of the novel has become a
successful, if unhappy, actress. "The wages of sin is death,"
she muses to a Salvation Army lassie, "but—the wages of sin—
well, it's sometimes a house on Fifth Avenue."[82]

In June 1915, *Hearst's Magazine,* catering to the renewed
public interest in prostitution, began to serialize the novel.
The editor and business manager of *Hearst's* were soon haled
into magistrates' court by the New York Vice Society, but the
case was promptly dismissed.[83] In 1917, however, when Appleton's published *Susan Lenox* in book form, the Vice Society
was prompted to try its luck once more. John Sumner's initial
move was a thinly veiled threat. "It is impossible to believe,"
he wrote the publisher, "that the firm of D. Appleton Company

desire to stand as sponsors for the publication of an objectionable book, and for that reason I bring the matter to . . . your serious consideration."[84] Joseph H. Sears, the head of Appleton's, was not intimidated. *Susan Lenox* had been published, he retorted, "to awaken the American people to a high moral sense, in order that the terrible evils going on daily about them might be eliminated. . . ."[85]

Appleton continued to promote the book, and Sumner instituted proceedings. Sears was prepared for a showdown, but Phillips' sister and literary executor, "eager to have this last product of her brother's genius reach as wide an audience as possible," persuaded him to compromise. An expurgated version of *Susan Lenox* was issued, and the Vice Society's complaint was withdrawn.[86] Aided by divisions within the opposing camp, Sumner had won a partial victory.

The last of these vice-society efforts to stanch the flow of books springing from the antiprostitution movement was completely abortive. Chronologically, *Madeleine* and its legal vicissitudes belong to the postwar period, but the book is so clearly linked to the Progressive social-purity impulse that it is best treated here.

Madeleine, published in 1919 under the prestigious Harper imprint, is the anonymous autobiography of a reformed prostitute and madam. The domestic details of bordello life are set forth in painstaking detail, but references to sex are veiled and infrequent. Indeed, the book exudes that moral zeal peculiar to the reclaimed sinner. The author sternly condemns "[t]he present-day craze for rag-time" and notes stiffly that in *her* day "[n]o 'decent' house . . . would have tolerated some of the styles . . . on the streets to-day." Nevertheless, a certain jaded cynicism does creep in. The only difference between prostitutes and wives, she comments, is that the prostitutes "do not cheat in the delivery of the merchandise for which they are paid."[87]

Reviewers who had survived the "white-slave" investigations were not particularly scandalized. The story was "well enough known to a generation ridden with vice commission reports," observed the *Nation*.[88] John S. Sumner, however, responded like a Pavlov dog to this affront to the familiar code. Charges were filed, and in January 1920 Clinton T. Brainard, the president of Harper's, was hauled into the court of special sessions, convicted, and fined $1,000.[89]

While *Madeleine* was undoubtedly offensive to the Vice Society, other factors were involved in the prosecution as well. Brainard, it developed, was also secretary of an Extraordinary Grand Jury investigating scandals in the administration of New York's Mayor John Hylan, a protégé of William Randolph Hearst, and Hearst's *New York American* had launched a vendetta against *Madeleine* at the moment it appeared, pointedly mentioning Brainard's name in each article. The conviction was front-page news in the *American*, whose story gleefully emphasized that Brainard had been "fingerprinted like any other common law-breaker."[90]

Charges of collusion between Hearst and the Vice Society were widespread, but Sumner stoutly maintained that he had been "actuated solely by considerations of public welfare. . . ." *Madeleine*, he said, was "one of the worst and most dangerous books that has come to our attention in a long time." Privately, he expressed irritation that Hearst had exploited the prosecution for his own purposes.[91]

Meanwhile, Brainard had appealed. His lawyers, emulating John Quinn's defense of *Hagar Revelly*, stressed the book's reformist intent. It had been given prepublication endorsements, they pointed out, by a minister, a physician, and two judges, one of whom, the famous Ben B. Lindsay of Denver, had written the foreword. Impressed by these arguments, the appellate court of New York, on July 9, 1920, reversed the lower-court conviction.[92] *Madeleine* was given a clean bill of health, and the Vice Society, by implication, was tendered a sharp rebuff.

These attacks on books of clearly reformist intent heightened the growing debate over censorship, obscenity, and the vice societies. In an unprecedented move, *Publishers' Weekly* in July 1916 devoted eight closely printed pages to a symposium on these subjects. Defending the strictest possible interpretation of the obscenity laws, John S. Sumner made the familiar Progressive appeal:

> Every growing child has the right to be protected, in so far as possible, in his environment against those things which tend to demoralize and degrade and corrupt.

The child and "the poor little half-educated reader," he said, must be shielded from "pessimistic scribblers who hold up humanity . . . as a thing of moral shreds and patches."[93]

Speaking for those no longer impressed by such arguments, James M. Morton, Jr., of the New York bar, declared that to permit solicitude for children and defectives to determine publishing standards was not only foolish, but allowed "the larger aspects of personal liberty . . . to disappear entirely from view." The courts, Morton charged, had too long been "docile and sheeplike" in the face of vice-society rhetoric and bluster. In a clear reference to such books as *Hagar Revelly*, Morton wrote:

> The sex question is one of the most complex and important subjects that concern the human race; yet any man . . . who undertakes to discuss any phase of it in public in the United States, does so at his peril. . . .

Echoing the *Arena* editorial of 1890, Morton declared that in attacking such works, "the dear chaperones of public morals" were merely "protecting the white slave trade from effective public exposure. . . ."[94]

In an editorial weighing these conflicting points of view, *Publishers' Weekly* summed up the prevailing attitude toward the problem on the eve of the First World War. The vice societies' work, it said, was "worthy" and "deserving of the support of every good citizen." Unquestionably, the "genuinely

obscene" should be rigorously suppressed. But, the editorial
went on,

> [T]here is a borderland in which the exact delimitation of the
> obscene is a very complex matter, and the excessive zeal
> sometimes displayed by semi-official or unofficial censorship
> in the suppression of 'borderland' literature has been often
> ludicrous, generally annoying and sometimes positively unjust.[95]

The debate that men like Robert Ingersoll and Theodore
Schroeder had been trying to provoke for years was at last
well under way. The vice societies, by mechanically applying
their code against serious works of reformist intent, had not
only alienated many uplifters whose support they could ill
afford to lose, but they had aroused uneasiness within the
literary and legal fraternities as well. The issue of censorship
was in the air, and publishers, courts, and the public could
no longer be expected to defer unquestioningly to the keener
moral sensibilities of the professional obscenity hunters. For
the vice societies, this was a gloomy prelude to the major
struggles that lay ahead.

THREE

The First World War

A perceptive observer of the American scene in 1916 might
well have predicted that a book-censorship conflict loomed
in the future. The identity of purpose between the vice societies
and the broader community was weakening. Publishers were
showing increasing willingness to adjust their standards to the
shifting whims of public taste. Even Progressivism, seemingly
so congenial to the vice-society outlook, had, in the antiprostitution crusade, spawned a literature that flouted the traditional
code. Nevertheless, the book-censorship explosion which did
occur in the 1920s, though a natural consequence of these
earlier trends, owed much of its intensity and bitterness to
an intervening crisis: the First World War.

Woodrow Wilson's war message in April 1917, with its moving evocation of the deeper meaning of the impending struggle, profoundly stirred the American people. The nation was swept by the conviction that the war was a just one, and that America's aims were pure. To drive home these verities to any doubters, a massive opinion-moulding campaign was soon under way. In its official form, this campaign was spearheaded by George Creel's Committee on Public Information with its torrent of pamphlets, traveling exhibits, posters, and "Four-Minute Men." In addition, religious organizations, woman's clubs, the Boy Scouts, the Y.M.C.A., the Salvation Army—even the American Library Association—set up war councils to reach their special constituencies. Newspapers and magazines joined wholeheartedly in what an awed Walter Lippmann described in 1922 as history's "largest and . . . most intensive effort to carry quickly a fairly uniform set of ideas to all the people of a nation."[1]

As with all attempts to sway great masses of people, this campaign dealt in stark issues of right and wrong, lurid villains, and shining heroes. "The struggle between good and evil . . . has been dramatized by the war," wrote John Jay Chapman early in 1918, "and the whole world has become the stage of a miracle play." The president of Oberlin College spoke of "a truly Holy War."[2]

A necessary element in this spiritualization of the war was a belief in the enemy's unqualified villainy, and nothing was spared in painting Germany as "the most absolute synonym for evil that the world has ever seen . . ., the blood-red Moloch of materialism." From hundreds of books, articles, and lectures—often delivered to "men only" audiences—Americans learned that the Hun was an obscene, lustful brute who laughed as he mutilated virgins and impaled infants on his bayonet.[3]

Standing in absolute contrast to this fiend was the American soldier, a paragon of moral excellence. A deluge of propaganda was devoted to the proposition that the American troops, purified in the fire of combat, were dwelling at last in

that state of virtue so long honored as an elusive ideal. One
important purveyor of this notion was the erstwhile Authors'
League secretary Harold Hersey, now an army lieutenant
whose public relations duties took him from camp to camp—
though never, it appears, into the battle zones. In a series of
lyrical articles in *Scribner's Magazine,* later published in book
form, Hersey assured the nation that the American soldier's
battle experience had so "moulded him along straight lines"
that he had been "recreated—an individual with a distinct
change of personality." Hersey's typical recruit, "swept into a
machine that requires cleanliness [a favorite euphemism of
the day] first, last, and all the time," soon becomes a man "of
clean motives and higher desires" eager to add his bit to "the
large mass of sincere good that is present everywhere." Army
life, in short, "changes men over night to superhuman beings."[4]

If the mere touch of khaki did not bring about the anticipated moral transformation, more conventional methods
were at hand. In April 1917, Secretary of War Newton D.
Baker issued an order banishing alcohol from all military
camps and barring bawdy houses from the surrounding neigh-
borhoods. Soon after, Baker established a Commission on
Training Camp Activities, made up of military men, Y.M.C.A.
officials, ministers, and social hygienists, to enforce these
regulations. This commission sponsored a flood of pamphlets,
posters, movies, slide programs, and lectures designed to dramatize the dangers of prostitution and venereal disease and to
elevate "the moral tone of camp life."[5]

For reformers who had made the nation's sexual behavior
their special province, these developments proved a heady
experience. "[R]ejoice with us," said the American Social
Hygiene Association in a communiqué to its members, ". . . that
the growing movement for social morality . . . is showing results in this important way. . . ." "[T]he government is putting
into the hands of social experts a million picked men," reported
one social hygienist excitedly, "to do with them in compulsory
regimen, protection and education what no so-called sane

government . . . would dare force upon the same men in time of peace."[6]

The vice societies, too, were infused with new confidence by the sudden national preoccupation with morality. The New York Vice Society in 1917 proudly reported that John S. Sumner was "somewhere in France" with the Y.M.C.A., helping to maintain "those standards of conduct which have given to the United States in this war . . . a reputation for high ideals and moral greatness."[7] Freed for the moment of nagging criticism and worrisome setbacks, the vice organizations trumpeted the significance of their work with a self-assurance reminiscent of an earlier day. "[L]argely due to the fact that this Society has existed . . . we have exhibited to the world at large an army which for spirituality and morale has never been equaled"—so asserted the New York Vice Society in 1917.[8]

The home front felt the edifying currents as well. "It is not an army that we must shape and train for war," the President had said, "it is a nation."[9] Gradually the belief took hold that the civilian population, deprived of the purification of the trenches, should nevertheless seek its own spiritual renewal. "How much sweeter and cleaner would our home lives be," mused Lieutenant Hersey, "if we were to live like these [army] boys do?" Horatio W. Dresser's *The Victorious Faith* (1917) described the struggle as a "beneficent illness" that would purge the national life of all impurities. A British journalist probing the war's impact on the United States found that the conflict had brought "a splendid height of exaltation" and "cleared the American air . . . of a multitude of unwholesome vapours." "[I]n entering the war to save democracy," he concluded, "America has also saved herself."[10]

As with the military, this elevation of the civilian moral level was helped along by official prodding. Secretary of War Baker vigorously exercised his authority to suppress loose moral behavior in the environs of military camps, and urged local

officials "to arouse the cities and towns to an appreciation of
their responsibility for clean conditions. . . ."[11] As a war
measure, Congress appropriated four million dollars to combat prostitution and venereal disease on the homefront, and
some of the literature published as part of this campaign
wandered rather far afield, with lengthy warnings against
"[t]hinking about or looking at things which excite the sex
feelings. . . ."[12]

In still another expression of the civilian purity campaign,
some sixty Y.W.C.A. lecturers toured the country for the Commission on Training Camp Activities, warning women and
girls not to permit soldiers any improper advances. Though
required to stress patriotic and medical considerations, these
"Y" lecturers also took pains to emphasize "the moral and
spiritual values of square conduct. . . ." By the war's end, they
had reached almost a million women, distributed countless
pamphlets—"Do Your Bit to Keep Him Fit" was one title—
and secured several hundred thousand feminine signatures on
a pledge to observe "the highest standards of character and
honor." In praising this program, the Commission declared
that it would not only help win the war but would also "foster
a higher standard of personal conduct and civic cleanliness."[13]

As a result of these attempts to channel wartime emo-
tionalism into the moral-purity movement, many citizens concluded that an impassioned crusade against domestic immorality was the natural corollary of the struggle against the
lustful Hun. A spate of municipal and antivice campaigns,
often characterized by intolerance and self-righteousness, broke
out across the country. In San Antonio the wartime purity
drive was led by "a lean, grey-haired Yankee type of lawyer"
who (said Social Hygiene) had been "waiting for years for the
people to be ready." At the organizational meeting, this thin,
aging Yankee set the tone at once: "I understand," he announced, "that we propose to fight vice and its allies with the
cold steel of the law and to drive in the steel from point to
hilt until the law's supremacy is acknowledged."[14]

❧

The deceptively easy task of routing a few prostitutes did not nearly exhaust the energies of towns seeking moral rejuvenation. "The universal cry issuing out of . . . such communities," wrote an official of the Commission on Training Camp Activities, "has been 'What shall we do next? We have complied with your requests to abolish our red light districts. What more do you want us to do?' "[15]

These unsatisfied purification impulses often found an outlet in attacks on "obscene literature"—a development which the vice societies worked strenuously to encourage. With "the other countries . . . meeting all kinds of losses and bearing all kinds of burdens," said a Watch and Ward speaker in 1917, "we over here . . . ought to be doing a great deal more than we have ever done in the way of cleaning house. . . ." A speaker at the 1918 meeting of the Boston-based vice society, alluding to the high moral standards of the military camps, added:

> It remains for the people of the country to do some house-cleaning at home, and to see to it that the surroundings and the atmosphere into which the soldier returning home on leave is introduced are as clean and wholesome as that which they leave behind in the camps.[16]

As casualty figures mounted, any suggestion of ribaldry, irreverence, or vulgarity in literature seemed increasingly offensive. At a time of such high resolve, Americans did not relish being reminded of the less exalted dimensions of their natures. In 1917 alone, bills directed against obscene literature were introduced in twelve states—a "phenomenal advance," reported *Social Hygiene*.[17]

This flurry of obscenity legislation was but one symptom of the wartime book-censorship impulse. The Espionage Act of 1917, the Trading-with-the-Enemy Act, and the 1918 Sedition Amendment were all used to suppress radical and pacifist publications as well as books that ran counter to the prevailing spirit of idealism, sacrifice, and purity. In the summer of 1918, for example, postal authorities informed a recently established New York publishing firm, Boni & Liveright, that its edition of Andreas Latzko's *Men in War* had been barred from the mails under the wartime legislation. This perfervid novel, similar in some respects to the more successful *All Quiet on the Western Front*, dismisses the war as a "wholesale cripple-and-corpse factory" and heaps scorn on those who view it "with a mixture of religious devotion, romantic longing and shy sympathy." The offices of Boni & Liveright were kept under surveillance by military intelligence officers to make sure the ban was enforced.[18]

Magazines were not exempt from the iron literary standards of a nation at war—as Margaret Anderson quickly learned. In October 1917, Miss Anderson's *Little Review* published "Cantelman's Spring-Mate," Wyndham Lewis's story of a British draftee's conquest of his fiancée Stella, a young lady who is obviously not doing her bit to keep him fit:

> On the warm earth consent flowed up into her body from all veins of the landscape. The nightingale sang ceaselessly in the small wood at the top of the field where they lay. He grinned up towards it, and once more turned to the devouring of his mate.

The story has a darker side, however, for as Cantelman seduced Stella "his thoughts and sensations all had, as a philosophic background, the prospect of death"; later, in combat, he kills a German "with the same impartial malignity that he had displayed in the English night with his Spring-mate." Both war-sanctioned killing and war-inspired copulation, in Lewis's dark view, turn men into repellant automatons. Such mordant reflections struck a sourly discordant note amid the organ swell of wartime idealism, and the offending issue of the *Little Review* was confiscated as obscene by the postal authorities. Attorney John Quinn appealed, but Federal Judge Augustus N. Hand upheld the ban.[19]

Another author to arouse suspicion was Sigmund Freud, whose *Reflections on War and Death* was published in New

York in 1918 by Moffat, Yard. To a citizen who filed a complaint with the Committee on Public Information, George Creel replied: "[Y]our report seems to be absolutely justified. I am calling it to the attention of the proper authorities." There is no record that an actual suppression was attempted, suggesting that the "proper authorities" dampened Creel's zeal, or that the end of the war intervened.[20]

The stringent wartime literary standards were enforced in a variety of less obvious ways as well. G. P. Putnam's Sons withdrew one of its books, Ellen Key's *War, Peace, and the Future,* under pressure from the National Security League, a powerful private group set up in 1915 to promote loyalty, patriotism, and universal military training. To prove that its repentance was genuine, Putnam's urged full support for the League's efforts to remove Miss Key's book from the library shelves of the nation.[21]

Librarians proved particularly vulnerable to the repressive spirit of 1917–18. In the summer of 1918 the War Department notified the American Library Association, which had accepted responsibility for conducting the servicemen's book program, that certain objectionable titles had been discovered in camp libraries and should be removed. Most were books by pacifists like Rufus Jones and David Starr Jordan, but a few "salacious or morbid" works of fiction were also barred. Among these were Ambrose Bierce's *In the Midst of Life* and *Can Such Things Be?* and Henri Barbusse's *Under Fire, the Story of a Squad,* a best-seller in France and winner of the 1916 Prix Goncourt. These library censorship lists, widely publicized in the press, were assumed to be relevant for the homefront as well. "[I]t is now correct to 'blacklist' " these writers, noted the *Boston Evening Transcript* punctiliously. The A.L.A., for its part, carried out the War Department edict with alacrity, protesting nervously that all the members of its selection committee were of "proved loyalty."[22]

The embryonic prewar assault on censorship was not completely forgotten, however, for in at least one notable instance the attempt to force literary expression into the rigid wartime straitjacket was frustrated in the courts. The book in question was Théophile Gautier's *Mademoiselle de Maupin,* which appeared in an English-language edition in New York City in 1917, some eighty years after its first publication in Paris. The novel outrageously affronts the whole spectrum of bourgeois sex taboos as it details Madeleine de Maupin's efforts to learn more about men by assuming a masculine disguise. Several passionate encounters between the heroine and another young lady who has fallen in love with "him" are described more or less explicitly, as is Madeleine de Maupin's voluptuous night of love with a young nobleman to whom she at last reveals her identity after a considerable period of confusion having obvious homosexual overtones. In a lengthy, bombastic, and platitudinous preface, the twenty-three-year-old Gautier heaped scorn on conventional morals, censorship, and the stuffiness of mid-nineteenth-century France. "The great affectation of morality which reigns at present would be very laughable," he wrote, "if it were not very tiresome."[23]

The publication of *Mademoiselle de Maupin* in America at the height of the war struck many people, including John S. Sumner, as an unsubtle jibe at the moral earnestness which lay over the land like a heavy blanket. In November, shortly before his departure for "somewhere in France," Sumner made his move. Purchasing a copy of the novel from McDevitt, Wilson & Co., a Manhattan bookstore, he brought legal proceedings against Raymond D. Halsey, the clerk who had made the sale. Even under the stress of war emotion, however, the court could not bring itself to outlaw an acknowledged, albeit somewhat scandalous, classic of eighty years' standing. Halsey was acquitted both in magistrates' court and, on appeal, in the court of special sessions.[24]

That the war did not bring an even greater outburst of book censorship on moral grounds is due, in part, to the sharp overall drop in wartime fiction production—nearly 20% below the prewar level. "[I]n the presence of such immense happen-

ings . . . one's own little imaginings seem trivial," observed
one literary figure explaining the decline.[25] Furthermore, of
those novels that were published, very few could have offended
even a hyper-moral public. The war crisis temporarily halted
the assault on Victorian standards of literary propriety. Most
of the established writers were themselves caught up in the
exaltation of the moment, and to the few who were not, publishers' doors were firmly closed. "So wisely was self-censorship
carried on in the publishing profession [during the war],"
notes an industry historian, ". . . that government censorship
was seldom invoked."[26] In a time of national stress, American
writers were expected either to offer superficial escape from
the realities of the crisis—Edward Streeter's *Dere Mable:
Love Letters of a Rookie* and Arthur Empey's *Over the Top*
nicely filled the bill—or to provide yet another channel for
glorifying the Allied cause and reënforcing the national impulse
toward a higher, purer life.

To the vice societies, all this seemed to be the realization
of their most fondly cherished dreams. Despite *Mademoiselle
de Maupin,* 1917–18 came to seem, in retrospect, a satisfying
interlude when their historic identification with the broader
purposes of society had been renewed and strengthened.

THE POSTWAR VISION

The impact of the First World War on the vice societies
did not end with the Armistice, for they shared the prevailing
conviction that the war ordeal would permanently elevate the
quality of American life. This belief—an integral part of the
wartime mystique—was summed up in a *Chicago Evening
Post* cartoon in which the figure of "Our Better Selves" gazes
at the dim, receding figure of "Our Old Selfish Existence" and
asks, "Is it possible we will go back to it?"[27] While the war
continued, few Americans doubted the answer to the cartoonist's rhetorical question. "[T]he faith [which the war] . . . has
evoked will outlast it, and will shine in the life of the world

forever," exulted John Jay Chapman. A Columbia professor predicted that as a result of the conflict, human nature would "change in the most radical, tremendous, cataclysmic way." An Episcopal bishop foresaw "a regenerate earth at the close of this war."[28]

For a brief post-armistice interlude, this bright dream lingered. "[N]ever before was victory so great, and so full of universal blessing," mused Frank Moss, ". . . a new spirit will have ascendancy in the world." Henry C. King of Oberlin declared that the German defeat offered "the largest single opportunity that the race has ever had for a great advance."[29] *A New Mind for the New Age; The Great Change; The New Frontier; For a New America in a New World; The War and the New Age*—such titles dominated publishers' lists in the immediate postwar period.[30] The triumph of the prohibition movement in 1919, after years of effort, seemed to many merely a harbinger of still more profound advances. A few Americans, perhaps, shared William Fitz-Gerald's uneasiness about the "insistence upon universal slaughter as a panacea for spiritual and social ills," but more common was the roseate outlook of the Y.M.C.A. pamphleteer who wrote lyrically: "As a woman forgets her travailing pains in the joy that comes with the birth of a son, so will mankind rejoice in the rebirth of the world as the result of this war."[31]

The returning soldier was to be the midwife of this rebirth. "No boy goes through the hell of fire and suffering and wounds that he does not come out newborn," wrote another Y.M.C.A. spokesman, "The old man is gone from him, and a new man is born in him. That is the great eternal compensation of war. . . ." An official of the United States Council of National Defense asserted that "the cost of the war is nothing" compared to the "civil advancement" it was bringing in its wake.[32] A leader in the social-purity movement declared:

> Young men of today . . . are nearer perfection in conduct, morals, and ideals than any similar generation of young men in the history of the world. Their minds have been raised to

ideals that would never have been attained save by the
heroism of . . . the World War.[33]

Such a tragically costly undertaking had to have com-
mensurate significance, and for an intense moment Americans
almost persuaded themselves that the war had, indeed, ushered
in a vast spiritual advance. Again the caustic pen of William
Fitz-Gerald delineated the national mood:

> The battle-field of France loomed as a new Sinai. . . . On that
> Mount of thunder new laws were being graved for the wiser
> ruling of the race. . . . Rainbows of Christ were seen gleaming
> from green clouds of poison-gas. Nests of new-born sweets
> were found in the shell craters; the perfect man would yet
> be gathered from horrid fragments that swung from the
> barbed wire.[34]

For the vice societies, the prospect of a continued postwar
upsurge of righteousness was particularly heartening. The
nation's renewed commitment to literary purity would survive
and even grow stronger! "[T]he 'new spirit' . . . of the returning
'crusader,'" declared the Watch and Ward Society, ". . . is a
prophecy of greater moral triumphs to come. . . ."[35]

One expression of these hopes was the League of Nations
conference on obscene literature convened in Geneva in 1923,
the fruit of planning that had begun soon after the war's end.
Although the deliberations proved inconclusive, the delegates
were deeply moved by the closing address of the chairman,
Gaston Deschamps of France, who declared that literary purity
was a solemn obligation of the postwar generation. As "sur-
vivors of a carnage which surpassed in horror the most savage
butcheries of the past," said Deschamps,

> we owe to the memory of the dead and to the sufferings of
> those victims who are only half alive some proof that we
> deserve to live by giving to life in the peace we have regained
> greater nobility and greater harmony and, if we can, greater
> beauty.

Anything less, he added feelingly, would be "a permanent
insult to the secret grief of countless homes and innumerable

bereaved families whose hearts have been pierced to the quick."[36] Such sentiments were already beginning to ring hollow by 1923, but Deschamps's appeal recalled for his audience the expectations that had prevailed only a few years before, when it had still been possible to believe that the literature of a war-scarred generation would be unprecedented in its lofty grandeur and purity.

Disillusionment soon set in. "The war-emotion did not deepen into abiding conviction," acknowledged *Christian Century* as early as January 1919,

> . . . Instead, the feeling now is that the loss must be made good. The bent-under bough returns with a swish. . . .[E]vils prohibited as a war measure confidently count upon returning . . . to feed the riot of appetite that flows like an ebb-tide back from the front.[37]

Soon it became clear to even the most hopeful that the moral surge of the war years would be sustained, if at all, only through the most strenuous effort. A harsh note began to tinge discussions about the prospective quality of postwar American life. *Zion's Herald,* the influential Methodist weekly which had vigorously supported the war as a salutary moral undertaking, was by 1920 calling for "a wave of Puritanism, even with its stern exactions. . . ."[38] The speeches of Oberlin's Henry King, vocal exponent of the idealistic view of the war's moral impact, began to betray a certain stridency. "Men of ideals—social, moral, and religious—have now their *great opportunity*," he wrote in 1919. "This is no time to 'pussyfoot,' to be 'mealy-mouthed' or apologetic on the great issues of faith and conduct. . . . *[T]he immeasurable cost of the peace* which has come makes any other view a blasphemy."[39]

Predictably, the vice societies were in the forefront of those who demanded stern measures to make the nation safe for morality. "[C]onstant vigilance only," declared the Watch and Ward, "will assure a permanency to the gains achieved."[40] The vice organizations were not particularly upset by the

knowledge that coercive methods might be necessary to preserve the moral advances of the war, for the lessons of 1917–18
had confirmed their long-held belief in society's far-reaching
mandate to control literary expression. To the vice societies,
the lesson taught by the wartime book suppressions—Latzko
and Lewis, Bierce and Barbusse—seemed clear: "Censorship"
was not only justifiable but even praiseworthy if the purpose
underlying it were of sufficient import. And, surely, measures
which had been applauded as a patriotic necessity during the
war would win equal acceptance if brought to bear in the
campaign to achieve a purer and finer peacetime society!

This lesson—that coercion was an acceptable method of
achieving moral reform—was driven home with particular
forcefulness to the New England Watch and Ward Society.
Early in the war, the Commission on Training Camp Activities
had invested the Watch and Ward, as well as several other
organizations, with hazy powers of "scrutiny and supervision"
over moral conditions in communities surrounding military
installations, and the vice organization's wartime reports enthusiastically describe its efforts to force upon the civilian
citizenry "the higher moral standard which Congress has raised
for the soldier and sailor." In 1918 the Watch and Ward report
recounted with obvious relish how twenty Watch and Ward
agents, beefed up by a contingent of troops, had staged a raid
on a brothel in a "largely foreign mill town" whose residents
"had not felt the thrill of the new public opinion. . . ." "[T]he
majesty of the law was vindicated," concludes the report in
grim triumph, after noting that "fifty-four pleasure seekers and
eight women inmates" had been driven into the streets.[41] The
Watch and Ward Society's semi-official powers were withdrawn in March 1918, but it carried on in much the same
fashion through a special committee on camps and barracks.
" 'War Emergency' has been the imperative factor in all the
work of this year," notes the 1918 report, chronicling the
"large moral advances" the war had brought.[42]

This lesson was reënforced, too, by A. Mitchell Palmer's

spectacular "Red raids" of January 1920, which involved not only the arrest of 4,000 suspected "radicals," but also the seizure of great quantities of books and magazines as well. In Boston, for example, without benefit of search warrant, "[p]rivate rooms were searched in omnibus fashion; trunks, bureaus, suit cases, and boxes broken open; books and papers seized."[43] The vice societies, so skilled at formulating plausible analogies, at once grasped the relevance of the "Red raids" to their own work. "Just as we have the parlor Anarchist and the parlor Bolshevist in political life," declared John S. Sumner,

> so we have the parlor Bolshevist in literary and art circles, and they are just as great a menace. . . . While the governmental authorities are struggling against foreign ideas and their advocates regarding political attack, we have had the same conflict with foreign ideas calculated and intended *to break down American standards of decency and morality*.[44]

The fleeting brushes with real power, coupled with the vivid demonstrations of official coercion and repression, established the mood in which the vice societies entered the postwar era. "The armed conflict is over," declared the New York Vice Society, but "the everlasting conflict continues . . . between right and wrong—vice and virtue. There can be no discharge in that war,' there can be no armistice with the enemy; there can be no terms except the unconditional surrender of wrong." The American army had demonstrated that to succeed in battle "blow upon blow must be delivered," and "[e]xactly similar methods must be used in combating the enemies of decency and morality."[45]

The same grim mood prevailed in Boston. Reviewing the wartime purity crusades in which the Watch and Ward had shared, the secretary of the Boston society observed:

> [T]he machinery, the methods and motives of the Federal forces were crushingly strong and wisely used for local good. Reforms which had been advocated by this Society for ten years were easily forced upon the authorities. . . . All this . . . was supported by a public opinion that would have annihilated

any one opposing it. This was especially true of sexual offenses.[46]

"Forced," "crushingly," "annihilated"—such words all too clearly reveal the vice societies' mood at war's end. The pre-occupation with force became sufficiently intense as to inspire reports on vice-society personnel injured in the line of duty. In 1918 the attrition in Boston was particularly severe: "[O]ne was shot through the lower leg, one was assaulted with a loaded gun pointed at his heart, one had his cheek bone laid open by a brick thrown in a dark cellar, and one was struck with a fist in the eye and had his glasses broken."[47] (One suspects from this sanguinary catalog that the Watch and Ward secretary had been secretly reading some of the dime novels confiscated by his predecessors in the 1880s!)

Refreshed by the spiritual exaltation of the war, exempt for the moment from legalistic criticism, and instructed by the official coercion which had silenced dissent and controlled public behavior through the magic of "War Emergency," the vice societies in 1918 set out to achieve the bright new age that was the nation's rightful wartime legacy. "If we could insist on character in khaki," asked a vice-society speaker, "could we not demand character in evening dress?"[48] The literary purity crusades which followed owed at least as much, in their bitter intensity, to the lofty rhetoric of Woodrow Wilson as to the nineteenth-century fulminations of Anthony Comstock.

FOUR

The First Postwar Clash—
1918-22

The Armistice did indeed usher in a new era; of that there could be little doubt. Far from bringing a triumphant reaffirmation of the traditional values, however, the postwar period witnessed their final collapse. The pipe dreams of 1917–18 faded rapidly as disillusionment with the high-flown rhetoric of the war set in. Prohibition proved not the harbinger of greater moral triumphs, but the final wave of an ebbing tide. "The pumped-up idealism and fervor of war-time was followed by cynicism, by a general smashing of idols, by skepticism of exalted motives"—so wrote Frederick Lewis Allen in 1930. Floyd Dell said the same thing more bluntly: "So much nonsense, and so many lies, were promulgated during that hysteri-

cal period in the guise of patriotic idealism, and rammed so
ruthlessly into people's minds, that there has been a violent
reaction. . . ."[1] A period in which "purity" had been elevated as a
war aim, an unofficial Fifteenth Point, yielded to one marked
by a wholesale retreat from idealism.

Indeed, a number of intellectual and technological currents converged in the 1920s to contribute to the dramatic
upheaval in taste and morals. Freudianism was first publicized
—and vulgarized—in this decade; the Nineteenth Amendment
helped remove the American woman from her pedestal; the
mushrooming movie industry transmitted the latest standards
of dress and behavior to every corner of the nation; and the
enormous jump in automobile ownership—2.5 million registra-
tions in 1915, 26.7 million by 1930—enabled young people
to put into practice what they were viewing on the screen.[2]

This social upheaval found expression in a burst of intense
literary creativity. Hardly had the boys come marching home
before the bookstores began to fill up with books that repudiated, ridiculed, or—worst of all—simply ignored the values and
ideals which the doughboys had fought to defend. The scope
of this outpouring may be suggested simply by setting down a
shopping list of familiar titles:

> 1919   Sherwood Anderson, *Winesburg, Ohio*
>   James Branch Cabell, *Jurgen*
>   Waldo Frank, *Our America*
>   Joseph Hergesheimer, *Java Head*
>   Henry L. Mencken, *Prejudices—First Series*
>
> 1920   Floyd Dell, *Moon-calf*
>   F. Scott Fitzgerald, *This Side of Paradise*
>   James Gibbons Hunecker, *Painted Veils*
>   Sinclair Lewis, *Main Street*
>   John Dos Passos, *One Man's Initiation*
>
> 1921   John Dos Passos, *Three Soldiers*
>   Ben Hecht, *Erik Dorn*
>   Eugene O'Neill, *Anna Christie; The Hairy Ape*
>   Harold E. Stearns, *America and the Young Intellectual*

1922   E. E. Cummings, *The Enormous Room*
       F. Scott Fitzgerald, *The Beautiful and the Damned;*
        Tales of the Jazz Age
       Sinclair Lewis, *Babbitt*
       Harold Stearns (ed.), *Civilization in the United States*

Implicitly, and often explicitly, the authors of these books were engaged in a massive assault upon the comfortable assumptions with which most Americans had grown up. "[T]he reformistic and 'uplift' tendencies of our national life—the Pollyanna optimism; prohibition; blue laws; exaggerated reverence for women; home and foreign missions; Protestant clericalism—" declared Harold Stearns rather breathlessly in 1921, were nothing but "the fine flower of timidity and fear and ignorance."[3] With a wave of the pen, a century of reform and philanthropy was airily swept aside. "If a single phrase could characterize all the widely-read books which have been published since the Armistice," wrote Frank Stockbridge in 1928, "I should term them the literature of disillusion."[4]

A somewhat less familiar feature of the American literary upheaval of the 1920s was the simultaneous turmoil in the book-publishing profession. The near-absolute hegemony of the staid old nineteenth-century houses, whose genteel standards had been so congenial to the vice societies, had begun to crumble before the war, but it was in the 1920s that the publishing revolution (which is of central importance to book-censorship history) reached its culmination. As a fresh group of authors arose in the wake of the First World War, there emerged a new generation of publishers eager to make the writings of these authors available to the public. Horace Liveright (Boni & Liveright), Thomas Seltzer (Thomas Seltzer, Inc.), Richard Simon and Max Schuster (Simon and Schuster), Alfred Harcourt and Donald Brace (Harcourt, Brace and Company), Thomas R. Coward and James McCann (Coward-McCann Company), Harold K. Guinzburg and George S. Oppenheimer (The Viking Press), Bennett Cerf and Donald

Klopfer (Random House), Pascal Covici and Donald Friede
(Covici-Friede), W. W. Norton (W. W. Norton & Company),
William Morrow (William Morrow & Company), Lincoln Mac-
Veagh (The Dial Press)—the roll of publishers who began
their independent careers during this flush era is long and
impressive. Other newcomers like Ben W. Huebsch (later of
The Viking Press), Alfred A. Knopf (Alfred A. Knopf, Inc.),
and the Boni brothers, Charles and Albert, whose initial offerings antedate the war, first rose to prominence in the favorable climate of the 1920s. These young upstarts left a certain
amount of organizational chaos in their wake, as partnerships
sprang up, dissolved, and reëmerged in new combinations, but
at least fifteen viable and enduring book-publishing firms were
founded from 1917 to 1929.[5]

Young and eager to make places for themselves, these
newcomers were temperamentally receptive to manuscripts
reflecting the iconoclasm of the postwar generation. Themselves in many instances immigrants or of recent immigrant
background, they were less intimidated by the taboos of the
older America, more attuned to the tastes and needs of the
newer groups, and often far more at home with the polyglot
European literary traditions. It is no coincidence that in the
1920s novels representing the whole spectrum of modern
European culture were for the first time systematically translated and published in the United States.

Under these changed circumstances, the standards of the
older firms proved remarkably elastic. Some of these companies,
falling upon evil days, came into the hands of new owners
who retained only the prestigious names. Others through the
natural process of time passed to younger, less hidebound
members of the controlling family. The venerable G. P. Putnam's Sons is a case in point. Established before the Civil War
by the family patriarch George Palmer Putnam, it was for many
years firmly and conservatively managed by his son Major
George Haven Putnam. As crusty old Major Putnam advanced
in years, a whole group of younger Putnams took over, among

them George Palmer Putnam, namesake of the founder, who
joined the firm as treasurer in 1919, at thirty-two, and remained its guiding force for eleven years. Young Putnam
prized authors like Ben Hecht, whom his ancestors would
certainly have thrown out of their offices, and in 1922 he
compiled and published *Nonsenseorship*, a breezy and sophisticated attack on book censorship in all its manifestations. What
happened at Putnam's was symptomatic of changes that were
occurring throughout the book-publishing industry.[6]

The breakdown of the old taboos and ideals did not infuse
the vice societies with quite the exhilaration it brought to
literary and publishing circles. "The ebbtide of moral laxity,
as a result of the great war, has revealed itself ominously,"
declared the New York Vice Society glumly; in Boston, the
Watch and Ward reported "a recrudescence of obscenity" and
blamed "[t]he visit of so many of our young men to countries
where obscenity laws are not enforced. . . ."[7]

As the vice organizations struggled to keep alive the
vision of a postwar age of purity, their utterances came to
sound like parodies of Wilsonian rhetoric. Denouncing those
who dealt in "pain-producing sarcasm" and were preoccupied
with "social sores," John S. Sumner declared that American
literature should radiate "joy and adventure, wholesome
physique and sane mentality, clear vision and buoyancy, genial
criticism, and whimsical humor."[8] As the appalling outlines of
the postwar literary world unfolded, the vice-society reaction
hardened. The optimistic tone in which they had once proclaimed their devotion to reform was replaced by a crabbed
insistence on the *status quo*. "I am not a reformer," Sumner
testily told a reporter in 1922, "I am a conservative."[9]

The idea of coercive social control, always implicit in
the vice-society movement though masked by the rhetoric
of philanthropy and Progressivism, had been given fresh impetus by the war. Now, in an era of apparent moral collapse,

it moved decisively to the fore. Between 1918 and 1922 the
New York Society for the Suppression of Vice, while carrying
on the interminable battle against "hard core" pornography,
attempted on repeated occasions to censor books written by
recognized authors and published by respected houses. (The
situation in Boston, where unique conditions prevailed, will
be taken up in Chapter VII.) Viewed broadly, these prosecutions represent a futile attempt to dam up, or at least to divert
into familiar channels, the onrushing current of postwar literature and society. The net result was humiliating failure.
The *Madeleine* decision of 1920 (see page 50), proved only
the first in a dismal series of vice-society setbacks which left
the venerable organization frustrated and angry.

The best-known of the early postwar censorship cases
involved a book which at first glance seems far removed from
the iconoclastic and rebellious mood of the decade: James
Branch Cabell's *Jurgen*. With a full panoply of legendary
heroes and heroines, this mythic fantasy recounts the pere-
grinations of Jurgen, a medieval pawnbroker miraculously
restored to youthful vigor, through the earth, heaven, and
the nether regions. Beneath the persiflage, however, *Jurgen*
is a highly topical work, full of pungent observations on the
state of American life. The piety and enforced conformity of
the war years, for example, are given short shrift. "I have
actually heard," says an incredulous St. Peter to Jurgen, "that
in war-time, prayers are put up to the Lord God to back His
favorites and take part in the murdering." When a rather
harried Satan enquires what to do about pro-celestial elements
in his domain, Jurgen responds with familiar advice: "The
patriotic people of Hell are not in a temper to be trifled with,
now that they are at war. Conviction for offences against the
nation should not be hedged about with technicalities devised
for over-refined peacetime jurisprudence."[10]

On a deeper level, *Jurgen* may also be read as a spiritual
autobiography. After reliving his youthful dreams of romantic

love and poetic achievement, the middle-aged pawnbroker—
"the remnant of a poet"—resignedly returns to his mean profession and his shrewish wife.[11] Coming from the forty-two-
year-old author of ten undistinguished novels, this is a sad
and revealing conclusion.

With supreme irony, this testament of failure remains
Cabell's one famous and successful work—for reasons other
than he might have hoped. Published in 1919 by New York's
Robert M. McBride and Co., *Jurgen* at first drifted toward
the obscurity which had enveloped Cabell's earlier novels.
Gradually, however, rumor began to circulate that the book
contained more than met the eye; that it was, in fact, chock
full of sex. Columnist Heywood Broun informed his *New York
Tribune* readers that it was nothing but "a . . . nasty . . .
barroom story refurbished for the boudoir," and published a
letter which charged that the novel treated "in thinly veiled
episodes . . . all the perversities, abnormalities, and dam-
foolishness of sex." Broun commented in another column that
the book was a best-seller among New York chorus girls, who
were competing to discover the greatest number of *double-
entendres.*[12]

The gossip had some basis in fact. *Jurgen* unquestionably
has a number of delicately conveyed but nevertheless ribald
scenes—in one amusing and clever passage the hero gives a
highly unorthodox arithmetic lesson to a complaisant young
lady. Indeed, Cabell wrote in somewhat boastful exaggeration
to his friend Burton Rascoe that *Jurgen* was "a jungle of phallic
hints and references" that would "shock nobody because nobody will understand them."[13]

This latter expectation was sadly misplaced, however,
thanks to Heywood Broun. John Sumner was evidently among
Broun's faithful readers, for he now took a second look at
Jurgen and realized that what had at first seemed an irritating,
but hardly illegal, book, was in fact a prime candidate for
censorship. In a January 1920 police raid instigated by the vice-
society head, the printing plates, unbound sheets, and remain-

ing copies of *Jurgen* were seized and Robert McBride and his editor Guy Holt cited to appear in special sessions court. (Guy Holt, fearing just this outcome, had made—by Cabell's painstaking count—783 changes and expurgations in the manuscript of *Jurgen,* but had remained most uneasy about the book's prospects.)[14]

The feared prosecution having become a fact, McBride retained John Quinn, the Tammany lawyer who was by now a veteran of several obscenity battles. A fundamentally cautious man, Quinn decided that conviction was inevitable unless the court could be persuaded to be lenient. Accordingly, he advised McBride to withdraw *Jurgen* from sale at once, as evidence of his good intentions. McBride complied. Quinn's further strategy was to secure a delay, in hopes that both the book and the prosecution would be forgotten. To this end, he arranged for the case to be transferred from special sessions to general sessions court, where a log jam of cases assured a long delay before trial. Having accomplished this feat, reputedly through masterful use of his extensive political connections, Quinn withdrew from the case, collecting a $1000 fee.[15]

After a preliminary hearing on May 17, 1920 (at which McBride and Holt pled not guilty),[16] the *Jurgen* case did, indeed, enter a judicial limbo where it remained for over two years. The book itself, however, was not to be forgotten. Indeed, as the months rolled by it gained in fame. Second-hand copies brought up to $30, and a bootleg British edition sold briskly. McBride, still under the influence of Quinn's advice, made no effort to translate this interest into public support for his cause.[17]

James Branch Cabell, too, remained aloof. ". . . I refuse to defend *Jurgen* on any count," he wrote. "The book must speak for itself: and those who don't like it can go to hell."[18] Cabell did, however, condescend to write *Taboo,* a parody account of the case that is as full of double meanings as *Jurgen* itself. After a mocking dedication to John S. Sumner, *Taboo* goes on to describe its hero's adventures in the land of

Philistia, where he has inadvertently violated a rule against talking about *food*—a taboo he finds particularly mystifying in view of the fact that "[e]verywhere maids were passing hot dishes, and forks were being thrust into these dishes, and each was eating according to his ability and condition." A lawyer he consults merely joins in the condemnation "by reason of the fact that age had impaired his digestive organs."[19]

In a limited edition of 1,000 copies, *Taboo* had no discernible public effect on the *Jurgen* case, but it doubtless did serve to relieve Cabell's feelings and, one must in fairness record, it provides a refreshing interlude for the historian making his way through the records of the case.

In sharp contrast to McBride's cautious silence and Cabell's sardonic resignation was the "Emergency Committee" organized by Barrett H. Clark, a young actor and drama critic, to protest the *Jurgen* suppression. A protest manifesto drawn up by Clark was signed by some 160 authors and critics; others contributed indignant letters of their own. Ernest Boyd, for example, called *Jurgen* a "charmingly sophisticated fairy tale" to which "the crude solemnities of Methodist morality" were irrelevant. These responses, together with a review of the case, were published by the committee late in 1920 as *Jurgen and the Censor*. But aside from a sympathetic review in the *Nation*, it attracted little notice.[20]

A turning point came in the autumn of 1921, however, when McBride retained a new lawyer, Garrard Glenn of Goodbody, Danforth, and Glenn. Though a specialist in corporate law, Glenn enthusiastically took up *Jurgen*'s defense. Moving for a directed verdict of not guilty, he filed a long and persuasive brief defending (somewhat disingenuously) each passage objected to by the Vice Society. He buttressed his argument with citations from the *Madeleine* decision and other favorable precedents and with a sheaf of letters and reviews lauding Cabell and his work.[21]

Glenn's efforts were given a timely and powerful boost by a decision of the New York court of appeals (the state's highest) in a suit arising from the *Mademoiselle de Maupin* case of 1918. The bookseller Raymond D. Halsey had filed suit against the New York Vice Society after his acquittal, charging malicious prosecution, and in April 1919 had been awarded $2500 by a state supreme court jury. In July 1922, after various legal vicissitudes, this award was upheld in the appeals court in an important and wide-ranging decision which established that in New York obscenity cases a book "must be considered broadly as a whole," and that expert testimony to an author's reputation and a book's literary merit constituted admissible evidence.[22]

For *Jurgen*'s partisans, this was good news indeed! In October 1922, guided by Glenn's brief and the *Maupin* decision, Judge Charles C. Nott directed the general-sessions jury to acquit McBride and Holt. Nott went out of his way to praise *Jurgen* as a "brilliant" work of "unusual literary merit," whose erotic allusions were so "delicately conveyed" as to be "free from the evils accompanying suggestiveness in more realistic works."[23] Though hardly encouraging to a writer like Dreiser, Nott's decision was generally greeted with approval, and Garrard Glenn won high praise for his efforts. Among those applauding was Harlan Fiske Stone, dean of Columbia Law School. "[T]he whole country is in danger of being ruined by a smug Puritanism," he wrote Glenn, "and . . . intelligent people with liberal ideas, especially lawyers, ought to fight this tendency."[24] A small group of New York attorneys, led by Arthur Garfield Hays and Morris Ernst, would soon emerge to lead the fight Stone envisioned.

As for *Jurgen*, it was promptly reissued by McBride and became a runaway best-seller—easily Cabell's most successful book.

Two further censorship efforts of 1922 suggest that John Sumner's particular aim was to divide the publishing industry by concentrating his fire on the newer publishers who seemed especially involved in the postwar breakdown of standards.

If this was Sumner's aim he was not, as we shall see, wholly unsuccessful. The two victims of his design were Thomas Seltzer and Horace Liveright.

Thomas Seltzer (an uncle of Albert and Charles Boni, two other new publishers of the 1920s) was born in Russia in 1875 and emigrated with his parents to New York City as a boy. After several years in a sweatshop, he began translating Russian and Polish works for Mitchell Kennerley, B. W. Huebsch, and Alfred Knopf, taking time off in 1911 to serve briefly as first editor of *The Masses*. He commenced publishing books in 1920, and continued for six years until mounting money troubles forced him to sell out.[25] Seltzer issued some notable titles during this brief span. His first list included D. H. Lawrence's *Women in Love*, which had been refused by several publishers because of an earlier British obscenity conviction against Lawrence's *The Rainbow*. In 1921 came Arthur Schnitzler's *Casanova's Homecoming* and the anonymous *A Young Girl's Diary* with a preface by Sigmund Freud.

The theme of sex was central to each of these works. "Let us hesitate no longer to announce that the sensual passions and mysteries are equally sacred with the spiritual mysteries and passions," wrote Lawrence in his Foreword to *Women in Love*.[26] The Lawrence novel, wrote a *Dial* reviewer, was characteristic of a postwar generation in search of immediacy, to whom sex, "the most immediate experience of the individual, presents the greatest revelation."[27] *Casanova's Homecoming* depicts the waning of sexual desire through an imaginative re-creation of the aged Casanova's final conquest, contemptible to others and disgusting to himself. As for the language employed, a few delicate references to "firm little breasts" represent the limits of Schnitzler's daring. *A Young Girl's Diary*, the charmingly unselfconscious journal of an adolescent Austrian girl, is awash with naive but earnest reflections about sex. "Berta Franke says that when one is dark under the eyes one has *it* and that when one gets a baby then one doesn't have it any more until one gets another. She told us too how one gets

it, but I didn't really believe what she said. . . . She said it
must happen every night, for if not they don't have a baby. . . .
That's why they have their beds so close together. People call
them *marriage beds*! ! ! ." The climax, as it were, comes when
the young girl happens to observe a young couple next door
engaged in intercourse, and sets down her excited, hazy impression of what is going on. In his preface, Freud wrote:
"This diary is a gem. Never before, I believe, has anything
been written enabling us to see so clearly into the soul of a
young girl, belonging to our social and cultural stratum, during
the years of puberal development."[28]

John Sumner did not agree. Sex in childhood, sex in
maturity, sex in old age! Here was a trio of books which seemed
to epitomize the erotic obsession of the postwar world. Thomas
Seltzer, an obscure immigrant, was clearly one of the culprits
responsible for shattering the dream of a finer, "cleaner"
America. On July 11, 1922, armed with the appropriate war-
rants, Sumner descended on Seltzer's offices and seized nearly
800 copies of the offending titles. Adding insult to injury, he
forced Seltzer to transport the books to police headquarters in
his own truck.[29]

In contrast to Robert McBride, Seltzer showed a disposition to fight. With attorney Jonah J. Goldstein he organized
a thoroughgoing yet dignified defense campaign. Newspaper
publicity was encouraged; letters praising the three books
were secured from literary figures and psychologists. Soon
"[a] great tide of public discussion came into the press"—
most of it favorable to Seltzer.[30] Present in magistrates' court
to testify for Seltzer when the case was heard on July 31 were
Adolph Stern, a psychiatrist; Carl Van Doren, Columbia Professor and literary editor of the *Nation;* Gilbert Seldes of the
Dial; and Mrs. Dorothea Brand, a contributing editor of the
New Republic. "Mr. Seltzer added to the importance of his
trial by producing witnesses of the first order," noted *Publishers' Weekly.*[31] For the first time since the war the press
gave attention to such thorny questions as the wisdom of

using isolated passages as the basis for an obscenity prosecution, the admissibility of expert testimony, and whether it made sense to ban a book because of its putative effect on immature readers.

On September 12, 1922, Magistrate George W. Simpson gave his decision. Praising the Lawrence and Schnitzler novels and *A Young Girl's Diary* as "a distinct contribution to the literature of the present day," Simpson dismissed all charges against Seltzer. In a pointed aside to the Vice Society he added:

> It has been said, with some justice, that the policy of pouncing upon books too frank for contemporary taste, without regard to the motive or purpose for which they were written, or the use to which they are to be put, is objectionable and should be curbed.[32]

To Seltzer, who promptly filed a damage suit for $30,000, the decision represented a heavy blow to the Vice Society's "dictatorship" over the reading public. The *New York Times* welcomed the verdict, and *Publishers' Weekly* called it "the worst defeat that the New York [Vice] Society . . . ever suffered." A certain hopefulness began to stir; the venerable vice organization was not invincible. Sumner, however, remained philosophical: "We cannot win every case," he said.[33]

John Sumner's next foray was against the publisher who typified, even more than Seltzer, the ferment of the 1920s. Horace Liveright, an improbable mixture of genius and charlatan and one of the most colorful figures in American book-publishing history, was born in Pennsylvania in 1886. He left high school after a year, came to New York, and worked for a time as a bond salesman. In 1918 he entered book publishing in partnership with Albert Boni. The latter soon withdrew to begin a separate venture with his brother, while Liveright, now on his own, rapidly emerged as a leader among the new publishers who welcomed the manuscripts of younger writers.[34] At its apogee, Liveright's impressive list included Dreiser, Faulkner, O'Neill, Sherwood Anderson, Gertrude Atherton,

Ludwig Lewisohn, and Robinson Jeffers. Of all the publishers
of the fertile 1920s, Liveright, with his significantly titled
Modern Library, was perhaps the most in tune with a generation "hungry for what was sophisticated, subversive, avant-
garde in literature."[35] Very much in the Jazz Age tradition,
Liveright's amatory adventures and his wild parties were nearly
as famous as his distinguished list. "Authors in the waiting
room were often outnumbered by bootleggers," recalled Bennett Cerf.[36]

Horace Liveright, epitomizing all that John S. Sumner,
and those who thought as he did, found most reprehensible
in the postwar world, was kept under careful scrutiny. The
1918 suppression of *Men in War* was only the first of many
brushes with the law.[37] A golden opportunity for Sumner
seemed to offer itself in 1922 when Liveright published, in
a two-volume $20 limited edition, an idiomatic English trans-
lation of the *Satyricon* of Petronius Arbiter, a well-known if
somewhat notorious Roman classic of the first century, A.D.

Sumner promptly instituted obscenity proceedings. He
was doomed to frustration once again, however, for on September 27, 1922, Magistrate Charles A. Oberwager dismissed
the charge. After establishing that the *Satyricon*, despite admittedly lewd passages, was a recognized classic and a significant historical document, Oberwager pointed out that the
obscenity statute was not intended "to anathematize all historical manners and morals different from our own, or to close
the treasure house of the past." Furthermore, he added, no
individual or private organization should be permitted to exercise "general powers of censorship over literary works. . . ."[38]
For the second time in a month, the New York Vice Society
had been sharply reprimanded from the bench.

Liveright was jubilant. Through his attorney, Arthur
Garfield Hays (later of the American Civil Liberties Union),
he announced his intention of suing Sumner for $25,000.
Liveright later issued an expurgated and quite innocuous
trade edition of the *Satyricon*, which sold briskly.[39]

John Sumner's reaction suggests his growing frustration. If the *Satyricon* decision stood, he declared, nothing would be too indecent for publication: "The *Decameron* is a Sunday School book beside it." Elsewhere Sumner added that the decision "condemns the public . . . to receive all the literary garbage of ancient and modern Europe, and some domestic decadence. . . ."[40]

Resorting to his custom of "shopping around" for a conviction (a technique publishers justifiably found infuriating), Sumner tried to bring action against Liveright in another magistrate's court, but was thwarted by Chief City Magistrate William G. McAdoo, who warned Sumner that his influence was being eroded by his attacks on "inert publications, which are . . . at once historic, classical, and erotogenic. . . ."[41] McAdoo missed the point; the *Satyricon* may have been an inert publication, but Horace Liveright was far from being an inert publisher, and he was the real target of Sumner's action.

Trying yet another angle, Sumner persuaded District Attorney Joab A. Banton, a warm vice-society supporter, to seek a grand-jury indictment of Liveright. When the jurors learned that they would be subjected to a reading of the entire two-volume *Satyricon,* however, they quickly turned down Banton's request.[42] The Vice Society, in its efforts to keep American literature safely enmeshed in outgrown swaddling clothes, had suffered a series of damaging reverses. The coercive methods so widely accepted in 1917–18 had proven dismally ineffective as a peacetime weapon.

Not all was darkness on the legal front. Sumner could still secure convictions against the furtive peddlers of crude erotica, and in 1921 he was even able to win another case against the troublesome *Little Review.* This prosecution, though an exception to the pattern of postwar vice-society failures, is of interest as the first skirmish in the long battle between the forces of purity and James Joyce's *Ulysses.*

Margaret Anderson had begun to publish extracts from *Ulysses* in the *Little Review* in 1918, at the suggestion of Ezra Pound. All went well until July 1920, when the episode describing Leo Bloom's erotic musings about Gertie McDowell made its appearance. John Sumner, egged on by District Attorney Banton, filed a complaint, and Miss Anderson and her co-editor Jane Heap were arrested.[43] Undaunted, they not only published the next issue on schedule, but struck back at their tormentors. "It was the poet, the artist, who discovered love, created the lover, made sex everything that it is beyond a function," wrote Miss Heap indignantly. "It is the Mr. Sumners who have made obscenity."[44]

The ubiquitous John Quinn, having recently withdrawn from the *Jurgen* case, agreed to handle the defense, primarily out of friendship for Pound and Joyce. The trial, held in February 1921 before a three-judge panel in the court of special sessions, was not without absurd overtones. The arcane testimony of three defense witnesses—Scofield Thayer of the *Dial*, Phillip Moeller of the Theatre Guild, and John Cowper Powys—delighted the Greenwich Villagers who crowded the court, but merely puzzled the elderly justices, one of whom commented that *Ulysses* struck him as "the ravings of a disordered mind." At this, Margaret Anderson leaped up in protest, only to be forcibly restrained by her co-editor. An attempt to read the offending episode into the record was forbidden by the judges out of consideration for the ladies present—who, of course, had published it in the first place. An assistant district attorney thereupon cautiously explained that the objectionable passage contained "a too frank expression concerning a woman's dress when the woman was in the clothes described."[45]

On February 21, 1921, the court found the defendants guilty and imposed a $50 fine. More annoying than the fine to the fastidious female editors was the police fingerprinting to which they were subjected.[46] The conviction attracted little notice; the *New York Times* declared that the decision was "a condemnation with which most people would agree in substance if not in detail," but argued that *Ulysses* was so intrinsically insignificant that to dignify it by legal action was foolish. "To make martyrs, even pseudo-martyrs, unnecessarily is not wise," observed the *Times* sagely.[47]

The *Little Review* case left bitterness on all sides. Margaret Anderson felt that Quinn had not made a strong defense, and Otto Kahn, a financial angel of the magazine, agreed. In a comment which anticipated the more flamboyant tactics of anticensorship lawyers later in the decade, Kahn wrote to Miss Anderson:

> Of course your "Ulysses" affair was badly managed. John Quinn is rather old-fashioned, I'm afraid. I should have given you Morris Gest as a publicity agent and had the case on all the front pages. That would have helped you.[48]

James Joyce alone remained unperturbed. "This is the second time I have had the pleasure of being burned while on earth," he wrote, "so that I hope I shall pass through the fires of purgatory as quickly as my patron S. Aloysius."[49]

The only happy aspect of the case was that it gave Miss Anderson opportunity to talk at length with John S. Sumner, and to form an impression of the notorious censor:

> I found him charming. . . . He was shy and sensitive and he believed in his ideas as intensely as I did in mine. He loved to talk. He was full of quotations from Victor Hugo and other second-rate minds. He had been brought up this way and there was in his arguments a half-acknowledged eagerness to be convinced that he was wrong.

Given several weeks of conversation, she thought, one could easily "capture John Sumner's mental imagination and set it to work under the magnetic influence of ideas more hardy than his own."[50] But, alas, she could spare no time for such a philanthropic venture, and Sumner continued his unenlightened and increasingly rugged course through the 1920s.

Despite the *Little Review* success, the Vice Society's postwar record appeared, by mid-1922, distressingly bleak. In

October of that year Sumner to his chagrin was unable to
secure even a warrant against Robert Keable's *Simon Called
Peter*, an inconsequential novel about a renegade clergyman's
love affairs which was then creating something of a stir.[51]
The magistrate to whom Sumner applied agreed that the
book was "nasty," but said that in view of recent court decisions he could do nothing. As Guy Holt of McBride & Co.
wrote shortly after: "[T]he courts, of late, with gratifying accord have failed to detect obscenity in a number of volumes at
which professional righteousness has taken offense. . . ."[52]

❧

In contrast to the judicial reverses suffered by the New
York Vice Society in 1918–22 was the wide respect it continued to command. "Any feeling of antagonism heretofore
existing has disappeared," announced John Sumner in 1921.
Accepted for half a century as a worthy reformist organization,
its reputation did not collapse overnight. Most publishers
retained a healthy respect for the Vice Society, viewing a
prosecution, whether successful or not, as "extremely harmful
to their standing."[53] Maxwell Perkins of Scribner's expressed a
common attitude toward the vice organizations when he wrote
to F. Scott Fitzgerald: "Even when people are wrong you
cannot but respect those who speak with such passionate
sincerity. . . ." (Fitzgerald was not impressed: *"be intimidated
by"* should be substituted for *"respect,"* he replied.)[54]
Even Henry L. Mencken, often portrayed as the scourge
of the comstocks, stood in considerable awe of them in the
early 1920s. "A publisher who takes any unnecessary chances
[of prosecution]," he wrote in 1921, "is not brave; he is simply
silly."[55] Mencken, indeed, was the principal actor in a little
1922 drama which strikingly illustrates the Vice Society's continued latent power. Early that year, contemplating a reissue
of *The "Genius"* (whose earlier vicissitudes were described in
Chapter II), Theodore Dreiser asked Mencken to approach
John Sumner with a view toward preparing an expurgated
text which could be published with the Vice Society's blessing.

The negotiations began in May, Sumner pointing out "obscene" pages, Mencken defending them. Among the passages salvaged were:

> He drew her to him and turned her face up by her chin in spite of her. 'Open your eyes,' he pleaded. 'Oh God! That this should come to me! Now I could die. Life can hold no more. Oh, Flower Face! Oh, Silver Feet! Oh, Myrtle Bloom! Divine Fire! How perfect you are. How perfect! And to think you love me.'

Sumner stoutly refused, however, to approve a paragraph including the sentences: "The flower-like face of Suzanne came back to him—her supple body, her wondrous grace and beauty," and "She was like the budding woods in spring, like little white and blue flowers growing. If life now for once would only be kind and give him her!"[56]

These high-level negotiations, extending over several weeks, were dutifully reported by Mencken to Dreiser, who urged his friend to persevere. On one blue-ribbon day Mencken wrote triumphantly: "Sumner agrees to let pages 445 and 446 stand. . . . [T]o give him something I have suggested cutting out one sentence. It is unimportant."[57] It was Horace Liveright who brought this spectacle to an end several months later by publishing an unexpurgated edition of The "Genius." Sumner took no action. Although the venture proved abortive, the heady experience of sitting down with H. L. Mencken to expurgate Theodore Dreiser must have convinced Sumner that he might yet be granted the benevolent supervision of literary morals for which he felt himself so eminently fitted.

Whatever happened in the courts, the New York Vice Society in 1922 was still a factor to be reckoned with. A former New York governor served as chairman of its Fiftieth Anniversary Committee that year, and Warren G. Harding (his own moral standing not yet a subject of national scandal) sent a warm telegram. "My own sentiments," declared the President, ". . . strongly coincide with the purposes of your organization. . . ."[58]

The religious press was almost unanimous in its enthusiasm

for the vice societies, and the newspapers and general-circula-
tion magazines, while occasionally questioning a specific
prosecution, most notably in the Seltzer case, still expressed
general approval of Sumner's broad aims. Writing late in 1920
in the *New York Times Book Review,* Lucas Lexow expressed
(somewhat incoherently) the dominant viewpoint. Acknowledging sadly that "human beings . . . take to immorality, in
and out of fiction, as a duck takes to water," Lexow declared:

> The extra-legal associations which exist to protect the morality
> of each community must and should continue to call the at-
> tention of the courts to instances which in their opinion break
> the [obscenity] law. . . . No one can or should attempt to
> destroy this framework of defense against a lowering of the
> standards of the community. It has been suggested that there
> should be no censorship whatever, that art is free and should
> be left unfettered; but this dodges the question, since the
> good taste of the community will still remain, but will have no
> specific way in which it can assert itself. . . . This is only
> another way of saying that the majority should rule not only
> itself but the minority as well. . . .[59]

With such views still in ascendancy, "censorship" remained
in these years a greater threat to creative expression than
Sumner's conviction record might suggest. The power of a
vice-society prosecution—even an unsuccessful one—to discourage and demoralize was expressed in 1921 by an unnamed
young author quoted in the *Nation*:

> I write a passage that I believe to be as true as it is important.
> I know what will be thought of it in certain quarters. A thin
> psychical slime seems to creep over it right here in the
> quietude of my study. . . . Between it and myself has fallen
> the shadow of the Comstockery, of my publisher's mingled
> bravado and desire to avoid trouble. . . . We must destroy
> the censorship not because it forbids books, but because it
> corrupts souls.[60]

The continued influence of the Vice Society in these early
postwar years was based not only on its lingering prestige, but
also on the fact that within the literary community itself a

great many people shared Sumner's outlook and covertly supported his suppressive efforts. The new writers of the 1920s
won the field only gradually, and amid much bitterness. The
literary generation that had reached maturity in the pre-1914
world had passionately supported the war as a defense of
living ideals, and they experienced a painful wrench upon
seeing these ideals casually cast aside.[61] The voice of Albert
Jay Nock was only one of many urging the younger writers
to return once more to "great emotions, great spiritual experiences, great actions."[62]

Aging purveyors of popular fiction, jostled off the best-
seller lists, raised against the young upstarts a condemnatory
chorus far more vitriolic than Nock's mild lament. Sixty-three-
year-old Irving Bacheller, whose *Eben Holden: A Tale of the
North Country* had been a great success in 1900, declared in
1922 that the "sellers of sex passion done up in glittering
phrases" were "doomed to go to the garbage heap" for following "a pathway of muck covered with tinted and perfumed
sand." "I would rather have a serpent in my home than the
unclean literature of the present," he told Detroit's Twentieth
Century Club.[63] Booth Tarkington suggested that "most of the
young realists are realists for revenue only," and Lloyd C.
Douglas, on the threshold of his career as a writer of such
popular religious novels as *Magnificent Obsession,* lashed out
at the negativism of postwar fiction and denounced "Dreiser's
sour and bitter diatribes."[64]

Women novelists seemed particularly vehement. Alice
Hegan Rice, well known for her *Mrs. Wiggs of the Cabbage
Patch* (1901) and other prewar best-sellers, was deeply resentful of the literary upheaval which had swept her aside. "Those
of us who learned to write when taste was a thing to be
reckoned with are under a serious handicap today," she later
wrote. Gene Stratton-Porter, nearly sixty years old in 1922,
author of the 1909 best-seller *A Girl of the Limberlost,* denounced the "prurient . . . and suggestive" novels that glorified
loose-living modern habits. Margaret Deland, sixty-five, author

of *The Voice* (1912) and some ten other popular prewar novels, categorically asserted that "any story which makes wickedness attractive (or even commonplace and not reprehensible) is a wicked book." "[T]here are such things as sewers in human life," she also declared, "but human life is not made up of sewers!" The popular mystery writer Mary Roberts Rinehart labeled the iconoclastic writer "The Hun of literature," and excoriated the "cynical and disillusioned school of writing" as "morbid, introspective . . ., materialistic . . ., pessimistic, despondent, [and] astigmatic." In a crowning indictment of the new authors Miss Rinehart declared: "[T]hey violate the sanctuary of the human mind, and expose it in print."[65] What greater indecency!

At times, these attacks took on unpleasant nativist overtones. Irving Bacheller observed that the books he disliked were "mostly published by men of the European spirit." The aging author and critic Brander Matthews in 1920 reviewed unfavorably a recently published anthology of American literary criticism on the sole grounds that the critics represented were predominantly immigrants, and hence could not hope to understand the literature, language, and ideals "which are the precious possession of the English-speaking commonwealths." And Stuart Pratt Sherman, writing in the *Bookman*, rhetorically inquired whether the deplorable postwar literary situation had not been created by "writers whose blood and breeding are as hostile to the English strain as a cat to water."[66] Symptomatic of this embittered conflict was the attitude prevailing in the prestigious Authors Club of New York. Richly endowed by Andrew Carnegie, for decades a gathering place of such literary giants as Richard Watson Gilder and Henry Van Dyke, the club in the 1920s became a refuge for old men who intensely resented the new literary wave. "So far as the influence of the Authors Club is concerned," declared a spokesman, "American literature will be free from radicalism either in content or form."[67]

Some of the established book publishers, too, were distressed by the turbulent winds buffeting their profession. Typical of this group was George H. Doran, who had founded his own firm in 1908 after a long apprenticeship with Fleming H. Revell, the publisher of D. L. Moody's sermons. Doran spent the war years with the British Ministry of Information working (as he later wrote) for "the survival and supremacy of the Anglo-Saxon . . . race." The post-Armistice period, a time of such heady excitement for some, was to Doran profoundly depressing:

> The war was over; a strange and almost appalling calm came over the publishing situation. The vitality had evaporated from books which a few hours before had seemed of tremendous importance. . . . I was overcome by a great sense of desolation and vacuity.

Doran had little sympathy with the iconoclasm of postwar literature. He published an expurgated version of John Dos Passos' *Three Soldiers* with serious misgivings, and refused altogether to publish Dos Passos' second book, *Manhattan Transfer*. It reduced sex to its "commonest nomenclature," Doran later explained, and would have been offensive to the "finer sensibilities" of women—particularly those who were mothers, sisters, or daughters.[68]

To the writers, publishers, and critics who experienced little but repugnance for the innovators of the 1920s, an occasional vice-society prosecution was something less than an unmitigated disaster. Of thirty publishers asked to sign the *Jurgen* protest, only seven complied.[69] Some leading critics held out as well. "The harm done by the [Vice] Society seems to me very slight," wrote Paul Elmer More, "whereas the harm done by the self-styled artists may be very great." "[I]s freedom to injure the mind more precious than freedom to injure the health?" demanded William Lyon Phelps of Yale in 1922, echoing the frayed vice-society analogy between book censorship and pure-food legislation. If stringent censorship should come, Phelps continued, "it will not be the fault of the prudes

and the reformers and the bigots. It will be the fault of those
. . . who wrote so abominably that in order to silence them the
army of wise and high-minded authors had to wear fetters."[70]

Publishers' Weekly, the bible of the book trade, occasionally expressed qualified satisfaction when specific titles were
cleared in the courts, as in the Seltzer prosecution, but *PW*
made no move to combat censorship in general. Late in 1922,
reprinting an inflammatory *Zion's Herald* editorial which
sweepingly attacked modern fiction and suggested the need
for a more rigid censorship, *Publishers' Weekly* raised no
objections, simply observing pointedly that this reflected the
opinion "of the intelligent leaders in church circles."[71]

Nor did the newly organized National Association of Book
Publishers take a stand against censorship in the early 1920s.
Early in 1922 the N.A.B.P. set up a "censorship committee"—
not, as one might surmise, to fight suppression, but to begin
preliminary discussions as to the feasibility of establishing
self-regulatory machinery, on the theory that "it is better
to censor than be censored."[72] Although the idea was shelved,
the fact that it was seriously considered suggests that the
libertarian flame was flickering somewhat low in book-publishing circles.

The Authors' League of America (not to be confused with
the Authors Club of New York), whose prewar intervention
in *The "Genius"* case had created such a storm, remained
strictly aloof from the censorship issue in the early postwar
years. The League refused to endorse the *Jurgen* protest, declaring that "it would be inadvisable . . . to take issue on the
censorship question in an individual's case."[73] Even those
authors to whom censorship was a real menace tended to
emulate James Branch Cabell's studied unconcern. "The dis-
tiller must make his beverage, I presume, and not worry about
an occasional caught bootlegger," nonchalantly observed Sherwood Anderson when his *Many Marriages* was threatened with
suppression.[74]

Among librarians, the mood remained cautious. In 1922

Louis N. Feipel of the Brooklyn Public Library asked librarians across the country to describe their handling of "questionable books," and, by implication, to discuss their views on censorship. Some could make no clear statement; "Our present state of mind in regard to it is so chaotic, and subject to change, that there would be no use in trying to record it," sighed one. Of those who did respond, most deplored "censorship" while making clear their determination to protect readers from what Feipel described as "'suggestive' fiction . . . of which many examples from authors of repute are but too well known. . . ." A Minnesota librarian reported that the "least objectionable" among such titles were kept on a special shelf where they could be watched at all times, while the "more objectionable" were kept under lock and key to be issued "only to those who do not seem to be asking for them just from curiosity."[75]

The nearest approach to an official library position on censorship came in 1922 when the influential *Library Journal* praised editorially a British library editorial which declared:

> We librarians do not like to pose as moralists, but we have no objection to taking upon ourselves the duties of the physician. And as doctors, we can have no hesitation in sterilizing our shelves, in cutting out and casting from us the morbid, neurotic, wrongheaded, decadent books, of which there are too many written nowadays.[76]

Librarians, clearly, were in no mood to lead a crusade against book censorship.

Nor did the American Civil Liberties Union, later such an anticensorship bulwark, display any inclination to involve itself in the obscenity cases of the early 1920s. Founded during the war to defend conscientious objectors, pacifists, and radicals, the A.C.L.U. in the early postwar period continued to be interested almost exclusively in protecting the rights of political and economic nonconformists; censorship fell within its purview only when it was related to these issues.[77]

The most sustained criticism of book censorship in this period came from the liberal weeklies. Oswald Garrison

Villard's *Nation*, in particular, was unremitting in its blasts at the depredations of the "smut-hunting society" and the "illiterate constable."[78] Even among the liberals, however, there existed a certain immobilizing ambivalence toward censorship. Contemptuous of John Sumner and his ilk, they nevertheless felt considerable affinity with the philosophy upon which the vice societies operated. A 1923 *New Republic* editorial suggests the nature of this conflict. While attacking the vice societies' "tory" view of censorship as a device "to keep the world just as it is, with all its virtues and vices unimpaired," the *New Republic* also said:

> [L]iberals are not persons who were born in blinkers. They know that there are and always have been artists and writers who seek deliberately to trade in perverted tastes and desires. . . . Nor is there anything in liberalism that is repugnant to positive action for the curbing of degrading influences. It is safe to assume that a liberal state would maintain a censorship, and very likely a more drastic one than conservative states maintain.[79]

New Republic liberals, vintage 1923, might regret that the censorship initiative was in the hands of dolts, but the *existence* of the machinery caused them little concern.

Interesting in this connection is Walter Lippmann's *Public Opinion*, a book of 1922 which challenged the classic libertarian notion that free and open debate inevitably produces wise national policy. So complex are the decisions of modern statecraft, argues Lippmann, that "intuition, conscience, or the accidents of casual opinion" can no longer be trusted to produce a "reliable picture of the world" in the average citizen's mind. The solution, he concludes, is for the government to assemble a cadre of social scientists and other experts to formulate and transmit to the public such a reliable worldpicture. The goal would be "not to burden every citizen with expert opinions on all questions, but to push that burden away from him towards the responsible administrator." *Public Opinion* is not directly concerned with literary censorship, nor does it overtly challenge the rights of free speech and a free press—indeed Lippmann affirms that "the human spirit is in jeopardy" when these liberties are curtailed.[80] Yet one wonders what controls, if any, are envisioned for the journalist, novelist, or poet who stubbornly persists in creating a "picture of the world" which the official opinion-molders deem false and meretricious. Lippmann leaves this problem unexamined and unresolved, but one gains the impression that he and John Sumner, light-years apart in most respects, were in essential agreement on the need for a greater degree of social guidance and supervision over the vagaries of individual expression, on the printed page and otherwise.

By 1922, the New York Vice Society found itself in a difficult and anomalous situation. Its influence remained powerful, its hostility to postwar literature found answering echoes within the literary community, and in liberal and civil-libertarian circles the priorities and preoccupations were such that literary censorship was not an issue of central concern. And yet, despite all this, court convictions were proving more and more elusive. One damage suit had been lost and others were pending.

One obvious ploy for Sumner, which he exploited fully, was to exacerbate the tensions already present within the literary and publishing communities. If these hostilities could be increased sufficiently, perhaps authors and publishers themselves would crack down on their more daring colleagues. No literary skirmish escaped Sumner's notice, and in speeches and reports he quoted approvingly the writers and critics who attacked postwar novels. He repeatedly urged "decent authors and publishers" to repudiate the "malodorous activities of a few." The Watch and Ward Society was similarly at pains to praise the "fine old publishing houses" while condemning the troublesome newcomers. Sumner also offered covert support to those who introduced ethnic and nationalistic considerations into literary debate. "There are a great many people in this country who like to bring forward something 'foreign' and hold it forth as an example of the way things should be done over here," he declared. Most vice-society critics, he noted pointedly, were "persons of alien origin."[81]

Sumner made his divisive aim explicit in mid-1922 when he proposed to the Authors' League and to the twenty leading New York book publishers a complicated plan of extralegal censorship. Why not, asked Sumner, establish a panel of 500 representative citizens, nominated by civic and religious groups as well as by the professional associations of authors and publishers, from which would be chosen "book juries" whose task would be to approve, expurgate, or reject manuscripts submitted by publishers. By implication, Sumner agreed to abide by favorable jury findings, but he warned that publication of a manuscript after its blacklisting by a "jury" would be "excellent ground for sustaining a complaint of immorality." He had decided to suggest the idea, he added, because of the "self-censorship" plan discussed by the N.A.B.P. itself a few months before, and because three different publishers had recently, and voluntarily, submitted manuscripts to him for evaluation.[82]

Sumner proved exceedingly maladroit in promoting his pet scheme, informing the newspapers that what he ultimately envisioned for the book trade was a "committee on ethics . . . with a possible arbiter or dictator at the head" as in baseball and the movies. He added that by supporting the jury plan "decent" writers and publishers could undermine the "authors of the so-called 'younger school'" who were making "cheap reputations by turning to salacity after failing to command attention by legitimate work."[83]

Reaction to the "book jury" idea was immediate and uniformly adverse. The executive secretary of the N.A.B.P., Frederic G. Melcher, dismissed it as "preposterous," adding that Sumner's blast at young authors had ended all possibility of cooperation.[84] Eric Schuler, secretary of the Authors' League, declared his organization "unalterably opposed" to Sumner's plan, and Waldo Frank wrote:

> No man with the slightest understanding of literary values would serve on a censorship committee, for any such man knows too well the delicate problem of spiritual expression to exercise a veto of life or death over any book, however alien it might be to his own taste.[85]

Publishers' Weekly noted of Sumner, somewhat wistfully, that "with every step it becomes increasingly difficult for sensibly minded people to work with him." New York newspapers swamped the scheme in "a flood of hostile comment." "We do not see how any self-respecting publisher can accept this proposal," said the *Times,* "unless forced to it by fear of a censorship. . . ."[86]

In the face of such unwonted unanimity, Sumner quietly shelved the "book jury" plan and gave way to intemperate outbursts that betrayed his frustration. Addressing the New York Catholic Club, he heaped scorn on "literary infants" who "seek to be shocking and succeed only in being loathsome." "Decency will prevail," he asserted a few weeks later, adding menacingly: "The result to defiant and law-breaking publishers is certain. The problem is: What will be the effect on reputable publishers?"[87]

To carry out such threats, however, posed a problem. The collapse of the "book jury" scheme confronted Sumner once again with his stubborn dilemma: how to translate the Vice Society's latent power into a more impressive court record. He believed firmly that "the chance of being convicted" was "the chief deterrent against a flood of still more vicious books,"[88] yet clearly the credibility of this deterrent would soon vanish if the pattern of acquittals continued. With the Vice Society's reserve of respect and goodwill seriously depleted in the abrasive "book jury" clash, Sumner found it particularly urgent to reëstablish the potency of the legal threat.

Perhaps the answer lay in tightening the New York obscenity statute. If the law could be made strong enough, judges and juries would have no alternative but to uphold vice-society prosecutions. The climate certainly seemed favorable for a "decency" crusade. In considerations such as these, growing out of the frustrations and setbacks of the early postwar years, the epochal "Clean Books" campaign of 1923–25 took shape.

1. Anthony Comstock, best known of the early censors and a founder of the New York Society for the Suppression of Vice.

2. (below) Comstock's 1875 Commission as a Special Agent for the Post Office Department; and (right) the seal of the New York Vice Society: a literary malefactor is being jailed and a layman burns harmful books.

Anthony Comstock BY HEYWOOD BROUN AND MARGARET LEECH. BONI. NEW YORK. 1927

3. Two cartoons of Comstock: (right) in the *New York World* of January 7, 1898, Comstock is seen trampling contemporary, questionable classics and pocketing certain standard authors; (below) in *Life* for December 10, 1898, Comstock disapproves the Venus de Milo, who thumbs her nose back at him.

SANCTUM
TALKS.

4. Prominent members of Vice Societies: (above, left) J. Franklin Chase of Boston; (above) Morris K. Jesup of New York; and (left) the Reverend Philip Yarrow of Chicago.

5. Senator Reed Smoot of Utah, a prime opponent of legislation to liberalize Customs regulations on foreign books.

6. William Allen White, Progressive editor of the Emporia *Gazette*, who found Remarque's *All Quiet on the Western Front* objectionable in 1929.

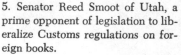

7. John Sumner (center), head of the New York Vice Society, oversees the burning of confiscated literature in the company of a Deputy Police Commissioner, 1935.

8. Judge John Ford, an important backer of the "Clean Books" crusade, as he was depicted in *The New York Times* for March 18, 1923.

Names and Record of Persons Arrested on Complaint of the New York

Date of Arrest	NAME & RESIDENCE OF PRISONER	Age	ALIASES	Nationality	Religion	Education	Married or single	No. of Children	Occupation	Warrant Issued by	OFFENCE	Committed	
June 15	Jacob Goldstein 706 Belmont Ave. Bklyn		Summons case 4th St. 7-6 Ave.	Russian	Jew				Immediate	J. M. D. Sevine	Sell ind. mag.		
June 15	Ramer Review Inc. 110 W. 47 St.		Summons case	N.Y. Corp.					Pub.	3d D.	Pub. art & mag.		
" 26	Esau Sevine 166 Hngl St. Bx	26		U.S.	Jew	S			Agent	1st D.	Ind. books "My Life" by Frank Harris		
"	Nathan Pomerantz 1042-45 88 St. Bx	40	Up-to-Date Ptg. Company	Russia	"		M.		Pres.	"	Frank Harris		
"	Harry Neushund 1665 Weeks Ave.	48		Russia	"		M.		mgr.	"	"		
"	Hyman Melleton 1943 Clinton Ave.	49		Russia	"		M.		Foreman	"	"		
" 30	Boni & Liveright 61 W. 48 St.	8	corporation	N.Y.S.					Pub.		Pub. ind. book "Replenishing Jessica"		
"	Horace B. Liveright			U.S.	Jew		M.		Pub.		"		
"	Thomas R. Smith			W.S.	Prot.				Lit. Dir.	"	"		
"	Maxwell Bodenheim	31		U.S.	Jew				author	"	"		

9. A page from the record book of the New York Vice Society. The last four entries show arrests in the case involving Maxwell Bodenheim's *Replenishing Jessica*.

10. Hamlin Garland, an author considered daring in the 1890s, supported the "Clean Books" crusade in the 1920s.

11. Elinor Glyn, author of *Three Weeks,* the object of a censorship case in 1907.

12. James Branch Cabell, with the jacket of his controversial novel, *Jurgen.*

13. H. L. Mencken and George Jean Nathan, editors of *The American Mercury*, in 1928.

14. Theodore Dreiser, long a target of the Vice Societies, in 1917.

15. Una Lady Troubridge and Radclyffe Hall in 1923, and (below) the jacket of Miss Hall's controversial novel.

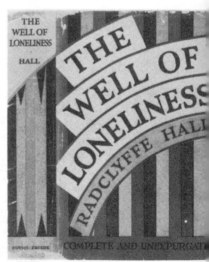

16. A cartoonist opponent of the "Clean Books" Bill saw it as a potential Trojan Horse.

UPI PHOTO

17. H. L. Mencken displays the banner of the Maryland Free State Association at Harvard, 1926, during the "Hatrack" controversy.

18. Upton Sinclair sells the "fig leaf" edition of *Oil* to Miss Florence Leiscomb at Tremont and Boylston Streets, Boston, 1927.

19. Margaret Anderson's *The Little Review*, cover and contents page. This 1920 issue included an installment from Joyce's *Ulysses*.

THE LITTLE REVIEW

VOL. VII   JULY-AUGUST   No. 2

CONTENTS

Subscription price, payable in advance, in the United States and Territories, $2.50 per year; Single copy, 25c; Canada, $2.75; Foreign, $3.00. Published monthly and copyrighted, 1920, by Margaret C. Anderson.
Manuscripts must be submitted at author's risk, with return postage.
Entered as second class matter March 16, 1917, at the Post Office at New York, N. Y., under the act of March 3, 1879.

MARGARET C. ANDERSON, Publisher
27 West Eighth Street, New York, N. Y.
Foreign Office: 43 Belsize Park Gardens, London, N. W. 3

Vol · VII   APRIL 1926   No · 28

THE AMERICAN MERCURY

A MONTHLY REVIEW

EDITED BY H · L · MENCKEN

50¢
FOR ONE COPY

$5.00
BY THE YEAR

ALFRED · A · KNOPF · PUBLISHER

20. *The American Mercury,* cover and contents page of the 1926 issue that included Herbert Asbury's story "Hatrack".

The AMERICAN MERCURY

VOLUME VII   April 1926   NUMBER 28

TABLE OF CONTENTS

ANNUAL BANQUET and FROLIC

OF THE

FORD HALL FORUM
BOSTON'S MOST UNDESIRABLE INSTITUTION

FORD HALL, TUESDAY EVENING, APRIL 16

BY UNDESIRABLES — FOR UNDESIRABLES.

NO ONE ADMITTED UNLESS UNDESIRABLE and can convince the Committee of this fact.

A Membership in the Ford Hall Forum is the surest way (though not the only way) to be considered undesirable and makes you eligible to attend.

GREATEST COLLECTION OF ARTISTIC TEMPERAMENTS EVER ASSEMBLED UNDER ONE ROOF AND ALL FOR THE PRICE OF ONE BANQUET TICKET, $2.50.

PROF. ARTHUR M. SCHLESINGER
Master of Rebelry

Author of "New Viewpoints in American History"— undesirable teacher of American history at Harvard. Undesirable because he teaches history as a scientist rather than as a propagandist.

HENRY L. MENCKEN

We asked The Mencken himself to disGrace our city on this most undesirable occasion. He replied, "I picked up a sinus infection on the Smith tour and have been wobbly ever since. At the moment it is exacerbated (a dangerous word) and so I feel like — (We just don't dare to repeat this one.) Thus, I hesitate to promise to come to Boston in April. The chances are that if I am alive by then, I'll be at some resort for the senile trying to pull

DARROW and HAYS
in

"..

MARGARET SANGER
in
"Rocking the Cradle of Liberty"
(A Silent Movie)

As she looks in other parts of Free America.

As we are a law-abiding bunch of Undesirables,—and as long as Those Who Sit in High Places insist that we must be protected from this dangerous woman, she will make no Speech. We would be permitted to listen to her for hours if she were on the other side of the B.C. Problem. T.W.S.I.H.P. have decreed that any public hall in which this woman is scheduled to speak will suddenly be found violating the fire laws or the building laws.

As she will look in our enlightened city.

MARGARET SANGER, author of "Happiness in Marriage," is the outstanding social warrior of the century. In her campaign, she has fought ignorance, disease, and smug convention and suffered calumny, persecution, arrest, and almost superhuman opposition without flinching. Even those who do not sympathize with her aim admire and respect her courage and unswerving devotion to the cause she upholds. Margaret Sanger's speeches always arouse tremendous interest. They are not the narrow and exclusive pleas of the fanatic. Her cool, rational arguments are inspired by a passionate devotion to the betterment of mankind. She deals with pressing questions of international scope and concern, the position and welfare of woman in the modern world, overpopulation as a cause of war, marriage and morality, and others of a like nature. Her vigorous personality, extraordinary breadth of outlook, and logical mind cannot fail to stir and provoke endless discussion among her audiences. BUT SHE WILL NOT SPEAK. N.B.—Although Mrs. Sanger is muzzled, she will not be handcuffed. This may have some significance

BOSTON'S OWN BRAND OF UNDESIRABLES WILL BE PRESENT

INVITATIONS HAVE ALSO BEEN SENT TO ALL THESE AUTHORS WHOSE BOOKS HAVE BEEN SUPPRESSED IN BOSTON: (PARTIAL LIST)

H. G. Wells, Author of "The World of William Clissold."
Count Keyserling, Author of "Twilight."
Conrad Aiken, Author of "Blue Voyage."
John Dos Passos, Author of "Manhattan Transfer."
Theodore Dreiser, Author of "An American Tragedy."
Sherwood Anderson, "Dark Laughter."
St. John Ervine, Author of "The Wayward Man."
Sinclair Lewis, Author of "Elmer Gantry."
May Sinclair, Author of "The Allinghams."

Ernest Hemingway, Author of "The Sun Also Rises."
Warwick Deeping, Author of "Doomsday."
Upton Sinclair, Author of "Oil."
Robert W. Service, Author of "Master of the Microbe."
Feuchtwanger, Author of "Power."
Julia Peterkin, Author of "Black April."
Babette Deutsch, Author of "In Such a Night."
Ernest Pascal, Author of "Marriage Bed."
Frances Newman, Author of "Hard Boiled Virgin."

Maybe some of them will come in person! If so, you will be told about it later. If they cannot come in person, we have asked them to send us something to be read at the banquet.

Warning: Not every book suppressed in Boston is worth reading.

UPTON SINCLAIR SAYS, "WE AUTHORS ARE USING AMERICA AS OUR SALES TERRITORY, AND BOSTON IS OUR ADVERTISING DEPARTMENT."

21. Announcement of the Ford Hall Forum "frolic," 1927. Participants included Morris Ernst, besides those shown here.

22. Horace Liveright, publisher of many books opposed by the Vice Societies, in 1930.

23. Alfred A. Knopf in a 1932 photograph by Carl Van Vechten.

24. Donald Friede (center), Vice-President of Boni and Liveright, being arrested for selling Dreiser's *An American Tragedy* in 1927.

25. Morris L. Ernst, the lawyer long associated with anti-censorship cases.

26. A meeting of prominent literary personalities of the twenties. Seated are Ezra Pound, Ford Madox Ford and James Joyce; the lawyer John Quinn is standing.

FIVE

The "Clean Books" Crusade

Reeling from a series of hostile court decisions, yet convinced of the existence of great latent support for its suppressive efforts, the New York Society for the Suppression of Vice concluded that the obscenity law was at fault and would have to be tightened. This conclusion was confirmed by a particularly intense flurry of censorship sentiment which reached its peak late in 1922. The result was the "Clean Books" crusade of 1923–25, the most far-reaching challenge to American literary freedom in the 1920s, if not in this century. The outcome, however, was quite different from what its instigators had hoped, for it was in the heated "Clean Books" controversy that an articulate anticensorship coalition, so markedly absent in the early postwar years, at last began to take shape.

❦

The vice societies had never been alone in their belief that censorship was needed to combat the alarming literary trends of the 1920s, and as the magnitude of the postwar upheaval became apparent, the demands for stern measures grew still more widespread. The religious press was particularly insistent. *The Baptist* denounced the "coarseness and vileness" of current fiction; the Presbyterian *Union Seminary Review* of Richmond, Virginia, likened it to "vile mud"; and *The Lutheran* deplored the modern literary stress on the "odd and abnormal" and nostalgically urged a revival of "the old masters of fiction." The *American Church Monthly*, an Episcopal publication, called for "a crusade against plausible immorality in our 'Best Sellers.' . . ." The December 1922 *Catholic World* warned that recent Vice Society defeats indicated a national "obliteration of the moral sense," and declared:

> The more brazen offenders against decency, be they authors, publishers, or critics, may finally go to such extremes that the American people will be driven to some such drastic measure as a federal censorship law.[1]

The bitterest of these outbursts came from *Zion's Herald*, that venerable and influential voice of Methodism, which in October 1922 published an impassioned editorial excoriating postwar fiction as a "sea of filth" and many recent books as "literary garbage wagons" fit for "the jungle and the sty." "A book censorship," it concluded ominously,

> . . . is not a very appealing proposition to lovers of freedom; but if some such measure should become necessary for the protection of the young life in our midst, upon what reasonable grounds could it be opposed? Publishers and authors have it within their power to avert a situation that ultimately will compel all good citizens to unite in demanding a literary censorship.[2]

This editorial produced a small torrent of letters, including responses from twenty-eight Methodist ministers and church officials. Eighteen of these urged a "book censorship" (the term was never precisely defined)—nine enthusiastically, and nine "if necessary." Seven others said public denunciation would probably be more effective than legal suppression. Only three rejected censorship as a matter of principle.

The merest sampling of these letters is enough to suggest their flavor. "Go to it. Hit the thing hard. Scorch it with flame—vitriolic acid may reach it. . . . It looks as if this ferment of putridity was a new eruption of phallic worship"— so wrote the Reverend Robert L. Roberts of Norwich, Connecticut. Others expressed themselves in a similar vein:

> We muzzle mad dogs. Why should we give literary charlatans unbridled license to prey upon our people?
>
> Books that leave a "bad taste" for adults should be burned. . . . It may be that we need another Anthony Comstock . . . and he should be backed either with such publicity as will deal a death-blow to its sale, or with such legislation as will tie the publishers' hands. . . . Give us the censorship.
>
> Authors of literary filth ought to have treatment similar to the purveyors of deadly disease germs, call it "book censorship" or anything else.

Other ministers spoke of "poison gas" and "the bubonic plague" in discussing current fiction. A California Methodist leader, denouncing the "literary ghoul" with his "slimy tracks," declared: "A militant censorship should at once be established, which will not only destroy their works but [will] deal peremptorily with the human rats themselves who produce such things." Another minister expressed the hope that the *Zion's Herald* editorial would be "the torch to start a great conflagration." "Nothing less," he said, "will suffice to purge away some very undesirable elements in our modern life."[3] The conflagration—or at any rate a fairly impressive blaze— was not long in coming.

Indignation over postwar literature, and frustration over John Sumner's inability to control it, were reaching a critical level. "A great deal will be heard during the next few months

about censorship," prophesied *Current Opinion* late in 1922.
"Those who believe in it, and those who don't, have for some
time been lining themselves up into opposing camps."[4] John
Sumner, only slightly chastened by the failure of his "book
jury" scheme, sensed this trend and became more aggressive.
"If a certain element in the publishing business continues to
publish degrading matter," he told the National Arts Club
in November,

> and the other element complacently sits back and takes no
> steps to discourage these harmful activities, it is possible to
> imagine that a revenue-producing measure might be enacted
> providing for the licensing of book and periodical publishers,
> the requirement of a bond in connection therewith, and the
> forfeiture of a license where an act is committed . . . inimical
> to the best interests of the state.[5]

A major book-censorship drive was gathering force.

At this crucial juncture, Sumner gained a powerful ally
in the person of John Ford, a sixty-year-old justice of the
New York State Supreme Court. The Roman Catholic son
of Irish immigrant parents, Ford had been raised in a small
western New York town where his father had worked on the
Erie Canal. After attending Cornell University on scholarship,
he had read law by night and passed the bar exam in 1893.
He then entered the state legislature as a reform Republican,
and in 1906 won election to the Supreme Court on a ticket
backed by both William Randolph Hearst and Tammany Hall.
In 1920 he was reëlected with strong bipartisan backing.[6]

The even tenor of John Ford's judicial career was rudely
jolted late in 1922 when a Manhattan book dealer gave Ford's
sixteen-year-old daughter a copy of D. H. Lawrence's *Women
in Love* from his lending library stock. The girl, coming upon
some puzzling passages, took the book to her mother; Mrs.
Ford, "in high perturbation," passed it along to her husband,
a man whose firm jaw, precisely parted steel-gray hair, thin
mustache, and bristling eyebrows bespoke a firm will and a
ready temper. "If that book dealer had been within reach of

my hands at that moment, I have little doubt I should have done him bodily harm," he later recalled grimly.[7]

Stymied in his impulse to commit mayhem, Ford instead went to the police. He was dumbfounded to learn, however, that not only had *Women in Love* recently been given a clean bill of health in magistrates' court (in the Seltzer case) but that, in the *Madeleine* decision, the appellate court had set forth a series of principles which, it seemed to Ford, "practically wiped from the statue books" New York's venerable obscenity law.[8]

Not one to suffer such reverses lightly, Ford at once concluded that the law must be strengthened. Unfamiliar with the subject, he contacted John S. Sumner, who quickly perceived that Ford's outraged sense of decency represented a highly valuable asset. With Sumner's encouragement, Ford mailed invitations to some fifty civic, fraternal, and religious organizations to meet with him on February 24, 1923, in the Nimrod Room of the Astor Hotel. The response was heartening. District Attorney Joab A. Banton sent a representative, as did the Roman Catholic Archdiocese, the Protestant Episcopal Diocese, the Lord's Day Alliance, the Boy Scouts and Girl Scouts, the Catholic Club, the antiprostitution Committee of Fourteen, the Knights of Columbus, the Girls' Friendly Society, the Episcopal Social Service Commission, the Salvation Army, Fordham University, the New York Civic Federation, the Colonial Dames of America, the Daughters of 1812, and some ten other groups.[9]

To this motley but impressive assemblage Judge Ford related the story of his encounter with *Women in Love*, vividly portrayed the mounting threat of obscenity, and flourished, as his *pièce de résistance*, a newspaper clipping which reported that the seniors at City College had just voted the *Decameron* and *Jurgen* their two favorite books—a revelation which aroused "the greatest indignation." Having thus demonstrated a humorlessness so complete as to disqualify them for any public purpose, the delegates proceeded to the main business at hand. Judge Ford, having consulted with the district attorney's office, outlined his ideas as to how the obscenity law should be tightened. When his proposals had been set forth and discussed, Ford offered final words of exhortation to his crusaders. Despite the machinations of "powerful publishing interests" and "blasé literati" eager to "pollute the minds of our children, undermine the teachings of Church and parent, and desecrate the family shrine of purity and innocence," he told them, the "moral sentiment" massed in the Nimrod Room would surely triumph.[10]

Two weeks later, a more select group met in John Ford's judicial chambers and formed a "Clean Books League" to direct the legislative campaign. The members included the New York [Protestant] Church Federation, the Roman Catholic Archdiocese, the Salvation Army, the Knights of Columbus, the Y.M.C.A., the Lord's Day Alliance, and the Episcopal Social Service Commission. Rabbi Stephen S. Wise, founder of Manhattan's Free Synagogue, was subsequently added to the roster. Martin Conboy, a socially prominent attorney and Catholic Club president, became chairman. John Ford, declaring that the obscenity law should be made "horse-high, pig-tight, and bull-strong," asked John Sumner and Anson Phelps Atterbury, retired minister of Park Presbyterian Church and a Vice Society stalwart, to join with the district attorney's office in drawing up the desired legislation.[11]

Sumner worked quickly, and on March 22, 1923, the long-promised bill was introduced at Albany by Representative George N. Jesse, a Republican, and by Senator Salvatore A. Cotillo, Democratic chairman of the Judiciary Committee. Both men were lawyers from New York City.[12]

The Jesse-Cotillo bill, as it was called, proposed to amend New York's obscenity law (Sec. 1141 of the Criminal Code) in four ways:

1. By providing that an obscenity indictment could be based on any *part* of a book, and that only this part could be admitted in evidence.

2. By making it explicit that "filthy" and "disgusting" books (two of the adjectives used in Sec. 1141) could be suppressed even if they were not sexually stimulating.
3. By making jury trials mandatory in obscenity cases.
4. By barring the introduction of expert testimony in obscenity trials "for any purpose whatever."

John Sumner and his friends had indeed made their bill "horsehigh, pig-tight, and bull-strong"! To the Clean Books League, the amendment seemed perfect. Was it not self-evident, asked John Ford, that the "ordinary, common sense, straight-out mind" of the average juryman, uncorrupted by a "coterie of literati," should decide a book's fate? John Sumner found it only fair to permit the suppression of books on the basis of isolated passages "because they are circulated on the strength of their worst passages."[13]

A few voices were immediately raised in protest. D. H. Lawrence sent a satirical telegram from New Mexico; Henry Seidel Canby declared in the New York *Evening Post* that any nation enacting such a law "would deserve no literature worth survival"; and the *New York Times* warned that the proposed amendment would give John Sumner "more power than Anthony Comstock ever dreamed of."[14] Yet, broadly speaking, the initial response was curiously passive. The prevailing tendency was to make light of the whole "Clean Books" phenomenon. Attorney Jonah J. Goldstein, a veteran of the Seltzer case, pledged "strenuous opposition," but noted that the amendment in any case was doomed to defeat. Practically no one, as a *Times* reporter later recalled, had the "slightest expectation" that the bill would get anywhere. At a routine Assembly hearing, not a single person appeared in opposition.[15]

This equanimity quickly faded when the Jesse-Cotillo bill sailed through the Assembly by a large majority and passed its first and second readings in the Senate with equal ease. With the "Clean Books" campaign now a serious and immediate threat, opposition began to emerge. The man who first sounded the alarm was Dennis Tilden Lynch, Albany cor-

respondent of the *New York Tribune,* who had followed the
progress of the bill carefully. Early in April, Lynch notified
the publisher Horace Liveright that Senate passage was im-
minent. Liveright at once began to speak and write against the
"Clean Books" bill and patched together an *ad hoc* anticensorship coalition of magazine and newspaper publishers
and printers' unions. Attorney Francis Gallatin, the New York
City parks commissioner, was retained to represent this group.[16]

Senator Cotillo, reached in Albany, expressed surprise
that there should be any opposition to such a worthwhile
measure, but he nevertheless agreed to a Judiciary Committee
hearing. Despite Liveright's feverish efforts, the turnout for
this last-minute hearing on April 18 revealed the perilous
weakness of the opposition. Only Gallatin, the novelist Gertrude Atherton, a psychology instructor from Union Theological
Seminary, *New York American* editorial writer Max Fleischer,
a Hearst representative, and Liveright himself were present to
challenge the bill. Opposing them was a host of witnesses
representing religious, welfare, and patriotic groups; the strong
Catholic contingent, led by Judge Ford himself, included
representatives of the Holy Name Society, the League of
Catholic Women, the Knights of Columbus, the Federated
Catholic Societies, and a personal emissary from Archbishop
Patrick J. Hayes.[17]

Despite its numerical disadvantage, the opposition group
presented a vigorous case. Max Fleischer read a *New York
Times* editorial (timed to appear on the day of the hearing)
which declared that the Jesse-Cotillo amendment would make
the Vice Society "an absolute and irresponsible censor of all
modern literature." Miss Atherton suggested that the proposed
law would merely "make New Jersey the most flourishing mart
for prohibited books." Francis Gallatin earnestly warned that
"Reds and Communists" might use a tighter obscenity law to
ban the Bible. Somewhat more relevantly, the Hearst spokesman said that the bill could destroy New York as a magazine-
publishing center, since owners of mass-circulation periodicals

would move elsewhere rather than risk capricious and potentially disastrous prosecutions.

John Ford damaged his own cause at the hearing by an intemperate attack on literary critics—particularly Heywood Broun, whom he accused of cynically puffing worthless books merely because they were advertised in the *World*. Ford also characterized book publishers as concerned only about "the dirty profits from their own filthy books." Gertrude Atherton's calm reply—"This is perfectly absurd and . . . entirely unfair"— set Ford's intemperate outburst in sharp relief. As a dramatic finale, John S. Sumner placed in the hands of each committee member a dozen sealed envelopes containing, like Chinese fortune cookies, shocking excerpts from recent novels. These, he said, would prove beyond question the need for a tighter law.[18]

Despite the mystery envelopes, the legislators were impressed by the arguments of the opposition. What had seemed like certain passage a few days earlier was now in doubt. Governor Alfred E. Smith, while maintaining a careful neutrality on the Jesse-Cotillo bill, was sympathetic toward those who urged a further delay so the opposing viewpoints might be aired more fully.[19] Liveright and his associates seized the opportunity to consolidate their position. On April 20, a more formal anti-"Clean Books" alliance, again comprised primarily of newspaper and magazine publishers and printers' associations, filed a brief with the Judiciary Committee denouncing the Jesse-Cotillo bill as "revolutionary" and "dangerous to the rights of publishers as a class." It would, the brief continued, "empower laymen, whipped and driven by fixed prejudices and opinions, to shackle knowledge at its source, in the name of social welfare, morality and religion."[20]

These efforts to organize an opposition to the "Clean Books" amendment forced into the open the uneasiness and distress over the trend of postwar fiction pervading large segments of the literary and publishing communities, and revealed that many key figures were unwilling to take a decisive stand against censorship. Five leading New York book publishers, including John W. Hiltman of Appleton's, president of the National Association of Book Publishers, flatly rejected Liveright's request to join his opposition delegation at the crucial April hearing. Liveright later charged that at least two "influential and prominent" publishers had *assisted* the Clean Books League in drawing up the bill, and that a number of others had covertly aided the movement. Sumner himself claimed the support of several "reputable" publishers, though he did not identify them.[21]

In mid-April, the five-member executive committee of the National Association of Book Publishers, the principal trade organization in the field, rejected a recommendation from its censorship committee that the N.A.B.P. fight the Jesse-Cotillo bill. Such opposition, declared the executive committee, "would be a misstatement of the general attitude of the publishers." In angry protest, two of the three members of the censorship committee, Alfred Harcourt and George Palmer Putnam, submitted their resignations, Putnam simultaneously announcing his support of Liveright's coalition. Two pillars of the establishment, George H. Doran and Frank N. Doubleday, were named to fill the vacancies. (The chairman and third member of the censorship committee, Arthur H. Scribner, fully supported the hands-off policy of the executive committee.) Further, the executive committee of the N.A.B.P. chose this moment officially to deplore "the growing tendency on the part of some publishers unduly to exploit books of a salacious character for purely pecuniary gain."[22] The Vice Society's oft-repeated appeals to the publishers, assuring them that safety for the conventional majority lay in ostracizing the unconventional few, had had their effect.

The divided state of the book-publishing industry was mirrored in the indecisive stance of its trade journal, *Publishers' Weekly*. Early in March *PW* expressed disapproval of Judge Ford's crusade, but also reprimanded the bookseller who had precipitated the crisis, and declared that each publisher and bookdealer should "re-examine his attitude" and "accept a personal responsibility for cleaning his own business. . . ." This effort at cautious compromise became still more evident after the N.A.B.P. refused to take a stand on the Jesse-Cotillo bill. While continuing to raise objections to the proposed amendment, *Publishers' Weekly* attributed it to a wave of "unfortunate" book promotion deprecated by "all the better elements in the trade." In a tortuous justification of the N.A.B.P.'s neutrality, this editorial continued:

> Many book publishers have felt so keenly the discredit on the profession by such selling methods that they have taken the position that this Bill was only intended by its sponsors to meet just that type of publication and that the books of honest character had nothing to fear from the revision. They have felt that to line themselves with the opposition would be to bring false interpretation on their real attitude toward objectionable books. This point of view, taken by the majority of the members of the Publishers' Association, brought about the position of non-action adopted by the Association.[23]

This line of reasoning was deplored by the *New York Times,* which warned of the risk "[i]f A and B stand calmly by and allow themselves to be made criminals, under the impression that the law will be enforced only against X and Y. . . ."[24] Few heeded this cautionary advice, however, and most leading book publishers, individually and through their trade association, did stand passively aside as the battle raged over one of the harshest literary censorship laws ever seriously proposed in America.

Writers, too, were hesitant to identify themselves as opponents of the "Clean Books" amendment. The Authors' League, having remained aloof from censorship matters since its much-criticized involvement in the *"Genius"* case of 1916, initially showed little inclination to alter this stand in the Jesse-Cotillo fight. Despite Liveright's urgent requests, no Authors' League representative appeared at the April hearing, a fact which caused pointed comment among the legislators. "Where," the *New York Times* later asked, "were the organizations of publishers and authors whose occupation, whether regarded as a business or as an art, was gravely threatened by this outrageous measure?"[25] The League later permitted its name to be appended to the brief filed with the Judiciary Committee by Liveright's coalition, but otherwise took little active part in the early phases of the struggle. This passivity was the subject of an acrimonious public quarrel late in May 1923 when Theodore Dreiser wrote Rex Beach, a League founder, that such inaction was "deplorable." In a newspaper reply, Gelett Burgess, vice-president of the League, accused Dreiser of "seeking personal publicity" and warned him not to expect the League "to help protect his dubious sex-fiction." Dreiser retorted that the apparent indifference of the Authors' League toward "the ever increasing and censorious band of vice-crusaders" was evidence of its exclusive concern with "the safer and more popular forms of light fiction."[26]

A few of the older literary figures chose the crucial summer of 1923 to resume, with even greater vehemence, their attacks upon modern fiction. Writing in *Current History* for August, the seventy-one-year-old poet Edwin Markham, popular author of "The Man With the Hoe" (1899), lashed out at "The Decadent Tendency in Current Fiction" and asked plaintively: "Why this recrudescence of sex-excess when we have so much progress in other directions?" "[T]hese young radicals in fiction," he concluded, using familiar vice-society rhetoric, ". . . are spreading a contagion that will tend to corrupt youth and to engender an enervating cynicism in all minds."[27]

In an *Independent* symposium that spring, Henry Walcott Boynton, well-known editor and anthologist of the standard English classics, declared that the "most offensive" of the recent American and British novels were "mongrels" written either by "persons with alien names and frankly alien standards" or by their native-born emulators. In the same vein, John Farrar, editor of the *Bookman* and a Doran executive, suggested that such writers as Mencken, Hecht, Dos Passos, and Waldo Frank were "insoluble alien influences" who were "simply foisting surface transcriptions of their own creeds, some of them shoddy and outworn, upon us."[28]

Discussing "Sex in American Literature" in June 1923, Mary Austin, a fifty-year-old writer whose highly successful novel of the Southwest, *The Land of Little Rain,* had appeared twenty-five years before, announced, as her opening premise, that "the love tradition of the Anglo-American strain . . . touches more and higher planes of consciousness, than the love life of any other socially coordinated group." But, Miss Austin warned, the literary expression of this love tradition was being "asphyxiated in the fumes of half-assimilated and fermenting racial contributions." Particularly to be deplored, she suggested, was the "peasant" sexuality of the nation's Baltic and Slavic writers, and the unhealthy eroticism she found characteristic of "Semitic" authors: "Neither the Russian nor the Jew has ever been able to understand . . . that not to have had any seriously upsetting sex adventures may be the end of an intelligently achieved life standard." It was these unfortunate alien forces, she implied, which accounted for the present "muddled stream of sex literature."[29]

To some of this older generation of writers, the censoring of an occasional risqué novel seemed a regrettable but necessary expedient. George Barr McCutcheon, the author of *Graustark* and other popular turn-of-the-century romances, deplored literary suppression but added, "[I]f there is no other way to clean our rapidly spreading Augean stables . . . I am for the censorship." Henry Boynton found censorship a natural, if ineffective, response to the abysmal alien standards of propriety. Booth Tarkington declared: "If we could get a man like Will H. Hays, or Augustus Thomas, to act as a censor of books, I would approve of it very heartily, for I know these two men and know they . . . can be trusted with power." Agnes Repplier, the sixty-five-year-old essayist who had written eloquently for the Allied cause during the war, unqualifiedly endorsed literary censorship as "a moral preservation that saves right-minded people from being thrown into a cesspool of immorality."[80]

In a widely publicized address on "Pernicious Books" delivered to Boston's Watch and Ward Society in April 1923, the respected Harvard professor Bliss Perry, biographer of Emerson, Whittier, and Whitman, member of the American Academy of Arts and Letters and of the Authors Club of New York, declared that the postwar rash of "unclean books" published by once-reputable firms constituted a "clear and present danger." Professor Perry praised legislative efforts "to protect the public from the moral contamination of rotten books," and declared that the vice societies, while not perfect, were doing good work and should be supported in their "constructive effort."[31]

One of the most embittered of this company of literary displaced persons was Hamlin Garland, sixty-three years old in 1923, his *Main-Travelled Roads* more than thirty years in the past. Writing in the *New York Times Book Review* late that year, when the "Clean Books" movement was still very much alive, Garland declared that the collapse of literary standards reflected the baleful influence of Manhattan, "a city of aliens, with a vast and growing colony of European peasants, merchants, and newly rich, who know little and care less for American tradition." Garland's proposed solution to this problem had at least the virtue of forthrightness:

> I believe in censorship. Over and over again I have been asked to sign a protest against the suppression of some indecent book, but I have always refused to do so, for I am certain that, on the whole, the restraining force is salutary. Censorship is, after all, only the organized collective protest against debasing forms of art. . . . I am quite certain that I can say anything worth saying under such laws.[32]

Garland had come far since 1890, when one of his own early novels had been rejected by Scribner's because of its slang, vulgarity, and radicalism![33]

The bitterness of such attacks, and the open avowal of censorship which they sometimes entailed, jolted even those accustomed to literary in-fighting. Henry Seidel Canby, hitherto inclined to make light of this squabbling between the literary generations, was forced by the "anger, the personal grievance" of writers like Hamlin Garland to revise his opinion. "I began to see," he later wrote,

> that far more was involved than I had supposed. . . . [T]hose who fought for the old tabus were really fighting against a tide that seemed to be swirling them from old moorings. Their violence was personal.[34]

Whether reflecting petty jealousies or deep-seated anxieties, these outbursts unquestionably contributed to the suppressive climate which very nearly made the "Clean Books" bill a reality.

The controversy touched off by Judge Ford's campaign swept also into the tidy world of booksellers, whipping up a bitter debate at the Detroit convention of the American Booksellers' Association in May 1923. The issue was raised by Henry S. Hutchinson, an elderly bookstore operator from New Bedford, Massachusetts. Speaking on "The Bookseller's Responsibility for the Book He Sells," Hutchinson denounced "certain publishers" for the "epidemic" of questionable books, and declared: "It behooves each one of us . . . to take a stand for clean books . . ., to sell nothing but wholesome books."

Soon thereafter, a young Detroit bookseller named Arthur Proctor arose in spirited protest. Hutchinson, he suggested, was sadly out of touch with the generation of the 1920s. "We don't want wholesome books; we don't want 'Pollyanna' books," he said, "but we do want books . . . that will portray life as it really is. . . ." "The younger people of today," he continued,

> are demanding books that may seem to some of you who are over thirty years of age as revolutionary. . . . [They] are demanding those books not from any motive of immorality, but from what they can learn about life.

A bookseller's duty to his customers, Proctor concluded, is "not just to sell books that have a sweet ending, but . . . to get them the books in spite of the censorship, in spite of . . . such men as Mr. John Sumner. . . ."

Proctor's libertarian outburst aroused great consternation. "There is no room in the United States for such literature as

that," cried one delegate amid "applause and cheers." Richard
F. Fuller, a highly influential Boston bookman, declared that
Proctor was typical of the booksellers and publishers who
were "attempting to ruin our business." The delegates seemed
particularly inflamed by Proctor's use of the word "revolution-
ary," though he clearly had intended no political connotation.
An Atlanta man found it "astonishing . . . to come up here to
Detroit, Michigan, and hear a bolsheviki speech like that. . . ."
H. H. Herr of Wilmington, Delaware, moved that Proctor's
remarks be "stricken from the records, because they are not
the kind that the American booksellers are in sympathy with."
This motion was supported by Boston's Thomas B. Ticknor
who noted somberly: "We all heard what he [Proctor] said.
The laws forbid anything referring to Reds or anarchy. . . ."
Despite the protestations of A.B.A. president Simon L. Nye
and of Frederic G. Melcher of *Publishers' Weekly,* Herr's motion carried, and Proctor's anticensorship plea was expunged
from the records.

The next day a Detroit Rotary Club leader, addressing the
convention on "Books and the Business Man," aroused great
applause when he declared: "I admire the gentleman who
addressed you yesterday and made the plea for clean books. . . .
[T]here is nothing in the world the businessman wants more
than a clean book." Warming to his subject, he added:

> [T]he man who stood up here afterwards and made a plea
> for this damnable bolsheviki stuff is wrong and we are going
> to drown that kind out before we are through.
>   There is one thing in the world that a businessman wants,
> and he wants decency, he wants cleanliness; he wants the
> square, right-thinking type of people around him, and it is
> up to your kind of people to help. If you continue to sell the
> best there is to make a living, the less we will have of this
> bolshevik and soviet stuff, the better off we will be. I hope
> you will drive it so far that you will never hear of it again.

With such an atmosphere prevailing, it need hardly be
said that the 1923 booksellers' convention took no stand against

censorship or the "Clean Books" movement. Indeed, the one resolution that touched on the subject was a terse denunciation of "the tendency to publish unwholesome literature."[35]

A similar, though more temperate, controversy broke out at the 1923 convention of the American Library Association, also held in May. The debate began when Miss Mary Rothrock, a young Knoxville librarian, declared in an address that librarians should not consider it part of their duty to exclude books "on the grounds of their possible moral effect on mature readers." Instead of hastily condemning "coarseness, vulgarity, [and] triviality" as immoral, she said, librarians should concentrate on "bringing to all the people the books that belong to them."

Her seemingly mild observations set off a "heated discussion." George F. Bowerman of Washington, D.C., a partisan of Miss Rothrock's position, and in any event "a kindly man, given to easy enthusiasms," suggested that her speech be "given to the publishers as the librarians' contribution" toward stemming "the tide of censorship." Strongly opposed to Bowerman's proposal was Miss M. E. Ahern, the editor of *Public Libraries*, who warned somewhat cryptically that this "would put a weapon in the hands of publishers. . . ." (She did not discuss the question of whom the librarians by their silence might be aiding.)

Pursuing the debate in a *Public Libraries* editorial, Miss Ahern asserted that "few, very few" librarians would agree with Miss Rothrock and Mr. Bowerman. With the appearance of so many novels of "neurotic exploration" and of so much fiction that made no contribution to the "happiness of mankind," she said, "it is to be expected that the question of censorship . . . will enter the minds of very many people." This need not trouble librarians, she suggested, since "the presence or absence of such books" was a matter of indifference to the "vast majority" of library patrons. Rejecting Bowerman's call for involvement in the censorship struggle, Miss Ahern exhorted librarians to remember "the old, old bulwark of what is true,"

and to "walk in lofty purpose and valuable service unmoved
by the roar of distasteful ideas around them."[36]

The professional associations of publishers, authors, booksellers, and librarians responded in strikingly similar fashion
to the issue so sharply posed by the "Clean Books" crusade.
Within each group, a deep antagonism toward the new literary
currents was forced into the open, and the resultant conflicts
for a time made impossible the emergence of a clear-cut,
united stand against literary suppression. In each group, however, an undercurrent of dissatisfaction with the dominant
policy gave promise that the literary community might yet
take up arms against censorship. "[A] few of us down here were
'Young Turks' . . ., and rather eager to challenge the *status quo,*"
Miss Rothrock has recalled.

With the book world itself vacillating in its attitude toward
the "Clean Books" amendment, it is not surprising that few
other voices should have been raised in opposition. The
American Civil Liberties Union, still focusing on other issues,
played no part in the "Clean Books" fight. Except in New York
City, where newspapers spoke out unanimously and effectively
against John Ford's purity drive, many newspapers and magazines found much to praise in what they viewed as simply
a high-minded crusade against the "filth," "nastiness," and
"sensuality" of postwar fiction. "[F]or centuries men and
women wrote splendid novels that knew nothing of psycho-
analysis, gland grafting and the allied arts," observed the
Newark News, adding: "Let the public turn back the clock
a little. . . ."[37] The *Ladies' Home Journal* attacked "The Filth
Uplifters," and the editor of *Current History* (a *New York
Times* publication) warmly endorsed the Jesse-Cotillo bill,
predicting eloquently that "the blazing wrath of aroused public
opinion from a people befouled and insulted will yet compel
the authorities to dam up the polluted streams of abomination."
Christian Century, hopefully viewing the New York censorship
drive as the overture to an even more ambitious crusade, declared that "a national censorship" was the only way to purify
"the fountain of literature and the drama."[38]

In mid-1923 the *Literary Digest* queried a small sampling of ministers, authors, publishers, and "moral uplift" leaders as to their opinions on the "Clean Books" agitation and other suppressive movements, and found that "the generality" favored "some form of censorship."[39] As the nation learned in 1936, *Literary Digest* surveys were not models of scientific accuracy, but in this instance the magazine's conclusion may be taken as one more straw in what had become a rather fearsome wind.

Meanwhile, the legislative struggle went forward in Albany. Having won a respite after the April hearing, Horace Liveright and his chief editor T. R. Smith, a former editor of *Century Magazine,* made repeated lobbying trips to the capital. Informal polls indicated at times that a majority of senators were prepared to support the bill, but the opposition managed to stave off a vote while the persuasive efforts went on. Liveright, not willing to place all his trust in principled appeals to literary freedom, spent at least one evening playing poker with important senators, taking care to lose heavily.[40] The periodical publishers, notably William Randolph Hearst and Bernarr MacFadden, conducted an effective campaign. Frederick Hume of the National Association of Periodical Publishers and William A. Deford, a Hearst attorney, presented their case to key legislators, while MacFadden, veteran of skirmishes with Anthony Comstock, warned that passage of the "Clean Books" bill would force him to "immediately consider" moving his vast pulp-magazine empire to another state.[41]

As for the Clean Books League, it was showing signs of internal strain. The Y.M.C.A. was said to be wavering in its enthusiasm for the Jesse-Cotillo bill, and several Episcopal clergymen were reported as sharply critical of their church's close identification with the book-purity movement. A serious defection came late in April when Rabbi Stephen S. Wise, a founding member of the Clean Books League, attacked its bill in an address before his Free Synagogue Congregation at

Carnegie Hall as "one of the stupid stratagems of democracy
to find a way out of responsibility." While still alarmed by
"dirty publishers" and the "cesspool" of indecent literature,
Wise had concluded that legal control was not the answer.
Even Henry Ford's anti-Semitic *Dearborn Independent,* said
Wise, should be given full freedom.[42]

On May 3, 1923, the Senate took up the Cotillo bill. In
a last-minute editorial, the *Times* warned once again of "Censorship Gone Daft." Opponents of the bill were led in the
floor debate by Jimmy Walker, then the Democratic majority
leader, who immortalized himself on this occasion by observing
that "No woman was ever ruined by a book." In a less frequently quoted passage, Walker completed the thought:

> It is . . . these strong men who are worrying about salacious
> books in the hands of little girls who are ruining them. . . .
> Some of the best tellers of shabby stories in this Senate have
> been worrying their hearts out during the debate today. . . .[43]

When the vote came, an unlikely coalition of conservative
upstate Republicans and Tammany Democrats produced fifteen
votes for the measure. Thirty-one senators, however, voted
in the negative.[44] The "Clean Books" drive had, for the moment,
been stalled. A combination of forces—including threats of
economic reprisal by powerful periodical publishers, the editorials of the major Manhattan dailies, the efforts of a small
but persistent band of authors and book publishers led by
Horace Liveright, and the excesses and misjudgments of Judge
Ford and his allies—had dealt the Vice Society a decisive
reverse.

The *New York Times* hailed the outcome and consoled
the defeated with the reminder that "purity did not become
wholly extinct in the several thousand years during which the
human race has got along without a clean books bill." A few
weeks later, H. L. Mencken, Ernest Boyd of the *Dial,* Jimmy
Walker, and others gathered at the Brevoort Hotel in Greenwich Village for a testimonial dinner in honor of Horace

Liveright, who took the occasion to announce his resignation from the National Association of Book Publishers.[45]

THE SECOND "CLEAN BOOKS" CRUSADE—1924

Undaunted by defeat, the New York Society for the Suppression of Vice and the Clean Books League at once mapped plans for a renewed legislative campaign. "We are going to arouse the decent people in all of the churches," Judge Ford announced, as he began a round of meetings with the men's groups of various congregations. (This raised the ticklish problem of how to maintain proper decorum while proving that modern literature was, indeed, drenched in obscenity. Ford's solution was to give the ministers at these meetings ample copies of a mimeographed compilation of spicy extracts from recent novels, which they could later distribute to their flocks.)[46] Ford's strenuous missionary efforts bore fruit. After some months he was able to report that both Protestant and Catholic churches were responding in a gratifying manner and that the religious press was conducting a "splendid campaign." "Unfortunately," he added, "we have been unable to interest Jewish organizations."[47]

Judge Ford, emboldened by the neutrality of the book publishers in the 1923 censorship fight, confidently assured the public that "a number of publishers . . ., for the sake of the reputation of their business," favored a more stringent obscenity law. Book publishing, he observed, was a "noble business" which had unfortunately been "prostituted" by a "small coterie" of newcomers. "The great majority of publishers have nothing to fear from our bill," he said soothingly, so long as they did not seek to "make common cause with the purveyors of debasing smut. . . ."[48]

But the opposition was at last finding its bearings. Those who had fought the bill from the first redoubled their efforts. Bernarr MacFadden, never one to do things by halves, announced a one-month fast in opposition to the "Clean Books" movement. Forming the "Americanism Protective League" early in January 1924, MacFadden drew 3,500 people to Madison Square Garden for a great anticensorship rally.[49] Significantly, too, the literary and book-publishing communities, divided and impotent in the April campaign, were moving hesitantly toward a greater involvement in the censorship fight. Ford's tactic of alternating cajolery with threats was producing diminishing results. When the new model of the "Clean Books" bill was unveiled late in 1923—and proved remarkably like its predecessor—*Publishers' Weekly* with unusual celerity and forthrightness denounced it as "entirely wrong" and predicted "a chorus of protest."[50]

The new tone of *Publishers' Weekly* reflected a changed attitude in the industry. A few months earlier the National Association of Book Publishers had quietly retained Harlan Fiske Stone of the prestigious law firm Sullivan & Cromwell to make a broad study of the problem of obscenity legislation. A former dean of the Columbia Law School (and soon to become a justice of the United States Supreme Court), Stone was not only a highly respected jurist but also a known opponent of censorship. On December 8, the N.A.B.P. broke its long silence and issued a statement on censorship, based on Stone's brief. Not precisely a ringing manifesto, this statement reiterated the familiar call for higher publishing standards and conceded society's right to repress "obscenity" by due process of law. Indeed, it went so far as to imply criticism of organized movements to defend specific books and publishers, arguing somewhat illogically that this might mean "defense without discrimination." Having expressed these sentiments, however, the N.A.B.P. proceeded to condemn censorship by "private initiative"—so much for the vice societies!—and to denounce the "Clean Books" amendment and related measures in every particular:

> Expert witnesses should by no means be considered incompetent to testify. Not all writing is intended for the immature,

and no state ought to consider restricting book publication to such volumes as are suitable for the immature. No book can be judged by a brief isolated passage and no statute should make it imperative for the court to do so. The intent or purpose of the work should be regarded.[51]

With this widely circulated manifesto, the National Association of Book Publishers brought an impressive new force to bear in the censorship battle. That the Association did indeed intend to take a more active role was confirmed in March 1924 when Harlan F. Stone himself appeared before a joint Senate-House hearing in Albany to testify against the recently reintroduced "Clean Books" amendment.[52]

Other vacillating organizations concluded, belatedly, that the "Clean Books" threat demanded united opposition. As a consequence, the 1924 hearing presented a sharp contrast to that of the previous year. The chairman of the American Library Association's committee on federal and state relations testified against the bill. The Authors' League was represented by the well-known playwright Augustus Thomas, whose remarks were both persuasive and witty:

> Words are the vehicle of art. They must be free. They cannot be . . . put within bounds by sectarian bigots. Under this bill you could throw out a book because it contained a description of a man eating corn beef and cabbage with his fingers. That might be called "disgusting."[53]

Only the hard core of the Clean Books League—John Ford, John Sumner, Anson Phelps Atterbury, Martin Conboy, and a few others—appeared at the 1924 hearing. There was, however, one newcomer: Herbert A. Goldstein, a Manhattan rabbi who presumably had replaced the defector Stephen Wise. "I wish we were back in Puritan days," mused Rabbi Goldstein, "when there was respect for the law of the state and everybody belonged to a church."[54]

The novelty having worn off, the second "Clean Books" campaign generated less interest than its predecessor. But this time apathy worked against, rather than in favor of, the bill.

It was not even called for a vote in the House, and early in
April the Senate defeated it by the crushing margin of forty-
seven to four.[55]

The issue continued to reverberate through the literary
world. When the American Booksellers' Association met in
New York City for its annual convention a few weeks after
the Senate vote, the atmosphere was entirely different from
that of 1923. The author Thomas Dixon was given "prolonged
applause" when he made a fervent attack on literary suppression. A Southern orator of the old school, Dixon described
censorship as "the most odious word in the English language,"
and declared:

> It comes down to us from Europe, wet with tears, reeking
> with the groans and anguish of martyrs through the centuries.
> . . . I . . . believe with every fiber of my soul and body, that
> God Almighty never made a man or woman big enough, broad
> enough, wise enough, strong enough, to be entrusted with the
> tremendous power that is put in the hands of a censor.

Swayed by such rhetoric, the 300 delegates unanimously declared their opposition "to federal, state, and municipal censorship"; to all "except the censorship of intelligent public
opinion."[56] Booksellers, too, were jumping aboard the (by now
rather crowded) anticensorship bandwagon.

The Clean Books League renewed the battle in 1925,
heartened by a fresh recruit in the person of William Sheafe
Chase, the sixty-seven-year-old rector of Brooklyn's Christ
Episcopal Church, who made an emotional appeal for purity
at the annual Albany hearing. A special feature of the 1925
hearing was a reading by Senator William Love, the Brooklyn
physician who had introduced the bill, of shocking excerpts
from an unidentified recent novel. The impact of this was
somewhat blunted, however, when an opposition witness,
recognizing the passages, pointed out that the book from
which the excerpts came had already been suppressed under
the very law which supposedly stood in such need of strength-
ening.

The National Association of Book Publishers, having recently reiterated its stand against any tightening of the obscenity law, was represented in force at the 1925 hearing by some twenty individual publishers, who traveled to Albany in a special delegation. These included not only men from the newer houses, but also from Harper's, Macmillan's, Century, Oxford, Lippincott, Dutton, Holt, and Doran. Also present for the first time was a representative from the Association of the Bar of the City of New York. Within two years' time, opposition to censorship excesses, from being considered dangerously radical, had become fashionable. Impressed by the serried ranks of publishers, the committee hastily killed the Love bill, and it never reached the Senate floor.[57]

John Ford was unable to see the handwriting on the wall. Through the rest of the decade—indeed, until his death in 1941—he carried on his increasingly lonely campaign. In 1926 Fleming H. Revell published Ford's *Criminal Obscenity—A Plea for Its Suppression,* a sad, rambling, scissors-and-paste denunciation of bad books. The dedication of *Criminal Obscenity* suggests that Ford's own literary taste ran to the floridly sentimental:

> To my infant granddaughter, VIRGINIA, in the fond hope that throughout her girlhood her pure soul may not be tainted or her innocent mind defiled through contact with impure prints, plays, or pictures; and that her young life may unfold into noble womanhood immaculate as the heart of a rose unsullied by mortal touch.

The "Clean Books" bill reappeared annually, but its defeat was now a foregone conclusion. By 1929 the Clean Books League had faded into obscurity and *Publishers' Weekly* could casually dismiss its bill as "that perennial irritant."[58]

❧

The "Clean Books" crusade was the most sustained and formidable attempt in the 1920s to convert the obscenity law into a fool-proof instrument for the emasculation of serious

literary expression. A well-organized movement with clearly
defined aims, it represented a greater threat than the better-
remembered but essentially parochial suppressive flurries which
shook Boston later in the decade.

The decisive defeat of John Ford's campaign had an
immediate effect upon would-be censors. John S. Sumner, in
his report for 1924, said cautiously that henceforth his organization would be "less punitive" and more "preventive and constructive" in its approach. This pledge is borne out by Vice
Society statistics. In 1924 the number of Vice Society arrests
for all causes dropped to twenty-four, the lowest figure in
years.[59] Except for so-called "hard core" pornography, book
prosecutions in the New York courts after 1923 were increasingly rare.

In a series of postwar obscenity cases, the New York
judiciary, sensing the changed literary and social climate, had
liberalized the obscenity law by formulating a set of careful
procedural restraints on book prosecutions: a book must be
judged in its entirety, expert opinion may be admitted in evidence, the book's effect upon adults rather than upon the immature must be the test. In setting out to destroy these troublesome restraints, John Sumner and Judge Ford had, ironically,
merely succeeded in giving them wide publicity and hastening
their general acceptance. Some taboos, of course, still remained
—a few four-letter words, explicit discussion of sexual perversion, detailed descriptions of coitus—to provide challenges
for future libertarian crusades, but this should not obscure the
fact that a wide new terrain had been occupied (perhaps
reoccupied would be more accurate) in the name of literary
freedom and had been successfully defended against formidable counterattack. "Despite the wails that are still lifted
whenever censorship is mentioned," wrote H. L. Mencken and
George Jean Nathan in the *American Mercury* in November
1924,

> it should be clear to a man with cinders in both eyes that
> never before in the history of American literature and drama

have things been so happily free from interference by busy-bodies as they are at the present time. Books are published today that so little as three years ago would have been raided before the ink was dry. . . .

The literary editor of *The Outlook* agreed. "[I]t takes just as much courage to write a book dealing frankly with sex," he wrote early in 1925, "as it does to wave the American flag in a musical comedy."[80]

As no single case had been able to do, the "Clean Books" controversy alerted the public—particularly in New York State—to some of the issues involved in book censorship. The debate over censorship, eclipsed during the war, had been resumed with a vengeance. The countless speeches, articles, editorials, and hearings sparked by the "Clean Books" issue constituted a massive exercise in popular education—with Sumner and Ford and their vociferous supporters the unwitting deans of instruction. As a consequence, the obscenity law was shorn of some of its sacrosanct quality; rather than an immutable and clear-cut moral guide, it was now seen as simply an archaic, wordy, and rather vague legislative formulation, readily subject to manipulation and varying interpretations.

The 1923–25 censorship battle also had a far-reaching impact upon publishers, authors, critics, booksellers, and librarians—that uneasy alliance comprising "the world of books"—many of whom had in the early postwar years covertly supported censorship as a useful check upon writers who seemed to be trampling underfoot all the hallowed canons of propriety. The blatant challenge of the "Clean Books" crusade forced these temporizers off the fence. A few, like Hamlin Garland, simply became more outspoken in their advocacy of repression, but the broader literary community, goaded by mavericks like Horace Liveright, gradually drew together in the beginnings of a firm anticensorship coalition.

The new climate is evident in the fact that after the "Clean Books" crisis, even those who attacked the new literary trends most strongly took care to avoid the slightest appearance of sympathy for legal suppression. One sees the change, for example, in the writings of the conservative critic Stuart Pratt Sherman. In the immediate postwar period Sherman had made repeated intemperate attacks on the newer writers which, probably unintentionally, had given considerable aid and comfort to the vice societies. Sherman had, indeed, on occasion been quoted with approval by John Summer. However, in an essay published a few months after the "Clean Books" drive had so nearly succeeded, Sherman pointedly described censorship, when directed against regularly published books, as "futile and mischievous." The "only proper instrument" for modifying the "temper and character of our literature," he declared, is "an independent and dispassionate criticism." As for such outbursts as the "Clean Books" crusade, Sherman found them beneath serious discussion:

> A country clergyman writes in that he has not read the book in question, but that he knows that our modern authors are a "bad lot." . . . An irate judge declares that he and his daughter *have* read the book, and he only wishes that he could "get it before the public"! An Outraged Parent says that he would like to read it; and in this wish he is joined by the association of Y.M.C.A. secretaries, the Associated Mothers' Club, the Boy Scouts, and the Camp Fire Girls. Members of any or all these organizations are prepared to affirm, after a careful perusal of the objectionable book, that it is not fit for them to read.[61]

Clearly, it was going to be increasingly difficult for the knights of book suppression to find any sympathy even in the most conservative corners of the literary world.

Finally, the "Clean Books" crusade drastically affected the reputation of the New York Society for the Suppression of Vice and, indirectly, that of vice societies in other cities. Indeed, it triggered a serious decline in vice-society fortunes which was to continue with increasing precipitousness throughout the decade. John S. Sumner had tried to use the impulsive Judge Ford to advance his own ends, and when Ford, returning year after year to the fray, became the butt of ridicule, Sumner and his organization suffered as well. The alliance between Clean Books League and Vice Society had been a union of enthusiast and professional, and as the public became successively alarmed, amused, and finally bored by the frenetic outbursts of the enthusiast, the professional paid a heavy toll in popular esteem. The image of "Censorship" began to crowd aside the more positive images—"Social Reform," "Urban Uplift," "Child Welfare"—which the vice societies had so sedulously cultivated. "To be a censor today," drily observed Mencken and Nathan late in 1924, ". . . a man must be not only an idiot; he must be also a man courageous enough in his imbecility to endure the low guffaws of his next-door neighbors."[62]

SIX

The Latter 1920s

It is by now a historical cliché to observe that the 1920s generated more froth than any other ten-year period in American
history, and that as the decade rushed to its climax the
froth billowed higher than ever. Confident in the knowledge that Calvin Coolidge and then Herbert Hoover were
minding the store, Americans settled down to enjoy themselves.
Radio sales statistics, Florida land prices, and stock-market
quotations joined Lindbergh in the stratosphere, while on
earth Tunney, Valentino, and Jolson, flagpole sitters and mara-
thon dancers, offered a dizzying kaleidoscope of distractions.

To their intense frustration, the New York Society for
the Suppression of Vice and similar organizations elsewhere
found themselves increasingly shunted to the sidelines amid

all this activity. With so much going on, it was harder to make the headlines. Too often now, when the newspapers did turn their attention to the vice societies, it was to report another defeat. Only rarely after 1924 did the vice organizations succeed in suppressing an over-the-counter book. (An important exception to this generalization will be taken up in the next chapter.) By 1930, John Sumner's dream of becoming a benign literary czar had vanished; he was, indeed, hard put simply to hold his organization together. Meanwhile, the libertarian coalition called forth by the "Clean Books" crusade grew firmer, and the anticensorship position was elaborated and hedged about with persuasive arguments. But, paradoxically, the period which saw a steady reduction in the pressure against books also brought a sharp intensification in censorship activity directed at magazines and the stage.

BOOK CENSORSHIP ON THE WANE

Numerous cases attest to the dismal regularity with which John Sumner's ventures in the literary realm in the later 1920s proved abortive. In June 1927, for example, he failed ignominiously to suppress *The President's Daughter*, Nan Britton's lurid exposé of her alleged relations with the late President Harding, whom she named as the father of her daughter. Shocked by this profanation of "the memory of a deceased statesman," particularly one who had praised the Vice Society so warmly only four years before, Sumner personally led six Manhattan policemen in a raid on the offices of the publisher, A. & C. Boni, seizing the printing plates and all remaining copies of the book. A magistrate refused to indict, however, and Sumner was forced to return the seized property and give up his efforts to silence the embarrassing Miss Britton.[1]

A second defeat came in 1928 at the hands of Sumner's old nemesis, Horace Liveright. Earlier in the decade Liveright had paid Maxwell Bodenheim $1000 for a still-unwritten novel. When Bodenheim delivered the manuscript, Liveright found it "filthy" even by his own permissive standards. In several acrimonious sessions with the author, Liveright and his editor T. R. Smith cleaned up the more glaring passages, and the book was published in 1925 as *Replenishing Jessica*.

Despite his efforts at purification, Liveright was soon slapped with a grand jury obscenity indictment—secured by Sumner. Retaining Arthur Garfield Hays, he loyally defended Bodenheim's novel as a "highly moral" work by "a great author and poet." The case hung fire until March 1928, when it was heard in general sessions court. Although Sumner offered damaging testimony as to Liveright's private opinion of *Replenishing Jessica*, the jury, after listening in considerable boredom to a reading of the 272–page book, took only fifteen minutes to return a verdict of not guilty.[2]

This series of setbacks, so depressing to John Sumner, reached its nadir in *The Well of Loneliness* case of 1929. *The Well of Loneliness* was written in 1927 by Radclyffe Hall, a Britisher known up to that time as the author of several quite conventional novels. In a perhaps idealized recollection, her longtime companion Una Vincenzo has described how Miss Hall came to her one day "with unusual gravity" seeking advice in a difficult decision:

> [S]he had long wanted to write a book on sexual inversion, a novel that would be accessible to the general public. . . . It was her absolute conviction that such a book could only be written by a sexual invert, who alone could be qualified by personal knowledge and experience to speak on behalf of a misunderstood and misjudged minority.
>
> . . . I told her to write what was in her heart, that . . . I was sick to death of ambiguities, and only wished to be known for what I was. . . .[3]

The novel which Radclyffe Hall proceeded to write traces the life of its autobiographical heroine from early childhood as she recognizes, struggles against, and finally accepts, her homosexual impulses. Physical encounters are passed over with

Victorian delicacy. "[T]hat night they were not divided," concludes a chapter describing a growing erotic attachment. The next chapter begins:

> A strange, though to them a very natural thing it seemed, this new and ardent fulfillment; having something fine and urgent about it that lay almost beyond the range of their wills. Something primitive and age-old as Nature herself. . . . For now they were in the grip of Creation, of Creation's terrific urge to create; the urge that will sometimes sweep forward blindly alike into fruitful and sterile channels. That wellnigh intolerable life force would grip them, making them a part of its own existence; so that they who might never create a new life, were yet one at such moments with the fountain of living.[4]

The Well of Loneliness, published in England by Jonathan Cape in 1928, won high praise from many literary and scientific figures, including Havelock Ellis. But when the London *Sunday Express* denounced it as "a challenge to every instinct of social sanity and moral decency which distinguishes Christian civilization from the corruptions of paganism," Cape bowed to a personal request from the Home Secretary, Sir William Joynson-Hicks, and withdrew it. In a subsequent test case, London Magistrate Sir Charles Biron found the novel legally obscene.[5]

Meanwhile, Mrs. Alfred A. Knopf, fully aware of its theme, had contracted to publish *The Well of Loneliness* in the United States. Several Knopf editors concurred in her judgment, finding that while the book dealt with "a very delicate subject . . . that might be regarded by many as taboo, it did so without offense." During the interval of informal suppression in Britain, Alfred A. Knopf announced to the trade his continued determination to publish the book; indeed, he had it set up in type. After Magistrate Biron's decision, however, Knopf tersely announced his withdrawal. "We didn't see anything heroic about publishing it here after what had happened in England," he later commented.[6]

With Knopf out of the picture, the American rights to *The Well of Loneliness* were taken over by Covici-Friede, a small, newly established publishing house. Like Horace Liveright, Pascal Covici and Donald Friede were the very personification of that young and "alien" publishing generation so obnoxious to John Sumner. Covici, a Roumanian brought as a child to the United States, grew up in Chicago, where, in the early 1920s, he managed an *avant-garde* bookstore. His first brush with the censors had come in 1922 when he and W. F. McGee had published a limited edition of Ben Hecht's *Fantazius Mallare*, a work notable primarily for its ingeniously suggestive (but in fact quite innocent) *art nouveau* illustrations by Wallace Smith. Covici, McGee, and Hecht had at once been charged with violation of the postal obscenity statute, and when Hecht's efforts to secure critical endorsement of his book met with failure, the trio pled *nolo contendere*. In February 1924, despite the efforts of attorney Clarence Darrow, they were convicted and fined $1000. Ben Hecht, like James Branch Cabell before him, retaliated by writing a satire on censorship. Entitled *Cutie, A Warm Mamma*, it describes the downfall of Herman Pupick, a vice crusader so pure he assumes "torso" is a bull-fighting term. Two hundred copies of *Cutie* were printed for private distribution.

Another, more significant, result of the *Fantazius Mallare* conviction was that Pascal Covici decided to abandon Chicago for the more tolerant atmosphere of New York. Here he soon encountered a kindred spirit: Donald Friede.[7] A twenty-seven-year-old playboy of Russian parentage, a dropout from several colleges, and a veteran of nine short-lived jobs, Friede had recently been advised by his analyst to go into book publishing. After a brief apprenticeship with Knopf and Liveright he joined forces with Covici in 1928.[8]

It was thus two brash and exuberant beginners who decided to publish *The Well of Loneliness* and thereby risk a tangle with John Sumner. Their first move was to retain Morris Ernst, a New York attorney whose book on censorship,

To the Pure, had appeared earlier in the year. At Ernst's suggestion they informed Sumner of their plans and invited a test case. The Vice Society head, who considered Miss Hall's book "literary refuse," needed no urging. He thought *The Well of Loneliness* especially "vicious" because the sympathetic presentation of its characters implied that they should be "accepted on the same plane as persons normally constituted. . . ."[9]

In December 1928, shortly after the appearance of the Covici-Friede edition of Miss Hall's book, Sumner purchased a copy from Donald Friede. Several weeks later, Manhattan police arrested Friede and seized over 800 copies of the book. On February 21, 1929, Magistrate Hyman Bushel found Friede guilty and *The Well of Loneliness* obscene; it "idealized and extolled" perversion, he said, and thus would "debauch public morals" and "deprave and corrupt minds," especially of "the weaker members of society." Ernst at once appealed.[10]

With the legal wheels in motion, Ernst began a massive publicity campaign on behalf of his clients. Letters and telegrams by the hundred were dispatched to authors, journalists, psychiatrists, clergymen—anyone of influence who might respond with an endorsement. Newspaper coverage was heavy. Covici-Friede, meanwhile, did not falter in supplying the heavy demand for what was rapidly becoming a runaway best-seller. Printing operations were transferred to Massachusetts, with distribution from New Jersey. Friede, believing that "any publicity was good publicity if they spelled your name right," was delighted by Morris Ernst's flamboyant tactics and the resultant columns of free newspaper advertising. He attempted to compound his good fortune by duping the Watch and Ward Society into prosecuting as well, but without success. "They assured me that they saw nothing wrong with the book," he later wrote. "This was very definitely not what I wanted to hear, but I had to be satisfied with it."[11]

On April 19, 1929, a three-judge special sessions court reversed the lower-court conviction and cleared *The Well of*

Loneliness. Covici-Friede at once placed a full-page advertisement in *Publishers' Weekly.* "[N]ow that *the law has spoken,*" it ran,

> our big advertising campaign is about to be launched. This campaign had just been mapped out, when the Powers of Darkness swooped down upon the book. The plans then laid are now to be carried out. The only difference is that, thanks to Mr. Sumner, our campaign may now exhibit a little more gusto. . . .

The ad went on to announce a "VICTORY EDITION" of "*The Well,* as the book is now affectionately known." This $25 edition featured Miss Hall's autograph and Morris Ernst's summary of the court proceedings. "Wire your orders now at our expense," urged the jubilant publishers.[12]

Advertising in this vein proceeded with such "gusto" that over 100,000 copies of *The Well of Loneliness* were sold within a year, for which a royalty check in excess of $60,000 went to Radclyffe Hall.[13] What had begun with Miss Hall's simple decision to tell the truth of her own experience, had ended in an extravaganza of publicity and commercial exploitation.

In later years, Donald Friede came to view his role in *The Well of Loneliness* case somewhat ruefully. Writing in 1964, shortly before his death, he said:

> [W]hen I see some of the books published today, I cannot help but wonder if our fight against censorship in the twenties was really wise. . . . *Fanny Hill* in paper! And *Naked Lunch* in any form! . . . But I suppose there are some people still willing to play the piano in the literary brothel. Certainly the pay is good.[14]

The Well of Loneliness defeat merely underscored the erosion of the Vice Society's prestige. Only a few years earlier, a Vice Society prosecution had represented a stigma to be avoided at all costs; now a prosecution was welcomed—by some publishers at least—as a valuable adjunct to advertising campaigns. John Sumner was forced to realize that he exerted an influence over serious American literature only insofar as lawyers and publishers chose to exploit his prosecutions. In 1930, having meanwhile won two more victories over the Vice Society, Morris Ernst wrote:

> In recent years *there has not been a single instance* where a book generally accepted by the public, the press, literary critics, the reading public, and the community at large, and openly dealt with by the publishers and the book trade, was ultimately condemned by the courts. . . .

H. V. Kaltenborn succinctly made the same point at the 1930 American Booksellers' Association convention: "Censorship is to the book business," he said, "what the flea is to the dog."[15]

Some publishers, it is true, remained willing to go to almost any lengths to avoid an obscenity prosecution, and over these Sumner still had considerable power. Alfred A. Knopf, as the *Homo Sapiens* and *The Well of Loneliness* cases would suggest, consistently yielded before Vice Society bluster. In 1924, when the New York City district attorney, at Sumner's prodding, threatened to prosecute Knopf for publishing Floyd Dell's *Janet March*, Knopf at once withdrew the book, "rather than have it attain a large sale through a possible censorship court action." Dell initially accepted Knopf's high-minded explanation, but he later became convinced that his publisher had let him down badly. Knopf has said in his own behalf that Sumner's omnipotence in the 1920s made surrender the only feasible course; but neither the Vice Society's dismal record in the courts nor the decisive "Clean Books" defeat of 1923 bears out this pessimistic view.[16]

Knopf's role in the *American Mercury* case of 1926 (see Chapter VII) was somewhat ambiguous. As publisher of the attacked periodical he joined editor H. L. Mencken and attorney Arthur Garfield Hays in a Washington trip to protest the postal ban. Later, however, it was Knopf's wish to "fade out of this business," together with other considerations, which discouraged Mencken and Hays from following up their Boston victory over the Watch and Ward Society with a damage suit. In Mencken's view, Knopf was annoyed because Hays was also representing Horace Liveright, whom Knopf "detested."[17]

As an anticensorship warrior, Alfred Knopf's characteristic stance was one of dignified retreat. One must in fairness record, however, that the imprint which Knopf went to such lengths to protect survived to become one of the most distinguished in American publishing history, while Seltzer, Liveright, Friede, Covici, and other impetuous adventurers ready to rush into a censorship fight at the drop of a hat, early fell into bankruptcy and oblivion.

The isolated *Janet March* success offered but little solace to John Sumner. Frustrated in his attacks on books of general circulation, he sought more vulnerable targets. In December 1923, two New York booksellers, Maurice Inman and Max Gottschalk, were arrested for selling *A Night in a Moorish Harem, Only a Boy,* and John Cleland's *Fanny Hill*—three hoary classics of the literary underworld. They had sold the books to Charles J. Bamberger, a venerable Vice Society agent whose talent for simulating a connoisseur's interest in erotica was, for over forty years, of inestimable aid to Anthony Comstock and John Sumner. In March 1924, the hapless Inman and Gottschalk were convicted in special sessions court and fined $250 each. *Publishers' Weekly,* for all its new-found outspokenness on the censorship question, had no quarrel with these convictions. The suppression of "such admittedly obscene books," it said, was a "salutary" measure of which "the book trade may well approve. . . ."[18]

Another book decidedly beyond the pale in the 1920s, and thus easy game for the Vice Society even in its twilight years, was Frank Harris's three-volume *My Life and Loves,* published in Germany between 1923 and 1927. In June 1925, Manhattan police raided the Up-To-Date Printing Company, where an American edition was on the presses, seizing about 300 copies of Volume II. They arrested Nathan Pomerantz, president of Up-To-Date; two of his employees; and Harris's

United States agent, one Esar Levine. John Sumner, pronouncing *My Life* "the most obscene book published in the present century," soon joined the campaign against it. In August 1925 he led a raid on a bindery where another 680 copies of the book were seized, and two more men, Jacob Sidowsky and Harry J. Lebovit, arrested. The following March, Lebovit and Pomerantz were fined a total of $750, and Levine was given a 90-day workhouse sentence. Once again, *Publishers' Weekly* acquiesced; Harris's book it found "unfit for publication under the standards of any country."[19]

Further Vice Society successes against obscure erotica punctuated the latter years of the decade. A 1928 raid on Frances Steloff's Gotham Book Mart netted over 400 books, including George Lewys's privately printed *Temple of Pallas-Athenae* (Los Angeles, 1924), and resulted in a conviction and fine for bookseller David Moss. In a 1929 Vice Society prosecution, Joseph Seiffer was convicted in magistrates' court for selling *The Adventures of Hsi Men Ching;* Earl B. Marks was convicted in 1930 for selling Pierre Louys' *Aphrodite;* and Alfred B. Risden met a like fate a year later in the sale of *One Hundred Merry and Delightful Tales.*[20]

But even against books of this description, Sumner could no longer be assured of success. His complaint against Isadore Lhevinne, an enterprising high-school French teacher who had published a novel of his own called *Ariadne,* was dismissed in 1929. In 1931 a prosecution of Frances Steloff for selling *Hsi Men Ching* and *A Night in a Moorish Harem* ended in the same fashion.[21]

The New York Vice Society, which long had fallen on evil books, now fell on evil days. Fast disappearing was the era when publishers, authors, and editors paid it the tribute of cautious deference. In a 1927 biography of Comstock, Heywood Broun and Margaret Leech discussed the Vice Society with that tolerant indulgence reserved for yesterday's bugaboos. Sumner's annual reports were now largely given over to financial appeals. The Depression revealed how tenuous his support

had become; by 1932 annual contributions had dropped to
$5,000 from a 1929 high of $12,000, and the Society was dipping
into capital to meet current expenses.[22]

The grimy midtown brownstone which housed the Vice
Society suggested the organization's fallen estate. The atmosphere was gloomy, the golden-oak furnishings dark and massive. A large portrait of Anthony Comstock dominated the
cluttered office, and a dusty cuspidor provided a further reminder of the Founder's brooding presence. In the bare yard,
a scrawny ailanthus tree struggled toward the sun. John Sumner, in late middle age now, paunchy and growing puffy
through the jowls, carried on his routine of work at an old-
fashioned roll-top desk. The idealistic young attorney who had
assumed the fallen leader's mantle twenty years before had
had a trying career. The era which was to have carried the
Vice Society to new heights had witnessed its slow decay.[23]

A similar fate overtook the vice organizations of other
cities. The Western Society for the Suppression of Vice, never
as robust as its eastern prototypes, in 1922 secured a Federal
conviction against Cincinnati bookseller John G. Kidd for
mailing a copy of Rabelais' works, but, evidently overcome by
this triumph, the westerners soon dropped from view.[24] In
Boston, as we shall see, the once-respected Watch and Ward
Society was wholly discredited by the end of the decade, and
in Chicago a spectacular 1930 case left the Illinois Vigilance
Association a shambles.

The Illinois Vigilance Association, it will be recalled, had
been founded in a burst of Progressive energy in 1908 to fight
both prostitution and bad books. Its leader in the 1920s was
the Reverend Philip Yarrow, a native of Great Britain who had
been brought to America in 1876 at four years of age. After
graduation from Princeton and Hartford Theological Seminary,
he had become minister of a Chicago Congregational church.
During the First World War he headed the Dry Chicago
Federation, and in 1922, with Prohibition achieved, he became
director of the Vigilance Association. In this capacity he raided

speakeasies and bookie joints, spoke widely on "white slavery," operated a home for erring girls, denounced corrupt city politicians, and fought for purity on the printed page. Owing to a unique feature of the Illinois obscenity law, Yarrow as "informant" was paid one-half of all fines imposed in the obscenity cases he brought to court.[25]

In 1929, Philip Yarrow launched a campaign which resulted in the arrest of nine Chicago booksellers. Among them was the elderly manager of Brentano's medical section, an employee of twenty-seven-years' standing, who had unsuspectingly sold a Vigilance Association agent a copy of a well-known marriage manual.[26]

Three of the indicted booksellers were convicted. But when the fourth, Walter Shaver, the owner of a chain of Chicago bookstores, was tried in municipal court in January 1930, he offered a vigorous defense based on a plea of entrapment. Yarrow's agent, he testified, had badgered him into ordering the indicted book, *A Night in a Moorish Harem*. The jury returned a verdict of not guilty.[27]

Shaver's attorney, Cameron Latter, at once filed a damage suit against Yarrow. The vice crusader fought back through his newspaper, *Vigilance*, declaring that "classical smut has no more standing under the law than low-down smut." *Christian Century* (published in Chicago) warmly praised Yarrow's "moral policing" of the "beasts" who specialized in distributing "moral sewage."[28] But the *Chicago Evening Post*, in a muckraking series by reporter Milton Fairman, exposed Yarrow's entrapment methods and published photographs of checks paid him as his "informant's fee" in obscenity convictions. Faculty members at the University of Chicago, including Robert Morss Lovett, issued a statement condemning the Vigilance Association.[29] As Milton Fairman was also Chicago correspondent for *Publishers' Weekly*, his exposé was widely publicized. The revulsion against Yarrow intensified when Walter Shaver went into bankruptcy, a misfortune he readily blamed on his prosecution, although the Depression was probably a more important factor.[30]

In April 1931 a Chicago superior court jury, after hearing
Shaver's attorney denounce Yarrow as an "un-American
snooper" and a "wolf in sheep's clothing," awarded Shaver
damages of $5000. Refusing either to pay or to post bail,
Yarrow was imprisoned in the county jail for nineteen days.
"I am simply a humble minister," he said. "This flesh of mine
will be putrid before I pay a nickel of the judgment against
me." In this prediction he was correct, for the judgment was
ultimately reversed on appeal.[31] But this was a hollow victory
for Yarrow, who had been hopelessly discredited. He continued to thunder against evil literature, finally from a wheel
chair in a Congregationalist home for the aged, until his death
in 1954, but after 1930 he and his Vigilance Association were
little more than quaint reminders of a bygone day.

The handwriting was on the wall, but the vice societies
tried to forestall the inevitable. In former days they had dis-
armed criticism by identifying themselves with a dominant
social current of the day—genteel reformism, Progressivism,
wartime idealism, etc.—and now in the business climate of
the 1920s they tried to do the same. As John Sumner told a
reporter in 1922: "I am not a reformer, I am a conservative."
Several years later the Watch and Ward secretary declared
that the vice-society emphasis on "personal responsibility" was
especially needed "[i]n these days when socialism is being
emphasized as a cure for human ills. . . ."[32]

For a time it seemed that this tack might succeed. In
1925 the Watch and Ward expressed gratification at "the way
in which big business interests have come forward and accepted our leadership in the matter of suppressing obscenity."[33]
But as one "questionable" novel after another succeeded in
the marketplace, it became evident that efforts to interfere
with free enterprise on nebulous grounds of "literary purity"
would win little but lip service from the business community.
Indeed, when vice-society ardor exposed an entire community

to ridicule—as in Boston—business leaders could quickly turn actively hostile.

Increasingly isolated and estranged, the vice societies tried to conjure up once more the aura of the years when they had been accepted and honored. "This organization was founded by such men as Edward Everett Hale and Phillips Brooks," declared an embattled Watch and Ward Society in 1929. "Some of Boston's best citizens have been in its service. . . . It is entitled to be treated with some respect." In 1927 an elderly New Yorker who had helped found the city's vice organization over fifty years before wrote to the *Times* protesting the universal ridicule of Anthony Comstock and recalling the social prominence and philanthropic bent of Comstock's first supporters. Somewhat later the president of the New York Vice Society noted almost wistfully that in its early years his organization had attracted "many of the most prominent men of that day."[34]

Memories of the ebullient Progressive years were invoked as well. Book censorship, declared the Watch and Ward secretary in 1926, was simply an effort to give "a moral square deal" to everyone. The vice societies' hero was "[n]ot Myles Standish," he added, "but Theodore Roosevelt."[35]

When their appeals to bygone loyalties fell on deaf ears, vice-society spokesmen sometimes assumed an aggrieved and peevish tone. "I am simply a humble minister," said Philip Yarrow, the erstwhile Savonarola of State Street, from his jail cell. "[S]ometimes," observed Anson Phelps Atterbury of the New York Vice Society in 1929, "we are tempted to feel as Elijah felt when, in his 'protest against a corrupt civilization,' he thought himself alone."[36]

More typically, however, the fading of real power led the vice societies to indulge in vitriolic denunciations of their enemies and in grandiose visions of future retribution. At the annual Watch and Ward Society gathering in 1924 the principal speaker exhorted the "Christian Forces of America" to gird for a "Holy War" against the "mighty organized forces which

threaten the nation with decay." He envisioned a "Law Enforcement Committee in every church . . . in union with the
Police, or better still, in union with some central Christian
Law Enforcement Body. . . ." A few years later John Sumner
was declaring: "[I]f we can't have public decency through a
sense of decency, let's have it through fear of punishment. If
we can't have governmental, orderly, standardized and ap-
pealable control because politicians are afraid of a word ['censorship'], then let's have control with a club."[37]

With the passing years, Sumner became increasingly
splenetic in his attacks, until by 1931 he seemed nearly to have
lost touch with reality. "A curse of the times is that there are
too many publishers . . . just as there are too many theatres,"
he burst out in the midst of a speech before the American
Booksellers' Association;

> [A]ny tramp can find an outlet in print for his trampish
> writings. Any hobo temporarily sober can find a publisher
> [for] . . . an epic of hobodom provided there is sufficient . . .
> lechery, blasphemy, profanity, and filth.

Once launched, Sumner seemed unable to control his tirade:

> Any alleged soldier of the late war . . . can find a publisher
> for his wartime experiences provided there is enough of yellow-
> back theorizing and sufficient defamation of war [!] and the
> army set forth in gutter language.[38]

In addition to a growing intemperateness of language,
another consequence of the setbacks of the 1920s was a marked
change in the vice societies' view of their mission. The postwar decade saw the evaporation of the idealistic concern for
community well-being which had once provided a rationale
for book censorship. In its place came a narrow exclusive-
ness and blatant appeals to fear. In a 1925 newsletter to his
supporters John Sumner declared that the fight against bad
books and wicked publishers "is your fight if you have in your
veins any of the blood which coursed in the veins of those who
founded and maintained this as a nation of high moral stan-

dards in former generations." A later New York Vice Society
report described objectionable books as a threat to "the Anglo-
Saxon standard" of decency. In Chicago, the Reverend Yarrow
inveighed against the "foreign invaders" who were undermining the nation's morals.[39] Sumner regularly published in his
annual reports a table showing the religious affiliations of
everyone prosecuted by the New York Vice Society. In a typical
year—1928—two Protestants, three Catholics, and nineteen
Jews were caught in the Vice Society's nets. Toward the end
of the decade, this religious tabulation was regularly accompanied by a statement declaring that "the very large percentage
of offenders of foreign origin" demonstrated the need for
"more stringent laws regulating the admission of immigrants
to the United States and their distribution in the interests of
assimilation."[40] One gains the impression that particular care
was taken to record the religious data on Jewish culprits. In
the Vice Society office record book (now in the Library of
Congress) for 1925, for example, the religious affiliation of
those arrested was recorded rather sporadically, but after the
names of Horace Liveright and Maxwell Bodenheim (arrested
in the *Replenishing Jessica* case) the word "Jew" is written in
a firm hand.[41]

Unwonted humility, nostalgia, verbal belligerence, narrow ethnic and religious appeals—all bear witness to the root
fact that the vice societies' influence was steadily diminishing
as the 1920s wore on. And as their utterances and accusations
grew more extreme, their alienation from the world about them
became more complete.

As the vice societies sought to come to terms with unaccustomed weakness, their opponents grew more confident and
articulate. The anti-"Clean Books" coalition not only held
firm, but grew stronger. In the summer of 1927 a group of
forty authors, forming a "Committee for the Suppression of
Irresponsible Censorship," issued a vigorous denunciation of

censorious meddling. In 1933 the Authors' League, confirming
the trend of a decade, attacked "all forms of censorship" and
denounced the New York Vice Society by name.[42]

The National Association of Book Publishers periodically
reiterated its stand against privately initiated censorship.
Publishers' Weekly became increasingly eloquent on the subject, eventually even finding the courage to omit the ritual calls
for literary purity that long were the concluding feature of
every editorial on censorship. In 1927 *PW* approvingly reprinted an editorial which sharply questioned whether such
a nebulous concept as "obscenity" could ever provide a sufficient basis for proceedings at law.[43] Though still capable of
being shocked by authors like Frank Harris and John Cleland,
Publishers' Weekly had come a long way from its temporizing,
ineffectual stance of the early 1920s.

The American Booksellers' Association, after the bitter
debates of 1923, moved steadily toward unequivocal opposition to censorship. "Intelligence, good taste, a sense of humor,
and common sense," declared the A.B.A. in 1927, constituted
the only "board of censorship" whose authority booksellers
recognized. In the same year they pointedly elected as president John G. Kidd, the Cincinnati bookseller earlier convicted
for mailing a copy of Rabelais' works.[44]

Librarians, too, contributed to the yeasty anticensorship
ferment of the later 1920s. Stirred by the "Clean Books" fight
and by other suppressive flurries, they took a fresh look at those
shocking postwar novels and concluded that what had seemed
a "symptom of disease" was perhaps "simply the stamp of
life itself."[45] Simultaneously, librarians began to reexamine
their traditional role as guardians of the middle-class pieties.
Perhaps, after all, their Gibraltarlike stance between the reading public and "questionable" literature was a bit presump-
tuous. Speaking in 1931 to a group of her colleagues, one
thoughtful librarian summed up the change that had occurred.
While recognizing the human impulse to "guide and control"
the lives and morals of others, she warned that librarians—
often unmarried ladies from sheltered backgrounds—could no

longer expect to play the role of moral arbiter in a rapidly changing society. "Who, after all, are we," she asked,

> to set ourselves up as capable of saying what will or will not harm another person? We have thought that upon us lay the heavy burden of guarding the morals of youth, 90 per cent of whom could tell us many things! . . . And the way we tried to help our young people was to weigh them down with the same narrowing shackles of ignorance and limited experience that we ourselves were struggling with.[46]

Increasingly outspoken in opposing literary suppression, librarians would play an important part in the censorship controversies which broke out in Massachusetts toward the end of the decade.

The changed climate was felt as well by church leaders, many of whom had vigorously supported the early postwar efforts to censor "immoral" and "blasphemous" books. Admittedly, some groups—notably the Methodist Board of Temperance, Prohibition, and Public Morals—never wavered in their enthusiasm for the vice societies, but they grew fewer in number as the decade wore on. More typical of the new outlook was the United Society of Christian Endeavor, the influential Protestant youth organization, whose secretary in 1927 issued a strong condemnation of book censorship; to suppress a book merely aroused curiosity in it, he said. In 1930 none other than the editor of *Zion's Herald* sweepingly denounced literary censorship as a hindrance to "the intellectual development of our race." Religious leaders seemed to be realizing that fretful demands for censorship exhibited remarkably little faith in the power of their own message. "Is the church going to gain in prestige, respect, and influence," asked *The Congregationalist* in 1926, "by appealing to the police in a situation that she ought to be meeting by the strength and power of her own witness?"[47]

Since the days of Theodore Schroeder early in the century, few except judges impelled by the exigencies of specific cases had given much thought to "obscenity" and censorship viewed in the abstract. With the emergence of a *de facto* anticensorship consensus, the theoretical aspects of the question attracted renewed attention. For every column on censorship by a Heywood Broun or an Oswald Villard in the early postwar years there were now dozens of books, editorials, pamphlets, and articles. Books and essays on the subject by such varied figures as Aldous Huxley, Mary Ware Dennett, Arthur Garfield Hays, Victor F. Calverton, Havelock Ellis, D. H. Lawrence, and H. L. Mencken were widely circulated.[48] Earlier contributions like Galsworthy's censorship essay in *The Inn of Tranquility* (1909) and Pareto's *Le Mythe Vertuïste et la Littérature Immorale* (1911) were revived and read with fresh interest.

In 1932, in keeping with the radicalism of the day, Victor F. Calverton's *The Liberation of American Literature* contributed a Marxist interpretation of American censorship to the growing library on the subject. In the nineteenth century, runs Calverton's argument, the moral fibre of the American ruling class was so debilitated by its role as exploiter that only the petty bourgeoisie was left to uphold the genteel taboos of the day. Faced in the twentieth century with a working-class revolt against these taboos, the petty bourgeoisie resorted to desperate efforts at legal censorship, but "victory was no more possible . . . in the literary field than in the economic or political," and "after three hundred years . . . the dictatorship of the bourgeoisie in the moral field was broken down at last." (One is reminded of the 1929 *Daily Worker* headline when a Boston jury composed of two machinists, two clerks, a hatter, a treasurer, a painter, an automobile washer, a shipper, two salesmen, and a janitor upheld an obscenity conviction against *An American Tragedy*: "BLUE STOCKING BOSTON JURY FINDS DREISER'S BOOK BAD FOR YOUTH.")[49]

Considerably more influential than Calverton's analysis was *To the Pure . . . A Study of Obscenity and the Censor,* a work published in 1928 by two little-known Manhattan lawyers,

William Seagle and Morris Ernst. Seagle, thirty years old in
1928, had practiced law only briefly prior to 1924 when he
became a free-lance writer on legal subjects for the *American
Mercury*, the *Nation*, and other periodicals. The dominant
figure in the collaboration was the forty-year-old Morris Ernst.
Ernst had been brought at an early age to New York City from
Alabama, where his father had been a country storekeeper.
Graduating from Williams College, he attended New York Law
School by night while selling shirts and furniture by day. He
began to practice law in 1915, but not until 1927 did he become
interested in book censorship. Galled by his defeat in a Customs
censorship case, he determined to master the subject. With
Seagle he studied the relevant laws and the available literature,
applied his own breezy iconoclasm to the problem, and produced *To the Pure*. The book attracted immediate attention
and brought to Ernst the succession of celebrated censorship
cases, from *The Well of Loneliness* to *Ulysses*, which made
him famous. Ernst's great gift as a censorship lawyer, which
also pervades *To the Pure*, was his flamboyant ability to
dramatize and publicize issues. "Very quickly I realized the
inadequacy of my part-time preparation," he once said in a
rare introspective moment; "I started to make up for it by
exhibitionism and have never recovered."[50]

As with Robert Ingersoll and Theodore Schroeder, the
principal weapon in Ernst's and Seagle's anticensorship arsenal
is ridicule. "Obscenity" is invariably viewed as a creation of
prudish, repressed, or otherwise emotionally crippled people.
The censors are seen as evil and ignorant persons whose
motives and techniques may be analyzed *in vacuo*, apart from
their specific historical or social context. Focusing almost
entirely upon those censorship cases which established significant libertarian precedents, the authors pay scant attention to
cases which did not produce landmark decisions. Such a
centrally important phenomenon as the "Clean Books" crusade
is ignored.

While Ernst and Seagle vigorously attack legal suppres-

sion in *To the Pure,* they have no hesitancy in invoking the
coercive power of public opinion. When the "modern teacher"
is asked about the vulgar term for sexual intercourse, they
advise, she should calmly inform the enquiring child that *fuck*
is a perfectly innocent word of Anglo-Saxon agricultural
derivation. But, they hastily add, the teacher should impress
upon the child that its "present disrepute . . . dictates the
wisdom of its avoidance by those who do not care to become
objectionable to friends and neighbors."[51] Legal freedom; social
tyranny. For all its insistence on modernity, *To the Pure* has
much in common with the attitude—at once aggressively
libertarian and hypersensitive to the opinions of others—
which de Tocqueville had described a century earlier* as
typically American.

For all its limitations, *To the Pure* unquestionably achieved
its immediate polemical purpose: the vagueness of the word
"obscene" and its synonyms, and the risks in making them the
basis of proceedings in a court of law, were repeatedly ham-
mered home. Perhaps as significant as the substance of *To the
Pure* is its jaunty, confident tone. Ernst and Seagle are clearly
speaking for a group which has ceased to feel on the defensive,
and which is now energetically consolidating its position. *To
the Pure* was a further reminder that the assault on literary
censorship was rapidly turning into a rout.

All these books and essays gradually generated—on both
sides of the Atlantic—a new attitude toward the vexed problems of censorship and obscenity. "The obscene" ceased to
be the immutable, instantly recognizable entity it had been
for the Victorians. Obscenity was now felt to be considerably

* In Volume I of *Democracy in America* (1835), in describing the
manner by which extralegal social pressures were utilized to suppress
unpopular or minority opinions in the United States, de Tocqueville
writes: "Attempts have been made by some governments to protect
morality by prohibiting licentious books. In the United States no one
is punished for this sort of books, but no one is induced to write them;
not because all the citizens are immaculate in conduct, but because the
majority of the community is decent and orderly."

more elusive—"a matter of changing conventions" and of "personal predilections"; "in people's minds and feelings, not in words or actions."[52] This almost oppressive awareness of the hazy nature of "obscenity" was certainly heightened by the Freudians' stress on the subconscious as well as by cultural anthropologists like Malinowski and Evans-Pritchard who in the later 1920s were beginning to point out that among African tribes or Trobriand Islanders the "obscene" was often quite different from what it was for the average American.[53] As the intellectual climate changed, fewer and fewer thoughtful people could be found who were willing to defend the banning of a book which to someone of another social group, or to some future generation, might seem completely innocuous or even supremely moral.

Furthermore, serious doubts began to be voiced as to the value of suppressing a book even in the unlikely event that its "obscenity" could be universally agreed upon. The presumed dire effects of "obscene" books—effects which the vice societies had chronicled in such loving detail for decades—no longer appeared quite so heinous. A British Home Secretary could still denounce an erotic novel because "two young people, who had been perfectly pure up till that time, after reading this book went and had sexual intercourse together"—but to D. H. Lawrence this seemed a happy and certainly a non-world-shaking outcome. Perhaps, suggested Lawrence, the Home Secretary would have been happier "if they had murdered one another, or worn each other to rags of nervous prostration."[54] Even autoerotism, the great peril of Comstock's generation, was losing its power to terrify. Morris Ernst acknowledged that erotic books "may lead to onanism," but added: "Medical science, of late, has tended to the view that its evil effects have been exaggerated. At any rate, it is not yet a crime to fall into this indulgence."[55]

If "obscenity" were indefinable and probably harmless, it followed that the effort to suppress it by law was futile at best. "Abolish the obscenity laws!" was the essential message

of *To the Pure,* and many emphatically agreed. The author
Ben Ray Redman, after discussing the hazy nature of "obscenity" in a *Scribner's* article, concluded:

> [D]oes this mean that . . . any piece of writing, however lewd,
> lascivious, obscene, salacious and pornographic, within or
> without the meaning of any statute, might just as well be
> printed anywhere at any time? For all practical purposes, yes.[56]

Some even contended that the free circulation of "obscenity" would accomplish a positive good in undermining
the furtiveness upon which taboos thrive. "[T]he effect of
abolishing censorship completely," argued the *Nation,*
". . . would ultimately be to demolish the notion . . . that the
natural processes of the human body . . . are essentially shameful and degrading." Arthur Garfield Hays considered it a "fair
deduction" that if the "mysteries" surrounding sex were removed "society would become so clean-minded that there
would be no such thing as 'obscenity'—in the present sense."
"[W]hy not," asked Mary Ware Dennett at the 1930 booksellers' convention,

> put all the lids in the trash barrel and give what has been
> under the lid a good sunning and airing and see to it that
> every one possible is spared from acquiring the dirty feelings
> that are the foundation of indecency.[57]

Most people hesitated to go quite this far. Many who
advocated the broadest possible freedom for books still favored strict limitations upon the more widely read magazines.
And even on the matter of books, the publisher M. Lincoln
Schuster expressed a common viewpoint when he distinguished
between "the broad highway of distinguished creative literature" and the "back alleys of filth" made up of books "offered
in dark places and under suspicious circumstances." The latter,
Schuster felt, should continue to be rigidly suppressed. Even
D. H. Lawrence declared he would "censor pornography,
rigorously." In this category he placed not only the "hard-core"
material with its "insult . . . to sex, and to the human spirit,"

but also "our glorious popular literature of pretty pornography, which rubs on the dirty secret without letting you know what is happening."[58]

In all this discussion there was universal agreement on one point: the vice societies had outlived their day. Nothing could have been more alien to the emerging consensus than the vice societies' tiresome insistence (as in John Sumner's 1929 annual report) that "certain fundamental principles of morality and decency" had been "incorporated by 'sane and sound' legislators in the body of our laws."[59] By the end of the decade the vice-society leaders had become the very epitome of D. H. Lawrence's "grey elderly ones"; Sumner and his partners in other cities had been written off as relics of "the eunuch century, the century of the mealy-mouthed lie, the century that . . . tried to destroy humanity, the nineteenth century."[60]

The repudiation of the vice societies was closely tied to the nation's experience during the 1920s with another experiment in social control: Prohibition. Initially, the ratification of the Eighteenth Amendment in 1919 had seemed likely to strengthen the book censorship forces by diverting a certain amount of antisaloon zeal into other moralistic causes and crusades. Indeed, the temperance boards of several denominations announced that henceforth they would broaden their field of interest to include the whole spectrum of public morality.

To many of these erstwhile temperance crusaders, sex was the next great area demanding attention. In 1919 the Boston social worker Robert A. Woods predicted that Prohibition would "profoundly stimulate a vast process of national purification" by hastening "the sublimation of the sex instinct upon which the next stage of progress for the human race so largely depends."[61] For decades the antiliquor champions had warmly supported the vice-society movement, and now, in their search for new dragons to slay, many were drawn into the

crusade against bad books. In 1922 *Zion's Herald* exhorted
Christians to battle sordid literature "just as reformers have
fought the saloon. . . ." A Presbyterian official, hailing Prohibition as a major forward step, cited "obscene literature" as
another evil which must now be vanquished. The W.C.T.U.
continued throughout the 1920s its close cooperation with the
New York Vice Society; the Methodist Board of Temperance,
Prohibition, and Public Morals not only strongly supported
the vice organizations but in 1926 organized its own crusade
against evil literature.[62]

The well-worn Prohibitionist arguments proved remarkably applicable to books. The procensorship letters in *Zion's
Herald* in 1922 were saturated with logic and rhetoric left over
from the Eighteenth Amendment fight. "[A] sensational book
intoxicates the imagination," observed one minister, adding
that censorship was therefore clearly "as truly American" as
Prohibition. It remained for the *Christian Century* to push the
analogy remorselessly to its conclusion:

> [P]rohibition is the censorship of beverages, and censorship
> is the prohibition of harmful literature and spectacles. . . .[I]n
> general principle the two problems are one. . . . Both . . .
> undertake to protect individuals against their own unwise
> or vicious choices. . . .[63]

The flaws in this appealing equation—the most obvious
being that a book's obscenity-quotient is considerably harder
to measure than a beverage's alcoholic content—did not go
unrecognized. All the same, memories of the heroic Prohibition
struggle continued to inspire champions of literary suppression
throughout the 1920s. As late as 1929, in a Senate debate on
Customs censorship, Arthur Robinson of Indiana demolished
some mildly libertarian sentiment expressed by a colleague
with the remark:

> I understood the Senator . . . to say . . . that nobody can
> tell him what he shall read; but the United States Government,
> and even the people of the country, have undertaken to tell
> him what he may drink; and I see no objection to that.[64]

This equation of alcohol and obscenity produced some bizarre results. In 1927 the Chicago Collector of Customs, one Anthony Czarnecki, devised a scheme whereby local Customs officials would forward "questionable" imported books to General Lincoln C. Andrews, head of the Prohibition Unit of the Treasury Department, for a ruling. The *New York Times* found Czarnecki's idea "fantastic" but warned:

> [L]et no one think . . . it has no chance of being adopted. The passion for censorship is so deep-seated in many minds that to link it with the passion for prohibition will not seem to them absurd. They may easily come to believe that somehow pure liquor is related to pure literature; that a man keen at smelling out poisoned whiskey is just the one to detect immorality where no one else can perceive it.[65]

The whimsical possibilities in such a link between books and bottles had already occurred to *Publishers' Weekly*:

> Think of picking up your morning paper and reading that Frank Doubleday was lying off Sandy Hook with a carload of Conrads in their original wrappers! And in the next column that Horace Liveright had been shot in the Hudson Terminal while attempting to escape with a case of Ben Hecht manuscripts.[66]

But the effort to couple the censorship caboose to the Prohibition locomotive had its perils. As more and more people became disillusioned with Volsteadism, their irritation often extended to literary prohibition as well. Book censorship, observed a disgruntled letter writer in the *New York Times* in 1923, "is in no real sense different from the decision of another group of reformers that certain beverages are to be prohibited for the benefit of our morals." In 1930 the Watch and Ward Society blamed its troubles on "[r]esentment against any form of prohibition, whether of free speech, of liquor, or of literature. . . ."[67]

The increasing problems of Prohibition enforcement supplied powerful ammunition to the anticensorship forces. The subject came up frequently during the "Clean Books" fight in New York. Gertrude Atherton declared that Judge Ford's bill "would fall as short of what its advocates are seeking to accomplish as does the Prohibition law." "This debate makes me think of the Volstead Act," jeered Jimmy Walker, ". . . of how many vote one way and drink another."[68]

As the breakdown of Prohibition became more apparent, the argument by analogy boomeranged. "Has [Prohibition] . . . made the Republic dry?" asked H. L. Mencken rhetorically in a 1926 essay on the uselessness of obscenity laws. A New York State senator argued that the legal suppression of indecency was pointless since "ways will be found to bootleg it." In 1929 the *Nation* warned: "The time is rapidly approaching when the problem of enforcing the literary censorship will be as complicated as the problem of enforcing prohibition."[69]

With Prohibition and book censorship so often linked throughout the 1920s, there is a singular appropriateness in the fact that the same week in 1933 brought both repeal of the Eighteenth Amendment and the legal vindication of *Ulysses,* the most famous of the bootleg classics. Morris Ernst noted the juxtaposition, and observed that now Americans could "imbibe freely of the contents of bottles and forthright books." Added a tongue-in-cheek *Nation* editor:

> All lovers of law and order, all upholders of true temperance, will pray that there be no orgies. Youth must show that it knows how to use its liberties, and it will be an ill augury if the streets are filled with young men and maidens drunk upon immoderate drafts of Mrs. Bloom's meditation.[70]

THE CENSORS SEEK NEW TARGETS

The emergence of an articulate opposition, and the failure of Volsteadism, were not the only factors in the marked decline of book censorship in the later 1920s. Developments in other media of communication—notably magazines, the theater, and the movies—made the peril of evil books come to seem less urgent and dramatic.

Since Anthony Comstock's heyday, magazines like the

shocking *Police Gazette* had been a thorn in the flesh of the vice societies. Not until the 1920s, however, did frankly erotic and sensational magazines become big business in the United States. In 1919 Bernarr MacFadden—who for twenty years had been using his "Physical Culture" crusade to justify ample displays of male and female epidermis—founded *True Story Magazine,* a periodical devoted to repentant tales of sexual misdeeds. *True Story* was an immediate success, and by 1930 a dozen such MacFadden magazines were enjoying astronomical circulation. Other entrepreneurs quickly entered the field. Shortly after the war, Wilford H. Fawcett founded *Captain Billy's Whiz Bang,* a monthly compilation of bawdy jokes and cartoons; by 1923 circulation reached 425,000, and the vast Fawcett empire, including *True Confession, Screen Secrets,* and a host of similar periodicals, was well launched. In 1921 George T. Delacorte, Jr., formed Dell Publishing Company, and soon *I Confess, Modern Romance,* and dozens of other Dell titles were jostling for space on crowded newsstand shelves. The newspaper tabloids, never noted for their decorum, struck back with lurid and prurient coverage of such stories as the Hall-Mills murder, the Snyder-Gray case, and the "Peaches" Browning separation suit.[71]

Amidst this carnival of journalistic vulgarity, the inevitable reaction soon set in. Laments over the collapse of American society, if not of Western Civilization itself, were heard on all sides. Established and respectable periodicals like *Woman's Home Companion, Collier's, Ladies' Home Journal,* and the *Literary Digest* led the hue and cry.[72] In the *Independent* Frank Kent of the Baltimore *Sun* reported after a nationwide tour that the country was "drenched with smut" from "pornographic periodicals and dirty fiction magazines." The *New Republic* condemned "Gutter Literature"; H. W. Van Loon, writing in *Commonweal,* denounced the pulp magazines as "a putrid stream of the most despicable, the most iniquitous, and on the whole the most dangerous form of a degraded variety of literature. . . ."[73] Newspapers joined the fray as well. In 1925 a Watch and Ward official happily reported that clipping bureaus were each day receiving scores of editorials and articles attacking sensational magazines. In that same year the *New York Evening World,* after consulting John S. Sumner, launched a fervent crusade against evil periodicals.[74] (Perhaps not all of this journalistic tut-tutting over the sensational periodicals was entirely disinterested. *Christian Century* observed that the established magazines had been "quick to understand that the growth of the illegitimate publication endangers their own investment." In the same vein, *Publishers' Weekly* noted in annoyance that "Other publishers must continue to take second place in the display facilities of the newsstands, while the notably vulgar are flaunted.")[75]

Social-purity enthusiasts, generally silent during earlier attacks on books, exhibited no such restraint toward the pulps. *Social Hygiene* denounced "Vicious Magazines" in 1923 as "sex-steeped, aphrodisiac, poorly-written rubbish"; a few years later it added "unsavory, unsound, and unwholesome" to the list of damning adjectives.[76]

Most of these jeremiads concluded with explicit or oblique references to the (of course, regrettable) need for censorship if conditions did not improve. "[N]o authority, public or otherwise, seems to be willing or able to stop the dissemination of this literary garbage," wrote Van Loon in *Commonweal.* Frank Kent observed that "[a] more fruitful field for a moral crusade would be hard to conceive," while the *Ladies' Home Journal* had "little doubt" that the worst of the pulps should be legally suppressed and only lamented that the "respectable filth" in postwar literature had evidently "stifled the courts and chloroformed the censors."[77] Certain metropolitan newspapers, too, were to be found in the unaccustomed role of censorship champions. "[I]f we fail to regulate a little and intelligently," declared the *Evening World,* "we shall in the end be regulated a lot and very stupidly." Added the *Daily News* unctuously:

> We hate the suppression of free speech. But unless the minds of the children of New York are to be drenched in obscenity, it seems to us that a censorship of the press . . . must come.[78]

The national government contributed to this groundswell of pressure for magazine censorship. In 1925 Postmaster General Harry S. New proudly reported that his Department had applied the postal obscenity statute so strictly that several periodicals had been "forced to completely alter the character of their publications in order to secure the admission of same to the mails." Not only the content, New added, but "general appearance and even the titles" had been altered. In 1926 New noted that under Post Office prodding many "questionable" magazines had "entirely changed their policy and viewpoint," that a number of "suggestive" titles had been abandoned "in favor of more conservative ones," and that this had produced "a corresponding tendency to conservatism in . . . text and illustration." The Postmaster General pointedly noted that the "rigid" enforcement of state obscenity laws "would do much to help clear the field of such objectionable matter."[79]

A few warnings were sounded against this precipitous rush to ban offensive magazines. Oswald Garrison Villard, though a gentleman of the old school who found the pulps vulgar and distasteful, cautioned that

> anything like wholesale suppression would be a fatal mistake. It is better that *Love Stories, I Confess,* and *Art Lovers* should run their course than that a permanent censorship should be fastened upon the country, which could so easily be extended to cover opinions and political doctrines in addition to racy stories and suggestive pictures.[80]

But such cautionary sentiments were rare. Even those who most strongly opposed book censorship seemed hesitant to extend their brave principles to the ephemeral sex magazines with their mass-produced eroticism; Morris Ernst and William Seagle in *To the Pure* had little to say about periodical censorship—a more immediate issue in 1928 than book censorship—beyond noting that "the daily and periodical press presents the hardest dilemma" for the opponent of legal suppression.[81]

Nor did the book industry do much to discourage the

tendency to shift to magazines the opprobrium which had
earlier been directed against shocking books. "With public
interest centered on the subject of censorship," said *Publishers'*
Weekly disingenuously in 1924, "it seems too bad that there
should not be some special interest roused in keeping these
[pulp] magazines out of the hands of children." Later, "speaking not as publishers, but as an old friend of the American
parent and a jealous defender of American youth," *PW* praised
"the present attack on bad magazines" and offered its "heartiest
support" to all those "fighting dirty literature." While standing
firm against any "craze of censorship" which would eventuate
in more stringent obscenity laws, it urged that the existing
statutes be strictly enforced—against magazines.[82]

With such pressures building, there was no lack of eager
crusaders ready to lead grass-roots campaigns against offensive
magazines. As early as 1923 *Social Hygiene* reported that civic
leaders in many cities were considering "ways and means by
which [periodical] publishers may be forced to either clean up
or go out of business." In 1924 the General Federation of
Women's Clubs urged its local affiliates to "take immediate
action . . . to stop the sale and distribution" of bad magazines.
Mrs. Nellie B. Miller, "Chairman of Literature" of the G.F.W.C.
declared that sex-magazine publishers were "slaughtering good
American forests" to get paper for their nefarious purposes—
a charge presumably framed to appeal equally to pacifists,
patriots, Puritans, and preservationists.[83] The Knights of Columbus instituted a similar crusade against "immoral and
harmful literature," with specific reference to magazines, and in
St. Louis a 3,000-signature petition circulated by the local
Board of Religious Organizations spurred the district attorney
to issue a list of forbidden periodicals. "[T]he magazine situation is much better than it was twelve months ago," said
Publishers' Weekly of the St. Louis campaign. In Washington,
the Methodist Board of Temperance, Prohibition, and Public
Morals succeeded in banishing some thirty magazines from
the city's newsstands. Encouraged by this local triumph, the

Methodists called a secret "Literature Conference" for January 1926 in the nation's capital. At this gathering representatives of interested organizations discussed how to promote the suppression of objectionable books and magazines "without incurring the odium of 'censorship.'" A list of seventy-three condemned magazines drawn up by this conference was distributed confidentially to Methodist ministers "for advisory purposes."[84]

The vice societies, with their role in book censorship so diminished, were delighted by this furore over bad magazines. In its 1925 report the New England Watch and Ward Society pronounced offensive periodicals "the alarming peril of the past year," and their suppression "the task to which we have given most time and thought." The report also noted that the New England sale of "hundreds of thousands of copies" of certain obnoxious magazines had been stopped through the prosecution of several large distributors and of seventeen individual newsdealers.[85]

At about the same time, the Rev. Mr. Yarrow of the Illinois Vigilance Association (still several years away from his jail cell) undertook a successful and widely praised Chicago campaign against bad magazines.[86] The indefatigable John Sumner devoted increasing space to "pornographic magazines" in his annual reports, and in a 1925 article in the *American City*—a journal normally devoted to such prosaic subjects as traffic lights and sewage disposal—Sumner pictured the nation as "literally flooded with periodical publications of a degrading type." In smaller communities, Sumner said, the problem could be "readily handled" by "a warning from the chief of police or the prosecuting attorney." For the large cities, he advocated publicity as the first step to legal suppression:

> [T]he more these publications are attacked and the more noise that is made, the sooner will some of our judiciary be aroused to the fact that the safeguarding of public morals is much more important than upholding some alleged 'freedom of expression' or 'freedom of the press.' . . .[87]

The vice societies played an active role in the Methodist
"Literature Conference" of 1926, and a few months later, "with
a view to accelerating this aroused public opinion," the New
York Vice Society and the Watch and Ward Society sent joint
letters to the chambers of commerce and church federations
of twenty major cities suggesting further local campaigns
against newsstand corruption.[88]

As with books earlier in the decade, the crusade against
pulp magazines and tabloid newspapers eventually reached the
legislative halls. In 1927 a bill was introduced in Congress by
Representative Thomas W. Wilson of Coldwater, Mississippi,
proposing the establishment of a National Board of Magazine
Censorship. In a long, applause-punctuated harangue, Wilson
denounced over sixty magazines, including not only the Mac-
Fadden, Dell, and Fawcett variety, but also *Scribner's*,
Harper's Bazaar, the *American Mercury*, and *Vanity Fair*. "I
do not propose that any magazine shall escape," he cried.

> . . . Let the dirty dog in human form who dare [sic] publish . . .
> these vile publications . . . feel the lash of outraged authority.
> . . . Let us . . . drive from our Christian land every salacious,
> indecent magazine, even as Jesus drove from his Father's
> house all those who sought to defile it.[89]

Congressman Albert Johnson, a Republican from Washington
State, strongly endorsed Wilson's bill. Asserting that "the
moral life of the Nation is threatened through printing-press
poison," Johnson blamed this frightening condition on "the
newly arrived people of the last quarter of a century. . . ."[90]

Early in 1928 a similar bill was introduced by John N.
Tillman, a sixty-nine-year-old Arkansas congressman and former president of the state university. "There are many abuses
that we can not control, but we can end this sorry practice,"
Tillman declared, waving aloft a copy of *Telling Tales* with a
scantily clad "flapper" on the cover. Such magazines, he said,
were to blame for the alarming moral collapse in the colleges,
where couples shamelessly "walk hand in hand, often with
arms intertwined." "I may be old-fashioned," Tillman added,

"but I think of the Virginia reel, and the stately minuet as preferable to the twisting, wiggling modern dance."[91]

Despite such persuasive oratory, these bills died in committee. By 1929, the heated public outcry against bad magazines had largely subsided. This reflects in part the natural ebb-and-flow of such movements, and in part an evolutionary development within the pulp-magazine industry. As circulation had leveled off and even declined, editors had begun to substitute innocuous household features and human-interest stories for lurid "confessions" and racy stories. Fruitcake recipes had replaced cheesecake photographs.[92]

While it lasted, the crusade against vulgar magazines eased the pressure on books. Confronted with *True Confession* or *Whiz Bang* at 25¢, it was hard to become excited about a $20 limited edition of the *Satyricon*. In 1926, while expatiating upon "pornographic magazines," John Sumner reported "an improvement in the tone of book publications"; the leaders of the 1927 "Clean Books" campaign largely ignored books to concentrate "a good deal of their attention on magazines"; and in 1929 *Zion's Herald* argued that it was pointless to ban books "while the newsstands literally wallow in sex magazines a thousand times more dangerous because they are bought, read, and absorbed by a class of people infinitely more susceptible to their evil influence than would be the readers of the longer novels."[93]

Alarming developments on the stage in the mid-1920s similarly diverted attention from the relatively sedate printed page. Ever since the abortive "play jury" scheme of 1922, the issue of theater censorship had remained a lively one in New York. In 1923 Sholem Asch's *The God of Vengeance* was closed by the police, and the theater owner and leading man (Rudolph Schildkraut) heavily fined. Eugene O'Neill's *Desire Under the Elms* suffered a similar fate in 1925, after having aroused widespread denunciation. *Social Hygiene* approved this action as a step toward cleaning "the muck from American stages."[94]

The vice societies, ever alert to the shifting tides of popular indignation, quickly joined in. "The stage is headed for a censorship," John Sumner announced in 1924, "if those in control don't clean up the situation themselves." In his *American City* article Sumner suggested that an "aggressive prosecuting official by a word of warning can frequently bring about the withdrawal or substantial cleaning-up of an objectionable public show."[95] In Boston in the 1920s the Watch and Ward warmly endorsed the mayor's unofficial theater censor, a political hack whose right arm and career as a drummer for burlesque shows had been simultaneously cut short in an accident some years before. The Boston play censorship was carried out under cover of a municipal statute which permitted the revocation of a theater's license if "structural defects" were discovered in the building.[96]

It was the 1926–27 Broadway season—what George Jean Nathan, writing in *Vanity Fair,* called "the dirtiest lot of shows . . . ever . . . put on view in the New York legitimate theaters"—which turned the smoldering stage-censorship movement into a full-fledged conflagration. With varying degrees of artistic integrity, the plays of that year described prostitution in China (*The Shanghai Gesture*), portrayed the seduction of a Negro by a white woman (*Lulu Belle*), presented adultery and prostitution as praiseworthy (*The Constant Wife* and *Virgin Man*), and treated homosexuality as a subject of farce (*The Drag*). Also opening in New York that season was *The Captive,* Edouard Bourdet's drama about lesbianism.[97]

These offerings aroused the predictable outcry. Booth Tarkington in *Collier's* dismissed the whole lot of plays as "sheer dirt," and a number of newspapers, including the *Evening World* and the *Daily News* in New York, called for a purification of the stage as well as a cleanup of the newsstands. Even V. F. Calverton, arch-opponent of bourgeois book censorship, lashed out at the "putrescent . . ., smirking, insinuating pornography" of the stage.[98]

The authorities responded with alacrity. On February 10, 1927, Manhattan police raided *Virgin Man, The Captive,* and *Sex*—the latter a comedy preoccupied with the subject hinted at in its title. Little protest was heard when convictions were secured against *Virgin Man* and *Sex,* but when *The Captive* closed rather than face prosecution, the protests were vigorous. Both the play and the production, starring Basil Rathbone and Helen Menken, had won critical praise. In the wake of the police raid Horace Liveright stepped in as producer of *The Captive,* but the owners of the Waldorf Theater refused his request to reopen the play. Liveright's attorney, Arthur Garfield Hays, tried to secure a legal ruling on the play by obtaining an injunction against the theater managers, but a chain of complications developed, and *The Captive* remained closed.[99]

In addition to the suppression of individual plays, the familiar demands for a more stringent law were heard anew. Declared the *New Republic*:

> Good people, as well as people ready to stand for a great deal in the cause of freedom of expression, are up in arms. Many of them, who would violently have opposed any kind of censorship a year ago, seem ready to accept it now.

John Sumner, paying increasing attention to the theater in his annual reports, became particularly vocal in his demands for state control over the stage. In February 1927 a New York state senator, citing in particular the growing alarm over conditions on the stage and in the tabloids, observed that the state was "rushing . . . toward a censorship with the speed of a hurricane."[100]

The hurricane struck Albany that March in the form of a bill providing for the prior examination and licensing of all stage plays by a special commission of the Board of Regents. This measure won quick support from the New York Vice Society and the usual panoply of clerics. Such a prior censorship, said an enthusiastic supporter in *Commonweal*, "would avoid all publicity and all delay." The proponents of the bill aired their views at a crowded Senate hearing in mid-March, but the lawmakers proved cool to the proposal, and it remained in committee.[101]

The New York legislature did, however, pass an amendment to the state's obscenity law permitting municipal license commissioners to close for up to a year any theater convicted of staging an obscene play. In addition, plays dealing with "sex degeneracy or sex perversion"—whether seriously or frivolously—were explicitly prohibited. Signed into law by Governor Al Smith on April 5, 1927, this "Padlock Law" represents one of the few tangible legislative results of the many censorship crusades of the 1920s.[102]

Even this legislation did not end the outcry against the theater, and in 1930 Flo Ziegfeld quite seriously proposed that Calvin Coolidge be appointed "czar" of the American stage at an annual salary of $150,000. Coolidge, said Ziegfeld, was "ideally fitted for the job, both in character and experience." Unfortunately the idea came to nothing, and Coolidge was prevented from adding this capstone to a distinguished career in the public service.[103]

The growth of the movies, too, influenced censorship attitudes in the 1920s. Since the days of such turn-of-the-century thrillers as *The Great Train Robbery*, the movies had attracted a large and devoted audience. It was in the 1920s, however, that the real surge of popularity occurred. By the end of the decade, an estimated 100,000,000 admissions each week were being registered by the nation's 23,000 motion-picture houses.[104]

That the late 1920s did not witness a movie-censorship crusade comparable to those directed against magazines and the stage is attributable to shrewd preventive action by the industry. In 1922, to forestall the spread of state and municipal censorship boards (several had been set up before the war and more were proposed in the early postwar period), the Motion

Picture Producers and Distributors Association with great fan-
fare appointed Postmaster General Will H. Hays as its president (at $100,000 a year), supposedly with a mandate to
"police" movie morals. Hays's role as "czar" proved largely
illusory, but the public was persuaded that the industry was
genuinely striving for self-regulation, and the censorship demands accordingly subsided.[105]

Nevertheless, the ubiquitous spread of the movies figured
in the decline of book-censorship pressures. The number of
Americans reached by the movies was so vast that the influence
of the printed page paled by comparison. "There is no instance
in history," wrote a Jesuit scholar in 1927, "of a popular
amusement which has . . . gained so deep a hold in such a brief
time on the public taste. . . ." It was quickly recognized that
a new era in the communication of ideas was unfolding. "When
we read, there is time for thought, reasoning, and the formation
of judgment," wrote a social-work leader in 1921, "but motion
pictures progress so swiftly as to permit almost no cerebral
action—little more than percept."[106] Booth Tarkington was
gloomy about the prospects of maintaining genteel literary
standards in the age of the movies. "[W]e can't," he said,
"propose to furnish good taste to the twenty million who frequent the movies and demand 'close-ups' of the hero and heroine 'locked in a passionate embrace.'" A Princeton English
professor in 1922 urged complete freedom for books but demanded strict control of the movies, basing his distinction on
the incomparably greater sensual power of the films—their
ability to "create new experiences."[107]

Such considerations placed the whole book-censorship
discussion in a new perspective. The belief in the fearsome
corruptive power of the printed page—the belief which for
decades had spurred the vice societies to ever greater feats
of book suppression—was drained of its potency as millions
of Americans gathered each week in darkened halls to *see*
reality, corrupt or otherwise, recreated on the flickering screen.
When the myriad censorship battles of the 1920s have all

been recounted, the sobering fact remains that the increasing
freedom permitted to authors as the decade wore on was due,
in part at least, to the simple fact that books were not considered quite so important any more.

SEVEN

"Banned in Boston"

Massachusetts censorship came over on the *Mayflower*. When Governor William Bradford of Plymouth discovered in 1628 that the renegade Thomas Morton had, with his other misdeeds, "composed sundry rhymes and verses, some tending to lasciviousness" the only solution was to send a military expedition to break up Morton's high-living settlement at Merrymount.[1] During the latter nineteenth century, and through the Progressive years, the Watch and Ward Society worked diligently at the Sisyphean labor of making Boston a fit habitation for the descendents of the Puritans.

It was not until the mid-1920s, however, that "Banned in Boston" became a national joke. Many viewed the goings-on

in the Hub with exasperated amusement, as simply a pic-
turesque part of the local scene, like the cobblestone streets and
the Indian pudding. Looking on tolerantly from sophisticated
New York, the *Herald Tribune* found "[t]he tyrannies of Boston's censorship, like those of its weather . . ., merely another
misfortune of the unhappy people who have to live there. . . ."
The easiest way to react to the whole problem, suggested a
writer in *Outlook*, might be simply to "turn over the page and
forget it, merely reflecting that poor, dear, old Boston is making
itself ridiculous again." "It has become so tiresome to reproach Boston for its constant repression of creative work,"
sighed a world-weary editor of the *Harvard Crimson* in 1929,
"that we are beginning to surrender in despair."[2] Despite such
pessimistic contemporary counsel, one must attempt, at least,
to understand the circumstances which conspired to make Boston, briefly, the censorship capital of America.

In New York, the years 1918–24 were a time of turbulent
censorship activity. The New York Vice Society, driven by
war-inspired expectations of moral reform, tried through courts
and legislature to impose its waning authority upon wayward
writers and publishers. Massachusetts, by contrast, largely
escaped these early postwar controversies. Few books were
prosecuted, and the state's obscenity statute was rarely a subject of discussion. To all outward appearances, the Watch and
Ward Society continued to function as a respected agency of
reform and uplift, fighting prostitution, narcotics, gambling,
and municipal corruption. Its annual report for 1923 noted
with quiet pride that the Watch and Ward had been behind a
successful and widely praised effort to remove a corrupt district attorney. The Society's founder, the venerable Frederick
B. Allen, enjoyed great public esteem, and the list of officers
still shone with such names as Charles W. Eliot, William Lawrence, Endicott Peabody, Godfrey Cabot, Thomas Dudley
Cabot, Julian T. Coolidge, Francis J. Moors, and John H.

Storer. Estimable public figures, including presidents and well-known professors from New England universities, regularly addressed the well-attended annual public meeting. In 1922 the president of Boston University was the guest speaker. The Watch and Ward Society had escaped the faint aura of foolishness which had been Anthony Comstock's principal legacy to the New York Vice Society.

The Watch and Ward leaders felt no less repugnance toward the literary trend of the 1920s than did their New York counterparts, but the people of Boston shared their sentiments to a far greater degree than was possible in heterogeneous Manhattan. Having long since ceased to be a wellspring of literary creativity, Boston lacked the intellectual ferment generated by a resident community of authors, editors, publishers, and critics. The staid Boston publishing houses and venerable periodicals such as the *Atlantic Monthly* adapted only painfully to the iconoclasm and freedom of expression of postwar literature, while the enclaves where such writing *was* greeted with sympathy and even enthusiasm—notably the Harvard community—remained generally aloof from local preoccupations. The newspapers, except for the fading *Transcript*, were determinedly philistine and parochial; in 1923 Oswald Garrison Villard with justice dismissed Boston as a "journalistic poor-farm."[3]

This left the public to find its own level of literary taste, and, as it happened, the major social groupings of the city were all, for varying reasons, hostile to the novelistic tendencies of the twenties. As for the Brahmins, these old Yankee families of wealth and cultivation, finding themselves rudely jostled by immigrant newcomers, turned with nostalgia to the age of Lowell, Longfellow, and Dr. Holmes, of Ticknor & Fields and Howells's *Atlantic*, when Boston's literary ascendancy had matched their own rank in the social firmament. Prizing as family heirlooms the great nineteenth-century literary giants, they reacted with personal affront when a brash New York-based generation dismissed their favorites as hopelessly out-

moded. After all, as a journalist noted, "one does not melt
down his family silver or revarnish his family portraits to
suit the passing style."[4]

The less affluent, less distinguished Yankees, the shop-
keepers and accountants whose names were not redolent of
inherited gentility, continued as always to look to the Brahmins
for literary and cultural leadership. Faithful attendants at such
evangelical bastions as Park Street Church and Tremont Temple, readers of perfervid diatribes against modern literature
in *Zion's Herald* and *The Baptist,* they deplored radicalism
in art as in politics, applauded the "Red Raids," kept cool
with Coolidge, and viewed the shocking novels of the decade
as unpardonably lewd and sacrilegious.

Boston's numerically dominant group, the Irish Catholics,
shared the Brahmin hostility to Dreiser, Joyce, and their ilk.
They looked with nostalgia to Ireland and Irish ways, and,
as it happened, the Irish Free State passed through a particularly virulent wave of censorship sentiment in the 1920s. Early
in 1926 the legislature at Dublin created an "Evil Literature
Committee" whose recommendations gave rise to a law establishing a "Censorship of Publications Board" with absolute
control over the importation and sale of books and periodicals;
"the most cruel and silly censorship law," said Heywood Broun,
"which any civilized country has ever known." Further, the
leadership of the Boston diocese during the 1920s was particularly suspicious of the new and unfamiliar. The autobiography of the popular primate, William Cardinal O'Connell, reveals all too clearly his strident anti-intellectualism, and the
diocesan newspaper, *The Pilot,* faithfully echoed O'Connell's
viewpoint.[5]

The various ethnic and religious enclaves which made
up the Boston of the 1920s were thus united on at least one
point: many of the novels issuing from New York were threats
to morality and tradition and deserved the severest censure by
all decent people. "Back of the Watch and Ward," wrote a Massachusetts reporter in 1925, ". . . stands the prestige of the

Brahmins of the Commonwealth, and to it is added the vast influence of the Roman Catholic hierarchy, and the jury services of the Mc's and O's of South Boston and points west."[6]

Boston's apparatus for book suppression reflected this near unanimity. In 1915 the Watch and Ward Society, in collaboration with Richard F. Fuller of the historic Old Corner Bookstore, had set up the so-called "Boston Booksellers' Committee" to eliminate the publicity which had characterized the *Three Weeks* case and other prosecutions. The committee was composed of Fuller, two other booksellers appointed by him, and three Watch and Ward directors. Their task was to read and evaluate current novels. If they found a book acceptable, bookstores could sell it without fear of prosecution. If not, all Massachusetts book dealers were so notified, and anyone selling the condemned book after forty-eight hours had elapsed was liable to a Watch and Ward prosecution, with little hope of sympathy from his colleagues. Boston's newspapers refused to advertise or review a condemned title, and the police rarely prosecuted a book not already proscribed by the Watch and Ward's committee. If the committee members disagreed, the book was submitted to the district attorney or a magistrate for an informal ruling.

The system was very nearly air-tight. "[I]f the bookseller won't sell and the reviewer won't review, the book might as well never have been written," boasted Fuller, ". . . in two weeks nobody is talking about . . . [it] at all."[7] A deliberate obscurity surrounded the precise number and titles of the books suppressed. To reveal these details, Fuller explained, would only "open a discussion." Members of the committee gave broadly varying estimates, but it is likely that in the 1918–26 period from fifty to seventy-five books, sold freely elsewhere, were suppressed by the Boston Booksellers' Committee. Not surprisingly, the city stood in the early 1920s as a beacon of hope for those alarmed by the general collapse elsewhere. "Just look at

good old Massachusetts!" wrote Judge John Ford of "Clean
Books" fame. "[S]he keeps herself clean from the filth that
circulates around her. . . ."[8]

Most Bostonians did not perceive as "censorship" an unobtrusive literary control exercised by men whose standards
so closely matched their own. As for the booksellers, they
were, as *World's Work* noted, "concerned not so much with
the morals of the reading public as with the health and prosperity of the book trade." If the route to prosperity lay in cooperating with the Watch and Ward, then so be it. Even those Bostonians whose interest in literature was presumably more
deep-seated proved complaisant under the protective Watch
and Ward blanket. At the A.L.A. convention of 1924 a Boston
librarian spoke in high praise of the Boston Booksellers' Committee, "which for ten years has kept the worst books . . . out
of the bookstores. . . ."[9] Nor did the New York publishers,
preoccupied by more immediate and spectacular censorship
problems, give much notice to the state of affairs in Boston.

The Booksellers' Committee assiduously avoided any hint
of fanaticism, and Richard Fuller was careful to stress the
reasonableness of his benevolent dictatorship:

> [W]e consider the book as a whole and we consider the
> author's motive in writing the story, and the probable effect
> it will have on the public. We are neither prudish nor
> prurient. . . .

Apologists for the system repeatedly portrayed it as the embodiment of the "self-censorship" so frequently advocated as the
democratic alternative to legal suppression. Fuller's committee, said *World's Work*, "is not and never has been a legal
censor in any way, shape, or manner."[10]

In actual fact, the system permitted one powerful and
conservative bookseller—a "sedulous stooge" of the Vice Society, in H. L. Mencken's opinion—in league with the Watch and
Ward Society, to coerce the mavericks of his profession with
threats of imprisonment and heavy fines. Said Richard Fuller
bluntly at the A.B.A. convention in 1923:

We have had a few black sheep. Some of the bookleggers have slipped thru the lines and there is where you have got to have a strong organization that will hold them in line. If the Watch and Ward catches them, it means going to the court, and . . . the courts are backing us up in this move. . . . Massachusetts stands today as the cleanest state in the Union . . . and I hope that everybody here will go back home and form some kind of a league. . . .[11]

As the postwar period wore on, however, the "bookleggers" proved increasingly nettlesome, and even in Boston the calls for suppressed titles grew more insistent. "[D]uring the last two years we have had hell," Fuller admitted in 1923. "There has been an awful lot of work." In October 1922 Mrs. Edith G. Law, owner of a Boston rental library, was convicted and fined on complaint of the Watch and Ward Society for circulating Robert Keable's *Simon Called Peter*, a trivial novel about the illicit loves of a Baptist preacher. The demand for *Simon Called Peter* had become irresistible, Mrs. Law explained, following newspaper reports that the book had been the favorite reading of Mrs. James Mills and her minister/lover, the Reverend Edward Hall, victims of a sensational double murder in September 1922.[12]

More disturbing to the Watch and Ward Society than such occasional transgressions was the realization that its very status as the accepted instrument for enforcing Boston's literary standards was growing less secure. The link with the Brahmin aristocracy was weakening. The old families, to be sure, still sent in their annual contributions, and some of the more ardent among them were as outspoken as ever in their enthusiasm. But as the philanthropic, reformist spirit waned, the instinct to avoid a commitment which might involve ridicule or suggest a boorish fanaticism grew more powerful. The Brahmin support became cautious and watchful; a certain distance was maintained.

Symptomatic was the gradual fading from public view of Frederick B. Allen (he died in 1925) and the emergence of

Jason Frank Chase as the principal spokesman for the Watch
and Ward. Allen, a Harvard graduate and an Episcopal leader,
had moved on terms of easy equality with people like Edward
Everett Hale, Julia Ward Howe, and Phillips Brooks. Dignified
and cultivated, with wide-ranging philanthropic interests, he
had for decades infused the Watch and Ward with something
of his own patrician respectability and *noblesse oblige* outlook.
The Reverend Mr. Chase, who came to his new job from a succession of obscure Methodist parishes in the less affluent Boston
suburbs, was a man of more limited horizons. A hail fellow well
met, he could usually be found in the Watch and Ward office,
feet on desk, a Between-the-Acts cigar beneath his bushy T.R.
mustache.

This is not to say that Chase's soul was devoid of romance
and poetry. In 1923, recalling his decision to go into the anti-
obscenity business, he wrote: "Fifteen years ago, at the foot of
Giotto's campanile at Florence, Italy, after repulsing an insistent peddler of degenerate photographs, I acquired the conviction that took me out of a pulpit and put me in a forum."
How reminiscent of Edward Gibbon's 1764 decision, as he
watched the barefooted friars singing vespers in the ruins of
the temple of Jupiter in Rome, to record the decline and fall of
the Roman Empire! But there were, alas, few who penetrated
these inner reaches of J. Frank Chase's personality. "He was a
Pecksniff, and despite all his burly geniality, he looked and
acted the part"—such was H. L. Mencken's harsh judgment.[13]
Chase was tolerated, but hardly respected, by the cultivated
residents of Back Bay and the wealthier suburbs.

Fading Brahmin support was not the only problem. There
were also the Irish. Though in sympathy with the stringent
literary standards of the Watch and Ward Society, the Catholic
immigrants sensed and resented their exclusion from its councils, which remained Protestant and Yankee. The Irish understood the fortuitous nature of their alliance with the Vice Society. Friendly but unconsciously patronizing gestures by J. Frank
Chase only emphasized the gulf. "The Spirit of the Puritan,"

said Chase in 1926, "has been inoculated into the aliens who
have swarmed our shores, and the Boston of the Cabots, the
Ameses, the Lowells, and the Lodges, has not essentially
changed in becoming the Boston of the Sullivans, the Fitz-
geralds, the Galvins, and the Walshes."[14]

The Watch and Ward Society, often portrayed as the all-
powerful arbiter of Boston's morals, in fact survived more on
suffrance than through any deep-seated loyalty among its supporters. Wisely, it pursued a quiet and unobtrusive course, for
any sudden publicity, any crisis of public confidence, could
reveal how shaky its foundations had become with the passage
of time.

❧

Such a crisis was precisely what lay in store. Censorship
was receiving increasing national attention, and with the
defeat of the "Clean Books" crusade in New York, Boston's interesting arrangement began to attract notice. The first exposé
came in September 1925 when Henry L. Mencken's *American
Mercury* published "Keeping the Puritans Pure," a slashing,
scornful attack on the Watch and Ward Society, J. Frank Chase,
and the so-called Boston Booksellers' Committee. Three months
later, in an *American Mercury* article lamenting Boston's
cultural decline, Charles Angoff again ridiculed the Watch and
Ward and attacked Boston's "Irish-Catholic anthropoids" as
"immigrant morons" who "spread everywhere, multiplying like
rabbits" and "have no more interest in ideas than a guinea pig
has in Kant's *Critique of Pure Reason* or a donkey in Goethe's
Faust." Boston's rebirth, Angoff concluded, "will not take place
until they are exterminated."[15]

J. Frank Chase, understandably furious over the September
article, evidently concluded that Angoff's strident blast had
sufficiently enraged Boston that a counterattack against the
American Mercury stood a good chance of success. The national
alarm over improper magazines, then at its peak, made the
climate for a showdown still more favorable. Chase's oppor-

tunity came early in 1926 when Mencken published "Hatrack," a story about a small-town prostitute who was publicly ostracized but privately patronized by the upright. The author, Herbert Asbury, *New York Herald Tribune* reporter, said the story was true, and the fact was reluctantly acknowledged by the citizens of Farmington, Missouri, where Asbury had grown up.[16]

On March eighth, Chase notified the New England News Company, local distributors of the *American Mercury*, that sale of the "Hatrack" issue would constitute grounds for legal action. As if by magic, the issue disappeared from the newsstands. The warning was ignored, however, by Felix Caragianes, operator of "Felix's," a Harvard Square magazine stand popular with the college crowd. On March 30, Caragianes was arrested. Said he resignedly:

> I honestly think from my heart it is a good magazine. Fine people buy it. Professors from the college and like that. . . . Oh well, that man from the Watch and Ward, he has his job, and I got mine.[17]

Mencken was at first inclined to pass off the arrest with a verbal blast. In consultation with Alfred A. Knopf, publisher of the *American Mercury*, however, he decided to retain Arthur Garfield Hays, whom he had met the year before in Dayton, Tennessee, during the Scopes trial. Hays, who thrived on *causes célèbres,* accepted with alacrity and urged Mencken to seek a direct confrontation with Chase. Hays warned of the possibility of a jail sentence, but Mencken, free of family responsibilities since the recent death of his mother, was inclined to take the risk.

Accordingly, the pair took the train to Boston, where Mencken publicly offered to sell to Chase a copy of the offending magazine. Chase reluctantly agreed, and Mencken, with a sense of history, chose to consummate the transaction in front of the Park Street Church at the foot of the Boston Common, where the Watch and Ward Society had been founded years before. On April fifth (having prudently secured a peddler's license), Mencken met Chase before a milling crowd of reporters and some 5,000 spectators, including a good percentage of the Harvard student body. Mencken later stoutly affirmed the truth of the story that he tested Chase's fifty-cent piece with his teeth before handing over the magazine. In any event, the sale was completed.[18]

Mencken was at once arrested, taken to the station house, and booked by Lieutenant Daniel J. Hines of the vice squad. A conviction seemed likely. The *Herald* and the *Post* published hostile editorials, and Mencken heard, via the journalistic grapevine, that the Suffolk County district attorney, Thomas O'Brien, was infuriated by the Angoff attack on the Boston Irish and determined to secure a conviction. At the municipal court trial on April sixth, a Watch and Ward attorney, described by Mencken as "tall, gaunt, seedy-looking . . ., stuffy and obviously stupid," confidently urged a conviction. There was thus general surprise the next day when Judge James P. Parmenter, sixty-seven years old, a Yankee and a Unitarian, found Mencken not guilty. Escorted by Felix Frankfurter and Zechariah Chafee, Jr., of the Harvard Law School, Mencken at once traveled to Cambridge where he spoke to 600 cheering students. That night he was the guest of Ferris Greenslet of Houghton Mifflin Company and Edward W. Weeks, Jr., assistant editor of the *Atlantic Monthly*, at a St. Botolph Club dinner.[19]

Arthur G. Hays, pursuing the legal angles, promptly filed suit in federal court in Boston to enjoin the Watch and Ward and the news companies from further harassment of the *American Mercury*. "No one has the right to interfere with the business of another except as part of an economic dispute," he declared at the hearing. On the key question of whether Watch and Ward "advice" constituted just such interference, Chase himself made a damaging admission from the witness stand:

> Hays: [W]hen a bookseller gets a notice of this sort, according to your practice, it means, if he doesn't follow

your judgment, he is going to be taken into court, doesn't it?

Chase: Yes, sir.

When the Watch and Ward lawyer, evidently trying to strike a conciliatory note, promised that ". . . if they will submit to us the May number [of the *Mercury*] in plenty of time, we will notify them whether it is objectionable or not," Hays was on his feet at once. "That is an outrageous presumption," he declared,

> That is what I object to, that we should have to submit our magazine to these people, to find out whether we can distribute it in Massachusetts. It shows the whole situation. They want to be censors of our business, and they have no right to do it. We will put in what we want, and we ask you to have us arrested if there is anything in it that is improper, and nothing more.[20]

On April 14, 1926, Judge James M. Morton, Jr., issued the injunction. Branding as "clearly illegal" the coercive tactics employed in the "Hatrack" case, Morton granted the Watch and Ward Society and its various committees "the right of every citizen to come to the courts with complaints of crime," but "no right to impose their opinions on the book and magazine trade by threats of prosecution if their views are not accepted."[21]

Mencken's satisfaction in this victory was somewhat dampened by other developments. Two days before the Morton ruling, Felix Caragianes was convicted and fined one hundred dollars by Judge Arthur P. Stone in Cambridge district court. As Caragianes was reluctant to appeal, Knopf paid the fine and the conviction was allowed to stand unchallenged. More serious was the counterattack launched by J. Frank Chase. Seeking to recoup his Boston setback, he persuaded the New York City postmaster ("a notorious ignoramus," Mencken assures us) to submit the April *American Mercury* to his superiors in Washington for an obscenity ruling on the "Hatrack" story. On April 15, Post Office Solicitor Horace J. Donnelly—a man famous for his marked resemblance to Calvin Coolidge and remembered by Mencken as "the perfect model of the third-rate bureaucrat; vain, cocksure, and unintelligent"—declared the April issue nonmailable. He was encouraged in this decision by Postmaster General Harry S. New, who had received a communication from (of all places!) the Farmington, Missouri, Chamber of Commerce urging just such a ban. When a personal appeal by Mencken, Hays, and Knopf failed to sway Donnelly, Hays secured an injunction ordering the postal authorities to show cause why the ruling should not be reversed. The injunction was set aside on appeal, however, on the grounds that since the April issue had in fact already passed freely through the mails the matter was moot. This very fact—that the postal ban was so obviously "gratuitous and malicious"—made it particularly obnoxious to Mencken and heightened his desire to have it reversed. His apprehension was increased by the knowledge that during the First World War the Post Office Department had at times used the expedient of banning several issues of a radical periodical and then withdrawing its second-class mailing privilege on the grounds that two or more consecutive issues had been missed.

Thrown off balance by these developments, Mencken concluded that prudence was the better part of valor. The May issue of the *American Mercury* had already gone to press with an article on "Sex and the College Girl" by "John August"—a pseudonym for Bernard DeVoto. Although the burden of the article was that the libertine "flapper" was largely a myth, Mencken and Knopf concluded that any references to sex at that juncture would be ill-advised. The entire press run was destroyed, and in place of the DeVoto piece Mencken inserted "On Learning to Play the Cello," an innocuous article of unimpeachable morality.[22]

The convolutions of the "Hatrack" case generated enormous national publicity. Boats and bicycles were named after it, and parties held in its honor. In thousands of newspaper and magazine articles, editorials, photographs, and cartoons the issue of censorship was dramatized as never before. Most papers deplored the attempted suppression, but many editors, particularly in the South and Midwest, were also sharply critical of Mencken as a publicity hunter. Said Mencken of these: "[T]hey resented, if only subconsciously, my appropriation of a job that they should, in honor, have taken on themselves."[23]

The net effect was to make the average citizen keenly aware of an issue which had hitherto been debated in more limited circles. "We have seldom enough called censorship the thing it evidently is, a comedy," observed the *Nation;* "here is one who acts it out as such." Mencken himself had no doubts about the significance of his effort. "The general success of our attack," he later wrote briskly, ". . . inspired many other persons to resist the fiats of organized wowserism. . . ."[24]

The most dramatic and lasting results were in Boston itself. After Judge Parmenter's decision the city's newspapers (prodded by Mencken's pointed hints at possible libel suits) unceremoniously reversed themselves and hailed Mencken's great blow for freedom of the press. Even the *Herald*, swallowing hard, joined in the acclaim. As for the Watch and Ward, it had suffered a severe blow, both legally and in public esteem. Will Rogers in his nationally syndicated column described the Watch and Ward's supporters as "the Ku Kluxers of Boston literature."[25] To the Brahmins, Chase's encounter with Mencken could have seemed only a vulgar sideshow. The *Transcript* spoke for them when it dismissed Chase and his ilk as "sanctimonious . . ., semi-official meddlers." And the Irish-Catholic population, hitherto only vaguely aware of the Watch and Ward Society, now saw it at its ridiculous worst. The *Telegram*, a small newspaper popular among the Boston Irish, declared that the Watch and Ward "does not represent the people of Boston." The *Telegram* grew increasingly vitriolic in its attacks on "Chase and his brother bandits" whom it eventually denounced as "the scum of society."[26]

The Watch and Ward Society board members salvaged a modicum of respect by blaming the whole unfortunate incident on the misguided zeal of Chase. Richard F. Fuller completely turned against his erstwhile colleague. "Chase is licked— bungled the job—made a damned fool of himself," he told a Knopf salesman. As if to ratify this judgment, Chase died unexpectedly of pneumonia four months later. "Now he was dead at last in defeat and dismay, and we were rid of him," H. L. Mencken grimly wrote of his fallen adversary. Chase was succeeded by Charles S. Bodwell, a dim figure who had formerly been engaged in Anti-Saloon League activity in Boston and "Americanization" work in Lawrence, Massachusetts.[27]

So ended the "Hatrack" case. Mencken's foray had focused nationwide attention on the suppressive climate in Boston, and made certain that any future censorship conflicts would be played out in the full glare of publicity. The Watch and Ward Society, if not totally discredited, had been seriously weakened, and the way prepared for another spectacular case which finished the job four years later.

The revulsion against the Watch and Ward Society growing from the "Hatrack" case did not imply a principled rejection of censorship in Boston. It simply meant that the censorship initiative was shifting to conform to Boston's social and religious configurations. After 1926 the authority which had been wrested from the Protestant Watch and Ward was assumed by municipal officials more representative of the Catholic majority.

This development was hastened in May 1927 when the Vatican launched a widely publicized war on immoral literature, invoking "the aid of the Bishops and diocesan clergy in reading and banning books whose number is too great to permit detailed examinations by the authorities of the Holy See." The papal campaign won enthusiastic support in Boston. "His Holiness awakened the conscience of the world to a moral disorder of which it was apparently oblivious," said *The Pilot*. "Most

readers suspected that there was something wrong with the
fiction of the day, but few realized the extent of its corrupting
influence until the Holy Father spoke." In another editorial
endorsing this campaign *The Pilot* noted:

> Some . . . seem unaware that there is any prohibition at all
> in the matter of reading the moral offal that passes for the
> best sellers of the day. They think that because a book is not
> on the Index they are allowed to read it, forgetful of the fact
> that most of the evil literature they read is forbidden by the
> natural law. . . . Presumably there will be the usual hue and
> cry . . . against the tyranny of the Church in interfering
> with human liberty and the freedom of the press, but the
> good Catholic heeds not such ill-natured and unwarranted
> criticism.[28]

The central aim of this crusade was to increase ecclesiastical
supervision over the reading of Catholics, but the Catholics
who held municipal office in Boston absorbed some of its fervor
and moved against evil literature with the secular weapons at
their command.

Occasionally prior to 1926 the Boston police had acted
independently when the Watch and Ward apparatus failed to
suppress a book they found objectionable. In 1923 Helen V.
Brooks, a Back Bay bookdealer, was arrested for selling Elliot
Paul's *Impromptu* even though the Booksellers' Committee had
taken no action on the book. The fact that the arrest was made
from Station 16 was probably related to the fact that *Impromptu* mentions Station 16 unfavorably in a discussion of
prostitution in Boston.[29]

But such police initiative was rare during the period when
the extralegal Watch and Ward system remained in effective
operation. With the *American Mercury* decision, however,
municipal authorities unversed in literature and inexperienced
in the enforcement of the obscenity statute assumed a suppressive role they had long delegated to others. During the
period of collaboration between booksellers and the Vice
Society, a modicum of discretion and good sense had generally

prevented the more absurd or flagrantly unjust suppressions. With this partnership ended, the police were thrown on their own resources, and these proved slender indeed.

The first sign of the new order came late in 1926, when two drugstore clerks in Dorchester, a heavily Catholic section of Boston, were arrested for selling Percy Marks's *The Plastic Age*, a novel about college high-life dimly reminiscent of Fitzgerald's *This Side of Paradise*. The following February, in consultation with Suffolk County District Attorney William J. Foley, Police Superintendent Michael Crowley notified Boston booksellers of eight books he considered obscene. In addition to *The Plastic Age*, they were:

Jean DeVanny, *The Butcher Shop*
Edwin Granberry, *The Ancient Hunger*
Frances Newman, *The Hard-Boiled Virgin*
Ernest Pascal, *The Marriage Bed*
"Diana Patrick" [Desemea N. Wilson], *The Rebel Bird*
Pauline Smith, *The Beadle*
"H.T." [Helen N. Thomas], *As It Was*

Except for *The Plastic Age*, published in 1924, these novels had all appeared within the past few months. A varied group of publishers was involved: Boni & Liveright, Century, Doran, Dutton, Harcourt Brace, Harper's, and Macaulay. All of these books—reputably published, openly advertised, freely sold elsewhere—disappeared from Boston's bookstores.[30]

"I have read these books, and I think they are bad," said the police chief. "I have a duty to protect the morals of the people of this county, so far as I am able," said the district attorney. "[F]renzied moralists," said H. L. Mencken.[31]

None of the affected publishers fought the ban. Alfred Harcourt saw no reason "why the publishers ... should concern themselves with the matter, especially when such proceedings do not seem to affect business adversely." "[T]he situation will take care of itself," said John Macrae of Dutton cryptically. Arthur Garfield Hays, after sampling the Boston mood for

Horace Liveright, advised against making a test case of *The Hard-Boiled Virgin.*[32] A suppression in New York was a serious matter, disrupting the very process of publishing and distributing a book, but a Boston ban was evidently considered insufficient justification for serious protest—particularly when the dividends in publicity and added sales elsewhere were so great.

Nor did the booksellers show any inclination to remonstrate. Indeed, Richard Fuller praised the police for their "common sense and tolerance." As *Publishers' Weekly* noted, the suppressed volumes were "of slight significance and their value in trade to any one individual bookseller slight."[33] In March 1927 the Boston booksellers, through their attorney, issued a response to criticism of their supine position. The police had acted, the statement said, because authors and publishers had persisted in producing books that "affront the feelings of large sections of our population." As for the booksellers' attitude:

> Their position as business men is one of neutrality . . . and their first care is to conduct their business according to law. They are not concerned either with the censorship of public morals or with the defense of art from the assault of puritanism. Their problem is to protect themselves and they can only do so by heeding any warning from the constituted authorities. . . . [W]here is the courage or sense in taking the position that some small shopkeeper . . . who has no interest either way shall wear the crown of martyrdom?[34]

Where indeed? Dismissing the suggestion that a "small shopkeeper" might possess interests or influence beyond the confines of his store, the Boston booksellers washed their hands of the censorship issue and turned once more to promoting the works of Mary Roberts Rinehart, Harold Bell Wright, and Bruce Barton. Petrified by the prospect of "unsought martyrdom and two years in the hoosegow," they were "afraid of the Watch and Ward Society, afraid of . . . the more powerful booksellers, afraid of Catholic sentiment, afraid of . . . their customers, afraid someone [would] . . . say 'Boo!'"[35]

A turning point came in April 1927, however, when District Attorney Foley, pointing out that the obscenity law barred books endangering "the morals of youth," notified Suffolk County booksellers that the sale of Sinclair Lewis's *Elmer Gantry*, recently published by Harcourt Brace, would be deemed grounds for prosecution. At this, even the long-suffering Boston booksellers threw up their hands. Through Richard F. Fuller, they shipped off to Foley a crate of fifty-seven bestsellers, asking advice as to their saleability. Returning the package unopened, Foley testily replied that no more advance rulings would be given by his office. Booksellers would simply have to use their own judgment, he said, and take the consequences. At the same time, he announced that jail sentences would be demanded in any future obscenity prosecutions. In an accompanying letter, Police Superintendent Crowley gave a "broad hint" that the further sale of Theodore Dreiser's *An American Tragedy* (published by Liveright in 1925) and Warwick Deeping's *Doomsday* (Knopf, 1927) would be considered grounds for prosecution.[36]

Foley's action was roundly condemned by Boston's secular press, and even by the Watch and Ward Society, but *The Pilot* strongly endorsed it. *Elmer Gantry*, said the editor of *The Pilot*, "casts the unworthy suspicion of hypocrisy upon the noblest profession in the world."[37]

The audacity of the Boston authorities in taking on bestsellers like *An American Tragedy* and *Elmer Gantry* was discussed in front-page stories in the New York newspapers. A challenge of this magnitude could hardly be ignored, but when Alfred Harcourt visited Boston and found that Foley's action was "backed by the opinion of the Catholic Church" and "popular with a considerable section of the voters," he abandoned his hope of precipitating a test case à la Mencken. *Elmer Gantry* thus remained under a cloud, and Boston bookstores sold it furtively, or not at all.[38]

Horace Liveright was not so easily dissuaded. He sent Arthur Garfield Hays and Donald Friede (who had not yet left Liveright to establish his own firm) to Boston, where

on April 15 Friede sold a copy of *An American Tragedy* to
Lieutenant Hines of the vice squad. "Hello old pal; I see you've
got your gang with you," said Hines, by now a veteran of such
affairs, upon recognizing Hays and his entourage of reporters.
When Hays tried to persuade the lieutenant to buy *The Scarlet
Letter* and the Bible as well, Police Superintendent Crowley,
who was supervising proceedings, put his foot down. "Now
don't go ahead wholesale. We are not running a bookstore
here," he said sourly.[39]

Friede was duly arrested, booked, and released on bail,
"confident that the case would be thrown out in quick order."
Publishers' Weekly reported that acquittal "seems likely."
That this confidence was misplaced, however, soon became apparent. On April 22, the case came before Municipal Judge
James H. Devlin. Evidence was introduced confirming Dreiser's
high literary reputation and establishing that his novel was
assigned reading at Harvard. Richard F. Fuller testified for the
defense. Nevertheless, Devlin found Friede guilty and imposed
a one-hundred-dollar fine. Magnanimously, he refrained from
imposing a jail sentence because, as he said, this was Friede's
first offense.[40]

Hays's appeal was not heard for two years, and during this
period *An American Tragedy* could not legally be purchased in
Boston, though it was freely sold across the Charles River in
Cambridge. "It is not a book which is before the bar now, but a
city," declared *Publishers' Weekly*.[41]

Another literary celebrity was drawn into the deepening
Boston imbroglio late in May 1927 when Richard F. Fuller, on
his own initiative, removed from the shelves of his Old Corner
Bookstore Upton Sinclair's *Oil*, a novel about the Harding ad-
ministration scandals published that year by A. & C. Boni. The
Boston police forthwith arrested a young clerk at Smith & Mc-
Cance, another Boston bookstore, for selling *Oil*. The reason for
the action, according to the police, was that *Oil* contained a
reference to birth control. A few weeks later, the clerk, John
Gritz, was found guilty and fined in municipal court.[42] Upton
Sinclair hastened from California to Boston to defend his good

name. He was indignant that the Boston censors, in digging for dirt, had struck *Oil*. "I have never written an indecent book, and resent the charge that I have done so," he wrote to Oswald Garrison Villard.[43] Now began a comedy of errors as Sinclair sought martyrdom and the police resolutely tried to prevent any such outcome. At a hearing before John Gritz's conviction, Sinclair tried to have his own name substituted on the indictment, only to be informed by the judge that this was impossible. At a Boston Common rally on June 12, the author tried in vain to sell copies of *Oil* to the mystified patrolmen. During a later protest meeting he did persuade an officer to buy an *Oil*-jacketed book which proved upon inspection to be a Bible. Sinclair next appeared on the streets of Boston wearing a large fig-leaf-shaped sandwich board, peddling copies of *Oil* from which the offending passages had been cut. "We authors are using America as our sales territory, and Boston is our advertising department," he boasted. At last the long-suffering Lieutenant Hines agreed to purchase a copy of *Oil*, but a municipal court judge refused to issue a warrant. In frustration, Upton Sinclair returned to the West Coast.[44]

By 1928 the Boston book situation seemed hopeless. *An American Tragedy* and *Oil* were under a legal ban, some fourteen other titles had been suppressed by the police without judicial procedure, and many more had simply been withdrawn by booksellers. The city was in the grip of a suppressive spirit which few defended but many resignedly accepted. A *New York Times* reporter spoke of "a sort of moral panic."[45]

This unhappy state of affairs had been reached as the censorship initiative shifted from the Watch and Ward Society into the hands of the new majority. Bitterness and a sense of waning authority had led the Watch and Ward into damaging excesses, while inexperience and perhaps a certain giddiness in the exercise of new-found power produced similar extremes on the part of the police. As Elmer Davis wrote perceptively in January 1928:

> [O]ld and new share the responsibility for the great crusade against current literature which has been going on in the

past year; the Puritans forged the sword and the Irish are wielding it. . . . Now that the Protestants have lost control of the secular arm, Boston, which was chastised with whips, is likely to be chastised with scorpions.[46]

❦

Beneath the surface, however, there was growing restiveness over the Boston situation. "[T]he city has become extremely conscious of its difficulties and the citizens are looking about for a way to . . . a more reasonable situation," noted *Publishers' Weekly* in mid-1927. Cultural and intellectual leaders who had tolerated the genteel Watch and Ward censorship rebelled at the municipal variety. On April 14, 1927, Ellery Sedgwick, Mark A. DeWolfe Howe, and MacGregor Jenkins, all of the *Atlantic Monthly*, together with three officials of Little, Brown and Company, issued a widely publicized statement attacking the "high-handed, erratic, and ill-advised" police censorship as repugnant to the "best sentiment of this community" and "definitely injurious to organizations, both religious and secular, with which the current prosecution becomes inevitably associated in the public mind." "It is difficult," they concluded, "for men of self respect to keep silent in the face of this violation of the historic tradition of Boston and New England."[47]

The major Boston newspapers, despite their reputation for pusillanimity, likewise condemned the literary ventures of the police. Said the *Globe:* "Censorship of books by public officials is a dangerous business, as well as, generally, a stupid one." "Do not make us ridiculous," the *Herald* admonished the police censors. "Do not imply to the world that those whom we elect to office have no comprehension of . . . intellectual freedom. . . ." Only *The Pilot* and the tabloid *Post* defended the police, the latter heaping scorn on the typical opponent of censorship as a "literary genius" or a "college professor"— evidently two of the strongest epithets in its arsenal.[48]

Gradually an anticensorship consensus, like that triggered

by the "Clean Books" crusade in New York, began to emerge in Massachusetts. In May 1927 the Women's City Club under the leadership of Mrs. William Z. Ripley, wife of a Harvard economist, sponsored a censorship discussion at the venerable Ford Hall. An audience of over a thousand heard Arthur Harcourt and the Reverend Dr. Raymond Calkins, president of the Watch and Ward Society, join in deploring the current situation. The keynote was struck by Hiller C. Wellman, a Springfield librarian and an outspoken opponent of censorship, who urged greater tolerance for literary innovators and suggested a revision of the state's obscenity law.[49]

Under the leadership of Wellman and others, library meetings became important forums for censorship discussion. In March 1927, addressing the Massachusetts Library Club (the state's leading professional association), Robert E. Rogers, professor of English at the Massachusetts Institute of Technology, urged librarians to be more outspoken in defense of books—even "radical" ones—that were unpopular with the majority of the public. In October, the Western Massachusetts Library Club heard the critic Walter Prichard Eaton vigorously denounce the Boston suppressions. The librarians responded hesitantly; was not "safety first" the best policy, one of them asked Professor Rogers. The *Library Journal* reported "considerable difference of opinion" among Massachusetts librarians on the subject, but said that most, while eager to elevate reading standards, were "not generally of the opinion that it is altogether practicable to do this by law. . . ."[50] Like their colleagues elsewhere, Massachusetts librarians were moving cautiously toward active participation in the struggle against book censorship.

The most powerful voice added to the growing demand for reform was that of the Boston business community. In December 1927 the influential Babson Business Conference at nearby Wellesley, in a rather unusual step, invited Professor Daniel Evans of Andover Theological Seminary in Cambridge to discuss Boston's censorship. Defending the "great free,

frank, vitalizing" books that deal with the "primal passions,"
Evans urged his business audience to speak out against censorship and "save Boston from being the laughing stock of
the country at large." A few days later the *Transcript* published
a long letter on this subject from A. Lincoln Filene of the
Boston department-store family. New England, declared Filene,
was losing out economically to "younger and perhaps more
vigorous sections," and this made it imperative for all business
leaders to ask themselves: "What price Boston's literary censorship?" Pointing out that the city's reputation for prudery
had aroused ridicule throughout the country, he went on:

> It is an easy step from scoffing at New England's Puritanic
> tradition to believing that if New England is "slow" in adjust-
> ing herself to an era of greater frankness in the discussion of
> sex relations, she is probably slow in business matters also.
> . . . This belief hurts New England badly. . . . Have the censors
> weighed against their moral triumphs the economic losses
> which they entail? Perhaps it's up to those business men who
> have been laughing at the book censorship to take it a little
> more seriously. Perhaps something can really be done about
> it.[51]

The censorship issue, reported a somewhat awed *Zion's Herald*,
had become "serious enough to engage the attention of leading
business men. . . ." With recruits of the stature of A. Lincoln
Filene, the anticensorship movement began to gain ground.
Even Richard F. Fuller, no flaming radical, noted the disturbing fact that many Boston book buyers had done their 1927
Christmas shopping in other cities, and that many of them
had opened accounts with New York City bookstores.[52]

The solution most frequently advanced was to amend the
state's obscenity statute, one of the nation's most stringent.
Not only did it open the door to frivolous suppressions and
demagogic appeals by outlawing all publications "manifestly
tending to corrupt the morals of youth," but it further barred
all books "containing obscene, indecent, or impure *language*,"
thus inviting prosecution on the strength of a single shocking
word.[53]

Some argued cogently that the fundamental problem in Boston was one of personnel rather than the precise wording of the law. Nevertheless, a statewide legislative campaign offered a possible means of bringing a countervailing force to bear on the Boston officials. Accordingly, the issue of book censorship, as in New York in 1923, moved from the courts to the legislature. In New York the procensorship forces had initiated the move after setbacks in the courts. In Massachusetts it was the frustrated *anti*censorship group which now sought relief.

A hastily organized attempt to liberalize the law came during the 1927–28 session. Representative Henry Shattuck, treasurer of Harvard College, introduced a bill to amend the obscenity statute by removing the reference to youthful morals and adding the requirement that a book's language be "considered in connection with its entire context and theme or with the entire context and theme of any complete component part. . . ." Shattuck's bill was the work of a citizens' committee headed by Ellery Sedgwick and including the state education commissioner, a former president of the Women's City Club, A. Lincoln Filene, eight librarians, and three booksellers. The Boston booksellers, however, introduced a divisive bill of their own which changed the mechanics of suppression so as to reduce the risk to the bookseller, but which left the stringent definition of "obscenity" unchanged. In April 1928 the legislature adjourned without taking action on either bill.[54]

The Massachusetts Library Club, which came out for a liberalized book law in November 1928, was designated to spearhead the next attempt at legislative reform. The so-called "Massachusetts Library Club bill," introduced the following January, was essentially the old Shattuck bill, with the added proviso that only a person who sold a book "knowing" it to be obscene could be prosecuted. This clause, which assumed some type of preliminary judgment in equity, was added to please the booksellers and to take advantage of a rift which had developed between the Boston booksellers, dominated by the conservative Richard F. Fuller, and those in western

Massachusetts, several of whom were actively cooperating with
the reform group. Under the prodding of these western dissidents, who threatened to set up a rival statewide booksellers' organization, the Boston booksellers, through Fuller,
announced their support of the Library Club bill.[55]

A hearing was held in February 1929 by the Joint Committee on Legal Affairs. Testifying for the proposal were
Fuller, Edward Weeks of the *Atlantic*, a vice-president of the
First National Bank of Boston, and no fewer than five librarians.
The Reverend Dr. Calkins of the Watch and Ward Society
appeared in opposition, but he "made such an effort to be
fair in his criticism that he seemed to create a feeling in favor
of rather than against the bill." In late March, by a unanimous
vote, the bill was reported favorably by the committee.[56]

The rapid progress of the amendment campaign generated
overconfidence. The librarians congratulated themselves that
"their personal knowledge of the situation and their freedom
from any selfish interest" had carried great weight with the
legislators. Opposition to the reform remained deeply entrenched, however, and a lull on the Boston censorship front
in 1929 encouraged those who wished to let the issue quietly
subside. The leaders of the amendment campaign made little
effort to follow up the favorable impression their spokesmen
had created at the hearing, and on April 16, 1929, the "Massachusetts Library Club bill" was defeated in the Senate by a
fifteen to thirteen vote.[57]

The peaceful interlude in the Boston censorship situation
was soon shattered by a series of well-publicized cases which
gave a fresh and decisive impetus to the reform movement.
While the legislators were still pondering the obscenity amendment, Donald Friede's appeal of his 1927 conviction in the
American Tragedy case was heard in superior criminal court.
With attorney Arthur Garfield Hays at the helm, the trial became a stage for dramatizing once again the suppressive con-

ditions prevailing in Boston. Hundreds of spectators crowded the courtroom as the aging Clarence Darrow read a chapter of *An American Tragedy* to the jury. Dreiser himself appeared on the stand, although his testimony was severely limited by the presiding judge. The prosecution, led by Assistant District Attorney Frederick T. Doyle, based its case primarily on the book's references to birth control, which were read to the jury.[58]

The attempt by the defense to heighten the symbolic quality of the trial did not end at the courthouse walls. On April 16, while the case was still being heard, 700 persons jammed Ford Hall for a great anticensorship, free-speech rally. The speakers included Darrow, Hays, Morris Ernst, Gardner Jackson, Oswald Garrison Villard, and other celebrated liberals. Presiding as "Chief Roastmaster and Master of Rebelry" was the dignified Harvard professor of history, Arthur M. Schlesinger. Massachusetts' censorship law was "lampooned, ridiculed, and pilloried." Students costumed to resemble the characters in banned novels roamed the hall carrying placards bearing book titles with the word "SUP-PRESSED" printed over them. Margaret Sanger, forbidden to speak in Boston because of her advocacy of birth control, sat with a large tape across her mouth while Professor Schlesinger read her speech. In a skit called "The Suppressed Book Shop" a clerk cannily refused to sell either a history of Middle*sex* County or a collection of Mother Goose stories ("Do you realize the things that are in that book? Take Jack and Jill. . . . [T]hey went up the hill ostensibly to get a pail of water and then tumbled down. Think of the conclusion that can be drawn!"). He was arrested all the same, however, for neglecting to get a customer's fingerprints before selling a geometry book full of "all sorts of triangles."[59]

Along with such witty thrusts, an undertone of intellectual condescension was in evidence throughout the evening. When one "customer" in the bookshop skit was asked why she wished to buy a certain title she replied: "I want to be intelligent, even if I do live in Boston." Arthur Garfield Hays poked fun at the intellectual calibre of the jury before which he was at that moment trying the *American Tragedy* case, and Clarence Darrow quoted Voltaire: "Fools are serious so intelligent men can laugh." A pugnacious radicalism was symbolized by the prevalence of lapel buttons bearing the slogan "Red But Not Dictated."[60]

The "Ford Hall Frolic," as it was promptly dubbed by the newspapers, provided a needed fillip to local anticensorship champions after their legislative setbacks, and again reminded the nation of Boston's unenviable reputation. "[W]e did not see how we could lose," wrote Donald Friede later, "Boston had been held up to ridicule all over the world. . . ." For this very reason, however, the immediate local reaction was distinctly hostile. Representatives of various civic and fraternal groups filled the newspapers with denunciations. The feeling that the city was being exploited grew stronger when Hays and Darrow, having used the local judicial system, as it seemed, for their own purposes, abruptly departed for New York, leaving Friede's defense in the hands of Thomas Lavelle, a local attorney. Reporters covering the trial told Friede privately that the Ford Hall affair had been the "last straw" and that his conviction was now certain. Sensing the hostility, Lavelle requested a new trial. Said he: ". . . Mr. Friede is the victim of his friends, or if not, is the victim of those people at Ford Hall." The motion was denied.[61]

District Attorney Doyle shrewdly played upon the feelings of resentment. "The only thing missing in their act is Tex Guinan," he said of the Ford Hall performers in his summation, sarcastically thanking the "imported attorneys" for their efforts to entertain the "little village" of Boston. On April 18, 1929, the jury, a cross section of working-class Boston, upheld the Friede conviction.[62] The stringency of the still-unrevised obscenity law, the intense Catholic feeling on the subject of birth control, and the tactical errors of the defense had produced an unexpected setback for the increasingly confident opponents of Boston's censorship. *An American Tragedy* was still "banned in Boston."

The pot continued to boil throughout 1929. In June, the Boston police chief banned an issue of *Scribner's Magazine* containing a serialized episode from Hemingway's *A Farewell to Arms.* ("[M]any readers had doubtless missed Mr. Hemingway's powerful story," commented the *New York Herald Tribune,* "and they will be grateful to the chief for calling their attention to it.")[63] In September Mayor Malcolm A. Nichols (Harvard, Class of 1899) refused to permit Boston's Hollis Theater to stage a scheduled engagement of O'Neill's *Strange Interlude,* thereby disappointing 7,000 Theatre Guild subscribers. "As far as the Catholics of Boston are concerned," said *The Pilot* of the play, "they are plainly disgusted with it, and commend the fearless stand of the municipal authorities. . . ." The production was transferred to nearby Quincy, where it won praise from religious and civic leaders and had a successful run.[64]

The now-widespread controversy over Boston censorship intensified still further in October with the revelation that the Christian Science Church, with headquarters in Boston, was attempting by threats of economic boycott to suppress Edwin F. Dakin's recently published biography of Mary Baker Eddy. The publisher, Charles Scribner's Sons, fought back vigorously. "[I]t would be extremely dangerous to the interest of intellectual freedom," declared Scribner's in a press statement,

> if publishers should refrain from publishing or booksellers from bringing forward such books as this . . . because they fear the hostility of a particular sect. . . . We reaffirm our belief in the essential integrity of the [Dakin] book [and] . . . intend to support it unfalteringly. . . .

As frequently occurs, the attacked book became a best-seller. In 1930 Dakin's biography was reissued by Scribner's in an inexpensive edition together with a pamphlet on the attempted suppression, "The Blight That Failed."[65]

These suppressive flurries of the summer and autumn of 1929 culminated in a spectacular censorship case which eclipsed all the others: the Dunster House Bookshop prosecution. The most important Boston censorship incident since "Hatrack," this trial significantly affected both the legislative reform movement and the fate of the Watch and Ward Society.

The book in question was a newcomer on the censorship scene: D. H. Lawrence's *Lady Chatterley's Lover*. Modestly described by Lawrence as "the most improper novel ever written," *Lady Chatterley's Lover* had been privately printed in Florence in 1928 and at once pirated in Paris and New York. Among the bookstores which began to receive requests for the work was the Dunster House Bookshop, a Cambridge establishment catering to Harvard students and faculty. The proprietor was James A. DeLacey, a bibliophile and former Yale librarian whose personal distaste for modern literary frankness was well known to his friends. His bookstore was housed in a gracious old residence on the site now occupied by Elsie's, a popular undergraduate eating spot.[66]

Early in October 1929 John S. Sumner in New York learned that DeLacey had ordered five copies of *Lady Chatterley's Lover*, and he made haste to notify the Watch and Ward Society. Since the *American Mercury* fiasco, the Watch and Ward had confined its activities to the narrower and less controversial field of "hard-core pornography." Believing the Lawrence novel to be safely within this category, the Watch and Ward secretary dispatched an elderly agent, John Tait Slaymaker, to the Dunster House Bookshop to purchase a copy. At first both the clerk, Joseph Sullivan, and DeLacey himself refused Slaymaker's importunities, but when Slaymaker (who was using a false name) returned the next day, DeLacey agreed to sell him a copy of *Lady Chatterley's Lover* at a later date. Slaymaker returned a third time two weeks later and purchased the book for fifteen dollars.

The Watch and Ward at once instituted legal proceedings. On November 25, in Cambridge district court, Judge Arthur P. Stone (who had convicted Felix Caragianes in 1926) found both DeLacey and Sullivan guilty. DeLacey was fined eight hundred dollars and sentenced to four months in jail, Sullivan two hundred dollars and two weeks. Their attorney, Herbert Parker, a distinguished Boston lawyer and former state attorney general, at once appealed.[67]

When the superior court trial opened on December 19, it was evident that DeLacey and Sullivan had many sympathizers. The Harvard community in particular rallied around, and the courtroom was filled with college students as the poet Robert Hillyer (then an assistant professor of English at Harvard), George P. Winship of the Harvard University Library, and Stewart Mitchell of the Massachusetts Historical Society testified to DeLacey's good character.[68]

The Watch and Ward leaders soon realized to their dismay that they were in for another storm of public denunciation. Not only did attorney Parker attack them as "miserable false pretenders who pose brazenly as protectors of public morals," but the young prosecuting attorney, Robert T. Bushnell, made plain his distaste for the "falsifiers" and "procurers" whose cause he was representing. When the presiding judge, Frederick W. Fosdick, added his criticism of the Society's entrapment methods, the *Boston Herald* was moved to observe:

> These three men, one young, one middle-aged, one old, representing the three great branches of the law, have voiced public opinion more effectively than it has been voiced for years. They have done a genuine public service.

Whatever useful "scavenging" the Watch and Ward may have done in the past, concluded the *Herald*, it had long outlived its day.[69] The case aroused intense public interest, and all the Boston papers (again excepting the *Post*) joined in excoriating the hapless Watch and Ward. *The Pilot* remained silent. The Vice Society keenly felt this journalistic barrage which, it said, "for bias, prejudice, disregard of fact, and total absence of any sense of justice and fair dealing has rarely been duplicated. . . ."[70]

For all the contempt heaped on the Watch and Ward Society and the outpouring of sympathy for DeLacey and

Sullivan, few defended *Lady Chatterley's Lover.* District Attorney Bushnell described Lawrence as "a filthy degenerate
with a sewer brain," and Robert Hillyer conceded that he personally would not mention the novel to his students.[71]

On December 20, 1929, Judge Fosdick, despite his expressed hostility to the Watch and Ward Society, upheld the
lower court conviction of DeLacey and Sullivan. His ruling
was in turn confirmed several months later by the state supreme
court. Although DeLacey's jail sentence was suspended on
motion of the district attorney and his fine paid by contributions from the Harvard community, he was emotionally shattered by his experience. His bookshop failed, his wife left him,
and—so say the older Harvard Square booksellers—he died
in obscurity some years later, a hopeless alcoholic.[72]

For the Watch and Ward Society, it was a Pyrrhic victory.
A certain good-natured carnival atmosphere had pervaded the
American Mercury episode, but the Dunster House Bookshop
case generated nothing but bitterness. Few found it amusing
that a man of DeLacey's standing had fallen victim to a vice
society *agent provocateur.* Indulgent chuckles gave way to
harsh condemnation. One of the sharpest rebukes came from
the urbane and normally gentle Bernard DeVoto, then a member of the Harvard faculty. "With the benignantly strabismic
innocence of reformers everywhere," wrote DeVoto in the
Harvard Graduates' Magazine, the Watch and Ward had
assumed that "to convict any one of any kind of crime under
any law was virtuous and would receive the reward of virtue."
"To read the list of books 'Banned in Boston,'" he went on,

> is to be shocked, not by the content of the books, but by the
> festering disease of the minds that find evil in them. Such
> minds have all the stigmata of the sexual invalid. . . . It does
> not seem desirable to abandon to such invalids the control
> of literature.[73]

The Watch and Ward defended its course in a pamphlet
setting forth its version of the DeLacey case and citing its
"over fifty years of useful service." Watch and Ward President Raymond Calkins argued that "no efficient state detective"

would have hesitated to employ the entrapment method used in the Dunster House Bookshop case. In any event, noted Calkins, replying to an attack in the *Nation:* "Compared with our work in other directions, the recent Book Shop case was the merest incident."[74]

Perhaps; but the tide of obloquy which the case had set off was not to be so easily turned aside. Serious defections from the ranks of the Watch and Ward's honorary vice-presidents and directors began to occur. Among those resigning were Professor Julian T. Coolidge of Harvard; Dean Henry B. Washburn of the Episcopal Theological School; Dr. David D. Scannel, a prominent Boston surgeon; and Episcopal Bishop William Lawrence. "When a Lawrence resigns," commented *Outlook,* ". . . his action carries with it a significance that it would be difficult for a New Yorker to appreciate." In 1931, Dr. Calkins himself quietly resigned as Watch and Ward president.[75]

Some of these defectors denied that their departure was linked to the Dunster House Bookshop case, but their protests were unconvincing. "Obviously the strength of the Society is crumbling fast," observed the *New York Sunday World* with satisfaction. Annual contributions, which had hovered around eight thousand dollars throughout the 1920s, dropped to less than 40% of that figure by 1931. Disillusionment as well as the Depression was taking its toll. "[M]any of the original supporters have in the natural course of events been removed by death," noted the Watch and Ward report sadly in 1932, adding: "We would emphasize the importance of having the surviving members of these families continue the support of our organization. . . ."[76]

But such pleas fell on deaf ears, and the venerable organization fell prey to the petty indignities which are the fate of the once-powerful. In December 1929 a Massachusetts legislator introduced a bill requiring all would-be censors to "submit to the state Department of Public Health satisfactory evidence of normal sex experience."[77] Soon even ridicule palled, and the New England Watch and Ward Society, like its

counterparts in other cities across the country, drifted into
shadowed obscurity. However, thanks to the impressive lar-
gesse of Mrs. Martha R. Hunt, who had bequeathed the
Society over $100,000 in 1911, the Watch and Ward was able
to weather this crisis more successfully than the vice societies
of New York, Chicago, and elsewhere. Indeed, as the "New
England Citizens Crime Commission" it still survives, operating from a comfortable Beacon Hill office. The Commission
now concentrates on such matters as illegal gambling and
school vandalism, holding itself firmly aloof from any involvement with book censorship.[78]

The recrudescence of suppressive activity in 1929 brought
the issue of Boston censorship once again into the limelight.
After the *Scribner's Magazine* and *Strange Interlude* bans the
New York World reported that "the apathy previously displayed by local residents" had given way to demands for action
from "clergymen, bankers, businessmen, publishers, literary
societies, women's clubs, librarians, editors, and scores of
other men and women." In an unusual gesture of involvement
in local affairs, a group of fifty Harvard professors publicly protested the *Strange Interlude* ban.[79]

Dissatisfaction intensified as the Dunster House Bookshop
case once again made Boston the butt of national ridicule.
Even the staid *Publishers' Weekly* printed a poetic joke at
Boston's expense, one verse of which went:

> If a mother would know, where her children should go,
> Or what is the book they may read,
> The cop on the beat, with the number twelve feet,
> Can supply every artistic need.[80]

Shafts of this sort found their mark. "I am sick and tired,"
said District Attorney Bushnell after the DeLacey prosecution,
"of having Boston and Massachusetts represented as backwoods
sections populated by yokels without backbone and spirit. . . ."
As 1929 drew to its close, the *Boston Globe* was able to report:

"The little snowball of protest against book and play bannings in Boston has rolled itself into a very solid and sizeable mountain. . . ."[81]

Proponents of the stalled movement for legislative reform seized the moment. Informed that the legislature was willing to hold only one more full-scale hearing on an obscenity bill, they organized their campaign carefully. The librarians having failed in their effort to spearhead a successful amendment drive, a more broadly based "Massachusetts Citizens' Committee for Revision of the Book Law" was set up under the chairmanship of Edward W. Weeks, Jr., of the *Atlantic Monthly*, a leader of the amendment campaign from the beginning. This committee, of almost stifling respectability, included: Ellery Sedgwick; Walter Prichard Eaton; Bliss Perry; the Episcopal Bishop of Massachusetts; the presidents of Mount Holyoke, Smith, Tufts, and Wellesley; the head of the Episcopal Theological School; and—the secretary of the Massachusetts Bible Society![82]

Sedgwick and Weeks made the *Atlantic Monthly* a forum for the reformist cause. In the January 1930 issue President Neilson of Smith College poked holes in "The Theory of Censorship" and Weeks himself detailed the absurdities of "The Practice of Censorship." Only a revision of the obscenity law, Weeks declared, could end "[t]he hypocrisy of the present situation, the injury which it does to literature, the notoriety which it too often bestows on cheap books, [and] . . . the contempt for law which it encourages. . . ."[83]

The reformers were heartened in their efforts by evidences of a changing climate of opinion in the Boston Catholic community. *The Pilot*, to be sure, continued throughout 1929 to excoriate bad books and occasionally to defend rigid suppression. "The banning of books and plays that are notoriously indecent and that menace the morals of the community," it said of the *Strange Interlude* incident, demands the praise of all "right-minded and right-thinking people."[84] But as criticism of censorship mounted, a more positive note began to be heard.

In October 1929 the Diocese of Boston launched a "Catholic Literature Campaign" under the Reverend Father Francis L. Phelan, who traveled from parish to parish establishing "Reading Clubs" pledged to reading recommended Catholic books. Rejecting imputations of censorship, Father Phelan said that his program was "simply a matter of direction touching a question of conscience." Strongly endorsing this undertaking (one aspect of which involved securing more subscriptions to the diocesan weekly), *The Pilot* praised Catholic literature as possessing "an essential beauty deeper and sweeter than anything that ever flowed from a tainted pen." The conclusion was inevitable: "[T]he easiest way to avoid bad books is to read only Catholic books."[85]

To a degree, at least, the "Catholic Literature Campaign" diverted ecclesiastical authorities from an excessive preoccupation with suppression through the secular agencies of enforcement. "[T]he wise counsel of the church" was now seen as a more effective way of preserving Catholics from "the literary morass." While continuing in theory to support stringent legal suppression, *The Pilot* admitted that this approach was only "partially effective" and the arguments against it "clamorous and plausible." Belatedly recognizing that censorship efforts usually trigger "a resentful counterattack waged with the weapons of ridicule and satire which largely nullify the good of the prohibition," *The Pilot* in November 1929 concluded that "civil law is not a cure-all adapted to remedy this evil."[86] With this conclusion all those who were battling the Boston censorship could heartily agree.

The amendment campaign was further strengthened in 1929 by the addition of strong support from the American Civil Liberties Union. Since 1920 a weak "New England Committee" of the A.C.L.U. had been functioning under Boston attorney John S. Codman, but it had not concerned itself with literary censorship. Compared with the Sacco-Vanzetti case, which aroused such all-absorbing concern within the A.C.L.U. and among liberals generally, a few book suppressions paled into insignificance.[87] Further, there were strategic reasons for the A.C.L.U.'s noninvolvement in censorship issues. Early in 1927, when Hiller C. Wellman, the Springfield librarian who was active in the Massachusetts anticensorship fight, urged the A.C.L.U. to take up the cause, he received a somewhat tortuous but essentially discouraging reply from Forrest Bailey, co-director of the Union:

> I hope you will not be too greatly disappointed when I tell you we cannot go into the "anti-obscenity" campaign in Boston. That is a phase of free speech which we have kept clear of because of our wish to avoid complicating our main issues. Usually these spasms of morbid conscience die down quickly. While they are on they are extremely disagreeable and the feeling they generate is likely to run high. The issue of free speech in its larger aspects—those affecting criticism of the status quo—appears to us to be so much more important, that it would be inexpedient for us to involve ourselves in controversies where questions of morals are present.[88]

Roger Baldwin, co-director with Bailey of the A.C.L.U. in this period, has suggested in retrospect that the Union's position was adopted not so much from a fear of prejudicing its other activities, but simply because no censorship case of sufficient interest presented itself. Obscenity cases "just didn't come to enough public notice to challenge us," he has written.[89]

Some of the internal conflicts underlying the A.C.L.U.'s stand on literary censorship are suggested by the 1929 reply of Dr. Richard C. Cabot, Harvard Social Ethics professor and a pillar of the civil liberties movement, when Roger Baldwin asked for his cooperation in a campaign against Boston censorship which the A.C.L.U. was at long last contemplating. "I should resign from the Civil Liberties Union if the proposed extension of its activities is carried out," wrote Cabot. "I am wholly in favor of censorship of books, plays, and movies, and the fact that it is now rather badly done . . . does not seem to me a good reason to abolish it."[90]

By 1929, Arthur Garfield Hays and Morris Ernst had become co-counsel of the A.C.L.U., and the Union was moving closer to an all-out identification with the campaign to liberalize the Massachusetts obscenity law. The New York office strongly condemned the *Strange Interlude* ban, and later in 1929 a reorganized and strengthened Massachusetts Civil Liberties Committee prepared and published *The Censorship in Boston*, a hard-hitting pamphlet to which Zechariah Chafee, Jr., of the Harvard Law School lent his name as author. After describing both the police and the Watch-and-Ward varieties of censorship, the pamphlet urged enactment of the proposed liberalizing revision of the obscenity law.[91] In October the Massachusetts Civil Liberties Committee sponsored a Ford Hall anticensorship rally which proved to be a considerably more sedate affair than the April "Frolic." John S. Codman presided, and the principal speakers were Weeks, Chafee, a Tufts psychiatrist, and an erstwhile director of the Watch and Ward Society. In a meeting the following month at Old South Church, Roger Baldwin scored the "scandalous record" of censorship attributable to the "extraordinary combination of the Catholic, Puritan, and Victorian spirit," and declared that the A.C.L.U. would not rest "until all this censorship is abolished in Boston."[92]

As more and more groups and individuals swung over to the anticensorship side, the defense of the procensorship position was left to a hard-core minority. Sensing defeat, these die-hards resorted to arguments of a bizarre vacuity remarkable even for censorship champions. "[A]s one moth may destroy a tree, one page may destroy a home," declared one alarmed opponent of the reform movement.[93] And Police Chief Crowley, who had preserved Boston from *Elmer Gantry*, responded with devastating scorn when he was informed that an M.I.T. professor had said unkind words about his censorship proclivities:

> Man, God's highest creation, learns by imitation and our actions betray the examples inherited from those under whose guidance we receive our knowledge. Consequently, I cannot quite comprehend how a distinguished and learned exponent

of knowledge and right-thinking can expect to make such criticisms of public officials, without resulting in no small influence upon the receptive minds of his pupils in making them critical cynics of the sincerity and capability of public officials in the latter's action against things detrimental to the welfare of our youth and society in general.[94]

Despite such rhetorical diversions, the reform campaign was now moving steadily forward. Late in 1929 the Weeks amendment was introduced in the legislature. More modest in scope than earlier versions, it retained the passage alluding to the morals of youth but eliminated the most egregious feature of the old law, the reference to obscene *language*. Again all Boston newspapers except the ineffable *Post* endorsed the bill. After protracted negotiations between Weeks and Fuller, the Boston booksellers once more agreed not to introduce a divisive separate bill.[95]

On January 23, 1930, over four hundred persons crowded the Statehouse for the hearing before the Joint Committee on Legal Affairs. Among those testifying for the bill were the editor of *Zion's Herald*, Boston business leader Carl Dreyfus, Robert Bushnell (the attorney who had prosecuted the De-Lacey case), and Weeks himself. In splendid isolation, a Watch and Ward official spoke against the measure. By a unanimous vote, the committee reported the amendment favorably to the House and Senate.[96]

Mindful of the overconfidence of earlier years, the backers of the measure did not slacken their efforts after this preliminary victory, and the momentum of the campaign continued to build. Additional groups and organizations—the Massachusetts Federation of Women's Clubs among them—announced their support. In mid-March, the Senate passed the Weeks bill, and on a close vote—one hundred and twenty-one to eighty-nine—the House followed suit. With the affixing of the governor's signature, the long campaign to liberalize Massachusetts' archaic obscenity law reached its goal.[97]

The impulse to suppress "bad books" did not therefore

suddenly vanish from the Bay State. It is never wholly absent from any society. But the legislative reform did put a damper on the excessive indulgence of that impulse by overzealous authorities and private groups. Boston "book massacres" were a thing of the past. "Since the change in the law," reported the Massachusetts Civil Liberties Committee in 1938, "no prosecution of any book published by an established publishing house has been brought." The Watch and Ward Society, the report added, had "completely withdrawn from the field."[98] The anticensorship consensus forged in the Massachusetts legislative campaigns of the late 1920s long remained viable, ready to challenge the aspirations of any who might be tempted to breath new life into the faded slogan "Banned in Boston."

This is the Cartoon Which Was Censored By The Mayor of Santa Fe

Who prevented its inclusion in
LAUGHING HORSE NO. 17

NAUGHTY NAUGHTY BOY!

CENSOR

LITERATURE

Chronic Appendicitis, of course!   *By Will Shuster*

27. Senator Bronson M. Cutting of New Mexico, author of legislation to liberalize Customs regulations on literature.

28. A cartoon suppressed by the printer of the satirical magazine, *Laughing Horse*. The "Censor" resembles Senator Smoot.

29. Two views of the Nazi book-burning, 1933.

30. Washington, D.C., 1954: Roy Cohn (left) and G. David Schine (right), aides to Senator Joseph R. McCarthy (center). In the spring of 1953, Cohn and Schine toured Europe investigating libraries maintained by the U.S. Information Administration (USIA) to enforce a State Department ban on books by "controversial persons, Communists, fellow travelers, etc."

31. Ruth Brown, dismissed in 1950 as director of the Bartlesville, Oklahoma, Public Library after thirty years of service, when a forty-member "citizens' committee" and the American Legion protest her subscription selections, including *The Nation, The New Republic,* and *Soviet Russia Today.*

COURTESY OF LOUISE S. ROBBINS

NEW YORK TIMES

32. Charles Rembar, New York attorney who from 1959–61 successfully defended the publishers of *Lady Chatterley's Lover, Fanny Hill,* and *Tropic of Cancer* in high-profile cases, which he described in his optimistically titled 1968 book *The End of Obscenity.*

33. Charles H. Keating, Jr. (right), leaving federal court in Los Angeles in 1998 with his attorney. Keating served five years in a federal penitentiary after his 1991 conviction for fraud in the Lincoln Savings & Loan scandal, in which 23,000 uninsured customers lost their savings. For many years, Keating's Citizens for Decent Literature organization, founded in 1957, loomed large in the anti-obscenity campaign.

34. The Summer 1962 issue of Ralph Ginzburg's short-lived magazine *Eros*, which led to his obscenity conviction and imprisonment. Bouncing back, Ginzburg in 1970 started a consumer financial advice magazine, *Moneysworth,* that proved highly successful.

REPRINTED BY PERMISSION OF RALPH GINZBURG

COURTESY OF RALPH GINZBURG

35. Publisher Ralph Ginzburg on March 9, 1972, when he entered the U.S. Penitentiary in Lewisburg, Pennsylvania, after exhausting all appeals of his 1966 conviction on obscenity charges for publishing *Eros* magazine. After serving eight months of a five-year sentence, Ginzburg was released on parole.

PHOTOGRAPH BY ROBERT S. OAKES AND VIC BOSWELL, COLLECTION OF THE SUPREME
COURT OF THE UNITED STATES, OFFICE OF THE CURATOR

36. The Supreme Court in 1970. Beneath the black robes lay deep divisions over censorship issues. Chief Justice Warren Burger (front row, center), would soon lead the court toward a more repressive position. Sitting beside Burger are First Amendment absolutists Hugo Black (left) and William O. Douglas (right). Thurgood Marshall (back row, left), John Marshall Harlan II (front row, left), and especially William J. Brennan, Jr. (front row, right), all wrote opinions in important censorship cases of the 1950s and beyond.

AP/WIDE WORLD PHOTOS

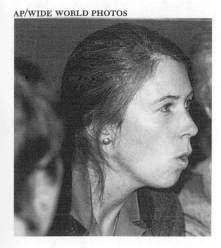

37. Catherine A. MacKinnon, speaking in Cambridge, Massachusetts, in October 1985 in support of an antipornography ordinance drafted by herself and Andrea Dworkin.

38. Nico Jacobellis, manager of an art-house theater in Cleveland Heights, Ohio, arrested and jailed in 1959 for showing the mildly erotic French film *Les Amants*. The Supreme Court overturned his conviction in 1964, but not before his life had been seriously disrupted by legal expenses, anonymous harassment, and deportation threats.

EIGHT

The Onslaught Against Federal Censorship

By 1929, literary censorship was decidedly on the wane all over America. The high tide of the "Clean Books" movement was six years in the past. The drive to liberalize Massachusetts' obscenity law was moving toward success. The vice societies lay in disarray. And the suppression of literature by private moralists or by overzealous local officials was accomplished, if at all, only under the keen scrutiny of a vocal anticensorship contingent with powerful weapons of law and publicity at its command. As the urgency of battle at the state and local levels diminished, attention shifted to a censorship issue hitherto largely unexamined and uncriticized: the administrative power held by the federal government over the free circulation of books. The first manifestation of this shift came late in 1929 with a vigorous campaign against the long-established censorship powers of the United States Customs Bureau.

The authority of the government to bar "obscene" matter from American shores, dating from the Tariff of 1842, had been renewed in each subsequent tariff, most recently in the Fordney-McCumber Tariff of 1922. By the 1920s, the administration of this archaic censorship power had become bogged down in a bureaucratic morass. In the great majority of cases, the decision of the local inspector at the port of entry was final. Local ruling could, however, be appealed to the so-called United States Customs Court sitting in New York City. This group of appraisers, having little time or stomach for literary disputes, almost invariably upheld the ruling of the local Customs officer. In the mid-1920s, to promote uniformity at the various ports, the Customs Court began occasionally to promulgate rulings which placed certain titles under a general ban.[1]

A local obscenity decision could also be appealed to the federal courts. This was rarely done, however, because the presumption was strongly against the appellant. In 1927 Morris Ernst (in his first obscenity case) took to the federal courts a Customs ban on John Hermann's *What Happens*, an exposé of high life among postwar youth published that year in France by an American expatriate. The judge was distinctly hostile, barring both the proffered expert testimony (by Heywood Broun and H. L. Mencken) and Ernst's efforts to introduce certain passages from Shakespeare into the record. The jury upheld the Customs ruling, and three hundred copies of *What Happens* were destroyed.[2]

Further to confuse matters, Customs rulings were also subject to review by the Treasury Department. Puzzled local inspectors regularly forwarded doubtful books to Washington, where an *ad hoc* group of Treasury officials rendered an opinion. Early in 1927, for example, Washington reversed a ruling by New York's Customs inspectors and admitted 250 copies of Boccaccio's *Decameron*, imported by A. & C. Boni, and 500 unbound sets of *A Thousand and One Nights*, on the reasonable grounds that these titles had always been admitted in the past. Similarly, a May 1929 ban by the Boston Customs authorities against Voltaire's *Candide* was quietly reversed in Washington, although not before the incident had become a national joke.[3]

In short, local Customs inspectors held wide powers, subject to sporadic review by a variety of higher authorities. Under such conditions, decisions were erratic and enforcement unpredictable. Books banned at one port might enter at another, works excluded in certain translations or editions were admitted in other guises, and a local ruling might be upset weeks or months later by an anonymous higher authority. The broad discretionary power held by local inspectors made the entire system vulnerable to the limitations of its weakest functionaries. "A classic is a dirty book somebody is trying to get by me," one of these local examiners confided to a reporter early in 1930, boasting at the same time that in the preceding two years he had read and barred "272 different titles—thousands of volumes."[4]

The bureaucratic nature of the system invited manipulation by special-interest groups. In 1923, French erotica was excluded with special diligence, not from a sudden access of prudery among Customs inspectors, but because the Franco-American Board of Commerce and Industry, suspecting that such books were giving Americans a distorted idea of France, had secured the cooperation of the Customs Bureau in a campaign to bar them at the ports.[5]

Such erratic practices make it difficult to speak with precision about the extent of Customs censorship in the 1920s, but it is clear that throughout the decade certain classics and works of recognized literary significance were frequently excluded. Among the condemned authors were Balzac, Boccaccio, Rabelais, Apuleius (*The Golden Ass*), Casanova, Ovid,

Aristophanes (*Lysistrata*), Rousseau (*Confessions*), and certain Restoration dramatists. James Joyce, D. H. Lawrence, George Moore, and Radclyffe Hall headed the list of more recent writers who were taboo.[6]

Protest against federal censorship throughout the 1920s was surprisingly infrequent. While the suppressive activity of vice societies and municipal officials was an immediate irritant which aroused sharp opposition, the more remote and impersonal postal and Customs censorship was generally conceded to be a legitimate and relatively innocuous governmental function. In 1928, despite his defeat in the *What Happens* case, Morris Ernst could write in *To the Pure* of the "greater humanism" of the Customs censorship as compared to other forms.[7]

But even as Ernst's book appeared, federal Customs censorship was entering a new and more intense phase. In August 1928, succumbing to a common bureaucratic impulse, authorities in Washington undertook to bring greater rationality into the government's censorship activities. In that month, lawyers from the Customs Bureau and the Post Office Department held a conference at which they drew up a stringent "blacklist" of over 700 books henceforth to be considered both nonimportable and nonmailable. Most of the above-mentioned authors were included, together with hundreds of others of varying literary merit. For reasons not entirely clear, 379 of the blacklisted works were in Spanish. Distributed to local Customs and postal officials, this list became the basic document guiding the enforcement of federal obscenity legislation.[8] While at the state and local levels censorship was on the decline, Washington appeared to be moving in the opposite direction.

As a new tariff bill wended its way through Congress in the spring of 1929, there seemed little reason to expect that the usual ban on obscene books would encounter any serious challenge. In House and Senate committee hearings, the National Association of Book Publishers and the American

Booksellers' Association offered no criticism of the Customs censorship. In the Senate Finance Committee hearing (according to a somewhat jaundiced report in *Publishers' Weekly* several months later) the N.A.B.P. spokesman "pointed out that book publishing was in good shape . . ., that the total production was increasing, that imports had not increased as rapidly as home production and finally that conditions were such that no thought-of change could possibly be recommended."[9] Despite their belated conclusion that domestic censorship was a dangerous threat, book publishers found no reason to be unduly alarmed over barriers placed in the path of foreign competitors.

This tranquil atmosphere was rudely shattered in May, however, when the House of Representatives voted to extend Sec. 305 of the tariff bill (the section dealing with obscenity) to include books or other printed matter "advocating or urging treason, insurrection, or forcible resistance to any law of the United States, or containing any threat to take the life or inflict bodily harm upon the President of the United States." This amendment was rooted in the wish of the Customs authorities to bring the tariff law into conformity with the postal code, which since the First World War had barred such matter from the mails.[10]

This amendment aroused immediate protest from the same groups and individuals who had fought the wartime sedition legislation. The American Civil Liberties Union and Professor Chafee of Harvard were among those who issued sharply worded warnings on the menace of political censorship. The liberal weeklies joined in remonstrance, as did a number of newspapers, including the Baltimore *Sun*, the *Chicago Tribune*, the *St. Louis Post-Dispatch*, and the *Washington Daily News*, which derided the amendment's "jackassity." *Publishers' Weekly* perceived a "grave danger to public liberties" and urged that protests be "immediate and stinging."[11]

This outcry was directed against the proposed *extension* of Sec. 305 to include political matter. Few if any critics questioned the law itself, with its ban on obscene books. Something of a sensation, therefore, was created on July 28, 1929, when Senator Bronson M. Cutting of New Mexico issued a press statement attacking not only the "treason" amendment, but also the entire Sec. 305 as "irrational, unsound, and un-American." He warned of the "danger and folly" of permitting Customs officers "to dictate what the American people may or may not read." To buttress his charges, Cutting reported that the unexpurgated British edition of Erich Maria Remarque's "intensely moving and accurate" war novel, *All Quiet on the Western Front*, had recently been banned by the United States Customs Bureau.[12]

In retrospect, Cutting's statement seems a natural next step in the evolving anticensorship movement, but it did not, in fact, grow out of any participation in, or even detailed knowledge of, the censorship battles of the decade. It was simply an annoyed outburst from a senator who by temperament and training was repelled by bureaucratic meddling with the arts. Scion of an old New York family linked to the Livingstons and the Bayards, and a distant cousin of Franklin D. Roosevelt, Cutting had gone from Groton to Harvard, where his fellows in the celebrated Class of 1910 included T. S. Eliot, Walter Lippmann, and John Reed. Elected to Phi Beta Kappa in his junior year, he received straight A's in his courses in philology, literary history, Greek philosophy, and Hellenistic culture. Among his professors were George Santayana, Hugo Münsterberg, and William James. A severe attack of asthma prevented his return to muggy Cambridge for his final year and took him instead to the more salubrious climate of Santa Fe, New Mexico.

In 1912, an ardent twenty-two-year-old Bull Mooser, Cutting purchased a daily newspaper, *The Santa Fe New Mexican*, and two weeklies, one of them a Spanish-language paper, to promote the candidacy of Theodore Roosevelt. After service in the First World War as a military attaché in London, he returned to New Mexico where, through his newspapers, through numerous friendships in the Spanish-American community, and through active participation in the American Legion, he soon built a solid political organization. His aesthetic bent remained strong, however, and he was thoroughly at home with the artists and writers who frequented Santa Fe and Taos, D. H. Lawrence among them. The library at "Los Siete Burros," his Spanish-style home, included almost a thousand volumes.[13]

Appointed to a Senate vacancy in 1927, Cutting won election in his own right the following year. A bachelor, he lived in Georgetown with his widowed mother, to whom he was devoted. Conscientious if somewhat languid in the performance of his legislative duties, he took greater delight in his reading, in his library of classical recordings, and in an extensive correspondence with literary and academic friends. He wrote felicitously, and on one occasion struck off, evidently for his own amusement, a short drama, involving a pair of miraculous golden balls, which is of considerable interest. Though a connoisseur of classical literature, his penchant for acquiring such items as a "Nudies Catalog" on trips abroad occasionally presented the Customs Bureau with delicate problems. Cutting was happiest when his senatorial prerogatives could be made to serve his cultural interests. He liberally availed himself of his Library of Congress privileges, and readily accepted an invitation to a reception at the Italian embassy when it afforded the opportunity to meet Toscanini.[14]

Quite naturally, then, Bronson Cutting was delighted by the opportunity to bring his political prestige to bear against literary censorship. The immediate impetus for his July 1929 statement was that most powerful of motivations: the complaint of an irate constituent. Early in 1929 a Santa Fe friend named Walter Willard Johnson (better known as Spud Johnson) had reported to Cutting that three copies of *Lady Chatterley's Lover* which Johnson had ordered from Florence had been seized by the Customs authorities. When Cutting's protest to Secretary of the Treasury Andrew W. Mellon was curtly dismissed with the statement that the Customs Bureau made "no exception in favor of the so-called classics or of the work of leading writers of the day," Cutting decided to take the whole issue of Customs censorship to the public. Early in July he asked Mercer G. Johnston of the People's Legislative Service, a Washington publicity and fact-finding agency linked to the bloc of progressive Republican senators, to supply him with more details on the subject. In a subsequent exchange of letters and telegrams between Washington and Santa Fe, the substance of Cutting's July 28 statement was formulated.[15]

Although the seizure of *Lady Chatterley's Lover* had been the immediate cause of Cutting's ire, he realized that the Lawrence novel was hardly the best flagpole from which to fly the anticensorship banner. Instead, at the suggestion of Mercer Johnston, he chose the less controversial *All Quiet on the Western Front* to illustrate the evils of Customs censorship. To Cutting, the issue was clear-cut; "[T]he Customs officers have denied our people the right to read the complete version," he charged in his public statement. In reality, the "censorship" of Remarque's novel was a somewhat more complex affair which, when examined in detail, provides a useful corrective to the simplistic notion that literary censorship invariably pits embattled publishers against prudish vice crusaders and unintelligent bureaucrats.

Im Westen Nichts Neues was published in Germany in January 1929 and rapidly sold three-quarters of a million copies. Written by a disabled German veteran, its skepticism of high-flown rhetoric, scorn for false sentimentality, and graphic portrayal of battle and violent death inevitably drew comparison with Ernest Hemingway's *A Farewell to Arms*, published the same year. Wrote Remarque in a frontispiece:

> This book is to be neither an accusation nor a confession, and least of all an adventure, for death is not an adventure to those who stand face to face with it. It will try simply to tell of a generation of men who, even though they may have escaped its shells, were destroyed by the war.

An English translation was published in March by the London office of G. P. Putnam's Sons, and sales in Great Britain soon mounted to hundreds of thousands of copies. In June, Little, Brown and Company of Boston brought out an American edition based on the same translation, on which it secured an *ad interim* copyright.[16]

Careful readers soon noted differences between the Putnam and Little, Brown editions. Some sixteen deletions and alterations had been made by the American publisher. Most were trivial, involving the softening of earthy phrases—"cow dung" replaced "cow shit," etc. In a description of the smells of a field hospital, "ether" was substituted for "pus." A few sentences were dropped entirely, including one which discussed the prevalence of masturbation among prisoners of war.[17]

More significant was the elimination of two lengthy sections, totalling eight pages. The first describes the camp latrines and recounts somewhat effulgently the hours spent in them— playing cards, gossiping, and gazing at the sky. The second excised passage relates a hospital incident. When Johann Lewandowski, a forty-year-old Pole, is visited by his wife whom he has not seen for two years, his wardmates collaborate to help him satisfy a natural urge:

> The time is favorable, the doctor's visit is over, at the most one of the sisters might come in. So one of us goes out to prospect. He comes back and nods. "Not a soul to be seen. Now's your chance, Johann, set to."
>
> The two speak together in an undertone. The woman turns a little red and looks embarrassed. We grin good-naturedly and make pooh-poohing gestures, what does it matter! The devil take all the conventions, they were made for other times; here lies the carpenter Johann Lewandowski, a soldier shot to a cripple, and there is his wife; who knows when he will see her again? He wants to have her, and he should have her, good.
>
> Two men stand at the door to forestall the sisters and keep them occupied if they chance to come along. They agree to stand guard for a quarter of an hour or thereabouts.
>
> Lewandowski can only lie on his side, so one of us props

a couple of pillows against his back. Albert gets the child to
hold, we all turn round a bit, the black mantilla disappears
under the bed-clothes, we make a great clatter and play skat
noisily.

All goes well. I hold a club solo with four jacks which
nearly goes the round. In the process we almost forget
Lewandowski. After a while the child begins to squall, although Albert, in desperation, rocks it to and fro. There is a
bit of creaking and rustling, and as we look up casually we
see that the child has the bottle in its mouth, and is back again
with its mother. The business is over.

We now feel ourselves like one big family, the woman is
happy, and Lewandowski lies there sweating and beaming.

He unpacks an embroidered handbag, and some good
sausages come to light; Lewandowski takes up the knife with
a flourish and saws the meat into slices.

With a handsome gesture he waves toward us—and the
little woman goes from one to the other and smiles at us and
hands round the sausage; she now looks quite handsome. We
call her Mother, she is pleased and shakes up our pillows for
us.[18]

In a book abounding in scenes of agony and gore—none
of which were altered by Little, Brown—this is one of the
few episodes in which the prevailing mood is of love and
tenderness.[19] In the structure of the novel, it stands in contrast to an earlier episode (also retained in the Little, Brown
edition) depicting a furtive front-line encounter between German soldiers and French girls willing to barter sex for bread.

The expurgation of *All Quiet on the Western Front* had
occurred in two stages. Little, Brown had initially made several
changes which it deemed necessary to avoid running afoul of
federal and state obscenity laws. Then the Book-of-the-Month
Club, having chosen the novel as its selection for June 1929,
informed Little, Brown that several members of its panel of
judges, particularly William Allen White, editor of the Emporia, Kansas, *Gazette*, had "advanced the thought" that some
passages were "distinctly too Elizabethan, too much on the
old free and easy Anglo-Saxon order," and had "suggested

the use of Latin equivalents. . . ."[20] (Linguistic authorities were doubtless interested to learn that "ether" was the Latin equivalent of "pus.")

These additional expurgations were "cheerfully" accepted by Little, Brown, an official of the publishing house later said, in the belief that they would "enlarge the market for the book." "The book was not damaged," said a vice-president of the Boston firm. "It is different only in the slightest degree." Among the 100,000 members of the Book-of-the-Month Club, he said, were "a lot of persons who are easily offended when they hear strong language or read of certain phases of a soldier's life." Further defending Little, Brown's decision, he pointed out that a "too-robust episode" in Joan Lowell's *The Cradle of the Deep* had been expunged by Simon & Schuster earlier in the year, similarly at the suggestion of the Book-of-the-Month Club. Speaking for the Book Club, Vice-President Harry Scherman described the expurgations in *All Quiet on the Western Front* as "trivial" and said it would not have made the "slightest difference" if Little, Brown had rejected its suggestions.[21]

Wishing to have its cake and eat it too, Little, Brown in its advertising presented its expurgated edition as a faithful rendition of Remarque's text. "The man in the trenches, the 'Tommy,' the under-dog, at last speaks out," boasted Little, Brown in a *Publishers' Weekly* advertisement. "Word for word it is his speech and his thought."[22]

The issue of federal censorship entered this confusing picture when local Customs inspectors, on orders from Washington, began confiscating shipments from London of Putnam's unexpurgated edition. When Cutting's protest appeared, Little, Brown announced that the seizures were being made at its request, on grounds of copyright infringement! This was promptly confirmed to Cutting by an aggrieved Commissioner of Customs who added that he himself had "read the story in the original text in German and takes pleasure in recommending same to his friends."[23]

In defending its effort to suppress the Putnam edition,

Little, Brown said of its own version: "[W]e know of no reason why we should sit back and permit serious interference with its sale through illegal importation in large quantities of the unexpurgated English edition."[24] Anyone preferring to read the book as Remarque had written it, added Little, Brown reasonably, could order it at retail from London without interference. (This, of course, would have meant payment of perhaps a 25% premium in shipping charges.)

Despite the protestations of publisher, book club, and Customs Bureau, many people felt that covert literary censorship was the basic issue. "It is as though we were not allowed to purchase reproductions of some foreign painting, but had to content ourselves with one in which the figures were modestly draped *à la* Boston" someone complained in a letter to *Publishers' Weekly*.[25] Whatever the legal technicalities, the ethics of Little, Brown's invoking the law to defend its emasculated version of *All Quiet on the Western Front* against competition from the unexpurgated text had raised disturbing questions.

Bronson Cutting understandably chose not to go into the technicalities of this complex situation, if indeed he ever knew of them, but simply presented the detention of Remarque's novel at the ports as a prime example of inane bureaucratic censorship. His July protest was widely reported, many editors giving it front-page coverage. From Cherrydale, Virginia, a citizen wrote to Cutting that his statement had come as "a ray of sunshine in the present murks of Puritanism." The Senator's literary and academic friends were equally enthusiastic. Encouraged, Cutting studied the issue further and in consultation with Mercer Johnston worked out a legislative strategy.[26]

On October 10, 1929, when the Senate debate of the tariff bill reached Sec. 305, Cutting offered an amendment to strike out the section entirely. This maneuver had but slight hope of success, for Sec. 305 was a legislative grab bag which also barred obscene photographs, lottery tickets, instruments of abortion, and contraceptive materials and information. Hardly prepared to face the storm which removal of the ban on such a variety of objectionable matter would have aroused, Cutting soon offered a substitute that would simply have removed "books" from this catalog. In addition, he proposed that the House-added "treason" clause be dropped.[27]

As his colleagues in the Senate chamber moved closer to hear his soft, cultivated voice, Bronson Cutting spoke on behalf of his amendment. "In the opinion of some of us," he said, "the question of free speech and free thought is of such great importance to this Republic that it even outweighs the effect of the tariff bill as a whole." Speaking intermittently over the next two days, with frequent reference to Milton, Dante, Pietro Aretino, and others rarely cited in Congressional discourse, Cutting placed on the record an eloquent plea against censorship.[28]

Cutting acknowledged that many proponents of censorship were asking plausibly enough: "[I]f there are sincere and intelligent persons among us capable of charting out our destinies in advance, capable of laying out a high road . . . and fencing the road in advance so that no man can miss the way, why should they not be allowed to do so?" But he cautioned against such seductive reasoning:

> [T]he road to enlightenment is not a Federal highway. It can not be surveyed in advance. It can not be graded or surfaced. It is not properly policed or guarded. It leads sometimes through trackless deserts and at other times over the roughest mountain trails. There are no signposts on it. Each man who travels on that road has got to find the way for himself.[29]

Cutting was given persuasive support by Senator Millard Tydings, who was incensed over the ban on the unexpurgated *All Quiet on the Western Front*. "It simply tells what a soldier does, and it tells the truth," he said. The salty Marylander ridiculed the pious breast-beating of senators who were attack-

ing Cutting's proposed liberalization of the Customs law.
"We are like a bunch of children in a kindergarten," he said.
"I do not think we are running a Sunday School here; I think
we are running a government. . . ." Tydings urged his fellow-
legislators to stop viewing themselves as "super-moralists who
can tell the dear common people what they have the mentality
to absorb and what they have not the mentality to absorb."[30]
Other senators concurred. "My books are my friends, my associates," said William E. Borah of Idaho. "I do not propose
that anybody shall choose my friends or my associates."[31]

But Reed Smoot of Utah, Finance Committee chairman
and a principal architect of the tariff bill, although caught un-
prepared by Cutting's proposal, made his position clear:

> I know it is said . . . that foreign classics die along with the
> . . . immoral. . . . Well . . . let the dead bury the dead. It
> were better, to my mind, that a few classics suffer the applica-
> tion of the expurgating shears than that this country be flooded
> with the books, pamphlets, pictures, and other articles that are
> wholly indecent both in purpose and tendency. . . .[32]

Cutting's largest single bloc of support came from senators
such as Borah, Thomas Walsh and Burton K. Wheeler of Montana, George Norris of Nebraska, and Thaddeus Caraway of
Arkansas, who had opposed the wartime espionage and sedition
legislation, and saw in the attempt to add a "treason" clause
to Sec. 305 a resurgence of the same suppressive spirit. "I feel
quite keenly about it," said Wheeler, "because . . . during the
war I saw how the sedition act worked. . . ."[33] As in 1917 and
1918, however, these legislators were in the minority, and
Cutting's amendment was defeated by a vote of thirty-three
to forty-eight.[34]

Prepared for this setback, Cutting at once offered another
amendment. Like its predecessor, this, too, removed "books"
from the obscenity clause of Sec. 305. But now, instead of
eliminating the House's "treason" amendment completely,
Cutting proposed that the vague and sweeping references to
"treason" and "insurrection" be dropped, limiting the ban to

printed material urging forcible resistence to the law or threatening the life of the President.[35]

This gesture of compromise seemed only to inflame the opposition. Tom Heflin of Alabama, asserting that "The home is the bedrock upon which the Republic rests," urged the "Christian, intelligent people of America" to rise up against "obscene, treasonable, and murderous literature." To Heflin a rigid Customs censorship seemed the obvious corollary to the recently enacted restrictive immigration laws:

> I have voted to keep America from becoming the dumping ground for . . . unfit foreigners, and I am going to vote today to keep America from becoming the dumping ground of the obscene, treasonable, and murderous literature of the anarchistic foreigners.[36]

While Cutting rested, Senators Wheeler, Walsh, and Caraway upheld his side in the debate. "You can not make people think the way you want them to," observed Caraway, "simply because you have a statute which says, 'We will put you in jail if you do not think that way.'" Senator Hugo Black of Alabama also raised a strong voice for the Cutting amendment and against "shackling the human intellect." Free speech, he said, was a fundamental right "which must not be overlooked or overstepped."[37]

When the vote came on October 11, 1929, at the close of two days of debate, Cutting's amendment was approved by the narrowest of margins: thirty-eight to thirty-six. Seven senators who had opposed the earlier amendment switched sides to provide the winning votes. The tariff bill was still in its preliminary stages, however, and Senator Smoot tempered the enthusiasm of Cutting's partisans when he announced: "I reserve the right to have a vote upon this amendment when the bill reaches the Senate."[38]

The initial public response to Cutting's apparent victory was enthusiastic. "If Senator Cutting . . . can persuade Congress to civilize the Customs laws," said the *New York Times*, ". . . he will have distinguished himself."[39] From England, Cutting's novelist friend Gordon Gardiner, writing to thank Cutting for a copy of the *Congressional Record* containing the censorship debate, observed:

> I suppose that to some of those apparently very old-fashioned . . . gentlemen your views were very shocking, and I thought they behaved very nicely. . . . [I]t all read more like a Bernard Shaw fantasy of elderly nineteenth-century notables trying, kindly and tolerantly, to understand a brilliant but dangerous young iconoclast of today. . . . I'm going to pass it on to . . . the Chairman of the Board of Customs (from whom I borrow the works of Joyce and Lawrence when I want to see what they're like!). I'm sure he'll be interested because of course we are just as silly over here.[40]

Many groups quickly moved to rally opinion behind Cutting's reform. The American Library Association sent a strongly worded pro-Cutting resolution to every senator, and urged state and local library groups to do the same. *Publishers' Weekly* hailed October 11, 1929, as a "day of new hope" and the Cutting amendment as "a great victory for sanity." The editor of *PW*, Frederic Melcher, urged booksellers, publishers, and "all liberal groups in the country" to make their views known. Henry Seidel Canby and his *Saturday Review* colleagues telegraphed both Smoot and Cutting expressing their pleasure at the liberalization of Sec. 305 and their hope that it would be preserved. Cutting himself kept the issue alive by addressing various interested groups, including the influential Manhattan P.E.N. club.[41]

The forms of pressure brought to bear in the controversy over Customs censorship were many and varied. In opposition to Cutting's reform, the vice societies of New York, Boston, and other cities deluged senators with demands for continued rigid federal censorship, buttressing their pleas with samples of particularly shocking foreign erotica. From the other side, the bemused lawmakers received copies of *The Innocensored*

Mother Goose, a 1926 anticensorship spoof, and *Censorship and the United States Senate,* a pamphlet prepared by the People's Legislative Service. This latter effort ridiculed Smoot's efforts to assure tariff protection to "the infant industry of American thought," and warned that the continued exclusion of foreign obscenity might only "stimulate production and extend consumption in the home market."[42]

In Santa Fe, Spud Johnson, whose difficulty in securing *Lady Chatterley's Lover* had triggered Cutting's crusade, responded with alacrity to the Senator's suggestion that he prepare a special censorship issue of his literary magazine, *The Laughing Horse,* for senatorial distribution. Johnson readily secured anticensorship statements from Carl Sandburg, John Dewey, Alfred Knopf, Maxwell Perkins, and some twenty-five other notables, but he ran into trouble in his efforts to illustrate the planned issue. A Santa Fe artist produced a cartoon depicting "Literature" as a naked baby boy from whom a "daisy" is about to be snipped by a Smoot-like physician wielding a pair of scissors labeled "Censorship." The title of the cartoon was: "Appendicitis, of course." Spud Johnson was delighted, but the printer quietly buried the cartoon in his desk drawer and published *The Laughing Horse* without artistic embellishment. Unabashed, Johnson had the illustration secretly printed elsewhere, and enclosed with each copy of *The Laughing Horse* an insert which declared: "We are humiliated, albeit somewhat amused, that in an issue devoted to the cause of fighting stupid censorship, we must acknowledge ourselves the victims of it." Explaining what had happened, Johnson offered a copy of the suppressed cartoon to anyone who requested it.[43] There is no record of how many senators availed themselves of this opportunity. For Cutting's sake the suppression was perhaps just as well. As one of his New Mexico friends wrote him: "If Mr. Smoot had seen that in the *Horse* it would not have been so good."[44]

These diverse efforts to focus attention on Customs censorship had a telling effect. "There is more interest in the cen-

sorship fight here now than ever before," Cutting's Washington
assistant wrote him in January 1930; "In fact," he added, "I
have never seen such interest displayed in any subject, since I
have been in Washington. It is all favorable from the newspaper
point of view."[45]

The Customs Bureau, in its own fashion, also contributed
to the debate. A few of its rulings during this 1929–30 period
suggest a desire to soothe libertarian critics. Shortly after Cutting's July statement, the United States Customs Court, in a
case appealed to it by Morris Ernst, reversed its ban on *The
Well of Loneliness*.[46] And a few weeks after the October debate
the same body released three erotic works which had been held
by the Baltimore Customs for over a year. "[A] literary work
can not be called obscene if here and there may be found some
expression which is obscene,"[47] declared the court in this ruling.

Local inspectors, however, seemed determined to destroy
the image of cultivated tolerance which their superiors were
trying to create. Among the books seized late in 1929 and
early in 1930 were the *Decameron*, Rabelais' *Gargantua*, De-
foe's *Roxana* and *Moll Flanders*, and Kanhaya Lai Gauba's
Uncle Sham, an amateurish exposé of vice conditions in America written in retaliation against Katherine Mayo's *Mother
India*. The New York *World* was incredulous over the latter ruling; "Are we so soft-skinned or so desperately self-righteous that
we cannot read an ill-word spoken of us on the Ganges?" it
asked.[48]

Particular interest was generated by two Baltimore Customs cases. In the first, a valuable four-volume set of Rabelais'
works was seized from an attorney who had purchased the
books in the United States and taken them to Paris for re-
binding. The *Sun* urged the deprived owner to take comfort in
the knowledge that he could still read the French satirist "in
such remaining American sinks of wickedness as great universities, and great public libraries, and that particular repository of
licentiousness, the Library of Congress. . . ."[49]

In the second Baltimore case, an autographed first edition of George Moore's *A Story Teller's Holiday* imported by Paul Hyde Bonner, a local bibliophile, was seized and marked up by the Customs inspectors. Bonner's attorney vigorously protested both the seizure and the "prudish vandalism" of the authorities.[50] *A Story Teller's Holiday* was precisely the kind of book whose seizure most infuriated the opponents of censorship. In language invariably delicate and restrained, Moore's rambling 500-page work relates dozens of Irish folk stories and legends, many describing amorous goings-on in convents and monasteries. Much is suggested, perhaps, but little is made explicit in Moore's allusive prose. The story of Adam and Eve in the Garden, from which the following is an excerpt, is typical:

> [I]n spite of her silence, perhaps because of it, he [Adam] began to speak once more of Iahveh's providence and his design, saying: Eve, if it be within his design that we beget children the secret how we shall beget them will not be withheld from us. Adam, she answered, I cannot talk any more, and fell back amid the mosses, and his joy was so great that he could not get a word past his teeth, and when relief came they lay side by side, enchanted lovers, listening to the breeze that raised the leaves of the fig-tree, letting the moonlight through.[51]

The suppression of *A Story Teller's Holiday*, and other excesses by local Customs inspectors, largely negated the more liberal policy suggested by the United States Customs Court rulings, and the outcry against Sec. 305 continued undiminished. Early in March 1930, a 500-signature petition urging the legislators to stand by their October vote was presented to the Senate by Bronson Cutting.[52] Among the well-known educators, authors, publishers, and librarians who signed were Zechariah Chafee, Jr., Charles A. Beard, John Dewey, Roscoe Pound—and William Allen White, whose squeamishness over *All Quiet on the Western Front* had helped precipitate the whole controversy!

While Senator Cutting had become the cynosure of the

anticensorship movement, Reed Smoot had emerged as the
spokesman for those who desired continued rigid federal control over the circulation of "questionable" books. The two men
differed sharply in their approach to the problem. Cutting
preferred to deal in broad principles and concepts, winning
converts through the persuasiveness of his rhetoric. Smoot's
technique was to master the intricacies of a given problem so
thoroughly that his colleagues, intimidated by his factual
grasp, would accept his conclusions as well. In this instance,
as always, he went to the experts: the New York Society for
the Suppression of Vice and the Customs Bureau, both of which
plied him with alarming facts and figures. Customs officials,
grateful to find a champion when they seemed to be under
attack on all sides, turned over to him a small library of banned
books, with the worst passages marked. Smoot (who in the
judgment of his biographer probably did not read a single
work of imaginative literature in the last half-century of his
life[53]) devoted the Christmas holidays to examining these
volumes. In the classic manner of purity champions, he could
not resist sharing the filth, a fact soon reported by embarrassed
newsmen. He further threatened to give a detailed report of
his findings before a closed session of the Senate, which at once
aroused speculation about a "Senatorial stag party." *Publishers'
Weekly* was sharply critical of this concentration on the "sensational aspects" of the censorship problem, and commented:
"[I]t does not sound as though Senator Smoot . . . wished to
do anything more than bring about an acrimonious and misleading debate in the excitement of which his point can be
carried."[54]

In October, Cutting had seized the initiative, but now
it was Smoot's turn. On March 17, 1930, at Smoot's request,
the Senate undertook a reconsideration of Sec. 305. The Utah
Senator had prepared for the debate by piling high on his
desk a display of the more sizzling books from the Customs
Bureau collection: *Lady Chatterley's Lover*, Frank Harris's
My Life and Loves, *A Story Teller's Holiday*, the *Kama Sutra*,

Balzac, Casanova, Rabelais, and the unexpurgated poems of Robert Burns. The senators, as they had gathered around Cutting three months earlier, now clustered about Smoot, reading the passages he pointed out to them.[55]

After this overture, the amendment Smoot offered came as something of a surprise. While returning to Sec. 305 the prohibition against "obscene" books, it stipulated that any doubtful book should be judged "as a whole" and that its effect on "the moral sense of the average person" should be the test of exclusion. A further clause granted the Secretary of the Treasury discretionary power to admit "so-called classics or books of recognized and established literary or scientific merit . . . when imported for noncommercial purposes."[56] Despite his heavy schedule of holiday reading, Smoot had evidently not remained oblivious to the support which had welled up behind Cutting.

But that Smoot in fact intended no liberalization in the law—or at best a minimal concession to the anticensorship forces—became evident when he launched into his speech. He made repeated references to isolated passages in the various books on his desk, admitted that he had read only brief extracts from them, and constantly warned of their effect on immature juveniles. "[T]hrow the arms of protection around the army of boys and girls," he urged.[57]

Declaring himself "saddened by the disclosure of laxity of views developed during the debate," the tall, dour Smoot, his severity accentuated by small, steel-rimmed spectacles, proceeded to deliver a harangue which at times dissolved into a stream of hardly coherent expletives. "I did not believe there were such books printed in the world," "lower than the beasts," "disgusting," "vile and rotten," "damnable," "beastly, beastly." In a voice described variously by reporters as a shout or a scream, he denounced the books before him as "the rottenest kind of stuff that can be thought of by a human being." D. H. Lawrence, he burst out, shaking his fist, had "a diseased

mind and a soul so black that he would even obscure the darkness of hell."[58]

Not only his senatorial colleagues, but also the nation at
large, was surprised by the ferocity of Smoot's tirade. "The
Senator is less cucumber than cauldron," said *Outlook*. "His
feelings boil and bubble like the very dickens."[59]

Even foreign observers were intrigued. Aldous Huxley
took note of Smoot's assertion that he would "rather have a
child . . . use opium than read these books," and recalled that
James Douglas had once made a similar statement *vis-à-vis*
prussic acid and *The Well of Loneliness*. "In an article written
at the time," observed Huxley, "I offered to provide Mr. Douglas with a child, a bottle of prussic acid, a copy of *The Well of
Loneliness*, and (if he kept his word and chose to administer the
acid) a handsome memorial in marble to be erected wherever
he might appoint, after his execution. The offer, I regret to
say, was not accepted."[60]

Reed Smoot's explosive turbulence suggests a personal
animus lying deeper than the immediate issue, and this indeed
appears to have been the case. Smoot was born in Salt Lake
City in 1862. His father, an early Mormon convert, was one of
the Twelve Apostles (ruling elders) of the Church and mayor
of Salt Lake City in 1857–58 when federal troops besieged the
city. Young Smoot was himself elected an Apostle in 1900—
a post he held until his death forty-one years later. His election
to the Senate in 1903 triggered an intense furore among millions
of Americans who still considered Mormonism wickedly immoral. Though himself monogamous, Smoot was the son of a
polygamist, and thus the object of bitter attack from women's
groups, church leaders, and unctuous newspaper editors. The
W.C.T.U. denounced him and other Mormons as "moral lepers";
an estimated three million people signed anti-Smoot petitions;
and in 1906, after lengthy hearings, the Senate Committee on
Privileges and Elections recommended that he be declared
unfit to sit in the Senate. In the debate on this resolution Smoot
emotionally defended his morality and denied any sympathy

with polygamy. At last in 1907, before a gallery of women, "the witch-burning element to the fore," the Senate—by fourteen votes—declared that Reed Smoot might, after all, take his seat.[61]

This humiliating ordeal was seared into Smoot's memory. In his old age he recalled it as "the most important and significant" episode of his life. His wife, too, suffered acutely at the bandying-about of her husband's sexual and moral standards, and is said never to have fully recovered emotionally. The principal effect upon Smoot was to intensify an already considerable self-righteousness. "I will be known throughout the United States as a man who has lived above reproach," he pledged in a letter of 1904.[62]

Having learned through painful experience that danger lay in expressing deeply held personal values and controversial social views, Smoot shunned such commitment and applied himself assiduously to finance, taxation, the tariff, and bureaucratic detail. "He persistently endeavored to make an efficient machine of the government," notes a biographical sketch approvingly. He may have disavowed polygamy, but he plunged into business ventures with wanton profligacy. Among the corporations which he served as president were the Provo Commercial and Savings Bank, the Utah Fuel Company, the Electric Company of Provo, the Home Fire Insurance Company, the Hotel Utah, the Western Pacific Rairoad, the Utah-Idaho Sugar Company, the Deseret National Bank, Zion's Co-operative Mercantile Institution, and the Beneficial Life Insurance Company.[63]

Smoot's demonstrations of virtue, when they came, tended to be embarrassingly self-conscious. When Congress declared war in 1917, he ostentatiously knelt in prayer on the Senate floor—the first man, it is said, ever to do so. Now, in 1930, the Utah Senator was passing through a difficult period. He was nearing seventy. His wife, the mother of their six children, had died some months before. The market collapse had seriously undermined his fortune.[64] Perhaps in some obscure way

the censorship debate seemed to him yet another occasion to
convince a suspicious Senate and nation that the virtue of Reed
Smoot, son of a polygamist, remained unsullied.

If so, there is irony in the fact that his moralistic tirade
merely served to stir memories of the time when his name had
been touched by scandal and gossip. The ever-busy Mercer
Johnston of the People's Legislative Service made a collection
of comments on polygamy and politics from the *Discourses of
Brigham Young*, and, in a widely publicized press release,
suggested that Smoot read these at his "Senatorial stag party."
Living Age quoted amused references to "the esteemed leader
of Mormonism"; the *Nation* poked fun at "the Mormon from
Utah"; and the *Saturday Review* pictured "Brigham Young,
leaning from the Mormon heaven, with his seventeen wives
beside him," laughing at Smoot's diatribe. Burton K. Wheeler
produced the *Discourses* on the Senate floor and asked Smoot
if the book might not be suspect under Sec. 305. The Mormons,
Wheeler said, "ought to be the last ones to stand upon this
floor and become intolerant." Senator Black observed that
"There are people . . . who think that the *Book of Mormon*
is a dangerous book."[65]

Faced with this unexpected turn in the debate, Smoot
could only seek refuge in a rambling defense of his faith and
a recitation of the ordeals his people had endured. "I am proud
of the record of the Mormon people. I know they are . . . honest
. . . industrious . . . virtuous. . . . [I]f I should lose my virtue,
the first thing I would do would be to leave the Mormon
Church."[66] A debate which had seemed to offer a promising
opportunity for a grandiloquent show of righteousness had instead revived memories best forgotten and once again exposed Reed Smoot and his religion to profane ridicule.

Meanwhile, the discussion of the main issue went forward,
and Senator Cutting again took the floor to renew his eloquent
plea for literary freedom. A veritable encyclopedia of anti-

censorship arguments, Cutting's wide-ranging speech cited recent liberalizing court decisions; mentioned a social-hygiene study showing that the principal sources of sex information for children were the Bible and the dictionary; and quoted authorities ranging from William A. Neilson of Smith College ("The saving of a man's soul, which one must presume is the object of a censorship, is, after all, a man's own affair. . . .") to Tacitus, who observes of certain forbidden books of antiquity:

So long as the possession of those writings was attended by danger, they were eagerly sought and read; when there was no longer any difficulty in securing them, they fell into oblivion.[67]

The urbane New Mexican twitted his Utah colleague for "filling the press of the country with his experiences in these realms of art," and ridiculed Smoot's contention that Customs inspectors were qualified as censors by their "knowledge of the world." Said Cutting:

The "knowledge of the world" which is requisite to enable a man to hold the office of Customs inspector . . . is exactly the knowledge which it takes to get from your home on the Bowery to the pier on the Hudson river, and then to open travelers' trunks, remove the contents from the trunks, and, after thoroughly confusing it, to replace it in such order as may be possible under the circumstances.[68]

Cutting also took note, in passing, of the penchant of Customs inspectors for defacing books with bold red pencil marks, "so that one can easily skip from one obscenity to another, like Eliza crossing the ice."[69]

Smoot rather ineffectually attempted to reply, but he was no match for Cutting when the subject was literature rather than finance. When Cutting urged him to read D. H. Lawrence's essay on obscenity, Smoot replied: "Anything that the Senator will recommend to me . . . I would hesitate even to think of reading." Shot back Cutting: "I am very sorry . . ., I was just going to refer to the Bible."[70]

Reed Smoot was not the only senator whose deeper feelings were touched by the debate. Senator Park Trammell of Florida emotionally recalled his boyhood when his "God-loving and country-loving parents" had barred obscene literature from the "home . . . and fireside." And Senator Cole Blease (of whom a British journalist once observed: "In fairness . . . it must be said that he has the unique distinction of combining in his sole person *all* the disadvantages attaching to the democratic form of government") declared that he would be ashamed to inflict the "dirty, filthy trash" defended by Cutting upon the "purer type of womanhood and manhood" to be found in South Carolina; "I love womanhood," he pointed out.[71] Blease also expressed satisfaction that no South Carolinian had signed Cutting's anticensorship petition, but when Senator Wheeler drew his attention to the name of Josiah Morse, a teacher at the state university, Blease said:

> [I]f he is a professor in the University of South Carolina, and if he will express publicly that he is in favor of putting in circulation in this country such books as the Senator from Utah showed upon this floor and such books as I have in my desk [!], I will guarantee . . . that he will not be a professor in that university 30 days. I will see that he is put out.[72]

For more than one senator, the debate provided occasion for a spiteful attack on intellectuals. "I suggest to some of these high brows who are so fond of this European literature," said Tom Heflin, ". . . that they go over to Europe . . . and stay just as long as they choose. . . ." Park Trammell assured the Senate that the opinions of "high brows" could safely be ignored, because "when they delve . . . into the field of commerce, away from their educational institutions, nine times out of ten they are failures."[73]

For Senator Heflin, too, the debate offered yet another opportunity to vent an all-consuming fear of foreigners and Negroes:

> Aliens, by the hundreds of thousands . . . infest the land. . . . [W]hat are we doing to stop it? Let us build the dike . . . be-

tween us and foreign countries so compact and strong that none of this filthy literature can come here. . . . One of the dangerous and shameful things they teach is that the dead line pertaining to social and marriage relations between the white and black races should be abolished. Race pride and purity and the protection of the great white race is absolutely essential. . . .[74]

While some senators aired their private preoccupations and obsessions, others were engaged in the more prosaic task of formulating a compromise which would reconcile their opposition to "censorship" with their fear of "obscenity." As the debate progressed, attention centered increasingly on the fact that Customs censorship procedures operated entirely within the bureaucratic framework of the Treasury Department, with no recourse to the courts of law except in the rare instances when the importer instituted an appeal. To remedy this situation, Senator Hugo Black suggested that the banning of a book under Sec. 305 be permitted only after regular judicial proceedings in which the role of the Customs Bureau would merely be that of instituting the action. Said Black: "I have an inherent, well-grounded opposition against vesting in the hands of an individual judicial powers on matters of supreme importance with reference to the dissemination of human knowledge."[75]

But pitfalls lay in this direction, too, as became apparent when Senator Walsh of Montana hurriedly drew up an amendment incorporating, as he thought, Black's proposal. To assure due process, Walsh proposed that an infraction under Sec. 305 be made a criminal offense punishable by a fine of up to five thousand dollars and imprisonment of up to ten years.[76] Hitherto, Customs censorship had involved destruction of the condemned books, but no action against the importer. Under Walsh's amendment, a person could in all innocence import a book subsequently declared obscene, and suffer heavy punishment for his misjudgment. Senator Cutting's liberalization campaign was moving in a strange direction indeed!

Reed Smoot welcomed Walsh's amendment. "I am per-

fectly willing to accept it, and, indeed, am glad to accept it,"
he said. Senator Guy Goff of West Virginia was equally enthusiastic; "I think we should enlarge the laws of this country
. . . wherever we can," he declared. Other legislators, however,
were alarmed by the Walsh amendment. Senator Bratton said
it would make "criminals" of legitimate importers. Hiram Johnson of California warned against "the habit of creating new
crimes." The strongest opposition came from the hitherto
silent Walter George of Georgia, who spoke of the potential
misuse of such a law in a time of national hysteria, and contrasted Jeffersonian libertarianism with the twentieth-century
impulse "to create and define crime, and . . . to throw people
into jails." "[T]here is . . . a just and a necessary limitation
upon law making," declared George, announcing his determination to "oppose the amendment as it stands until 10 o'clock
tonight and then further tomorrow morning."[77]

In the face of such resolve Senator Walsh withdrew his
amendment. In its place, he offered another which provided
that Customs obscenity cases involving books be tried in the
federal courts in *civil* forfeiture proceedings, with full guarantee of the right of jury trial and appeal.

Reluctantly, Smoot agreed to this amendment,[78] and his
original amendment to Sec. 305, as revised by Walsh, moved
toward a vote. Walter George raised a final point, expressing
his reservations over the phrase "the moral sense of the average
person" in Smoot's amendment. Who is this "average person,"
he asked; "an average layman, easily offended, perhaps . . ., or
. . . a normal scientist, or man of average culture in polite
literature?" In response to these difficult questions, Smoot simply struck the ambiguous phrase from his proposal.[79]

At last, after two days of debate, the Smoot amendment
passed the Senate on an unrecorded vote. It was accepted by
the Senate-House conference committee, and with the final enactment of the Smoot-Hawley Tariff on June 17, 1930, it became law.[80]

❧

The outcome of the Customs censorship controversy was not an unqualified triumph for either side. Indeed, both the New York Vice Society and the New England Watch and Ward Society professed satisfaction, since the ban on importing "obscene" books *had* been retained. Senator Black on the other hand, hailed the "great improvement" in the Customs law as "a forward step and . . . a progressive step." The American Civil Liberties Union emphatically agreed.[81]

The claim of victory by the anticensorship leaders was based on several considerations. Books were now to be judged in their entirety; the Secretary of the Treasury had been given discretionary power to admit "so-called classics" and books of "literary or scientific merit"; and, above all, the final authority had been shifted from anonymous Customs Bureau functionaries to the courts. There was no guarantee, of course, that judges—and still less, juries—would be more lenient than the Customs authorities, as Morris Ernst's experience with *What Happens* had shown. Nevertheless, the new procedure did draw a sharp line between books and the general run of imported merchandise, suggesting that special importance attached to their fate and that special care should be exercised where they were concerned. The awareness that decisions involving books were now subject to judicial review would, it was hoped, bring a restraining influence to bear upon local Customs personnel. And if proceedings did reach the courts, the importer was assured that the weapon of publicity—always a key element in censorship cases—could more readily be brought into action.

Of equal importance with these procedural reforms was the educational value of the debate itself. For nearly four days—taking the October and March debates together—the United States Senate had devoted itself to an unprecedented exploration of the issue of book censorship. Newspaper coverage had been extensive. The debate, commented *Publishers' Weekly,* had "immensely" increased "the public's understanding of the problems. . . ."[82] The "Hatrack" case of 1926 had had a similar national impact, but in that instance the issues had been overshadowed by H. L. Mencken's own colorful personality and keen sense of showmanship. Senator Cutting, a more retiring person, had shifted attention from himself to the principles at stake.

The 1929–30 debates had a bracing effect on the anticensorship consensus which had been forged in the heat of the decade's censorship battles. Those who had fought local attempts at suppression in New York, Boston, or Chicago now felt themselves part of a broader movement. "Your statements will find their way to many sympathizers who have wondered why their sentiments had never before found a spokesman in Washington," wrote one of Cutting's supporters.[83]

The contrast between the calibre of the senators who rallied behind Cutting and those attracted by Smoot's position was not lost on the public. "I cannot comprehend what Senator Smoot is driving at," a former president of the National Association of Book Publishers wrote to Cutting. "His fight seems so foreign to the Senator Smoot I used to know. . . . It seems strange that . . . [he] should ally himself with . . . such blatherskites as Blease of South Carolina and Heflin of Alabama."[84]

That this reform and national discussion should have occurred when it did was due almost entirely to Senator Cutting's efforts. The Customs fight was Cutting's "personal project," recalls Roger Baldwin of the American Civil Liberties Union. "We cheered him on from the sidelines. He needed no help." Hugo Black, who had himself figured importantly in the debate, said generously after it was over that he wished "to give credit where credit is due. . . . That credit, in my judgment, goes directly to the Senator from New Mexico for the great fight he has made. . . ."[85]

As for Reed Smoot, the ridicule called forth by his tirade did not quickly abate. Typical of the public's response was a poem published in the *Chicago Daily News:*

> Auld Georgie crossed the Delaware,
> His brave troops on tae lead;
> An' young Hale for his country died,
> Ah, what a breathless deed!
>
> Oor army an' oor navy baith,
> O' fame hae had thir cut;
> But a' thir glory's faded by
> Smoot smellin' oot the smut.[86]

Looking back in later years, Smoot could hardly have recalled with much satisfaction this phase of the debate over the tariff law which bears his name.

Both friends and foes of Cutting's crusade recognized that the true test of its significance would be whether or not books would be allowed to pass more freely through the Customs, and by this test it soon became apparent that a major liberalization had indeed been achieved. The first evidence was the Treasury Department's use of the "so-called classics" option. In 1931 the Department rescinded the ban on *The Arabian Nights*, Casanova's *Memoirs*, Rabelais' *Gargantua*, Boccaccio's *Decameron*, and Apuleius's *The Golden Ass*. In January 1933, on appeal from the A.C.L.U., *A Story Teller's Holiday* was cleared.[87]

By 1934 a new administration was in power, and Secretary of the Treasury Henry Morgenthau decided to utilize still more fully the discretionary power vested in him under Sec. 305. "Find me a lawyer who has read a book," he told an aide. This happy combination was discovered in Huntington Cairns, a young Baltimore attorney who four years earlier had represented Baltimore's Peabody Bookshop in a successful appeal to the United States Customs Court of a ban on Longus's *Daphnis and Chloe*. In that case Cairns had introduced, to good effect, testimony by a psychiatrist, an English professor, and a Baltimore *Sun* editor. "A distinguished liberal [and] a cultivated gentleman" (in Roger Baldwin's view), Cairns was

widely respected in civil libertarian circles.[88] He brought the
same broad outlook to his position as a "special legal advisor"
to the Treasury Department with responsibility for deciding
whether a questioned book should be admitted or challenged
in the courts. By 1935 the A.C.L.U. could report that "practically every book bearing the imprint of an established publisher" was being freely admitted. "Every appeal I made to
him was promptly and favorably decided," Roger Baldwin
later recalled. Soon all doubtful titles were automatically being
referred to Cairns, and he very rarely decided to challenge
books of any conceivable literary merit.[89]

On the infrequent occasions after 1930 when the Customs
Bureau did resort to a court test, the results offered further
confirmation that a genuine reform had been achieved. The
most famous test case to arise under the revised Sec. 305—
that involving James Joyce's *Ulysses*—is discussed in the next
chapter. Suffice it to say that when this celebrated work was
cleared in December 1933 it marked the dramatic culmination
of a crusade inaugurated by Bronson Cutting four years before.

POSTAL CENSORSHIP

Senator Cutting's efforts to publicize the Customs censorship served to arouse interest also in the related problem of
censorship by the Post Office Department—an interest intensified by a particularly egregious case of postal censorship in
1929. But the effort to attack this problem by legislative means
did not prove as successful as had the drive to reform the
Customs procedures, and it was ultimately by the judicial
rather than the legislative route that the postal censorship was
successfully brought within precise and narrow limits.

In the decades since the first postal obscenity legislation
in the Civil War and the "Comstock Law" of 1873, the Post
Office Department's censorship prerogatives had become firmly

entrenched. As with the Customs censorship, "[t]he citizen denied access to the mails could always go to court—if he was prepared to pay the cost and bear the possible stigma of defending a book which the government denounced as obscene."[90]

In the censorship controversies of the 1920s, the Post Office played a distinct if minor role. In 1924 the literary magazine *Broom*, already operating on a shoestring, was hastened toward extinction when it was banned from the mails because the word "breasts" had appeared in a story.[91] Later, as we have seen, Postmaster General Harry New worked zealously to force pulp magazines into a more "conservative" mold. On occasion, as in the *Little Review* and *American Mercury* cases, postal officials and vice-society men functioned in close cooperation. (Another instance of such collaboration came in 1929, when René Fülop-Miller's scholarly study *Rasputin, the Holy Devil* was barred from the mails at about the same time that John S. Sumner was prosecuting a secretary of the New York Free Thought Press for distributing circulars advertising the book.[92]) In actuality, however, postal censorship was exercised with considerably less force in the 1920s than the vice societies wished. In 1926 the head of the Watch and Ward Society complained that his fight against bad literature was hampered because "the great force of the Federal government at Washington through its postal laws has practically broken down."[93] Under these circumstances, libertarians found other suppressive threats more urgent, and the censorship power of the Post Office Department, like that of the Customs Bureau, generated little protest through most of the decade.

In 1929, however, a spectacular prosecution attracted nationwide attention and provided the needed catalyst for a movement to liberalize the postal censorship. At issue was a pamphlet, *The Sex Side of Life—An Explanation for Young People*, which Mrs. Mary Ware Dennett of Brooklyn had written some years earlier for her two sons. It contained straightforward descriptions of the human sex organs and their functions; spoke of the pleasures of sexual intercourse in fervent but delicate terms; and, while discouraging masturbation, denied that the habit was necessarily harmful. Published first as an article in the *Medical Review of Reviews* in 1918, Mrs. Dennett's work had subsequently been widely circulated in pamphlet form by Y.M.C.A.'s and similar groups.[94]

As early as 1922 *The Sex Side of Life* had been banned from the mails under Sec. 211 of the postal code (the section dealing with obscenity), but Mrs. Dennett had continued to mail it under first-class seal. In 1928, allegedly upon the complaint of a Daughter of the American Revolution, the Post Office Department brought court action against Mrs. Dennett. (Subsequent testimony established that a spurious request for the pamphlet and a decoy address had been used to secure evidence of mailing.) The case, heard in April 1929 before a judge clearly hostile to Mrs. Dennett, was prosecuted by a remarkably vindictive and obtuse government attorney. Despite the able efforts of Morris Ernst, the jury found Mrs. Dennett guilty, and a fine of three hundred dollars was imposed. Ernst at once appealed.[95]

Sympathy for Mrs. Dennett in her plight was overwhelming. "In not many cases has public opinion come so quickly and so unanimously on the side of a convicted person," commented a Missouri editor. Comic relief was provided by William Sheafe Chase, a Brooklyn clergyman and a veteran of the "Clean Books" crusade. Vehemently attacking the claim in Mrs. Dennett's pamphlet that sexual intercourse was "the very greatest physical pleasure to be had in all human experience," Chase declared that nursing a baby was far more delightful. Asked how he knew this to be true, Chase replied that his wife had told him! Chase's further assertion that "the joy of winning an athletic contest" rated higher than sex on the pleasure scale was vigorously disputed by Heywood Broun, who established his right to express an opinion on the matter by noting that as a Harvard freshman he had won a tennis cup for the north entry of Thayer Hall.[96]

The Sex Side of Life was so clearly rational and praise-worthy in intent that its suppression aroused the ire of many people whose interest in earlier censorship conflicts had been less than overwhelming. In a revealing editorial, the *New Republic* contrasted the suppression of *The Sex Side of Life* with that of *An American Tragedy*. The harm of the latter, it said, was "chiefly in principle," since the Dreiser novel could be "completely expunged from the memory of the nation" without "irreparable loss." But the ban on Mrs. Dennett's little pamphlet, said *New Republic*, was "a frightful injury not only to a principle, but to the children of the nation and to society itself." The Dennett conviction, the editorial concluded, "demonstrates why, in other cases where our sympathies may not be so thoroughly involved, it is necessary to fight for civil liberty."[97] Belatedly, an important lesson had been learned.

The reaction of the American Civil Liberties Union was similar. As we have noted, the A.C.L.U. had remained uninvolved in the literary censorship skirmishes of the 1920s. Postal suppression of "obscenity" had troubled it only when used as a pretext to silence unpopular political or economic views, as in the 1923 prosecution and jailing of Carlo Tresca, editor of *Il Martello,* an Italian-language radical periodical published in New York. *Il Martello* was suppressed ostensibly because of some advertisements for birth-control books, but in reality because the Italian ambassador to the United States had publicly complained about Tresca's vigorous stand against Mussolini.[98]

By 1929, however, the A.C.L.U. was deeply involved in the Massachusetts anticensorship fight, and it found the Dennett case another challenge too direct to ignore. The A.C.L.U. set up a "National Mary Ware Dennett Defense Committee" to publicize the case and to raise funds, and Morris Ernst's defense of Mrs. Dennett was undertaken in collaboration with the Union.[99]

These efforts bore fruit in March 1930 when a United States district court, in a decision written by Augustus N. Hand, overturned the lower court conviction and exonerated Mrs. Dennett and her pamphlet. [100]

Having won this victory in a case involving a sex-instruction pamphlet, the A.C.L.U. had no wish to retire from the field. At the same time, the Union remained wary of becoming too closely identified with cases in which works of imaginative literature were attacked as obscene. Accordingly, a "National Council on Freedom from Censorship" was created in 1931 "to appeal to a different and more specialized following." The chairman was Barrett H. Clark, organizer of the *Jurgen* defense committee a decade before. The Council's first order of business was a legislative assault on Post Office censorship.[101]

Senator Cutting, meanwhile, capitalizing upon the interest aroused by his Customs fight, announced in October 1929 that if the Customs effort proved successful he would move on to challenge the postal censorship. He was encouraged in this by a series of hortatory letters from the poet Ezra Pound, who for years had been scandalized that "filth like Article 211 of the U.S. Penal Code" should be allowed "to lie around empesting the atmosphere." Writing in *Poetry*, Pound declared that if Cutting took on the postal censorship as he had that of the Customs Bureau, he would make "a permanent mark in our history." [102]

While Cutting's initial attack on Customs censorship had been an impulsive and independent gesture, the Senator carefully coordinated his Post Office effort with other interested groups. Early in 1932 he introduced a bill drawn up by the National Council on Freedom from Censorship. Frankly modeled on the revised Customs law, Cutting's bill would have transferred all postal obscenity cases to federal courts and guaranteed the right of a jury trial. Among its innovations were the provisions that no ban could be enforced for more than five years and that copies of all suppressed publications should be deposited in the Library of Congress. [103]

The National Council on Freedom from Censorship did its best to generate public interest. In a pamphlet called *The Post Of-*

fice Censor it attacked postal censorship as an amalgam of "personal notions" and "political pressure" intensified by "occasional periods of public hysteria," and cited numerous meritorious works which at one time or another had been banned from the mails. [104]

But times had changed, and the electric drama of the Customs fight could not be revived. Cutting's bill was unable to compete for attention in a Congress and nation preoccupied with the Depression and the 1932 presidential campaign. After 1933 Cutting was himself too distracted by political problems in New Mexico to give much attention to the issue, and his bill died in committee.[105]

Nevertheless, postal censorship, like Customs suppression, declined markedly in the decade following 1930. In 1933 the American Civil Liberties Union reported a "changed and far more liberal attitude" in the Post Office Department.[106]

The man who had played such a significant catalytic role in the achievement of this new and more tolerant climate did not long survive its coming. When Bronson Cutting died in an airplane crash in 1935, at the age of forty-seven, the United States Senate lost one of its most humane and sensitive members, and the cause of literary freedom, one of its most eloquent defenders.

NINE

The Thirties

When H. L. Mencken glanced through an autobiographical work by James Branch Cabell in 1934, he was momentarily puzzled by a reference to a censorship case in which Cabell said he had once been involved. Finally Mencken remembered: *Jurgen*, the *cause célèbre* of 1922! "How much water has gone under the bridges since those insane days!" he wrote Cabell. "The Comstocks are now down and out."[1] The decade of the 1920s was already receding in a haze of legend and nostalgia, its heroic censorship battles growing remote.

"The Comstocks"—that loosely defined assortment of ogres, were indeed down, if not quite out. Vice-society reports from New York, Boston, and Chicago were little more than mournful recitals of declining income and rising public hostility. In 1930 the sponsor of a bill introduced in Albany to curb the New York Society for the Suppression of Vice described John Sumner's organization as "a self-constituted group of authoritarians." "In the past year we were abused far more than we have been in recent years," wrote the president of the New York Vice Society in 1939, with a hint of masochistic pride.[2]

Shafts of hope occasionally pierced the gloom. In 1938, when the New York Vice Society observed its sixty-fifth birthday, a scattering of social workers together with the customary ecclesiastical trinity—minister, rabbi, and priest—were on hand to laud its good work. "[T]he community is deeply in your debt," wrote the young District Attorney, Thomas E. Dewey, in a congratulatory letter.[3] The phrase must have caused a twinge, for debt—in its most literal sense—had become a painful subject in vice-society circles.

Sporadic attempts were made to regain public favor. John Sumner struggled to counter the prevailing suspicion that he had become a bit old-fashioned, even going so far as to dismiss his famed predecessor Comstock as "somewhat of a religious fanatic who also loved notoriety."[4] And in the mid-thirties, in a long-overdue move, the traditional emblem of the New York Vice Society, a top-hatted gentleman purposefully throwing a pile of books into a blazing bonfire, was removed from the cover of the annual reports. Vice-society objectives were defined more and more narrowly. "Times have changed, and we must change with them," noted the 1935 report of Sumner's organization, disclaiming any designs upon books "that simply offend good taste and are hopelessly vulgar." A year later the New York Vice Society again denied any hostility toward "realistic books when realism is within reasonable bounds," and expressed its abhorrence of "Puritanical prying or snooping."[5]

In keeping with this new and self-conscious posture of urbane tolerance, Sumner's book-censorship activities (and those of his counterparts in Boston, Chicago, and Cincinnati) grew more and more restrained. His last major effort came in 1933 against Donald Henderson Clarke's *Female* (Vanguard

Press) and Erskine Caldwell's *God's Little Acre* (Viking Press). After the *Female* prosecution was thrown out of a Manhattan magistrate's court, Sumner brought another action on Long Island and eventually was able to secure a conviction.[6] The *God's Little Acre* case, however, was more vigorously defended and resulted in a decisive vice-society defeat. Harold A. Guinzburg of Viking and attorney Wolfgang S. Schwabacher marshaled the opinions of forty authors and critics in defense of the book—evidence which Magistrate Benjamin Greenspan found overwhelming. In dismissing the case, Greenspan stressed the value of informed criticism in obscenity cases, reaffirmed the principle that books must be judged as a whole, and observed that authors should not be required by law "to put refined language in the mouths of primitive people." In a thinly veiled slap at the Vice Society, he criticized persons "who see the ugliness and not the beauty in a piece of work" and suggested that the very process of dragging a book to court "leads readers to endeavor to find licentiousness where none was intended." John Sumner bitterly but impotently protested Greenspan's verdict, particularly his reliance on expert opinion; "These matters must be judged by normal people and not by the abnormal," he complained.[7]

Only once after 1933 did Sumner venture against a book offered for general sale: James T. Farrell's *A World I Never Made*. This 1937 case was dismissed in short order by a Manhattan magistrate who declared that unvarnished language was preferable to asterisks which made the printed page "look like a rail fence."[8]

By the end of the decade, the once powerful vice-society movement was a mere shadow of its former self. In New York, the sole surviving link with the heroic Comstockian era, the superannuated vice-society agent Charles J. Bamberger, retired in 1940 after forty-six years of service; he was not replaced. Struggling on through years of diminished activity, the New York Society for the Suppression of Vice finally gave up the ghost in the mid-1950s when the aging John S. Sumner decided to seek Florida's more inviting climes.[9]

So dramatically had the power of the vice societies declined and the restraining legal barriers fallen that anguished protests reminiscent of the early 1920s were occasionally to be heard. In 1929 Gilbert Seldes, the erstwhile *Dial* editor, appalled to realize that the champions of free expression had "fought for Ibsen and *Mrs. Warren's Profession*—and got Mae West," took a more cordial view of censorship than he once had done.[10] In the same year the venerable editor of *Publishers' Weekly*, R. R. Bowker, criticized "certain tendencies" of modern literature, particularly the "questionable details" appearing in too many novels, and revived the familiar warning that "[u]nless carefulness is practiced within the publishing trade" a severe censorship would soon follow. The stern tone of Bowker's comments, unusual in *Publishers' Weekly* by this time, was in part a reaction to Will Rogers' remarks at a recent N.A.B.P. luncheon in which he "congratulated publishers that since 'sex stuff' came into vogue in recent years prosperity has been their lot." His audience was not amused.[11] In 1931 the vice-president of the Doubleday-Doran bookstore chain—a gentleman bearing a striking physical resemblance to Reed Smoot—issued an angry blast at publishers who specialized in "the *filth* of human experience" and who did not understand "the simple code of good taste." If persuasion failed, he declared, such offenders should be reported "to the officially constituted authorities, local, state, or national." A *Nation* editorial of November 25, 1931, which urged the wisdom of "permitting grown-ups to decide for themselves what books they shall buy, what plays they shall see, and even what pictures of undressed females they shall look upon" stirred *Christian Century* to denounce "the glib rationalizing of liberals of this kind—found in large numbers in the Manhattan sector."[12]

But such isolated expostulations merely underscored the change which had occurred. One expression of the new attitude prevailing in the 1930s was Judge John Woolsey's 1933 Customs decision admitting James Joyce's *Ulysses* to the United States. This famous case has often been used to exemplify, in short-hand fashion, the entire censorship history of the two or three decades which preceded it, leaving the impression that "comstockery" remained in full vigor until struck down by the Woolsey decision. One recent work, in discussing book censorship in America, mentions the *Hagar Revelly* decision of 1913, and then proceeds briskly: "The next considerable step forward in the United States took place in 1933. . . ."[13] As the foregoing chapters have suggested, such a view is, to say the least, oversimplified. Yet the *Ulysses* decision *is* significant, both for the immediate effect it had upon the circulation of an important work of literature and for the emblematic role it has come to play in twentieth-century censorship history.

From the first publication of certain *Ulysses* episodes in the *Little Review*, the book exhibited a remarkable ability to stir up the tidy world of bureaucratic officialdom. Extracts which were circulated privately during the First World War alarmed military censors, who assumed they represented an elaborate code.[14] Except for clandestine copies (which brought up to fifty dollars), *Ulysses* was not imported, mailed, or sold in the United States in the 1920s—a marked exception to the increasing freedom permitted literary expression as the decade progressed. In the *Little Review* case, as we have seen, the suppression was based on a whole segment considered unacceptably erotic in tone.[15] The publication of the full text by Sylvia Beach in Paris in 1922 revealed that Joyce had not refrained from the use of any English word, including *fuck*, and thereafter this factor became the major barrier to free circulation. In a 1928 Customs Court decision upholding the *Ulysses* ban, the judge explicitly cited the presence of obscenity "of the rottenest and vilest character."[16]

Few voices, even from within the literary community, were raised in protest against this suppression during the post-war decade. Joyce's friend T. S. Eliot in 1923 hailed *Ulysses* as "the most important expression which the present age has found" and "a book to which we are all indebted, and one from which none of us can escape"[17]—but this was not the accepted verdict. Henry Seidel Canby (a sensitive barometer of the outlook of the reading public at any given moment) in 1922 found *Ulysses* "an extravaganza of erratic genius in which literally hundreds of pages are driven into an insane indecency by an obsession with inflamed or perverted sex. . . ."[18] Arnold Bennett called it "more indecent, obscene, scatological, and licentious than the majority of professedly pornographic books," and added that its publication "must cause reflection in the minds of all those of us who have hitherto held and preached that honest works of art ought to be exempt from police interference." While praising the book's "finest passages," Bennett concluded that, on balance, its "staggering indecency" was "not justified by results obtained."[19] In 1927 the critic and anthologist Frederic Cooper called *Ulysses* a "Hymn of Hate" and Molly Bloom's famous reverie a mass of "slime and ordure." As late as 1929 Harvey Wickham could speak of Joyce's "instinct to soil clean paper."[20]

Slowly, however, the opposite point of view began to make itself felt. Stuart Gilbert's monumental analysis of the book appeared in 1930. Edmund Wilson's 1931 study of recent literary trends, *Axel's Castle,* simply assumed the central importance of *Ulysses* and described its author as "the great poet of a new phase of the human consciousness." In such a work, Wilson implied, the appearance of "certain words ordinarily excluded today from English literature" was a trifling matter.[21]

The fate of the book itself stood in ironic contrast to this growing critical acceptance. As a legally proscribed work it could not be copyrighted, and this attracted the unprincipled. The first attempted American publication after the *Little Review* conviction was by Samuel Roth, an unscrupulous literary pirate who in 1926 rearranged and edited parts of *Ulysses* and published them in his *Two Worlds Monthly*. The *New Statesman* condemned Roth's "offense against the unwritten laws and the decencies of his profession," and Ezra Pound succinctly

dismissed him as "a skunk."[22] An obscenity action against Roth
was brought by "The Clean Books Committee of the Federation of Hungarian Jews in America." This improbably named
organization, which does not otherwise appear in the censorship records of the decade, had evidently been hastily set up
to avenge what its sponsors took to be Joyce's unflattering
portrayal of Leopold Bloom, a principal character in *Ulysses*
and, as it happens, a Hungarian Jew.[23]

Samuel Roth responded with brave talk of his crusade
against Puritanism, and his lawyer, one Nathan Padgug, announced a plan to call "a battery of distinguished literary
figures" to testify, but the cause won few supporters, and
Roth's subsequent conviction was not widely lamented.[24]

As one book after another broke the legal barriers, interest
in the legitimate American publication of *Ulysses* grew more
intense. Viking, Harcourt Brace, Morrow, and Covici-Friede
all vied for the privilege, but were turned down in preference
to "Mr. Bennett Serf," whom Joyce announced to T. S. Eliot
as a possible choice in February 1932.[25]

Cerf was a junior member of that brash publishing generation of the 1920s which had thrust so many thorns into
the flesh of John S. Sumner. The grandson of Nathan Wise,
a wealthy tobacco wholesaler, he had come into a $100,000
fortune at the age of twelve. Graduating from Columbia University, he worked for several years on Wall Street before
becoming a Boni & Liveright vice-president in 1923. Two years
later, with Donald S. Klopfer, he purchased the Modern Library
from Liveright and established Random House, a publishing
firm of which in 1928, at thirty, he became president.[26]

Having won the competition to publish *Ulysses*, Cerf
prudently consulted Morris Ernst as to the next step. Ernst
suggested that the book's legal status could most safely be
tested by instituting a test case under Sec. 305 of the new
tariff law, recently liberalized through the efforts of Senator
Cutting. No works of fiction had yet reached the federal
courts under the new procedures governing Customs cases,

but the way had been paved in 1931 by the clearing of several nonfictional works objected to by the Customs Bureau including *The Sexual Life In Its Biological Significance* by Dr. Joannes Rutgers of the Netherlands and *Married Love* by the British birth-control champion Dr. Marie C. Stopes.[27]

A copy of *Ulysses* was accordingly imported by Random House and duly seized by the Customs inspectors. The Customs Bureau, no less eager than Cerf to have a definitive legal judgment on the book, brought action in federal court. Ernst represented Random House, while attorney Nicholas Atlas shouldered the government's case. It was quickly and amicably agreed that the action would be heard without a jury and before a single judge, John Munro Woolsey.[28]

Woolsey, who had also presided in the *Married Love* case two years earlier, was fifty years old in 1933. A native of South Carolina, he was a product of Phillips Andover Academy, Yale, and Columbia Law School. Before his elevation to the bench in 1929 he had developed a successful private practice, specializing in maritime law. Known as "the literary jurist," he was a knowledgeable collector of paintings and rare books.[29]

The hearings (on cross motions of dismissal) took place in December 1933, after Woolsey had spent a good portion of his summer holiday reading and rereading *Ulysses*. Attorney Atlas, assisted by Samuel C. Coleman, presented the case for suppression with an evident lack of enthusiasm, while Morris Ernst, in a series of informal and cordial conversations with Woolsey, eagerly seized the occasion to elucidate the etymology of the taboo words, explain Joyce's literary techniques, and explode the theory and practice of book censorship. On December 6, Woolsey handed down his verdict: *Ulysses* was absolved of the obscenity charge! The news was phoned to Cerf, linotypers were at work within ten minutes, and a few days later Random House published *Ulysses* in the bulky Modern Library edition which would become familiar to a generation of readers. Thirty-three thousand copies were sold in a few weeks' time.[30]

Not everyone was pleased by this outcome. John Sumner groused about the "sociable and very friendly" relations prevailing between Ernst and Woolsey at the hearings, and observed somewhat stiffly that the decision would make it "more difficult to keep obscene books out of circulation in the future." A Notre Dame English professor, writing in *Catholic World*, dismissed *Ulysses* as "absolutely nothing but a sewer left open for smut-hounds to wade in," and complained (accurately enough) that "the Dublin of James Joyce [is not] the Dublin of poetry and so much of the world's song." Woolsey's decision, this article continued, proved only that "certain American publishers must prove their rapacity even at the cost of the reading public's morals and taste. . . ."[31]

In most quarters, however, the decision was welcomed. The A.C.L.U. distributed it widely, and even attorney Coleman praised the verdict as "thoroughly wholesome" and pronounced Woolsey's ruling "a masterpiece."[32] Indeed, Woolsey's felicitous style was the subject of much admiring comment. Passages such as this were singled out for mention: "Joyce has attempted—it seems to me, with astonishing success—to show how the screen of consciousness with its ever-shifting kaleidoscopic impressions carries, as it were on a plastic palimpsest, not only what is in the focus of each man's observation of the actual things about him, but also in a penumbral zone residua of past impressions, some recent and some drawn up by association from the domain of the subconscious." Witty epigrams also brightened the judicial prose; in evaluating the "recurrent emergence of the theme of sex in the minds of [Joyce's] . . . characters," noted Woolsey, "it must always be remembered that his locale was Celtic and his season Spring."[33]

Everyone praised Woolsey's limpid prose. "The world, it seems, lost a fine essayist when Judge Woolsey turned his style and taste to the writing of legal opinions," observed the *New Republic*.[34] There was, however, considerably less agreement over the *significance* of his decision, beyond its obvious and immediate effect on the fate of *Ulysses* and the fortunes of Random House. Morris Ernst quite naturally viewed the document as only slightly less momentous than *Magna Carta* in the progress of human freedom. "The New Deal in the law of letters is here," he exulted, "a major event in the history of the struggle for free expression."[35]

Not everyone found the decision so revolutionary. It was obvious, of course, that henceforth it would be difficult to suppress a book solely for its use of four-letter words. On that Woolsey was clear:

> The words which are criticized as dirty [in *Ulysses*] are old Saxon words known to almost all men and, I venture, to many women, and are such words as would be naturally and habitually used, I believe, by the types of folk whose life, physical and mental, Joyce is seeking to describe.[36]

The author Ben Ray Redman, writing in *Scribner's*, expressed satisfaction that these verbal taboos had been lifted, especially the one barring the word which "refers to an act which has directly or indirectly . . . inspired much of the world's loveliest poetry; without which, indeed, there would soon cease to be any poets at all."[37]

In addition, the Woolsey decision ratified, at a high judicial level, those adages which for at least a decade had been the commonplaces of censorship discussions: that a book should be judged "in its entirety" and in its effect upon "a person with average sex instincts."

Beyond these points, one is hard put to find the basis of Morris Ernst's further claim that the Woolsey ruling marked "the repeal of the sex taboo in letters."[38] Woolsey explicitly stated in his decision that one of the tests he had applied to *Ulysses* was its capacity "to stir the sex impulses," and that on the strength of readings by himself and two friends he had concluded that the book did not have an erotic effect. Although "somewhat emetic" in places, he said, "nowhere does it tend to be an aphrodisiac."[39]

The *Nation* was appalled by this stringent and hoary test, which, strictly applied, would rule out "[a]t least half the recognized diversions of civilized mankind. . . ." Ben Ray Redman found Woolsey's antierotic premise "just plain tommyrot" because it "hypocritically ignores the facts of life and the realities of literature." Added Redman: "To deny literature the right of stirring the sex impulses of man is to deny it one of its prime and proper functions; for these impulses are fundamental, necessary, and energizing, and there are no strings within us more vital and vitalizing upon which art can play."[40]

Nor did the decision by a stroke of the pen revolutionize the censorship situation. In retrospect, it is clear that Judge Woolsey only confirmed a change in popular attitudes and standards which had occurred gradually over a number of years. The piety with which the *Ulysses* ruling has been dissected, probed, analyzed, and enshrined has led some skeptics to question whether the role of such famous cases has not been consistently exaggerated in censorship history. Among the doubters is Eric Larrabee, an editor of *Harper's Magazine*, who in a 1955 contribution to a symposium on "Obscenity and the Arts" noted that those who see the *Ulysses* decision as a milestone have "the flattering illusion (for lawyers) that society takes its erotic cues from the bench. . . ." In fact, Larrabee adds, "the so-called 'advances' within the law can very quickly be cancelled by retrogression outside it—a point less appreciated by the literati than by the philistines, who are not so bedazzled by legality."[41]

Even granting the force of this view, however, such well-publicized confrontations do have a barometric value, and the *Ulysses* case accurately reflects the temper of a society ready, at last, to accept a book whose suppression had come to symbolize the whole phenomenon of book censorship. John Woolsey and Morris Ernst played their roles in the drama of acceptance with a flair sufficient to win for themselves a justified and lasting fame.

❦

That the clearing of *Ulysses* and other books in the 1930s grew naturally from the events of the preceding decade, including a succession of censorship defeats and the emergence of an articulate anticensorship consensus, seems clear enough. Yet attitudes regarding censorship and the proper bounds of literary freedom can change very rapidly—as the vice societies had discovered!—and it is not inconceivable that, under different circumstances, the decade of the 1930s could have witnessed a powerful resurgence of the suppressive spirit. To what factors, other than the continued force of trends already established in the 1920s, shall we attribute the fact that it did not?

In the first place, there was the impact of the Depression upon the literary imagination. Even before the stock-market crash, the portrayal of the individual consciousness struggling to free itself from the lingering trammels and taboos of the pre-1914 world—a theme which had underlain so much innovative and controversial writing in the twenties—had begun to pall as a source of literary inspiration. "Self-expression is not enough; experiment is not enough; the recording of special moments or cases is not enough. All of the arts have broken faith or lost connection with their origin and function"—so wrote a disheartened Jane Heap early in 1929, in a farewell editorial explaining the demise of the *Little Review*.[42] At about the same time Sherwood Anderson, whose *Many Marriages* had aroused the British censors in 1923, said of the fiction of the 1920s: "It is all involved in sex. I think my generation went a little nuts on that, myself with them. We rather centered all feeling in sex."[43]

The shock of the Depression gave focus to the search for fresh themes and deepened the oppressive sense that the literary output of the 1920s, however vigorous and creative, had been the product of an impaired social vision. From the vantage point of the thirties the decade just ended not only seemed (as F. Scott Fitzgerald wrote in 1931) "as dead as were the Yellow Nineties in 1901," but it also, in Malcolm Cowley's image, came to be viewed as an interlude when writers had lived "in a mist, on what seemed to be level ground, but with nothing visible beyond a few yards." With the economic emer-

gency the mist rose, revealing that "chasms lay on all sides. . . ."
The campaign to expand the limits of legally permissible literary expression, which had seemed such a vital and worthwhile
pursuit, now appeared less momentous, "like a hunter's zest for
game when there is a forest fire in the woods."[44]

As national complacency followed prosperity into limbo,
ideas about which literary themes most merited attention
underwent a corresponding change. ". . . I'm through with
the ordinary problem of middle-class people in love, etc.,"
wrote Sherwood Anderson to Horace Liveright. "I've got an
interest, though. . . . It is working people . . . in the mills in the
South."[45] Not all writers followed Anderson, Dos Passos, and
Dreiser in exploring mill towns and strikebound cities, and the
overtly "radical" novelists produced mainly manifestoes and
interminable discussion, but the entire literary community was
brought by the swirl of social crisis into a new relationship with
the wider society about them. The goal now became not to jolt
a self-satisfied booboisie, but to understand and portray the
common trouble. Even Maxwell Bodenheim, whose *Replenishing Jessica* had been prosecuted as obscene in the 1920s, managed to produce two certified "proletarian" novels in the Depression decade.[46]

Under these conditions, the kinds of books which had
been such a source of outrage and alarm in the twenties were
simply no longer written. Of course, the newer literary wave—
the hard-boiled fiction of the Caldwells and the Farrells—
could itself arouse the senescent vice societies to feeble repressive efforts, but the mood of the nation was now wholly in
sympathy with those who set out to portray the life of the
submerged classes.

Publishers, too, were profoundly shaken by the Depression. The prosperous twenties had been a time of exciting
growth and experimentation. Young newcomers with a fresh
outlook had infused the staid old industry with new life and
vigor. The speculative, get-rich-quick mood of the decade had
spawned many marginal publishing ventures and eased the way

for "questionable" manuscripts which in a more cautious time would have been rejected.

In the 1930s, by contrast, book publishing became a far more chancy and calculating enterprise. In 1935 only 8,766 new titles were published in the United States, a drop of over 1,400 from 1929.[47] To remain solvent now became the overriding concern. It is true that books still sold reasonably well, as the public gave up more expensive diversions. Robert and Helen Lynd, revisiting "Middletown" (Muncie, Indiana) in the mid-1930s, found that reading had become considerably more important as a leisure-time activity than it had been in the 1920s. Adult library use, for example, was up 145%. But Middletown readers now wanted either escapist literature—historical romance, light fiction, mysteries, travel—or books on economics and politics.[48] Retail book outlets strove to meet these preferences. The bankruptcy of so large a bookstore chain as Brentano's (in 1933) sent a chill down the spines of booksellers all over the country, intensifying an already ingrained tendency to play it safe.[49]

Publishers who wished to survive gave due weight to these considerations. Manuscripts were nervously evaluated in the light of Depression tastes. In a time of financial stringency, the mass distribution of broadly popular books became the goal. Production procedures and advertising methods grew more highly professionalized and streamlined. Department stores replaced musty bookshops as the major channels of distribution. And, though rarely so overtly as in the *All Quiet on the Western Front* incident, the mass-market standards of the book clubs continued subtly to influence the editorial judgments of publishers with an eye on this lucrative source of sales.[50]

Those publishers who could adapt to the changed circumstances of the Depression years survived and even prospered; others fell by the wayside. Among the latter were some of the houses which had been the most frequent targets of censorship efforts in the 1920s. Samuel Roth, convicted for publishing parts of *Ulysses* in 1927, and source of many books (as *Publishers' Weekly* delicately put it) "on the borderline of decency," went bankrupt in 1933. Covici-Friede, publisher of *The Well of Loneliness*, was in a state of financial crisis throughout the 1930s, and eventually fell in 1938. The firm of A. & C. Boni, source of *The President's Daughter* and other shockers of the 1920s, similarly went under during the Depression. And G. P. Putnam's Sons, which under the influence of the younger George Palmer Putnam had shown a marked affinity for Ben Hecht and other young and controversial writers of the twenties, was on the brink of bankruptcy in 1930 when it came under new management. A number of other houses specializing in limited editions and small issues of exotic and off-beat works were among the first Depression casualties.[51]

The fate of Horace Liveright, stormy petrel of so many censorship battles of the twenties, is illuminating. In deep financial trouble by 1930, Liveright was forced to relinquish control of his own company. Three years later it was in bankruptcy. Now nearly penniless, Liveright spent his final months in a Manhattan hotel, sick and alone, living on money supplied by publishing friends ostensibly as an advance on his autobiography. He died of pneumonia in October 1933, at forty-nine. At the funeral, in New York's Universal Chapel, a "straggling handful of people" listened as Upton Sinclair, "fearfully embarrassed, mumbled inadequate nothings. . . ." In a letter to *Publishers' Weekly*, Bennett Cerf pronounced an epitaph which might have been applied to more than one publisher of the 1920s facing the harsher realities of the Depression decade:

> Intensified competition, the rise of young men who breathed fresh life into doddering, but financially impregnable, old houses, and, above all, the spectre of diminishing outlets and narrower profit margins, left no chance for a madhouse like Liveright's.[52]

To be a publisher in the 1930s was to be haunted by the shadow of failure. This was no time to shock the public, to blaze unknown trails, or to expose one's investment to even

the remote possibility of an obscenity conviction. Even had
the vice societies survived into the Depression decade in full
strength and vigor, one suspects they would have found little
to occupy their attention among the offerings of the American
publishing industry.

Amid these trying domestic circumstances, frightening
developments abroad served further to diminish the potential
for an outbreak of literary suppression in the 1930s, and to
infuse the anticensorship cause with a far greater seriousness
and immediacy than had hitherto characterized it.

Throughout the twenties, reports of literary censorship
in other countries had periodically reached the United States:
Walt Whitman banned in Hungary in 1922, Austrian books
excluded from various new Balkan states in 1923, a Turkish
author prosecuted in Istanbul for a book critical of Islam, an
Indian jailed for publishing a book called *India in Bondage*.[53]
These and similar stories had been reported routinely, arousing
no great interest.

When such incidents were linked to stories of the rise
of Fascism, however, they could not be passed off so lightly.
Mussolini's Italy underwent a sharp diminution of literary
freedom. "I do intend that liberty shall not degenerate into
license," was *Il Duce*'s familiar rationalization. Benedetto
Croce's highly respected *Storia D'Italia* was among the works
suppressed.[54]

The literary ramifications of the Fascist triumph in Germany seemed particularly relevant to Americans, because the
two nations had in certain respects followed similar paths in the
1920s. The Americans had expected that the First World War
would be a cleansing experience, and in Germany, too, as
Walter Z. Laqueur has written, it was "commonly assumed
that [the war's] . . . moral effect would be that of a great
purifying fire; it would destroy everything that was rotten and
decaying." Declared Franz von Papen: "August, 1914, saw

the opening of a fight against the . . . de-spiritualization of our national life. . . ."⁵⁵

In both countries, disillusionment over the failure of this dream had spawned efforts to coerce the unregenerate into purity. In Germany, this impulse had found particular expression in the *Jugend* movement, a phenomenon dating from the early 1900s, when wandering bands of middle-class youngsters had sought through vagabondage and the revival of German folk culture to recapture the presumed purity and simplicity of peasant life. Surviving the war, the various loose-knit *Jugend* groups, while singularly lacking in specific aims or ideology, still attempted "to remedy the discontents of modern society by reverting to the irrecoverable past. . . ."⁵⁶ To such youth, the disillusionment, eroticism, and brittle sophistication of postwar German literature seemed the very antithesis of the purity for which they longed. They were prepared to tolerate considerable sexual freedom of a hearty, outdoorsy sort, but they thoroughly disapproved of the decadent sensuality they assumed to be typical of the intellectuals and literati of the big cities.⁵⁷

The *Jugend* expressed these sentiments through a variety of direct-action techniques. They distributed pamphlets and posters denouncing bad books, broke up objectionable stage performances, and boycotted and occasionally raided offending bookshops. "[M]any a cobbled market-place was strangely lit up with a bonfire of collected literary refuse," commented a sympathetic reporter in 1927 of the early postwar period.⁵⁸ The German Y.M.C.A. played a part in fomenting these activities through its *Schundkampf* (anti-trash) campaign.⁵⁹

Reports of these do-it-yourself censorship efforts by juveniles received a generally favorable reception in the United States. *Survey*, the social-work weekly, highly approved, and in 1922 the *New York Times*-sponsored magazine *Current History* praised "The Moral Revolt of Germany's Youth." The vigilante methods of these "doughty champions of public morality," wrote Lilian Eagle in *Current History*, was a move "in the right direction." Her article was illustrated with a photograph of Berlin police "burning wagon loads of trashy juvenile fiction which school teachers have collected in an effort to suppress the evils of bad literature."[60]

Gradually, as *Survey* reported in 1927, "more reasonable methods prevailed, and the young crusaders discovered allies in the book trade and in the social welfare organizations. . . ." The purity crusade now found a focus in the "Act for the Protection of Youth Against Trashy and Smutty Literature,"[61] a national censorship bill proposed to the Reichstag late in 1926. This *Schmutz und Schund* (Smut and Trash) bill, as it was dubbed, aroused fears in German literary and intellectual circles, but the Minister of the Interior soothed the apprehensive with assurances that it "threatens in no way the freedom of literature, [the] arts, or [the] sciences," having been designed solely for "the protection of the younger generations." It was aimed only at works which "undermine culture" and purvey "moral dirt," he added, and had been devised "not by reactionaries, but by men holding liberal views. . . ."[62] On December 18, 1926, after a bitter debate, the *Schmutz und Schund* bill passed the Reichstag by a large majority. The Catholic Center and Nationalist parties were strong in its support, the Socialists divided. In accordance with the provisions of the new law, the Interior Minister appointed boards of censorship for each of the Federal states. These eight-member panels, including representatives from publishers', authors', and booksellers' groups as well as from youth, welfare, and educational organizations, were empowered to prohibit the advertising, display, or sale to minors of any book deemed morally objectionable. Periodicals could also be barred, and any magazine falling under the ban twice could be suspended from sale in that state for up to one year.[63]

Little attention was paid to these developments in the United States, although the *Literary Digest* and *Living Age* carried fairly extensive stories about the new law and the circumstances surrounding its passage. A *Survey* editor, after interviewing members of the new German censorship boards, issued a highly positive report: "They admit that in some cases their decision may hit a work of partially artistic qualities," he wrote, "but they are not appointed to make artistic distinctions, merely to safeguard the morals of youth."[64]

The rising Nazi Party, meanwhile, was providing ample evidence of its attitude toward objectionable books. Hitler's original 25-point program of February 1920 included a demand for action against literature "having a disruptive effect upon the life of the people. . . ." Throughout the Weimar period his followers seized every opportunity to denounce the urban literati (usually Jewish) who had polluted the pure stream of Aryan literature with corrupt books and plays.[65]

In 1930 the Thuringian education minister, a Nazi, banned *Im Westen Nichts Neues* from all school libraries, and in 1931 the Prussian Diet passed similar legislation. The Nazi legislators were joined on this occasion by the Catholic Centrists who, reported the *New York Times*, "stated that although they did not want to criticize the book's contents in general, they thought certain 'indecent' parts . . . were not fit for youths to read."[66] The Nazi bid for supreme power shrewdly capitalized on the youthful longings for "purity" which had underlain the *Jugend* book crusades of the early 1920s and the *Schmutz und Schund* law. Hitler "lost few opportunities of declaring that his movement was *inter alia* a revolt of the coming generation against all that was senile and rotten with decay."[67]

The Nazis came to power in January 1933, and the literary world soon felt the full fury of the purifying lash. Early reports were sporadic but ominous. In March the Berlin residence of Lion Feuchtwanger, who had imprudently ridiculed *Mein Kampf* on a New York trip earlier in the year, was raided and some of his manuscripts destroyed. In April, reports filtered out of the country that the head of the respected Ullstein Verlag, a major German publishing firm, had died following an S.A. beating.[68] Early in May, Propaganda Minister Joseph Goebbels set forth the aesthetic principles of the new régime:

Only that art which draws its inspiration from the body of the people can be good art in the last analysis and mean something to the people for whom it has been created. There must be no art in the absolute sense, such as liberal democracy acknowledges. An attempt to serve such art would end in the people's losing all internal contact therewith and the artist's becoming isolated in a vacuum of art for art's sake.[69]

An uneasy quiet pervaded the literary community. "Very few books are now appearing in Germany," noted the *New Republic* tersely.[70]

Goebbels' pronouncement laid the groundwork for the great orgy of book burning which occurred in university towns across Germany on the night of May 10, 1933. The most impressive and elaborate of these pageants was staged in Berlin. It began with a torchlight parade of 5,000 singing students along *Unter den Linden*. When the marchers reached Franz Josef Platz, a large square lying between the university and the opera, they threw their torches on a great pile of firewood which quickly became a blazing pyre. Despite a slight drizzle, a crowd of 25,000 gathered as book-laden trucks backed into the square and their contents were systematically thrown into the flames. Included in the conflagration were works of Einstein, Freud, Marx, Gide, Proust, Mann, Zola, Wells, Remarque, Schnitzler, and Havelock Ellis. Among the American authors included were Hemingway, Jack London, Upton Sinclair, Ben B. Lindsay, Margaret Sanger, Franz Boas, and Helen Keller, who had written a pamphlet espousing socialism.[71]

The spectacle was staged by and for juveniles. The *New York Times* correspondent who wrote that "it savored strongly of the childish" was in fact pinpointing its great strength. The thousands of youngsters in the crowd were given small Nazi flags to wave. Young boys were flattered to be chosen to make up the human chains passing the books from the trucks to the fire. (One observant reporter noted the good-humored competition which developed among them.)[72] A succession of well-primed youths explained over loudspeakers why the various condemned authors were so obnoxious. Thomas Mann was "un-German and enfeebling," Freud dwelt on "the animal qualities of human nature," Emil Ludwig was guilty of "literary rascality," Remarque of "degrading the German language."[73]

The guiding hand of a skilled publicist was evident behind the student groups ostensibly responsible for the event. The participants wore colorful regional costumes, the flames were hypnotic in the darkness, and powerful searchlights played on a giant Nazi flag fluttering overhead. At midnight, when all the books had been burned, Joseph Goebbels, who had been sitting, a benign presiding eminence, on a podium overlooking the fire, approached the microphone and drew the moral for the listening children: "Jewish intellectualism is dead. . . . The German folk soul can again express itself. These flames not only illuminate the final end of the old era; they also light up the new."[74]

For a few of the witnesses, the drama had a significance quite different from that proclaimed by Goebbels. One who was present, the American journalist Mary Heaton Vorse, reported in the *New Republic* her thoughts as she watched leaves of books blown upward by the hot column of air:

> Bright as fire they mount upwards, farther and farther they soar, high above the blaze. One page goes on and on; it mounts bright and defiant as if it said, 'You can't burn me. You can't burn thought.' Far in the air flickers the unburned page—a symbol of the uselessness of the bonfire below.[75]

Similar ceremonies were held in Breslau, Munich, Kiel, Heidelberg, and Frankfurt, where Chopin's *Funeral March* was played in mocking accompaniment. The task of collecting the books for these demonstrations had been handled by student organizations who had circulated form letters asking librarians to contribute from their shelves any book "that works subversively on family life, married life or love, or the ethics of our youth, or our future, or strikes at the roots of German thought, the German home and the driving forces in our people; any works of those who would subordinate the soul to the material, anything that serves the purpose of lies." From the resultant miscellaneous tide a four-page typewritten list, comprising 160 authors, was compiled of those to be burned. Since many more books were received than were needed for the ceremonies, the surplus was thriftily sold to a paper mill for $3.00 a ton, and the proceeds used to help defray the cost of torches, firewood, and other incidental expenses.[76]

It soon became clear that the book burnings had been no temporary aberration. A few weeks afterwards, the German *Dichter Akademie* was purged of Jews, political dissidents, and pacifists, and in September the activities of all persons involved in literary endeavor—writers, publishers, booksellers, librarians—were placed under Goebbels' direct control. The direct responsibility for book censorship went to Alfred Rosenberg, who drew up and circulated a *schwarze Bücherliste* of forbidden titles.[77]

The Hitler régime made a deliberate effort to portray these measures as a natural culmination of the impulse which had underlain the *Jugend* purity campaigns and the *Schmutz und Schund* law. "The fire of the pyres which flared up in the German lands in May 1933," wrote a Nazi literary historian in 1934,

> is to us the sign and symbol of an inflexible will to purity. . . . The nests of corruption shall be destroyed and the haunts of degeneration purified. Youth, prizing its human dignity, presses forward to the light, to the sun.
>
> In the flaming words that rang out whilst intellectual filth was burning lay the sacred rage of o'erwhelmed and outraged human hearts. O thou eternal longing of the soul to be free from degrading smut and trash![78]

In the United States, Goebbels' bonfire and the events which followed caused a profound emotional shock. Newspapers gave it extensive front-page coverage. Upwards of 100,000 people in New York City and 50,000 in Chicago marched in a mass protest timed to coincide with the event.[79] Literary people expressed the deepest forebodings. "They

burned the books, but there remains a red glow in the sky,"
wrote Heywood Broun, marveling at "the most amazing demonstration of national neuroticism the world has seen in our
time." Walter Lippmann issued dark warnings, and Thomas
Mann, a refugee in America, spoke of Germany's "St. Vitus
dance of fanaticism."[80] The *New York Times* was reminded
of Caligula's mad effort to destroy the Roman classics, and
cautioned against dismissing as a mere "passing freak of school-
boys" a display so "plainly touched with insanity." *Zion's
Herald* (whose blazing book-purity crusade of 1922 now seemed
remote indeed) deplored as a literary and cultural catastrophe
"the narrowing impulsions of Nazi 'unity.'" Ludwig Lewisohn
wrote in *Harper's* of an entire society in "revolt against the
whole inner meaning of Western civilization" and sinking "to
a pagan, pre-Christian level."[81]

The impact of the German book burnings took many forms.
In 1934 William Saroyan published a story, probably autobiographical, of a poor young writer living in an unheated
room in San Francisco. On one particularly cold morning he
devises a plan for starting a fire in a tub in his room and burning some of his old and unwanted books to keep warm. The
first candidate for the flames is a six-pound German anatomy
text acquired for a nickel at a forgotten book sale. "But," says
Saroyan's hero,

> I couldn't do it. There were over a thousand pages in the
> book and I planned to burn one page at a time and see the fire
> of each page, but when I thought of all that print being
> effaced by fire and all that accurate language being removed
> from my library, I couldn't do it. . . .

After trying with no more success to persuade himself to ignite
a pile of cheap novels, he concludes:

> It is simply this: that if you have any respect for the mere
> idea of books, what they stand for in life, if you believe in
> paper and print, you cannot burn any page of any book. Even
> if you are freezing. Even if you are trying to do a bit of
> writing yourself. You can't do it. It is asking too much.[82]

Inevitably, the Fascist assault on literary freedom became a factor in American censorship cases. A few days after the Berlin bonfire, the attorney defending *God's Little Acre* reminded the court of "Hitler's purification of German literature," and urged the judge to take a stand against similar tendencies in the United States. And the *Ulysses* decision, coming as the full magnitude of the Nazi attack on books unfolded, was widely seen as America's answer to Hitler's repressions. Judge Woolsey and Morris Ernst made the point explicit a few days after the clearing of *Ulysses* when they made a joint speaking appearance at the inauguration of a Manhattan exhibit of the titles destroyed in the German book burnings. In 1937, after *A World I Never Made* had been exonerated, James T. Farrell observed: "There are few enough countries left where a writer can strive to write seriously and frankly. I am glad that America still remains one of them."[83]

The book burnings, and the rise of European Fascism generally, also importantly influenced the nation's retrospective understanding of the censorship battles of the 1920s. At the time, these had often seemed ludicrous and annoying, but essentially harmless. The vaporings of the Sumners, the Chases, and the Yarrows about "so-called intellectuals," "clannish publishers," "alien influences," and "over-sophisticated literati" had been passed off as the rhetoric of isolated fanatics.

A few observers, it is true, had been made uneasy by this casual attitude toward the suppressive tendencies of the decade. In 1927, when an aide of "Big Bill" Thompson, the demagogic mayor of Chicago, had symbolically burned one of Arthur M. Schlesinger's history books on the steps of the Chicago Public Library, Henry Seidel Canby had been distressed by the lighthearted derision with which this gesture had been greeted. Wrote Canby in the *Saturday Review*:

> There are some words that mean far more than they seem to say because they echo back and back and back into the history of the race. . . . They have power to stir anger or fear without further context or argument because their possible

meanings are felt long before they are understood. A sense of
insecurity follows them and for the moment complacency
opens a tiny crack. This happens when they talk of burning
our books. . . .

Take warning, therefore, you who love books because
you believe in free opinion and free fact circulating where
they can be known, discussed, affirmed, or denied. You are
not as safe as you think. The Mayor Thompsons of the world
are shrewder than you are. . . . The black forces of intolerance
are always ready just below the surface. . . . There will always
be a mob with a torch ready when someone cries "Burn
those books!"[84]

Such somber reflections seemed out of place in 1927; six
years later they appeared prophetic. Book censorship, one more
diversion for the amusement-hungry twenties, took on a new
and somber significance in the shadow of Goebbels. The American delegates to the 1933 conference of P.E.N., the international writers' organization, held late in May at Dubrovnic,
Yugoslavia, were witnesses to a vivid demonstration of the
changed mood. When the outlawed German-Jewish playwright
Ernst Toller rose to speak, Edgar von Schmidt-Pauli, Hitler's
sycophantic biographer and head of the German P.E.N. delegation, protested violently. Again it was Henry Seidel Canby
who sensed the significance of the moment:

I felt rather than saw a chill spreading . . ., visible fear rising
like cold fire. And I realized with a shock that what was a row
over principle for English and Americans, and an affirmation
of faith, was for these Europeans, imaginative men and women
all of them, a quick vision of armies in their cities and bombs
on their homes.[85]

Even when the obvious differences in the American situation had been taken into account, few sensitive observers after
May 1933 could be certain beyond the shadow of a doubt that
the United States had at no time in the twenties been itself
in danger of a Yankee version of the Franz Josef Platz holo-
caust, with domestic "Clean Books" champions at last gratify-

ing their frustrated, festering desire to rid the country of all that smut and trash.

From the perspective of the 1930s, the odd vignettes remembered from the censorship battles of the preceding decade —John Ford's rustic fulminations, Margaret Anderson's delicate shudder as she was fingerprinted, Morris Ernst's brash dialogues with judges, H. L. Mencken's jaunty performance on the Boston Common, Upton Sinclair and his fig-leaf edition of *Oil*—seemed freighted with a significance unrecognized at the time. After May 1933 the anticensorship impulse was infused with a new and passionate intensity. The new depth of feeling was expressed by Howard Mumford Jones when he addressed the American Library Association in October 1933. "Over the greater part of the surface of the earth," he said, "active and violent movements are at work designed to mold the minds of men into a single set of ideas. . . . The barbarities of Hitlerism have been equalled only by its stupidities, among which I count the childish burning of books. . . ." Added Jones:

> The charter of our freedom is that the people shall have the right freely to receive and freely to discuss ideas regarding themselves and the state to which they belong; and the frail shield which we have to interpose between this hard won political platitude and the storm of absolutism which is sweeping the world is the thin and perishable leaf of the printed book.[86]

The Shifting Rhythms of Censorship from the 1950s to the 1970s

The history of print censorship in America from World War II through the Nixon era presents divergent and seemingly contradictory trends. As we have seen, judicial and public attitudes toward censorship shifted dramatically in the 1920s and 1930s, as profound changes in U.S. society and culture brought a distinctly more permissive view of what could be expressed in print, culminating in the liberalization of the Customs law and the landmark *Ulysses* decision of 1933. Assaults on free expression by dictatorial governments elsewhere, especially the Nazi book burnings of 1933, added emotional intensity to the swelling tide of anticensorship sentiment.

These developments shaped the post–World War II censorship climate. Through the mid-1960s, the ongoing conflict between the liberal principle of free expression, enshrined in the First Amendment, and the impulse to suppress books or periodicals deemed obscene under prevailing cultural norms—or the norms of dominant social groups—was increasingly resolved in favor of free expression.

But censorship wars are not waged in a vacuum. We have seen how censorship history from the Gilded Age through the 1930s unfolded against a larger social and political background, and this remained true after World War II. In the early postwar era, even as the courts extended First Amendment protection to works once banned as obscene, the Cold War gave rise to an upsurge of politically motivated censorship. In the 1960s, unsettling social changes, cultural upheavals, and domestic unrest caused public and judicial views of obscenity to harden, spawning a resurgence of censorship pressure that would intensify in the 1970s and beyond.

DEBATING CENSORSHIP DURING
WORLD WAR II AND THE EARLY POSTWAR ERA

In contrast to World War I, when heavy-handed government censorship at the federal, state, and local level fell on socialists, pacifists, German Americans, and other critics of the war, the World War II homefront saw fewer and far less egregious efforts to stifle dissent. To be sure, official Washington worked behind the scenes to assure that Hollywood movies supported U.S.

war aims, and the Office of War Information oversaw the flow of war news and photographs. Under Attorney General Robert Jackson, the Justice Department's Special War Policies Unit vigorously cracked down on propaganda disseminated by foreign governments considered a threat. The 1938 Foreign Agent Registration Act and the 1940 Voorhis Act required foreign-governments' agents to register and "propaganda" publications financed from abroad to be so labeled. The Federal District Court for the District of Columbia upheld the constitutionality of the former law in *U.S.* v. *Rush* (1939). Under these laws, historian Brett Gary notes, the wartime Justice Department successfully prosecuted more than fifty cases against agents or propaganda offices of the German, Soviet, Spanish, and Japanese governments, with the defendants including "booksellers, journalists, news services, libraries of information, official consuls, and front organizations (such as labor organizations and fraternal groups) with financial connections to foreign governments."[1]

Nevertheless, domestic censorship in 1941–45 was conducted much less recklessly than in the hyperpatriotic climate of 1917–18. In part, this reflected the higher level of national unity during World War II, and the comparative rarity of vocal dissent. But it also related to changing attitudes regarding censorship. As Gary observes, Justice Department lawyers charged with enforcing the wartime propaganda-control laws operated on the premise that "registration and disclosure were more tolerant and more constitutionally sound than censorship." Testifying before Congress in 1941, the head of the Special Defense Unit, Lawrence Smith, described the labeling requirement for foreign "propaganda" as a "democractic" approach, and not an instance of the suppression of ideas.[2] The marketplace of ideas remained open; it was simply being monitored more closely than usual as a consumer-protection measure.

As in World War I, although to a lesser degree, World War II also saw official efforts to exploit wartime patriotism to enforce threatened standards of moral propriety and purity in print. But the attempts ultimately failed in the courts, further underscoring the sea change in opinion about censorship. The most important initiative originated in the Post Office Department, the source of several notable censorship efforts from the 1940s through the 1960s. As we saw in chapter 8, tariff-law reform in 1930 and Judge James Woolsey's 1933 *Ulysses* decision had restricted the censorship powers of Customs officials. The authority of the Post Office in this area remained in force, however, rooted in the 1873 Comstock law prohibiting the mailing of obscene materials. In 1942, soon after Pearl Harbor, Postmaster General Frank C. Walker chose what seemed an auspicious moment to crack down on *Esquire* magazine and other somewhat risqué periodicals for failing in what he called their "positive duty to contribute to the public good and public welfare." Walker withdrew *Esquire*'s second-class mail permit, which he described as "a certificate of good moral character." This wartime measure recalls not only the moral-purity and anti-obscenity campaigns of World War I, but also the alarm over the scandalous publications reaching Union troops during the Civil War that had helped build support for the Comstock law. If Walker's ruling stood, *Esquire* faced a death sentence, since lower second-class rates were essential to any magazine's survival.

But 1942 was not 1917, and Walker's crusade soon ran afoul of the courts. The American Civil Liberties Union, born in the civil-rights struggles of World War I, joined *Esquire* in a legal challenge, and won. In 1943, a U.S. Court of Appeals, reversing a lower-court decision, rescinded Walker's action and restored *Esquire*'s second-class mailing privileges. Congress had never intended, declared the court, to grant the Post Office "the power first to determine what is good for the public to read and then to force compliance." Moral supervision of the mails, it said, suffers from "utter confusion and lack of intelligible standards." As a final fillip, the court observed drily that postal officials might well "experience a feeling of relief if they are limited to the more prosaic function of seeing to it that 'neither snow nor rain nor heat nor gloom of night stays these couriers from the swift completion of their appointed rounds.'" On appeal, the U.S. Supreme Court upheld the decision.[3]

Despite liberalizing trends, censorship pressures persisted as the nation entered the Cold War era. With political leaders and opinion molders calling for national consensus as America mobilized for an all-out struggle with the Soviet Union, the repression of dissident voices and radical ideologies often seemed a natural corollary. In this tense and uneasy climate, marked by powerful and contradictory cultural pressures, the courts struggled to draw the line between the permissible and the impermissible under the First Amendment.

A series of early postwar cases produced sharply varying outcomes, depending on how specific judges assessed a particular work's literary merit or degree of indecency, which suggested high levels of ambivalence in cultural attitudes toward censorship. For example, in 1945, the Supreme Judicial Court of Massachusetts—reinforcing the old "Banned in Boston" stereotype—confirmed an obscenity conviction against Lillian Smith's *Strange Fruit* (1944), a novel dealing with interracial sex in the South. In 1950, the same court upheld a ban on Erskine Caldwell's *God's Little Acre* (1933), a bawdy comic novel set in rural Georgia, which had been cleared in 1933 by a New York magistrate. In 1946, Doubleday and Co. was convicted under New York State's obscenity statute for publishing *Memoirs of Hecate County* (1946), a novel about the turbulent domestic lives of New York's intelligentsia by the literary critic Edmund Wilson. One chapter of Wilson's novel, entitled "The Princess with the Golden Hair," dealt with a sexual relationship delicately but quite explicitly for the time. In 1948, the Supreme Court divided four-four on the case (Justice Felix Frankfurter did not participate), and the lower-court ban stood.[4]

By contrast, the same Massachusetts court that condemned *Strange Fruit* and *God's Little Acre* ruled in 1948 that Kathleen Winsor's *Forever Amber* (1944), a torrid potboiler set in Restoration England, was not obscene. And in *Commonwealth* v. *Gordon*, a notable 1949 case later upheld by the Pennsylvania Supreme Court, Judge Curtis Bok of Philadelphia's Court of Quarter Sessions dismissed indictments against a group of modern novels including *God's Little Acre*; James T. Farrell's *Studs Lonigan* trilogy

(1932–35), a portrayal of an Irish American youth's bleak life in Depression-era Chicago; and William Faulkner's *Sanctuary* (1931), a gothic, Mississippi-based tale of rape, murder, bootlegging, prostitution, and lynching. Bok rejected the view that the arousal of sexual desire was sufficient basis for finding a work obscene. He also challenged the long-unexamined assumption of a causal link between the printed word and criminal conduct. For this claim to be relevant in a specific obscenity case, he declared, "the causal connection between the book and the criminal behavior must appear beyond a reasonable doubt."[5]

ROTH/ALBERTS AND BEYOND:
THE LIBERALIZING TREND CONTINUES

The U.S. Supreme Court attempted to introduce some definitional clarity into this constitutional twilight zone in two landmark cases of June 1957, for which the court wrote a single decision: *U.S. v. Roth* and *Alberts v. California*. In its *Roth/Alberts* ruling, the high court for the first time explicitly and substantively addressed the First Amendment issues posed by federal, state, and local obscenity laws. In doing so, the court drew upon a liberalized definition of obscenity recently proposed in a Model Penal Code drafted by the American Law Institute, a nongovernmental body of jurists, attorneys, and law scholars.[6]

In the specific cases at hand, the court upheld the convictions of Samuel Roth of New York and David Alberts of California, both commercial purveyors of sexually explicit material. Roth, with eight arrests and a prison term behind him, had been tangling with the obscenity laws since at least 1927, when he had issued pirated excerpts from James Joyce's *Ulysses*. A poet and something of an idealist who published both pornography and works of recognized literary merit, Roth, according to attorney Charles Rembar, believed that "reading itself is a great good, that any kind of reading is better than no reading and that some people will read only rather low material, which he was willing to supply."[7]

The majority opinion (which upheld the convictions of Roth and Alberts), written by Justice William J. Brennan, began by affirming that certain publications lay outside the charmed circle of constitutional protection: "[I]mplicit in the history of the First Amendment is the rejection of obscenity as utterly without redeeming social importance. . . . We hold that obscenity is not within the area of constitutionally protected speech or press." But it went on to define the scope of First Amendment protection very broadly, and to hedge in quite narrowly the realm of the "obscene" that could be legally suppressed:

> All ideas having even the slightest redeeming social importance—unorthodox ideas, controversial ideas, even ideas hateful to the prevailing climate of opinion—have the full protection of the [First Amendment's] guarantees, unless excludable because they encroach upon the limited area of more important interests.[8]

The Court went on to offer a definition of obscenity to supplant Victorian-era definitions, which, like the 1868 *Hicklin* rule, were filled with impossibly vague and circular terminology ("deprave," "corrupt," "immoral," "lewd," "lascivious," etc.); were preoccupied with specific words and passages; and focused their concerns on children, youth, and other groups deemed especially susceptible, rather than on normal adults. First, as we have seen, the Court held that even the slightest "redeeming social importance" created a presumption of First Amendment protection. Further, mere sexual content did not prove obscenity: "Sex and obscenity are not synonymous. Obscene material is material which deals with sex in a manner appealing to prurient interest. The portrayal of sex, e.g., in art, literature and scientific works, is not itself sufficient reason to deny . . . constitutional protection." Building on these principles, the Court offered its definition: a work could be found legally obscene, and therefore outside the realm of constitutional protection, if "to the average person, applying contemporary community standards, the dominant theme of the material taken as a whole appeals to prurient interests."[9]

Despite the apparent clarity of this ruling, the range of opinions offered in the *Roth/Alberts* decision illustrates how contentious the issue remained, and the strength of support for maintaining a stricter stance toward obscenity. To be sure, justices William Douglas and Hugo Black, as First Amendment absolutists, dissented from the conviction of Roth and Alberts because, in their view, the First Amendment prohibited *all* censorship, except in rare cases where the material in question was "so closely brigaded with illegal action as to be an inseparable part of it."[10] Chief Justice Earl Warren, however, argued that Roth and Alberts were so clearly guilty that a broad declaration of First Amendment principles was unnecessary.[11] Warren had reason for caution. The Supreme Court was already under heavy conservative attack for the *Brown* v. *Board of Education* school-desegregation decision of 1954. Further, in *Yates* v. *U.S.*, another controversial decision issued a week before *Roth/Alberts*, the Supreme Court held that the government's aggressive prosecution of U.S. communists had violated their First Amendment rights. In this context, Warren may well have concluded that wading into the obscenity issue so boldly, in a ruling clearly intended to whittle down the scope of federal and state anti-obscenity laws, would only embolden the court's critics—as indeed it did.

Warren objected to Brennan's opinion on substantive grounds as well. The key factor in such cases, he argued, should not be the content of the material, but the circumstances of its production and distribution. "The conduct of the defendant is the central issue," he said, "not the obscenity of a book or a picture." From this perspective, the guilt of Roth and Alberts lay in the fact that they had promoted their wares "to appeal to the erotic interest of their customers. They were plainly engaged in the commercial exploitation of the morbid and shameful craving for materials with prurient interest."[12] Little noticed at the time, Warren's approach, opening new possibilities for censorship, would prove influential in future cases.

Justice John Marshall Harlan concurred in the conviction of Alberts, who had been tried under California law, but dissented in Roth's conviction under the federal postal-obscenity law. Like Warren, Harlan advanced an argument welcomed by pro-censorship

forces. On the one hand, he said, the courts should rigorously uphold First Amendment standards in *federal* obscenity cases; indeed, federal obscenity prosecutions should be extremely rare. But
Harlan went on to argue that the courts should adopt a presumption in favor of *state* obscenity convictions, since protecting public
morality was mainly a state and local function. As states experi-
mented with different standards, some more permissive, some
stricter, works banned in one jurisdiction could still circulate elsewhere. The *Roth/Alberts* ruling, Harlan feared, could limit states'
freedom to regulate obscenity.[13] This laissez-faire approach, of
course, would open book publishers, periodical dealers, movie distributors, and others to multiple local prosecutions, with minimal
recourse to the federal courts. As we shall see, Harlan, in fact, anticipated future developments: as the twentieth century wore on,
federal censorship of print materials largely disappeared, while
censorship efforts and repressive impulses remained vigorously
alive at the grassroots level.

Although the cautionary notes from Warren and Harlan
suggested possible changes ahead, the *Roth/Alberts* decision,
still a cornerstone of U.S. obscenity law, was the culmination of
a process of liberalization extending back to the 1920s and earlier. While affirming the state's power to censor obscenity, the
Court sharply constrained that power, acknowledging a decades-
long transition, in the law and the larger culture, toward greater
tolerance of sexual candor in print.

Taking advantage of the seemingly more permissive climate, Barney Rosset's Grove Press of New York in 1959 published the first unexpurgated U.S. edition of D. H. Lawrence's
long-banned *Lady Chatterley's Lover*. New York postal authorities, despite the clear message of Brennan's ruling in *Roth/
Alberts*, confiscated copies of the book from the mails and
brought action against Rosset. Grove's lawyer, Charles Rembar,
appealed, and Judge Frederick van Pelt Bryan of the U.S. District Court for the Southern District of New York overrode the
post office, finding Lawrence's novel not obscene under the
Supreme Court's definition in *Roth/Alberts*. Despite Lawrence's

use of Anglo-Saxon sexual and excretory terms, his explicit if romanticized descriptions of intercourse, and his condoning of adultery, wrote Bryan (echoing Judge Woolsey's ruling in the *Ulysses* case twenty-six years earlier), "The book is replete with fine writing and with descriptive passages of rare beauty. There is no doubt of its literary merit." When Bryan's ruling was upheld in the U.S. Court of Appeals, a major work of twentieth-century literature that had languished in legal limbo for three decades could at last circulate freely.[14]

Revisiting the censorship issue in 1962, the Supreme Court further narrowed its definition of the legally obscene in *Manual Enterprises* v. *Day*, a case arising from a ban by the postmaster in Alexandria, Virginia, on three magazines published for homosexuals. *MANual, Trim,* and *Grecian Guild Pictorial* consisted mainly of artfully posed nude or semi-nude photographs of male models. In *Roth/Alberts*, the Supreme Court had cited "prurience" in its definition of the obscene, echoing older definitions in which works describing sexual pleasure, or seeking to arouse sexual desire, were banned for that reason alone. (Deriving from the Latin *prurire*, to itch or to crave, "prurient" is defined in *Merriam Webster's Collegiate Dictionary* as "marked by or arousing an immoderate or unwholesome interest or desire, *esp.,* . . . unusual sexual desire.") In *Manual Enterprises*, the Court, by a six-to-one vote, cleared the publications in question, and in the process backed away from the fraught word "prurience," with all its problems of subjectivity (precisely when does sexual desire become "immoderate"?). Writing for the majority, Justice Harlan—true to his principle that federal censorship must meet a particularly high constitutional standard—noted that while the target audience might find the magazines arousing, the contents were not presented with "patent offensiveness"—that is, "so offensive on their face as to affront current community standards of decency." In the wake of *Manual Enterprises*—or so it appeared in the hopeful climate of 1962—the culturally relativistic standard of "current community standards" would replace the judgmental moralism and even prudery of older tests.[15]

The Supreme Court's next broadside against censorship came in 1964, in a case involving Henry Miller's bawdy sexual memoir *Tropic of Cancer*, first published in Paris in 1934. A longstanding U.S. Customs ban on the book was upheld in 1953 by a California court and, in a fiercely hostile ruling, by a federal appellate court. But the times were changing, and in 1961, encouraged by its victory in the *Lady Chatterley* case, Grove Press published the first U.S. edition of *Tropic of Cancer*. The postal authorities, having at last absorbed the Supreme Court's message, took no action, but local authorities in various jurisdictions did prosecute, and the busy Charles Rembar again led the defense team. Some sixty cases in twenty-one states produced a mixed outcome: Massachusetts cleared the book; New York banned it. In Rhode Island, the state attorney general simply visited the local book wholesalers and persuaded them "voluntarily" to return the more than three thousand copies of Miller's book they had ordered. The wave of prosecutions ended abruptly in June 1964, however, when the Supreme Court, on a five-to-four vote, without written opinions, reversed a ban by the Florida Supreme Court, and cleared Miller's novel.[16]

The postwar liberalizing trend crested on March 21, 1966, when the Supreme Court, by a six-to-three vote, reversed a Massachusetts ban on John Cleland's *Memoirs of a Woman of Pleasure* (1749), more commonly known by the name of its heroine, *Fanny Hill*. It recounted the sexual adventures of a young orphan who arrives in London at the age of fifteen. *Fanny Hill* holds pride of place in American censorship history for provoking the first known U.S. obscenity prosecution, in Massachusetts in 1821, against Peter Holmes, described in the indictment as "a scandalous and evil disposed person, contriving . . . to debauch and corrupt, and . . . to create in [the minds of youth and others] . . . inordinate and lustful desires."[17] G.P. Putnam's Sons had published the edition at issue in the 1966 case in 1963. Charles Rembar represented the publisher.

In its ruling, the Supreme Court acknowledged that Cleland's long-suppressed *tour de force* was prurient through and through, but also found it significant in literary history, and thus possessed of "redeeming social importance"—a key test in the post-*Roth/Alberts* era. (In the Boston trial, Rembar had introduced literary scholars from Harvard, Brandeis, Boston University, and other institutions, who testified to the work's importance in literary and social history.) Justice Brennan stated the position forcefully: "[A] book cannot be proscribed unless it is found to be *utterly* without redeeming social value. This is so even though the book is found to possess the requisite prurient appeal and to be patently offensive."[18]

From a legal-history perspective, the successive judicial blows against print censorship from the 1933 *Ulysses* decision through *Roth/Alberts* of 1957 and on to the *Lady Chatterley*, *Manual Enterprises*, *Tropic of Cancer*, and *Fanny Hill* cases appeared to offer overwhelming evidence that the censors were on the run. It seemed that the First Amendment umbrella would soon protect almost any publication that could plausibly be shown to have even a scintilla of "redeeming social value," however explicit its treatment of once-taboo sexual themes. Reviewing the key cases in 1964, Morris Ernst and Alan Schwartz declared confidently that very soon "the censorship department of the Post Office may well be out of business." Charles Rembar offered a similar prediction in *The End of Obscenity* (1968): "[S]o far as writing is concerned . . . , not only in our law but in our culture, obscenity will soon be gone." When John S. Sumner, the longtime head of the New York Society for the Suppression of Vice, died in 1971 at ninety-four, he must have felt that his old censorship battles for "decency" and "purity" had been in vain.[19]

But Sumner need not have despaired. In fact, public opinion was shifting in his favor. In the early postwar period, as the courts adopted an increasingly permissive stance in the sexual arena, repressive efforts rooted in Cold War fears of radicalism and subversion characterized the nation's public life. Even in the realm of sexual expression, the Supreme Court's permissive rulings, coupled with mass-culture products offering more and more explicit descriptions and representations, triggered a sharp reaction in conservative and religious circles. This, in turn, stimulated renewed demands for censorship. This cultural turnaround, well underway by the later 1960s, gained momentum in the 1970s.

THE TIDE TURNS:
THE PERSISTENCE AND RESURGENCE
OF CENSORSHIP IN POSTWAR AMERICA

Without question, the courts dealt sharp blows to obscenity censorship in the rulings from the mid-1950s through the mid-1960s that we have just examined. The ramifying effect of these cases surely inhibited censorship on obscenity grounds at all governmental levels. But the repressive impulse remained strong in early Cold War America, and in the turbulent and divisive 1960s an upsurge of censorship pressure, much of it coordinated by well-organized groups, expressed itself in a variety of ways, including a partial retreat by the Supreme Court from the strongly libertarian position it had staked out in *Roth/Alberts* and other rulings.

Stifling Political Ideas in the Early Cold War. As many historians have documented, in the early 1950s when Cold War alarms were at a fever pitch, political radicals' First Amendment rights faced challenges on many fronts. From 1950 to his downfall in 1954, Senator Joseph McCarthy's many targets included the freedom of the press. In February 1953, McCarthy hauled writer and Communist party member Howard Fast, author of *The Unvanquished* (1942), *Citizen Tom Paine* (1943), *Spartacus* (1952), and many other works, before his committee. Responding to McCarthy's pressure, the day after Fast's appearance a nervous State Department instructed the overseas libraries of the United States Information Administration (USIA) to remove books by "any controversial persons, Communists, fellow travelers, et cetera." Unmollified, McCarthy aides Roy Cohn and G.

David Schine rampaged across Europe that spring "investigating" USIA libraries for books by allegedly radical authors. The targets included many well-known writers, among them John Dewey, Henry Steele Commager, Bernard DeVoto, W. H. Auden, and even a 1946 issue of the *Annals of the American Academy of Political and Social Science* that included an article about the United Nations. As McCarthy grew more reckless, opposition grew. Even President Dwight Eisenhower, who generally kept his contempt for the Wisconsin senator well hidden, finally spoke out. Addressing the Dartmouth College commencement in June 1953, in the midst of the Cohn and Schine junket, Eisenhower declared: "Don't join the book-burners. . . . Don't be afraid to go into the library and read every book, so long as that document does not offend our own ideas of decency—that should be the only censorship." Though Ike denied that he had McCarthy in mind, his comments—including the term "book-burners," evoking the Nazi book bonfires of twenty years before—were widely read as a rebuke to his fellow Republican. (The State Department, pressured from all directions, nervously issued another directive instructing USIA librarians that books purged from the shelves should be "stored, not burned.")[20]

The McCarthyite assault on civil liberties provided the context, too, of Ray Bradbury's *Fahrenheit 451*, a dystopian science-fiction story in which the government controls nearly all thought by means of television. Books are strictly banned, and, if discovered, burned by "firemen," whose duty is not to extinguish fires, but to ignite them. (451° F is the temperature at which paper burns.) Expanding a story that had appeared in *Galaxy Science Fiction* in 1950, Bradbury published the full-length novel in 1953, as the Cohn-Schine European junket made headlines.

While McCarthy and other congressional communist-hunters like Democratic Senator Pat McCarran of Nevada, author of the draconian Internal Security Act of 1950, and the members of the House Committee on Un-American Activities attracted the publicity, a more systematic attack on the First Amendment had been undertaken earlier by the Truman Administration under the Alien

Registration Act of 1940, commonly known as the Smith Act. This measure, designed to check domestic subversion, made it a crime to advocate or teach the overthrow of the government by force, or to organize or join any group that taught such doctrines. During the early Cold War, it became a major weapon against the expression of radical political views, culminating in the 1949 conviction of eleven leaders of the U.S. Communist Party on the charge that in 1945, when the party was founded, they had conspired to promote Marxist-Leninist doctrines by recruiting members, operating schools and classes, and "publish[ing] books, magazines, and newspapers." In 1949, when government lawyers introduced Stalin's *Foundations of Leninism* and *The History of the Communist Party of the Soviet Union* as evidence in the trial before the U.S. Court of Appeals, defense attorney George Crockett objected that the defendants' possession of the books was "protected . . . by the First Amendment." Another defense attorney, Abraham Isserman, protested: "We are putting a book on trial." But the presiding judge firmly, if somewhat incoherently, dismissed the objection:

> If the contents of this book and these other pamphlets and documents of one kind or another, that were handed around, and people were told to study them and to teach other people what to do, and how they were to go around and do the things that have been testified to here. I can scarcely believe that it is trying a book. It is trying those persons who used the book and other means to allegedly commit a crime, and that is part of the paraphernalia of the crime.[21]

In *Dennis* v. *U.S.* (1951), which historian Ellen Schrecker has called "the main free speech case of the cold war," the U.S. Supreme Court, by a six-to-two vote, upheld the Smith Act and the conviction of the Communist Party leaders. The majority opinion by Chief Justice Fred M. Vinson oozed Cold War paranoia. Citing Justice Oliver Wendell Holmes's "clear and present danger" rule of 1919, Vinson dismissed constitutional objections to the Smith Act: "Speech is not an absolute. . . . To those who would paralyze our Government in the face of impending threat by encasing it in a semantic straitjacket we must reply that all concepts are relative. . . . Overthrow of the Government by force and violence is certainly a substantial enough interest for the Government to limit speech."[22]

A stinging dissent by Hugo Black, joined by William Douglas, dismissed the majority opinion as a gross misapplication of the "clear and present danger" principle: "These petitioners [the convicted communists] were not charged with an attempt to overthrow the government," Black insisted. "They were not charged with overt acts of any kind designed to overthrow the Government. They were not even charged with saying anything or writing anything designed to overthrow the Government. The charge was that they agreed to assemble and to talk and publish certain ideas at a later date." If the majority position became established precedent, warned Black, "The [First] Amendment as so construed is not likely to protect any but those 'safe' or orthodox views which rarely need its protection."[23]

Over the next few years, the government secured nearly one hundred convictions and issued many more indictments under the Smith Act. This wholesale assault on the advocacy of unpopular ideas continued at least until 1957, when the Supreme Court, in *Yates* v. *U.S.*, revisited the Smith Act. This time it ruled that advocating the forcible overthrow of the government as a general principle, absent overt actions to achieve that end, enjoyed constitutional protection. The *Yates* ruling, coming as Cold War tensions eased after Stalin's death, largely halted at least the federal assault on radical or revolutionary political ideas. In its heyday, however, the domestic anticommunism campaign, involving all three branches of the federal government, local governments, and various private organizations, resulted in gross and sustained violations of many citizens' First Amendment rights, including freedom of speech and freedom of the press. In a 1953 Gallup Poll that asked whether a person "known to favor communism" should be permitted to deliver a speech, 29 percent of Americans said yes, 67 percent, no.[24]

McCarthy's bumbling campaign against politically suspect books and authors, and the government's more systematic

Smith Act prosecutions, were matched by grassroots, do-it-yourself repressive efforts, often directed at libraries. In Chicago, the American Legion demanded the purging of "subversive" books from school libraries. The San Antonio Public Library faced demands that it affix a large red warning stamp in the front of all works deemed communistic or subversive. In Galion, Ohio, the school board adopted a plan, narrowly reversed by last-minute opposition, to remove all fiction from the school libraries for "screening." In Marin County, California, a prominent citizen called a news conference and alerted a grand jury to publicize a list of "subversive" titles she had found in the local high-school library.[25]

In Bartlesville, Oklahoma, in 1950, a forty-member "citizens' committee," abetted by the American Legion, instigated the firing of Ruth Brown, the director of the public library for thirty years, for subscribing to such "subversive" periodicals as the *Nation* (described by the citizens' committee as publishing "the prattle of the Communists" as well as articles on "sexology and homosexuality"); the *New Republic* (denounced for "offering the views of the pro-Communist press, along with erotic literature and atheist books"); and a New York–based magazine called *Soviet Russia Today*. Brown's real offense, in that deeply racist time and place, as historian Louise S. Robbins has made clear, was her advocacy of racial integration and her support for the Congress of Racial Equality.[26]

As Robbins has also documented, the library profession, having moved far beyond its timid and uncertain posture of the 1920s, resisted such campaigns vigorously. A 1948 *Library Journal* editorial urged librarians to report censorship pressures and to make available "books and periodicals of all shades of opinion, to the end that our citizens may continue to be educated and not indoctrinated."[27] The council of the American Library Association (ALA) and the ALA's Intellectual Freedom Committee (IFC), created in 1939, issued a series of statements insisting that libraries be left free to offer a wide array of reading matter.[28]

Early in 1953, with McCarthyite hysteria at its height, some four hundred librarians attended an IFC conference on "Book

Selection in Defense of Freedom." At the ALA's Los Angeles conference that spring, president Robert Downs warned of the "virulent disease" of McCarthyism and cautioned: "Censorship directives, issued in the atmosphere of fear, hysteria, and repression now prevailing in Washington, threaten to place the entire information library system in jeopardy." Around the same time, the ALA and the American Book Publishers Council issued "The Freedom to Read," a powerful anticensorship manifesto. The library profession also publicized a June 1953 letter from President Eisenhower to the ALA lauding librarians' role in preserving "the precious liberties of our nation: freedom of inquiry, freedom of the spoken and written word, freedom of exchange of ideas." Deploring repressive efforts by "zealots . . . with more wrath than wisdom," the president declared: "A democracy chronically fearful of new ideas would be a dying democracy." (This ringing pronouncement was elicited from Eisenhower by a friend, Douglas Black, the president of Doubleday and Company and also president of the Book Publishers Council.) In 1960, the ALA published Robert Downs' *The First Freedom: Liberty and Justice in the World of Books*, an anthology of anticensorship writings.[29]

This activism by librarians, book publishers, and other groups underscores how seriously politically motivated censorship was perceived as a threat in these years. Despite the "big publicity battle for intellectual freedom in libraries," noted the head of the IFC late in 1954, "[t]he fear and intimidation in small public and in school libraries, particularly those in small communities, is greater today than it was a year ago."[30]

The Anti-Obscenity Wars Revive. Even on the obscenity front, greater judicial tolerance did not necessarily translate into a dramatic shift in public attitudes. Despite the Supreme Court's liberalization of the obscenity laws, censorship sentiment remained strong. A series of congressional hearings in the 1950s reflected many Americans' continuing preoccupation with sex and violence in print and other cultural media. In 1952, Democratic Congressman Ezekiel C. Gathings of Arkansas chaired a "select committee on current pornographic materials." The highly publicized 1954 hearings on juvenile delinquency conducted by Senator Estes Kefauver of Tennessee devoted much attention to pornography, including violent and salacious comic books, issuing an alarming report on *Obscene and Pornographic Materials*. Putting a dollar figure on the menace, it estimated the annual traffic in mail-order pornography at $500 million. Congresswoman Kathryn E. Granahan of Pennsylvania conducted another round of pornography hearings in 1959, and produced a report that doubled Kefauver's figure to a round $1 billion. Citing post office sources, the Granahan report charged that over a million children a year were receiving ads for "lewd and obscene materials." At the state level, Rhode Island in the mid-1950s set up a Commission to Encourage Morality in Youth, which, until the U.S. Supreme Court curbed its activities in 1963, periodically sent booksellers blacklists of books it found objectionable.[31]

Charles Rembar, a perceptive cultural observer as well as resourceful anticensorship lawyer, well understood the difference between the courtroom and society at large. Citing poll data to prove his point, Rembar asserted in his 1968 account of his legal victories over sex censorship: "Most of you who read this book belong to a minority. In each of the three cases I tell about, the decision would have gone the other way if it had been put to a popular vote. . . . The majority does not really accept the [First] Amendment. . . . [I]t was the United States Constitution that saved these books, and not the will of the people." Rembar also noted New York City mayor Robert Wagner's 1965 demand for tougher anti-obscenity laws. It was the mayor's response to a campaign by the tabloid *New York Daily News* (the nation's second-largest newspaper) featuring screaming headlines such as "BLAME COURTS FOR FLOOD OF PRINTED FILTH."[32]

In part, this resurgence of demands for more censorship—or aggressive reassertion of popular attitudes that had never really gone away—represented a predictable response to the more sexually explicit books and periodicals of these years. As in the 1920s, the post–World War II years saw changes in the publishing world as newcomers like Barney Rosset, who started Grove Press in 1951, entered the field. At the same time, the paperback explosion brought books into new venues such as drug stores and within the price range of more people. (Local censorship attacks on *Tropic of Cancer* shot up, Charles Rembar recalled, when Grove issued a paperback edition.[33]) Encouraged by the Supreme Court's more permissive stance, Rosset and other publishers offered general trade books that exceeded formerly accepted limits in their sexual explicitness and use of taboo words. Rosset published not only *Lady Chatterley's Lover* and *Tropic of Cancer*, but also classic erotica such as the *Kama Sutra* and the first U.S. editions of Frank Harris's three-volume sexual autobiography *My Life and Loves* (Paris, 1923–27; Grove, 1963), and *Story of O* (French-language edition, Paris, 1954; Grove's English translation, 1966), by the pseudonymous "Pauline Réage," a novel of sexual obsession and the narrator's sadomasochistic dominance by men. Rosset's list also included contemporary writers who dealt in graphic detail with drug addiction and sexual deviance, such as William Burroughs's *Naked Lunch* (Paris, 1959; Grove, 1962), John Rechy's *City of Night* (1963), and Hubert Selby's *Last Exit to Brooklyn* (1964). He also issued many erotic and sexually explicit titles from Jack Kahane's Obelisk Press in Paris and its successor Olympia Press, founded in 1953 by Kahane's son, Maurice Girodias.[34] Like publishers of the 1920s, Rosset used censorship prosecutions to sell books. The 1966 paperback edition of *Naked Lunch*, for example, prominently featured a statement from the recent decision by the Massachusetts Supreme Court clearing the work.

Other publishers joined in, including some old-line houses whose offerings surely sent their nineteenth-century founders spinning in their graves. As we have seen, G. P. Putnam's Sons, that pillar of the Gilded Age literary establishment, published the first openly sold U.S. edition of John Cleland's *Fanny Hill*, as well as Norman Mailer's *The Deer Park* (1955), and Terry Southern's and Mason Hoffenberg's erotic spoof, *Candy* (1964). Other books that shocked many readers included Grace Metalious's steamy *Peyton Place* (Simon & Schuster, 1956); J.P. Donleavy's *The Ginger Man* (Paris, 1955; U.S. edition, McDowell, Oblensky, 1958); and Anthony Burgess's *A Clockwork Orange* (London, Heinemann, 1962; New York, Ballantine, 1965).[35] The print culture of these years also included a flood of cheap paperbacks with titles like *Instant Love*, *High-School Scandal*, *Cheater's Paradise*, *Campus Mistress*, *Orgy Club*, *Sin Whisper*, *Lust Pool*, *Shame Agent*, and *Born to Be Made*. In the aftermath of *Roth* and other decisions, notes Felice Flanery Lewis, "the publishers and distributors of pulp books now had reason to believe they could win their pleas [against local censorship convictions], as indeed they frequently did."[36]

Hugh Hefner's *Playboy*, with its famous nude centerfolds, was launched in 1953 and reported total sales of 64 million copies by 1969.[37] (Comedian Mort Sahl said Hefner taught a generation of teenage boys to expect their girlfriends to have staples in their navels.) Bob Guccione's *Penthouse* was founded in England in 1965 and came to America in 1969. Larry Flynt's far raunchier *Hustler* appeared in 1972.

On other cultural fronts, Broadway playgoers saw unprecedented expanses of naked flesh in such plays and musicals as *Hair* (1967), *Ché* (1969), and *Oh! Calcutta* (1969). As for the movies, nudity and more explicit sex moved from X-rated venues to neighborhood theaters in such films as *Blowup* (1966), the Swedish import *I Am Curious—Yellow* (1967), *Rosemary's Baby* (1968), *Easy Rider*, *Midnight Cowboy*, *Myra Breckenridge*, and *Women in Love* (all 1969), *Tropic of Cancer* (1970), *Last Tango in Paris* and *The Last Picture Show* (both 1973), and many others. At the same time, the makers of hard-core pornographic movies, long confined to the furtive realm of the "stag party," moved from the underground into the cultural mainstream. The explicitly pornographic films *Deep Throat* (1972) and *The Devil*

in Miss Jones (1973), both by the same director, Gerard Damiano, were widely reviewed and screened in general theaters.
Both proved highly successful moneymakers.

As the world of print and the mass culture in general
moved toward greater sexual explicitness, many Americans reacted in dismay and revulsion. Laments about the nation's "sex-
drenched culture" proliferated in pulpits and the religious press.
In 1971, the Boston evangelical leader Harold John Ockenga declared, "Between 1965 and 1970 the moral dam gave way, and
. . . the resulting flood has played havoc with civilization." America, warned another religious writer in 1972, was rapidly sinking
into "a quagmire of wickedness and lasciviousness, immorality
and debauchery." In 1974, the Rev. David Wilkerson of the As-
semblies of God Church foresaw a "moral landslide" of "nudity,
perversion, and . . . filth" engulfing the nation.[38]

Not all the warnings came from churchmen or conservative
activists. It found voice on the Supreme Court in various dissents, notably Justice Tom Clark's angry outburst in the 1966
Fanny Hill case: "I have 'stomached' past cases for almost ten
years without much outcry. Though I am not known to be a
purist—or a shrinking violet—this book is too much even for
me. . . . [T]he repetition of sexual episode after episode and the
candor with which they are described renders the book 'patently
offensive.'"[39]

These years also saw much discussion of obscenity and censorship issues in journals of opinion quite different in tone from
the discourse of the 1920s, when untrammeled free expression
had seemed an entirely worthy goal to be championed without
reservation and anyone with a kind word for the censors had
been ridiculed as hopelessly reactionary by cultural arbiters like
H. L. Mencken. Some intellectuals of the 1960s, notably Susan
Sontag, defended pornography, but many had reservations.
Writer Cleveland Amory (quoting liberally from the books he deplored) lambasted "Paperback Pornography" in a 1963 *Saturday
Evening Post* article. Novelist George P. Elliott, writing in
Harper's Magazine in 1965, issued a warning reminiscent of ear-

lier eras: "Decent people had better learn now to censor moderately, or the licentiousness released by liberal zealots may arouse their brothers the puritan zealots to censorship by fire." Postage cancellation messages urged citizens to report obscene mail to their postmaster. In Boston, bright yellow bumper stickers called on the motoring public to "FIGHT SMUT."[40]

In an influential two-page feature entitled, "The New Pornography," published in 1965, *Time* magazine declared that while the old pornography had celebrated sex, the current version, as practiced by Burroughs, Genet, Selby, and Rechy, was "a pornography of nausea" and "homosexual nihilism" and was fundamentally antisex. "[J]ust about anything is printable in the U.S. today," *Time* declared. "[A]ll kinds of respectable hardcover books now contain subject matter and language that would have brought police raids only a few years ago." The magazine went on to quote British writer Malcolm Muggeridge, *Partisan Review* editor William Phillips, critics Leslie Fiedler and John Wain, and novelists Saul Bellow and Joseph Heller all expressing various degrees of frustration or dismay with the excesses of contemporary literature.[41]

Even Charles Rembar had second thoughts about what his courtroom victories had wrought. "The current uses of the new freedom are not all to the good," he wrote in 1968. "There is an acne on our culture. Books enter the best-seller lists distinguished only by the fact that once they would have put their publishers in jail. . . . This is indeed a lip-licking, damp-palmed age." (Rembar, of course, did not advocate a return to censorship. The mass culture's obsession with sex would pass, he predicted, as the novelty wore off.)[42]

Alexis de Tocqueville had long ago noted Americans' penchant for forming voluntary societies to achieve their purposes; this impulse manifested itself as the reaction against permissiveness gained momentum. Citizens for Decent Literature, founded in 1957 by Cincinnati attorney Charles H. Keating, Jr., soon had three hundred chapters nationwide. (Years later, Keating would win notoriety as a central figure in the savings and loan scandals of the 1980s. Convicted in both state and federal court on fraud, racketeering, and conspiracy charges after the $3.4 billion collapse of his Lincoln Savings & Loan of Irvine, California, he spent nearly five years in federal prison before his release in 1996. One of Keating's properties seized in the case was the elegant Crescent Hotel resort in Scottsdale, Arizona, where management took pride in its refusal to sell magazines like *Playboy* or to include erotic films among the selection available to guests for viewing in their rooms.) A Churchmen's Committee for Decent Publications sprang up as a Protestant equivalent of the Roman Catholic National Organization for Decent Literature. On the West Coast, the California League Enlisting Action Now (CLEAN) campaigned for a tougher state obscenity law. Another California group sought to remove Eric Partridge's scholarly *Dictionary of American Slang* from public school libraries. (Certain words, it appeared, especially interested inquiring young minds.) In Philadelphia, the police commissioner and school superintendent attended a ceremonial burning of offensive magazines organized by a local minister. In 1965, *Time* magazine reported "a distinct reaction against permissiveness [in the printed word]." A 1969 Gallup poll found that 85 percent of U.S. adults supported "stricter laws on pornography."[43]

Despite the objective reasons for this resurgence of censorship enthusiasm, larger factors entered the picture as well. This latest cycle of America's censorship history unfolded against a background of increasing political and social conflict. Familiar as it is, this larger history merits notice because it was the crucial matrix of the anti-obscenity campaigns of these years. In the later 1950s and early 1960s, civil-rights conflicts and protests against nuclear tests unsettled the deceptive placidity of the Eisenhower years. The African American freedom movement soon spread to the urban North, accompanied by alarming rhetoric by militant blacks. Elvis and rock and roll, James Dean and Marlon Brando, and Beat writers like Allen Ginsberg and Jack Kerouac all challenged the bland surface of 1950s culture. The

sense of deepening unrest accelerated in the mid- and later
1960s as campus antiwar protests escalated. Riots, arson, and
police violence rocked the inner cities, and a highly visible counterculture outraged conservatives and mocked mainstream values. Through its casual sex, pop music, recreational drug use,
unconventional clothing and hair styles, rejection of traditional
religion in favor of New Age mysticism, this counterculture displayed its contempt for "the Establishment" and middle-class
notions of propriety and decorum.

As in the 1920s, the heightened preoccupation with obscenity and censorship cannot be separated from the larger anxieties swirling through a society wracked by political and cultural
conflict. As Judge Curtis Bok had observed in 1949, in the area
of obscenity, "[i]t is the prevailing social consciousness that matters quite as much as the law." Instructed by conservative opinion molders, many Americans became convinced that there was
a clear causal link between the mass culture's explicit treatment
of sex and the broader social and cultural changes they found so
troubling. The British sociologist Alan Hunt, in *Governing
Morals: A Social History of Moral Regulation* (1999), argues that
"crisis tendencies" in societies at particular historical moments
can generate powerful moral-regulation projects that, in turn,
"become arenas in which fierce political and cultural battles are
fought out."[44] The United States from the late 1950s into the
1980s offers a classic instance of this phenomenon. The 1959
Granahan report, for example, while ostensibly about pornography, was in reality a sweeping conservative critique of contemporary American culture. It deplored the "false moral standards"
fostered by prurient paperbacks, and quoted approvingly a
broad-brush condemnation by a Lutheran church body of much
contemporary literature for its "flippant, lewd, low tone toward
marital infidelity," and its view that "sex is for personal enjoy-
ment, a biological necessity like eating and drinking." In such
works, the Lutherans concluded, and the Granahan report
agreed, "[b]asic moral principles of honesty, integrity, forthrightness, purity, respect for authority, and regard for person, life,

property, and good name are ridiculed as antiquated relics of a simple era."[45]

The line between sexual provocation and political radicalism was often blurred in these years. Barney Rosset, whose Grove Press pioneered the new explicitness in print, was also a political leftist who celebrated Fidel Castro and published the 1965 autobiography of Malcolm X, widely reviled in white America for his incendiary pronouncements. Rosset also published books by such radicals as Franz Fanon, Bertolt Brecht, Alain Robbe-Grillet, and LeRoi Jones (Imamu Amiri Baraka). Ralph Ginzburg, jailed in 1972 for publishing the erotic magazine *Eros*, was a Vietnam War opponent who in 1967 joined a movement of writers and editors pledged to withhhold a portion of their federal income taxes as a war protest.[46] Jerry Rubin's *Do It! Scenarios of the Revolution* (Simon & Schuster, 1970), with an introduction by black radical Eldridge Cleaver, combined its attacks on the Vietnam War and corporate "Amerika" with praise of drugs, incessant use of four-letter words, photographs of young women with psychedelically-painted breasts, male protesters urinating in the streets, and flauntingly nude counterculture communards. In one photograph that leaves nothing to the imagination, a naked young woman carries a platter with a pig's head into a political gathering of affluent and well-dressed men and women.

Throughout the years covered in this chapter, many censorship cases involved a complex tangle of issues beyond the overt charge of obscenity, with the sexually transgressive, politically subversive, and culturally outrageous blending into one threatening whole, as in Rubin's *Do It!*. Lillian Smith's *Strange Fruit* of 1944, although prosecuted for obscenity (including its use of the ultimate taboo word *fuck*), was especially vulnerable because the plot involved interracial sex—still an explosive subject in the 1940s.[47] *God's Little Acre*, targeted by the censors in the 1950s for its raunchy sex, also dealt with rural poverty and cultural deviance—unwelcome themes in a decade that prized conformity and celebrated American affluence. As we have seen, the underlying threat posed by Ruth Brown, the Oklahoma librarian dismissed in 1950 for acquiring allegedly "subversive" periodicals, was her outspoken opposition to racial segregation. Fanny Hill, Lady Chatterley, and the eponymous heroine of *Candy* were all sexually autonomous women at a time when soaring divorce rates, premarital sex among the young, and the counterculture's boldly transgressive sexuality were causing intense uneasiness in conservative and religious circles. Terry Southern, widely denounced as a pornographer when the novel *Candy* appeared, also co-authored the screenplay of Stanley Kubrick's 1963 film, *Dr. Strangelove*, a devastating satire of U.S. nuclear policies and the military mind in general. Southern, in turn, wrote a glowing blurb for the paperback edition of William Burroughs' *Naked Lunch*, which was prosecuted (unsuccessfully) for obscenity in Massachusetts and California. He praised it for its "absolutely devastating ridicule of all that is false, primitive, and vicious in current American life: the abuses of power, hero worship, aimless violence, materialistic obsession, intolerance, and every form of hypocrisy."[48] On both sides of the cultural divide, talking about books became a way of talking about America.

Clive Barnes of the *New York Times* noted that of all the late-1960s plays featuring nudity, the one singled out for prosecution was Lennox Raphael's *Ché*, which combined sexual explicitness with a ferocious attack on U.S. government policies. The play opened at the Free Store Theater in Manhattan on March 22, 1969, and closed two days later when the police arrested the entire cast. Barnes further observed that the underground press, a major conduit of New Left and counterculture perspectives, often combined "lightweight obscenity with heavyweight political opinion." "It would be a bad day for America if these papers were banned," he commented. "We need dissent—it is part of the pattern of democracy. And if this dissent comes in packages that we do not always find acceptable to our taste, we must remember that it is more honorable, and democratically more useful, to honor dissent rather than ban it."[49]

The intersection of rising censorship pressures with deeper social and political issues is vividly illustrated in the case of Newton Arvin, a professor of American literature at Smith College, and 1951 winner of a National Book Award for his biography of Herman Melville. Arvin was an active homosexual (Truman Capote was an early lover), but like other gays in the 1950s, revealed his sexual orientation only to a few intimates. On September 2, 1960, however, five Massachusetts state policemen raided Arvin's apartment in Northampton; combed through his possessions; and seized some mildly erotic male beefcake magazines of the type the Supreme Court would clear in the *Manual Enterprises* case two years later. The raid was led by John ("Dirty Pictures") Regan, an Irish-Catholic officer in charge of a special unit charged with enforcing a recent Massachusetts statute criminalizing the possession of "obscene pictures" with the intent of showing them to others. The Massachusetts law, in turn, was inspired by a campaign by President Eisenhower's postmaster general, former Chevrolet-dealer Arthur Summerfield, against "pornographic filth in the family mailbox." The media, trumpeting details of the Arvin raid, quickly exposed his sexual orientation and the "sex ring" he allegedly led at Smith. "Suspect's Diary Studied for Clues to Smut Traffic," brayed the *Boston Herald*. Passing along gossip supplied by Regan, who was an avid publicity hound, newspapers described "orgies" in Arvin's apartment. While this case ostensibly concerned obscenity, cultural anxieties about homosexuality lurked near the surface.

So, too, did Cold War anticommunist fears. Arvin had been a political radical in the 1920s and 1930s, and in 1954 had been among a group of five Smith professors denounced by alumna Aloise Heath, the older sister of rising conservative superstar William F. Buckley, Jr. In a letter to several thousand Smith alumnae, Heath charged that Arvin and the others "have been or are presently affiliated with many organizations cited as Communist or Communist-front . . . by the Committee on Un-American Activities." Although the Department of Justice reported "nothing of interest" in Arvin's file, two members of the Massachusetts

Committee to Investigate Communism, an official body, had traveled to Northampton and interrogated Arvin under oath.

Seven men were arrested following the Arvin raid, including several of his younger colleagues at Smith and young academics at other Massachusetts schools. (Upset by the surprise raid, Arvin had named names.) All were convicted and received suspended sentences. In some cases, the damage to their careers and psyches was severe. "We caused a lot of goddamn misery," Regan's top aide, Gerald Crowley, would later concede. Arvin was dismissed by Smith (on an "early retirement" arrangement at half pay), and after an interval at Northampton State Hospital, gradually resumed the threads of his career. He died of cancer in 1963.[50]

Harry Clor, a political science professor at Kenyon College, also illustrates the links between the 1960s censorship debate and the turmoil of the era in his 1969 study, *Obscenity and Public Morality: Censorship in a Liberal Society*. This thoughtful critique of the Supreme Court's position on obscenity was also clearly a conservative response to the larger crisis of the day. The political scientist and legal scholar C. Herman Pritchett of the University of California at Santa Barbara set the tone in his foreword. Asserting that "the current flooding of book stalls, mails, and movie theaters with pornography or near pornography raises major problems of public policy," and seeking a middle way between the "extreme libertarians and the extreme moralists," Pritchett called for "an intelligent and restrained use of controls [that] can promote public standards of civility essential to our democracy." The last phrase is a key to the book. For Clor, as for Pritchett, the restoration of "public standards of civility" was the urgent priority, with an "intelligent and restrained" censorship a step toward this larger goal. Censorship is essential if society is to uphold standards of decorum and defend itself against the forces of disintegration, Clor argued, but it must be conducted "in such a way that real moral evils are attacked, genuine literature is protected, and community convictions are respected." Under this standard, he contended, obvious pornography such as *Fanny Hill*, "some of the more lurid sensationalist tabloids and 'exploitation films,' " and "some of the writings of Mickey Spillane" (the author of hardboiled detective novels featuring fairly explicit sex and extreme violence, such as *I the Jury* of 1947) would fail the test. Rejecting the "contemporary community standards" approach as an evasion of judicial responsibility, Clor argued that the courts must forthrightly recognize that "[o]bscenity can contribute to the debasement of moral standards and ultimately of character," and make decisions accordingly.[51]

Writing as the headlines screamed of protest marches, the assassination of public figures, inner-city rioting, the collapse of the Johnson presidency, and police brutality at the 1968 Democratic convention, Clor readily conceded that in focusing on censorship, he was really addressing what seemed to him a desperate threat to the survival of civil society itself. "The problem of obscenity . . . has much in common with many of the issues that we face," he wrote, and concluded earnestly:

> The dilemma of Vietnam will be resolved, one way or another; someday we will be free of it. But the dilemma of free expression, public morality, and the law will not be resolved; we will not be free of it someday. This is a pervasive and permanent problem of civilized society. The controversies and opposing attitudes . . . associated with this problem reflect fundamental controversies of political life and typical alternative political postures within liberal democracy. Do we not see how the libertarian and the moderate democrat confront each other today on so many battlefronts, present and potential? Do we not see reflected in so many of these battles those underlying issues concerning the functions of law, the importance of public standards, and the prerequisites and limits of liberty? Serious exploration of the problem of obscenity and the law can contribute to our understanding of much more than that problem.[52]

As the 1960s wore on, the increasing support for censorship that was given voice by Harry Clor and others, and rooted in the larger history of this turbulent decade, soon found expression at the national political and judicial level. The 1964 Republican Party platform pledged "enactment of legislation, despite Democratic opposition, to curb the flow through our

mails of obscene material which has flourished into a multi-
million dollar obscenity racket." In the 1968 presidential contest, amid the distraction of domestic unrest, assassinations,
and Vietnam War protests, Republican candidate Richard
Nixon, campaigning in California, found time to call for
tougher obscenity laws and to accuse the Cub Scouts of selling
their mailing lists to pornographers. (The Boy Scouts of America vehemently denied the charge.) By 1969, the year Clor's
book appeared (and the year when nudity on stage and screen
appears to have peaked, if such things can be quantified),
eleven U.S. senators, 124 Congressmen, and four governors,
together with three university presidents, the New York City
superintendent of schools, and an array of bishops and other
notables had signed on as honorary members of Charles Keating's Citizens for Decent Literature.[53]

Ginzburg *to* Miller: *Growing Judicial Repressiveness,
Pornography-Commission Battles.* The Supreme Court, too,
proved sensitive to the surge of public concern about obscenity. As early as 1966, on the same day it cleared *Fanny Hill*, the
court in *Ginzburg* v. *United States* reached a quite different
conclusion that foreshadowed a conservative shift on censorship issues.[54] The case involved the appeal of a five-year prison
sentence imposed by New York courts on the flamboyant
Ralph Ginzburg, publisher of the magazine *Eros* (launched in
1962), as well as an allegedly autobiographical book, *The
Housewife's Handbook on Selective Promiscuity*, and a
newsletter, *Liaison. Eros*, a glossy periodical bound in hard
covers and selling for ten dollars a copy, featured erotic paintings, photographs, stories, and poems, and articles on various
topics. In Charles Rembar's words, it "combined elements of
Playboy, Captain Billy's Whiz Bang, and *American Heritage*,
and suggested the coffee table at least as much as the bed
table."[55] Early issues included reproductions of Hindu temple
carvings; Correggio's "Venus and Cupid"; Hogarth's comic en-

gravings of a before-and-after seduction scene; poems by the Earl of Rochester; a Maupassant story set in a brothel, illustrated by Degas; a photo essay by Garry Winograd of couples embracing in the subway; and Mark Twain's ribald *1601; or Conversation as It Was by the Social Fireside in the Time of the Tudors*. Among the articles were an essay on the blues by jazz critic Nat Hentoff and "We All Love Jack [Kennedy]" by TV personality Faye Emerson. (One issue, significantly, included a nude art photograph of a black man and a white woman embracing.) A sense of humor was much in evidence, including a selection of ads for virility restorers from nineteenth-century magazines; the inventor's description and alarmingly detailed drawing of a "male chastity belt" patented in 1897; and "Mother Goose Censored," in which innocent words were blacked out, leaving the mind free to imagine all kinds of indecencies. (In the first issue of *Liaison*, insisting that he would never publish taboo words "merely to titillate gross palates *à la* Henry Miller," Ginzburg helpfully appended a list of the words that he promised never ever to use.)⁵⁶

Postal authorities, alerted to *Eros* by Congresswoman Kathryn Granahan (who had conducted her own pornography hearings in 1959), and under direct instructions from President Kennedy's postmaster general, J. Edward Day, prosecuted Ginzburg for violating the Comstock Law. A federal district judge in Philadelphia sentenced Ginzburg to five years in prison and imposed a $42,000 fine; the U.S. Court of Appeals affirmed the conviction. To general surprise, the Supreme Court, too, upheld Ginzburg's conviction, by a five-to-four vote, on the grounds that his promotional techniques had involved "the sordid business of pandering." Documenting the "brazenness" of Ginzburg's methods, the justices solemnly described his efforts to mail promotional material for *Eros* from such places as Middlesex, New Jersey; Blue Balls, Montana; and Intercourse, Pennsylvania—a hamlet in Amish country.⁵⁷ (Another nearby town is Paradise, and a local joke has it that you must go through Intercourse to get to Paradise.) Ginzburg's fatal error, it seemed, was not in publishing erotica, but in doing so with flair and a sense of humor.

The Ginzburg ruling made little sense in terms of recent Court decisions. As we have seen, in *Manual Enterprises* the Court had moved away from the judgmental "prurience" test toward a flexible "contemporary community standards" rule; now in *Ginzburg*, the "prurience" test returned as a denunciation of Ginzburg's "pandering" advertising. Adopting Earl Warren's argument in the *Roth/Alberts* case, the Court now held that the circumstances of promotion can render legally obscene a work that would otherwise enjoy First Amendment protection. The justices' pose of shock at Ginzburg's promotional techniques was particularly bizarre in an advertising culture notorious for using sex to sell everything from cars to beer. Indeed, in the *Lady Chatterley* case, to illustrate the pervasiveness of erotica in contemporary culture, Charles Rembar had introduced ads from recent issues of *Life*, *Look*, and the *Saturday Evening Post*, as well as a cigarette advertising poster, featuring sensuously posed women.[58]

To jail Ralph Ginzburg while on the same day clearing *Fanny Hill*, wrote Yale law professor Alexander Bickel, left obscenity law an "utter shambles." Short of a "broadly permissive constitutional rule," which the public would not tolerate, he concluded, "there is no coherent and consistent constitutional principle on which to rest judicial judgment." The four dissenting justices (Black, Harlan, Douglas, and Stewart) heartily agreed. Harlan called the majority opinion "an astonishing piece of judicial improvisation." To uphold Ginzburg's conviction on the basis of his "pandering" advertising was to create a new crime not found in any statute. In fact, he went on, the "pandering" charge was "a mere euphemism for allowing punishment of a person who mails otherwise constitutionally protected material just because a jury or a judge may not find him or his business agreeable." Justice Stewart was even more eloquent, finding Orwellian implications in the majority decision. "[T]he First Amendment protects us all with an even hand," he wrote. "It applies to Ralph Ginzburg with no less completeness than to G. P. Putnam's Sons [the publisher of *Fanny Hill*]. In upholding and enforcing the Bill of Rights this Court has no power to pick or choose. When we lose sight of that fixed star of constitutional adjudication, we lose our way. For we then forsake a government of law and are left with government of Big Brother." The *Nation* simply found the ruling "beyond comprehension." A few weeks later, the court's newest member, Abe Fortas, having voted to uphold Ginzburg's conviction, confessed to his fellow justice William Douglas, "I think I was wrong." He had, Fortas said, been "[s]ubconsciously . . . affected by [Ginzburg's] slimy qualities." "Well, live and learn," he added philosophically. On February 17, 1972, having exhausted the appeals process, Ginzburg, as prisoner #38124-134, entered Allenwood penitentiary, a minimum-security federal prison near Lewisburg, Pennsylvania. Together with a former congressional legislative aide convicted of conspiracy, bribery, and forgery, he was assigned to organize and file prisoners' records. (He seized the opportunity to smuggle out extra copies of his mug shot—see illustration.) Only weekly visits from his wife and monthly visits with his children broke the tedium. He served eight months, until his parole on October 10, 1972. Abandoning the risky arena of erotica, he devoted his energies to a new venture, *Moneysworth*, a magazine of consumer financial advice he had launched in 1970. It quickly attracted 2.4 million subscribers, replenishing his own finances depleted by years of litigation.[59]

The Ginzburg case and confessions such as that of Fortas underscore how little obscenity law follows the more typical judicial process of what is for the most part a rational development based on precedent and generally agreed-upon principles and concepts. Even more than most, this area of legal history must be approached with continual attention to social context and shifts in public opinion. Ever-more-precise legal definitions of the obscene are always subject to upset as prevailing attitudes change. In few other areas, perhaps, does the law remain so close to its roots in the raw feelings of the social group. Prose-

cutor Richard Kuh made the point forcefully in his 1967 study
of sex censorship, *Foolish Figleaves?* Nowhere else in the criminal law, he wrote,

> are the public emotions on each side so strong, so widely
> shared, and so persistent as they are concerning obscenity
> and censorship; in none have the words of the statutes
> proven so inadequate; in none has the impact of the United
> States Constitution remained so uncertain despite so many
> rulings from our nation's highest Court; and in none do the
> decisions of the judges throughout America so unrelent-
> ingly defy consistency.[60]

This is not to suggest that legal formulas are irrelevant, or
that the celebrated "landmark cases" are unimportant. Precedent plays some role, of course, and as these rulings themselves
enter the stream of cultural discourse, they help mold public attitudes. But in the shadow land of obscenity law, where judges
looking at the same materials and applying the same statutes and
precedents regularly arrive at wildly different conclusions, the
legal picture can change abruptly in response to shifting social,
cultural, and political realities.

If one turns from the legal realm to the larger mid-1960s
context—vehement denunciations of obscenity, attacks on judicial "permissiveness," a rising tempo of civic unrest and cultural
conflict—*Ginzburg* becomes more comprehensible. Alexander
Bickel noted that with this ruling, the Supreme Court signaled
"a concerted, collective change of attitude, a hardening of attitude."[61] Ginzburg himself provided evidence of the surly public
mood that lay behind the court's harsh action. In the advance
publicity for *Eros*, he had sent out three million brochures announcing a new magazine "devoted to the joy of love and sex."[62]
The mailing, which included a prepaid subscription postcard,
produced a deluge of some ten thousand unsolicited responses
including handwritten missives deploring vice and obscenity;
formally typed letters informing Ginzburg that the authorities
had been alerted to his plans; scrawled notes on the return post-

card spewing hate. In the second issue of *Eros*, before turning the whole mass over to Alfred Kinsey's sex-research institute at Indiana University, Ginzberg reprinted some fifty of these responses, of which the following are typical:

"Thank God there's a real man like Senator Kefauver in Washington to take care of bastards like you."

"Since you seem to believe so strongly in free speech, you won't mind if I tell you to take this worthless shit and jam it up your ass!"

"Keep your wretchedness for those who have never known the saving grace of Jesus Christ."

"Your filthy trash should put you in prison. If I lived in New York, I'd come personally to your office and spit in your face for insulting the public with your filthy mail."

"Persons who sell literature of this type are . . . similar in moral level to those who traffic in heroin and certain rock-and-roll music."

"Without doubt the most *diabolical, vulgar, indecent, immoral*, and *devilish* magazine ever conceived by the evil mind of Satan's Chosen People."

"Everyone I know of who received your insulting offer is up in arms. They are bombarding their Congressmen and Senators to protest your vile action. They will keep on until they obtain a reversal of the laws."

"It was predictable that a magazine like *Eros* would be the product of a cheap, lousy, rotten Hebe."[63]

Both civil libertarians and anti-obscenity crusaders quickly grasped that *Ginzburg* signaled a significant shift in the court's position. The *New Republic* called it "a grim day in the temple of justice." Charles Keating of Citizens for Decent Literature, writing in his newsletter, *The National Decency Reporter*, called *Ginzburg* "a major defeat for the smut industry," and exulted: "Now we are on the offensive. We intend the attack to be as brutal and unremitting as was the attack on society by pornographers in pushing their stuff. We will have no regard as to whom, what, or where. We have the weapon—the law." Even the *New York Times*, generally strong on First Amendment issues, commented only that justice had been meted out to "an entrepreneur in a disreputable business who took his chances on the borderline of the law and lost."[64]

Politicians got into the act in October 1967, when the heavily Democratic Ninetieth Congress, perhaps tired of Republican charges that Democrats were soft on pornography, declared "the traffic in obscenity and pornography . . . a matter of national concern," and called for a presidential Commission on Obscenity and Pornography to study the problem and make recommendations "to regulate the flow of such traffic without interfering with constitutional rights." A conservative Democratic senator, John McClellan of Arkansas, introduced the motion.[65]

The resulting eighteen-member commission, appointed by President Lyndon B. Johnson, was chaired by William B. Lockhart, dean of the University of Minnesota law school. Other members included psychiatrists, sociologists, California's attorney general, a Catholic priest, a Methodist minister, and a rabbi. The gender breakdown was fifteen men and three women. (President Richard Nixon, filling a vacancy, appointed one member in 1969: Charles H. Keating, Jr.) With a budget that eventually exceeded $2 million, the commissioners appointed an executive director (W. Cody Wilson, a 1961 Harvard Ph.D. in social psychology), a general counsel, an administrative officer, a nine-member professional staff, and a ten-member support staff. Public hearings were held, and four subpanels reviewed the legal record and the research literature, including studies by social scientists. In one study conducted under commission auspices, twenty-three male university students were exposed to sexually explicit materials and their responses measured by means of a thermometer attached to the right earlobe; a photoplethysmograph attached to the left earlobe to gauge blood flow, a chest device to measure respiration, and a mercury-filled rubber tube capped with electrodes slipped over the penis. (Whether this technological arsenal in itself was likely to increase or diminish the subjects' sexual response, quite apart from the pornography, remained a disputed point.)[66]

The commission's 700-page report appeared in 1970. Initially, it seemed to offer a soothing balm to a society trapped in bitter divisions, including angry differences over censorship and obscenity. Citing studies discounting allegations that pornography posed a grave national problem, it found "no evidence that exposure to or use of explicit sexual materials play a significant role in the causation of social or individual harms such as crime, delinquency, sexual or nonsexual deviancy or severe emotional disturbances." The increase of sexually explicit materials in the culture, it said, was a byproduct of larger and generally healthy changes in sexual behavior and attitudes. Commenting on the proliferation of citizen-action groups, the report found that they often lacked knowledge of the law; assumed that their restrictive views were more widely shared than they were; had little impact on the flow of sexually explicit materials; and were mainly of symbolic importance in giving citizens a way to "demonstrate . . . support for an enduring set of basic values in the face of threatened change." Discussing the campaigns by such groups to influence publishers, broadcasters, and moviemakers, the commission said: "It is very possible that self-regulation, often reinforced by pressures from a vigilant minority, not only . . . [reduces the volume of] material deemed offensive, but also inhibits experimentation with new ideas, dampens response to social change, and limits the sources of cultural variety."[67]

Having made these points, the commission recommended that "federal, state, and local legislation should not seek to interfere with the right of adults who wish to do so to read, obtain, or view explicit sexual materials." (It did recommend the retention of laws banning the sale of sexually explicit pictorial representations to minors without parental permission, as well as restrictions on the public display or unsolicited mailing of such materials.) In the therapeutic mode characteristic of late-twentieth-century social prescriptions by the "helping professions," the commission declared: "A large majority of sex educators and

counselors are of the opinion that most adolescents are interested in explicit sexual materials, and that this interest is a product of natural curiosity about sex. They also feel that if adolescents had access to adequate information regarding sex, through
appropriate sex education, their interest in pornography would
be reduced." In this spirit, the report recommended "a massive
sex education effort . . . to contribute to healthy attitudes and
orientations to sexual relationships so as to provide a sound
foundation for our society's basic institutions of marriage and
family . . . [and] an acceptance of sex as a normal and natural
part of life and of oneself as a sexual being."[68]

Any hopes the commission had of lowering the decibel
level of the obscenity debate and blunting the growing calls for
censorship proved sadly misplaced. By 1970, Richard Nixon was
in the White House and the political climate was turning increasingly conservative. In these circumstances, the report simply added fuel to the fire. Six of the commissioners refused to
sign it. Three—California attorney general Thomas Lynch,
Rabbi Irving Lehrman of Miami Beach, and South Dakota educator Cathryn Spelts—supported much of the report, but found
the research data insufficient to justify any wholesale repeal of
obscenity laws. Three others, however—Charles H. Keating, Jr.;
the Rev. Morton Hill, S.J., head of Morality in Media; and Rev.
Winfrey C. Link, manager of a Methodist retirement home in
Tennessee—went much further by issuing a stinging minority
report that blasted the majority's recommendations as "a Magna
Carta for the pornographer." The pervasiveness of sexually oriented material posed a grave national danger, they insisted, and
obscenity laws, far from being repealed, should be tightened.[69]

Charles Keating, having refused even to participate in the
commission's deliberations, not only concurred in the minority report, but also issued a separate denunciation of his own. Bristling
with quotations from Arnold Toynbee, psychoanalyst Bruno Bet-
telheim, sociologist Pitirim Sorokin, and novelist Marcel Proust
("Oh, the stream of hell that undermined my adolescence"), Keating's denunciation of the majority report ridiculed the commis-

sion's staff and insisted on the gravity of the obscenity problem. "[O]ur nation is imperiled by a poison which is all-pervasive," he proclaimed. "Credit the American public with enough common sense to know that one who wallows in filth is going to get dirty. This is intuitive knowledge. Those who spend millions of dollars to tell us otherwise must be malicious or misguided, or both." The "shocking and anarchistic" proposal to repeal all anti-obscenity laws affecting consenting adults, he thundered, was a formula for "moral anarchy!"[70]

For good measure, Keating added the damning fact that chairman William Lockhart had once belonged to the ACLU and had criticized censorship in published essays. Dismissing judges' efforts to move beyond specific words and phrases in defining the obscene, he declared: "If courts are to merit the confidence of our citizens, it can no longer be pretended that four-letter-word substitutes for fecal matter and copulation are not obscene merely by veiling them with such hocus-pocus phrasing as 'redeeming social value' and the like."[71]

All told, the dissenters' inflammatory comments, complete with attachments and appendices, took up some 250 pages, or well over one-third of the total report. President Nixon, for his part, contemptuously dismissed the majority report as "morally bankrupt." Vice President Spiro T. Agnew, still three years from his resignation in disgrace, declared: "As long as Richard Nixon is President, Main Street is not going to turn into Smut Alley." The Senate, in a rare moment of near-unanimity, voted sixty to five on a motion introduced by Senator McClellan to reject the report. Declared Senator Robert Griffin of Michigan: "The Commission's report should be tossed into the trash can along with all the foul and corrupting pornographic material that it would make available to the public." The conservative American Enterprise Institute issued a hostile analysis focusing especially on weakness and contradictions in the research data. (The commission cited polling data, for example, showing *both* that 60 percent of Americans believed that "adults should be allowed to read or see any explicit sexual materials that they want to" *and* that 73 percent of

Americans believed that gratuitous sexual scenes in movies should "definitely not be allowed.")[72]

The critic Clive Barnes, introducing a paperback edition of the report, offered a mixed assessment. He detected among censorship advocates confusion between pornography, which he agreed should be suppressed, and eroticism, which should be cherished: "Eroticism is to the artist the expression of a very precious part of life. The artist's intention is not pornography but truth. Eroticism is woven into the web of his words and offered as part of life." On the other hand, Barnes warned that cultural production was increasingly dominated by "a comparatively small group of highly sophisticated men in New York, Los Angeles, and London" whose standards "may well . . . diverge from those of the nation as a whole." Artists should not be subjected to censorship, he continued, "but neither should they imagine that their own standards of taste are universal. To impose such standards unilaterally without concern or regard for the audience, savors rather nastily of fascism. Our arts must be free, but they also must be careful."[73] Overall, an effort to call a truce in the censorship wars through sweet reason and social science objectivity had simply widened the cultural divide and made the debate more rancorous than ever.

Three years after the Obscenity and Pornography Commission fiasco, the Supreme Court's shift toward a more repressive position on obscenity, already evident in the 1966 *Ginzburg* decision, emerged with stark clarity when, on June 21, 1973, the Court upheld, in a series of five-to-four decisions, lower-court convictions in five separate obscenity cases. The Court now had a new and more conservative chief justice, Nixon-nominee Warren Burger, and three other conservative justices chosen by Nixon (Harry Blackmun, Lewis Powell, and William Rehnquist). First Amendment absolutist Hugo Black had died in 1971. These shifts proved decisive: the majority in each case consisted of the four Nixon appointees plus Byron White, a Kennedy appointee.

While the cases differed among themselves and generated a variety of opinions, the net effect was to slow if not reverse a forty-year judicial liberalizing trend on obscenity cases. The key

case, in terms of obscenity law, was *Miller* v. *California*, involving
a sexually explicit film, four books (*Intercourse, Man-Woman, Sex
Orgies Illustrated*, and *An Illustrated History of Pornography*),
and unsolicited advertisements featuring explicit pictures and
drawings.[74] Writing for the majority, Chief Justice Burger rejected the "utterly without redeeming social value" test established in *Roth/Alberts* and invoked in the *Lady Chatterley* and
Fanny Hill cases. Such a rule, he declared, imposed on prosecutors "a burden almost impossible to discharge under our criminal
standards of proof." (For Hugo Black and other civil libertarians,
of course, this "almost impossible" burden was precisely what
prosecutors *should* face in First Amendment cases.) Instead,
Burger substituted an easier test: to be found obscene, a work
"taken as a whole" must lack "serious literary, artistic, political, or
scientific value."[75]

In a second important move, the *Miller* decision redefined
the rule that to be found obscene, a work must violate "contemporary community standards." In *Roth/Alberts* and *Manual Enterprises*, the Court had implicitly understood this to mean a *national* standard. In *Miller*, however, Burger called the idea of a
national standard an "abstract formulation" and dismissed any
effort to establish one as "unrealistic." Instead, picking up on
Justice Harlan's argument in *Roth/Alberts*, he said that "contemporary community standards" could mean state or presumably even local standards. Nixon administration officials intent
on combating obscenity quickly took advantage of the narrowed
definition of "community standards" in *Miller*, and initiated
cases in conservative local jurisdictions. In one notorious instance, for example, federal officials in 1975 intercepted a ship-
ment of allegedly obscene materials being mailed from California to New York, and secured a conviction in Louisiana. The
Supreme Court declined to review the conviction.[76]

Burger's passionately argued opinion, endorsed by four
other justices, illustrates yet again the way amorphous concerns
over disturbing cultural changes and social problems influence
attitudes toward obscenity. Simply noting the ways it modified
earlier definitions of the obscene does not capture the emotional

intensity of Burger's ruling in *Miller* v. *California*, and thus its larger cultural significance. The opinion reveals Burger's anger and dismay, which he shared with many other Americans, toward the threatening cultural changes that seemed to be rushing the entire nation at headlong speed toward some kind of precipice. Even if "the 'sexual revolution' of recent years" had served a beneficial purpose in breaking down excessive prudery, said the chief justice, this was no excuse for tolerating pornography. Pursuing his comparison of pornography and healthy sexual candor, he managed to bring in the issue of illicit drugs: "[C]ivilized people do not allow unregulated access to heroin because it is a derivative of medicinal morphine." Figuratively shaking a finger at Broadway producers, Hollywood filmmakers, and publishers of erotica, Burger declared: "Sex and nudity may not be exploited without limit by films or pictures exhibited or sold in places of public accommodation any more than live sex and nudity can be exhibited or sold without limit in such public places."[77]

Displaying a disappointing unawareness of the first edition of *Purity in Print* (published five years earlier), Burger claimed to find "no evidence, empirical or historical, that the stern 19th century American censorship of public distribution and display of material relating to sex . . . in any way limited or affected expression of serious literary, artistic, political, or scientific ideas." In another sweeping obiter dictum, he added: "To equate the free and robust exchange of ideas and political debate with commercial exploitation of obscene material demeans the grand conception of the First Amendment and its high purpose in the historic struggle for freedom."[78] This high-sounding pronouncement blurred the fact that apart from the 1950s cases involving the Smith Act, the key First Amendment rulings of recent decades had dealt not with the "robust exchange of ideas and political debate," but with sexual material. Critics quickly pointed out that historically it has been cases involving publications that many people found deeply repugnant or disgusting that have elicited the landmark First Amendment decisions. Obscenity cases that reach the Supreme Court are not popularity contests, but occasions to explore the meaning and risks of freedom. As Hugo Black observed in *Dennis* v. *U.S.*, "'safe' or orthodox views . . . rarely need protection."

In *Kaplan* v. *California*, another of the cases decided on June 21, 1973, the Supreme Court upheld a jury's conviction of Murray Kaplan, a Los Angeles bookstore proprietor, for selling a sexually explicit work called *Suite 69* to an undercover police officer. In this case (reminiscent of the Dunster House Book-shop case of 1929, which also involved entrapment), the Court explicitly rejected expert testimony as irrelevant. Burger, again writing the majority opinion, acknowledged that books "[seem] to have a different and preferred place in our hierarchy of values," but saw no reason to grant constitutional protection to the specific book in question. Evoking nineteenth-century judicial opinions that had justified censorship on the grounds that innocent youth might be corrupted, Burger wrote: "For good or ill, a book has a continuing life. It is passed hand to hand, and we can take note of the tendency of widely circulated books of this category to reach the impressionable young and have a continuing impact."[79]

Hammering home their new get-tough approach to obscenity, the five-member majority on that same day, in *Paris Adult Theatre I* v. *Slaton*, upheld the conviction of the operators of an adult theater in Atlanta. In another blistering opinion, Chief Justice Burger cited approvingly the minority's views in the 1970 pornography-commission report, and insisted that the constitutional right of privacy, newly articulated in the abortion decision *Roe* v. *Wade*, did not protect the operators of a movie theater. In more nostalgia-inducing Victorian language, Burger denounced obscenity's "corrupting and debasing" power, and insisted on the courts' duty to protect "the weak, the uninformed, the unsuspecting, and the gullible from the exercise of their own volition." So grave was the danger, he asserted, that lawmakers had a right to assume a connection between obscenity and a host of undesirable consequences even in the absence of evidence, and

judges should defer to their opinions. Echoing Harry Clor's
themes of 1969, Burger wrote:

> The sum of experience, including that of the past two de-
> cades, affords an ample basis for legislatures to conclude
> that a sensitive, key relationship of human existence, cen-
> tral to family life, community welfare, and the development
> of human personality, can be debased and distorted by
> crass commercial exploitation of sex. Nothing in the Con-
> stitution prohibits a State from reaching such a conclusion
> and acting on it legislatively simply because there is no con-
> clusive evidence or empirical data.[80]

In an equally impassioned dissent, Justice Brennan, joined
by Potter Stewart and Thurgood Marshall, warned that the majority's direction gravely jeopardized First Amendment freedom.[81]
These rulings elicited an array of commentary reflecting the
cultural divisions of the day. To William F. Buckley, Jr., they simply
meant that "a commerce in pornography and obscenity" existed,
and that "it was never a commitment of the First Amendment to
protect that commerce against legislation by a self-ruling people."
Liberals, civil libertarians, publishers, librarians, and persons in the
media, by contrast, expressed dismay. "These rulings set the
United States of America back twenty years," declared one columnist.[82] The shift from national to local "community standards," critics warned, would encourage censors to "shop around" and institute selective prosecutions in particularly conservative localities.
The *New York Times*, speaking for a cosmopolitan publishing and
culture-production center (and striking a note quite different from
its blasé response to Ralph Ginzburg's conviction seven years earlier), warned that the *Miller* decision made "every local community
and every state the arbiter of acceptability, thereby adjusting all
sex-related literary, artistic, and entertainment productions to the
lowest common denominator of toleration." What constituted a
"community" for censorship purposes, asked *Publisher's Weekly*,
"the state? the city? the town? the block?"[83]
        Again, historical context is crucial. In the years leading up
to these 1973 rulings and the tight-lipped anger so evident in

Chief Justice Burger's majority opinions, the cultural reaction against the antiwar protesters, the inner-city rioters, and the counter-culture rebels had coalesced into a powerful political movement. Alabama's racist governor, George Wallace, moving northward from his southern base, had exploited the resentments of millions of white lower middle class and blue-collar ethnics, while Richard Nixon had won the presidency in 1968 by appealing to a disaffected "silent majority." The religious right, mobilized by Jerry Falwell and other televangelists, would soon coalesce around Falwell's Moral Majority as a "pro-life, pro-family, pro-moral, and pro-America" conservative movement. The *Ginzburg*, *Miller*, *Kaplan*, and *Paris Theatre* rulings, as well as the ferocious repudiation of the 1970 obscenity-commission report, unfolded amidst this sea change in public attitudes.

From the 1920s through the mid-1960s, a slowly increasing acceptance of erotic themes and even explicit sexual descriptions in print, with a concomitant extension of First Amendment protection to books and periodicals once considered beyond the pale, reflected the nation's greater cultural and social diversity and a growing cosmopolitanism linked to urbanization and the spread of the mass culture. By the same token, the recrudescence of censorship sentiment that crested in the early 1970s reflected larger trends as well: not only the sheer volume and greater explicitness of sexually oriented books, magazines, plays, and films—though this was certainly a factor—but also the troubled response to urban riots, racial conflict, assassinations, bitter divisions over Vietnam, radical critiques of consumer capitalism, and the rejection of middle-class values by a highly visible sector of privileged middle-class youth. All these developments provoked a cultural turmoil that added a sharp edge of urgency to the debate over obscenity and pornography. (Even the words themselves became weapons in the culture wars of the era: the bombing and killing in Vietnam and Cambodia and the sacrifice of thousands of American lives by the Johnson and Nixon administrations was the real "obscenity" of these years, the war's opponents would charge; TV images of maimed children and burning villages the real "pornography."[84]) From this perspective, as Harry Clor observed in 1969, court rulings in obscenity cases became important not only in themselves, but as indicators of larger tectonic shifts and stress points in the culture.

As I have tried to show in this chapter, in the three decades from 1945 through the mid-1970s, public attitudes and legal rulings in the U.S. relating to censorship followed two interrelated and partially contradictory trajectories. On the one hand, through the mid-1960s the courts, and to a more limited extent the public at large, grew more tolerant of cultural material dealing with sex, and more willing to extend First Amendment protection to a wider range of materials. In response, the volume and explicitness of such material entering the cultural mainstream increased exponentially. Simultaneously, a counter-trend of repressiveness, present throughout the period, grew in momentum from the mid-1960s on, culminating in the Supreme Court decisions we have just examined. This did not mean, of course, that the legal situation after 1973 simply reverted to what it had been decades earlier. The liberalizing trend expressed in the *Ulysses*, *Roth/Alberts*, *Lady Chatterley*, *Fanny Hill*, and *Manual Enterprises* rulings (and others at lower court levels) remained powerful. And despite the fulminations of censorship advocates like Charles Keating, and the willingness of citizens to vent their repressive impulses to public-opinion pollsters, the broad current of opinion in a more diverse and cosmopolitan America, even in the 1970s, at least grudgingly accepted a far more capacious view of what was acceptable, or tolerable, in print than had been true in, say, the 1920s.

Nevertheless, as the 1970s ended, the Supreme Court's greater tolerance of censorship, coupled with continued worries within the general public—inflamed by the religious right— about the growing cultural visibility of pornography and obscenity, guaranteed that this issue would not soon fade. Indeed, it would remain very much alive in the years that followed, although, as we shall see, the censors' targets, the location of the battles, and the alignment of forces would all undergo some surprising changes.

ELEVEN

1980 to the Present

Symbolic Crusades, Embattled Libraries,
Feminist Interventions, New Technologies

The resurgence of censorship pressures that began in the later
1960s intensified in the 1970s and beyond. But simply to speak
of periodic "waves" of censorship, or a "cyclical pattern" of repressive outbursts suggesting a mechanical process like the
swing of a pendulum, is, as sociologist Alan Hunt reminds us,
misleading and simplistic.[1] In fact, the upsurge of repressiveness
at century's end differed markedly from what had gone before,
reflecting the particular political, cultural, and technological realities of these years.

Foremost among these realities was the conservative political resurgence that culminated in Ronald Reagan's election as president in 1980, and the culture wars that ensued. Reagan's victory laid the groundwork for another federal pornography study, very different in tone from the 1970 report. The Reagan-era study, personally initiated by President Reagan and carried out under the auspices of Attorney General Edwin Meese, was released in 1986. In the manner of such reports, it cited various studies, testimony by citizens who showed up at its three hundred hours of hearings in various cities, and the views of interested organizations to buttress a predetermined conclusion. One member was James C. Dobson, founder of the conservative action group Focus on the Family. The report endorsed and added fuel to the censorship demands that had been building for years, and warned that a vast outpouring of pornography threatened the foundations of society. Wading into a particularly murky area, it cited clinical studies that, in its view, demonstrated beyond doubt that pornography, especially of a sexually violent nature, causes criminal or harmful behavior. Significantly, however, the report did not call for any extension of the legal tests of the obscene, and in fact, argued that the First Amendment should protect the printed word in all cases. "There remains a difference between reading a book and looking at pictures, even pictures printed on a page," it noted.[2] Despite the Supreme Court's repressive turn and the conservative political climate, decades of liberalizing court rulings and the emergence of new visual and electronic technologies, had clearly reshaped definitions of the legally obscene. From the perspective of *print* censorship—the principal focus of this book—the Meese report illustrates how completely, even for conservatives, this issue had been resolved in favor of First Amendment protection.

But the overall tone of the Meese report exacerbated the growing preoccupation with obscenity, feeding public alarm and encouraging a broad range of repressive efforts. Critics quickly pointed out its many flaws and polemical biases: it not only cited the research literature selectively, drew misleading conclusions from that literature, and assumed that findings in research settings could be extrapolated to "real world" behavior, but it also asserted without evidence that violent pornography and child pornography were increasing at an explosive rate, and included pages of undigested, unexamined anecdotal accounts of the harm allegedly caused by pornography, including amorphous psychological effects (e.g., "The Commission heard testimony from many witnesses who described feelings of worthlessness, guilt and shame which they attributed to experiences involving pornographic materials"). The commission urged relentless enforcement of existing obscenity laws and tough measures short of outright censorship to regulate pornography, particularly representations of sexual violence. In ninety-two numbered suggestions, federal, state, and local authorities were advised on ways to combat obscenity (e.g., "The Attorney General should direct the United States Attorneys to examine the obscenity problem in their respective districts, identify offenders, initiate investigations, and commence prosecution without further delay").[3]

As historian William E. Brigman has documented, the Meese report was only one particularly visible component of a sustained war on obscenity by the Department of Justice in the Reagan-Bush years. As Reagan's second term began, the Justice Department established an Obscenity Unit with a staff of prosecutors that eventually grew to thirteen. Organizing "Project Porn" and "Operation Porn Sweep," this unit battled the producers and marketers of sexually explicit material, especially of films and videos. In a process of "litigation by attrition," simultaneous prosecutions were launched against target companies in multiple jurisdictions, particularly conservative ones, to wear them down and drain their resources. Prosecutors also set up fake video-rental companies in conservative areas, ordered videos from the California producers, and then prosecuted the companies locally.[4]

The Obscenity Unit also made use of the 1970 Racketeer Influenced Corrupt Organization (RICO) law aimed at organized crime, which provided for the seizure of all the assets of convicted persons. In a 1990 obscenity case, a couple convicted under the RICO law lost assets in excess of $1 million, even though the material seized as evidence was worth under $100. Justice Department prosecutors also pressured indicted distributors to avoid trial through plea bargains in which they would agree to stop selling all erotic material, whether legally obscene or not. In one case, a company distributing sexually explicit material was pressured to accept a plea bargain by which it would cease handling even *Playboy*, *Penthouse*, and Dr. Alex Comfort's bestselling *The Joy of Sex*. When the company publicized these tactics, the Justice Department retaliated by prosecuting them in Mormon Utah, a deeply conservative state. A federal Court of Appeals threw out the government's case in 1992, however, finding that the Justice Department had engaged in "a persistent and widespread campaign to coerce [the company owners] into surrendering their First Amendment rights." Despite such setbacks, the Obscenity Unit conducted 222 adult-pornography investigations between 1987 and 1991 and, using the tactics described above, secured 135 convictions.[5]

Surveying this full-court press by the Justice Department, the *Wall Street Journal* in 1989 announced: "Pornography . . . on the Decline." In fact, despite the flurry of governmental activity, sales and rentals of sexually explicit videos actually exploded in this same five-year period, 1987–1991, growing from $992 million to $1.6 billion, according to *Adult Video News*. As William Brigman observes, this heavily publicized antipornography campaign was largely symbolic, as a conservative administration sought to dramatize the seriousness of its determination to shore up traditional values. The entire episode, Brigman writes, illustrates how "pornography . . . can be used as a symbol—a lightning rod—for those threatened by changing attitudes regarding proper sexual behavior, abortion, homosexuality, and other lifestyle issues."[6]

On another front in this Kabuki-theater crusade against pornography, North Carolina senator Jesse Helms and other conservatives in the late 1980s and early '90s denounced as obscene the work of various performance artists, and of photographers Robert Mapplethorpe and Andres Serrano. Some of Mapplethorpe's homoerotic photographs of male nudes highlighted their genitalia or featured simulations of sadomasochistic acts, while Serrano won notoriety with *Piss Christ*, a photograph of a cross submerged in an aquarium-like container of urine-colored liquid. Helms and his allies, including the evangelical American Family Association and many other conservative action groups, used such work to attack a favorite target, the National Endowment for the Arts, which they loathed. Winning control of Congress in 1994, Republicans cut NEA funding sharply, though the institution survived.[7]

In one widely publicized censorship incident early in 1990, police and sheriff's deputies closed a Mapplethorpe retrospective at Cincinnati's Contemporary Arts Center. (Mapplethorpe had died of AIDS in 1989.) The show, exhibited without incident in other cities, was open only to persons over eighteen, with the sexually explicit photos segregated in a separate room. In well-coordinated demonstrations before the forced closing, protesters waved posters proclaiming "We Want Decency in Cincinnati." Supporters responded by denouncing censorship and invoking artistic freedom. The Cincinnati Institute of Fine Arts dropped funding for the Contemporary Arts Center, and a grand jury indicted the Center's director, Dennis Barrie, on obscenity charges. (He was acquitted six months later, but meanwhile had left Cincinnati for another job.) The protest organizers called themselves "Citizens for Community Values," deliberately invoking the Supreme Court's "community standards" test for obscenity. Interviewed ten years later, the protest leader declared the effort a success, since the Contemporary Arts Center had "acted responsibly" in the intervening decade.[8]

In his perceptive 1991 study, *Culture Wars: The Struggle to Define America*, James Davison Hunter treated censorship as simply one battleground in a larger struggle between two parties: the "orthodox" and the "progressivists," each holding radically different views on many emotion-laden topics. On First

Amendment issues, Hunter writes, the "progressivists," led by liberal intellectuals and opinion molders in academia and the media, as well as by groups like the American Civil Liberties Union and TV producer Norman Lear's People for the American Way, insisted on nearly untrammeled free speech. They denounced their opponents as "bigots," "literary death squads," and "cultural terrorists," and found whiffs of Nazism in every protest against the latest cultural provocation.[9] The "orthodox," by contrast, saw nothing less at stake than the survival of morality and civilization in the upsurge of explicit sex, and dismissed First Amendment appeals as a mere smokescreen for pornographers, perverts, and political leftists.[10] In one of the more temperate expressions of this view, in 1990, the evangelical magazine *Christianity Today* accused media elitists of using "freedom of speech as a means to flout standards of common decency," and went on:

> We must not throw in the towel. Christians must unite in mounting a counteroffensive through our families, churches, schools, and other institutions. The legal issues surrounding public standards may be complex, but the moral imperatives are not. We must not abandon the ring of public debate to those who would use freedom of speech as an excuse to be as morally offensive as they "wanna" be.

Turning the tables on their opponents, cultural conservatives accused the "liberal elite" of "censorship" for ignoring religious faith—especially evangelical Christianity—in their mass-culture productions, for airbrushing the Founding Fathers and religion out of U.S. history textbooks, and for failing to give Creationism equal billing with Darwinism in science textbooks.[11]

While Hunter focused on the extremes and downplayed the middle ground in late-twentieth century cultural discourse to prepare the way for his concluding section, "Toward Resolution," he did capture the intensity of the *Kulturkampf* of these years—the essential context for understanding the era's censorship battles. Energized by, and contributing to, the rightward turn in U.S. public life, rapidly growing evangelical and fundamentalist churches mobilized politically, along with an elaborate network of national conservative organizations, including the American Family Association, Morality in Media, Falwell's Moral Majority, Pat Robertson's Christian Coalition, Tim LaHaye's American Coalition for Traditional Values, Beverly LaHaye's Concerned Women for America, James Dobson's Focus on the Family, Phyllis Schlafly's Eagle Forum, Donald Wildmon's National Federation for Decency, Mel and Norma Gabler's Texas-based Educational Research Analysts, which claimed to be able to measure the patriotism-and-traditional-values quotient of school textbooks, and Tipper Gore's blandly named Parents' Music Resource Center, which campaigned to force record companies to add warning labels to CDs containing objectionable lyrics. A 1984 strategy conference of such groups in Cincinnati adopted a stringent "Resolution on Pornography" and issued a "Call to National Righteousness."[12]

But while highly visible confrontations involving lightning-rod figures like Helms and Mapplethorpe loom large in the cultural history of the period, and thus in the history of censorship, they are not the whole story. In contrast to the earlier censorship cases involving nationally known battlers like Anthony Comstock, Upton Sinclair, H. L. Mencken, Morris Ernst, and Bronson Cutting, and often ending in "landmark" court decisions, the contests now typically involved bitter local skirmishes that unfolded out of the public eye and often never really ended, but simply entered a kind of latent stage as the combatants gathered strength for the next round.

THE LIBRARY AS CENSORSHIP BATTLEGROUND

In one important but little-publicized arena of conflict, librarians faced intensified censorship pressures. These initiatives often came from the religious right or from local foot soldiers of the conservative organizations mentioned above. Across the nation, schools and public libraries confronted a rash of demands to purge their curricula and shelves of books that allegedly advocated "Secular Humanism," promoted witchcraft and the occult, endorsed "globalism," provided candid sex information, treated religious faith with skepticism, condoned homosexuality, or taught evolution without equal billing to creationism. Most frequently attacked were books containing "dirty words." Surveying the censorship scene in 1988, an official of the ALA's Office for Intellectual Freedom noted that repressive efforts had "increased dramatically" in recent years, and observed: "[T]he past decade has been a time of controversy and, occasionally, fear." As the *New Republic* somewhat belatedly announced in 1997: "The culture wars have spread to a new front: the library."[13]

This trend, as we have so often seen, reflected broader social anxieties. In 1987, a handout distributed by a local group in Michigan charging school libraries with promoting witchcraft said rather poignantly: "[T]hese are times of violence, drugs, broken homes, AIDS, and suicide among our young. As if this isn't enough for our precious young, we now add witchcraft. We let the other destroyers creep into our flock. Are we going to let witchcraft and indecent teachings, too, or . . . see this as a chance to reclaim a decent life style for our children?"[14] Feeling powerless in the face of unsettling social trends, citizens could at least monitor their local libraries—and monitor them they did!

Perennial targets included Judy Blume's stories for teenagers, particularly *Forever*, dealing with an adolescent girl's transition to womanhood, and J. D. Salinger's *The Catcher in the Rye*, an object of censorship attack since its publication in 1951. In 1981, an assiduous reader counted 785 profanities, obscenities, and vulgarisms in Salinger's book, and denounced it as "part of an overall communist plot." *Bloods*, an oral history featuring black Vietnam veterans, faced censorship demands for its raw language. Maya Angelou's autobiography, *I Know Why the Caged Bird Sings* (1970), led the list of besieged titles in the mid-1990s, along with Alice Walker's *The Color Purple* (1982), and older works such as John Steinbeck's *The Grapes of Wrath* and William Faulkner's *As*

I Lay Dying. At various times and places, school library vigilantes attacked works by Shakespeare, Saul Bellow, William Golding, John Updike, Norman Mailer, Vladimir Nabokov, Stephen Crane, Ernest Hemingway, Eugene O'Neill, Harper Lee, Mario Puzo, and many others. (One aggrieved citizen demanded the removal of a book called *Making It with Mademoiselle*, only to learn that it was a collection of dress patterns.)[15]

From 1966 into the 1980s, according to a longitudinal survey of several thousand high school librarians, censorship pressures increased steadily. The ALA's intellectual freedom office reported nearly a thousand such incidents in 1981. In Texas that year, the state board of education asked two dictionary publishers, Houghton Mifflin and Merriam Webster, to remove seven words from their dictionaries. Houghton Mifflin capitulated, Merriam Webster refused, so Texas schoolchildren found themselves using Houghton Mifflin's expurgated *American Heritage Dictionary*.[16]

In that same year, 1981, as the Reagan era began, the Nassau County, New York, school board ordered eleven books removed from all school libraries, including Bernard Malamud's *The Fixer*, Eldridge Cleaver's *Soul on Ice*, Kurt Vonnegut's *Slaughterhouse Five*, and Desmond Morris's *The Naked Ape*. A group of high school students sued to reverse the ban, and in 1982 the U.S. Supreme Court voted five-to-four to permit the suit go to trial. One of the minority, Justice Lewis F. Powell, Jr., a Nixon appointee, greeted this decision with "genuine dismay," warning that it would encourage student lawsuits and undermine school authority. (In the end the Nassau County board ordered the books returned to the shelves, thereby avoiding a trial.) Summing up the Supreme Court's general position on school censorship in 1992, legal scholar Mark Yudof wrote that while administrators could not impose "an official orthodoxy or ideology," they could remove library books "for good-faith educational reasons, including efforts to eliminate vulgar or obscene words."[17]

A few egregious cases attracted national notice. In 1987, for example, a U.S. Court of Appeals reversed an Alabama fed-

eral judge's order directing *all* public schools in the *state* to remove forty-four textbooks in social studies, history, and other
fields for promoting the "religion" of "secular humanism."[18]
More typically, however, these stealth campaigns unfolded beneath the radar of the national or even of the local media. Cu-
mulatively, however, they represented a major, ongoing manifestation of book-censorship pressure.

The 1990s brought no respite from grassroots efforts
to compel librarians to remove titles or accept restrictive
acquisition-and-access guidelines. *Publishers Weekly* reported
475 such attempts in forty-four states in 1995, the year Focus
on the Family, in a cover story in its magazine *Citizen*, attacked
the ALA for its policy of unrestricted access.[19] A new national
organization emerged in 1996, Family Friendly Libraries
(FFL), the brainchild of Karen Jo Gounaud of Springfield, Virginia. While rejecting the censorship label, Gounaud's organization called for parental access to children's borrowing records,
restrictions on children's access to "anti-family" books, and increased library holdings of "pro-family" works. That is, a library
could acquire children's books like *Daddy's Roommate* or
Heather Has Two Mommies, dealing with children with a gay or
lesbian parent, but it could not permit children to read them,
and would be required to "balance" them with titles like *You
Don't Have to Be Gay*, which treats homosexuality as a curable
psychological disorder.[20]

How did Gounaud interpret those amorphous terms "pro-
family" and "anti-family"? In 1997, shown a page from a book of
children's poems that pictured two men in bed together, with
the rhyme: "Robin and Richard were two pretty men, / They lay
in bed till the clock struck ten," she declared: "That's outside the
norm for a child's book. That is *definitely* the kind of book that
we would ask to be moved." The page was from a 1916 edition
of *The Original Mother Goose*.[21]

Librarians fought back. In 1988 the American Library Association (ALA) and the American Association of School Administrators (AASA) jointly published a handbook for school officials and librarians facing censorship pressures. It reviewed the

censorship situation; summarized key legal rulings; and offered a sample letter to send to complainants, tips on drafting a written selection policy, and advice on "Dealing with the News Media" and "Preparing for a Crisis."[22]

The library-censorship drive, a war by attrition paralleling the Justice Department's antipornography campaign, won some victories, as local libraries gave in to censorship pressures or yielded to parental demands for access to children's borrowing records (a violation of ALA policy on confidentiality, enacted into law in many states). The Loudoun County, Virginia, library board repudiated the ALA's Bill of Rights entirely, and adopted its own code; one board member denounced the ALA's "radical homosexual agenda that is disparaging of the traditional family."[23]

While most censorship demands came from the right, complaints also emanated from the other end of the ideological spectrum, reflecting the heightened ethnic sensitivities and identity politics of these years. African Americans attacked books that allegedly encouraged racism; feminists protested works that reinforced sexist stereotypes; liberal activists targeted conservative or superpatriotic textbooks; Hispanic Americans, Italian Americans, and other ethnic groups criticized publications that they felt demeaned their group. "The conservative censor has been joined by groups that want their own special group values recognized," noted the 1988 ALA/AASA handbook. "And these groups, too, may use the devices of censorship . . . [employing] tactics they are quick to condemn in others."[24]

The case against Samuel Clemens's *Huckleberry Finn* (1884), a work often praised as the great American novel, offers the paradigmatic example of censorship employed against perceived racism, addressing the novel's frequent use of the term "nigger." As early as 1957, New York City school officials withdrew an edition of the novel on these grounds, but under murky circumstances: the edition in question had substituted "negro" for "nigger," and the protests targeted the failure to capitalize "negro." (Harper and Brothers was apparently the first to publish a school edition of *Huckleberry Finn*, in 1931, that omitted

the inflammatory word.) Despite the claim by Clemens's defenders that he simply used the term that Huck would have
used at the time, and that his larger purpose was to *combat*
racism by stressing Huck's growing awareness of his common
humanity with the slave, Jim, the attacks went on; grassroots
censorship battles mirrored the larger fault lines in the culture
wars. The controversy erupted in earnest in 1982 when John H.
Wallace, a black educator at (ironically enough) the Mark Twain
Intermediate School in Fairfax, Virginia, attacked the book as
"racist trash," unfit for school use. Wallace soon issued his own
expurgated edition that not only eliminated "nigger," but also
"hell." The ensuing brouhaha, which continued with varying intensity for the next two decades, included many efforts to ban
the book from classrooms and even school libraries.[25]

Those unconvinced that *Huckleberry Finn* is an uplifting
plea for human brotherhood received support in 1997 from English professor Jonathan Arac. Attacking the work's "hyper-
canonization," Arac argued that the book's alleged "anti-racist"
message is murky at best, and he made a strong case against as-
signing it in classes because of Clemens's repeated use of the
still-potent racist slur. Noting that in the 1995 O. J. Simpson
murder trial, the media generally avoided printing the word
"nigger" used by detective Mark Fuhrman, Arac asked rhetorically: "[S]hould people of goodwill unhesitatingly maintain that
a word banned from CNN and *USA Today* must be required in
the eighth-grade schoolroom?"[26] Arac reprinted a letter by an
African American published in the *New York Times* in 1982,
apropos the *Huckleberry Finn* controversy:

> I can still recall the anger and pain I felt as my white class-
> mates read aloud the word "nigger." . . . I wanted to sink
> into my seat. Some of the whites snickered, others giggled.
> I can recall nothing of the literary merits of this work that
> you term the "greatest of all American novels." I only recall
> the sense of relief I felt when I would flip ahead a few
> pages and see that the word "nigger" would not be read
> that hour.[27]

On the question of library censorship and control of teachers' curriculum—the level at which the *Huckleberry Finn* debate was fought in the trenches—Arac wrote: "As a member of the ACLU, I hope . . . that my materials and arguments will persuade local chapters to seek discussion, not just confrontation, with protesting voices. . . . I do not want to ban *Huckleberry Finn*. I do want to see fairer, fuller, better-informed debates when the book comes into question."[28]

PORNOGRAPHY AS A FEMINIST ISSUE

The phenomenon of antipornography pressure from unexpected sources emerged with particular clarity in the most highly publicized and contentious censorship initiative of these years: the effort by some feminists to provide legal recourse for the alleged harm of pornography, not on the usual obscenity grounds, but as a violation of women's civil rights. The key figures, lawyer Catharine MacKinnon and writer Andrea Dworkin, argued that pornography subordinated, degraded, and dehumanized women as a class, as well as individual women, and promoted violence toward them, and therefore, violated their civil rights.[29] As early as 1970, in *Sexual Politics* (her Columbia University doctoral dissertation), Kate Millett had attacked D. H. Lawrence, Henry Miller, and other male writers as sexists whose work degraded women. In 1973, Susan Brownmiller denied that the defense of pornography constituted any part of the feminist agenda, and praised the Supreme Court's tougher stance on obscenity as consistent with the *Roe* v. *Wade* abortion-rights ruling and other decisions advancing women's rights. Robin Morgan wrote in an influential 1980 essay: "Pornography is the theory, and rape is the practice."[30]

In this same period, feminist activists had formed grassroots organizations such as Women Against Violence Against Women (1976) and the more concisely named Women Against Pornography (1979). As media historian Carolyn Bronstein has shown, these groups mobilized protests against hardcore sex magazines such as *Hustler* and *Penthouse*, pornographic films that featured violence against women, or that, in their view, reduced sex to purely mechanical interactions and privileged male fantasies, such as the phenomenally successful *Deep Throat* (1972). These activist groups also battled exploitative advertising, most notoriously ads for the Rolling Stones' album *Black and Blue* (1976), which featured a "bruised, trussed, and scantily clad woman." In the context of this broad feminist mobilization against pornography, and drawing out the legal and practical implication of the ideological positions articulated by Millet, Brownmiller, Morgan, and others, MacKinnon and Dworkin, in December 1983, while teaching at the University of Minnesota Law School, proposed to the Minneapolis City Council, at the council's request, an anti-pornography ordinance based on the civil rights claim. In defense of the ordinance, they cited concrete injuries to specific women allegedly caused by pornography.[31]

Defining pornography as "the sexually explicit subordination of women, graphically depicted, whether in pictures or in words," the ordinance authorized the city's civil rights commission, and the courts, to deal with cases that allegedly involved (1) coercing women to perform in pornography; (2) any "assault or physical attack" that could be shown to have been directly caused by pornography, with liability extending to the producers and/or distributors of the pornography in question; (3) displaying pornography to unwilling subjects; and (4) "trafficking" in the production, sale, exhibition, or distribution of material proscribed under the ordinance—a catch-all category under which any woman, as a member of the victimized class, could win relief if she could prove that the material had, indeed, caused harm. Despite *Roth* and other obscenity rulings, a work proven to cause these harms could be banned by court order, even on the basis of a single section, and regardless of artistic merit.[32]

In several days of emotional hearings that some found psychologically coercive, women testified under oath to sexual abuse by husbands and lovers, pimps, and fathers, as well as strangers, inflamed by pornography. A celebrity witness, Linda

Marchiano (Linda Lovelace), testified that she had been coerced into making the film *Deep Throat*. Critics of the measure, including a librarian, a bookstore owner, a gay activist, and a Minnesota Civil Liberties Union spokesman, also testified, sometimes to the accompaniment of boos, hissing, and weeping. A core group of proponents dominated the proceedings, writes Donald Downs on the basis of interviews with participants, "treat[ing] everyone outside the circle of believers with a disrespect which seemed at odds with their own goal of empowering the silenced." Finally, on a seven-to-six vote, the council passed the ordinance. Minneapolis mayor Donald Fraser vetoed it, however, as well as a second version passed in 1984.[33]

The movement spread to other cities, but continued to run afoul of politics and the law. In *Hudnut* v. *American Booksellers Association* (1985), a federal appeals court declared a version of the MacKinnon/Dworkin ordinance enacted in Indianapolis unconstitutional. Proponents in Madison, Wisconsin, withdrew their proposed legislation before final action by the county board, and a referendum in Cambridge, Massachusetts, was narrowly defeated. The Los Angeles Board of Supervisors rejected it on a three-to-two vote. Voters in Bellingham, Washington, passed the ordinance, but it was found unconstitutional under *Hudnut*.[34]

The antipornography initiative deeply divided the women's movement. Some feminists in the United States and abroad embraced it enthusiastically. In England, Catherine Itzin of the "Violence, Abuse, and Gender Relations Research Institute" at the University of Bradford published a 645-page collection of essays in defense of the feminist antipornography cause. Other feminists, however, attacked it on First Amendment grounds or even argued for pornography's positive benefits as a radical challenge to social taboos and class hierarchies, and as a means of liberation from sexual inhibition. A New York–based Feminist Anti-Censorship Task Force (FACT) was founded in 1984 specifically to combat the MacKinnon/Dworkin position. A few defiant feminist scholars offered college courses in pornography (provoking Pat Robertson to fulminate: "A feminist teaching pornography is like Scopes teaching evolution"), and Internet pornography sites operated by women attracted the notice of popular culture scholars.[35]

Feminist opponents also argued that the MacKinnon/ Dworkin initiative encouraged stereotypes of female helplessness, revived a Victorian view of sex as inherently dangerous, defined pornography too loosely, suggested a grim, anti-erotic regime of sexual correctness; and unwittingly furthered the cultural agenda of the religious right. Law professor and ACLU president Nadine Strossen, a particularly vehement critic of the "pornophobic feminists," declared: "So influential have the MacDworkinites become that all too many citizens and government officials believe that the suppression of sexually oriented materials is a high priority for all feminists or even for all women. Nothing could be further from the truth."[36]

As the critics charged, the MacKinnon/Dworkin view of pornography and its effects was, indeed, echoed if not exploited by censorship advocates on the right. Donald Wildmon of the National Federation for Decency, writing in 1987, claimed to find a "strong correlation between pornography and rape" and argued that TV-incited violence was "increasingly directed toward women and young girls." Antipornography arguments advanced by some feminists, and sweeping assertions of a causal link between pornography and violence toward women, figured prominently in Attorney General Meese's 1986 pornography report, while in heavily Republican Indianapolis, conservative politicians and civic leaders warmly supported the proposed ordinance. Feminist antipornography crusaders, William E. Brigman contends, "provided camouflage for conservatives in the Reagan administration" (MacKinnon and Dworkin in their 1997 account of the episode, *In Harm's Way,* and elsewhere, insisted that they never worked with the right and that the right as a whole never supported their ordinance or adopted their approach).[37]

Although thwarted in the legislative and judicial arenas, feminist efforts to redefine pornography as a civil rights issue attracted media attention and added fuel to the ongoing debate over censorship. In 1992, when lawyer Edward de Grazia published *Girls Lean Back Everywhere: The Law of Obscenity and the Assault on Genius*, an anticensorship polemic in the vein of earlier paeans to untrammeled free speech by Morris Ernst and others, some feminists attacked him for sexist bias and his failure to consider pornography's role in the oppression of women.[38]

While hostile critics charged that the feminist antipornography campaign gave aid and comfort to some of the most reactionary forces in the culture wars, the MacKinnon/Dworkin initiative also stimulated debate among academics and civil libertarians. As the University of Wisconsin political scientist Donald Downs observed a few years later: "[T]he ordinance . . . gained the respect of some intellectuals who had previously opposed censorship of sexual materials, thus weakening the long-standing broad consensus supporting the liberal doctrine of free expression. . . . [It] brought a usually avoided subject to public attention and forced society to confront its attitudes toward pornography and its effects."[39]

In their compelling and closely argued anticensorship work, *Pornography in a Free Society* (1988), Gordon Hawkins and Franklin E. Zimring of the Earl Warren Legal Institute at the University of California–Berkeley Law School felt it necessary to devote a full chapter to "Pornography and the Subjugation of Women: The Radical Feminist Challenge." Criticizing the definition of "pornography" offered by MacKinnon and Dworkin as idiosyncratic, they argued that the assumption of a causal connection between pornography and the physical abuse of women underlying the ordinance rested on unsubstantiated anecdotal evidence and controversial or inconclusive research findings in this field. Taking a broader cultural view, Hawkins and Zimring concluded: "A sexist society produces a pornography—and not only pornography—that reflects the relative position of men and women in that society. . . . [A]s sexism diminishes in our society and the relative position of women improves, the kind of pornography that consumers demand may change. . . . [A] society in

which males were less dominant would produce a pornography
that was less debased and less dehumanized." Meanwhile, they
suggested, efforts at legal repression based on such dubious assumptions and murky definitions were unlikely to be effective or
to be worth their cost in the infringement of First Amendment
rights.[40]

Donald Downs, in his 1989 book on the MacKinnon/
Dworkin initiative, *The New Politics of Pornography*, revealed a
degree of ambivalence in his overall assessment. As a civil libertarian, he criticized its "unprecedented scope," affirmed a strong
reading of the First Amendment ("We always should err on the
side of protecting free speech"), questioned the enforceability of
new antipornography laws, and endorsed the Meese commission's support of absolute constitutional protection of the printed
word. Public condemnation of pornography, he argued, would
likely be more effective than banning it.[41]

But Downs also observed: "Obscenity law . . . leaves out an
important element that feminists and academic researchers have
forced us to consider: violence. The evidence suggests that sexual violence is a social problem, and that certain forms of pornography are associated with violent sexual aggression." This conclusion came after an extended review of the research evidence
on whether violent pornography (usually in the form of visual images) "tends to desensitize men to sexual violence and increase
their inclination to engage in aggression against women." While
the Meese report strongly insisted upon such a causal relationship, overstating research findings and downplaying contrary evidence and dissident views on this controversial question, Downs
was more skeptical and cautious, noting, for example, the difference between the "contrived situations" of research experiments
and the real world, as well as the lack of any convincing evidence
of a simple, causal link. He nevertheless tentatively concluded
that the cumulative evidence, particularly experiments involving
visual representations of violence toward women in sexual con-
texts, did suggest a link, in the experimental context, "in the
sense of a non-deterministic, 'multiple,' or 'probabilistic' cause."[42]

In determining the legal status of visual representations (as opposed to the printed word, which should enjoy absolute protection), Downs concluded, the courts should pay special attention to pornographic material portraying violence against women in the context of explicit sexual depictions. (The 2000 movie *Quills*, about the Marquis de Sade, offered an interesting mass culture intervention in this debate: de Sade, imprisoned in the Charenton asylum and denied pen and paper, tells other inmates a graphic story involving the brutal rape and murder of a young woman. Aroused by de Sade's tale, one inmate acts it out, raping and mutilating a young female employee in the asylum.)

Positioning the censorship issue in a broader public policy context, Downs concluded: "'Self government' means more than simply the libertarian right to engage in self-regarding actions. . . . [V]alues of restraint based on the norms of civility and equal respect are necessary to foster a healthier society and cultural pluralism. . . . We must err on the side of freedom without forsaking our responsibility to maintain a decent and just society. Controversy and ambiguity cannot be avoided; the struggle . . . [over censorship] reflects the tensions in our natures and the conflict of legitimate values in society."[43]

The MacKinnon/Dworkin episode illustrates both the persistence of the censorship debate and its evolution over time, reflecting new political and social realities. While their initiative certainly intensified censorship pressures, it also forced First Amendment champions to think more deeply and critically about the social and gender implications of their position.

THE PROBLEM OF CENSORSHIP
IN AN ERA OF TECHNOLOGICAL CHANGE

Innovations in communications technology raised thorny new issues of regulation and oversight as the twentieth century ended, and this, in turn, profoundly affected public and judicial views of print censorship, the subject of this study. In a sense, this was nothing new: throughout the century, as we have noted

from time to time in the earlier chapters of this work, print censorship had proceeded in tandem with regulation of the new
electronic media—radio, the movies, and eventually, television—
with both processes following generally similar cycles of repressiveness and liberalization. A brief review of this background will
help place the late-twentieth developments in context.

*A Backward Glance: Regulating the Electronic Media in
the Pre-Internet Era.* Debates over what could properly be
broadcast arose with the rapid spread of radio in the 1920s. The
Federal Radio Commission (1927) and its successor the Federal
Communications Commission (1934) exercised licensing authority over broadcasting. This authority included the right to
adjudicate among competing applicants for licenses on the basis
of the type of programming they proposed, measured by a vague
"public interest" standard. These regulatory agencies were also
empowered to remove the licenses of stations broadcasting obscene material, even though the 1927 law creating the FRC, carried over to the 1934 FCC law, also explicitly forbade them from
censorship or restricting First Amendment rights.[44] With the
rise of television, the FCC's authority extended to the new
medium.

Aside from requiring broadcasters to present controversial
issues fairly and to serve the interests of special constituencies
such as farmers, the early FCC construed its regulatory power
narrowly. The Communications Act of 1934 creating the FCC
reaffirmed the anti-obscenity provision of the 1927 legislation.
Section 328 forbade the broadcast of "any obscene, indecent or
profane language," but the FCC rarely had occasion to enforce
this provision. The commission revoked only two radio station licenses in its first fifteen years, and neither case involved program content. In 1938, amid the activist regulatory climate of
the New Deal, FCC chairman Frank McNinch warned broadcasters that if they did not enforce Section 328 voluntarily, the
FCC would "do something about it," but in practice the agency's

hands-off policy continued. As historian James Baughman observes, station owners willingly accepted restrictions on their right of unlimited free expression in exchange for the routine renewal of their highly lucrative licenses. Accordingly, the FCC in these years, in Baughman's words, resembled less a "burly cop" than an "aging barely competent babysitter." Programming that offended some listeners, such as Mae West's sexually suggestive spoof of the Adam and Eve story on NBC's *Chase and Sanborn Hour* in 1937, might stir a flurry of protest, but did not lead to FCC intervention.

As the political climate grew more conservative in the late 1960s, however, the FCC became more politicized. In 1969, on instructions from the Nixon White House, FCC chairman Dean Buroh, a former head of the Republican National Committee, in an action described by historian William E. Porter as "simple harassment," telephoned the heads of the three major TV networks asking for transcripts of their reports and commentary on a recent Nixon speech about Vietnam. By 1973, Nixon had appointed six of the seven FCC commissioners, bypassing the rule that at least three members must be of the opposition party by appointing "Democrats" who were in fact Nixon supporters. When FCC commissioner Nicholas Johnson, a maverick critic, left the Commission in January 1974, he issued an angry blast at "excessive White House control." The Nixon administration itself, meanwhile, actively engaged in press intimidation. While ostentatiously battling obscenity (see Chapter 10), the administration's real target was its media critics. In 1969, Vice President Spiro Agnew attacked the TV network news agencies as "a tiny and closed fraternity of privileged men." In 1970, after pressuring top TV executives to tone down criticism of Nixon, White House staffer Charles Colson jubilantly wrote his boss, H. R. Haldeman: "The harder I pressed them, the more accommodating, cordial, and almost apologetic they became. . . . [T]hey are damned nervous, and we should continue to take a very tough line, face to face, and in other ways." In 1971, when the Long Island paper *Newsday* ran an

investigative series on the financial dealings of Nixon's friend
Bebe Rebozo, the administration floated talk of a possible anti-
trust suit against the *Los Angeles Times*, the flagship paper of
the Times Mirror Company, which also owned *Newsday*. At the
same time, on White House instructions, the Internal Revenue
Service audited the tax returns of the reporter who had written
the Rebozo series. Soon World Publishing Company, another
Times Mirror holding, dropped plans to publish the Rebozo series as a book. Also subjected to the hot breath of White House
displeasure was CBS-TV reporter Daniel Schorr, an outspoken
Nixon critic. In 1971, under the pretext that Schorr was being
considered for a high-level administration job, the FBI
launched a full-scale investigation of him. Joining in the full-
scale campaign of heavy-handed media bashing was the head of
the White House "Telecommunications Policy Office" (a Nixon
creation), Clay T. Whitehead, who in a December 1972 speech
to Midwestern journalists implicitly warned TV executives that
their FCC license renewals could be in jeopardy unless they
cracked down on commentators or newscasters who "stress or
suppress information in accordances with their beliefs." Grum-
bled one elderly journalist as he walked out: "That SOB wants
to curtail our freedom."[45] Only the distractions of Watergate
and Nixon's resignation in 1974 ended this extraordinary assault
on the electronic and print media by the executive branch of
the federal government.

Nevertheless, Washington's regulatory power over the electronic media remained in force. In *FCC* v. *Pacifica Foundation*
(1977), a case arising from a broadcast by WBAI, a New York
FM station, of a monologue entitled "Filthy Words" by satirist
George Carlin, the Supreme Court upheld, on a five-to-four
vote, the FCC's reprimand of the station for airing "indecent" (if
not legally obscene) sexual and excretory language that listeners
could find "patently offensive," and that children could hear.
That the broadcast had occurred in daytime, with minors more
likely to be listening, weighed heavily with some justices. Voic-
ing broader concerns about the power of the electronic media,
Justice John Paul Stevens alluded to its "uniquely pervasive

presence in the lives of all Americans," including "children, even those too young to read."[46]

In the heyday of radio and the early days of television, advertisers carefully monitored the content of programs they sponsored. Indeed, this oversight probably shaped program content more than the remote prospect of government censorship. Sponsor interference sometimes went to ridiculous extremes. As James Baughman has recorded, the Schick Corporation, makers of electric razors, once vetoed a scene in a TV historical drama that called for the character to shave with a straight razor.[47]

As profit-oriented businesses, radio and TV have always been sensitive to the prevailing cultural and political winds. During the Cold War, as the Justice Department prosecuted radicals under the Smith Act and McCarthy's minions investigated overseas libraries, anticommunist blacklists derailed the careers of many radio, TV, and film performers and writers, including the "Hollywood Ten" screenwriters, and radio humorist John Henry Faulk. Even the popular *I Love Lucy* TV show faced a crisis in 1953 when gossip-columnist Walter Winchell "revealed" that the star, Lucille Ball, had registered as a Communist in 1936. (Ball had testified to the fact as a friendly witness before the House Un-American Activities Committee.) In 1969, with Americans deeply divided over the Vietnam War, CBS cancelled "The Smothers Brothers," an iconoclastic show popular with the young that had featured antiwar performers like Joan Baez and Pete Seeger.[48] In 1998, ABC cancelled the TV sitcom *Ellen*, starring Ellen DeGeneres, in part because of protests over the open lesbianism of both DeGeneres and her character on the show.

Among the electronic media, the movies faced especially strong censorship pressures. With the emergence of the commercial motion-picture business in the early twentieth century, would-be censors soon raised the same objections they were leveling against "immoral" books and magazines, with the added argument that the movies conveyed their message even more compellingly than the printed word.[49]

Beginning with Chicago in 1907, cities and states set up licensing boards to ban or cut scenes from films deemed obscene or immoral. In 1915, at a time when censorship was widely viewed as a praiseworthy part of progressive reform, the Supreme Court in *Mutual Film Corp.* v. *Ohio* upheld such prior restraint. Since the movies were "a business pure and simple, originated and conducted for profit, like other spectacles, not to be regarded . . . as part of the press of the country, or as organs of public opinion," said the court, they did not enjoy First Amendment protection. Emboldened by this finding, local censorship boards proliferated.[50]

In 1952, however, reflecting its postwar permissive trend, the Supreme Court overturned a New York ban on *The Miracle*, an Italian film denounced as sacrilegious by Catholic officials. Made by Roberto Rossellini, it featured Anna Magnani as a peasant girl who becomes convinced that the child she has borne after being impregnated by a bearded stranger is Jesus Christ. Reversing its 1915 ruling, the Court now declared motion pictures "a significant medium of the communication of ideas" shielded by the First Amendment. In 1959, the same year it cleared *Lady Chatterley's Lover*, the Supreme Court unanimously reversed a ban by the New York State censorship board on a French movie based on Lawrence's novel. The New York courts, in upholding the ban, had introduced a new concept into censorship law by arguing that the film, while it had no explicit sex scenes, condoned adultery, and was thus guilty of "ideological obscenity." The Supreme Court had little difficulty extending First Amendment protection to the advocacy of ideas, even the idea of adultery.[51]

Several cases in the 1960s gave the *coup de grace* to moviecensorship boards. In 1961, the Supreme Court overturned a Chicago ordinance requiring theater owners to submit films for prior approval. In a wide-ranging opinion, Chief Justice Earl Warren offered examples of silly excess by movie censors, including the Chicago censors' ban on a buffalo birth scene in Walt Disney's *Vanishing Prairie*, and the ban on all of Ingrid Bergman's movies by a Memphis judge on the grounds that her affair with Roberto Rossellini proved that her soul was "black as the soot of hell." In a rare flash of eloquence, Warren declared: "The censor's sword pierces deeply into the heart of free expression."[52]

In *Jacobellis* v. *Ohio* (1964), the high court, by a six-to-three vote, overturned the conviction of Nico Jacobellis, the operator of an art theater in the upper-middle class suburb of Cleveland Heights, Ohio, for showing the French film *Les Amants* (*The Lovers*), about a married woman's adultery with a younger man. It included a sex scene so brief that, according to Justice Arthur Goldberg, only a censor was likely to spot it. This case is notable in the history of censorship law because Justice William J. Brennan, writing for the majority, insisted that "community standards" meant *national* standards: "society at large . . . the public, or people in general"—a position a more conservative court would soon reject. (This is also the case that elicited Justice Potter Stewart's much-quoted quip about pornography: "I know it when I see it.")[53]

The *Jacobellis* case, like the 1950 dismissal of the Oklahoma librarian Ruth Brown discussed in Chapter 10, vividly illustrates one of the central themes of this book: to understand how censorship actually functions in the culture, one must look beyond the courts to the larger social context. Nico Jacobellis, an Italian immigrant, was arrested on November 13, 1959, during a showing of *The Lovers* at his theater, on complaint of a local branch of Citizens for Decent Literature. He was fingerprinted and his photograph published in the *Cleveland Plain Dealer*, which subsequently refused to accept ads for his theater. In a nice Orwellian touch, the police official who authorized the arrest said, "We don't act as censors and we don't propose to." After his conviction, Jacobellis was fined $2,500 and imprisoned for six days, allegedly while probation arrangements were worked out. As the case wended its way through the judicial maze, Jacobellis was subjected to harassing telephone calls (including anti-Semitic ones, even though he was a Catholic). Taxis, repair trucks, and delivery vans summoned by cranks as part of the harassment campaign appeared at his door. He disconnected his phone and eventually left his apartment and began to sleep at the theater. Local Catholic priests refused to perform his wedding mass, made him unwelcome at church, and threatened to pursue deportation efforts. The 1964 Supreme Court decision clearing him, while hailed in First Amendment circles, was cold comfort. As political scientist Richard S. Randall wrote soon after: "Jacobellis' eventual exoneration . . . four and one half years after his arrest can offer slight encouragement to other exhibiters faced with coincident pressures of the local authorities and of powerful community religious groups."[54]

In *Freedman* v. *Maryland*, another 1964 case, the Supreme Court struck down the procedures of the Maryland censorship board as insufficiently attentive to exhibitors' First Amendment rights.[55] By the later 1960s, film censorship, like censorship of the printed word, seemed a thing of the past.

But as the ordeal of Nico Jacobellis makes clear, public attitudes toward obscenity were rapidly hardening in these years. We have already noted the harshly condemnatory language with which the Supreme Court in 1973 upheld the conviction of an Atlanta theater owner who featured sexually explicit films. In *Young* v. *American Mini Theatres* (1976), still in a full-throated anti-obscenity mode, the Supreme Court, on another five-to-four vote, upheld a Detroit zoning ban on "adult" movie theaters in certain parts of the city. Society's interest in protecting sexually explicit material, wrote Justice John Paul Stevens for the majority, is "of a wholly different, and lesser, magnitude than the interest in untrammeled political debate." Added Stevens sarcastically: "[F]ew of us would march our sons and daughters off to war to preserve the citizen's right to see . . . [explicit sex scenes] in the theaters of our choice."[56]

Deep Throat was banned in New York City in 1973 as part of Mayor John V. Lindsay's antismut campaign. In the aftermath of the *Miller* decision, *Deep Throat* faced local bans in many other cities as well, including Memphis, Atlanta, San Antonio, St. Paul, Fort Worth, Boston, and Houston. In each case, local district attorneys, citing the *Miller* ruling, based their action on the claim that the film violated local community standards. In that

same year, 1973, federal authorities, again taking advantage of
the "local community standards" principle, secured a conviction
in conservative Memphis of sixteen persons associated with the
production of *Deep Throat*, including the male lead, Harry
Reems. The assistant U.S. attorney who won the case, Larry Par-
rish, became something of a celebrity in national magazines and
on the talk-show circuit, helping make the antipornography campaign, in the words of the historian Jon Lewis, "the issue du jour
for politically ambitious and/or celebrity hungry local, state, and
federal prosecutors."[57]

Beginning as early as 1909, the motion-picture industry,
seeking to deflect censorship by governmental bodies, had
adopted various schemes of self-regulation. In 1922, as we saw
in Chapter 6, the Motion Picture Producers and Distributors of
America, reacting to growing criticism, appointed Will Hays to
oversee movie morals. Hays's Production Code, promulgated in
1930, was initially ineffective, but in 1934, under continued censorship and boycott threats by the Legion of Decency (later the
National Catholic Office for Motion Pictures) and other groups,
Hollywood created the more powerful Production Code Administration under Joseph Breen. But this code, too, lost effectiveness after World War II, as the movie industry became less
monolithic and at least a portion of the public grew more tolerant of what could be shown and said on screen. United Artists,
the producers of Otto Preminger's 1953 comedy, *The Moon Is
Blue*, which dealt with a possible adultery (which never takes
place), and included the taboo word "virgin," caused a stir when
they released it without Code approval. Preminger thumbed his
nose at the code again in 1955 with *The Man with the Golden
Arm*, based on a novel by Nelson Algren and starring Frank
Sinatra as a drug addict. In the later 1960s, however, as movies
featured nudity and more explicit sex, demands for censorship
again increased. To forestall these efforts, and feeling the chill
winds blowing from the Supreme Court, the Motion Picture Association of America under Jack Valenti, lately an advisor to
President Lyndon Johnson, adopted a rating system in 1968 in-

dicating each film's appropriateness for different age groups. Periodically revised, the rating system remained in place at the end
of the century, largely defusing movie censorship pressures and
influencing movie content in subtle ways. For example, Warner
Brothers, the distributor of Stanley Kubrick's last film *Eyes Wide
Shut* (1999) avoided a restrictive NC-17 rating by adding shadowy digitized figures to obscure the nudity in some of Kubrick's
scenes. Warner Brothers' parent company, the multinational
Time Warner Corporation, meanwhile, released the uncensored
version in other markets and in videotape and DVD format,
demonstrating the way new technologies could be employed simultaneously to both accommodate and circumvent censorship
constraints. [58]

*Regulatory Dilemmas in an Age of New Communications
Technologies.* Across the twentieth century, in short, while addressing censorship issues relating to the printed word, the courts
had also gained experience in dealing with the electronic media.
This, however, hardly prepared judges, legislators, or Americans
in general for the issues posed by the new communications technologies that arose as the century ended. The rise of cable TV
companies that transmitted programs to paying subscribers over
private telephone lines rather than broadcasting them, posed
new and thorny regulatory questions. In the Cable Communication Policy Act of 1984, the federal government yielded primary
jurisdiction and franchising authority in this area to states and
local municipalities.[59]

The regulatory scene changed still further with the rapid
spread of video cassette recorders (VCRs) in the 1980s, enabling
individuals to view movies—including sexually explicit films
readily available from video rental stores—in the privacy of their
homes. By the 1990s, many hotel and motel chains also offered
guests access (for a fee) to erotic and sexually explicit video
movies in their rooms. As technology outran the censors, home
VCRs largely killed off the more-easily-regulated "adult" the-

aters, which declined from around fifteen hundred in the mid-1970s to fewer than 250 by 1989. Even New York City, beginning in the 1970s and continuing in the 1990s under Mayor Rudolph Giuliani, transformed notorious Times Square, haven to prostitutes, sex shops, and X-rated movies, into a squeaky-clean center of Disney-style family entertainment and fast-food franchises. (In 1999, outraged by a Brooklyn Museum of Art exhibit he deemed sacrilegious, Giuliani tried—unsuccessfully—to cancel the museum's $7 million annual appropriation.)[60]

In the 1990s and beyond, as Americans—to the dismay of the religious right—displayed an avid taste for explicit videos catering to all sexual tastes, the already thriving "adult video" industry in California's San Fernando Valley, having survived largely unscathed the Reagan-era antipornography campaign, expanded rapidly. Producing eleven thousand videos a year of varying artistic quality, the industry had its own star system, trade association, a journal publishing four hundred reviews a month, Internet news portal (AVN.com), rating system (X, XX, and XXX), a large labor force of "sex workers" with employee-benefits packages, and an annual awards ceremony. (The 1996 award for Best Group Sex scene went to the "Staircase Orgy" segment of *New Wave Hookers 4*.) In 2000, Americans spent $4.2 billion renting or buying 700 million adult videos. Adding sexually explicit Web sites, cable channels, magazines, and so forth, analysts estimated the total size of the business at $10–14 billion. Wrote Frank Rich in the *New York Times Magazine* in 2001: "[P]ornography is a bigger business than professional football, basketball and baseball put together. People pay more money for pornography in America in a year than they do on movie tickets, more than they do on all the performing arts combined."[61] By century's end, the era when the police could padlock adult theaters and bring criminal proceedings against their owners with the Supreme Court's blessing, though still quite recent, seemed remote indeed.

Video and cable-TV sex raised First Amendment issues of a complexity that made earlier struggles over the printed word seem simple. In *Stanley* v. *Georgia* (1969), the Supreme Court had unanimously upheld citizens' right to possess sexually explicit movies in their own homes for private viewing. But the *Stanley* opinion, by Justice Thurgood Marshall, involved a confusing mélange of First and Fourth Amendment arguments with privacy rights thrown in, and had, in any event, been undercut by later decisions.[62] What regulations, if any, might apply to the burgeoning adult video industry remained unclear. As for cable TV, it served paid subscribers and used privately owned transmission lines, but did this free it of public oversight? For Donald Wildmon of the National Federation for Decency, the case for censoring cable posed no problems: "You might pay for it, but once the cable operator transmits pornography through that wire, it is released to the community. It becomes the community's business, and the community can legislate against it. . . . You might also want heroin in your home and pay for it, but it is against the law for the seller to sell it to you." The courts found the issue more complicated, however, for practical as well as constitutional reasons. In 1986, a Los Angeles cable company sued the City of Los Angeles, claiming that its First Amendment rights had been violated by the city's refusal to grant it a license. The Supreme Court ruled that different technologies raised different First Amendment issues, and in the case of cable, the practical problems of proliferating utility poles and underground lines were relevant considerations.[63]

The First Amendment issues posed by the Internet and the World Wide Web, byproducts of the computer revolution, proved even more intractable. Should they be free of regulation simply because the words and images they transmitted were ephemeral electronic impulses rather than printed on paper? If they *could* be regulated, precisely how? Even the issue of child pornography, for which even First Amendment absolutists made an exception, became more complex in the era of the Internet. The Meese commission stated flatly that images of children in sexual situations "necessarily includes the sexual abuse of a real child," and were, thus, obviously illegal.[64] But matters became complicated when, in the Child Pornography Prevention Act of 1996, Congress banned not only photographic representations of actual children engaging in sexual acts, but also any computer image that "appears to be" or "conveys the impression" of an actual child performing such acts. Was this constitutional? Were computer-generated virtual images really no different in the eyes of the law than representations of actual children? And who would determine the "appearances" and "impressions" on which this law relied? If a young adult in a sexually explicit representation "convey[ed] the impression" of being under-age, would this be actionable? The courts seemed as confused as everyone else. A federal trial judge upheld the law, only to have the 9th U.S. Circuit Court of Appeals in San Francisco reverse the decision in 1999, ruling the law too vague and therefore, unconstitutional. Once again the long-suffering Supreme Court faced the challenge of "drawing the line," this time in the murky shadow land of virtual reality. In April 2002, the Supreme Court upheld the lower court ruling. The law's ban on any computer-generated image or performance by an adult actor that "appear[ed]" to portray a person under eighteen engaging in sexually explicit conduct, declared Justice Anthony M. Kennedy for the majority, went far beyond accepted legal definitions of either child pornography or the criminally obscene.[65]

The resurgent anti-obscenity crusade, including conservative jeremiads demanding a return to "traditional values" and feminist recastings of pornography as a civil rights issue, ran head-on into these new technologies. With the wildfire spread of global communication systems, concern about pornography, sexual solicitation, and children's access to sexually explicit Web sites became a national obsession, echoing earlier moral panics over "indecent books." Responding to the public mood, the Republican Party's 1994 campaign document, the "Contract with America," pledged "stronger child pornography laws" as part of a larger commitment to the American family. Republicans won control of both houses of Congress that fall, and early in 1996 by overwhelming margins Congress passed the Communications Decency Act. President Bill Clinton, attuned to the public demand that "something must be done," signed it into law on February 8.[66] (The Child Pornography Prevention Act, discussed above, soon followed.)

The sponsors of the Communications Decency Act claimed that it would protect children and youth from TV and Internet violence, obscenity, and sexual exploitation. Attacking the media's assault on decency and family values, the measure blamed childhood TV-watching for contributing to "violent and aggressive behavior later in life" and asserted that "the pervasiveness and casual treatment of sexual material on television [erodes] the ability of parents to develop responsible attitudes and behavior in their children." All this, in turn, created "a compelling governmental interest in empowering parents to limit the negative influences of video programming that is harmful to children."[67]

A complex, hurriedly drafted revision of the Communications Act of 1934, the law required cable TV companies to "scramble" sexually-oriented channels at subscribers' request and securely block sex channels from nonsubscribers; it made it a crime to entice a minor sexually by means of the Internet. Troubled by the moral hazards posed by the new technologies, Congress looked to technology for the solution, instructing the FCC, in consultation with the TV and computer industries, to investigate technical means by which parents could block TV programs or Internet Web sites they deemed inappropriate for their children. Finally, the law made it a crime, punishable by two years in prison and a $250,000 fine, to transmit via the Internet, "in a manner available to a person under 18 years of age, any comment, request, suggestion, proposal, image, or other communication that, in context, depicts or describes, in terms patently offensive as measured by contemporary community standards, sexual or excretory activities or organs."[68]

While the sexual solicitation of children by pedophiles via the Internet and the access of very young children to pornographic Web sites were legitimate concerns, these issues also became a way of articulating more amorphous anxieties, including

not only the generalized parental worries present since time im-
memorial, but also anxieties specific to the 1990s as adults struggled with confusing new technologies that kids could master
with disconcerting ease. Reversing the usual pattern of knowledge transmission, bumbling grown-ups depended on their children to teach them the most rudimentary computer skills. Commenting on the argument that parents, not the government,
should monitor children's computer use, one writer observed in
1996: "In practice . . . this is difficult, particularly since many
children in this technological society are far more computer lit-
erate than their parents."[69]

The placement of children in the foreground of the obscenity discussions of the 1990s had deep historic roots. Since the
mid-nineteenth century, the need to protect innocent youth had
provided a compelling rationale for censorship of the printed
word, and this argument remained potent in the computer age as
it was marshaled by individuals and groups dismayed by changing sexual mores. A section of the 1986 Meese Report entitled
"The Special Horror of Child Pornography" made sweeping but
largely unsubstantiated claims regarding the vast scope and
frightening proliferation of the problem, and advocates of the
1996 legislation made similar assertions. As a Clinton administration official commented: "We all knew . . . that the Communications Decency Act was unconstitutional. This was purely politics. How could you be against a bill limiting the display of
pornography to children?"[70]

In their 1988 study *Pornography in a Free Society*, Gordon
Hawkins and Franklin E. Zimring of the University of California—
Berkeley commented on the "passionate emotions and frequent
political posturing" that the subject of child pornography invariably
elicited. Seeking to bring a degree of clarity to the discussion, they
noted the lack of precision in defining "children" and the loose definition of "child pornography" in the Meese Report and other pro-
censorship pronouncements. In discussing the issue, they argued,
one must distinguish between the use of minors as *subjects* in the
production of sexually explicit materials, the criminal nature of

which is universally accepted, and the *consumption* of sexually explicit material by teenagers, which raises quite a different set of legal and public policy issues. Echoing the findings of the much-maligned 1970 report of President Johnson's pornography commission, they noted the lack of evidence of long-term harm to adolescents from exposure to sexually explicit material. But if "the sexual stimulation of the young" is indeed assumed to be a serious social problem, they suggested, then "a more appropriate policy would be aimed at the minimization of the amount of sexually arousing content in the diet of childhood America" generally, rather an exclusive focus on pornography, despite the political popularity of the latter approach.[71]

While concern for the moral welfare of children certainly loomed large for many Americans, and for wholly understandable reasons, it is also true that some politicians and others used this volatile hot-button issue to mount a far broader attack on adults' freedom of expression in the age of explicit videos and Web sites and the de facto deregulation of most adult-oriented sexually explicit material. In 1993, noting that President Clinton's attorney general, Janet Reno, was scaling back the fervent antipornography crusade of the Reagan-Bush Justice Department, Republican congressman Christopher Smith of New Jersey declared: "This unholy alliance between Clinton and the porn peddler can only lead to the proliferation of child pornography and to the further exploitation of America's children." In this highly charged political atmosphere, as William Brigman observes, "anything carrying the imprimatur of child pornography, whether the designation was warranted or not . . . required vigorous opposition," and any measure claiming to oppose child pornography, "whether logical or ill-considered," demanded unquestioned support.[72]

The new law did, indeed, immediately raise constitutional red flags. The ACLU and liberal groups criticized it, and federal courts in Utah and Pennsylvania found it unconstitutional. In June 1997, the Supreme Court agreed, ruling unanimously that the law created "a content-based blanket restriction on speech" and that the "undefined terms 'indecent' and 'patently offensive' will provoke uncertainty among speakers about how the two standards relate to each other and just what they mean." In seeking to protect children, the Court held, Congress had ended by "suppressing a large amount of speech that adults have a constitutional right to send and receive." In response, Congress in 1998 enacted a new version of the law, renaming it the Child Online Protection Act, that sought to pass constitutional muster by limiting its restrictive provisions to commercial Web sites, excluding noncommercial sites such as chat rooms, and by adopting the Supreme Court's test for obscenity. But in 2000 this law, too, was found unconstitutional by the U.S. Court of Appeals for the Third District, sitting in Philadelphia, and the case passed on appeal to the U.S. Supreme Court. In its decision, the appeals court held that the effort to identify what was "harmful to minors" on the basis of "contemporary community standards" was an impossibly vague test to apply to a global medium, and could give "the most puritan of communities" power over the entire Internet—the same argument raised against the "contemporary community standards" test when the Supreme Court first promulgated this test in 1973.[73]

But as usual on the censorship front, this was only one development albeit an important one—in an endlessly unfolding process. While the Clinton administration advocated industry self-regulation as the answer, many states passed anti-obscenity Internet legislation. Civil libertarians, meanwhile, insisted that states had no authority to regulate a national, indeed, a global, communications medium. Republican Senator Charles Grassley of Iowa, a leading proponent of the Communications Decency Act, said of the Supreme Court's action: "Our objective hasn't changed. Some way, some how, we will have to find a constitutional way of doing this for kids, protecting them from [Internet] porn the way we did for printed material." [74]

While politicians and the courts wrestled with (or exploited) the censorship issues posed by the new media, as always, the full story involved the larger culture as well. In 2001, Yahoo, a giant

Internet service provider, dropped links to many sexually explicit
Web sites and the "Adult and Erotica" section of its video shopping area. Yahoo acted after being inundated with 100,000 e-mail
protests orchestrated by Donald Wildmon's American Family Association. The Free Speech Coalition, a trade association of companies providing "adult entertainment" on the Internet, criticized
Yahoo for denying its subscribers "routine adult material made for
and by consenting adults" that allowed people "to explore their
own sexuality and their own fantasies without hurting or intrud-
ing on anyone," and which offered greater privacy than video
rental stores.[75]

CONCLUSION

Thirty years after Charles Rembar had confidently predicted "the end of obscenity," the censorship impulse seemed as
strong as ever as the twentieth century ended. True, court-
enforced censorship of the printed word—Rembar's principal
concern, which looms so large in the earlier chapters of this
study, had diminished (though libraries and schools faced continuing pressures). This long-term development reflected, perhaps, less a heightened respect for publishers' and booksellers'
First Amendment rights than a sense that print seemed a much
less potent medium compared to film and TV, videos, and the
Internet in the era of new electronic technologies.

But taking a larger view, the perennial struggle between
freedom of expression (and the mass media's profit motive) on
the one hand, and society's need to uphold common standards
of propriety on the other, continued unabated. Even the printed
word could not be assumed to be permanently immune to censorship, despite the shift of focus to the electronic media. As
Donald Downs observed in 1989: "[B]ecause readers supply
their own pictures from their imaginations, the effects of written fantasy may be more personal and powerful than those of
still photographs or film. Thus, the written word may actually be
more harmful than pornographic pictures."[76]

In his 1989 study *Freedom and Taboo: Pornography and the Politics of a Self Divided*, political scientist Richard S. Randall reiterated a point made years before by Charles Rembar: all available data make clear that public support for censorship is almost always far greater than that of the judges charged with upholding the First Amendment. On the censorship–free speech continuum, he suggests, the social reality in contemporary America is not of "tolerance freely given," but of "grudging de facto tolerance" imposed by the courts on a "majority favoring greater social control."[77] If this is a correct assessment, as I believe it is, then it is hardly surprising that censorship pressures seem so impervious to liberalizing court rulings grounded in constitutional principles, and that the repressive impulse periodically spikes upward when the larger political/cultural climate is conducive to such a response.

Pushing the analysis beyond the usual polarity between would-be censors and civil libertarians, Randall roots the perennial nature of the struggle within the human psyche itself. Writing from a psychoanalytic perspective, he suggests that all human beings are simultaneously attracted by the transgressive lure of the sexually forbidden and alarmed by the danger inherent in yielding to such impulses. The universal "pornographic imagination" is thus continually monitored and thwarted by the superego. "Forbidden sexual fantasies—the pornographic within—tempt us with their promise of delight and impossible gratification and disturb us by their trespass and perversity. No external liberty can completely free us from anxiety about the latter, and no social censorship is so complete that it can obliterate the seductive invitation of the former." From this perspective, the endless legal and cultural struggle between repression and tolerance, always resulting in some compromise between the two, mirrors in the public sphere the divisions and conflicts inherent in each individual's psychological make-up.[78]

Assuming that Randall is correct, within that underlying psychological reality operate the political and cultural dynamics that shape the intensity and nature of repressive movements in successive time periods. As always, late-twentieth-century discussions of censorship reflected the larger political and cultural developments these years. Earlier debates had generally been sharply polarized between outspoken civil libertarians and easily caricatured moralists appalled by the corrupting power of bad books and sex-drenched movies. These two camps survived at the century's end, with groups like the ACLU and People for the American Way on one side and the National Federation for Decency and Morality in Media on the other. But one also found—as in the mid-1960s—a growing middle ground of intellectuals and cultural commentators opposed to censorship, but concerned about pornography's social effects. We have already examined the views of commentators troubled by pornography's alleged role in encouraging child abuse or violence against women. Others in this middle camp, however, harking back to Harry Clor's 1969 work *Obscenity and Public Morality*, focused less on such clear-cut (if sometimes difficult to prove) harms than on the more general debasement of the public sphere that they attributed in part to the flood of sexual material, explicit or merely titillating, sloshing through the culture.

A case in point is *The Repeal of Reticence* (1996), by the young historian and cultural critic Rochelle Gurstein. Her work is a study of the bitter war between "the party of reticence" and "the party of exposure" in late-nineteenth and twentieth century America, with censorship as a major battlefield. Praising the Gilded Age's "reticent sensibility," Gurstein argues that much was lost in the successive victories of the "party of exposure." In discussing book censorship from the 1870s through the 1930s, Gurstein casts a cold eye on the lawyers, judges, and others who challenged the legal and extra-legal censorship that so firmly buttressed the "culture of reticence." As that culture collapsed under repeated fusillades from civil libertarians in league with literary modernists, sex reformers, and others, argues Gurstein, "taste was among the first casualties" and the way was paved for "an ugly, vulgar world" characterized by "sheer triviality" and "devoid of legitimate standards of taste and judgment." The introduction of expert opinion about literary merit in censorship cases, she writes, was a slap at "common sense" and "a direct rebuttal of the position that public morals and decency took precedence over literary culture." While Comstock and his ilk were "severely limited by their prejudice, overwrought moralism, religious zeal, and . . . singular inability to appreciate [genuine art]," Gurstein insists, the cruel ridicule of Comstock and the portrayal of all censors "as prurient prude[s] and hypocrite[s]" by the "party of exposure" encouraged contempt for Gilded Age culture and its values of restraint, decorum, and respect for privacy.[79]

What must be done? The lost culture of reticence, Gurstein somewhat ambiguously observes, is something "we must recover—even if we reject it anew." First, conventional liberal ideas about censorship, personal freedom, the claims of decency, and the literary canon must be reappraised. In the battle to elevate the tone of public life, she contends, "either we recognize that certain activities and experiences require privacy to give our lives ballast, or the common world becomes literally shameless and our shared existence without consequence." While a reassertion of standards of taste and decorum are central, the law has a role as well. Deploring the Supreme Court's "extreme reluctance to regulate obscenity," Gurstein calls for "a rational program of censorship" that will require (here she approvingly quotes Harry Clor) "the exercise of political judgment in the broadest and deepest sense" and the ability "to reason rightly about fundamental principles, *and* to apply principles with intelligent sensitivity to changing circumstances." She is even prepared to reopen the censorship battles fought and won by earlier generations of readers and civil libertarians: "[I]t is worthwhile to reconsider whether the old defenses of modernist novels such as *Ulysses* or *Lady Chatterley's Lover* should continue to receive automatic endorsement."[80]

One might question whether recent experience—the rulings of the Burger court, the role of the religious right in the culture wars, the Meese Report, the 1996 censorship laws—offer hope that the American people and their leaders in their handling of obscenity issues will rise to the level of wisdom and discretion envisioned by Clor and Gurstein. But whether or not these authors' prescriptions could be achieved in the real world, their books, and others, clearly represented significant conservative interventions in the ongoing debate.

We've come a long way from the sepia-tinted world of Anthony Comstock, John Sumner, Morris Ernst, Upton Sinclair, the young Alfred Knopf, and the others who populate the earlier chapters of this study. Yet for the historian, the late-twentieth-century chapters in the nation's long struggle to balance the competing values of individual freedom, a due regard for public opinion, and the desire to uphold a decent and humane civic culture can only elicit a keen sense of *déjà vu*. As the twenty-first century began, one felt oneself in a kind of cultural echo chamber, in which issues that had been fiercely debated decades earlier once again gripped the public mind, albeit in new terms and involving new alignments of forces. Even the old metaphors were recycled. Echoing the public-health analogies of Progressive-era advocates of censorship, radio commentator Paul Harvey declared in the 1980s: "I am opposed to putting garbage on television for the same reason I would oppose open sewers in our streets. . . . [W]here . . . sewage flows unconfined, it breeds disease."[81]

America's long preoccupation with regulating the obscene and the subversive within the constraints of the First Amendment's free speech and free press protections was clearly in no danger of fading as the twentieth century ended. As a new century began, the odds seemed good that censorship efforts, together with the impassioned debate that such efforts always elicit, would continue—doubtless in new forms to address evolving technologies, changing domestic and global realities, and ever-shifting legislative actions and judicial interpretations.

With a mournful shake of the head or a derisive chuckle, both Anthony Comstock and H. L. Mencken, those quaintly dated yet quintessential embodiments of the two poles of Americans' divided thought on these matters, would probably not be surprised by this inconclusive conclusion. The issues involved are so fundamental, and the balance of competing public values—and even of contradictory impulses within the human psyche—so delicate and precarious, that they probably never will, and perhaps never should, be finally resolved. Meanwhile, the constantly evolving debate and the kaleidoscopic realignments of social forces arrayed in these struggles tell us much about the larger cultural realities of successive eras of American history. It is this larger context, and its role in shaping attitudes and public policies toward censorship and obscenity, that I have tried to position at the center of this history.

A NEW CENTURY BEGINS, THE STRUGGLE
CONTINUES: A PORTFOLIO OF VIGNETTES

New York Times, June 11, 2001

A new computer virus is reported that invades the victim's files, searches out sites deemed to be pornographic, and alerts the authorities.

BBC News report, July 20, 2001

The Chinese government shuts down thousands of Internet chat rooms and installs software to allow government officials to monitor Internet communications. Parents have complained, Beijing reports, that their teenage children are becoming addicted to the Internet.

Wisconsin State Journal, December 11, 2000

The mayor of Albany, New York, asks the city transit authority to remove from city buses lingerie ads featuring supermodel Claudia Schiffer. "I can't and won't advocate for censorship," she says, "but I can be an advocate for good taste, which is what this is all about."

New York Times, March 24, 2001

Paula Houston is appointed Utah's "Obscenity and Pornography Complaints Ombudsman," a $75,000-a-year position created by the state legislature to handle citizen complaints about obscenity and to advise local communities how to fight it.

❦

New York Times, July 14, 2001
In the first known case of a child-pornography conviction involving words rather than images, a jury in Columbus, Ohio, sentences Brian Dalton to ten years in prison for fictional stories he wrote in his journal describing fantasies of molesting and torturing children. The Franklin County prosecutor hails the case as a breakthrough in child-pornography prosecution.

❦

Wisconsin State Journal, June 15, 2001
A citizen in Sheboygan, Wisconsin, presumably under cover of night, staples towels over scantily clad models in two large billboards advertising Captain Morgan Spiced Rum.

❦

New Yorker, April 16, 2001
The American Civil Liberties Union warns of Echelon, a worldwide surveillance network created by the U.S. National Security Administration in cooperation with England, Canada, Australia, and New Zealand "to intercept virtually all forms of electronic communications" including cell phone transmissions, e-mail, and computer Web sites. The ACLU also notes an FBI wiretap system involving special hardware installed in the computers of all Internet service providers. In researching this chapter, I am about to launch an Internet search on "child pornography," but then I hesitate: could those red-flag words land me in some computer database of suspicious persons?

❦

July 2001
As a consultant in a copyright-infringement lawsuit involving a movie based on the Book of Revelation, I compose an e-

mail to a Los Angeles law firm quoting the biblical account of the Harlot of Babylon and her "fornications." When I click "Send," a warning appears on the screen: "This message may be offensive to some viewers. You may want to consider toning it down." Only when I click on "Send it Anyway" does the message go through. A few months later, when I e-mail the "Acknowledgements" for the second edition of *Purity in Print* to my editor at the University of Wisconsin Press, my ever vigilant e-mail nanny spots the shocking word "wantoness" in the Wislawa Szymborska poem and again sends me the same warning message.

September 2001

In the "Boondocks" comic strip, artist Aaron McGruder, with obvious satirical intent, portrays a character reciting the innuendo-filled titles of movies featuring actress Viveca Fox. The next day, the *Milwaukee Journal Sentinal*, citing readers' complaints, preempts two panels of the "Boondocks" strip to denounce the preceding day's strip as "unfit for the comics page"— while "firmly defend[ing] Mr. McGruder's right to free speech."

New York Times, September 14, 2001

The Rev. Jerry Falwell, appearing on the popular "700 Club" television program of the Rev. Pat Robertson, blames the American Civil Liberties Union and People for the American Way, among other groups, for the terrorist actions that destroyed the World Trade Center and heavily damaged the Pentagon the day before. Such groups plunged America so deeply into sin, Falwell suggests, that God withdrew his protective hand and permitted the terrorists to carry out their action.

New York Times, October 26, 2001

Congress approves and President George W. Bush signs into law an anti-terrorism bill, the USA PATRIOT Act, empow-

ering law-enforcement officials in certain cases to conduct surveillance of Internet communications without a court order. The
four-year sunset provision attached to some parts of the bill do
not apply to the section dealing with Internet surveillance. Only
one senator, Russell Feingold of Wisconsin, votes against the
bill, citing civil-liberties concerns.

St. Paul Pioneer Press, January 1, 2002
The Rev. Jack Brock, founder and pastor of Christ Community Church in Alamogordo, New Mexico, conducts a public
burning of J. K. Rowling's Harry Potter series, which he de-
nounces as "a masterpiece of satanic deception." As the ceremony
proceeds, hundreds of protesters shout "Stop burning books."

Notes
Index

Notes

INTRODUCTION

1. For more on the *Ginzburg* decision, see Chapter X.

2. *New York Times*, Jan. 17 and April 23, 1968; *Publishers' Weekly*, July 12, 1965.

3. *N. Y. Times*, Sept, 23, 1967.

4. George P. Elliott, "Against Pornography," *Harper's*, CCXXX (March 1965), pp. 51–60; Ernest van den Haag, "The Case for Pornography is the Case for Censorship," *Esquire*, May 1967, pp. 134–35; Sidney Hook, "Pornography and the Censor," *N.Y. Times Book Review*, April 12, 1964; Pamela Hansford Johnson, "Who's To Blame When a Murderer Strikes?" *Life*, Aug. 12, 1966, pp. 62 ff (This idea is more fully developed in her book, *On Iniquity*, Charles Scribner's Sons, N.Y., 1967); Norman Mailer, "A Note on Comparative Pornography," in *Advertisements for Myself* (Signet ed., N.Y., 1959), pp. 385–87; Norman Mailer, "On the Steps of the Pentagon," *Harper's*, March 1968, pp. 65, 129;

Howard Moody, "Towards a New Definition of Obscenity," *Christianity and Crisis*, XXIV (Jan. 25, 1965), pp. 284–88; Richard Schechner, "Pornography and the New Expression," *Atlantic*, Jan. 1967, pp. 74–78; Susan Sontag, "The Pornographic Imagination," *Partisan Review*, Spring 1967, pp. 181–212; George Steiner, "Night Words: High Pornography and Human Privacy," *Encounter*, Oct. 1965, reprinted in George Steiner, *Language and Silence* (N.Y., 1967), pp. 68–77; Gore Vidal, "On Pornography," *New York Review of Books*, Mar. 31, 1966.

5. Cited in Horace Judson, "The Critic Between," *Encounter*, XXX (March 1968), pp. 59–60.

CHAPTER I

1. The standard biography is Heywood Broun and Margaret Leech, *Anthony Comstock, Roundsman of the Lord* (N.Y., 1927). See also Charles G. Trumbull's highly sympathetic *Anthony Comstock, Fighter* (N.Y., 1913).

2. Margaret Anderson, ed., *The Little Review Anthology* (N.Y., 1953), p. 137.

3. Quoted in Anon. [Howard Potter], *In Memoriam: Death of Charles Loring Brace* [N.Y., 1890], p. 5.

4. [N.Y.] Children's Aid Society, *Annual Report* (1864), pp. 3, 4. On wartime unrest in Manhattan, see Br. Basil Leo Lee, F.S.C., *Discontent in New York City, 1861–1865 . . .* (Washington, 1943); on the 1863 riot: David M. Barnes, *The Draft Riots in New York, July 1863* (N.Y., 1863), esp. p. 6; Herbert Asbury, *The Gangs of New York* (N.Y., 1928), Chaps. VII–VIII. A contemporary pamphlet, "The Bloody Week" (N.Y., July 1863) conveys something of the intense alarm the riots stirred among the established citizenry.

5. Charles Loring Brace, *The Dangerous Classes of New York, and Twenty Years' Work Among Them* (N.Y., 1872), p. 30; [Anon.], *The Volcano Under the City, by a Volunteer Special* (N.Y., 1887), p. 316; William O. Stoddard, *The Battle of New York, A Story for All Young People* (N.Y., 1892), p. 201.

6. C. Howard Hopkins, *History of the Y.M.C.A. in North America* (N.Y., 1951), pp. 107, 384; Broun and Leech, *Comstock*, p. 18; New York Society for the Suppression of Vice, *Annual Report* (1876), Act of Incorporation printed on the inside front cover (hereafter: N.Y. Vice Soc., A.R.). For discussions of the Protestant response to urban industrial America, a response of which the vice-society movement was but a small part, see William W. Sweet, *The Story of Religion in America* (rev. ed., N.Y., 1950), Chap. XXIII, "The Church and the Rise of the City"; Henry F. May, *Protestant Churches and Industrial America* (Octagon Ed., N.Y., 1963), Part III, Chap. 2, "The Face of the City"; and Winthrop S. Hudson, *American Protestantism* (Chicago, 1961), pp. 111–12.

7. Broun and Leech, *Comstock*, p. 167. For a list of the vice-society officers in cities other than New York and Boston, see New England Watch and Ward Society, *Annual Report, 1887–88* (1888), pp. 25–26, "Kindred Societies" (hereafter: W. & W. Soc., A.R.).

8. The seventeen incorporators are listed in the N.Y. Vice Soc., A.R. (1876) and many later reports. Biographical data was found on thirteen of them, as follows: **Thatcher M. Adams**, thirty-six years old in 1873, prominent New York City attorney, son of a New Hampshire minister; **Cornelius R. Agnew**, forty-three, of Huguenot and Scotch-Irish ancestry, son of a New York City tobacco merchant and shipper, professor of ophthalmology at the College of Physicians and Surgeons; **Moses S. Beach**, of Connecticut background, proprietor of the New York *Sun*, a leading daily of the period; **Cephas Brainerd**, forty-two, native of Haddam, Conn., New York City lawyer, lecturer in international law at University of the City of New York; **John M. Cornell**, prominent merchant and real-estate developer, a founder of Mount Vernon, N.Y.; **William E. Dodge, Jr.**, forty-one, son of a native of Hartford, Conn., great-grandson of a Congregationalist minister, active in Phelps, Dodge & Co., the copper business founded by his father-in-law; **Morris K. Jesup** (see text); **Robert R. McBirney**, thirty-six, of devout Scotch-Irish parentage, came to New York City at eighteen, became general secretary of New York City Y.M.C.A. in 1862; **Elbert B. Monroe**, treasurer of Mercantile Safe Deposit Co., later a partner in Ball, Black & Co., a brokerage firm; **Howard Potter**, forty-six, son of the Episcopal Bishop of Pennsylvania, nephew of the Bishop of New York, prominent lawyer, partner in Brown Bros. & Co.; **J. P. Morgan**, thirty-six, native of Hartford, by 1873 well along in a banking and finance career; **Charles E. Whitehead**, senior partner in the law firm Whitehead, Dexter, and Osborn; **William H. S. Wood**, thirty-three, of Pennsylvania Quaker antecedents, president of the Bowery Savings Bank and of a medical publishing firm founded by his grandfather. Sources: Andrew N. Adams, *Genealogical History of Henry Adams of Braintree, Mass. and His Descendants* (Rutland, Vt., 1898), p 318; *Dict. Am. Biog.* (Agnew, Beach, McBirney, Morgan); *Nat. Cyc. Am. Biog.*, XIII, p. 352 (Dodge), XXIV, p. 389 (Wood); *Lamb's Biog. Dict. of the U.S.*, I, p. 45 (Agnew): I, p. 389 (Brainerd); Moses King, *Notable New Yorkers of 1869–1899* (N.Y., 1899), p. 584 (Whitehead); Hopkins, *Y.M.C.A.*, p. 384 (Brainerd), p. 409 (Monroe); *Boston Evening Transcript*, Apr. 19, 1888 (Agnew obit.); Dec. 17, 1910 (Brainerd obit.); Apr. 30, 1902 (Cornell obit.); and Mar. 26, 1897 (Potter obit.).

9. Barnes was a vice-president of the Vice Society, Van Rensselaer its treasurer for many years, and Beecher an executive-committee member from 1882 to 1897. *Nat. Cyc. Am. Biog.*, XIII, pp. 159–60 (Colgate); IV, p. 378 (Barnes); II, p. 251 (Van Rensselaer family); XXXI, p. 141 (Beecher).

10. William A. Brown, *Morris Ketchum Jesup, A Character Sketch* (N.Y., 1910), *passim*, esp. pp. 19, 42, 57, 113, and 137.

11. George M. Roe, *Cincinnati, The Queen City of the West* (Cincinnati, 1895), pp. 137–38; "William J. Breed, 1835–1908" (pamphlet privately printed by the Cincinnati Commercial Club, 1908); Cincinnati Chamber of Commerce, *Annual Report, 1908* (Cincinnati, 1908), p. 219.

12. W. & W. Soc., A.R., *1883–84* (1884), p. 2. The four other colleges were Amherst, Colby, Brown, and the University of Vermont.

13. Frederick Lewis Allen, *Frederick Baylies Allen, A Memoir* (Cambridge, 1929); *My Neighbor; A Journal of the Episcopal City Mission, the Archdeaconry of Boston,* XXXIV (Feb. 1925), p. 8; *Boston Evening Transcript,* Feb. 20, 1925.

14. W. & W. Soc., A.R., *1888–89* (1889), p. 21. Mary Baker Eddy and the publisher D. C. Heath also contributed in this year.

15. The Reverend Mr. James Eells, addressing the Watch and Ward Society in 1900—*ibid., 1899–1900* (1900), pp. 24–25; N.Y. Vice Soc., A.R., (1876), p. 3.

16. Trumbull, *Comstock,* p. 23.

17. Anthony Comstock, *Traps for the Young* (N.Y., 1883), p. 183; Anthony Comstock, *Frauds Exposed; or, How the People Are Deceived and Robbed, and Youth Corrupted* (N.Y., *ca.* 1880), p. 441.

18. N.Y. Vice Soc., A.R. (1876), p. 4. On the newspapers' attitude, see Broun and Leech, *Comstock,* pp. 93, 146.

19. "The substantial results of work [of the Watch and Ward] during the last three months justify its urgent appeal for a more generous support"—*Boston Evening Transcript,* Oct. 16, 1890. The Reverend Mr. Allen's comment is in W. & W. Soc., A.R., *1894–95* (1895), p. 6.

20. Other of these crusades were directed against De Robigne M. Bennett, editor of the *Truth Seeker,* imprisoned through Comstock's efforts, and Ida Craddock, a mentally disturbed woman who committed suicide when her pamphlet "The Wedding Night" was attacked by Comstock as obscene—Broun and Leech, *Comstock,* pp. 170, 175, and 211; *Dict. Am. Biog.* (Heywood and Bennett). On the "Comstock law" of 1873, which extended an 1865 postal obscenity act to include publications and materials relating to contraception and abortion, see James C. N. Paul and Murray L. Schwartz, *Federal Censorship; Obscenity in the Mail* (N.Y., 1961), pp. 16–18, 21–24, 343–44.

21. National Defense Association, *Words of Warning to Those Who Aid and Abet in the Suppression of Free Speech and Free Press* (N.Y., 1879), statement of objectives on back cover. The National Defense Association was founded by the Reverend Mr. A. L. Rawson and Mrs. Laura Kendrick of Boston. See also Broun and Leech, *Comstock,* p. 179.

22. Quoted in Comstock, *Traps,* pp. 189–90.

23. Comstock, *Frauds Exposed,* pp. 421–29.

24. *Woman's Journal,* May 2, 1891, p. 138.

25. Comstock, *Traps,* p. 137. For a record of the number of books suppressed through vice-society prosecutions in New York and Boston, see Comstock, "Vampire Literature," *North American Review,* CLIII

(Aug. 1891), p. 161, and W. & W. Soc., A.R., *1897–98* (1898), p. 3. The charter of the New York Vice Society directed the police to "aid this corporation . . . in the enforcement of all laws. . ." quoted in N.Y. Vice Soc., A.R., (1876), inside front cover. In addition, Comstock bore the title of Special Investigator for the Post Office Department. The Watch and Ward Society enjoyed similar, though less explicitly spelled-out, privileges.

26. The speaker was William F. Dodge—N.Y. Vice Soc., A.R. (1876), p. 3.

27. The progress of this campaign is set forth in the following (where the passages quoted may also be found): untitled Watch and Ward Society pamphlet dated Mar. 24, 1879, in the collection of miscellaneous Watch and Ward material in Widener Library, Harvard University; W. & W. Soc., A.R., *1897–98* (1898), p. 8; *ibid., 1884–85* (1885), p. 7; *ibid., 1885–86* (1886), p. 11 (italics added); *ibid., 1892–93* (1893), p. 7.

28. *Ibid., 1903–04* (1904), p. 6; *ibid., 1899–1900* (1900), p. 36. Mrs. Edwin D. Mead was the latter speaker.

29. *Ibid., 1884–85* (1885), p. 5; *ibid., 1898–99* (1899), pp. 5 and 6 (cigarette-vendor incident).

30. Comstock discusses this phase of his work almost interminably in the 576 pages of *Frauds Exposed.*

31. *The New York Charities Directory* (3rd ed., N.Y., 1888, and subsequent editions); William D. P. Bliss, *Encyclopedia of Social Reform* (N.Y., 1897), p. 318; National Congress of P.T.A., *Golden Jubilee History, 1897–1947* (Chicago, 1947), p. 20; *Union Signal* (W.C.T.U. organ), Nov. 26, 1885; *Minutes of the National W.C.T.U.* (1884), Appendix CL.

32. W. & W. Soc., A.R., *1897–98* (1898), pp. 41–42. On Peabody, see *Dict. Am. Biog.*

33. See above, Notes 8 and 10. Whitehead and Potter were, respectively, vice-president and a trustee of the Children's Aid Society. Potter was also a trustee of the Charity Organization Society, to which J. P. Morgan lent his name as treasurer. Brainerd was a leader in the N.Y. Prison Association. Wood (whose father founded the Society for the Prevention of Pauperism) supported a wide variety of charities. Barnes was active in the Association for Improving the Condition of the Poor, and a heavy contributor to several benevolent homes. It was Thatcher M. Adams who was aroused by dirty streets as well as by dirty books.

34. See above, Note 11.

35. The Watch and Ward executive committee in 1884, for example, included the following: **Robert Treat Paine,** founder of the Boston Associated Charities, the Workingmen's Housing Movement, and Wells Memorial Institute for Workingmen, and an active member of the Children's Aid Society and the American Prison Association; **Homer B. Sprague,** founder of the Martha's Vineyard Summer Institute, the first adult-

education center in the nation; **Loring F. Deland,** founder of the Wage-Earners' Theatre League, trustee of the Massachusetts Babies' Hospital and the Boston Dispensary; **Charles W. Dexter,** active in both the Wells Memorial Institute and the Associated Charities; **Arthur B. Ellis,** officer in the Improved Dwellings Association (and, in 1903, founder of a Utopian community, "Cooperative Brotherhood Industries," in the state of Washington.) Sources: W. & W. Soc., *A.R., 1883–84* (1884), p. 2; *Dict. Am. Biog.* (Paine, Sprague); *Boston Evening Transcript* (obits.): May 3, 1917 (Deland), June 29, 1915 (Dexter), Dec. 28, 1923 (Ellis).

36. See above, Note 13.

37. The Reverend Dr. Raymond Calkins, Belmont, to Paul S. Boyer, Mar. 12, 1961.

38. W. & W. Soc., *A.R., 1899–1900* (1900), p. 26; *ibid., 1887–88* (1888), p. 14.

39. Comstock, *Traps,* p. 219.

40. *My Neighbor,* XXXIV (Apr. 1925), p. 3.

41. *Boston Herald,* Dec. 21, 1929.

42. Morris L. Ernst and Allan U. Schwartz, *Censorship, The Search for the Obscene* (N.Y., 1964), p. 29.

43. Frederick P. Hier, Jr., "When Boston Censored Walt Whitman," *N.Y. Times Magazine,* June 19, 1927, p. 7; Charles A. Madison, *Book Publishing in America* (N.Y., 1966), pp. 116–17; Paul and Schwartz, *Federal Censorship,* pp. 30, 253; *The Critic,* XIV (Aug. 9, 1890), p. 71.

44. Thomas Beer, *The Mauve Decade* (Vintage Ed., N.Y., 1961), p. 170; Walter E. Houghton, *The Victorian Frame of Mind, 1830–1870* (Yale Paperbound Ed., New Haven, 1957), p. 358; George Moore, *Confessions of a Young Man* (N.Y., 1917 Ed. [first published in 1886]), p. 178. For more on the phalanx of "cultural custodians" guarding the genteel literary code, see Beer, *The Mauve Decade,* Chap. VI, "The American Magazines"; Henry F. May, *The End of American Innocence* (N.Y., 1959), pp. 50–79; Donald Sheehan, *This Was Publishing; A Chronicle of the Book Trade in the Gilded Age* (Bloomington, Ind., 1952), pp. 107–11; and Madeleine B. Stern, *Imprints on History, Book Publishers and American Frontiers* (Bloomington, Ind., 1956), p. 307, which points out the strikingly similar New England backgrounds of the leading late-nineteenth-century publishers.

45. The commissioner is quoted in Richard Jones, "The Moral and Literary Responsibility of Librarians in Selecting Books for a Public Library," *Journal of Proceedings and Addresses of the XXXVIth Annual Meeting, National Education Association* (Washington, D.C., 1897), p. 1027. For a British version of the genteel ideal, see "The Fleshly School of Poetry," Robert Buchanan's slashing attack on the poems of Rossetti. It appeared first in the *Contemporary Review* of October 1871, and is reprinted in Robert L. Peters, ed., *Victorians on Literature and Art* (N.Y., 1961), pp. 220–35.

46. Julia Ward Howe, "The Influence of Literature upon Crime," in

Papers and Letters Presented at the First Woman's Congress of the Association for the Advancement of Women, Held in Union League Theatre . . . New York, October 1873 (N.Y., 1874), pp. 13, 15, 17; Richard Hofstadter, *Anti-Intellectualism in American Life* (Vintage Ed., N.Y., 1966), pp. 94, 108 (Finney and Moody); Mrs. H. O. Ward, *Sensible Etiquette of the Best Society* (N.Y., 1878), p. 405; Eugene P. Link, "Abraham and Mary P. Jacobi, 'Humanitarian Physicians,'" *Jour. of the Hist. of Medicine* (Autumn 1949), p. 389; *Dict. Am. Biog.* (on Jacobi); Elizabeth Blackwell, *Counsel to Parents on the Moral Education of Their Children* (N.Y., 1879), pp. 116, 117.

47. J. Henry Harper, *The House of Harper* (N.Y., 1912), p. 620; Roger Burlingame, *Of Making Many Books; A Hundred Years of Reading, Writing and Publishing* (N.Y., 1946), p. 80 (a Scribner's house history); William S. Walsh to Jeanette L. Gilder, Feb. 2, 1889, Gilder Papers, XI, Schlesinger Library, Radcliffe College.

48. Justin Kaplan, *Mr. Clemens and Mark Twain* (N.Y., 1966), pp. 93, 221, 268; Madison, *Book Publishing in America*, p. 120.

49. Crane to Ripley Hitchcock, [Feb. 10, 1896], R.W. Stallman and Lillian Gilkes, eds., *Stephen Crane: Letters* (N.Y., 1960), p. 113. See also: *ibid.*, the footnotes on pp. 12, 13, 14, and 79; William M. Gibson, Introduction to Stephen Crane, *The Red Badge of Courage and Selected Prose* (Rinehart Ed., N.Y., 1962), esp. pp. v, xvi; and Robert W. Stallman, "Stephen Crane's Revision of *Maggie: A Girl of the Streets*," *American Lit.*, XXVI (Jan. 1955), pp. 528–36. *Library Journal* quoted in "Fiction in Public Libraries," *Review of Reviews*, XV (N.Y. Ed., May 1897), p. 604.

50. Page to Dreiser, July 19, 1900, Robert H. Elias, ed., *Letters of Theodore Dreiser, A Selection* (Philadelphia, 1959), Vol. I, p. 55. On the whole episode, see Robert H. Elias, *Theodore Dreiser, Apostle of Nature* (N.Y., 1949), pp. 110–17.

51. Dreiser, *Letters*, Vol. I, p. 210n.

52. W. & W. Soc., *A.R.*, *1885–86* (1886), p. 10.

53. *The Critic*, XIV (Aug. 9, 1890), p. 71.

54. W. & W. Soc., *A.R.*, *1899–1900* (1900), p. 42; Comstock, *Traps*, p. 240.

55. This potpourri of vice-society wisdom is from the following sources: N.Y. Vice Soc., *A.R.* (1900), p. 12; W. & W. Soc., *A.R.*, *1892–93* (1893), p. 6; Comstock, *Traps*, p. 133; Comstock, *Frauds*, p. 416; the Reverend Mr. J. M. Buckley, Introduction to Comstock, *Traps*, p. v; [Watch and Ward Soc.], "To Every Thoughtful Man Having the Care of Youth" [n.p., 1883?]. This pamphlet advised that any boy who had fallen victim to the "secret vice" through evil literature or other sources should be warned that he was in danger of becoming "an effeminate, weak-minded poltroon . . ., perhaps even an idiot or a maniac. . . ."

56. Comstock, "Vampire Literature," p. 165.

57. The Reverend J. L. Withrow, quoted in W. & W. Soc., A.R., *1898–99* (1899), pp. 7, 22.

CHAPTER II

1. New England Watch and Ward Society, *Annual Report, 1897–98* (1898), p. 40.

2. *Ibid., 1902–03* (1903), p. 48; William B. Forbush, *The Coming Generation* (N.Y., 1912), pp. vii, 93; W. & W. Soc., A.R., *1910–11* (1911), p. 36. Analogies to other aspects of Progressivism were frequent. In 1916, for example, Professor W. T. Sedgwick of M.I.T. referred to the conservation movement, and declared that the Watch and Ward's task was "the conservation of the morality and decency of the human race. . . ."—*ibid., 1915–16* (1916), p. 42.

3. Quoted in *ibid., 1906–07* (1907), p. 23. Jeffrey R. Brackett of the Boston School for Social Workers addressed the Watch and Ward Society in 1907. See also Jane Addams, *A New Conscience and an Ancient Evil* (N.Y., 1912) in which (p. 106) she deplores "the novels which form the sole reading of thousands of young men and girls," and Mary E. Richmond's influential *Friendly Visiting Among the Poor* (N.Y., 1899), which (p. 86) discusses "bad reading" as one cause of juvenile crime.

4. W. & W. Soc., A.R., *1914–15* (1915), pp. 5–6.

5. *Who Was Who,* I (Birtwell, Cole); *Dict. Am. Biog.,* Supp. II (Lee, Mead). Other officers at this time included the Reverend Dr. Raymond Calkins, a young Congregationalist minister active in many philanthropic movements, particularly housing legislation and prison reform, and the Reverend Dr. Rufus B. Tobey, who founded homes for unwed mothers and the aged in Revere, Mass., as well as the novel "Floating Hospital," which for many years docked at various Massachusetts port and river cities as a visiting clinic for tenement dwellers. (Raymond Calkins, Belmont, Mass., to Paul S. Boyer, Mar. 18, 1961; *Boston Evening Transcript,* Jan. 6, 1920, Tobey obit.)

6. N.Y. Vice Soc., A.R. (1903), p. 4.

7. Numerous works cover this aspect of Progressivism. Particularly helpful were Otto Wilson, *Fifty Years' Work with Girls, 1883–1933, A Story of the Florence Crittenton Homes* (Alexandria, 1933), esp. Chap. II, "Fifty Years' War on Vice"; Roy Lubove, "The Progressives and the Prostitute," *Historian,* XXIV (May 1962), pp. 308–30; Willoughby C. Waterman, *Prostitution and Its Repression in New York City, 1900–31* (N.Y., 1932), esp. Chap. III, "Privately Organized Groups"; Walter E. Houghton, *The Victorian Frame of Mind, 1830–1870* (Yale Paperbound Ed., New Haven, 1957), pp. 367–77, in which the depth and basis of the fears aroused by prostitution in the late nineteenth century are discussed; Louise C. Wade, *Graham Taylor, Pioneer for Social Justice,*

1851–1938 (Chicago, 1964), pp. 198–200, on the Chicago investigation. Jane Addams's *A New Conscience and an Ancient Evil* was another by-product of this crusade.

8. On the origins of the A.S.H.A. see William F. Snow, "Progress, 1900–1915," *Social Hygiene*, II (Jan. 1916), pp. 37–47. The prevalence of VD had been a particular cause for alarm since the appearance of Dr. Prince A. Morrow's *Social Disease and Marriage* in 1904.

9. William T. Foster, ed., *The Social Emergency; Studies in Sex Hygiene and Morals* (Boston, *ca.* 1914), p. v; Rt. Rev. William Lawrence, "Venereal Disease in the Army, Navy, and Community," *Social Hyg.*, IV (July 1918), p. 331.

10. Donald R. Hooker, "Social Hygiene—Another Great Social Movement," *ibid.*, II (Jan. 1916), p. 9.

11. William W. Sanger, *History of Prostitution* (N.Y., 1882), p. 21.

12. M. J. Exner, *Problems and Principles of Sex Education; A Study of 948 College Men* (N.Y., *ca.* 1915), pp. 8, 34.

13. Quoted in Snow, "Progress, 1900–1915," p. 40.

14. *The Social Evil in Chicago; A Study of Existing Conditions with Recommendations by the Vice Commission of Chicago* (Chicago, 1911), p. 249; *Report and Recommendations of the Wisconsin Legislative Committee to Investigate the White Slave Traffic and Kindred Subjects* (Madison, 1914), p. 173. This committee suggested consumer resistance as the best means of combatting these evils. The Chicago group listed (pp. 345–46) the Illinois obscenity statute in a compilation of laws combatting "the immoral influences and dangers which surround children and young people."

15. Information from an undated fund-raising letter of the Illinois Vigilance Association. Photocopy supplied courtesy Virgil W. Peterson, Operating Director, Chicago Crime Commission.

16. Eliot, "The American Social Hygiene Association," *Social Hyg.*, I (Dec. 1914), p. 3; "Social Hygiene Legislation in 1915," *ibid.*, II (Apr. 1916), p. 251.

17. G. Stanley Hall, *Adolescence; Its Psychology and Its Relations to Physiology, Anthropology, Sociology, Sex, Crime, Religion and Education* (N.Y., 1904), pp. 437, 465.

18. *The National Purity Congress, Its Papers, Addresses, Portraits* (N.Y., 1896), pp. 418–20; John Collier, "Anthony Comstock—Liberal," *Survey*, XXXV (Nov. 6, 1915), p. 128. Another speaker at the 1895 Congress was Theodore Roosevelt.

19. N.Y. Vice Soc., A.R. (1916), p. 6.

20. *Ibid.*, pp. 22ff. (Carnegie and his wife contributed $500 each); W. & W. Soc., A.R., *1898–99* (1899), p. 33 (Palmer); *ibid.*, *1901–02* (1902), p. 32 (Howe); *ibid.*, *1910–11* (1911), pp. 21 (Guild) and 35 (Eliot); *ibid.*, *1908–09* (1909), p. 28 (Hall).

21. N.Y. Vice Soc., A.R. (1906), pp. 16–17. Comstock's ire was aroused by *Mrs. Warren's Profession*, then playing on the New York stage.

22. *N.Y. Times,* Sept. 22, 1915, p. 1; "Anthony Comstock's Service," *ibid.,* Sept. 23, 1915, p. 12; *New Republic,* III (June 19, 1915), pp. 160–61; Collier, "Anthony Comstock—Liberal," p. 127; *Outlook,* CXI (Sept. 29, 1915), pp. 246–47. On June 14, 1915, the *Times* had written of Comstock (p. 8): "He has made [New York] . . . a city more decent than it was. . . . [H]is retirement from any of his activities would be something of a public calamity. . . ."

23. *Ibid.,* Oct. 4, 1915, p. 18; *Who's Who in New York* (N.Y., 1947), p. 1021.

24. Henry F. Pringle, "Comstock the Less," *American Mercury,* X (Jan. 1927), pp. 56–63, quote on p. 56.

25. Henry Van Dyke, *Essays in Application* (N.Y., 1905), pp. 166, 171. For Van Dyke's career and a list of his forty-odd books, see *Who Was Who,* I (1943). He was born in 1852 and died in 1933.

26. J. Henry Harper, *The House of Harper* (N.Y., 1912), p. 648; "Is There a 'Public'?" *Nation,* XCVII (Sept. 4, 1913), p. 205; Roosevelt's letter quoted in Alice Hegan Rice, *The Inky Way* (N.Y., 1940), pp. 69–70. *Cf.* Charles Scribner's comment in 1911: "So many of the well known English authors—like Wells, Arnold Bennett, George Moore, and others—are too free and coarse in their handling of delicate questions to suit us"—quoted in Roger Burlingame, *Of Making Many Books; A Hundred Years of Reading, Writing and Publishing* (N.Y., 1946), p. 86.

27. Arthur E. Bostwick, "The Librarian as Censor," *Library Jour.,* XXXIII (July 1908), pp. 257–64, quoted passages on p. 264.

28. Julia T. Rankin of Atlanta's Carnegie Library, quoted in "What Shall the Libraries Do About Bad Books?" *ibid.* (Sept. 1908), p. 351; *ibid.,* pp. 352 (Wisconsin) and 349 (N.Y.P.L.). The Cleveland Public Library was encouraged (*ibid.,* p. 352) by the fact that bookstores were joining "in the effort to suppress harmful literature." For the responses as a whole see pp. 349–54 of the Sept. issue and pp. 390–93 of the Oct. issue.

29. Corinne Bacon, *What Makes a Novel Immoral?* (Chicago, 1914), p. 20, quoted in Mary U. Rothrock, "Censorship of Fiction in the Public Library," *Library Jour.,* XLVIII (May 15, 1923), p. 455.

30. "Ignatius Phayre" [William G. Fitz-Gerald], *America's Day; Studies in Light and Shade* (London, 1918), p. 225.

31. Frank L. Mott, *Golden Multitudes; The Story of Best Sellers in the United States* (N.Y., 1947), p. 250; Elinor Glyn, *Three Weeks* (N.Y., 1907), p. 84.

32. *Academy,* LXXII (June 29, 1907), p. 635.

33. Quoted in *Publishers' Weekly,* LXXII (Dec. 21, 1907), p. 1996.

34. W. & W. Soc. A.R., *1908–09* (1909), p. 19.

35. *Pub. Wkly.,* LXIII (Feb. 15, 1908), p. 851; W. & W. Soc., A.R., *1907–08* (1908), pp. 9–10; *ibid., 1908–09* (1909), pp. 9, 19–22, where the court's decision is quoted.

36. *Ibid.,* p. 9.

37. *Ibid.*, *1907–08* (1908), pp. 9–10; "Censorship Par Excellence," *Pub. Wkly.*, LXXVIII (July 30, 1910), p. 597.

38. *Ibid.*, LXIV (Dec. 5, 1903), p. 1398; LXV (Jan. 23, 1904), p. 106. After Boston booksellers had subscribed $400 to a defense fund, the case was settled out of court with an agreement on the part of the indicted booksellers not to display the objectionable titles openly.

39. This plan is discussed at length in Chap. VII of this book.

40. *N.Y. Times*, Dec. 24, 1915, p. 6.

41. *Ibid.*

42. *Pub. Wkly.*, LXXXIX (Jan. 22, 1916), p. 280. Knopf has told his version of this incident a number of times, first in the *Publishers' Weekly* letter cited, and most recently in "Publishing's Past Fifty Years, A Balance Sheet—II," *Saturday Rev.*, XLVII (Nov. 28, 1964), pp. 17, 69.

43. " 'Homo Sapiens' is Obscene!" *Little Rev.*, II (Jan./Feb. 1916), p. 20.

44. Theodore Dreiser, *The "Genius"* (John Lane Ed., N.Y., 1915), p. 126. The word "Genius" was enclosed in quotation marks in the 1915 edition's title but not in later editions.

45. *Ibid.*, p. 161.

46. *Bookman*, XLII (Nov. 1915), p. 322; *Boston Evening Transcript*, Oct. 9, 1915, p. 9; *N.Y. Times*, Oct. 10, 1915; Stuart P. Sherman, "The Naturalism of Mr. Dreiser," *Nation*, CI (Dec. 2, 1915), p. 650; *Chicago Daily Tribune*, Dec. 4, 1915.

47. *Cincinnati Enquirer*, Sept. 14, 1916. Quoted in Robert H. Elias, *Theodore Dreiser; Apostle of Nature* (N.Y., 1949), p. 193.

48. John S. Sumner to George T. Keating, Nov. 22, 1916, and to Felix Shay, Nov. 24, 1916, quoted in Elias, *Dreiser*, p. 195.

49. *Ibid.*, pp. 194–96; Dreiser to H. L. Mencken, Nov. 4, 1916, in Robert H. Elias, ed., *Letters of Theodore Dreiser, A Selection* (3 vols., Philadelphia, 1959), I, 233–35. Later in the year Dreiser's attorneys, John Stanchfield and Louis Levy, devised a possible way out of this impasse. A breach of contract suit was filed against the John Lane Co. in the hope that the court would take the opportunity to express an opinion as to the obscenity or nonobscenity of *The "Genius"* under the New York statute. The suit was dismissed, however, the court declining to pass judgment on the book in the absence of a criminal action—Elias, *Dreiser*, p. 206; Ernst and Schwartz, *Censorship*, (N.Y., 1964), pp. 138–41.

50. Dreiser to Mencken, July 31, 1916, Dreiser, *Letters*, I, pp. 221–22; *N.Y. Sun*, Sept. 9, 1916, quoted in Elias, *Dreiser*, p. 198.

51. Mencken to Dreiser, Dec. 20, 1916, Dreiser, *Letters*, I, p. 242. See also *ibid.*, p. 226n.; Elias, *Dreiser*, p. 199; and *Pub. Wkly.*, XC (Sept. 23, 1916), p. 972, where the protest is printed in full.

52. Hamlin Garland to Eric Schuler, Oct. 2, 1916, cited in Elias, *Dreiser*, p. 200. For the nonsigners, see *ibid.*, pp. 200–01; Dreiser to

Mencken, Sept. 23 and Nov. 26, 1916, Dreiser, *Letters*, I, pp. 229, 236. W. A. White eventually signed under strong pressure from Mencken.

53. Mencken to Dreiser, Dec. 16 and Dec. 20, 1916, *ibid.*, pp. 239, 243.

54. Dreiser to Mencken, Dec. 21, 1916, *ibid.*, p. 245.

55. Quoted in W. & W. Soc., A.R., *1907–08* (1908), p. 10. On the changes within the publishing industry, discussed more fully in Chap. IV of this book, see Henry F. May, *The End of American Innocence; A Study of the First Years of Our Own Time, 1912–17* (N.Y., 1959), pp. 290–93. The rise of new publishing houses in this prewar period should not be overemphasized. In both the number of titles issued, and in best-sellers, publishing still remained very much in the hands of the old-line houses. See Alice P. Hackett, *Fifty Years of Best Sellers, 1895–1945* (N.Y., 1945), for the 1900–15 period, and *American Book Trade Manual, 1915* (N.Y., 1915), pp. 197–240, "Directory of Publishers," which gives statistics on the number of titles issued by each house during the foregoing year.

56. "The New England Watch and Ward Society—A Ten Year Record," n.p. [1912]. Arrests made at the Watch and Ward's instigation jumped from 42 to 146 in this eight-year period.

57. This oft-quoted decision, in *Queen v. Hicklin,* a case arising under the (British) Obscene Publications Act of 1857, is discussed at length in all studies of the legal aspects of book censorship. The best recent work is Paul and Schwartz, *Federal Censorship* (N.Y., 1961), pp. 12–17.

58. Joseph Ishill, *A New Concept of Liberty from an Evolutionary Psychologist: Theodore Schroeder, Selections from His Writings with a Biographical Outline* (Berkeley Heights, N.J., 1940), pp. ix-xxxiii, *passim.*

59. Theodore Schroeder, *"Obscene" Literature and Constitutional Law* (N.Y., 1911), pp. 30, 105. Schroeder (p. 27) assumes that only ignorance and "nasty-mindedness" underlie a social group's collective designation of certain words as "obscene."

60. *Ibid.*, pp. 130, 142, 204, 92.

61. W. & W. Soc., A.R., *1908–09* (1909), pp. 37–38. The speaker was Professor E. Carlton Black of Boston University.

62. *Ibid.*, *1905–06* (1906), p. 36. The Reverend John H. Denison made these remarks.

63. *Ibid.*, *1902–03* (1903), p. 36; *1908–09* (1909), p. 35 (Professor Black was the speaker); *1911–12* (1912), p. 18.

64. *Ibid.*, *1905–06* (1906), p. 32. The comment was made by Professor William T. Sedgwick of M.I.T.

65. *Ibid.*, p. 33. Another of Sedgwick's analogies: "When you vaccinate a human being you infringe his personal liberty, but it is an infringement which humanity demands and applauds. . . ."

66. *Ibid.*, p. 35.

67. *Ibid.*, *1907–08* (1908), p. 29. The spokesman on this occasion was the Reverend Carroll Perry of St. Peter's Church, Jamaica Plain.

68. "Filth on the Stage," *Nation*, XCVII (Sept. 11, 1913), p. 246.

69. This incident, witnessed by an amused Theodore Schroeder, is related in *"Obscene" Literature and Constitutional Law*, p. 121.

70, Charles W. Eliot, "The American Social Hygiene Association," p. 2; Exner, *Sex Education*, p. 34; Hall, *Adolescence*, p. 469.

71. Lubove, "Progressives and the Prostitute," p. 318.

72. "Sex O'Clock in America," *Current Opinion*, LV (Aug. 1913), p. 113; "Literary Censorship and the Novels of the Winter," *ibid.* (Nov. 1913), p. 353. *Current Opinion* explicitly attributed this development to the antiprostitution crusades. See also Lubove, "Progressives and the Prostitute," p. 328, and May, *End of American Innocence*, pp. 343–44.

73. Benjamin O. Flower, "Conservatism and Sensualism—An Unhallowed Alliance," *Arena*, III (Dec. 1890), p. 126.

74. Quoted in "Literary Censorship and the Novels of the Winter," p. 377. For biographical data on Goodman (1883–1957), see *Who Was Who*, III, and *Bookman*, XXXVII (1913), p. 622.

75. Daniel Carson Goodman, *Hagar Revelly* (N.Y., 1913), p. 324. Thatah's comments are on p. 381.

76. *Boston Evening Transcript*, June 25, 1913, p. 22; *Review of Reviews*, XLVIII (Oct. 1913), p. 502. On Kennerley, see Charles A. Madison, *Book Publishing in America* (N.Y., 1966) pp. 310–12.

77. "Literary Censorship and the Novels of the Winter," p. 353. In a separate action under the state obscenity law, Comstock prosecuted a clerk in Kennerley's Manhattan bookstore for selling *Hagar Revelly*. The clerk was found guilty in special session court—*Pub. Wkly.*, LXXXV (Jan. 3, 1914), p. 14. (This decision was, of course, superseded by the later Federal court decision.)

78. *N.Y. Times*, Dec. 3, 1913, p. 11; decision quoted in Paul and Schwartz, *Federal Censorship*, p. 52.

79. *N.Y. Times* obit., July 29, 1924; *The Library of John Quinn* (2 vols., N.Y., 1923–24), a listing for public auction purposes. Note on Widener Library, Harvard University, card entry: "The collection brought $226,358.85." For an idea of the scope of Quinn's correspondence with Irish literary figures, see the transcripts in the John Quinn Papers, Mss. Div., N.Y. Public Library. These are open to the public, but may not be quoted. Aline B. Saarinen, *The Proud Possessors* (N.Y., 1958), includes a chapter on Quinn.

80. *"Hagar Revelly* Not Immoral Says Jury," *Pub. Wkly.*, LXXXV (Feb. 14, 1914), pp. 515–16.

81. Daniel Carson Goodman, letter to the editor, *N.Y. Times*, June 20, 1915, II, p. 14.

82. Quoted in Isaac F. Marcosson, *David Graham Phillips and His Times* (N.Y., 1932), p. 250.

83. *Ibid.*, pp. 255–56.

84. John S. Sumner to Joseph H. Sears, Feb. 13, 1917, quoted in *ibid.*, pp. 257–58.

85. Sears to Sumner, quoted in *ibid.*, pp. 259–60.

86. *Ibid.*, pp. 260–61; *N.Y. Times*, Apr. 3, 1917, p. 9; *Pub. Wkly.*, XCI (May 12, 1917), p. 1565. While these proceedings were underway some New York City booksellers "voluntarily" withdrew *Susan Lenox* in response to a warning from Sumner. *Publishers' Weekly* pronounced this approach "a step in the right direction," and said "Mr. Sumner deserves the thanks of the retail book trade. . . ."—*ibid.* (Mar. 10, 1917), pp. 824, 834.

87. [Anon.], *Madeleine, an Autobiography* (N.Y., 1919), pp. 148, 326.

88. "Magdalen," *Nation*, CIX (Nov. 22, 1919), p. 660. See also *New Republic*, XXI (Dec. 24, 1919), p. 126. The *N.Y. Times* disapproved; *Madeleine*, it said (Nov. 16, 1919, VII, p. 662), offered "not the slightest ray of illumination to the social problem out of which it comes."

89. *Pub. Wkly.*, XCVI (Dec. 20, 1919), p. 1608; *N.Y. Times*, Jan. 24, 1920, p. 1, and Jan. 31, 1920, p. 14. A similar fine was imposed against Harper's as a corporation, co-defendant.

90. Pringle, "Comstock the Less," pp. 58–59. See also *Pub. Wkly.*, CXX (Jan. 17, 1920), p. 120, and *N.Y. Times*, Jan. 24, 1920, p. 1.

91. Quoted in *N.Y. Times*, Jan. 25, 1920, p. 18, and Pringle, "Comstock the Less," p. 59.

92. *N.Y. Times*, Jan. 31, 1920, p. 14; July 10, 1920, p. 14.

93. John S. Sumner, "Obscene Literature—Its Suppression," *Pub. Wkly.*, XC (July 8, 1916), pp. 94–97. Quoted passages on pp. 96 and 97.

94. James F. Morton, Jr., "Our Foolish Obscenity Laws," *ibid.*, pp. 97–100. Quoted passages on pp. 97, 98, 99, 100. Morton (p. 97) praised Theodore Schroeder's *"Obscene" Literature and Constitutional Law* as "unanswered and unanswerable." *Publishers' Weekly* reprinted the essays by Sumner and Morton from *Case and Comment*, a magazine for lawyers.

95. "Our Shadowy 'Obscenity' Laws," *Pub. Wkly.*, XC (July 8, 1916), pp. 93–94. Quoted passages on p. 93.

CHAPTER III

1. Walter Lippmann, *Public Opinion* (N.Y., 1922), p. 47. See also George Creel, *How We Advertised America* (N.Y., 1920); James R. Mock and Cedric Larson, *Words That Won the War; The Story of the Committee on Public Information, 1917–1919* (Princeton, 1939); Ray H. Abrams, *Preachers Present Arms; A Study of the Wartime Attitudes and Activities of the Churches and the Clergy in the United States* (Philadelphia, 1933).

2. John Jay Chapman, "The Bright Side of the War," *Atlantic Monthly*, CXXI (Jan. 1918), p. 138; President Henry C. King of

Oberlin quoted in Abrams, *Preachers Present Arms*, p. 50. Added Chapman: "The great crash of evil was followed by a counter-crash of sanctity and heroism—of faith in every form."

3. Henry C. King, *For a New America in a New World* (Paris, 1919), p. 13; Carl Vrooman, an official of the United States Department of Agriculture, quoted in Mock and Larson, *Words That Won the War*, p. 64. Abrams, *Preachers Present Arms*, pp. 99–102, deals with the atrocity stories and their wide circulation. As Henry F. May has observed, the assumption of total German depravity was especially necessary in 1917, for any other explanation of the war would have demanded a major reëxamination of the intellectual bulwarks of the Victorian world view: the belief in progress, in unchanging moral absolutes, and in the superiority of modern Western civilization. To avoid such a painful reëxamination, the leaders of American society undertook to portray the war as a defense of those ideals against an unaccountable German aberration. *End of American Innocence*, pp. 364–66.

4. Harold Hersey, *When the Boys Come Home* (N.Y., 1919), pp. 47, 141, 202, 203.

5. William F. Snow, "Social Hygiene and the War," *Social Hyg.*, III (July 1917), pp. 417–50, esp. p. 421; Raymond B. Fosdick, *Chronicle of a Generation; An Autobiography* (N.Y., 1958), Chap. VIII, "Training Camps in World War I" (pp. 142–86). Fosdick, a brother of the clergyman Harry Emerson Fosdick, was chairman of the Commission on Training Camp Activities. See also Walter Clarke, "Social Hygiene and the War," *Social Hyg.*, IV (Apr. 1918), pp. 259–306.

6. Snow, "Social Hygiene and the War," p. 442; Thomas D. Eliot, "Possible Effects of War upon the Future of the Social Hygiene Movement," *Social Hyg.*, IV (Apr. 1918), pp. 222–23. For some fifty additional articles on the impact of the war on the social-purity movement, see the indexes of Volumes III and IV (1917–18) of *Social Hygiene*.

7. N.Y. Vice Soc., A.R. (1917), p. 13.

8. *Ibid.* (1918), p. 6.

9. *The Messages and Papers of Woodrow Wilson*, ed. Albert Shaw (2 vols., N.Y., 1924), I, p. 397. This assertion was made by Wilson in proclaiming the Selective Service Act, May 18, 1917.

10. Hersey, *When the Boys Come Home*, p. 119; Horatio W. Dresser, *The Victorious Faith: Moral Ideals in Wartime* (N.Y., 1917), quoted in "The War as a Process of Moral Purification," *Current Opinion*, LXIV (Feb. 1917), p. 117; Sydney Brooks, "What the War Has Done for America," *Fortnightly Rev.*, CX (Nov. 1918), pp. 712, 714.

11. Newton D. Baker to all governors and chairmen of state councils of national defense, May 26, 1917, quoted in Snow, "Social Hygiene and the War," p. 434.

12. Gustavus Myers, "Fighting a Menace to Our Race," *Current Hist.*, XVI (June 1922), pp. 420–25; U.S. Public Health Service, "Fighting Venereal Diseases" (Washington, D.C., 1920), p. 23.

13. Social Morality Committee, War Work Council, National Board, Y.W.C.A., *Report* [N.Y.?, 1919?], pp. 1–3 (origins and purposes), 72 (pamphlets), 162–64 (lecture statistics). Quoted passages on pp. 3, 165. Vera Scott Cushman, "The War Work of the Y.W.C.A.," *Review of Reviews*, LVII (Feb. 1918), pp. 191–92 (pledge quoted on p. 192).

14. Harrol B. Ayres, "Democracy at Work—San Antonio Being Reborn," *Social Hyg.*, IV (Apr. 1918), pp. 211–17, esp. pp. 215–17. Fosdick, *Chronicle of a Generation*, pp. 146–47, discusses the role of the Commission on Training Camp Activities in these municipal antivice crusades. See also David Lawrence, "Washington—the Cleanest Capital in the World," *Social Hyg.*, III (July 1917), pp. 313–21, esp. p. 320. The indexes of *Social Hygiene* for the war years contain many additional references to these war-related municipal vice crusades.

15. Maj. Bascom Johnson, "Next Steps," *Social Hyg.*, IV (Jan. 1918), p. 9. Johnson was director of the Division of Law Enforcement of the Commission on Training Camp Activities.

16. New England Watch and Ward Society, *Annual Report, 1916–17* (1917), p. 44 (this alarm was sounded by the Reverend Paul Revere Frothingham); *ibid., 1917–18* (1918), p. 32. The speaker in 1918 was Colonel M. B. Stewart, chief of staff at Camp Devens.

17. Joseph Mayer, "Social Hygiene Legislation in 1917," *ibid.*, V (Jan. 1919), p. 67 and table following p. 68. The link between wartime emotion and a heightened hostility to "obscenity" was not limited to the First World War. The first postal obscenity law in the United States was enacted in 1865 after the Postmaster General had reported that "great numbers" of "obscene books and pictures" were being sent to the Union troops. Also, after a drop in censorship activity in the 1930s, there was an increase with the outbreak of World War II, when the Postmaster General set out to suppress "girlie" magazines such as *Esquire*, which had wide popularity in the armed forces. Paul and Schwartz, *Federal Censorship*, pp. 17, 71–77.

18. Horace Liveright to George Creel, Aug. 27, 1918, quoted in James R. Mock, *Censorship, 1917* (Princeton, 1941), p. 156; Andreas Latzko, *Men in War* (N.Y., 1918), p. 181. The book was published in both a regular and a Modern Library edition. For more on Boni & Liveright, see Chap. IV of this book; for more on the censorship carried out under the wartime espionage and sedition laws, see Zechariah Chafee, Jr., *Free Speech in the United States* (N.Y., 1940), pp. 37–100, and Mock, *Censorship, 1917, passim*. The Espionage Act, among its other provisions, empowered the Postmaster General to bar from the mails any publication considered a threat to the war effort; the Trading-with-the-Enemy Act set up a strict censorship of all mail coming from and going abroad, including published matter; and the Sedition Amendment to the Espionage Act barred any "disloyal, profane, scurrilous, or abusive" criticism of the government, the flag, or the war effort in either print or speech.

19. Wyndham Lewis, "Cantelman's Spring-Mate," *Little Review,* IV (Oct. 1917), pp. 8–14 (passages quoted on pp. 9, 13, and 14); "To Subscribers Who Did Not Receive Their October Issue," *ibid.* (Nov. 1917), pp. 43–44; "Judicial Opinion (Our Suppressed October Issue)," *ibid.* (Dec. 1917), pp. 46–49, which reprints Judge Hand's decision. Hand was obviously troubled by the case, wishing to avoid appearing puritanical yet afraid of undermining the government's position in wartime. He acknowledged that it is "very easy by a narrow and prudish construction of the statute to suppress literature of permanent merit," but added: "I do not think the complainant has made out a case for interfering with the discretion lodged in the Postmaster General whose decision must be regarded as conclusive by the courts unless it appears that it was clearly wrong."

20. Mock, *Censorship, 1917,* pp. 153–54; Creel quoted on p. 154.

21. *N.Y. Times,* May 31, 1918, p. 17. Miss Key's book had been published by Putnam's in 1916.

22. "Many Books Barred from Army Reading," *N.Y. Times,* Sept. 1, 1918, II, p. 2 (in which the A.L.A. statement is quoted): "The Army's Index," *Literary Digest,* LVIII (Sept. 21, 1918), p. 31 (where the *Transcript's* statement is reprinted); "More Condemned Books," *ibid.,* LIX (Oct. 12, 1918), p. 27; Mock, *Censorship, 1917,* pp. 159–71.

23. Théophile Gautier, *Mademoiselle de Maupin* (N.Y., Boni & Liveright [Modern Library Ed.], 1918), p. ii; John G. Palache, *Gautier and the Romantics* (London, 1927), p. 41.

24. *Pub. Wkly.,* CII (July 29, 1922), p. 404. The Halsey case is also discussed in: Emergency Committee for the Defense of James Branch Cabell's *Jurgen, Jurgen and the Censor* (N.Y., 1920), p. 26. Halsey filed a damage suit against the Vice Society upon his acquittal. The final successful outcome of this suit is discussed in Chap. IV of this book. It is not altogether clear who published the edition of *Mademoiselle de Maupin* which Sumner tried to suppress. Boni & Liveright issued a Modern Library edition in 1918, but the later appellate decision in Halsey's suit notes that "the work before us bears the name of no publisher"—quoted in Ernst and Schwartz, *Censorship* (N.Y., 1964), p. 61. The Modern Library Edition is an expurgated one, omitting such sentences as: "In an instant he undressed and flung himself beside her. The girl pressed herself against him and embraced him closely, for her two breasts were as cold and as white as snow," and "The divine moment approached. A supreme spasm convulsed the two lovers. . . ." (*cf.* p. 289 of the Modern Library Edition of 1918 and p. 295 of the Limited Editions Club version published in 1943, available at Houghton Library, Harvard University). It seems probable that the book Sumner prosecuted was an unexpurgated edition published by Boni & Liveright simultaneously with the Modern Library Edition, but without identifying imprint.

25. E. E. Hale, "American Literature, Nov. 15, 1917–Nov. 15,

1918," *American Year Book, A Record of Events and Progress, 1918* (N.Y., 1919), p. 767. Hale taught English at Union College. The *Year Book* records (p. 768) that an estimated 581 novels by Americans were published in 1918, as against 703 in 1916.

26. Isidor Schneider, "*Publishers' Weekly* and the Book Trade Since World War I," *Pub. Wkly.*, CLI (Jan. 18, 1947), p. 307.

27. The cartoon is described in King, *For a New America*, p. 4.

28. Chapman, "Bright Side of the War," p. 140; Professor Robert S. Woodworth of Columbia, quoted in Charles W. Wood, *The Great Change* (N.Y., 1918), pp. 148, 156; Bishop Fallows of the Episcopal Church quoted in Abrams, *Preachers Present Arms*, p. 234. Raymond Fosdick of the Commission on Training Camp Activities has written of the war: "The nation was united behind a compelling ideal. Before us stretched a shining prospect, and it seemed as if our generation by some divine providence had been specially chosen for great and determining events"—*Chronicle of a Generation*, p. 142.

29. Frank Moss, *America's Mission to Serve Humanity* (Boston, 1919), pp. 2, 3; Henry C. King, *A New Mind for the New Age* (N.Y., 1920), p. 39.

30. King, *For a New America*; Wood, *The Great Change*; Guy Emerson, *The New Frontier* (N.Y., 1920); Willis Mason West, *The War and the New Age* (Boston, 1919).

31. "Ignatius Phayre" [William G. Fitz-Gerald], *America's Day, Studies in Light and Shade* (N.Y., 1919), p. 256; George F. Pentecost, *Fighting for Faith, the Justice of Our Fight, the Reasons for Our Faith* (N.Y., 1918), p. 186, quoted in Abrams, *Preachers Present Arms*, p. 224.

32. William L. Stidger, *Soldier Silhouettes on Our Front* (N.Y., 1918), pp. 50–51; Council of National Defense press release, quoted in Snow, "Social Hygiene and the War," p. 430. Coningsby Dawson's *The Glory of the Trenches; An Interpretation* (N.Y., 1918) was widely read as representing the typical soldier's outlook: "[T]here's many a man who . . . has learnt to say, 'Thank God for this war,' . . . not because of the carnage, but because, when the winepress of new ideals was being trodden, he . . . could do his share" (pp. 55–56).

33. Kate Waller Barrett, head of the Florence Crittenton movement (unwed mothers), quoted in Otto Wilson, *Fifty Years' Work with Girls, 1883–1933, A Story of the Florence Crittenton Homes* (Alexandria, Va., 1933), p. 195.

34. "Phayre" [Fitz-Gerald], *America's Day*, p. 256.

35. W. & W. Soc., A.R., *1918–19* (1919), p. 5.

36. League of Nations, *Records of the International Conference for the Suppression of the Circulation of and Traffic in Obscene Publications, Held at Geneva from August 31st to Sept. 12th, 1923* (Geneva, 1923), p. 97 (copy in New York Public Library). The United States was represented at this conference by Alexander R. Magruder, who attended in an advisory capacity.

37. Quoted in "Moral Gains and Losses of the War," *Literary Digest*, LX (Jan. 11, 1919), p. 29. See also "Has Peace Brought Real Changes?," *Current Opinion*, LXVI (Apr. 1919), pp. 248–49, which in general takes a pessimistic view.

38. "A Review of Puritanism," *Zion's Herald*, XCVIII (Aug. 11, 1920), p. 1045.

39. King, *For a New America*, p. 2. "The Christian forces," King warned in 1920, ". . . may not run away from the full task of Christianizing our entire civilization"—King, *A New Mind*, p. 186.

40. W. & W. Soc., *A.R., 1917–18* (1918), p. 7.

41. New England Watch and Ward Society, "The First Corps of Moral Engineers" (Boston, 1917), pp. 9–10, 13; W. & W. Soc., *A.R., 1917–18* (1918), pp. 6–7.

42. *Ibid.*, p. 1.

43. This was the finding of Judge George W. Anderson in *Colyer et al. v. Skeffington*, a federal case arising from the Boston raids, quoted in Chafee, *Free Speech in the U.S.*, p. 207. See also Robert K. Murray, *Red Scare, A Study in National Hysteria, 1919–1920* (Minneapolis, 1955), esp. Chap. XIII, "The January Raids"; Stanley Coben, *A. Mitchell Palmer, Politician* (N.Y., 1963), Chap. XII, "The Palmer Raids."

44. N.Y. Vice Soc., *A.R.* (1919), pp. 5–6. This report was evidently written in early 1920, after the January raids.

45. *Ibid.* (1918), p. 5.

46. W. & W. Soc., *A.R., 1918–19* (1919), p. 10.

47. *Ibid.*, p. 14.

48. *Ibid.*, p. 3. The speaker was W. H. P. Faunce, president of Brown University.

CHAPTER IV

1. Frederick Lewis Allen, "The End of An Era," *Outlook and Independent*, CLIV (Feb. 5, 1930), p. 208; Floyd Dell, "In Defense of the New School," *Current History*, XXVI (Apr. 1927), p. 28.

2. For a brief survey of the moral revolution of the decade, see William E. Leuchtenburg, *The Perils of Prosperity, 1914–1932* (Chicago, 1958), pp. 158–79. The automobile statistic is from U.S. Bureau of the Census, *Historical Statistics of the United States, Colonial Times to 1957* (Washington, D.C., 1960), p. 462.

3. Harold Stearns, "America and the Young Intellectual," *Bookman*, LIII (Mar. 1921), p. 46.

4. Frank P. Stockbridge, "Main Street Wants to Know," *ibid.*, LXVI (Jan. 1928), p. 548.

5. Alfred Harcourt, "Publishing Since 1900," in *Bowker Lectures on Book Publishing* (N.Y., 1957), pp. 28–41; Isidor Schneider, "Publishers' Weekly and the Book Trade Since World War I," *Publishers'*

Weekly, LI (Jan. 18, 1947), pp. 307–24, esp. p. 308; Hellmut Lehmann-Haupt, *The Book In America* (N.Y., 1939), pp. 224–29; Charles A. Madison, *Book Publishing in America* (N.Y., 1966), pp. 188, 256, 303.

6. On the elder G. P. Putnam, see *Nat. Cyc. Am. Biog.*, II, p. 388; on George Haven Putnam (1844–1930), *ibid.*, II, p. 389; on the younger G. P. Putnam, *Who Was Who*, II, and his autobiography, *Wide Margins* (N.Y., 1942), esp. Chap. IX, "Censorship and Such," pp. 98–111. Another old established house which came under new control in this period was Harper & Bros. In 1921 Thomas B. Wells, a Harper's editor, effected a successful financial reorganization which saved the tottering firm. Among the books published during Wells's ascendancy was John Dos Passos' *Manhattan Transfer*, which had been indignantly rejected by George H. Doran (see below, p. 91). See, on this point, Madison, *Book Publishing in America*, p. 172.

7. N.Y. Vice Soc., A.R. (1922), p. 4; New England Watch and Ward Society, *Annual Report 1921–22* (1922), p. 8.

8. Quoted in Pringle, "Comstock the Less," *American Mercury*, X (Jan. 1927), p. 62.

9. Alva Johnston, " 'I'm no Reformer,' Says Sumner," *N.Y. Times Book Review and Magazine*, Aug. 20, 1922, p. 3.

10. James Branch Cabell, *Jurgen, A Comedy of Justice* (N.Y., 1919), pp. 313, 279.

11. *Ibid.*, p. 357.

12. *N.Y. Tribune*, Nov. 17, 1919 and Jan. 3, 1920, quoted in Emergency Committee Organized to Protest Against the Suppression of James Branch Cabell's "Jurgen," *Jurgen and the Censor* (N.Y., 1920), pp. 15–16. The reference to chorus girls, Broun said later, had seemed innocuous enough, since "it was easy to imagine ever so many ways in which chorus girls might be employed to worse advantage"—*N.Y. Tribune*, Oct. 21, 1922, quoted in *Between Friends; Letters of James Branch Cabell and Others*, ed. Padraic Colum and Margaret Freeman Cabell, with an introduction by Carl Van Vechten (N.Y., 1962), p. 271n. The publisher of *Jurgen*, Robert W. McBride, forty-one years old in 1920, had established his own firm shortly before the war. *Who's Who*, XII (1922–23).

13. Cabell, *Jurgen*, pp. 236–40; Cabell to Burton Rascoe, June 21, 1919, in *Between Friends*, p. 121.

14. Emergency Committee, *Jurgen and the Censor*, p. 17; *Between Friends*, pp. 95, 109.

15. Robert McBride to Cabell, Mar. 1, 1920, Holt to Cabell, May 8, 1920, in *Between Friends*, pp. 167, 173–74.

16. *N.Y. Times*, May 18, 1920, p. 9.

17. *Ibid.*, Oct. 20, 1922, p. 21; *Pub. Wkly.*, CII (Oct. 21, 1922), p. 144. The British edition was published in 1921 by John Lane, with an introduction by Hugh Walpole.

18. Cabell to Holt, May 11, 1920, in *Between Friends*, p. 175.

19. James Branch Cabell, *Taboo; A Legend Retold from the Dirghic*

of Saevius Nicanor (N.Y., 1921), pp. 11, 28, 36. As evidence that *Jurgen* was not the only book capable of being subjected to varying interpretations, Cabell quoted in *Taboo* several Mother Goose selections, e.g.:

"I had a little husband, no bigger than my thumb,
I put him in my pint-pot, and there I bid him drum."

20. Emergency Committee, *Jurgen and the Censor*, pp. 20–21, 37–39; Ernest Boyd to Guy Holt, Feb. 10, 1920, in *Between Friends*, p. 160; "Again the Literary Censor," *Nation*, CXI (Sept. 25, 1920), p. 343. The committee's protest denounced the suppression as an "arbitrary and unjustifiable" action by "an unrepresentative body of people exercising disproportionate influence. . . ." On Barrett H. Clark (1890–1953), see *Who Was Who*, III (1960).

21. The Glenn brief is reprinted in Guy Holt, *Jurgen and the Law* (N.Y., 1923), pp. 19–69. On Glenn (1878–1949), see *Who Was Who in America*, II (1950).

22. "Vice Society Loses Case," *Pub. Wkly.*, CII (July 29, 1922), p. 404. The text of the decision appears also in Morris Ernst and Alexander Lindey, *The Censor Marches On* (N.Y., 1940), pp. 273–81. On the earlier history of the *Mademoiselle de Maupin* case, see Chap. III of this book, pp. 60–61.

23. The Nott decision is set forth in Holt, *Jurgen and the Law*, pp. 73–74.

24. Quoted in Glenn to Cabell, Oct. 27, 1922, in *Between Friends*, p. 273.

25. Lehmann-Haupt, *The Book in America*, p. 225; *Pub. Wkly.*, CXLIV (Sept. 25, 1943); *N.Y. Times*, Sept. 29, 1943, p. 21; G. Thomas Tanselle, "The Thomas Seltzer Imprint," *Papers of the Bibliographical Society of America*, LVIII (Fourth Quarter, 1964), pp. 380–448. Among Seltzer's translations for Knopf was *Homo Sapiens*, suppressed by John Sumner. When Seltzer's business faltered in the mid-1920s, he was bought out by his nephews, the Boni brothers—*Pub. Wkly.*, CX (Aug. 28, 1926), p. 751.

26. D. H. Lawrence, *Women in Love* (Viking Ed., N.Y., 1960), p. vii.

27. Evelyn Scott, "A Philosopher of the Erotic," *Dial*, LXX (Apr. 1921), p. 460.

28. Anon., *A Young Girl's Diary, Prefaced with a Letter by Sigmund Freud* (London, 1921), pp. 5, 37, 118–19. The Seltzer edition was a United States reprint of this London edition. Both the *Diary* and *Casanova's Homecoming* were translated from the German by Eden and Cedar Paul.

29. *Pub. Wkly.*, CII (July 15, 1922), p. 118; *N.Y. Times*, July 12, 1922, p. 32. In a related action, Mary H. Marks, a clerk at Womrath's, a circulating library chain, was arrested for lending *A Young Girl's Diary* to a borrower—*Pub. Wkly.*, CII (Sept. 16, 1922), p. 801.

30. *Ibid.*

31. *Ibid.*, CII (Aug. 5, 1922), pp. 463–64. *Publishers' Weekly* noted later (Sept. 16, 1922, p. 801) that the Seltzer prosecution was "[o]ne of the most widely discussed cases in book censorship that has ever been before the courts."

32. Judge Simpson's decision is printed in *ibid.*, pp. 802–04. Miss Marks, who had been made co-defendant, was cleared at the same time.

33. *Ibid.*, p. 801; *ibid.*, CIII (Jan. 27, 1923), p. 222; *N.Y. Times*, Sept. 17, 1922, II, p. 1; "The Law and the Censor," *ibid.*, Sept. 14, 1922, p. 21. A second vice-society move against the Schnitzler book and *A Young Girl's Diary* came in 1923, when Sumner secured a grand jury indictment against the two titles. The case was never heard, however, and was dropped two years later when Seltzer, no longer active as a publisher, withdrew the two books. *N.Y. Times*, July 19, 1923, p. 2; Jan. 17, 1924, p. 13; and Feb. 3, 1925, p. 5.

34. *Dict. Am. Biog.*, Supp. I; Bennett Cerf, "Horace Liveright, an Obituary—Unedited," *Pub. Wkly.*, CXXIV (Oct. 7, 1933), pp. 1229–30.

35. Louis Kronenberger, "Gambler in Publishing: Horace Liveright," *Atlantic Monthly*, CCXV (Jan. 1965), p. 95. Kronenberger was a Boni & Liveright reader in the 1920s.

36. Cerf, "Liveright," p. 1229.

37. See Chap. III of this book, pp. 58–59. A 1920 obscenity prosecution against Liveright for publishing the anonymous *Story of a Lover* was dismissed in magistrates' court—*Pub. Wkly.*, XCVII (Mar. 27, 1920), p. 1033; *N.Y. Times*, Apr. 21, 1920, p. 8.

38. *Ibid.*, Sept. 28, 1922, p. 11, which quotes the Oberwager decision at length. See also *Pub. Wkly.*, CII (Oct. 7, 1922), p. 1292.

39. *N.Y. Times*, Sept. 28, 1922, p. 11; Oct. 1, 1922, p. 14. The suit was settled out of court—*Pub. Wkly.*, CXIII (Mar. 31, 1928), p. 1449. In 1927 Liveright published a one-volume *Satyricon* with a publisher's note as follows: "This edition . . . is adapted from the excellent idiomatic translation of Mr. W. C. Firebaugh originally issued in 1922. All changes or emendations varying from the original text are solely the responsibility of the publishers." This expurgated version contains little if anything which could be considered objectionable even by vice-society standards.

40. *N.Y. Times*, Sept. 29, 1922, p. 9; N.Y. Vice Soc., A.R. (1922), p. 14.

41. *Pub. Wkly.*, CII (Oct. 28, 1922), p. 1524.

42. *N.Y. Times*, Nov. 2, 1922, p. 19.

43. These failures in well-publicized cases seem to have affected all phases of the Vice Society's work. By 1923 its overall conviction rate, invariably well over 90% in the prewar years, had dropped to 55%, according to statistics quoted in Pringle, "Comstock the Less," p. 62.

44. Jane Heap, "Art and the Law," *Little Rev.*, VII (Sept.-Dec., 1920), p. 6, reprinted in Margaret Anderson, ed., *The Little Review Anthology* (N.Y., 1953), pp. 301–04. For the extract which elicited the prosecution, see "*Ulysses*, Episode XIII Concluded," *Little Rev.*,

VII (July-Aug. 1920), pp. 42–61. See also Anderson, *My Thirty Years' War*, pp. 174, 212–18; John S. Sumner, "The Truth About Literary Lynching," *Dial*, LXX (Apr. 1921), pp. 66–67, and his typed statement about the case in N.Y. Vice Soc. Mss., VIII, Library of Congress.

45. *N.Y. Times*, Feb. 22, 1921, p. 13. Also *N.Y. Times*, Feb. 15, 1921, p. 4; Margaret Anderson, "*Ulysses* in Court," *Little Rev.*, VII (Jan.-Mar. 1921), pp. 22–25 ("disordered mind" quote on p. 24); and Anderson, *My Thirty Years' War*, pp. 220–21.

46. *N.Y. Times*, Feb. 22, 1921; Anderson, *My Thirty Years' War*, p. 221.

47. "Taste, Not Morals, Violated," *N.Y. Times*, Feb. 23, 1921, p. 12. Wrote Miss Anderson: "[N]ot one New York newspaper came to our defense, not one spoke out for Joyce . . ."—*My Thirty Years' War*, p. 226.

48. *Ibid.*, p. 228.

49. Joyce to Harriet Shaw Weaver, Feb. 25, 1920 [evidently a misdate for 1921], Stuart Gilbert, ed., *Letters of James Joyce* (N.Y., 1957), p. 197. Joyce was referring to the fact that earlier, in Dublin, a wealthy and irate citizen had purchased and burned the entire edition of his first book, *Dubliners*.

50. Anderson, *My Thirty Years' War*, pp. 218–19.

51. *N.Y. Times*, Oct. 20, 1922, p. 3.

52. Holt, *Jurgen and the Law*, p. 8.

53. N.Y. Vice Soc., A.R. (1921), p. 4; John Sumner, quoted in *N.Y. Times*, Aug. 4, 1922, p. 7.

54. F. Scott Fitzgerald to Maxwell Perkins, "before Dec. 12, 1921" [editor's dating], Andrew Turnbull, ed., *The Letters of F. Scott Fitzgerald* (N.Y., 1963), p. 149.

55. Mencken to Theodore Dreiser, Mar. 27, 1921, in *Letters of H. L. Mencken*, selected and annotated by Guy J. Forgue (N.Y., 1961), p. 222.

56. Passages from pp. 534 and 541 of the 1915 John Lane ed. of *The "Genius"*; cited in Robert H. Elias, ed., *Letters of Theodore Dreiser, A Selection* (3 vols., Philadelphia, 1959), II, p. 402n. For the origins of the conferences, see *ibid.*, II, p. 396: "Mencken will see Sumner, get his views and make such changes as are necessary providing Dodd-Mead are interested to bring out *The "Genius"* (Dreiser to Arthur C. Hume of Dodd-Mead, Apr. 18, 1922); and *ibid.*, p. 400: "I'll be glad to see Sumner and to arrange the cuts. I doubt that he will insist on any of much concern. . . ." (Mencken to Dreiser, Apr. 25, 1922).

57. Mencken to Dreiser, June 16, 1922, Dreiser, *Letters*, II, p. 403n.

58. N.Y. Vice Soc., A.R. (1923), p. 5.

59. *N.Y. Times Book Review and Magazine*, Sept. 5, 1920, p. 9. Late in 1921 the *American Church Monthly*, an Episcopal publication, lashed out at the "vulgarity" and "salaciousness" of postwar books and said: "[W]e need a crusade against plausible immorality in our 'Best Sellers.' . . . The Church long fostered and controlled drama for her purposes. Is it impossible that she should attempt something of the kind

in the field of fiction?"—"The Idle Words of Fiction," *American Church Monthly*, X [Dec. 1921], pp. 355, 359.

60. "The Novelist Rebels," *Nation*, CXIII (Sept. 7, 1921), p. 256.

61. See, in this connection, Charles A. Fenton, "A Literary Fracture of World War I," *American Quarterly*, XII (Summer 1960), pp. 119–32.

62. Quoted in Stearns, "America and the Young Intellectual," p. 44.

63. N.Y. Vice Soc., A.R. (1922), p. 15; *N.Y. Times*, Nov. 3, 1922, p. 19.

64. Theodosia Walton, "Tarkington Looks at the Censor," *ibid.*, Aug. 20, 1922, III, 3; Lloyd C. Douglas, "A Stampede by the 'Literature of Despair,'" *Zion's Herald*, C (Nov. 1, 1922), p. 1392.

65. Alice Hegan Rice, *The Inky Way* (N.Y., 1940), p. 73; Stratton-Porter quoted in "Beware! Poison!" *The Baptist*, III (Aug. 5, 1922), p. 828; Deland quoted in *Zion's Herald*, C (Oct. 4, 1922), p. 1264 (on Mrs. Deland's prolific literary output see *Who Was Who*, II); Mary Roberts Rinehart, "The Unreality of Modern Realism," *Bookman*, LVI (Dec. 1922), pp. 462–64.

66. N.Y. Vice Soc., A.R. (1922), p. 15 (Bacheller); Brander Matthews, "Alien Views of American Literature," *N.Y. Times Book Review and Magazine*, Nov. 14, 1920, p. 2, a review of *On American Books, A Symposium by Five American Critics*, published by Huebsch; (on Matthews, see Lehmann-Haupt, *The Book in America*, p. 183, and *Who Was Who*, I); Stuart P. Sherman, "Is There Anything to Be Said for Literary Tradition?" *Bookman*, LII (Oct. 1920), p. 110.

67. Henry Francis Sherwood, "A Guild of Authors," *Bookman*, LXII (Nov. 1925), p. 298. See also Duffield Osborne, *The Authors Club, An Historical Sketch* (N.Y., 1913), pp. 3, 10.

68. George H. Doran, *Chronicles of Barabbas, 1884–1934* (N.Y., 1935), pp. 286, 400, and (on his early career) 19–48. Of interest in this connection is a letter from the aged publisher Henry Holt (1840–1926) in the *N.Y. Times*, May 3, 1922, declaring that "artificial titillation" of the sex instinct by literary or other means is "counter to the requirements of civilization . . ., maleficent and destructive," and "leads to more murders and suicides than all other causes put together." (Holt cited no statistics to buttress his assertion.)

69. *Jurgen and the Censor*, p. 22.

70. P. E. More quoted in Emergency Committee . . . , *Jurgen and the Censor*, p. 46, in justification of his refusal to sign the *Jurgen* protest; William Lyon Phelps, "As I Like It," *Scribner's Magazine*, LXXII (Nov. 1922), p. 631.

71. *Pub. Wkly.*, CII (Nov. 11, 1922), pp. 1785–86.

72. "The Voluntary Censorship Plan," *Pub. Wkly.*, CI (Apr. 8, 1922), p. 1043; "The Censorship Situation," *ibid.*, CIII (Apr. 28, 1923), p. 1323; Emergency Committee . . . , *Jurgen and the Censor*, p. 22. The members of the committee were Arthur H. Scribner (chairman), George Palmer Putnam, and Alfred Harcourt. The committee's purpose was evidently to discuss the feasibility of applying to the book publishing

industry a "jury" system proposed early in 1922 for the theater industry. This scheme, devised by the Authors' League and other interested groups to forestall a theater-censorship bill drawn up by Sumner, involved a citizens' panel from which "juries" would be selected to evaluate the decency of new plays. The system was tentatively scheduled to go into operation for the 1922–23 theater season, the city license commissioner having agreed to abide by the "jury" verdicts in granting theater licenses, but the hostility of "the drama fraternity," coupled with doubts as to its legality, killed it. The whole episode is recounted in the *N.Y. Times,* Feb. 26, 1923, p. 17. For more on drama censorship and its links with book censorship, see Chap. VI in this book.

73. Emergency Committee . . . , *Jurgen and the Censor,* p. 19n. The League added somewhat vaguely that it was "considering ways and means of taking up the general question of censorship in some effective way."

74. Sherwood Anderson to Karl Anderson, May 31, 1923, in *Letters of Sherwood Anderson,* Selected and Edited with an Introduction and Notes by Howard Mumford Jones in association with Walter B. Rideout (Boston, 1953), p. 98.

75. Louis N. Feipel, "Questionable Books in Public Libraries," *Library Jour.,* XLVII (Oct. 15, 1922), pp. 857–61; (Nov. 1, 1922), pp. 907–11. Quoted passages on pp. 857 and 908. In 1924, when the mood among librarians was changing rapidly (see Chap. V in this book), one of them wrote: "I know no more depressing indication of the librarian's attitude toward literature than may be found in Mr. Feipel's elaborate inquiries . . . [revealing] library energies all focussed on the detection of 'moral tendencies' and the modern novel pursued with stern suspicion by official inquisitors. . . ."—Helen H. Haines, "Modern Fiction and the Public Library," *ibid.,* XLIX (May 15, 1924), p. 458.

76. This editorial, appearing originally in the *Library World* for May 1922, was reprinted and commented upon approvingly by the *Library Journal,* XLVII (Nov. 1, 1922), p. 911.

77. The principal concerns of the A.C.L.U. in this period may be seen by examining its annual reports and its weekly (later monthly) bulletin, *Report on Civil Liberty Situation.* In neither does literary censorship make a significant appearance. See also Donald Johnson, *The Challenge to American Freedoms, World War I and the Rise of the American Civil Liberties Union* (Lexington, Ky., 1963).

78. "With Intent to Corrupt," *Nation,* CXV (July 26, 1922), p. 86. Villard in his autobiography, *Fighting Years; Memoirs of a Liberal Editor* (N.Y., 1939), speaks with justifiable pride (p. 522) of the *Nation's* long record of opposition to literary censorship.

79. "Liberalism and the Censor," *New Republic,* XXXIV (Apr. 4, 1923), pp. 148–49.

80. Walter Lippmann, *Public Opinion* (N.Y., 1922), pp. 249, 365, 399, 319.

81. *N.Y. Times,* Aug. 4, 1922, p. 7 (quoting Sumner); W. & W.

Soc., *A.R.*, *1922–23* (1923), p. 10; John S. Sumner, "The Truth About Literary Lynching," p. 68; N.Y. Vice Soc., *A.R.* (1920), p. 13; *ibid.* (1922), p. 8.

82. "Shall There Be a Censorship?" *Literary Digest*, LXXIV (Aug. 26, 1922), pp. 31–32; *N.Y. Times*, Aug. 4, 1922, pp. 1, 7. For the "play jury" idea, on which this plan was modeled, see above, Note 72.

83. Quoted in *N.Y. Times*, Aug. 4, 1922, p. 7.

84. Melcher's reaction, in a letter to the *N.Y. Tribune*, is quoted in *Literary Digest*, LXXIV (Aug. 26, 1922), p. 32.

85. Schuler and Frank quoted in *N.Y. Times*, Aug. 5, 1922, p. 20.

86. "Censorship Discussion," *Pub. Wkly.*, CII (Aug. 19, 1922), p. 581; "Book Censorship Condemned As Un-American and Undesirable," *Current Opinion*, LXXIII (Oct. 1922), p. 517; "Censorship for Books," *N.Y. Times*, Aug. 5, 1922, p. 10. The "policy of repression fostered in wartime and sanctioned by the American people because of the war is running its course," declared *Current Opinion* hopefully.

87. *N.Y. Times*, Aug. 11, 1922, p. 11; Oct. 15, 1922, II, 1.

88. *Ibid.*, Sept. 17, 1922, II, 1.

CHAPTER V

1. "Beware! Poison!" *The Baptist*, III (Aug. 5, 1922), p. 828; Thomas P. Harrison, "Recent Tendencies in Literature," *Union Seminary Review*, XXXIV (Oct. 1922), p. 23; *The Lutheran* quoted in *The Baptist*, IV (Sept. 1, 1923), p. 967; "The Idle Words of Fiction," *American Church Monthly*, X (Dec. 1921), p. 359; "Editorial Comment," *Catholic World*, CXVI (Dec. 1922), pp. 398–99.

2. "Polluting the Springs," *Zion's Herald*, C (Sept. 27, 1922), p. 1222.

3. *Ibid.*, Oct. 4, 1922 (pp. 1264–65); Oct. 11, 1922 (pp. 1294–95); Oct. 18, 1922 (p. 1314); Rev. C. M. Haines, "Movie Censorship and Questionable Literature," *ibid.* (Oct. 25, 1922), p. 1378.

4. "Censoring the Censors," *Current Opinion*, LXXIII (Oct. 1922), p. 451.

5. Quoted in *Pub. Wkly.*, CII (Nov. 18, 1922), p. 1858.

6. *Who Was Who*, I; *N.Y. Times*, July 26, 1941, p. 15 (obit.); "Ford Tells How to Purge Books," *ibid.*, Mar. 18, 1923, VIII, p. 2.

7. *Ibid.*, Feb. 25, 1923, p. 1. The *Times*, of which I have made extensive use in this chapter, gave exceptionally full coverage to the entire "Clean Books" crusade.

8. Quoted in "Ford Tells How to Purge Books," *ibid.*, Mar. 18, 1923, VIII, p. 2. "I had no idea that anything of the kind was tolerated," he said on another occasion (*ibid.*, Feb. 6, 1923, p. 23).

9. *Ibid.*, Feb. 25, 1923, p. 1.

10. *Ibid.*, pp. 1, 7. For the details of Ford's proposals, see pp. 104–05 in this book.

11. *N.Y. Times,* Mar. 9, 1923, p. 17. On Conboy (1878–1944), see *Who Was Who,* II; on Atterbury (1854–1931) see *ibid.,* I.

12. *N.Y. Times,* Mar. 23, 1923, p. 2. On Cotillo and Jesse, see *Manual for the Use of the Legislature, State of New York* (Albany, 1923).

13. Ford quoted in *N.Y. Times,* Mar. 18, 1923, VIII, p. 2, and Mar. 25, 1923, II, p. 1; Sumner in *ibid.,* Feb. 11, 1923, p. 18; the Jesse-Cotillo bill is printed in *Pub. Wkly.,* CIII (Mar. 31, 1923), p. 1078. The law which it was designed to change is printed in Holt, *Jurgen and the Law,* pp. 77–78, and in John Ford, *Criminal Obscenity* (N.Y., 1926), p. 134. The first-listed of these proposed changes was especially desired by District Attorney Banton, while the fourth had been added at the suggestion of Chief City Magistrate William McAdoo— *N.Y. Times,* Feb. 25, 1923, p. 1; Mar. 13, 1923, p. 5. As for the jury proviso, the framers of the amendment well knew that juries are notoriously harsher in obscenity cases than are judges.

14. *Pub. Wkly.,* CIII (Feb. 24, 1923), p. 580 (Lawrence); "A Preposterous Measure," *Literary Review of the N.Y. Evening Post,* Apr. 28, 1923, p. 641 (Canby); "Advertising Bad Books," *N.Y. Times,* Mar. 15, 1923, p. 18. See also "Censoring Books Again," *ibid.,* Feb. 27, 1923, p. 18.

15. *Ibid.,* Feb. 26, 1923, p. 17; Apr. 19, 1923, p. 1.

16. *Ibid.,* Apr. 19, 1923, p. 1; Theodore Dreiser to Gelett Burgess, [between May 19 and June 2, 1923], Dreiser, *Letters,* II, pp. 412–13; Horace B. Liveright, "The Absurdity of Censorship," *Independent,* CX (Mar. 17, 1923), pp. 92–93. Dreiser's letter, which contains much detail on the "Clean Books" fight, is hereafter cited as "Dreiser to Burgess." On Denis Lynch, a familiar and colorful figure on the New York journalistic scene for many years, see *Manual for the Use of the Legislature,* p. 541; and obituaries in the *N.Y. Times* and *N.Y. Herald Tribune,* Jan. 15, 1966.

17. *N.Y. Times,* Apr. 18, 1923, p. 7; Apr. 19, 1923, p. 1; Dreiser to Burgess, Dreiser, *Letters,* II, 412–13.

18. *N.Y. Times,* Apr. 19, 1923, p. 1; *Pub. Wkly.,* CIII (Apr. 21, 1923), p. 1262. As searches at the N.Y. Public Library and at the Legislative Reference Library of the N.Y. State Library in Albany failed to unearth a transcript of this hearing, I have relied on contemporary reports in the *Times* and *Publishers' Weekly.* The *Times* editorial read by Fleischer, "The Worst Bill Yet," is on p. 20 of the Apr. 18 issue.

19. *N.Y. Times,* Apr. 20, 1923, p. 2.

20. *Ibid.,* Apr. 24, 1923, p. 3. The formation of the Liveright group is reported in *ibid.,* Apr. 21, 1923, p. 6.

21. Dreiser to Burgess, Dreiser, *Letters,* II, p. 412; *Pub. Wkly.,* CIII (Jan. 20, 1923), p. 143; *N.Y. Times,* June 15, 1923, p. 6 (Liveright's resignation and charges); N.Y. Vice Soc., A.R. (1923), p. 9.

22. *Pub. Wkly.,* CIII (Apr. 28, 1923), pp. 1323–24; Madison, *Book Publishing in America,* p. 302. The members of the N.A.B.P.

executive committee at this time were: John W. Hiltman, sixty-one years old, president of Appleton's; Frederick A. Stokes, sixty-six; George H. Doran, fifty-four; W. E. Pulsifer, seventy-one, president of D. C. Heath & Co.; Edward Mills, forty, of Longmans Green & Co.; and Alexander Grosset, fifty-three years old. Sources: *Pub. Wkly.*, CIII (Jan. 20, 1923), p. 144; *Who Was Who*, I (Hiltman, Stokes, Pulsifer); *Who's Who in N.Y.*, 1924 (Mills); *Dict. Am. Biog.*, Supp. I (Grosset); George H. Doran, *Chronicles of Barabbas, 1884–1934* (N.Y., 1935). For a later summary review of this episode, see *Pub. Wkly.*, CV (Jan. 19, 1924), p. 165.

23. "Renewed Censorship Agitation," *Pub. Wkly.*, CIII (Mar. 3, 1923), pp. 627–28; "The Censorship Situation," *ibid.*, (Apr. 28, 1923), p. 1323.

24. *N.Y. Times*, Apr. 23, 1923, p. 14.

25. *Ibid.*; *Pub. Wkly.*, CIII (Apr. 28, 1923), p. 1323; Dreiser to Burgess, Dreiser, *Letters*, II, p. 413. The Authors' League did send two telegrams of protest to the committee (the effectiveness of which Dreiser and the *Times* discounted) and said in its own defense that Arthur Somers Roche had been designated to represent it at the Albany hearing but had not been able to attend (*ibid.*). The League was also marginally involved in the anticensorship fight as a member of the rather pretentiously named "Joint Committee for the Promotion and Protection of Art and Literature" founded in 1922 by George Creel primarily as a motion-picture-industry vehicle for opposing movie censorship, particularly in Massachusetts, where the issue was on the ballot that November. Except for a single letter from Creel to Cotillo, the "Joint Committee" took no recorded part in the "Clean Books" fight. Late in 1923 Creel's group transformed itself into the "National Council to Protect the Freedom of Art, Literature, and the Press." In 1925 it became the "National Council for the Protection of Literature and the Arts." Through all these permutations its role in book censorship matters remained negligible—*Pub. Wkly.*, CII (Aug. 19, 1922), pp. 587–88; CVII (Feb. 14, 1925), p. 528; *N.Y. Times*, Sept. 17, 1922, II, 13; Dec. 17, 1923, p. 11; Dreiser to Burgess, Dreiser, *Letters*, II, p. 413.

26. Dreiser to Beach, May 5, 1923; Dreiser to Burgess, [between May 19 and June 2, 1923], Dreiser, *Letters*, II, pp. 409, 411; *N.Y. Telegraph*, May 19, 1923, quoted in *ibid.* p. 410.

27. Edwin Markham, "The Decadent Tendency in Current Fiction," *Current History*, XVIII (Aug. 1923), pp. 719, 723.

28. Henry W. Boynton, "Native vs. Alien Standards," *Independent*, CX (Mar. 17, 1923), pp. 191–92, quoted passage on p. 192; John Farrar, "The American Tradition," *Bookman*, LVIII (Feb. 1924), p. 611; also see p. 614. Boynton's numerous works include *A Reader's History of American Literature* (N.Y., 1903) and *Selected Poems for Required Reading in Secondary Schools* (N.Y., 1911).

29. Mary Austin, "Sex in American Literature," *Bookman*, LVII (June 1923), pp. 386, 388, 389, 391, 392.

30. McCutcheon quoted in "Censorship or Not," *Literary Digest*, LXXVII (June 23, 1923), p. 58; Boynton, "Native vs. Alien Standards," pp. 191, 192; Theodosia Walton, "Tarkington Looks at the Censor," *N.Y. Times*, Aug. 20, 1922, III, p. 3; Repplier quoted in "Censorship as a Gesture," *N.Y. Times*, Apr. 26, 1923, p. 16. McCutcheon (1866–1928) was the author of the 1901 bestseller *Graustark* and other popular novels. Miss Repplier's resentment at the erosion of wartime idealism was especially keen because her own image of the struggle had been a particularly exalted one. "Christianity and war have walked together down the centuries," she wrote in 1916. "How could it be otherwise? . . . Nothing sacred and dear could have survived upon the earth had men not fought for their women, their homes, their individual honor, and their national life. . . . The wave of religious emotion which sweeps over a nation warring for its life . . . is part of man's responsiveness to the call of duty. . . ."—*Counter-Currents* (Boston, 1916), pp. 81–84, *passim*.

31. New England Watch and Ward Society, *Annual Report, 1922–23* (1923), pp. 19–30, esp. pp. 20, 21, 30. The speech was reported at length in the *N.Y. Times*, Apr. 23, 1923, p. 19; *Literary Digest*, June 23, 1923, p. 58; and elsewhere. On Perry (1860–1954), see *Who Was Who*, III, and his autobiography, *And Gladly Teach* (Boston, 1935), in which he writes (p. 279): "My wife, whose instinct in such matters is so often truer than mine, holds that the world war 'took it out of' our generation, exhausting our capacity for emotional and moral reactions to events."

32. Hamlin Garland, "Current Fiction Heroes," *N.Y. Times Book Review*, Dec. 23, 1923, pp. 2, 23, quoted at length in *Literary Digest*, LXXX (Jan. 19, 1924), p. 28. Garland renewed his attack in "Limitations of Authorship in America," *Bookman*, LIX (May 1924), pp. 257–62, in which he wrote (p. 259): "[A]n enormous mass of old world peasantry has been thrown into our social group . . . and the result is a production of millions of hot-blooded, half-educated, half-assimilated men and women . . . without literary taste or tradition or standards of any kind." The "crude, sensual, greedy demands" of such people, he went on, were corrupting American writers, editors, and publishers.

33. Robert E. Spiller, *et al.*, *Literary History of the United States* (rev. ed., N.Y., 1953), p. 953.

34. Henry Seidel Canby, *American Memoir* (Boston, 1947), pp. 298–99.

35. *Pub. Wkly.*, CIII (May 26, 1923), pp. 1621, 1622 (Hutchinson); pp. 1623–24 (Proctor); pp. 1624, 1625 (the protests of Fuller and others, and the vote to expunge); pp. 1640–41 (Jefferson R. Webb, "Books and the Business Man"), and p. 1653 (the resolution against "unwholesome literature"). In protesting the motion to expunge, Melcher, executive secretary of the N.A.B.P. and former secretary of the A.B.A., said: "I want to make plain my earnest feeling that we should not deny open discussion in these conventions. . . . [W]e have taken a step back-

wards in saying we cannot hear both sides of any question in the American Booksellers' Convention" (*ibid.*, p. 1626). Later in the convention, when passions had cooled, Melcher's advice was heeded and Proctor's speech was restored to the record—*ibid.* (May 19, 1923), p. 1513. On Melcher, see *Current Biog.* (1945), pp. 395–97.

36. "One Man's Meat Is Another's Poison," *Public Libraries*, XXVIII (June 1923), p. 296; Mary U. Rothrock, Knoxville, to Paul S. Boyer, Feb. 17, 1967. For Miss Rothrock's paper, and the ensuing discussion, see "Proceedings, Hot Springs Conference, 1923," *Bulletin of the American Library Association*, XVII (July 1923), pp. 244–45. After the debate the session voted to submit Miss Rothrock's paper to the A.L.A. executive council for possible publication. The council replied that it would try to place it "with some literary magazine." It eventually appeared as "Censorship of Fiction in a Public Library," in *Library Jour.*, XLVIII (May 15, 1923), pp. 454–56.

37. *Charleston* [S.C.] *News and Courier, Richmond* [Va.] *News Leader*, and *Newark News*, quoted in "A Crusade Against Unclean Books," *Literary Digest*, LXXVI (Mar. 31, 1923), p. 30. As for the New York City dailies, the *Times* has already been quoted extensively; Hearst's *Journal* was strongly opposed to the bill; and editorials of a similar intent from the *Tribune* and the *World* are reprinted in "Opinion on the Clean Books Bill," *Pub. Wkly.*, CIII (Apr. 28, 1923), pp. 1328–29.

38. "The Filth Uplifters," *Ladies' Home Journal*, XLI (Aug. 1924), p. 20; *Current History*'s editor, George W. Oakes, quoted in N.Y. Vice Soc., *A.R.* (1924), p. 14; "Censorship and Prohibition," *Christian Century*, XL (July 19, 1923), pp. 901–03, quoted passage on p. 903.

39. "Censorship or Not?" *Literary Digest*, LXXVII (June 23, 1923), p. 27.

40. Dreiser to Burgess, Dreiser, *Letters*, II, p. 414; Madison, *Book Publishing in America*, p. 333.

41. Dreiser to Burgess, Dreiser, *Letters*, II, p. 414; *N.Y. Times*, Apr. 22, 1923, p. 19 (MacFadden).

42. *N.Y. Times*, Apr. 23, 1923, p. 19 (Rabbi Wise). Although the Y.M.C.A. had been listed as a charter member of the Clean Books League, the *Times* later stated (Apr. 19, 1923, p. 1) that two "Y" officials were at the Albany hearing in opposition to the Jesse-Cotillo bill. If so, they evidently did not testify or otherwise make their presence known.

43. *N.Y. Times*, May 3, 1923, p. 1; "Censorship Gone Daft," May 2, 1923, p. 18. "As for Justice Ford," said this editorial, "he is only the conjurer's handkerchief that distracts the eye of the audience during the decisive instant when the rabbits are being deposited in the hat. . . ."

44. N.Y. State, *Journal of the Senate, 146th Session*, 1923, II, p. 1432. On the party affiliation and home districts of the senators who supported the bill, see *Manual for the Use of the Legislature*, pp. 535–37.

45. "A Danger Deferred," *N.Y. Times,* May 4, 1923, p. 16; June 15, 1923, p. 6.

46. *Ibid.,* May 14, 1923, p. 6; Dec. 3, 1923, p. 6.

47. "A New 'Clean Books' Bill," *Pub. Wkly.,* CIV (Dec. 1, 1923), p. 1783.

48. *Ibid.,* (Dec. 8, 1923), p. 1840; *N.Y. Times,* Dec. 3, 1923, p. 6.

49. *Ibid.,* May 24, 1923, p. 22; Jan. 15, 1924, p. 23.

50. "Judging Books By Paragraphs," *Pub. Wkly.,* CIV (Dec. 1, 1923), p. 1768.

51. "Publishers Outline Stand on Censorship," *ibid.* (Dec. 8, 1923), p. 1837. On the background of Stone's appointment, see *ibid.,* CV (Jan. 19, 1924), p. 165, and (Apr. 12, 1924), p. 1267.

52. *Ibid.* (Mar. 22, 1924), p. 1048. The 1924 bill, introduced in the Senate by Ellwood M. Rabenold, a Manhattan Democrat, and in the Assembly by Edmund B. Jenks, was modified in only one respect from the 1923 bill: it would have permitted judges, at their discretion, to admit an entire book in evidence in obscenity trials—*ibid.* (Mar. 8, 1924), p. 832; *N.Y. Times,* Mar. 3, 1924, p. 19.

53. "Little Support for 'Clean Books' Bill," *Pub. Wkly.,* CV (Mar. 22, 1924), p. 1048. For evidence of the changing climate among librarians, see Helen H. Haines, "Modern Fiction and the Public Library," *Library Jour.,* XLIX (May 15, 1924), pp. 457 61, in which (p. 459) the "Clean Books" movement is criticized as one symptom of "our national disease of regulatory and supervisory fever," and book censorship in general is dismissed as "futile, impracticable and dangerous. . . ."

54. *N.Y. Times,* Mar. 19, 1924, p. 23.

55. N.Y. State, *Jour. of the Senate, 147th Session,* 1924, II, p. 951.

56. *Pub. Wkly.,* CV (May 24, 1924), pp. 1698–1701 (Dixon's speech); pp. 1659, 1728 (the anticensorship resolution). The 1923 reference to "salacious books" was repeated, but now the emphasis was on the new anticensorship part of the resolution.

57. *N.Y. Times,* Mar. 2 and 19, 1925; *Pub. Wkly.,* CVII (Feb. 28, 1925), pp. 717–18. On Canon Chase, who also contributed some fiery sermons in support of the bill, see *Who Was Who,* I.

58. *Pub. Wkly.,* CXV (Mar. 16, 1929), p. 1406. See also, for reports of the periodic recurrence of the "Clean Books" bill, *ibid.,* CIX (Feb. 20, 1926), p. 596; (Apr. 24, 1926), p. 1395; CXI (Apr. 16, 1927), p. 1568; *N.Y. Times,* Jan. 26, 1928, p. 12, and Mar. 7, 1928, p. 7.

59. N.Y. Vice Soc., *A.R.* (1924), p. 6; "Arrests 1920–1950," N.Y. Vice Society Mss., V, Library of Congress.

60. "Clinical Notes," *American Mercury,* III (Nov. 1924), p. 311; "Rough Stuff," *Outlook,* CXXXIX (Feb. 4, 1925), p. 193.

61. Stuart P. Sherman, "Unprintable," *Atlantic Monthly,* CXXXII (July 1923), pp. 12, 13, 14, 18, 19. Similarly, one O. W. Firkins in 1926

heatedly arraigned the modern generation of writers for various crimes, but carefully pointed out that he was urging "[O]bloquy only, not suppression." "The bounds we set are destined for the critic," he said, "not the legislator"—O. W. Firkins, "The Irresponsible Power of Realism," *North American Review,* CCXXIII (Mar.–Apr.–May 1926), p. 142.

62. "Clinical Notes," *American Mercury,* III (Nov. 1924), p. 312.

CHAPTER VI

1. N.Y. Vice Soc., A.R. (1927), p. 15; Morris Ernst and William Seagle, *To the Pure . . . A Study of Obscenity and the Censor* (N.Y., 1928), p. 15.

2. *N.Y. Times,* Mar. 21, 1928, p. 28 (background); *Pub. Wkly,* CVIII (July 4, 1925), p. 32 (Liveright comment); Arthur Garfield Hays, *City Lawyer; The Autobiography of a Law Practice* (N.Y., 1942), pp. 238–39; *N.Y. Times,* Mar. 22, 1928, p. 18, and Mar. 24, 1928, p. 30 (outcome).

3. Una, Lady Troubridge, *The Life of Radclyffe Hall* (London, 1961), p. 81.

4. Radclyffe Hall, *The Well of Loneliness* (N.Y., 1928), pp. 358, 359.

5. *Pub. Wkly.,* CXIV (Sept. 1, 1928), p. 683; *ibid.* (Nov. 24, 1928), p. 2194; *N.Y. Times,* Jan. 12, 1929, p. 3.

6. Interview with Alfred A. Knopf, May 13, 1964; interview with Morris Ernst, May 14, 1964; *Pub. Wkly.,* CXIV (Sept. 1, 1928), p. 683 ("The book is scheduled for publication in this country on October 5th by Knopf. According to them the withdrawal of the book in England will not affect their publishing of the book as planned."); *ibid.,* CXIV (Nov. 10, 1928), p. 1988.

7. On Covici: *N.Y. Times,* Oct. 15, 1964 (obit.); on the *Fantazius Mallare* case: *Pub. Wkly.,* CII (Oct. 14, 1922), p. 1356; *ibid.,* CV (Mar. 1, 1924), p. 674; *N.Y. Times,* Feb. 5, 1924, p. 21; Ben Hecht, *A Child of the Century* (N.Y., 1954), p. 180; Donald Friede, "Getting Started," in Gerald Gross, ed., *Publishers on Publishing* (N.Y., 1961), p. 338; Ben Hecht and Maxwell Bodenheim, *Cutie; A Warm Mamma* (Chicago, 1924).

8. Donald Friede, *The Mechanical Angel* (N.Y., 1948), pp. 4–15; *N.Y. Times,* May 31, 1965 (obit.).

9. N.Y. Vice Soc., A.R. (1928), p. 9; N.Y. Vice Soc., Periodical Letter, Mar. 12, 1929 (N.Y. Public Library); Friede, "Getting Started," p. 346. In his autobiography Friede states (*Mechanical Angel,* p. 91) that Ernst demanded as his fee a 25¢ royalty on each copy of *The Well of Loneliness* sold by Covici-Friede. Ernst has denied this (interview, May 14, 1964), and Friede, replying to a query on this discrepancy,

wrote: ". . . Mr. Ernst's records would be clearer than my recollection, and I would accept his statement as fact" (Donald Friede to Paul Boyer, Oct. 28, 1964).

10. *N.Y. Times*, Jan. 23, 1929, p. 7; Feb. 22, 1929, p. 11; *Pub. Wkly.*, CXV (Mar. 2, 1929), pp. 962–63.

11. Friede, *Mechanical Angel*, pp. 50, 94; interview with Alfred A. Knopf, May 13, 1964. On Ernst's publicity campaign: Friede, "Getting Started," p. 347; *N.Y. World*, Jan. 20, 1929; *N.Y. Evening Post*, Jan. 19, 1927.

12. *Pub. Wkly.*, CXV (Apr. 27, 1929), p. 1990; *N.Y. Times*, Apr. 20, 1923, p. 20 (the verdict).

13. Friede, "Getting Started," p. 339.

14. Donald Friede to Paul Boyer, Oct. 28, 1964.

15. "Obscenity in Court," *Nation*, CXXX (June 4, 1930), p. 642 (Ernst quote); *Pub. Wkly.*, CXVII (May 31, 1930), p. 2737; *Patterson* [N.J.] *Call*, May 22, 1930 (Kaltenborn). Ernst's two further victories following *The Well of Loneliness* case were in defense of Nathan Asch's *Pay Day* (N.Y., 1930) and Schnitzler's *Casanova's Homecoming*, reissued by Simon & Schuster in 1930. On *Pay Day*: *Pub. Wkly.*, CXVII (Apr. 19, 1930), p. 2117; (May 3, 1930), p. 2323; (May 24, 1930), p. 2622. On *Casanova's Homecoming*: Morris Ernst, *The Best is Yet . . .* (N.Y., 1945), p. 119; *N.Y. Morning World*, Aug. 8, 1930; *N.Y. Herald Tribune*, Sept. 28, 1930 (clippings in American Civil Liberties Union Archives, Princeton Univ., Vol. CCCLXXXV).

16. *Pub. Wkly.*, CV (Jan. 5, 1924), p. 24 (*Janet March* case); interview with Alfred A. Knopf, May 13, 1964; Floyd Dell, *Homecoming; An Autobiography* (N.Y., 1933), p. 361. Published in October 1923, *Janet March* sold 13,000 copies before its suppression.

17. Alfred A. Knopf to H. L. Mencken, Feb. 19, 1927, in H. L. Mencken, "The 'Hatrack' Case, 1926–27. *The American Mercury* vs. the New England Watch and Ward Society, the Postmaster-General of the United States, *et al.* . . . with Newspaper Reports and Other Documents" (8 vols., H. L. Mencken Room, Enoch Pratt Free Library, Baltimore, Md., 1937), VII, Appendix LVII–aaa, and *ibid.*, I, p. 122. This unpublished record, hereafter cited as "The 'Hatrack' Case," was prepared by Mencken in 1937. For more on the *American Mercury* case see Chapter VII in this book.

18. *Pub. Wkly.*, CIV (Dec. 22, 1923), p. 1919; *ibid.* (Dec. 29, 1923), p. 1974 (editorial comments). *Pub. Wkly.*, CIV (Dec. 22, 1923), p. 1938; *ibid.*, CV (Mar. 8, 1924), p. 834 (report of case).

19. E. Merrill Root, *Frank Harris* (N.Y., 1947), p. 282; *N.Y. Times*, June 27, 1925, p. 3; Aug. 21, 1925, p. 15; *Pub. Wkly.*, CIX (Mar. 27, 1926), p. 1136 (report of case); N.Y. Vice Soc., *A.R.* (1925), p. 10 (Sumner quote); *Pub. Wkly.*, CVIII (July 4, 1925), p. 32 (editorial comment).

20. *N.Y. Times*, June 27, 1928, p. 26; *ibid.*, Sept. 22, 1928, p. 22 (Steloff); *Pub. Wkly.*, CXX (Nov. 14, 1931), p. 2234 (Seiffer); *ibid.*, CXVII (June 21, 1930), p. 3010 (Marks); *ibid.*, CXIX (Jan. 31, 1931), p. 575 (Risden).

21. *N.Y. Times*, Jan. 17, 1929, p. 14, and June 5, 1929, p. 12 (Lhevinne); *Pub. Wkly.*, CXX (Nov. 14, 1931), p. 2234 (Steloff).

22. Broun and Leech, *Comstock*; N.Y. Vice Soc., *A.R.* (1931), p. 8; *ibid.*, 1932, p. 6.

23. S. J. Woolf, "A Vice Suppressor Looks at Our Morals," *N.Y. Times*, Oct. 9, 1932, VIII, p. 2, with a pencil sketch of Sumner by Mr. Woolf.

24. *Pub. Wkly.*, CI (May 13, 1922), p. 1337; *ibid.*, CII (July 15, 1922), p. 118; *ibid.*, CIII (Jan. 27, 1923), p. 221. Under Frederick L. Rowe, publisher of the *Christian Leader*, the Cincinnati organization continued to exist, at least on paper, until 1938, when it disappears from the Cincinnati directories—John Mullane, Public Library of Cincinnati and Hamilton County, to Paul Boyer, Nov. 7, 1964.

25. The Illinois obscenity statute may be found in Ford, *Criminal Obscenity*, pp. 136–37. On Yarrow, see biographical article in *Chicago Sun*, Aug. 4, 1946, and obit., *Chicago Daily News*, June 16, 1954.

26. *Pub. Wkly.*, CXVII (Feb. 1, 1930), pp. 567–68.

27. *Vigilance*, Jan. 1930, p. 3; *Pub. Wkly.*, CXVII (Feb. 1, 1930), p. 567; *Chicago Tribune*, Mar. 28, 1931.

28. *Vigilance*, Jan. 1930, p. 3; "Neither Censorship nor Puritanism Involved," *Christian Century*, XLVII (Mar. 19, 1930), pp. 357–58; "Battling the Wolves," *ibid.*, XLVIII (Apr. 8, 1931), pp. 470–71.

29. "Trapping the Booksellers," *Pub. Wkly.*, CXXXV (Jan. 25, 1930), p. 435; "Booksellers Victorious in Chicago Reformer's Campaign," *ibid.*, CXVII (Feb. 1, 1930), p. 567; *N.Y. Sunday World*, Mar. 23, 1930.

30. *Chicago Tribune*, June 28, 1931.

31. "Chicago Bookseller Wins Case," *Pub. Wkly.*, CXIX (Apr. 4, 1931), p. 1790; *Chicago Tribune*, Mar. 28, 1931; *ibid.*, June 28, 1931 (quoting Yarrow); *Chicago Evening Post*, Dec. 28, 1931 (reversal of judgment).

32. J. Frank Chase, "The New Puritanism," *Harvard Advocate*, CXII (May 1926), p. 15.

33. New England Watch and Ward Society, *Annual Report, 1924–25* (1925), p. 12.

34. Watch and Ward spokesman quoted in *Boston Herald*, Dec. 25, 1929; "H. L." to *N.Y. Times*, Mar. 16, 1927, p. 24; N.Y. Vice Soc., *A.R.* (1932), p. 7.

35. Chase, "The New Puritanism," p. 11.

36. N.Y. Vice Soc., *A.R.* (1929), p. 6. Atterbury, an Episcopal leader, was a brother-in-law of Killaen Van Rensselaer, Vice Society treasurer from 1881 to 1906.

37. W. & W. Soc., A.R., *1923–24* (1924), pp. 31–32; John Sumner to *N.Y. Times,* May 13, 1927, p. 22.

38. Quoted in *N.Y. Times,* May 21, 1930, p. 29. The contrary point of view at this A.B.A. session on censorship was ably upheld by Mary Ware Dennett, H. V. Kaltenborn, and Morris Ernst—*Pub. Wkly.,* CXVII (May 31, 1930), pp. 2734–37.

39. N.Y. Vice Soc., Periodical Letter (N.Y.P.L.), Dec. 10, 1926; N.Y. Vice Soc., A.R. (1931), p. 6; *Chicago Sun,* Aug. 4, 1946 (repeating a Yarrow comment dating from the 1920s).

40. *E.g.,* N.Y. Vice Soc., A.R. (1931), p. 17. The same statement was used in earlier reports.

41. "Arrests, 1920–50," N.Y. Vice Soc. Records, Library of Congress, Vol. V, p. 44.

42. *Pub. Wkly.,* CXI (May 21, 1927), p. 2063; *ibid.,* CXXIII (May 6, 1933), p. 1471. Founders of the Committee for the Suppression of Irresponsible Censorship included Joseph Hergesheimer, Owen Davis, Walter P. Eaton, Will Irwin, Fannie Hurst, Edgar Lee Masters, and Meredith Nicholson.

43. *Pub. Wkly.,* CXI (June 4, 1927), pp. 2178–79. The editorial first appeared in *Legal Notes.*

44. *N.Y. Times,* May 10, 1927, p. 22; May 13, 1927, p. 28.

45. Mrs. J. Wells Smith, "Values in Fiction," *Libraries,* XXXIII (Oct. 1928), p. 404.

46. Margery Bedinger, "Censorship of Books by the Library," *ibid.,* XXXVI (Nov. 1931), pp. 391, 393, 394.

47. *N.Y. Times,* May 6, 1927, p. 16 (*Christian Endeavor*); *Boston Evening Transcript,* Jan. 23, 1930 (quoting testimony of the editor of *Zion's Herald* at a Massachusetts legislative hearing on a bill to liberalize the state's obscenity law); *The Congregationalist,* Apr. 8, 1926.

48. Aldous Huxley, *Vulgarity in Literature* (London, 1930); Mary Ware Dennett, *Who's Obscene?* (N.Y., 1930); Arthur Garfield Hays, *Let Freedom Ring* (N.Y., 1928); Victor F. Calverton [George Goetz], *Sex Expression in Literature* (N.Y., 1926); Havelock Ellis, "Obscenity and the Censor," *Saturday Rev.* [London], CXVLI (Nov. 17, 1928), pp. 642–43, and "The Revaluation of Obscenity," in *More Essays of Love and Virtue* (N.Y., 1931); D. H. Lawrence, *Pornography and Obscenity* (London, 1929); H. L. Mencken, "Comstockery," in *Prejudices: Fifth Series* (N.Y., 1926). See also Horace M. Kallen, ed., *Freedom in the Modern World* (N.Y., 1928) and *Indecency and the Seven Arts* (N.Y., 1930); Leon Whipple, *Story of Civil Liberty in the United States* (N.Y., 1927); Walter Lippmann, *American Inquisitors* (N.Y., 1928); and John Cowper Powys, *In Defense of Sensuality* (N.Y., 1930). The legal profession contributed to the remarkable outpouring of censorship literature as well; see, *e.g.: Columbia Law Review,* XXVIII (Nov. 1928), pp. 950–57; *Indiana Law Journal,* IV (Apr. 1929), pp.

445–55; and *Law Notes*, XXX (Feb. 1927), p. 204; XXXI (July 1927), p. 63; and XXII (June–July 1928), pp. 67–70.

49. Victor F. Calverton [George Goetz], *The Liberation of American Literature* (N.Y., 1932), pp. 402–06, *passim*; *Daily Worker* [N.Y.], Apr. 19, 1929.

50. *Current Biog.* (1940), pp. 281–83 (Ernst quote on p. 282); interview with Ernst, May 14, 1964. On Ernst and William Seagle: *Who's Who in America, 1964–65.*

51. Ernst and Seagle, *To the Pure . . ., passim,* esp. pp. 133, 151, and 275. Recognizing the limitations of *To the Pure*, a number of otherwise favorably disposed reviewers made rather severely negative comments about the book. See, *e.g., Saturday Rev.,* V (Nov. 10, 1928), pp. 333–34 (Ferris Greenslet); *Pub. Wkly.,* CXIV (Nov. 10, 1928), pp. 1983–85 ("A Librarian"); *Nation and Athenaeum* [London] XLV (Apr. 20, 1929), p. 77 (Leonard Woolf). For contrasts to the Ernst-Seagle treatment of the subject, see Huntington Cairns, "Freedom of Expression in Literature," *Annals of the American Academy of Political and Social Science,* CC (Nov. 1938), esp. pp. 78–79, and David Riesman, "Civil Liberties in a Period of Transition," *Public Policy* [Harvard Graduate School of Public Administration], III (1942), esp. p. 72. Cairns stresses that all social groups, not merely "prudish" ones, evolve taboos and conceptions of the obscene, while Riesman goes beyond legalism to consider the wide variety of "apparently petty and often anonymous forms of control" by which these taboos are enforced. De Tocqueville's remark may be found in Alexis de Tocqueville, *Democracy in America* (Vintage Ed., N.Y., 1945), I, 275.

52. Joseph Wood Krutch, "The Indecency of Censorship," *Nation,* CXXIV (Feb. 16, 1927), p. 162; *Pub. Wkly.,* CXI (June 4, 1927), pp. 2178–79; *ibid.,* CXVII (May 31, 1930), p. 275 (quoting Mary Ware Dennett).

53. Bronislaw Malinowski, *Sex and Repression in Savage Society* (N.Y., 1927), esp. Part II, Chap. 4, "Obscenity and Myth"; E. E. Evans-Pritchard, "Some Collective Expressions of Obscenity in Africa," *Journal of the Royal Anthropological Inst. of Great Britain and Ireland,* LIX (1929), pp. 31 *ff.*

54. D. H. Lawrence, "Pornography and Obscenity," reprinted in Lawrence, *Sex, Literature and Censorship; Essays* (Compasss Ed., N.Y., 1959), pp. 68–69.

55. Ernst and Seagle, *To the Pure . . .,* p. 197.

56. Ben Ray Redman, "Is Censorship Possible?" *Scribner's Magazine,* LXXXVII (May 1930), p. 517.

57. "Who's Obscene?" *Nation,* CXXX (Feb. 26, 1930), p. 236; Hays, *Let Freedom Ring,* pp. 163–64; *Pub. Wkly.,* CXVII (May 31, 1930), p. 2735 (Dennett).

58. Schuster to *N.Y. Herald Tribune,* Nov. 9, 1930; Lawrence, "Pornography and Obscenity," pp. 69, 72.

59. N.Y. Vice Soc., *A.R.* (1929), p. 6.

60. Lawrence, "Pornography and Obscenity," p. 77.

61. Robert A. Woods, "Prohibition and Social Hygiene," *Social Hyg.*, V (Apr. 1919), pp. 143–44. On the denominational temperance boards which expanded their purview after Prohibition was achieved, see *New Era Magazine*, XXV (Aug. 1919), p. 424 (Presbyterian Board of Temperance, Prohibition and Moral Welfare); and *Zion's Herald*, CI (Dec. 10, 1924), p. 1585 (Methodist Board of Temperance, Prohibition, and Public Morals).

62. "Polluting the Springs," *Zion's Herald*, C (Sept. 27, 1922), p. 1222; Arthur F. Southwick, "Moral Welfare: Its Problems and Its Place in Society," *Presbyterian Magazine*, XXVIII (May 1922), p. 291 (Southwick was associate secretary of the Presbyterian Board of Temperance, Prohibition, and Moral Welfare); W.C.T.U., *Annual Report, 1920; ibid., 1927*.

63. *Zion's Herald*, C (Oct. 4, 1922), p. 1265; "Censorship and Prohibition," *Christian Century*, XL (July 19, 1923), pp. 901–02.

64. *Congressional Record*, LXXI, 71 Cong., 1 Sess. (Oct. 11, 1929), p. 4463.

65. *N.Y. Times*, May 8, 1927, p. 26 (report of plan); May 9, 1927, p. 20 (editorial).

66. William J. Flynn, "Verboten," *Pub. Wkly.*, CV (June 14, 1924), p. 1916.

67. Edward Blakeley to *N.Y. Times*, Mar. 6, 1923, p. 20; *The Dunster House Bookshop Case: A Statement by the Directors of the New England Watch and Ward Society* [Boston, 1930], p. 11.

68. *N.Y. Times*, Apr. 19, 1923, p. 4; *ibid.*, May 3, 1923, p. 1.

69. Mencken, "Comstockery," p. 21; Benjamin Antin, "Demand for Censorship Grows," *N.Y. Times*, Feb. 20, 1927, VIII, p. 4; "Which Law?" *Nation*, CXXVIII (June 19, 1929), p. 729.

70. Morris Ernst, Foreword to James Joyce, *Ulysses* (Modern Library Ed., N.Y., 1934), p. viii; "Another Repeal," *Nation*, CXXXVII (Dec. 20, 1933), p. 693.

71. Theodore Peterson, *Magazines in the Twentieth Century* (Urbana, Ill., 1958), pp. 243–81; Frederick Lewis Allen, *Only Yesterday* (Bantam Ed., N.Y., 1959), pp. 131–34.

72. William L. Chenery, "This Is the Age of Dirt," *Collier's*, LXXVII (Apr. 3, 1926), p. 21; "The Filth Uplifters," *Ladies' Home Journal*, XLI (Aug. 1924), p. 20; "Muckraking the Newsstands," *Literary Digest*, LXXIV (Feb. 21, 1925), pp. 31–32; the *Woman's Home Companion* editorial is reported in *Pub. Wkly.*, CVIII (Sept. 19, 1925), p. 870.

73. Frank R. Kent, "Filth on Main Street," *Independent*, CXIV (June 20, 1925), pp. 686, 688; Ernest W. Mandeville, "Gutter Literature," *New Republic*, XLV (Feb. 17, 1926), pp. 350–52; H. W. Van Loon, "Uplift Journals Please Copy!" *Commonweal*, I (Dec. 31, 1924), pp. 202–03, quoted passages on p. 203.

74. J. Frank Chase, quoted in "America First—in Lewd Literature," *Literary Digest,* LXXXVI (Sept. 19, 1925), p. 35; N.Y. Vice Soc., A.R. (1926), p. 6. The *Evening World* should not be confused with the morning *World,* a much more distinguished newspaper.

75. "Opposition to Dirty Magazines Brings Quick Results," *Christian Century,* XLII (Nov. 5, 1925), pp. 1362–63; *Pub. Wkly.,* CXI (Apr. 16, 1927), p. 1568.

76. "Vicious Magazines," *Social Hyg.,* IX (Oct. 1923), pp. 424–25; "Mental Prostitution," *ibid.,* XII (June 1926), pp. 357–58.

77. For references, see above, Notes 72 and 73.

78. *Evening World* quoted in *Social Hyg.,* XII (June 1926), p. 358; *Daily News* in *Literary Digest,* XCII (Feb. 19, 1927), p. 32.

79. *Annual Report of the Postmaster General for the Fiscal Year Ended June 30, 1925* (Washington, D.C., 1925), p. 63; *ibid. . . . 1926* (Washington, D.C., 1926), pp. 62, 63.

80. Oswald Garrison Villard, "Sex, Art, Truth, and Magazines," *Atlantic Monthly,* CXXXVII (Mar. 1926), p. 398.

81. Ernst and Seagle, *To the Pure . . .,* pp. 34, 35.

82. *Pub. Wkly.,* CV (Mar. 22, 1924), p. 1046; *ibid.,* CVIII (Sept. 19, 1925), p. 870.

83. "Vicious Magazines," *Social Hyg.,* IX (Oct. 1923), p. 424; Nellie B. Miller, "Fighting Filth on Main Street," *Independent,* CXV (Oct. 10, 1925), pp. 411–12, quote on p. 412.

84. *N.Y. Times,* Aug. 8, 1924, p. 16; *Pub. Wkly.,* CX (Aug. 28, 1926), p. 749; *ibid.,* CVII (June 13, 1925), p. 1937; "Suggested Program for Meeting of Conference on Salacious Literature to Be Held in the Methodist Building, Washington, D.C., Jan. 13, 1926" (mimeographed, N.Y. Vice Soc. Records, VIII, Library of Congress; *The Voice* [Methodist Board of Temperance, Prohibition, and Public Morals], Feb. 1926; Mencken, "The 'Hatrack' Case," VII, p. 29 (Appendix L–a), contains a copy of the letter sent by the board to the ministers who requested a report of the conference. Lists of both objectionable books and magazines were attached, but the main thrust of the conference seems to have been against magazines. The mimeographed conference program concludes: "No announcement has been made of this meeting. Those invited have been asked to hold the matter confidential. No one attending need fear he will be unwillingly identified with public utterance."

85. W. & W. Soc., A.R., *1924–25* (1925), pp. 13–14.

86. "Peddling Obscenity to Children," *Literary Digest,* LXXXVII (Dec. 12, 1925), p. 34; *Pub. Wkly.,* CIX (Mar. 27, 1926), p. 1136.

87. John S. Sumner, "Effective Action Against Salacious Plays and Magazines," *American City,* XXXIII (Nov. 1925), p. 555.

88. N.Y. Vice Soc., Periodical Letter, Oct. 31, 1927 (N.Y.P.L.).

89. *Cong. Record,* LXVIII, 69 Cong., 2 Sess. (Feb. 8, 1927), pp. 3264–67, quoted passages on pp. 3264 and 3267.

90. *Ibid.*, p. 3276.

91. *Ibid.*, LXIX, 70 Cong., 1 Session (Jan. 20, 1928), p. 1833; *ibid.* (Jan. 26, 1928), pp. 2077–79, esp. pp. 2078, 2079. Biog. information on Tillman: *Biog. Directory of the Am. Congress, 1774–1949* (Washington, D.C., 1950).

92. Peterson, *Magazines in the Twentieth Century*, p. 277.

93. N.Y. Vice Soc., A.R. (1926), p. 9; *Pub. Wkly.*, CXI (Mar. 3, 1927), p. 860; *Zion's Herald*, CVII (Apr. 10, 1929), p. 453.

94. *God of Vengeance*: N.Y. *Times*, Mar. 7, 1923, p. 6, and May 29, 1923, p. 2. (The play is about a brothel owner who tries to keep his daughter pure, only to have her perverted by one of the prostitutes in his establishment). *Desire Under the Elms*: *Nation*, CXX (Mar. 4, 1925), p. 233; "Muck is Muck," *Social Hyg.*, XI (Apr. 1925), pp. 224–25. *The Times*, in a bantering editorial (Mar. 1), said the play's "primitive passions" were "essentially un-American."

95. N.Y. *Times*, Mar. 9, 1924, II, p. 1; Sumner, "Effective Action . . .," p. 553.

96. W. & W. Soc., A.R., 1929–30 (1930), p. 19; interview with Charles W. Morton of the *Atlantic Monthly*, Mar. 10, 1961.

97. *Pub. Wkly.*, CXI (Apr. 2, 1927), p. 1417; Hays, *Let Freedom Ring*, pp. 237–39; Nathan quoted in *Cong. Record*, LXVIII, 69 Cong., 2 Sess. (Feb. 8, 1927), p. 3266.

98. Booth Tarkington, "When Is It Dirt?" *Collier's*, LXXIX (May 14, 1927), p. 48; Calverton, *Sex Expression in Literature*, p. 307.

99. Hays, *Let Freedom Ring*, pp. 239–62, *passim*. Note that *The Captive* was closed at about the same time that *The Well of Loneliness*, on the same theme, was being cleared.

100. "Is the Censor Coming?" *New Republic*, XLIX (Feb. 16, 1927), p. 344; Benjamin Antin, "Demand for Censorship Grows," N.Y. *Times*, Feb. 20, 1927, VIII, p. 4. For a typical outburst by Sumner on the subject see *ibid.*, Jan. 19, 1927, p. 25.

101. *Pub. Wkly.*, CXI (Mar. 19, 1927), p. 1255; *ibid.* (Apr. 16, 1927), p. 1566; N.Y. *Times*, Mar. 16, 1927, p. 12; *Commonweal* quoted in N.Y. *Times*, Mar. 15, 1927, p. 15.

102. *Ibid.*, Mar. 18, 1927, p. 1; Mar. 24, 1927, p. 15; Mar. 26, 1927, p. 6; *Pub. Wkly.*, CXI (June 4, 1927), p. 2178; Hays, *Let Freedom Ring*, pp. 264–65.

103. N.Y. *Times*, Oct. 26, 1930, p. 27.

104. Malcolm M. Willey and Stuart A. Rice, "The Agencies of Communication," in President's Committee on Social Trends, *Recent Social Trends in the U.S.* (2 vols., N.Y., 1933), I, p. 208.

105. Ruth A. Inglis, *Freedom of the Movies, A Report on Self-Regulation from the Commission on Freedom of the Press* (Chicago, 1947), pp. 62–96, *passim*, esp. p. 71, 86–89, also pp. 100, 106. Only in 1933, when the formation of the Catholic Legion of Decency posed

the threat of damaging boycotts, was Hays given any real power (*ibid.,* pp. 116, 121, 125).

106. Edward F. Garresché, S.J., "The Parish Priest and Moving Pictures," *Ecclesiastical Review,* LXXVI (May 1927), p. 465; Rowland C. Shelton, "Moving Pictures, Books, and Child Crimes," *Bookman,* LIII (May 1921), p. 244. Shelton was head of the "Big Brother" organization.

107. Theodosia Walton, "Tarkington Looks at the Censor," *N.Y. Times,* Aug. 20, 1922, III, p. 3; Professor J. Duncan Spaeth, quoted in *N.Y. Times,* Dec. 5, 1922, p. 8. My ideas on the link between the movies and book censorship were also influenced by an exchange of ideas with Robert Sklar.

CHAPTER VII

1. William Bradford, *Of Plymouth Plantation, 1620–1647,* Samuel Eliot Morison, ed. (N.Y., 1952), pp. 206, 209.

2. *N.Y. Herald Tribune,* Sept. 21, 1929; Helena H. Smith, "Boston's Bogey Man," *Outlook,* XLIX (June 6, 1928), p. 214; *Harvard Crimson,* Sept. 30, 1929.

3. Oswald Garrison Villard, *Some Newspapers and Newspaper-men* (N.Y., 1923), Chap. VI, "Boston, A Journalistic Poor-Farm." Dismissing the *Post, Advertiser,* and *American* as crime-oriented tabloids, Villard found the *Globe* "as parochial as it knows how to be" and the corporation-owned *Herald* "without a soul, and . . . ruled by fear." Even the *Transcript's* relatively enlightened cultural outlook, he added, was vitiated by a reactionary political stance aimed at Brahmin readers "whose horizons are as limited as their prejudices are unnumbered" (pp. 99, 108, 111). My understanding of both the journalistic and social configurations of Boston in the 1920s was deepened by an interview with Louis Lyons, Curator of the Nieman Foundation, Mar. 13, 1961.

4. R. L. Duffus, "Our Changing Cities: Unruffled Boston," *N.Y. Times Magazine,* Jan. 30, 1927, p. 6. See also Katharine F. Gerould, "Boston Revisited," *Scribner's Magazine,* LXXI (Jan. 1922), pp. 100–05; and Elmer Davis, "Boston: Notes on an Immigrant Invasion," *Harper's Magazine,* CLVI (Jan. 1928), pp. 140–52. Writes Davis (p. 141): "Beacon Hill . . . is flawless, complete, finished, static, dead; it lies before you in an autumnal sunset splendor, like Rome under the Ostrogoths. The Irish have the Gothic roughness, the Gothic vigor and power; and the old Bostonians, like the old Romans, keep out of their way, hiding in the crumbling palaces, each race despising and envying the other."

5. "It Seems to Heywood Broun," *Nation,* CXXIX (Oct. 2, 1929), p. 345; William Cardinal O'Connell, *Recollections of Seventy Years* (Boston, 1934); Dorothy G. Wayman, *Cardinal O'Connell of Boston . . .*

1859–1944 (N.Y., [1955]). Writes the admiring Miss Wayman of the Cardinal's social views, *ca.* 1924: "He branded the Child Labor Amendment boldly as 'this soviet legislation' " (p. 220). In 1929, addressing a group of Catholic college students, O'Connell said: "What does all this worked up enthusiasm about Einstein mean? . . . I have never yet met a man who understood in the least what Einstein is driving at and . . . I very seriously doubt that Einstein himself knows really what he means." *The Pilot* editorially endorsed these sentiments and asked: "[I]f this wonderful [Einsteinian] theory is too far away from the average human being, what is the good of it?" (Apr. 13, 1929, pp. 1 and 4). For more on the Irish censorship see: "Irish Free State Censorship," *Pub. Wkly.*, CXIV (July 28, 1928), p. 322; Norman St. John-Stevas, *Obscenity and the Law* (London, 1956), pp. 179–87; and Walter Prichard Eaton, "New England in 1930," *Current History*, XXXIII (Nov. 1930), pp. 168–73, esp. p. 171.

6. A. L. S. Wood, "Keeping the Puritans Pure," *American Mercury*, VI (Sept. 1925), p. 75.

7. Cameron Rogers, "A Booksellers' Censorship," *World's Work*, L (June 1925), pp. 218–20, quote on p. 219. For further descriptions of the system, of which both the Watch and Ward and Fuller were inordinately proud, see: Richard F. Fuller, "How Boston Handles Problem," *Pub. Wkly.*, CIII (May 26, 1923), p. 1624; W. & W. Soc., *Annual Report, 1912–13* (1913), p. 7 (on the background of the idea); *ibid.*, *1922–23* (1923), pp. 7–11 (p. 11: "We intend to carry this Democratic Censorship throughout New England, and it is only a question of a short time before the publication of a libidinous book will be an unprofitable venture even for a New York publisher"); *ibid.*, *1924–25* (1925), p. 9; J. Frank Chase, "Literary Freedom and Its Limitations," *Zion's Herald*, CI (Jan. 31, 1923), pp. 160–61; and F. Lauriston Bullard, "Book Banning Issue Burning in Boston," *N.Y. Times*, July 3, 1927, II, p. 2.

8. Ford, *Criminal Obscenity*, p. 71; Fuller, "How Boston Handles Problem," p. 1625. In 1923 the Reverend J. Frank Chase of the Watch and Ward Society said that seven books had been suppressed in 1922 ("Literary Freedom," p. 160), while Fuller ("How Boston Handles Problem," p. 1624), set the figure at fourteen.

9. Frank H. Chase (not to be confused with J. Frank Chase of the Watch and Ward), "What People Are Reading in Boston," *Bulletin of the American Library Association*, XVIII (Aug. 1924), p. 172; Rogers, "A Booksellers' Censorship," p. 218.

10. *Ibid.*, p. 219; Fuller quoted in *ibid.*, p. 220.

11. Fuller, "How Boston Handles Problem," pp. 1624–25. H. L. Mencken made his comment about Fuller in "The 'Hatrack' Case" (8 vols. typescript, 1937, H. L. Mencken Room, Enoch Pratt Free Library, Baltimore), I, p. 109.

12. *Pub. Wkly.*, CII (Oct. 28, 1922), p. 1514; *N.Y. Times*, Oct.

19, 1922. Mrs. Law's fine was suspended by Judge Arthur P. Stone, but she was threatened with a jail sentence if she were ever again convicted in an obscenity case. A second Watch and Ward conviction for the sale of *Simon Called Peter* came in 1923 against Morris Honigbaum of Boston's Modern Bookshop. *Pub. Wkly.*, CIV (Oct. 27, 1923), p. 1435; *ibid.*, CV (Jan. 26, 1924), p. 240. Fuller's "we have had hell" comment is in "How Boston Handles Problem," p. 1624.

13. J. Frank Chase, "Literary Freedom," p. 160; Mencken, "The 'Hatrack' Case," I, p. 130. For more on Chase: "A Valiant Fighter," *Zion's Herald*, CIV (Nov. 10, 1926), p. 1424 (with photograph); Wood, "Keeping the Puritans Pure," p. 74; *Boston Herald*, Aug. 29, 1926; and obituaries in the *Herald* and the *Transcript*, Nov. 4, 1926. On Allen see Chap. I, Note 13 in this book.

14. J. Frank Chase, "The New Puritanism," *Harvard Advocate*, CXII (May 1926), p. 15.

15. Charles Angoff, "Boston's Twilight," *American Mercury*, VI (Dec. 1925), p. 444; Wood, "Keeping the Puritans Pure," pp. 74–78. Mencken tried unsuccessfully to persuade several Boston journalists to write the Watch and Ward article before he settled on Wood, a young reporter from Springfield, Mass. (Mencken, "The 'Hatrack' Case," I, pp. 6–7).

16. "The Case of the April *Mercury*," *Pub. Wkly.*, CIX (Apr. 10, 1926), pp. 1333–34. "Hatrack" appears as a chapter in Herbert Asbury's *Up from Methodism* (N.Y., 1926).

17. Quoted in Mary E. Prim, "Picking Up *Mercury*," *Boston Evening Transcript*, Apr. 8, 1926, p. 14. See also Mencken, "The 'Hatrack' Case," I, p. 11, and V, Appendix XII ("Stenographic Record of Hearing Apr. 12, 1926, before Judge Morton, U.S. Dist. Court, Dist. of Mass."), p. 9. The latter reprints the letter J. Frank Chase had written John T. Tracy of the New England News Company in which he stated his objection to the April *Mercury* and warned: "We shall seek for a warrant against anyone that violates the law." This was a more explicit threat than the usual Boston Booksellers' Committee warning letter which typically went as follows: "The Watch and Ward Society have informed us that they believe that there are passages in . . . which will be held by our courts to be in violation of our statutes. This information is passed along to you without comment and without assuming any obligation to furnish similar information in the future" (Mencken, "The 'Hatrack' Case," VII, Appendix, XXXIII-B). The explicit threat contained in Chase's *American Mercury* letter enabled other Watch and Ward officials later to claim that Chase had exceeded his authority in this case.

18. Mencken, "The 'Hatrack' Case," I, pp. 11–16. All the Boston newspapers carried lengthy stories, many with photographs.

19. Mencken, "The 'Hatrack' Case," I, pp. 17–20 (the booking); p. 21 (the district attorney's reported hostility); pp. 24, 27 (the trial,

and Mencken's description of the Watch and Ward lawyer); pp. 31–32 (the Parmenter decision); p. 30 (the St. Botolph Club reception); "To the Friends of the *American Mercury*, A Statement by the Editor" (4 pp., n.p., April 1926), containing the Parmenter decision, which was delivered *ad lib* but later written down at Hays's request; *New England Hist. and Geneol. Record*, XCI (July 1937), pp. 211–22 (on Parmenter); *Harvard Crimson*, Apr. 8, 1926 (the Harvard reception). On the newspapers' attitude: *Boston Herald*, Apr. 2, 3, and 5, 1926; *Boston Post*, Apr. 5, 1926 ("Peddling smut about, publicly or privately, is an offense here. . . . If censorship was ever justified, it surely is in the stopping of this publication"); *Boston Evening Transcript*, Apr. 5, 1926. The *Transcript*, while half believing that Mencken was merely hunting publicity, remained friendly throughout.

20. "Stenographic Record of Hearing . . ." in Mencken, "The 'Hatrack' Case," VII, Appendix XVI, pp. 9, 11. The hearing is discussed in some detail in Hays, *Let Freedom Ring*, pp. 171–79. Secondary sources covering the entire "Hatrack" incident include William Manchester, *Disturber of the Peace, The Life of H. L. Mencken* (N.Y., 1950), pp. 187–207; and M. K. Singleton, *H. L. Mencken and the American Mercury Adventure* (Durham, 1962), pp. 167–81.

21. Morton's decision is printed in Mencken's pamphlet about the case, "To the Friends of the *American Mercury*." Appendix II, and in Hays, *Let Freedom Ring*, pp. 176–79.

22. Mencken, "The 'Hatrack' Case," I, pp. 36–39, 42–44, 66, 90, 94–100. The characterizations of the New York City postmaster and Post Office Solicitor Donnelly are on pp. 39 and 66 and the injunction appears on pp. 99–100. See also "A Libertarian Laughs," *Nation*, CXXII (Apr. 2, 1926), p. 440; Hays, *Let Freedom Ring*, pp. 179–84; *Camden* [N.J.] *Courier*, May 27, 1926; and, on the wartime censorship, Paul and Schwartz, *Federal Censorship*, p. 35. A rare copy of the original May issue, containing "Sex and the College Girl," is in Mencken, "The 'Hatrack' Case," VI, Appendix II. On the Caragianes conviction, see *ibid.*, I, pp. 53–54 and 112 ff.

23. *Ibid.*, I, p. 77. See also Calverton, *Sex Expression in Literature*, p. 298, on the "Hatrack" vogue.

24. Mencken, "The 'Hatrack' Case," I, p. iii; "A Libertarian Laughs," p. 440.

25. Mencken, "The 'Hatrack' Case," I, pp. 70–71; the *Fort Wayne Journal-Gazette*, Apr. 18, 1926 (in *ibid.*, V, p. 703), contains the Will Rogers column.

26. *Boston Evening Transcript*, Apr. 3, 1926; *Boston Telegram*, Apr. 6 and 23, 1926 (clippings in Mencken, "The 'Hatrack' Case," I, p. 106 and V, p. 751). On the *Telegram*, see Villard, *Some Newspapers and Newspaper-men*, p. 103.

27. W. & W. Soc., A.R., *1926–27* (1927), p. 5 (on Bodwell);

Mencken, "The 'Hatrack' Case," I, p. 110 (Fuller's comment) and I, p. 131 (Mencken's comment). For Chase's obituaries, see above, Note 13.

28. "Pope Declares War on Immoral Books," *N.Y. Times,* May 11, 1927, p. 24; "The Evil of Immoral Literature," *The Pilot,* July 23, 1927, p. 4; "An Insidious Influence," *ibid.,* Aug. 20, 1927, p. 4.

29. *Pub. Wkly.,* CIV (Oct. 27, 1923), p. 1435. *Impromptu* was published by Knopf in 1923.

30. "The Banning of Books in Boston," *Pub. Wkly.,* CXI (Mar. 19, 1927), pp. 1254–55. On *The Plastic Age* case: Zechariah Chafee, Jr., *Censorship in Boston* (22 pp., Boston, 1929), p. 7; "Our Book Censorship—II," *Springfield* [Mass.] *Republican,* Feb. 14, 1928 (this valuable six-part series [Feb. 13–18, 1928] covers many aspects of the Boston censorship situation). In a feeble effort to reassert its prerogative, the Watch and Ward Society at about the same time let it be known that it found objectionable Hulbert Footner's *Antennae* (Doran & Co., N.Y., 1926), though it was careful not to threaten prosecution. It was reported that the ban on *The Marriage Bed* was also at Watch and Ward initiative, but the head of the Vice Society later said explicitly that *Antennae* was the only one of the current crop of banned books to which his organization objected—*Pub. Wkly.,* CXI (Mar. 19, 1927), pp. 1254–55; *Boston Evening Transcript,* Oct. 3, 1927.

31. *N.Y. Times,* Mar. 12, 1927, pp. 1 and 6; *ibid.,* Mar. 14, 1927, p. 14.

32. *Ibid.,* Mar. 13, 1927, p. 2 (Harcourt and Hays); *Pub. Wkly.,* CXI (Mar. 19, 1927), p. 1255 (Macrae).

33. *N.Y. Times,* Mar. 13, 1927, p. 2 (Fuller); *Pub. Wkly.,* CXI (Apr. 16, 1927), p. 1570.

34. "Boston Booksellers State Position on Censorship Law," *ibid.,* CXI (Mar. 26, 1927), p. 1332.

35. Helena H. Smith, "Boston's Bogey Man," pp. 214, 233. Indeed, the booksellers on their own initiative compiled what *Publishers' Weekly* called a "timidity list" of books they refused to sell—"Will Boston Find Its Way Out?" *Pub. Wkly.,* CXI (May 28, 1927), p. 2122.

36. "*Elmer Gantry* Banned in Boston," *Pub. Wkly.,* CXI (Apr. 16, 1927), pp. 1569–71. Foley's letter is quoted on p. 1569. A month later, the police notified booksellers that four more titles had been banned: Maurice Dekobra, *The Madonna of the Sleeping Cars* (Payson & Clarke, N.Y., 1927), a French best-seller; May Sinclair, *The Allinghams* (Macmillan, N.Y., 1927); Adelaide Phillpotts, *Tomek, the Sculptor* (Little, Brown, Boston, 1927); and Anthony Pryde [Agnes Russell Weekes], *Rowforest* (Dodd Mead, N.Y., 1927). The fact that these books had either just appeared or had not yet been placed on sale (*Rowforest*) suggested to *Publishers' Weekly* that the police were receiving expert advice from someone highly knowledgeable about the current literary scene—*Pub. Wkly.,* CXI (May 14, 1927), p. 1900. In 1928 Viña Delmar's

Bad Girl (Harcourt Brace, N.Y., 1928) was added to the list—*ibid.*, CXIII (May 12, 1928), p. 1963.

37. "Commercialized Bunk," *The Pilot*, Apr. 16, 1927, p. 4; a *Boston Herald* editorial of Apr. 14, 1927, criticizing Foley, is typical of the reaction of Boston's secular press.

38. Donald Brace to Sinclair Lewis, Apr. 22, 1927, *From Main Street to Stockholm, Letters of Sinclair Lewis, 1919–1930*, Harrison Smith, ed. (N.Y., 1952), p. 240. An alternative procedure was devised which seemed to promise the desired judicial ruling on *Elmer Gantry* without the risk of a criminal conviction. The idea was for the Old Corner Bookstore to return its stock of the Lewis novel to Harcourt Brace, who would then file an amicable suit against Old Corner. The outcome of this suit, it was hoped, would give a clue as to the book's legal status under the obscenity law. This idea was dropped when Harcourt concluded that intervention by an out-of-state publisher would only "embarrass" the embryonic movement to amend the Massachusetts obscenity law—*Pub. Wkly.*, CXI (May 14, 1927), p. 1900; Alfred Harcourt to Sinclair Lewis, June 1, 1927, *Main Street to Stockholm*, p. 242.

39. *Boston Evening Transcript*, Apr. 16, 1927, I, 6; "Test Case Made of Dreiser's Book," *Pub. Wkly.*, CXI (Apr. 23, 1927), p. 1651.

40. Donald Friede, "Getting Started," p. 345; *Pub. Wkly.*, CXI (Apr. 23, 1927), p. 1651; *ibid.*, (Apr. 30, 1927), p. 1712; *Boston Globe*, Apr. 22, 1927; *N.Y. Times*, Apr. 23, 1927.

41. "Will Boston Find Its Way Out?" *Pub. Wkly.*, CXI (May 28, 1927), p. 2122.

42. *Ibid.*, (June 4, 1927), p. 2190; *ibid.* (June 18, 1927), p. 2330.

43. Upton Sinclair Reminiscences (typescript), Oral History Project, Columbia University, I, p. 200; Sinclair to Villard, May 31, 1927, Upton Sinclair Folder, Villard Papers, Houghton Library, Harvard University.

44. *Pub. Wkly.*, CXI (June 18, 1927), p. 2330; *ibid.* (June 25, 1927), p. 2403; *Boston Herald*, June 13, 1927; Upton Sinclair, "Poor Me and Pure Boston," *Nation*, CXXIV (June 29, 1927), pp. 713–14; Sinclair Reminiscences, I, p. 200; Hays, *Let Freedom Ring*, pp. 191–92, quotes the Sinclair comment cited and also contains a photograph of Sinclair wearing his fig-leaf signboard.

45. *N.Y. Times*, Jan. 22, 1928, III, p. 6.

46. Elmer Davis, "Boston: Notes on an Immigrant Invasion," pp. 143–44.

47. "Boston Discusses Its Censorship Problem," *Pub. Wkly.*, CXI (May 28, 1927), p. 2118; *N.Y. Times*, Apr. 15, 1927, p. 2 (*Atlantic-Little, Brown* statement).

48. *Literary Digest*, XCIII (Apr. 2, 1927), p. 31 (quoting the *Globe* and the *Post*); *Boston Herald*, Apr. 14, 1927; *Boston Evening Transcript*, Apr. 2 and Nov. 11, 1927. On *The Pilot's* attitude, see Note 37.

49. *Pub. Wkly.*, CXI (May 18, 1927), pp. 2118–20.

50. *Libraries*, XXXII (Mar. 1927), p. 136 (Rogers' speech); *N.Y. Times*, Oct. 21, 1927, p. 26 (Eaton's speech); *Library Jour.*, LII (Apr. 1, 1927), p. 361; *ibid.* (May 1, 1927), p. 479.

51. A. Lincoln Filene to *Boston Evening Transcript*, Dec. 27, 1927; *Pub. Wkly.*, CXII (Dec. 10, 1927), p. 2112.

52. Edward H. Cotton, "When Is a Book Pernicious?" *Zion's Herald*, CVI (Feb. 22, 1928), pp. 238–39, quoted passage on p. 239. Fuller is also quoted in Cotton's article.

53. This statute (Chap. 272, Sec. 28 of the General Laws of the Commonwealth) is printed in *Pub. Wkly.*, CXI (May 18, 1927), p. 2120. Italics mine.

54. *Pub. Wkly.*, CXIII (Jan. 28, 1928), pp. 349–50 (the Shattuck bill is on p. 357); *ibid.* (May 12, 1928), pp. 1963–64; "Book Censorship in Massachusetts—A Responsible Statement" (a four-page pamphlet [1928] in Mencken, "The 'Hatrack' Case," VII Appendix XXXIX) contains a full listing of the leaders of the 1928 amendment movement. The Boston booksellers' bill, printed in *Pub. Wkly.*, CXIII (Jan. 28, 1928), pp. 357–58, provided that the attorney general, district attorneys, or any two adult Massachusetts citizens could proceed against a book by filing a petition in equity in superior court. After a "summary examination" a judge could issue a temporary (sixty-day) injunction prohibiting the book's sale in the state. During this interim the publisher would be given opportunity to defend his imprint in a civil action. If the verdict were negative, or if the publisher failed to appear, the injunction would become permanent and further sale of the book would constitute a criminal offense. Backers of the Shattuck bill strongly assailed the booksellers' bill. The "summary examination" provision and the lack of a jury at any point in the proceedings, they said, was a "reversion to the . . . Star Chamber" which would impose "a censorship more inexorable than this Commonwealth has yet known" ("Book Censorship in Massachusetts—A Responsible Statement"). In fact, this approach had much to recommend it, for it shifted the focus from criminal action against a bookseller to *in rem* proceedings against a book. In 1945, after a campaign led by Professor Zechariah Chafee, Jr., the Massachusetts obscenity law was, in fact, revised along these lines. The danger in 1929, however, was that the booksellers' bill would divide the reformers' strength and obscure the need to revise the statute's definition of obscenity. For a review of the whole issue see Sidney S. Grant and Samuel E. Angoff, "Massachusetts and Censorship," *Boston Univ. Law Review*, X (Jan. 1930), pp. 36–61; (April 1930), pp. 147–94; and (Nov. 1930), pp. 488–508. Also Civil Liberties Union of Massachusetts, *Civil Liberties Bulletin*, (Summer 1966), pp. 6, 7, on the 1945 revision.

55. *Library Jour.*, LIV (Jan. 15, 1929), p. 69; *Pub. Wkly.*, CXV (Jan. 12, 1929), p. 172; *ibid.* (Jan. 26, 1929), p. 411; "The Librarians'

Bill," A.C.L.U. Archives, Princeton Univ. CCCLXXIII. The librarians' bill differed from the Shattuck bill in that it was limited to books, leaving periodicals, prints, etc., under the more stringent provisions of the old law. On the conflict among the state's booksellers, see "Our Book Censorship," *Springfield* [Mass.] *Republican,* Feb. 18, 1928; *Library Jour.,* LIV (Jan. 15, 1929), p. 69; *Pub. Wkly.,* CXI (May 28, 1928), p. 2135; and *ibid.,* CXV (Jan. 12, 1929), p. 172. Marion Dodd of the Hampshire Bookshop in Northampton was a leader of those who opposed the dominance of the conservative clique of Boston booksellers led by Fuller.

56. *Pub. Wkly.,* CXV (Feb. 16, 1929), p. 761; *ibid.,* CXV (Mar. 23, 1929), p. 1504; Leslie T. Little (librarian of the Waltham Public Library) to A.C.L.U., A.C.L.U. Archives, Princeton Univ., CCCLXXIII (comment on Calkins).

57. *Library Jour.,* LIV (Mar. 1, 1929), p. 219 (quoted passage); *Pub. Wkly.,* CXV (Apr. 6, 1929), p. 1676. See also *Library Jour.,* LIV (May 1, 1929), p. 395: "Possibly because of over-confidence, the librarians of the State had not kept busy at the critical time."

58. *Boston Evening Transcript,* Apr. 17, 1929; *Boston Herald,* Apr. 18, 1929; Karl Schriftgiesser, "Boston Stays Pure," *New Republic,* LVIII (May 8, 1929), pp. 327–29.

59. *Boston Herald, Globe,* and *Post,* Apr. 17, 1929. A poster announcing the meeting ("No One Admitted Unless Undesirable") is in the A.C.L.U. Archives, Princeton Univ., CCCLXXIII.

60. Hays's statements and the lapel-button detail were played up in the *Post* story; Darrow was quoted in the *Herald.*

61. Friede, "Getting Started," pp. 349, 351; *Boston Herald,* Apr. 18 (quoting attacks on the "Frolic" by the head of the Massachusetts Civic League, the state V.F.W., and others) and Apr. 19, 1929.

62. *Boston Evening Transcript,* Apr. 16, 1929 (makeup of jury); *Boston Herald,* Apr. 18, 1929. For more on the jury, see Chap. VI, p. 146 of this book.

63. *Pub. Wkly.,* CXV (June 22, 1929), p. 2867; *N.Y. Herald Tribune,* June 22, 1929.

64. *Pub. Wkly.,* CXVI (Sept. 21, 1929), p. 1351; *ibid.* (Oct. 5, 1929), p. 1725; "The Strange Interlude," *The Pilot,* Sept. 28, 1929, p. 4. The other Boston newspapers generally condemned the ban; for extracts from their editorials see *Boston Herald,* Sept. 18, 1929. In December 1928 Mayor Nichols had banned the Harvard Dramatic Club's scheduled Boston performance of Michael Gold's *Fiesta*—A.C.L.U., "Report on Civil Liberty Situation," (mimeographed bulletin), Dec. 1928.

65. *Pub. Wkly.,* CXVI (Oct. 5, 1929), p. 1728 (report of boycott and Scribner's statement); *ibid.* (Dec. 14, 1929), p. 2760; and CXVII (Mar. 8, 1930), p. 1332. In its early years the Christian Science Church attempted with considerable success to bring the story of Mrs. Eddy's life under its exclusive control. In 1909 church authorities purchased and

destroyed the printing plates and all copies of an "unauthorized" biography by Georgine Milmine published by Doubleday. The *Memoirs of Mary Baker Eddy* by Adam Dickey, one of Mrs. Eddy's secretaries, privately printed in 1927, was also withdrawn under pressure. For the full story see the *Publishers' Weekly* articles cited above and Henry Raymond Mussey's four-part series, "The Christian Science Censor," *Nation*, CXXX (Feb. 5, 12, 26, and Mar. 12, 1930). When Vol. VI of the *Dictionary of American Biography* appeared in 1931, with a biographical sketch of Mrs. Eddy by Allen Johnson, the Christian Science Church authorities attempted without success to persuade the American Council of Learned Societies and the publisher (Scribner's) to withdraw the volume and issue a new one in which the Eddy article would reflect the Church's own view of her life—all this to be done at the expense of the Christian Science Church.

66. D. H. Lawrence to S. S. Koteliansky, Dec. 23, 1927, Harry T. Moore, ed., *The Collected Letters of D. H. Lawrence* (2 vols., London, 1962), II, p. 1028 (added Lawrence: "[Y]ou would probably find it sheer pornography. But it isn't. It's a declaration of the phallic reality. I doubt if it will ever be published"); on the pirated editions: *Pub. Wkly.*, CXVI (Nov. 30, 1929), p. 2603, and Warren Roberts, *A Bibliography of D. H. Lawrence* (London, 1963), pp. 98–99; *Boston Herald*, Dec. 20, 1929, p. 1; Bernard DeVoto, "Literary Censorship in Cambridge," *Harvard Graduates' Magazine*, XXXIX (Sept. 1930), pp. 31, 36 (on DeLacey); interview with Gordon Cairnie of the Grolier Bookshop, Cambridge, Jan. 10, 1966.

67. "Arrests 1920–1950," N.Y. Vice Soc. Mss., Library of Congress, V, p. 74 ("James A. DeLacey, Joseph Sullivan, Boston arrests result of our information"); *Boston Herald*, Dec. 20, 1929; Gardner Jackson, "My Brother's Peeper," *Nation*, CXXX (Jan. 15, 1930), p. 64; DeVoto, "Literary Censorship in Cambridge," *passim; The Dunster House Bookshop Case; A Statement by the Directors of the New England Watch and Ward Society* (Boston, July 1930), pp. 5, 6; *Pub. Wkly.*, CXVI (Nov. 30, 1929), p. 2603. On the Watch and Ward attitude after the *American Mercury* case see W. & W. Soc., A.R., *1926–27* (1927), p. 9: "Our main efforts are devoted to the suppression of the vilest kinds of pictures and pamphlets. . . ."

68. *Harvard Crimson*, Dec. 20, 1929; *Boston Herald*, Dec. 20, 1929.

69. *Boston Herald*, Dec. 21, 1929, news story and editorial, "The Watch and Ward Society."

70. *The Dunster House Bookshop Case*, p. 7. See also DeVoto, "Literary Censorship in Cambridge," p. 37, and Jackson, "My Brother's Peeper," p. 65.

71. *Boston Herald*, Dec. 20, 1929, p. 1.

72. Jackson, "My Brother's Peeper," p. 64; *Pub. Wkly.*, CXVI (Dec. 28, 1929), p. 2923, and CXVII (June 7, 1930), p. 2826; *N.Y. Times*,

Dec. 21, 1929, p. 1; *The Dunster House Bookshop Case*, pp. 10–11; DeVoto, "Literary Censorship in Cambridge," p. 36; interviews with Charles W. Morton of the *Atlantic Monthly*, Mar. 10, 1961; Eva Thurman of the Starr Bookshop, Cambridge; and Gordon Cairnie, Grolier Bookshop, Jan. 10, 1966.

73. DeVoto, "Literary Censorship in Cambridge," pp. 38, 41.

74. *The Dunster House Bookshop Case*, p. 13; *Boston Herald*, Dec. 25, 1929; Raymond Calkins to the *Nation*, CXXX (Feb. 12, 1930), p. 178. The Reverend Dr. Calkins, who lived to be a vigorous nonagenarian, subsequently modified his view of the Watch and Ward's book activities, acknowledging that this was "debatable territory." Raymond Calkins, Belmont, Mass., to Paul Boyer, Mar. 18, 1961.

75. *N.Y. Herald Tribune*, Jan. 14, 1930; *N.Y. Sunday World*, Jan. 13, 1930; *Boston Herald*, Dec. 24, 1929; Richard F. Warner, "Boston Sees the Joke," *Outlook and Independent*, CLIV (Feb. 5, 1930), p. 210; W. & W. Soc., A.R., 1931–32 (1932), p. 3.

76. *N.Y. Sunday World*, Jan. 13, 1930; W. & W. Soc., A.R., 1931–32 (1932), pp. 7, 30.

77. *Pub. Wkly.*, CXVI (Dec. 21, 1929), p. 2821.

78. Interview with Dwight S. Strong, Executive Secretary, New England Citizens Crime Commission, Boston, Mar. 9, 1961. For the bequest from Mrs. Hunt, see the financial reports in the Watch and Ward's annual reports for 1912 and after. Citizens Crime Commission investigations in 1961 led to a national C.B.S. television program, "Biography of a Bookie Joint," showing police involvement in bookie operations in Boston. The program produced a great furore in Boston, with the governor calling for the resignation of the police commissioner, and Richard Cardinal Cushing defending the police from allegations of corruption (*Christian Science Monitor*, Dec. 12, 1961).

79. *N.Y. World*, Sept. 19, 1929 (clipping in A.C.L.U. Archives, Princeton Univ., CCCLXIII); *Boston Herald*, Sept. 30, 1929.

80. H. R. Burgess, "Alice in Censorland," *Pub. Wkly.*, CXVII (Mar. 8, 1930), p. 1339.

81. Warner, "Boston Sees the Joke," p. 210; *Pub. Wkly.*, CXVII (Feb. 1, 1930), p. 568 (Bushnell); *Boston Globe*, Dec. 22, 1929.

82. *N.Y. World*, Dec. 14, 1929; *Pub. Wkly.*, CXVI (Dec. 21, 1929), pp. 2820–21; interview with Edward W. Weeks, Jr., Aug. 16, 1965.

83. Edward W. Weeks, Jr., "The Practice of Censorship," *Atlantic Monthly*, CVL (Jan. 1930), p. 25. President Neilson was very active in the amendment campaign. In September 1929 he addressed the Massachusetts Conference of Social Workers, persuasively urging their support for the reform (unidentified clipping dated Sept. 28, 1929, A.C.L.U. Archives, Princeton Univ., CCCLXIII).

84. "The Strange Interlude," *The Pilot*, Sept. 28, 1929. See also editorials of July 13, Aug. 24, and Nov. 16, 1929.

85. *The Pilot*, Oct. 26, 1929 (Phelan quote); "Good Reading," Nov. 2, 1929, p. 4; and "Literary Chaos," Aug. 24, 1929, p. 4 (editorial comments).

86. *Ibid.*, Aug. 31, Nov. 2, and Nov. 30, 1929.

87. On Aug. 24, 1927, the day after the execution of Sacco and Vanzetti, Forrest Bailey, A.C.L.U. co-director, wrote to John S. Codman that the A.C.L.U. had felt that while the two convicted men were alive, protests against other aspects of "the general Boston situation" would have been "out of place" because "there was a far more important fight making claim upon all of us"—A.C.L.U. Archives, Princeton Univ., CCCXXVII, p. 280. See also the A.C.L.U.'s mimeographed "Report on Civil Liberty Situation" for June–July–August 1927: "The tragic developments in the Sacco-Vanzetti case over-shadow all other events in the field of civil liberties." On the origins of the A.C.L.U.'s New England Committee see Anna N. Davis to Roger Baldwin, Aug. 19, 1920, A.C.L.U. Archives, Princeton Univ., CXIX, p. 124.

88. Forrest Bailey to Hiller C. Wellman, Mar. 31, 1927, *ibid.*, CCCXXVII.

89. Roger Baldwin, Rio Piedras, Puerto Rico, to Paul Boyer, Feb. 23, 1966. The A.C.L.U was occasionally mentioned in newspaper accounts of the "Hatrack" and early phases of the *American Tragedy* cases, but the Union did not in fact take part in these cases, although Arthur Garfield Hays, who did, later became an A.C.L.U. counsel.

90. Richard C. Cabot to Roger N. Baldwin, Feb. 15, 1929, A.C.L.U. Archives, Princeton Univ., CCCLXXIII.

91. *N.Y. Telegraph*, Sept. 19, 1929 ("It was announced by the Civil Liberites Union that the fight against the *Strange Interlude* edict was merely the first phase of a campaign the organization would wage against Boston censorship"); Zechariah Chafee, Jr., *Censorship in Boston*, esp. pp. 5–8; Roger Baldwin to John S. Codman, June 17, 1929, A.C.L.U. Archives, Princeton Univ., CCCLXXVIII (". . . Chafee has agreed, if the thing is put in satisfactory shape, to appear as the author of it . . .").

92. *Boston Herald*, Oct. 10 and Nov. 4, 1929; *Boston Post*, Nov. 4, 1929.

93. Eben Burnstead of the Massachusetts Civic League, quoted in *Boston Evening Transcript*, Jan. 23, 1930, p. 11.

94. Quoted in *Boston Herald*, Nov. 1, 1929.

95. *Pub. Wkly.*, CXVI (Dec. 21, 1929), pp. 2820–21; CXVII (Jan. 11, 1930), p. 222; (Mar. 22, 1930), p. 1670.

96. *Ibid.* (Feb. 1, 1930), p. 568.

97. *Boston Evening Transcript*, Jan. 23, 1930; *Pub. Wkly.*, CXVII (Mar. 22, 1930), p. 1670. Eighty of the eighty-nine opposition votes in the House came from Democrats, many of them from Greater Boston.

98. Civil Liberties Committee of Massachusetts, *Censorship in Boston* (14 pp., Boston, 1938), p. 9. At the same time, the Committee

noted that Boston booksellers were still showing a greater timidity than booksellers elsewhere in the state.

CHAPTER VIII

1. Paul and Schwartz, *Federal Censorship*, pp. 12, 40–41; William H. Futrell, *The History of American Customs Jurisprudence* (N.Y., 1941), pp. 133, 298–99; *Customs Regulations of the United States, Edition of 1923* (Washington, 1924), p. 314 (Article 586), p. 365 (Article 705). Prior to 1926 the United States Customs Court was known as the Board of General Appraisers, a title which more correctly describes its nature and function.

2. Schwartz and Paul, *Federal Censorship*, p. 42; *N.Y. Times*, Sept. 29, 1927, p. 17; Oct. 4, 1927, p. 10; Oct. 5, 1927, p. 28. Most reviewers (e.g., *Nation*, Aug. 11, 1926, p. 117) found *What Happens* not very well written, but commendably frank. It was Ernst's anger at this defeat which launched his career as an anticensorship attorney.

3. *Decameron* and *A Thousand and One Nights: Publishers' Weekly*, CXI (May 14, 1927), p. 1900; *N.Y. Times*, May 6, 1927, p. 23; May 13, 1927, p. 7. The edition of *A Thousand and One Nights* was the J. C. Mardrus translation, published in four volumes by the Casanova Society of London in 1923; the *Decameron* was J. M. Riggs' translation published in two volumes in London in 1921 by The Navarre Society. *Candide: Pub. Wkly.*, CXV (June 8, 1929), p. 2670; CXVI (July 13, 1929), p. 191. The books had been ordered for Professor André Morize of Harvard by W. B. Dumas, a Boston bookseller. Morize to Roger N. Baldwin, May 28, 1929, A.C.L.U. Archives, Princeton Univ., CCCLXXIII, which also contains numerous newspaper clippings about the incident. See also, "Our National Book Censor Finds His Work Is Growing," *N.Y. Times*, Dec. 8, 1929, XI, p. 9, a feature on J. D. Nevius, Deputy Customs Commissioner.

4. Perry Hobbs, "Dirty Hands, A Federal Customs Officer Looks at Art," *New Republic*, LXII (Apr. 2, 1930), pp. 188–90, quoted passages on pp. 189 and 190. This inspector, evidently at the port of Boston, was of the opinion that the ban on *Candide* had been lifted because "some sweet banker friend of Mellon's put up a howl." "The wealthy class is full of perverts," he pointed out.

5. *N.Y. Times*, Jan. 23, 1924, p. 9.

6. Schwartz and Paul, *Federal Censorship*, pp. 41–42, 46–47; *Pub. Wkly.*, CIX (Mar. 20, 1926), p. 1069; *N.Y. Times*, May 16, 1929, p. 18; Duff Gilfond, "The Customs Men Keep Us Pure," *New Republic*, LIX (July 3, 1929), pp. 176–77. Books dealing with sex information and contraception were also barred.

7. Ernst and Seagle, *To the Pure . . .*, p. 81.

8. Schwartz and Paul, *Federal Censorship*, p. 43; Gilfond, "Customs Men Keep Us Pure," p. 176; *Cong. Record*, LXXI, 71 Cong., 1 Session (Oct. 10, 1929), p. 4434 (Senate speech by Bronson Cutting).

9. "The Troublesome Tariff," *Pub. Wkly.*, CXVI (July 27, 1929), p. 354; *ibid.* (Aug. 24, 1929), p. 721.

10. The amendment is printed in *Cong. Record*, LXXI, 71 Cong., 1 Sess. (Oct. 11, 1929), p. 4446. For its origins see Senator Cutting's remarks in *ibid;* Gilfond, "Customs Men Keep Us Pure," p. 177; and *Washington News*, June 5, 1929 (clipping in Bronson Cutting Papers, Library of Congress, XCIV [hereafter: Cutting Papers]).

11. *N.Y. Times*, Sept. 15, 1929, p. 21; Sept. 28, 1929, p. 4; Gilfond, "Customs Men Keep Us Pure," p. 177; *Baltimore Sun*, May 31, 1929; *Chicago Tribune*, July 31, 1929; *St. Louis Post-Dispatch*, June 1, 1929; *Washington Daily News*, June 5, 1929; *Pub. Wkly.*, CXV (June 8, 1929), p. 2670; "Why These Tariff Changes?" *ibid.*, CXVI (Aug. 31, 1929), p. 837. (*Sun, Tribune,* and *Post-Dispatch* clippings in Zechariah Chafee, Jr., "Scrapbook 1928–37," Chafee Papers, Harvard Univ. Archives; *Washington News* in Cutting Papers, XCIV).

12. Quoted in *N.Y. Times*, July 29, 1929, p. 23.

13. C. O. Paullin, "Bronson Cutting," *Dict. Am. Biog., Supp. I* (1958); "Record of Bronson Murray Cutting [at Harvard]," Cutting Papers, XI; "Inventory of Contents of *Los Siete Burros*, Santa Fe, New Mexico," *ibid.*, XXII. Unaccountably, Paullin's sketch does not mention Cutting's anticensorship fight, certainly a high point of his Senate career. Correspondence with Mary Austin, Witter Bynner, Ezra Pound, the British novelist Gordon Gardiner, the poet Howard Phelps Putnam, the historian Frederick Manning, and others is scattered through the Cutting Papers.

14. Paullin, "Bronson Cutting," *Dict. Am. Biog.*; Herbert C. Plummer, "A Bystander in Washington," *Canton* [O.] *Repository*, Oct. 27, 1929 (clipping in Cutting Papers, XCIV); L. E. Seibold, Customs House Broker, to Edgar F. Puryear (Cutting's secretary), Oct. 25, 1933, *ibid.*, X; Cutting to his mother, Mrs. William Bayard Cutting, Mar. 10, 1930, *ibid.* (reference to Toscanini reception); overdue notices to Cutting from Library of Congress, *ibid.*, IX and CXIV. The little drama, pencilled on the stationery of Chicago's Blackstone Hotel, is in *ibid.*, IX.

15. Walter Willard (Spud) Johnson, Taos, to Paul Boyer, Jan. 19, 1965; Mellon's letter quoted by Cutting in *Cong. Record*, LXXI, 71 Cong., 1 Sess. (Oct. 10, 1929), p. 4435; Mercer G. Johnston to Cutting, July 17, 1929, Cutting Papers, XXI; and three telegrams: Cutting to Edgar F. Puryear, July 23, 1929; Puryear to Cutting, July 24 and 29, 1929, *ibid.*

16. *N.Y. Times*, July 29, 1929, p. 23 (Cutting statement); July 14, 1929, p. 19 (the Little, Brown edition); Erich Maria Remarque, *All Quiet on the Western Front* (G. P. Putnam's Sons, London, 1929), publication data opposite title page.

17. Remarque, *All Quiet on the Western Front* (Putnam Ed.), pp. 20, 88, 212. Also see pp. 25, 49, 55, 141, 156, 197, and 258; and *cf.* corresponding passages in the Little, Brown edition.

18. *Ibid.* (Putnam Ed.), pp. 13–17, 290–92.

19. *Cf.* Eric Larrabee's statement: "The true obscenities of American life lie in our vicious public consumption of human suffering, in virtually every form and every media. By comparison, the literature of sexual love would seem . . . vastly preferable"—Eric Larrabee, "The Cultural Context of Sex Censorship," *Law and Contemporary Problems*, XX (Autumn, 1955), p. 687. On this point see also Gershon Legman, *Love and Death* (privately printed, N.Y., 1949), and Howard Moody, "Toward a New Definition of Obscenity," *Christianity and Crisis*, XXIV (Jan. 25, 1965), pp. 284–88.

20. *N.Y. Times*, May 31, 1929, p. 23; Edward Weeks, "The Practice of Censorship," *Atlantic Monthly*, CXLV (Jan. 1930), p. 24. The members of the "jury" at this time were Henry Seidel Canby (Chairman), Heywood Broun, Dorothy Canfield, Christopher Morley, and White.

21. *N.Y. Times*, May 31, 1929, p. 23.

22. *Pub. Wkly.*, CXV (May 4, 1929), pp. 2082–83. Little, Brown was here quoting from a review of the original German edition, implying that it applied equally to the expurgated Little, Brown edition.

23. *N.Y. Times*, July 14, 1929, p. 19; F. X. A. Eble, Commissioner of Customs, to Cutting, July 31, 1929, Cutting Papers, XXI.

24. *Pub. Wkly.*, CXVI (Aug. 31, 1929), p. 845; (Nov. 2, 1929), pp. 2176–77.

25. F. A. Blossom to editor, *ibid.* (Oct. 26, 1929), p. 2088.

26. Clippings in Cutting Papers, XCIV; W. L. McAfee, Cherrydale, Va., to Cutting, Aug. 2, 1929, *ibid.*, XXI; Witter Bynner to Cutting, Aug. 5, 1929, *ibid.*, VIII; Cutting to Mercer Johnston, Aug. 5, 1929, *ibid.*; Johnston to Cutting, Sept. 19, 1929, *ibid.*

27. *Cong. Record*, LXXI, 71 Cong., 1 Sess. (Oct. 10, 1929), p. 4432; (Oct. 11, 1929), p. 4457.

28. *Ibid.* (Oct. 10, 1929), pp. 4432, 4434; (Oct. 11, 1929), p. 4445 (the entire speech covers pp. 4432–39 and 4445–57); *N.Y. Times*, Oct. 11, 1929, p. 1; Mrs. Vernon Kellogg to Mrs. William Bayard Cutting, n.d., Cutting Papers, XLIV: ". . . I have never before seen this in the Senate. Both sides crowding close, and that something in the faces that rises and shines out to leadership—mental and spiritual." Mrs. Kellogg may have overstated the case somewhat to please a doting mother.

29. *Cong. Record*, LXXI, 71 Cong., 1 Sess. (Oct. 10, 1929), p. 4456.

30. *Ibid.*, p. 4435; (Oct. 11, 1929), pp. 4458, 4459.

31. *Ibid.* (Oct. 11, 1929), p. 4454.

32. *Ibid.*, p. 4458.

33. *Ibid.*, p. 4465. See also remarks by Borah (p. 4454) and Caraway (p. 4467).

34. *Ibid.*, p. 4461.

35. *Ibid.*

36. *Ibid.*, pp. 4465, 4470.

37. *Ibid.*, pp. 4467, 4468–69.

38. *Ibid.*, p. 4472. The senators who switched were Broussard (Dem., La.), Connally (Dem., Tex.), Couzens (Rep., Mich.), Gillett (Rep., Mass.), Glenn (Rep., Ill.), Ransdell (Dem., La.), and Walcott (Rep., Conn.).

39. "Books on the Index," *N.Y. Times,* Oct. 12, 1929, p. 18.

40. Gordon Gardiner to Cutting, Nov. 25, 1929, Cutting Papers, VIII.

41. *Bulletin of the American Library Assn.*, XXIV (Jan. 1930), p. 16; (May 1930), p. 136; *Libraries*, XXXV (Jan. 1930), p. 8; *Library Jour.*, LIV (Nov. 15, 1929), p. 952; (Dec. 15, 1929), pp. 1024–26; *Pub. Wkly.*, CXVI (Oct. 26, 1929), p. 2068; (Nov., 1929), p. 2290; CXVII (Feb. 22, 1930), p. 985; F. G. Melcher to *N.Y. Times,* Oct. 19, 1929, p. 18; *Saturday Rev.*, VI (Nov. 30, 1929), p. 482; *N.Y. Times,* Feb. 16, 1930, II, p. 8 (Cutting's P.E.N. address). One hundred authors, editors, playwrights, and publishers were present at this meeting.

42. New England Watch and Ward Society, *Annual Report, 1929–30* (1930), p. 6; *Pub. Wkly.*, CXVI (Nov. 9, 1929), p. 2308; Richard W. Hogue, *Censorship and the U.S. Senate* (Washington, Feb. 5, 1930), p. 8.

43. *Laughing Horse*, XVII (Feb. 1930); Spud Johnson to Paul Boyer, Jan. 19, 1965; H. G. Baca, Santa Fe, to Cutting, Mar. 6, 1930, Cutting Papers, IX. A copy of the offending cartoon is in *ibid*. The *Laughing Horse*, founded at Berkeley in 1922 as an undergraduate satirical review, had caused the arrest and expulsion from college of one of its editors for an issue containing a book review by D. H. Lawrence and extracts from *The Goose-Step*, Upton Sinclair's as yet unpublished exposé of academic life. Later the magazine was moved to Santa Fe by Johnson and published sporadically until 1939.

44. H. G. Baca to Cutting, Mar. 6, 1930, Cutting Papers, IX.

45. Edgar Puryear to Cutting, Jan. 4, 1930, *ibid.*

46. *N.Y. Times,* May 16, 1929; July 27, 1929, p. 6.

47. *Pub. Wkly.*, CXVI (Nov. 9, 1929), p. 2302. The decision, handed down Oct. 31, 1929, was later quoted at length by Cutting— *Cong. Record*, LXXII, 71 Cong., 2 Sess. (Mar. 18, 1930), p. 5491. Counsel for the Peabody Bookshop of Baltimore was Huntington Cairns, later appointed special legal advisor to the Treasury Department on the admissibility of questioned books (see below, pp. 237–38). The books in this case were Hugh McCrae, *Satyrs and Sunlight* (London, 1928); Sophista Longus, *Daphnis and Chloe*, ed. Joseph Jacobs (London, 1890); and an issue of the short-lived (1928–29) periodical, *The London Aphrodite*, edited by Jack Lindsay and P. R. Stephensen. On the original seizure see undated Baltimore *Sun* clipping, A.C.L.U. Archives, Princeton Univ., CCCLXXXV.

48. *Pub. Wkly.*, CXVI (Nov. 9, 1929), p. 2302 (*Decameron*);

Saturday Rev., VI (Nov. 30, 1929), p. 482 (Rabelais); *Pub. Wkly.*, CXVI (Oct. 19, 1929), p. 1938 (*Moll Flanders, Roxana*); (Aug. 10, 1929), p. 535; *N.Y. World*, Aug. 2, 1929 (*Uncle Sham*).

49. Baltimore *Sun*, Feb. 28, 1930 (quoted passage) and undated Baltimore *Sun* clipping, A.C.L.U. Archives, Princeton Univ., CCCLXXXV.

50. *Pub. Wkly.*, CXVII (Apr. 26, 1930), p. 2226 (which dates the seizure as "last fall"); (May 17, 1930), p. 2537 (quoting Bonner's attorney, Mary Rehan).

51. George Moore, *A Story Teller's Holiday* (2 vols., London, 1928), I, p. 253.

52. *Pub. Wkly.*, CXVII (Mar. 15, 1930), p. 1557.

53. Milton R. Merrill, "Reed Smoot, Apostle in Politics," unpub. Ph.D. dissertation (Columbia, 1950), p. 211. By permission. Also N.Y. Vice Soc., *A.R.* (1929), p. 13; *N.Y. Times*, Dec. 24, 1929, p. 16.

54. *N.Y. Times*, Dec. 24, 1929, p. 16; *Pub. Wkly.*, CXVI (Dec. 28, 1929), p. 2919; CXVII (Mar. 8, 1930), p. 1331 ("Senatorial stag party" quote); (Jan. 11, 1930), p. 216 ("acrimonious and misleading" quote).

55. *N.Y. Times*, Mar. 18, 1930, p. 5.

56. *Cong. Record*, LXXII, 71 Cong., 2 Sess. (Mar. 17, 1930), p. 5414.

57. *Ibid.*, p. 5417.

58. *Cong. Record*, LXXII, 71 Cong., 2 Sess. (Mar. 17, 1930), pp. 5414, 5415, 5416, 5417; (Mar. 18, 1930), p. 5494; *Outlook*, CLIV (Apr. 2, 1930), p. 534, with photograph; "Mr. Smoot's Fight on Tainted Books," *Literary Digest*, CIV (Mar. 29, 1930), p. 11; *N.Y. Times*, Mar. 18, 1930, p. 5.

59. *Outlook*, CLIV (Apr. 2, 1930), p. 534.

60. Aldous Huxley, *Music at Night and Other Essays* (Penguin Ed., London, 1950), p. 120. First published in 1931. Senator Smoot's heroic assertion, which inspired Huxley's response, is in *Cong. Record*, LXXII, 71 Cong., 2 Sess. (Mar. 17, 1930), p. 5418.

61. *Nat. Cyc. Am. Biog.*, XXXV, p. 63; Merrill, "Reed Smoot," pp. 23–99, esp. pp. 45, 57, 87, 96; Alice Roosevelt Longworth, *Crowded Hours* (N.Y., 1935), p. 139 ("witch-burning element" quote).

62. Merrill, "Reed Smoot," p. 124 (by permission); Smoot to James Glove, Apr. 8, 1904, quoted in *ibid.*, pp. 59–60 (by permission). Also see *ibid.*, p. 39, on Mrs. Smoot.

63. *Nat. Cyc. Am. Biog.*, XXXV, p. 63.

64. *Ibid.*, Merrill, "Reed Smoot," p. 819 (by permission).

65. *N.Y. Times*, Feb. 24, 1930, p. 2; "Smoot and Smut," *Living Age*, CCCXXXIII (May 1, 1930), p. 317; "The Virtue of Reed Smoot," *Nation*, CXXX (Apr. 2, 1930), p. 384; "Minds Not Fit for Books," *Saturday Rev.*, VI (Mar. 29, 1930), p. 865; *Cong. Record*, LXXII, 71 Cong., 2 Sess. (Mar. 17, 1930), p. 5420 (Black); (Mar. 18, 1930), p. 5495 (Wheeler).

66. *Ibid.*, p. 5495.

67. *Ibid.*, pp. 5487–95, *passim*, esp. pp. 5488 (Neilson) and 5489 (Tacitus). Said the *N.Y. Times:* "Perhaps not since the passing of Henry Cabot Lodge has there been a Senator better read in literature, better able to discuss it with intelligence"—Oct. 12, 1929, p. 18.

68. *Cong. Record*, LXXII, 71 Cong., 2 Sess. (Mar. 18, 1930), p. 5492.

69. *Ibid.*, p. 5491. Once again Millard Tydings vigorously seconded Cutting: "[L]et us close every church from now on and make the Ten Commandments statutory. . . . Let us . . . call out the Army, and make righteousness compulsory"—*ibid.*, pp. 5511, 5513, 5514.

70. *Ibid.*, p. 5494.

71. *Ibid.*, pp. 5502, 5504; Karl E. Meyer, "The Washington Press Establishment," *Esquire*, April 1964, p. 158.

72. *Cong. Record*, LXXII, 71 Cong., 2 Sess. (Mar. 18, 1930), p. 5504.

73. *Ibid.*, pp. 5503 (Trammell), 5511 (Heflin).

74. *Ibid.*, pp. 5509–10.

75. *Ibid.* (Mar. 17, 1930), p. 5418.

76. *Ibid.*, p. 5421. The text of Walsh's amendment is on p. 5424.

77. *Ibid.*, pp. 5421 (Smoot), 5428 (Goff), 5426 (Bratton), 5424 (Johnson), 5429–30 (George).

78. *Ibid.*, pp. 5431, 5520.

79. *Ibid.*, p. 5430.

80. *Ibid.* (Mar. 18, 1930), p. 5520; *N.Y. Times*, Mar. 19, 1930. The March debate also involved further discussion of the House-added "treason" clause. Smoot retained it in his amended version of Sec. 305, but agreed to remove it under pressure from Cutting. Senator Broussard (Dem., La.) then moved that it be retained, and his motion was upheld by a 54–24 vote. *Cong. Record*, LXXII, 71 Cong., 2 Sess. (Mar. 17, 1930), p. 5414; (Mar. 18, 1930), pp. 5496, 5502, 5504, 5516.

81. N.Y. Vice Soc., *A.R.* (1929), p. 30; New England Watch and Ward Society, *Annual Report, 1929–30* (1930), pp. 6–7; *Cong. Record*, LXXII, 71 Cong., 2 Sess. (Mar. 18, 1930), p. 5518 (Black); Roger Baldwin Reminiscences, Columbia Univ. Oral History Project, I, p. 198.

82. "Signs of Clearing," *Pub. Wkly.*, CXVI (Oct. 26, 1929), p. 2068. See the numerous clippings in the A.C.L.U. Archives, Princeton Univ., CCCLXXXVI, and in the Cutting Papers, XCIV.

83. Emilie M. Baca, New York City, to Cutting, July 29, 1929, Cutting Papers, XXI.

84. John Macrae to Cutting, Mar. 25, 1930, in *ibid.; Who Was Who*, II. Macrae, head of E. P. Dutton and Co., was president of the N.A.B.P. from 1923 to 1927.

85. Baldwin Reminiscences, Columbia Univ. Oral History Project, I, p. 198 (by permission of Roger Baldwin); *Cong. Record*, LXXII, 71 Cong., 2 Sess. (Mar. 18, 1930), p. 5518.

86. *Chicago Daily News,* Jan. 2, 1930. Clipping in Cutting Papers, XCIV.

87. *Pub. Wkly.,* CXIX (Mar. 21, 1931), p. 1582; CXXIII (Jan. 7, 1933), p. 36. The seizure of *A Story Teller's Holiday* by Baltimore Customs inspectors late in 1929 had been appealed to the United States Customs Court before the new procedure laid down by the Congress became operative. The Customs Court upheld the ban in May 1930 (despite testimony by Donald Friede, Arthur Krock, John Macrae of the N.A.B.P., and E. W. Meyer of the A.B.A.), and it was this ruling which the Treasury Department reversed in 1933. *N.Y. Times,* May 13, 1930, p. 16; Feb. 5, 1932, p. 19.

88. Roger Baldwin Reminiscences, Columbia Univ. Oral History Project, I, p. 198 (by permission); Henry Morgenthau quoted ("Find me a lawyer who has read a book") in Don Whitehead, *Border Guard, the Story of the United States Customs Service* (N.Y., 1963), p. 237; *Who's Who in America, 1964–65* (entry on Cairns); Huntington Cairns, "Freedom of Expression in Literature," *Annals of the American Academy of Political and Social Science,* CC (Nov. 1938), pp. 76–94.

89. A.C.L.U., A.R., *1934–35* (1935), p. 42; Roger Baldwin Reminiscences, Columbia Univ. Oral History Project, I, p. 198; Paul and Schwartz, *Federal Censorship,* p. 68.

90. *Ibid.,* p. 39. See also pp. 17–18 and 25–49 *passim.*

91. Malcolm Cowley, *Exile's Return* (Compass Ed., N.Y., 1956), pp. 186–95.

92. *Pub. Wkly.,* CXV (Mar. 23, 1929), p. 1505. *Rasputin, the Holy Devil* was published in 1928 by Viking. The secretary of the Free Thought Press, Fannie Gitler, was found guilty, but sentence was suspended. A.C.L.U., *Report on Civil Liberty Situation, April 1929.*

93. J. Frank Chase, "The New Puritanism," p. 14.

94. Dennett, *Who's Obscene?* pp. 6–8. "The Sex Side of Life" is reprinted in its entirety in *ibid.,* pp. 140–60.

95. *Ibid.,* pp. 8–9, 33–34, 44–70, 130–35, 160–94; *Pub. Wkly.,* CXV (Feb. 9, 1929), p. 660; (Apr. 27, 1929), pp. 2016 and 2022.

96. *Neosho* [Mo.] *Democrat,* Mar. 22, 1930 (one of about forty clippings from different newspapers in the A.C.L.U. Archives, Princeton Univ., CCCLXXXV, nearly all of them supporting Mrs. Dennett); Dennett, *Who's Obscene?,* p. 150; Hays, *City Lawyer,* p. 205; Heywood Broun, "Canon Shocks Columnist," in *Collected Edition of Heywood Broun,* compiled by Heywood Hale Broun (N.Y., 1941), pp. 226–29.

97. "Enemies of Society," *New Republic,* LVIII (May 8, 1929), pp. 318–20, quoted passages on p. 319.

98. Dennett, *Who's Obscene?,* pp. 236–42; A.C.L.U., A.R., *1923–24,* (1924), *1924–25* (1925), and *1925–26* (1926). Tresca, an Italian immigrant who had lived in the United States for twenty years, served four months of a 366-day sentence in 1925 before receiving a Presidential pardon.

99. A.C.L.U., *A.R.*, *1928–29* (1929), pp. 25, 31. See also the Committee's full-page advertisement on the back cover of the *New Republic* of May 8, 1929.

100. *N.Y. Times,* Mar. 4, 1930; *Pub. Wkly.*, CXVII (Mar. 8, 1930), pp. 1336–38; Dennett, *Who's Obscene?*, pp. xx–xxxii, which reprints Judge Hand's decision.

101. A.C.L.U., *A.R.*, *1931–32* (1932), p. 31. Morris Ernst was, and remains, sharply critical of the decision to set up a separate organization, viewing it as an evasionary tactic. Interview with Ernst, May 14, 1964.

102. *N.Y. Times,* Oct. 11, 1929, p. 1; Ezra Pound to R. P. Blackmur, Nov. 30, 1924, *The Letters of Ezra Pound, 1907–1941,* D. D. Paige, ed. (N.Y., 1950), p. 190; Pound's letters to Cutting in Cutting Papers, XXXVI, *passim;* Ezra Pound, "Honor and the United States Senate," *Poetry,* XXXVI (June 1930), p.152.

103. The bill drawn up by the National Council on Freedom from Censorship is in Cutting Papers, XXI; the measure introduced by Cutting (S-3907), different in slight particulars, is printed in the N.C.F.C.'s pamphlet, *The Post Office Censor* (N.Y., 1932), and summarized in *Pub. Wkly.*, CCXXI (Apr. 2, 1932), p. 1561.

104. *The Post Office Censor,* p. 4.

105. A.C.L.U., *A.R.*, *1931–32* (1932), p. 1; *1932–33* (1933), p. 23; Paullin, "Bronson Cutting," *DAB, Supp. I;* Arthur M. Schlesinger, Jr., *The Politics of Upheaval: The Age of Roosevelt,* Vol. III (Boston, 1960), pp. 130–41 (on the political difficulties Cutting faced in this period). In 1937 the A.C.L.U. tried again, without success, to push postal reform legislation in the Senate. A.C.L.U., *A.R.*, *1936–37* (1937), p. 41.

106. A.C.L.U., *A.R.*, *1932–33* (1933), pp. 3–4. In 1929 there were over 200 prosecutions under Sec. 211, while by 1931 the figure had dropped to 118—*The Post Office Censor,* p. 5.

CHAPTER IX

1. H. L. Mencken to James Branch Cabell, [1934], in *Between Friends,* p. 285.

2. N.Y. Vice Soc., *A.R.* (1939), p. 5. On the 1930 Albany bill, which passed the Assembly but failed in the Senate, see *Pub. Wkly.*, CXVII (Mar. 22, 1930), p. 1683, and A.C.L.U., *A.R.*, *1931–32* (1932), p. 32.

3. N.Y. Vice Soc., *A.R.* (1938), pp. 5, 13.

4. S. J. Woolf, "A Vice Suppressor Looks at Our Morals," *N.Y. Times,* Oct. 9, 1932, VIII, p. 2.

5. N.Y. Vice Soc., *A.R.* (1935), p. 7; (1936), pp. 6, 10.

6. *Pub. Wkly.*, CXXIII (Apr. 22, 1933), p. 1344; (June 10, 1933), p. 1887; CXXIV (Sept. 2, 1933), p. 669. The decision was later upheld in the court of appeals—Ernst and Lindey, *The Censor Marches On,* pp. 290–91.

7. *Pub. Wkly.*, CXXIII (May 27, 1933), p. 1702. See also *ibid.* (Apr. 22, 1933), p. 1344; and (May 6, 1933), p. 1475, Sumner, following his usual *modus operandi,* next tried unsuccessfully to secure a grand jury indictment—*N.Y. Times,* June 27, 1933, p. 15.

8. A.C.L.U., *A.R., 1936–37* (1937), p. 40; Ernst and Lindey, *The Censor Marches On,* pp. 34–37, quoted passage on p. 36.

9. N.Y. Vice Soc., *A.R.* (1940), p. 4 (Bamberger); interview with Dwight S. Strong, Executive Secretary of the New England Citizens' Crime Commission (formerly the Watch and Ward Society), Mar. 26, 1964.

10. Gilbert Seldes, "The Censor," *Saturday Eve. Post,* Sept. 21, 1929, pp. 16 *ff.*, esp. p. 153.

11. R. R. Bowker, "As to 'Sex Stuff,'" *Pub. Wkly*, CXV (June 15, 1929) pp. 2757–58.

12. Cedric R. Crowell, "Publishers, Clean Up," *ibid.,* CXX (Aug. 1, 1931), p. 403, with photograph; "The Traffic in Smut," *Christian Century,* XLVIII (Dec. 9, 1931), pp. 1552–53, quoted passages on p. 1552.

13. H. Montgomery Hyde, *A History of Pornography* (London, 1964), p. 183.

14. Ezra Pound to James Joyce, [July?] 1920, *The Letters of Ezra Pound, 1907–1941,* ed. D. D. Paige, (N.Y., 1950), p. 154.

15. See above, pp. 83–85.

16. Ernst and Lindey, *The Censor Marches On,* p. 21.

17. T. S. Eliot, "*Ulysses,* Order, and Myth," *Dial,* LXXV (Nov. 1923), p. 480.

18. H. S. Canby, "Sex in Fiction," *Century,* CV (Nov. 1922), p. 100.

19. Arnold Bennett, "Concerning James Joyce's *Ulysses,*" *Bookman,* LV (Aug. 1922), p. 570.

20. Frederic T. Cooper, "The Twentieth Century Novel," *ibid.,* LXV (Mar. 1927), p. 44; Harvey Wickham, *The Impuritans* (N.Y., 1929), p. 253.

21. Stuart Gilbert, *James Joyce's* Ulysses: *A Study* (London, 1930); Edmund Wilson, *Axel's Castle, A Study in the Imaginative Literature of 1870–1930* (N.Y., 1931), pp. 221, 219.

22. *Pub. Wkly.*, CXI (Feb. 12, 1927), p. 608, quoting the *New Statesman;* Ezra Pound to James Joyce, Nov. 19, 1926, Pound, *Letters,* p. 204. See also Joyce to Bennett Cerf, Apr. 2, 1932, in James Joyce, *Ulysses* (Modern Library Ed., N.Y., 1934), pp. xiv–xv; Sylvia Beach to editor, *Pub. Wkly.*, CX (Dec. 11, 1926), p. 2213; Joyce to H. S. Weaver, Nov. 5, 1925; Feb. 1, Mar. 2, and May 31, 1927; and to Eric Pinker, [Autumn

1925?], *Letters of James Joyce,* ed. Stuart Gilbert (Vol. I) and Richard Ellmann (Vols. II–III), (N.Y., 1957–1966), I, pp. 236, 237, 249, 250, 255.

23. *N.Y. Times,* Mar. 10, 1927, p. 2.

24. *Ibid.*

25. T. S. Eliot, Feb. 13, 1932, Joyce, *Letters,* I, p. 314; see also Joyce to Ralph Pinker, Nov. 28, 1929; *ibid.,* I, pp. 275–76, and Joyce to T. S. Eliot, Mar. 4, 1932, *ibid.,* I, pp. 316.

26. *Nat. Cyc. Am. Biog.,* Current Vol. I, p. 256.

27. Mary Ware Dennett, " 'Married Love' and Censorship," *Nation,* CXXXII (May 27, 1931), pp. 579–80; *Pub. Wkly.,* CXIX (Mar. 14, 1931); *ibid.* (Apr. 11, 1931), p. 1907; Ernst and Lindey, *The Censor Marches On,* pp. 302–05; A.C.L.U., *A.R., 1931–32* (1932), p. 2.

28. *N.Y. Times,* June 24, 1933, p. 14; July 12, 1933, p. 15; *Pub. Wkly.,* CXXIV (July 15, 1933), p. 162; (Sept. 9, 1933), p. 749; Woolsey decision in Joyce, *Ulysses,* pp. vii–viii. (Hereafter: Woolsey decision.)

29. Obituaries in *N.Y. Times,* May 5, 1945, p. 15, and *Pub. Wkly.,* CXLVII (June 9, 1945), p. 2305. Also see *N.Y. Times,* Aug. 30, 1933, p. 16.

30. Woolsey decision, vii–xii; Ernst, *The Best is Yet . . . ,* pp. 115–17; Ernst and Schwartz, *Censorship,* pp. 94–96; N.Y. Vice Soc., *A.R.* (1934), p. 8; Richard Ellmann, *James Joyce* (N.Y., 1959), p. 678; Joyce to H. S. Weaver, Apr. 24, 1934, *Letters,* I, p. 340. In 1934 a new United States attorney, Martin Conboy, counsel to the New York Vice Society and a "Clean Books" veteran, decided to appeal the Woolsey decision. His effort was in vain, however, for the United States Court of Appeals, on a 2–1 vote, upheld Woolsey. The majority decision by Augustus N. Hand, is in Ernst and Lindey, *Censor Marches On,* pp. 281–90. See also N.Y. Vice Soc., *A.R.* (1934), p. 8.

31. N.Y. Vice Soc., *A.R.* (1934), pp. 8, 9; Camille McCole, *"Ulysses," Catholic World,* CXXXVIII (Mar. 1934), pp. 722, 724.

32. A.C.L.U., *A.R., 1933–34* (1934), p. 25; *N.Y. Times,* Dec. 7, 1933, p. 21.

33. Woolsey decision, pp. ix, x.

34. *New Republic,* LXXVII (Dec. 20, 1933), p. 154.

35. Morris Ernst, "Foreword," Joyce, *Ulysses,* p. v.

36. Woolsey decision, p. x.

37. Ben Ray Redman, "Obscenity and Censorship," *Scribner's Magazine,* XCV (May 1934), p. 342. At the same time, Redman made clear (pp. 342 and 344) his view that "no writer capable of good work was ever starved into anemia for want of a few forbidden words." The greatness of *Ulysses,* he added, "does not reside in its use of four-letter words. . . ."

38. Ernst, "Foreword," Joyce, *Ulysses,* p. vi.

39. Woolsey decision, pp. xi and xii.

40. "Another Repeal," *Nation*, CXXXVII (Dec. 20, 1933), p. 693; Redman, "Obscenity and Censorship," p. 343.

41. Eric Larrabee, "The Cultural Context of Sex Censorship," *Law and Contemporary Problems* [Duke University], XX (Autumn 1955), pp. 672–88, quoted passages on p. 675 and 677. The entire issue is of interest.

42. Jane Heap, "Lost: A Renaissance," reprinted in Anderson, *My Thirty Years' War*, p. 225.

43. Sherwood Anderson to John Anderson and Charles Bockler, [?Oct. 1929], *Letters of Sherwood Anderson*, Selected and Edited with an Introduction and Notes by Howard Mumford Jones in Association with Walter B. Rideout (Boston, 1953), p. 195.

44. F. Scott Fitzgerald, "Echoes of the Jazz Age" (November, 1931), reprinted in Fitzgerald, *The Crack-Up*, ed. Edmund Wilson (New Directions Ed., N.Y., 1956), p. 13; Malcolm Cowley, "A Remembrance of the Red Romance," *Esquire*, March 1964, p. 126; Henry Seidel Canby, *American Memoir* (Boston, 1947), p. 376. In this instance, Canby was describing the effect of the Depression on his interest in literary criticism.

45. Anderson to Horace Liveright, [?Jan. 2, 1930], *Letters*, pp. 202–03.

46. Walter B. Rideout, *The Radical Novel in the United States, 1900–1954* (American Century Ed., N.Y., 1966), pp. 135–254, 296. See also Willard Thorp, *American Writing in the Twentieth Century* (Cambridge, Mass., 1960), pp. 113–14; and Daniel Aaron, *Writers on the Left* (N.Y., 1961), pp. 173–90.

47. Alice P. Hackett, "Seventy-Five Years of Booklisting," *Pub. Wkly.*, CLI (Jan. 18, 1947), p. 336. See also Isidor Schneider, "*Publishers' Weekly* and the Book Trade Since World War I," *ibid.*, p. 308.

48. Robert S. and Helen M. Lynd, *Middletown in Transition; A Study in Cultural Conflicts* (N.Y., 1937), pp. 252–54.

49. On the bankruptcy and reorganization of Brentano's ("the largest retail outlet for books in the world") see *Pub. Wkly.*, CXXIII (Apr. 1, 1933), p. 1124; and *ibid.* (May 6, 1933), p. 1473.

50. Schneider, "*Publishers' Weekly* and the Book Trade," pp. 309, 312; William Miller, *The Book Industry, A Report of the Public Library Inquiry* (N.Y., 1949), p. 34; Harold K. Guinzberg, Robert W. Frase, and Theodore Walker, *Books and the Mass Market* (Urbana, Ill., 1953), p. 14.

51. *Pub. Wkly.*, CXXIV (July 1, 1933), p. 21 (Roth); *N.Y. Times* obituary of Donald Friede, May 31, 1965; Madison, *Book Publishing in America*, pp. 338 (Boni) and 187–88 (Putnam); Schneider, "*Publishers' Weekly* and the Book Trade," p. 308.

52. Cerf, "Liveright," p. 1229. Also Edwin F. Edgett, "Horace Brisbin Liveright," *Dict. Am. Biog.*, Supp. I (1944); Louis Kronenberger,

"Gambler in Publishing: Horace Liveright," *Atlantic Monthly*, CCXV (Jan. 1965), pp. 102–04; Henry W. Simon to Paul Boyer, Apr. 14, 1965.

53. *Pub. Wkly.*, CI (Mar. 25, 1922), p. 905 (Hungary); CIV (Aug. 11, 1923), p. 486 (Balkans); CXII (July 16, 1927), p. 209 (Turkey); CXVI (Aug. 24, 1929), p. 727 (India).

54. John A. R. Marriott, *Dictatorship and Democracy* (Oxford, 1935), p. 190; *Pub. Wkly.*, CXIII (Apr. 21, 1928), p. 1693.

55. Walter Z. Laqueur, *Young Germany: A History of the German Youth Movement* (N.Y., 1962), p. 90; von Papen quoted in Alice Hamilton, "The Plight of the German Intellectuals," *Harper's*, CLXVIII (Jan. 1934), p. 165.

56. Laqueur, *Young Germany*, p. 166. Also see *ibid.*, pp. 1–87, esp. 12, 17, 33, and Bruno Lasker, "The Youth Movement of Germany," *Survey*, XLVII (Dec. 31, 1921), pp. 487–93.

57. *Ibid.*, p. 537.

58. Bruno Lasker, "Youth Tilts at Smut and Trash," *Survey*, LVII (Feb. 15, 1927), p. 622. See also Lilian [sic] Eagle, "The Moral Revolt of Germany's Youth," *Current History*, XVI (June 1922), pp. 447–51; and Lasker, "Youth Movement of Germany," p. 490.

59. Lasker, "Youth Tilts at Smut and Trash," p. 622.

60. Lasker, "Youth Movement of Germany," p. 490; Eagle, "Moral Revolt of Germany's Youth," p. 451.

61. Lasker, "Youth Tilts at Smut and Trash," p. 622.

62. *Berliner Tageblatt* article quoted in *Literary Digest*, XCII (Jan. 22, 1927), pp. 28–29. See also Lasker, "Youth Tilts at Smut and Trash," p. 622, and *N.Y. Times*, Jan. 3, 1927, p. 18.

63. "German Censorship of 'Literary Trash and Mud,'" *Literary Digest*, XCII (Jan. 22, 1927), pp. 28–29; Lasker, "Youth Tilts at Smut and Trash," p. 622; "German and English Censorship," *Living Age*, CCCXXXII (Feb. 1, 1927), p. 270. For an analysis of the law's effect see Erich Sielaff, "Schülerbücherei und Schundbekämpfung," in *Bücherei und Bildungspflege*, X (1931), pp. 467–86, summarized in *Soc. Sci. Abstracts*, III (May 1931), p. 764. Sielaff found that German children were, indeed, reading less smut and trash, but he was uncertain whether this was owing to the effect of the law or to a growing interest in sports, movies, and radio.

64. Lasker, "Youth Tilts at Smut and Trash," p. 622. On the *Literary Digest* and *Living Age* reports, see above, Note 63. it is interesting to note that it was about six weeks after enactment of the *Schmutz und Schund* law that Congressman Thomas W. Wilson introduced his bill for a "National Board of Magazine Censorship" in America—see Chap. VI, p. 160, in this book.

65. Konrad Heiden, *A History of National Socialism* (N.Y., 1935), p. 17. See also H. G. Atkins, *German Literature Through Nazi Eyes* (Lon-

don, 1941), pp. 2, 18–22. Atkins was Emeritus Professor of German at the University of London.

66. *N.Y. Times,* Feb. 9, 1930, p. 15; July 10, 1931, p. 24.

67. Laqueur, *Young Germany,* p. 191.

68. *Pub. Wkly.,* CXXIII (Mar. 25, 1933), p. 1062; "The Arts Under Hitlerism," *New Republic,* LXXIV (Apr. 19, 1933), p. 268.

69. Quoted in "Putting Art in Its Place," *Nation,* CXXXVI (May 10, 1933), p. 519.

70. *New Republic,* LXXIV (Apr. 19, 1933), p. 268.

71. Mary Heaton Vorse, "Germany: The Twilight of Reason," *New Republic,* LXXV (June 14, 1933), pp. 117–19; *N.Y. Times,* May 10, 1933, pp. 1, 10–11; May 11, 1933, pp. 1, 12 (long Berlin dispatch by F. T. Birchall); May 19, 1933, p. 9; May 20, 1933, p. 3 (photograph). Estimates of the crowd varied from 25,000 to 40,000.

72. Vorse, "Germany: The Twilight of Reason," p. 118.

73. *Ibid.; N.Y. Times,* May 11, 1933, p. 12.

74. *Ibid.;* Vorse, "Germany: The Twilight of Reason," p. 118.

75. *Ibid.*

76. *N.Y. Times,* May 11, 1933, p. 12.

77. Atkins, *German Literature Through Nazi Eyes,* pp. 6–13; "Germany's Blacklisted Books," *Living Age,* CCCXCIV (July 1933), pp. 430–32; Hamilton, "Plight of the German Intellectuals," pp. 166–67.

78. F. E. May, *Neue deutsche Literaturgeschichte* (Leipzig, 1934), p. 5, translated and quoted by Atkins in *German Literature Through Nazi Eyes,* p. 4.

79. *N.Y. Times,* May 11, 1933, pp. 1, 10.

80. Heywood Broun, "The Burning of the Books," in *Collected Edition of Heywood Broun,* compiled by Heywood Hale Broun (N.Y., 1941), pp. 288 and 289; "Germany's Book Bonfire," *Literary Digest,* CXV (May 27, 1933), p. 14 (quoting Lippmann); Ludwig Lewisohn, "The German Revolt Against Civilization," *Harper's,* CLXVII (Aug. 1933), p. 275 (quoting Mann).

81. "Book-Burning Day," *N.Y. Times,* May 11, 1933, p. 16; "German Press Under Hitler," *Zion's Herald,* CXII (Feb. 28, 1934), p. 205; Lewisohn, "The German Revolt Against Civilization," pp. 278, 282.

82. William Saroyan, "A Cold Day," in *The Daring Young Man on the Flying Trapeze, and Other Stories* (N.Y., 1934), quoted in Robert B. Downs, ed., *The First Freedom, Liberty and Justice in the World of Books and Reading* (Chicago, American Library Association, 1960), pp. 281, 282.

83. *Pub. Wkly.,* CXXIII (May 6, 1933), p. 1474; Ernst, *The Best is Yet . . . ,* p. 118; Ernst and Lindey, *Censor Marches On,* p. 37.

84. "Burn the Books!" *Saturday Rev.,* IV (Nov. 5, 1927), p. 273. Thompson, a notorious Anglophobe, accused Schlesinger of pro-Bristish

sympathies. See Arthur M. Schlesinger, *In Retrospect: The History of a Historian* (N.Y., 1963), p. 105.

85. Canby, *American Memoir,* pp. 392, 393.

86. Howard Mumford Jones, "The Place of Books and Reading in Modern Society," *Bulletin of the American Library Association,* XXVII (Dec. 15, 1933), pp. 585–93, quoted passages on p. 592.

CHAPTER X

1.Brett Gary, "The Propaganda Prophylaxis: The U.S. Fights Poisonous Ideas during World War II," paper presented at the Organization of American Historians annual meeting, April 1997, quoted passage, p. 8. For a fuller discussion, see Brett Gary's book *The Nervous Liberals: Propaganda Anxieties from World War I to the Cold War* (New York: Columbia University Press, 1999). Richard W. Steele, *Free Speech in the Good War* (New York: St. Martin's Press, 1999) further documents government suppression of dissent in the years 1939–1945 through wiretaps, deportation, prosecution threats, and occasional postal censorship. See also Clayton R. Koppes and Gregory D. Black, *Hollywood Goes to War: How Politics, Profits and Propaganda Shaped World War II Movies* (New York: Free Press, 1987); George H. Roeder, Jr., *The Censored War: American Visual Experience during World War Two* (New Haven: Yale University Press, 1993).

2. Gary, "The Propaganda Prophylaxis," pp. 7, 8.

3. James C. N. Paul and Murray L. Schwartz, *Federal Censorship: Obscenity in the Mail* (New York: Free Press, 1961), pp. 71–77, quoted passage, p. 76. Roger Baldwin, *Reminiscences*, Columbia University Oral History Project, I, p. 200.

4. *Commonwealth* v. *Isenstadt*, 318 Mass. 543, 62 N.E. 2d (1945) [the *Strange Fruit* case]; *Doubleday & Co.* v. *New York*, 335 U.S. 848 (1948) [*Memoirs of Hecate County*]; Felice Flanery Lewis, *Literature, Obscenity and Law* (Carbondale: Southern Illinois University Press, 1976), pp. 120–24 (*God's Little Acre*); 148–52 (*Strange Fruit*); 162–66 (*Memoirs of Hecate County*). In this and other discussions of prosecuted books cited below, Lewis offers helpful critical assessments and plot summaries, including quotations from the passages that attracted the censors' attention.

5. *Commonwealth* v. *Gordon*, 66 Pa. D. & C. 101 (Philadelphia County Ct., 1949); Lewis, *Literature, Obscenity, & Law*, pp. 172–74, quoted phrase, p. 172.

6. Richard F. Hixson, *Pornography and the Justices: The Supreme Court and the Intractable Obscenity Problem* (Carbondale: Southern Illinois University Press, 1996), p. 21.

7. Charles Rembar, *The End of Obscenity: The Trials of Lady Chatterley, Tropic of Cancer, and Fanny Hill* (New York: Random House, 1968), p. 45. See also, on Samuel Roth, Lewis, *Literature, Obscenity, & Law*, pp. 126, 185.

8. *Roth v. United States; Alberts v. California*, 354 U.S. 476 (1957); Richard H. Kuh, *Foolish Figleaves? Pornography in—and out of—Court* (New York: Macmillan, 1967), p. 31 (quoted passages); Frederick Schauer, essay on the *Roth/Alberts* decision in Kermit L. Hall, ed., *The Oxford Companion to the Supreme Court of the United States* (New York: Oxford University Press, 1992), pp. 745–46.

9. Lewis, *Literature, Obscenity & Law*, pp. 187, 188.

10. Donald B. Sharp, "Obscenity Law and the Intransigent Threat of Ginzburg," in Donald B. Sharp, ed., *Commentaries on Obscenity* (Metuchen, N.J.: The Scarecrow Press, 1970), pp. 32–34, quoted phrase, p. 33.

11. *Ibid.*, pp. 24–25.

12. *Ibid.*, pp. 25, 26.

13. *Ibid.*, pp. 30–32.

14. Rembar, *The End of Obscenity*, pp. 59–160; Lewis, *Literature, Obscenity, & Law*, pp. 201–7, quoted passages, p. 202.

15. *Manual Enterprises v. Day, Postmaster General*, 370 U.S. 478 (1962); Rembar, *The End of Obscenity*, pp. 190–93 (Harlan quoted, p. 191); Jay E. Daily, *The Anatomy of Censorship* (New York: Marcel Dekker, Inc., 1973), pp. 97–101; Hixson, *Pornography and the Justices*, pp. 37–38.

16. Rembar, *The End of Obscenity*, pp. 168–215 (Rhode Island incident, p. 176; Supreme Court ruling, pp. 204–5); Lewis, *Literature, Obscenity, and Law*, pp. 208–13. See also E. R. Hutchison, *Tropic of Cancer on Trial* (New York: Grove Press, 1968).

17. Rembar, *The End of Obscenity*, pp. 460–61. Quoted passage, p. 461fn.

18. *Memoirs v. Massachusetts*, 383 U.S. 413 (1966); Rembar, *The End of Obscenity.*, pp. 477–90 (Brennan quote, p. 480), and *passim* for lower-court prosecutions in Massachusetts, New Jersey, and New York; Lewis, *Literature, Obscenity, & Law*, pp. 217–22.

19. Morris L. Ernst and Alan U. Schwartz, *Censorship: The Search for the Obscene* (New York: Macmillan, 1964), p. 229; Rembar, *The End of Obscenity*, p. 493; John S. Sumner obituary, *New York Times*, June 22, 1971.

20. Louise S. Robbins, *Censorship and the American Library: The American Library Association's Response to Threats to Intellectual Freedom, 1939–1969* (Westport, Conn.: Greenwood Press, 1996), pp. 75–76, quotes from directives, p. 76); James Gilbert, *Another Chance: Postwar*

America, 1945–1985, 2nd ed. (Chicago: Dorsey Press, 1986), pp. 140–41; Louise S. Robbins, *The Dismissal of Miss Ruth Brown: Civil Rights, Censorship, and the American Library* (Norman: University of Oklahoma Press, 2000), p. 143 (Eisenhower quoted).

21. Trial excerpts in Ellen Schrecker, ed., *The Age of McCarthyism: A Brief History with Documents* (Boston: Bedford/St. Martin's, 1994), quoted passages pp. 174, 179, 181.

22. *Ibid.*, pp. 182 (Schrecker), 184 (Vinson).

23. *Ibid.*, pp. 186, 187.

24. Rembar, *The End of Obscenity*, p. 9. Another mid-1950s national poll asked: "If a person wanted to make a speech in your community against churches and religion, should he be allowed to speak or not?" Thirty-seven percent of the respondents said yes, sixty percent, no (*ibid.*).

25. Robbins, *Censorship and the American Library*, pp. 31, 84, 86.

26. Robbins, *The Dismissal of Miss Ruth Brown*, quoted passages, pp. 55, 67.

27. "The Library's Stake in Freedom of the Press," *Library Journal*, 73 (January 1, 1948), 24, quoted in Robbins, *Censorship and the American Library*, p. 30.

28. See, e.g., the "Library Bill of Rights" adopted by the ALA Council in 1948. *Ibid.*, pp. 35–36.

29. *Ibid.*, pp. 78–80 (Downs quoted, pp. 79–80); "Letter from the White House" and "The Freedom to Read" statement included in four-page reprint from the Wilson Library Bulletin, vol. 28, no. 1 (September 1953); Douglas Black to "Dear Ike," June 15, 1953, Dwight D. Eisenhower Papers, Eisenhower Library, Abilene, Kansas. My thanks to Louise Robbins for providing copies of both these documents.

30. Paul Bixler, "The Librarian—Bureaucrat or Democrat," *Library Journal*, 79 (December 1, 1954), 2278, quoted in Robbins, *Censorship and the American Library*, p. 85.

31. Keisha L. Hoerrner, "The Forgotten Battles: Congressional Hearings on Television Violence in the 1950s," (June 1999), www.scripps. ohiou.edu/wjmcr/vol02/2-3a-B/htm (while these hearings did address TV, print culture loomed large as well); Harry M. Clor, *Obscenity and Public Morality: Censorship in a Liberal Society* (Chicago: University of Chicago Press, 1969), pp. 4–6, 281 fn. 1; American Civil Liberties Union, *Annual Report, 1963–64* (1964), pp. 17, 19, 20; *New York Times*, February 19, 1963, p. 7; *Bantam Books v. Sullivan*, 372 U.S. 58 (1963).

32. Rembar, *The End of Obscenity*, pp. 8–9, 174.

33. *Ibid.*, p. 171.

34. Kent Carroll, "In the Echoing Grove: Fifty Years of Avant-Garde Publishing in New York," *Times Literary Supplement*, January 12, 2001, p. 14.

35. For an account of a Canadian Tariff Board hearing on *Peyton Place*, see A. M. Beattie and Frank A. Underhill, "Sense and Censorship: On Behalf of *Peyton Place*," *Canadian Library Association Journal*, 15 (July 1958), pp. 9–16.

36. Lewis, *Literature, Obscenity & Law*, p. 197. Lewis discusses (pp. 193–97) a number of obscenity prosecutions in the 1960s involving paperbacks of this type.

37. *The Report of the Commission on Obscenity and Pornography* (New York: Bantam Books, 1970), p. 16.

38. Harold John Ockenga, "Fulfilled and Unfulfilled Prophecies," in Carl F. H. Henry, ed., *Prophecy in the Making* (Carol Stream, Ill: Creation House, 1971), pp. 305, 306; Charles R. Taylor, *The Destiny of America* (Van Nuys, Calif.: Time-Light Books, 1972), p. 72; David Wilkerson, *The Vision* (New York: Pyramid Books, 1974), pp. 43, 44, 50, 79.

39. Quoted in Rembar, *The End of Obscenity*, p. 479.

40. David Steigerwald, *The Sixties and the End of Modern America* (New York: St. Martin's Press, 1995), p. 169 (Sontag); Cleveland Amory, "Paperback Pornography," *Saturday Evening Post*, April 6, 1963, pp. 10–12; George P. Elliott, "Against Pornography," *Harper's Magazine*, March 1965, pp. 51–60, quoted passage p. 57; American Civil Liberties Union, *Annual Report, 1963–64* (1964), pp. 17, 19, 20; author's personal observations (postal cancellation messages; Boston bumper stickers).

41. "The New Pornography," *Time*, April 16, 1965, pp. 22–23.

42. Rembar, *The End of Obscenity*, p. 491.

43. *New York Times*, May 3, 1966 (Citizens for Decent Literature); *Boston Herald*, February 20, 1963, and *Civil Liberties*, October 1966, p. 3 (the California CLEAN movement); "The New Pornography," *Time*, April 16, 1965, pp. 28–29; *New York Times*, November 10, 1966, p. 36 (defeat of proposal to tighten California's obscenity law); Lane V. Sunderland, *Obscenity: The Court, the Congress, and the President's Commission* (Washington, D.C.: American Enterprise Institute for Public Policy Research, 1975), p. 77 (Gallup Poll data). "Savings and Loan Figure Released from Jail," *The Augusta Chronicle Online*, posted April 2, 1998, http://www.augustachronicle.com/stories/040298/bus124-2994.shtml; Skipp Porteous, "What's in a Name?", Institute for First Amendment Studies, Inc., *Freedom Writer*, November/December 1989. http://www.ifas.org/fw/8911/name.html.

44. Lewis, *Literature, Obscenity & Law*, p. 6 (Bok quote); Alan Hunt, *Governing Morals: A Social History of Moral Regulation* (Cambridge: Cambridge University Press, 1999), pp. 201–4 (quoted passages, pp. 201, 202).

45. Granahan report quoted in Clor, *Obscenity and Public Morality*, pp. 5–6.

46. Carroll, "In the Echoing Grove: Fifty Years of Avant Garde Publishing in New York," p. 14; Howard Brick, *Age of Contradiction: American Thought and Culture in the 1960s* (New York, Twayne, 1998), p. 12; *Facts on File, 1967*, Oct. 5–11, 1967, p. 418 (Ginzburg).

47. Smith took her title, "Strange Fruit," from an antilynching protest song written in the 1930s by Abel Meeropol, a New York City school teacher (and communist). Billie Holiday introduced the song in 1939 and sang it at nearly every performance thereafter. Smith's novel thus had associations with racial protest years before the civil rights movement. See David Margolick, *Strange Fruit: Billie Holliday, Cafe Society and an Early Cry for Civil Rights* (Edinburgh: Payback, 2001). See also Lewis, *Literature, Obscenity, & Law*, pp. 148–52.

48. *Ibid*, p. 269, n. 1.

49. Clive Barnes, "Special Introduction," *Report of the Commission on Obscenity and Pornography*, p. xv.

50. The full story is told in Barry Werth, *The Scarlet Professor: Newton Arvin: A Literary Life Shattered by Scandal* (New York: Doubleday, 2001). Quoted passages on pp. 145 (Summerfield), 140 (Heath), 233 (Crowley).

51. Clor, *Obscenity and Public Morality*, pp. x, xi, 174, 209, 245. Also see Harry M. Clor, *Public Morality and Liberal Society: Essays on Decency, Law, and Pornography* (Notre Dame: University of Notre Dame Press, 1996).

52. *Ibid.*, pp. 279–80. For another thoughtful (and witty!) late-1960s work urging censorship, but under precise limitations, see Richard H. Kuh, *Foolish Figleaves? Pornography in—and out of—Court* (New York: Macmillan, 1967). Kuh was a prosecutor in the office of New York County district attorney Frank S. Hogan.

53. *Civil Liberties*, October 1964, p. 2; *Report of the Commission on Obscenity and Pornography*, pp. 597–601 (list of honorary members of Citizens for Decent Literature); *New York Times*, October 10, 1968, p. 7 (Nixon).

54. In another obscenity case decided that day, *Mishkin* v. *New York*, the court upheld the conviction of the producer of furtively distributed paperbacks, crudely printed from photocopied typescripts and published under false names and addresses, involving bondage, torture, and various sadomasochistic practices. Lewis, *Literature, Obscenity & Law*, pp. 191, 196.

55. Rembar, *The End of Obscenity*, pp. 424–25.

56. *Eros*, vol. I, no. 1 (Spring 1962); vol. I, no. 2 (Summer 1962); Rembar, *The End of Obscenity*, pp. 425 (the interracial nude photo) and 424 (on *Liaison*).

57. *Ginzburg* v. *U.S.*, 383 U.S. 463 (1966), 837; Hixson, *Pornography and the Justices*, pp. 61–67 (quoted passage, p. 63); Rembar, *The End of Obscenity*, pp. 407–8, 424–28, 483–89. William E. Brigman, "Politics and the Pornography Wars," *Wide Angle*, vol. 19, no. 3 (1997), p. 152.

58. Rembar, *The End of Obscenity*, pp. 98–99.

59. Alexander M. Bickel, "Obscenity Cases," *New Republic*, May 27, 1967, pp. 15–17, quoted passage, p. 16; Harlan and Stewart dissents in *Supreme Court Reporter*, vol. 86A, October term, 1965 (St. Paul: West Publishing Co., 1967), pp. 953–58, quoted passages pp. 954, 958; Rembar, *The End of Obscenity*, p. 484 (*Nation* quote); Hixson, *Pornography and the Justices*, pp. 64 (Harlan), 69 (Fortas); Ralph Ginzburg, "Castrated: My Eight Months in Prison," *New York Times Magazine*, Decemer 3, 1972, pp. 38–39; *Contemporary Authors*, vols. 21–24, first revision (Detroit: Gale Research Co., 1977), pp. 335–36; author interview with Ralph Ginzburg, September 27, 2001.

60. Kuh, *Foolish Figleaves?*, p. x.

61. Bickel, "Obscenity Cases," p. 16.

62. Hixson, *Pornography and the Justices*, p. 61.

63. *Eros*, vol. I, no. 2 (Summer 1962), pp. 81ff.

64. Rembar, *The End of Obscenity*, pp. 484 (*National Decency Reporter* quote), 484 (*New Republic* quote); *New York Times*, May 3, 1966 (Keating quote), March 24, 1966, p. 36 (editorial on the *Ginzburg* decision).

65. Sunderland, *Obscenity: The Court, the Congress, and the President's Commission*, p. 72; Gorden Hawkins and Franklin E. Zimring, *Pornography in a Free Society* (Cambridge: Cambridge University Press, 1988), p. 9 (McClellan), see also pp. 7–13 *passim* ("The Johnson Commission").

66. *Ibid.*, pp. 73 (budget), 78 (experiment); *Report of the Commission on Obscenity and Pornography*, [xx] (list of commission members and staff), ix–x (information about the commissioners' professions).

67. *Ibid.*, quoted passages pp. 38, 41, 58. See also pp. 61, 585, 590. The commission funded a social-science study of two antipornography crusades to document its view that larger cultural anxieties underlay such movements. See Louis A. Zurcher, Jr., and R. George Kirkpatrick, *Citizens for Decency: Antipornography Crusades as Status Defense* (Austin: University of Texas Press, 1976).

68. *Ibid.*, quoted passages pp. 33, 54. See also pp. 57, 62, 64. On the increasing use of therapeutic strategies in late-twentieth-century moral regulation, see Hunt, *Governing Morals*, p. 216.

69. *Report of the Commission on Obscenity and Pornography*, pp. 456–505 ("Magna Carta" quote, p. 456).

70. *Ibid.*, pp. 578–623, quoted passages pp. ix, 578, 580, 581, 583.

71. *Ibid.*, p. 605. See also pp. 578, 580, 581, 583–84, 585, 586.

72. Sunderland, *Obscenity: The Court, the Congress, and the President's Commission*, chapter 3, "The Obscenity Commission," pp. 71–84, especially p. 77 (contradictory polling data); Joseph F. Kobylka, *The Politics of Obscenity: Group Litigation in a Time of Legal Change* (New York: Greenwood Press, 1999), p. xiii (Agnew quote); Lewis, *Literature, Obscenity & Law*, p. 226; Donald E. Wildmon, *The Home Invaders* (Wheaton, Ill.: Victor Books, 1987), p. 187 (Senate vote); Ray C. Rist, "Policy, Politics and Social Research: A Study in the Relationship of Federal Commissions and Social Science," in Ray C. Rist, ed., *The Pornography Controversy: Changing Moral Standards in American Life* (New Brunswick, N.J.: Transaction Books, 1975), pp. 244–68 (Griffin quoted, p. 261).

73. Clive Barnes, "Special Introduction," *Report of the Commission on Obscenity and Pornography*, pp. ix–xvii, quoted passages on p. xvi.

74. Lewis, *Literature, Obscenity & Law*, p. 230.

75. *Miller* v. *California*, 413 U.S. 15 (1973); Sunderland, *Obscenity: The Court, the Congress, and the President's Commission*, pp. 8–17, quoted passages, pp. 11, 15; Lewis, *Literature, Obscenity, and Law*, pp. 230–35 ("burden almost impossible" quote, p. 232).

76. Hixson, *Pornography and the Justices*, pp. 110–16, (Harlan quote, p. 115). See also Schauer, "*Miller* v. *California* and *Paris Adult Theatre* v. *Slaton*," in Hall, ed., *The Oxford Companion to the Supreme Court of the United States*, pp. 548–49. The obscenity case prosecuted in Louisiana, *Novick, Haim and Unique Specialties, Inc.* v. *U.S. District Court*, 423 U.S. 911 (1975), is discussed in William E. Brigman, "Politics and the Pornography Wars," *Wide Angle*, vol. 19, no. 3 (1997), p. 155, also at wysiwyg://12/http://muse.jhu.edu/journals/wide_angle/v019/19.3brigman.html.

77. Lewis, *Literature, Obscenity & Law*, pp. 232, 233; Hixson, *Pornography and the Justices*, p. 114.

78. Lewis, *Literature, Obscenity, & Law*, pp. 233.

79. *Kaplan* v. *California*, 413 U.S. 115 (1973); Lewis, *Literature, Obscenity, & Law.*, pp. 238–39, quoted passage, p. 239.

80. *Paris Adult Theater I* v. *Slaton*, 413 U.S., 49 (1973); Schauer, "*Miller* v. *California* and *Paris Adult Theater* v. *Slaton*"; Hixson, *Pornography and the Justices*, pp. 108, 117–30 (Burger quotes, pp. 108, 126).

81. *Ibid.*, pp. 128–29.

82. William F. Buckley, Jr., "Obscenity is Commerce" and Gerald Damiano, "Legislating Morality," *Chicago Tribune*, August 31, 1973, quoted in Sunderland, *Obscenity: The Court, the Congress, and the President's Commission*, pp. 1, 2.

83. *New York Times*, June 25, 1973, p. 32; Harriet F. Pilpel, "Obscenity and the Constitution," *Publishers' Weekly*, December 10, 1973, p. 26, quoted in Lewis, *Literature, Obscenity & the Law*, p. 240.

84. See, for example, Ralph Ginzburg's comment to *Playboy* after his conviction on obscenity charges: "I think photographs showing B-52s dropping napalm on Vietnamese civilians are vulgar. No let me make that stronger. They're grotesque, they're obscene." Ginzburg interview in *Playboy*, July 1966, quoted in *Contemporary Authors*, p. 336.

CHAPTER XI

1. Alan Hunt, *Governing Morals: A Social History of Moral Regulation* (Cambridge: Cambridge University Press, 1999), pp. 196, 200.

2. Gordon Hawkins and Franklin E. Zimring, *Pornography in a Free Society* (Cambridge: Cambridge University Press, 1988), pp. 13–16, "The Meese Commission" (Hawkins and Zimring adopt a valuable cross cultural approach, relating their study of U.S. pornography commissions to similar bodies in Canada and Great Britain); Carole S. Vance, "The Meese Commission on the Road," *The Nation*, August 2 and 9, 1986, pp. 76–80 (Vance describes the hearings as an "epiphany of prurient righteousness," p. 77); Attorney General's Commission on Pornography, *Final Report* (Washington, D.C.: U.S. Department of Justice, 1986), pp. 323–24, 383, as quoted in Donald Alexander Downs, *The New Politics of Pornography* (Chicago: University of Chicago Press, 1989), pp. 1–2, 163, 196 (quoted passage). On the Meese Commission's misleading use of studies on the relationship of violence and pornography, see the critique by three prominent researchers: Daniel Linz, Steven Penrod, and Edward Donnerstein, "The Attorney General's Commission on Pornography: The Gap Between 'Findings' and Facts," *American Bar Foundation Research Journal*, Fall 1987, No. 4, pp. 713–36.

3. Margaret C. Jasper, *The Law of Obscenity and Pornography* (Dobbs Ferry, N.Y.: Oceana Publications, 1996), quoted passages on pp. 41, 53. Appendix 2, pp. 40–51, reprints all ninety-two recommendations; Linz, Penrod, and Donnerstein, "The Attorney General's Commission on Pornography," *passim*; Donald Downs, "The Attorney General's Commission and the New Politics of Pornography," *American Bar Foundation Research Journal*, Fall 1987, No. 4, pp. 641–80. For a witty journalistic dissection of the Meese Commission report, see Hendrick Hertzberg, "Big Boobs: Ed Meese and His Pornography Commission," *New Republic*, 195 (July 14–21, 1986), 21–24.

4. William E. Brigman, "Politics and the Pornography Wars," *Wide Angle*, 19, 3 (1997), pp. 149–70 (also at wysiwyg://12http://muse.jhu.edu/

journals/wide_angle/vo19/19.3brigman.html), especially pp. 159, 160, 162 (quoted phrase, p. 160).

5. *Ibid.*, pp. 158, 160–62 (quoted passage p. 161).

6. *Ibid.*, pp. 150, 162 (quoted passage, p. 150).

7. James Davison Hunter, *Culture Wars: The Struggle to Define America* (N.Y., Basic Books, 1991), pp. 231, 240, 243; Jackie Demaline, "Mapplethorpe Battle Changed Art World," *Cincinnati Enquirer*, May 21, 2000 (at enquirer.com/editions/2000/5/21/loc_mapplethorpe_battle.html).

8. Hunter, *Culture Wars*, pp. 28–29; Demaline, "Mapplethorpe Battle Changed Art World."

9. Hunter, *Culture Wars*, pp. 239–42.

10. *Ibid.*, pp. 242–46.

11. Editorial, "Put Up Your Dukes," *Christianity Today*, 34 (December 17, 1990), p. 14, quoted in Hunter, *Culture Wars*, p. 242. For a conservative attack on the "censorship" of school textbook content by "the deeply entrenched liberal education establishment," see Paul C. Vitz, *Censorship: Evidence of Bias in Our Children's Textbooks* (Ann Arbor: Servant Books, 1986), quoted phrases, p. xiii.

12. Hunter, *Culture Wars*, pp. 48, 64, 91, 228, 243, 296.

13. Henry Reichman, *Censorship and Selection: Issues and Answers for Schools* (Chicago and Arlington, Va.: American Library Association and American Association of School Administrators, 1988), pp. 1 (quoted passage), 18, 27–45 (chapter 3, "Issues in Dispute"); Catherine Elton, "Balanced Books," *New Republic*, May 5, 1997, p. 10; Downs, *The New Politics of Pornography*, pp. 25–28 (1984 Cincinnati conference, p. 28).

14. Document reprinted in Reichman, *Censorship and Selection*, pp. 41–42, quoted passages p. 42.

15. Pamela Hunt Steinle, *In Cold Fear: The Catcher in the Rye Controversies and Postwar American Character* (Columbus: Ohio State University Press, 2000); *Los Angeles Times*, February 14, 1982, reprinted in *Facts on File, 1982*, p. 194; Calvin Reid and Bridget Kinsella, "In Banned Book Week, Censorship Still Thrives," *Publishers Weekly*, September 23, 1996, p. 12 (Angelou); Reichman, *Censorship and Selection*, pp. 11, 30, 32, 27, 34, 43.

16. *Ibid.*, p. 10; *Facts on File, 1982*, p. 194.

17. *Board of Education* v. *Pico*, 457 U.S. 853 (1982); *Facts on File, 1982*, pp. 166, 467–68; Mark G. Yudof, "Education," in Kermit L. Hall, ed., *The Oxford Companion to the Supreme Court of the United States* (New York: Oxford University Press, 1992), p. 245; Reichman, *Censorship and Selection*, pp. 73–75.

18. Reichman, *Censorship and Selection*, pp. 2–3.

19. Elton, "Balanced Books," p. 10; Reid and Kinsella, "In Banned Book Week, Censorship Still Thrives."

20. Elton, "Balanced Books," pp. 10–12.

21. *Ibid.*, p. 12.

22. Reichman, *Censorship and Selection*, pp. 64–66, 71–84, 97–106, 119–28.

23. Elton, "Balanced Books," p. 12.

24. Reichman, *Censorship and Selection*, pp. 12, 27.

25. *Ibid.*, pp. 44–45; Jonathan Arac, *Huckleberry Finn as Idol and Target: The Functions of Criticism in Our Time* (Madison: University of Wisconsin Press, 1997), pp. 63–64, 67–68.

26. *Ibid.*, p. 24.

27. *Ibid.*, p. 21.

28. *Ibid.*, p. viii.

29. The voluminous writings by McKinnon and Dworkin developing this argument include Dworkin, *Pornography: Men Possessing Women* (New York: Perigree Books, 1981); MacKinnon, "Pornography as Discrimination and Defamation," *Boston University Law Review*, 793 (1992), 71ff; *Feminism Unmodified: Discourses on Life and Law* (Cambridge: Harvard University Press, 1987); *Only Words* (Cambridge: Harvard University Press, 1993); and, by Dworkin and MacKinnon, *Pornography and Civil Rights: A New Day for Women's Equality* (Minneapolis: Organizing Against Pornography, 1988) and a co edited work, *In Harm's Way: The Pornography Civil Rights Hearings* (Cambridge: Harvard University Press, 1997). See also Susan Griffin, *Pornography and Silence: Culture's Revenge Against Nature* (New York: Harper & Row, 1981); Susanne Kappeler, *The Pornography of Representation* (Cambridge: Polity, 1986); Diana E. H. Russell, ed., *Making Violence Sexy: Feminist Views on Pornography* (New York: Teachers College Press, 1983); and Susan Gubar and Joan Hoff, eds., *For Adult Users Only: The Dilemma of Violent Pornography* (Bloomington: Indiana University Press, 1989).

30. Kate Millett, *Sexual Politics* (Garden City, N.Y.: Doubleday, 1970); *New York Times*, August 6, 1973, p. 31 (Brownmiller); Robin Morgan, "Theory and Practice: Pornography and Rape," in Laura Lederer, ed., *Take Back the Night: Women and Pornography* (New York: William Morrow, 1980), p. 139.

31. The MacKinnon/Dworkin initiative and its outcome is recounted in fascinating detail, and situated in its larger politico-legal context, in Downs, *The New Politics of Pornography*. See also Hunt, *Governing Morals*, pp. 204–11 ("Crisis in Gender Relations"), for interesting comments on the initiative and its context. For the larger context of the feminist antipornography movement of the 1970s and 1980s, see Carolyn Bronstein, "Porn Tours: The Rise and Fall of the American Feminist Anti-Pornography Movement, 1976–1986," University of Wisconsin–Madison, School of Journalism and Mass Communications, Ph.D., 2001, especially

chapters 1–5, (pp. 27–211) on the movement's theoretical roots and early activist manifestations. Quoted passage, p. 1.

32. The ordinance appears in MacKinnon and Dworkin, eds., *In Harm's Way*, pp. 426–32, quoted passage defining pornography, p. 428. See also Downs, *The New Politics of Pornography*, pp. 43–48 (content and administration of the proposed ordinance).

33. For the testimony in the Minneapolis hearings, as well as exhibits, telegrams, and letters introduced as evidence, see MacKinnon and Dworkin, eds., *In Harm's Way*, pp. 39–252 (Marchiano testimony, pp. 60–67, council vote, p. 432). For testimony in Indianapolis, Los Angeles, and Massachusetts, see pp. 269–89, 332–425. See also Downs *The New Politics of Pornography*, p. 93.

34. *Ibid.*, p. xiii, 95–143, (chapter 4, "Strange Bedfellows: The Politics of the Ordinance in Indianapolis"); See also Wendy Kaminer, "Courting Unsafe Speech," *The American Prospect*, June 18, 2001, p. 31, and Kaminer's testimony in the Massachusetts hearings on the MacKinnon/Dworkin initiative in MacKinnon and Dworkin, eds., *In Harm's Way*, pp. 378–80.

35. Laura Kipnis, *Bound and Gagged: Pornography and the Politics of Fantasy in America* (New York: Grove Press, 1996); M. G. Lord, "Pornutopia: How Feminist Scholars Learned to Love Dirty Pictures," *Lingua Franca*, May 1997, pp. 40–48 (Robertson quote, p. 42); Meredith Balderston, "Ladies! Ladies! Ladies! Representations of Women's Sexuality on Woman-Run Porn Sites," Popular Culture Association and the American Culture Association conference program, http://www.h-net.msu.edu/~pcaaaca/national/fri/2-4.htm; Catherine Itzin, ed., *Pornography: Women, Violence, and Civil Liberties* (Oxford: Oxford University Press, 1992); Gordon Hawkins and Franklin E. Zimring, *Pornography in a Free Society* (Cambridge: Cambridge University Press, 1988), p. 167 (Feminist Anti-Censorship Task Force).

36. Nadine Strossen, *Defending Pornography: Free Speech, Sex, and the Fight for Women's Rights* (New York: Scribner, 1995), quoted passages, p. 13. Other critical responses include Sarah Crichton, "Sexual Correctness: Has It Gone Too Far?" *Newsweek*, October 25, 1993; Carole S. Vance, ed. *Pleasure and Desire: Exploring Female Sexuality* (Boston: Routledge and K. Paul, 1984); Ann Snitow, Christine Stansell, and Sharon Thompson, eds., *Powers of Desire: The Politics of Sexuality* (New York: Monthly Review Press, 1983); Varda Burstyn, ed., *Women Against Censorship* (Vancouver: Douglas & McIntyre, 1985); and Linda Williams, *Hard Core: Power, Pleasure, and the Frenzy of the Visible* (Berkeley: University of California Press, 1989). See also Susan Fraiman, "Catharine MacKinnon and the Feminist Porn Debates," *American Quarterly*,

vol. 74, no. 4 (December 1995), pp. 743–49; and Karen Hand, "Feminism Divided: How Pornography and Censorship Have Split Feminism," *The Salad Bowl* [magazine of the American Studies Department, Rutgers University], vol. 21 (1996), pp. 53–57. Nearly twenty years after the MacKinnon/Dworkin initiative, the debate continued. See Drucilla Cornell, ed., *Feminism and Pornography* (New York: Oxford University Press, 2000).

37. Catharine A. MacKinnon, "The Roar on the Other Side of Silence," and "Memo on Proposed Ordinance on Pornography, December 26, 1983," in MacKinnon and Dworkin, eds., *In Harm's Way*, especially pp. 10, 256–59; Attorney General's Commission on Pornography, *Final Report*, chapter 5, "The Question of Harm," pp. 299–349; Donald E. Wildmon, *The Home Invaders* (Wheaton, Ill.: Victor Books, 1985), pp. 75, 89; Downs, *The New Politics of Pornography*, pp. 2, 95–143, *passim* (conservative support in Indianapolis); Brigman, "Politics and the Pornography Wars," p. 158.

38. See, for example, the highly critical review by Norma Basch of Rutgers Unversity–Newark in *American Historical Review*, vol. 98, no. 2 (April 1993), pp. 598–99.

39. Downs, *The New Politics of Pornography*, pp. xxiii, 198.

40. Hawkins and Zimring, *Pornography in a Free Society*, pp. 151–74, especially pp. 154–55, 163, 165–66; quoted phrases, p. 174.

41. Downs, *The New Politics of Pornography*, pp. 144, 192–93, 196, 198; quoted phrases on pp. 196, 198.

42. *Ibid.*, pp. 195, 165–72, 186–92; quoted passages pp. 167, 188. The case for a causal link between pornography and violence against women is made at great length in Itzin, ed., *Pornography*, part III, "Pornography and Evidence of Harm," pp. 201–397. For an introduction to this complex and disputed issue, see Edward Donnerstein, Daniel Linz, and Steven Penrod, *The Question of Pornography* (New York: Free Press, 1987); Neil M. Malamuth and Edward Donnerstein, eds., *Pornography and Sexual Aggression* (Orlando: Academic Press, 1984). As an example of the complexities of the matter, Donnerstein, Linz, and Penrod found in their experiments that while exposure to violent pornography seemed to increase male subjects' aggressiveness toward women in experimental settings, so did certain scenes from TV soap operas, popular Hollywood movies, and "many types of mass media" (*Question of Pornography*, p. 107, cited in Downs, *The New Politics of Pornography*, p. 191). For a critique of the use and misuse of the research evidence by pro-censorship advocates, including MacKinnon and Dworkin as well as by the Meese Commission, see Linz, Penrod, and Donnerstein, "The Attorney General's Commission on Pornography: The Gaps Between 'Findings' and Facts."

43. Downs, *The New Politics of Pornography*, pp. 197, 198.

44. Jasper, *The Law of Obscenity and Pornography*, p. 13; Jonathan W. Emord, *Freedom, Technology, and the First Amendment* (San Francisco: Pacific Research Institute for Public Policy, 1991), pp. 176, 177, 185. Emord provides examples (pp. 177–81, 189–91) of the exercise of this oversight and regulatory power by both the FRC and the FCC.

45. James L. Baughman, *The Republic of Mass Culture: Journalism, Filmmaking, and Broadcasting in America since 1941* (Baltimore: Johns Hopkins University Press, 1992), pp. 20, 116; James Baughman, "The Mother of Television," pp. 1–14, chapter 2 of his forthcoming book, *Medium of Compromise: American Television in the 1950s*. My thanks to Professor Baughman for sharing this manuscript chapter with me. *New York Times*, November 14, 1969, pp. 1, 24 (Agnew attack), December 19, 1973, p. 87, April 13, 1974, p. 87 (growing Nixon influence on FCC), January 29, 1974, p. 67 (Nicholas Johnson comment); William E. Porter, *Assault on the Media: The Nixon Years* (Ann Arbor: University of Michigan Press, 1976), pp. 45 (Dean Burch harassment of TV networks), 47 (Agnew speech), 70–72 (Colson), 126–29 (*Newsday* episode), 142–45 (Daniel Schorr), 173–74 (Clay Whitehead speech).

46. *Federal Communications Commission v. Pacifica Foundation*, 438 U.S. 726 (1978). The case is discussed in detail in Richard F. Hixson, *Pornography and the Justices: The Supreme Court and the Intractable Obscenity Problem* (Carbondale: Southern Illinois University Press, 1996), pp. 150–54; quoted passages p. 153.

47. Baughman, *The Republic of Mass Culture*, p. 45.

48. Stephen J. Whitfield, *The Culture of the Cold War* (Baltimore: Johns Hopkins University Press, 1991), pp. 166–69 (*I Love Lucy*); Baughman, *The Republic of Mass Culture*, pp. 111–12 (Smothers Brothers).

49. Richard A. Randall, *Censorship of the Movies: The Social and Political Control of a Mass Medium* (Madison: University of Wisconsin Press, 1968); Francis G. Couvares, ed., *Movie Censorship and American Culture* (Washington, D.C.: Smithsonian Institution Press, 1996).

50. *Mutual Film Corporation v. Industrial Commission of Ohio*, 236 U.S. 230 (1915). See also Randall, *Censorship of the Movies*, pp. 9–25; Rochelle Gurstein, *The Repeal of Reticence* (New York: Hill and Wang, 1996), p. 240 (quoted phrase); Jasper, *The Law of Obscenity and Pornography*, pp. 11–12; Jeffrey B. Morris and Richard B. Morris, eds., *Encyclopedia of American History*, 7th ed. (New York: HarperCollins, 1996), p. 883.

51. On the *Miracle* case, *Burstyn v. Wilson*, 343 U.S. 495 (1952), see Randall, *Censorship of the Movies*, pp. 25–32, quoted passage, p. 29. On the *Lady Chatterley's Lover* case, *Kingsley v. Regents of the State Univer-*

sity of New York, 360 U.S. 684 (1959), see *ibid.*, pp. 52–53 and Hixson, *Pornography and the Justices*, pp. 28–29.

52. *Times Film Corp* v. *Chicago*, 365 U.S. 43; Hixson, *Pornography and the Justices*, pp. 33–35, quoted passages p. 35.

53. *Jacobellis* v. *Ohio*, 378 U.S. 184 (1964); Hixson, *Pornography and the Justices*, pp. 41–45. Brennan quoted on p. 43, Stewart on p. 41.

54. Randall, *Censorship of the Movies*, pp. 163–66, quoted passage, p. 166.

55. *Ibid.*, p. 48.

56. *Ibid.*, p. 138.

57. *New York Times*, March 4, 1973, p. 8; March 11, 1973, p. 48. Jon Lewis, *Hollywood v. Hard Core: How the Struggle Over Censorship Saved the Modern Film Industry* (New York: New York University Press, 2000), pp. 195–208 (the early history of sexually explicit films), 208–13 (the success of *Deep Throat* and *The Devil in Miss Jones*), 263 (the local bans on *Deep Throat*), 353 n. 94 (the Memphis prosecution of *Deep Throat*).

58. Randall, *Censorship of the Movies*, pp. 10, 16, 198–214; Hixson, *Pornography and the Justices*, p. 82; http://moderntimes.com/palace/huac.htm (on *The Moon Is Blue* and *The Man with the Golden Arm*); *New York Times*, June 2, 1953, p. 34 (The Moon is Blue denied Production Code seal); Lewis, *Hollywood v. Hard Core*, pp. 1, 2, 297 (*Eyes Wide Shut*); for theoretical perspectives on censorship as a transnational, transhistorical cultural phenomenon, see Robert C. Post, ed., *Censorship and Silencing: Practices of Cultural Regulation* (Los Angeles: Getty Trust Publications, 1998).

59. Emord, *Freedom, Technology, and the First Amendment*, p. 259. See also 249–63 *passim* for an early (1991) effort to assess the First Amendment implications of the new electronic technologies.

60. Brigman, "Politics and the Pornography Wars," p. 157 (decline of "adult" movie theaters); "Giuliani Vows to Cut Subsidy Over 'Sick' Art," *New York Times*, September 23, 1999; "Giuliani Takes on Sex Industry Again, with Stricter Rules," *New York Times*, January 11, 2000.

61. Frank Rich, "Naked Capitalists," *New York Times Magazine*, May 20, 2001, pp. 51–56, 80–81, quote on p. 51. The 1997 film *Boogie Nights*, starring Burt Reynolds, evokes the "adult entertainment" industry as it was in the late 1970s and early 1980s.

62. Frederick Schaur, "*Stanley* v. *Georgia*, 394 U.S. 557 (1969)," in Hall, ed., *Oxford Companion to the Supreme Court*, pp. 821–22.

63. *Los Angeles* v. *Preferred Communications, Inc.*, 476 U.S. 488 (1986), discussed in Bill F. Chamberlin, "Speech and the Press," in *ibid.*, p. 812; Wildmon, *The Home Invaders*, p. 191.

64. Jasper, *The Law of Obscenity and Pornography*, p. 40.

65. Kaminer, "Courting Unsafe Speech," p. 31; Joan Biskupic, "High Court Takes on 'Virtual' Child Porn," *USA Today*, June 15, 2001, at www.usatoday.com/news/court/2001-01-22-porn-usat.htm. "Justices Weigh Law Barring Virtual Child Pornography," *New York Times*, October 31, 2001, p. A13. " 'Virtual' Child Pornography Ban Overturned," *New York Times*, April 17, 2002, pp. A1, A16. For historical context, see Philip Jenkins, *Moral Panic: Changing Concepts of the Child Molester in Modern America* (New Haven: Yale University Press, 1998).

66. Jasper, *The Law of Obscenity and Pornography*, p. 21.

67. The law is reprinted as Appendix 3 in Jasper, *The Law of Obscenity and Pornography*, pp. 59–77, quoted passages, p. 72.

68. *Ibid.*, quoted section, p. 61.

69. *Ibid.*, p. 21.

70. "White House Is Set to Ease Its Stance on Internet Smut," *New York Times*, June 16, 1997, pp. A1, A10, quoted passage p. A10. See also Marjorie Heins, *Not in Front of the Children: "Indecency," Censorship, and the Innocence of Youth* (New York: Hill & Wang, 2001).

71. Hawkins and Zimring, *Pornography in a Free Society*, chapter 7, "Pornography and Child Protection," pp. 175–97; quoted passages pp. 181, 186, 197.

72. Brigman, "Politics and the Pornography Wars," pp. 166, 167 (Smith quoted p. 166). See also Lawrence A. Stanley, "The Child Porn Storm," *Washington Post*, January 30, 1994, p. C3, cited by Brigman, f. 34.

73. The Supreme Court ruling is printed in full in "*Reno* v. *A.C.L.U.*: The Battle Over the Communications Decency Act," CNN Interactive, www.cnn.com/us/9703/cda.scotus. Seven justices concurred in the majority opinion ruling the law unconstitutional; Chief Justice William Rehnquist and Justice Sandra Day O'Connor concurred in part and dissented in part. On the Child Online Protection Act see "Justices Revisit the Issue of Child Protection in the Age of Internet Pornography," *New York Times*, November 29, 2001, p. A24.

74. "*Reno* v. *A.C.L.U.*: The Battle Over the Communications Decency Act."

75. "After Complaints, Yahoo to Close Access to Pornographic Sites," *New York Times*, April 14, 2001, p. B1. Interestingly, the *Times* carried this report not as a general news or cultural affairs story, but in the business section. For a thoughtful discussion of the public policy and First Amendment issues posed by Internet regulation, see Cass Sunstein, *Republic.com* (Princeton: Princeton University Press, 2001).

76. Downs, *The New Politics of Pornography*, p. 196.

77. Richard S. Randall, *Freedom and Taboo: Pornography and the Politics of a Self Divided* (Berkeley: University of California Press, 1989), pp. 256–58, quoted phrases p. 257. My thanks to Donald Downs for calling this work to my attention.

78. *Ibid.*, pp. 263–67, quoted passage p. 265.

79. Rochelle Gurstein, *The Repeal of Reticence: A History of America's Cultural and Legal Struggles over Free Speech, Obscenity, Sexual Liberation, and Modern Art* (New York: Hill and Wang, 1996), quoted passages pp. 3, 179, 197, 198, 200, 305, 306. See especially chapter 7, "The Legal Debate About Obscenity," pp. 179–212.

80. *Ibid.*, pp. 6, 38, 304. See also Alan Wolfe's review of *The Repeal of Reticence* in the *New Republic*, November 11, 1996, pp. 56–59 (Gurstein quoted on the need to recover the culture of reticence "even if we reject it anew," p. 58).

81. Harvey quoted in Wildmon, *The Home Invaders*, p. 124.

Index